LANDSCAPES
OF INJUSTICE

Rethinking Canada in the World
SERIES EDITORS: Ian McKay and Sean Mills

Supported by the Wilson Institute for Canadian History at McMaster University, this series is committed to books that rethink Canadian history from transnational and global perspectives. It enlarges approaches to the study of Canada in the world by exploring how Canadian history has long been a dynamic product of global currents and forces. The series will also reinvigorate understanding of Canada's role as an international actor and how Canadians have contributed to intellectual, political, cultural, social, and material exchanges around the world.

Volumes included in the series explore the ideas, movements, people, and institutions that have transcended political boundaries and territories to shape Canadian society and the state. These include both state and non-state actors, and phenomena such as international migration, diaspora politics, religious movements, evolving conceptions of human rights and civil society, popular culture, technology, epidemics, wars, and global finance and trade.

The series charts a new direction by exploring networks of transmission and exchange from a standpoint that is not solely national or international, expanding the history of Canada's engagement with the world.

http://wilson.humanities.mcmaster.ca

1 Canada and the United Nations
Legacies, Limits, Prospects
Edited by Colin McCullough and Robert Teigrob

2 Undiplomatic History
The New Study of Canada and the World
Edited by Asa McKercher and Philip Van Huizen

3 Revolutions across Borders
Jacksonian America and the Canadian Rebellion
Edited by Maxime Dagenais and Julien Mauduit

4 Left Transnationalism
The Communist International and the National, Colonial, and Racial Questions
Edited by Oleksa Drachewych and Ian McKay

5 Landscapes of Injustice
A New Perspective on the Internment and Dispossession of Japanese Canadians
Edited by Jordan Stanger-Ross

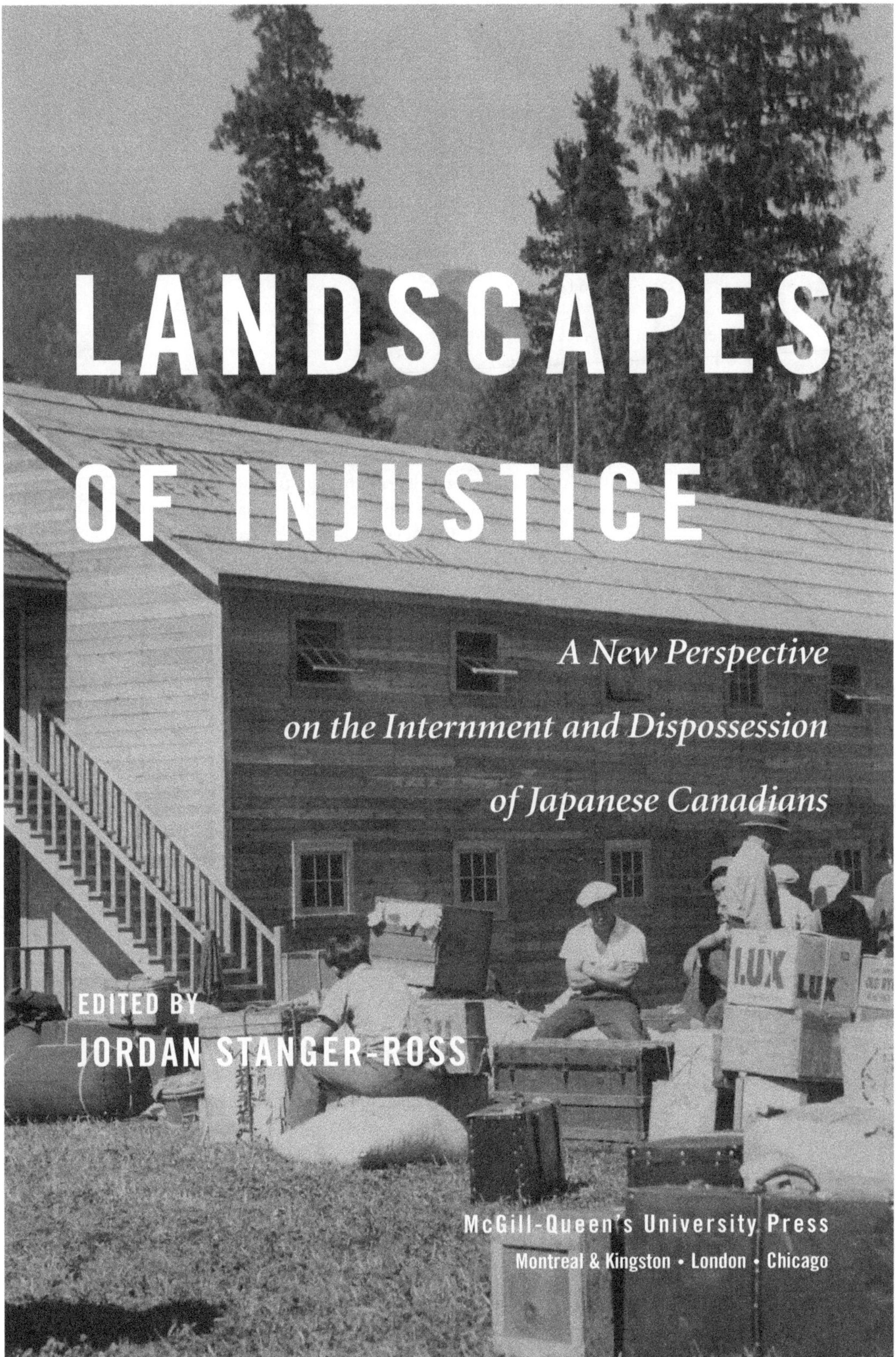

LANDSCAPES OF INJUSTICE

A New Perspective on the Internment and Dispossession of Japanese Canadians

EDITED BY
JORDAN STANGER-ROSS

McGill-Queen's University Press
Montreal & Kingston • London • Chicago

This book emerges from the work of the Landscapes of Injustice Research Collective.

ISBN 978-0-2280-0171-3 (cloth)
ISBN 978-0-2280-0172-0 (paper)
ISBN 978-0-2280-0307-6 (ePDF)

Legal deposit third quarter 2020
Bibliothèque nationale du Québec

This book has been published with the help of a grant from the Canadian Federation for the Humanities and Social Sciences, through the Awards to Scholarly Publications Program, using funds provided by the Social Sciences and Humanities Research Council of Canada. Funding was also received from the University of Victoria and the Landscapes of Injustice project.

Funded by the Government of Canada | Financé par le gouvernement du Canada | Canada

Canada Council for the Arts | Conseil des arts du Canada

We acknowledge the support of the Canada Council for the Arts.

Nous remercions le Conseil des arts du Canada de son soutien.

Library and Archives Canada Cataloguing in Publication

Title: Landscapes of injustice : a new perspective on the internment and dispossession of Japanese Canadians / edited by Jordan Stanger-Ross.
Names: Stanger-Ross, Jordan, editor.
Series: Rethinking Canada in the world ; 5.
Description: Series statement: Rethinking Canada in the world ; 5 | Includes bibliographical references and index.
Identifiers: Canadiana (print) 20200197592 | Canadiana (ebook) 20200197665 | ISBN 9780228001720 (softcover) | ISBN 9780228001713 (hardcover) | ISBN 9780228003076 (PDF)
Subjects: LCSH: Eviction—Canada—History—20th century. | LCSH: Canada—Race relations—History—20th century. | LCSH: Racism—Canada—History—20th century. | CSH: Japanese Canadians—Social conditions—20th century. | CSH: Japanese Canadians—Economic conditions—20th century. | CSH: Japanese Canadians—Canada—History—20th century. | CSH: Japanese Canadians—Evacuation and relocation, 1942-1945.

Classification: LCC FC106.J3 L36 2020 | DDC 971/.004956—dc23

CONTENTS

FIGURES

NOTE ON LANDSCAPES OF INJUSTICE

This book is the result of the collective work and resources of Landscapes of Injustice. Supported by a Partnership Grant of the Social Sciences and Humanities Research Council of Canada, Landscapes of Injustice is a seven-year project on the dispossession of Japanese Canadians. Our research collective is united by the conviction that this history still matters. The dispossession is a story about the violation of human and civil rights at a time of perceived insecurity, about measures taken in the name of national defence that made no one safer, about the enduring harms of mass displacement and the loss of home, and about the resilience of people confronting injustice.

We comprise dozens of individuals – academics, community leaders, museum professionals, programmers, students, and teachers – as well as institutions realizing the benefits of multidisciplinary and multisector collaboration. Participating institutions include the Canadian Museum of Immigration at Pier 21, the Immigration and Ethnic History Society, the Japanese Canadian Cultural Centre, Library and Archives Canada, the National Association of Japanese Canadians, the Nikkei National Museum and Cultural Centre, the OAH/JAAS Historians' Collaborative Committee, the Royal British Columbia Museum, Ryerson University, the Urban History Association, the University of Alberta, the University of Winnipeg, Simon Fraser University, the Vancouver Japanese Language School and Japanese Hall, and the University of Victoria, our host and headquarters. We are thankful to our community council, comprising established and emerging leaders in the Japanese Canadian community, and the members of our academic advisory board.

ABBREVIATIONS

BCA	British Columbia Archives, Victoria
CVA	City of Vancouver Archives
Buck Fonds	Frank E. Buck Fonds, UBC Archives, Vancouver
Héritage	Héritage Project, canadiana.ca
LoIOH	Landscapes of Injustice Oral History Collection, University of Victoria
LAC	Library and Archives Canada, Ottawa
NNM	Nikkei National Museum, Burnaby
Mackenzie Fonds	MG 27-IIB5, Library and Archives Canada
McPherson Fonds	Glenn W. McPherson Fonds, UBC Rare Books and Special Collections
Morishita Collection	Morishita Family Collection (Nikkei National Museum)
Shears Papers	Frank Gould Shears Papers, Thomas Fisher Rare Book Library, University of Toronto
RBSC	Rare Books and Special Collections, University of British Columbia
VLA	Veterans Land Act

LANDSCAPES
OF INJUSTICE

INTRODUCTION

Jordan Stanger-Ross with Kaitlin Findlay, Eiji Okawa, Yasmin Railton, Josh van Es, and Trevor Wideman and the Landscapes of Injustice Research Collective

In 1942, the Canadian government uprooted and interned all people of Japanese descent living in coastal British Columbia. The following year, it authorized the sale of everything that they had been forced to leave behind. As a result, when Canada's internment era finally ended in 1949, Japanese Canadians had nothing to return to. Their homes, farms, businesses, fishing vessels, cars, family pets, personal belongings – in short, everything that they had been unable to take with them – were gone. Because of the forced sale of real estate, no historic Japanese Canadian neighbourhoods remain. The loss of all of their personal belongings obliterated the sense of home that Japanese Canadians had built over generations. The uprooting and dispossession transformed the geography of British Columbia: hundreds of localities where Japanese Canadians had made their lives would, without the dispossession, have been very differently comprised, understood, and remembered.[1]

This book emerges from a collective effort to observe, from a new perspective, Canada's mass uprooting and internment of Japanese Canadians on the basis of race. This perspective centres on the dispossession – by theft, vandalism, neglect, and forced sale – of property. All forms of property, not just real estate, were taken. Families lost heirlooms and everyday possessions. They lost decades of investment and labour. As a result of the dispossession, Japanese Canadians also lost opportunities, neighbourhoods, and communities. They lost retirements, livelihoods, and educations. But, Japanese Canadians also responded. They responded by preserving and rebuilding home in the face of dispossession. They responded by sneaking aboard trains to internment more luggage and money than was officially permitted. They sometimes cultivated relationships with the officials responsible for their material well-being and sometimes exploded in outrage. Japanese Canadians responded in court, in print, and in public. They demanded an accounting of state wrongdoing that exceeded any exigencies of war.

When their property was forcibly sold by government officials, Japanese Canadians were credited with the funds. Officials opened thousands of files, one for each dispossessed person, and recorded in massive ledger books the debits and credits against their accounts. But owners had no role in setting the terms of the sales and lost the autonomy to decide not to sell. In a further indignity and injustice, long remembered within the community, they were denied any government relief until they first exhausted virtually all of their remaining capital. Forcibly isolated in places of scarce employment and barred from reinvesting in real estate, they were required to use the funds from the sale of their property to cover their basic sustenance in sites of internment.[2] Japanese Canadians thus saw one of their worst fears realized: all of their assets would "dwindle and vanish" during the internment leaving them destitute and forced to begin from nothing in the reconstruction of their material lives.[3]

Many people are implicated in this wrongdoing. Ian Mackenzie, member of Parliament for Vancouver Centre and the British Columbia representative in Canada's wartime cabinet, was perhaps the most influential political advocate of the dispossession. First as a provincial politician and then federally, Mackenzie for decades sought the exclusion of Asians from the province. "Economically we cannot combat with them; racially we cannot assimilate them," he told local newspapers in 1922, "hence we must exclude them from our midst and prohibit them for owning land."[4] Two decades later, the war in the Pacific gave Mackenzie the opportunity to pursue in federal policy these longstanding aspirations. In early 1942, he was a key advocate in cabinet for the uprooting, internment, and incarceration of the entire Japanese Canadian population from coastal British Columbia, later assuring the public that he "would not remain 24 hours in any government or any party which allows the Japanese on BC shores."[5] In April 1942, as Japanese Canadian farmers scrambled to lease or sell their lands in advance of their impending uprooting, Mackenzie instead pushed for the federal acquisition of hundreds of their properties, which he hoped to see distributed to veterans returning from war.[6] Following directly from his suggestion, cabinet passed Order in Council 5523 in June 1942, threatening a fine of $1,000 and six months in prison for any Japanese Canadian making private arrangements for the disposition of their own farms and authorizing officers of the Soldier Settlement Board to appraise them.[7] Justifying the policies to a constituent, Mackenzie explained that, "their country should never have been Canada ... I do not believe the Japanese are an assimilable race."[8] The dispossession cannot be understood without an account of such views, the people who espoused them, and the role they played in moving policy.[9]

In perpetrating these harms, elected officials like Mackenzie acted with significant public support, particularly in British Columbia. Citizens wrote to their representatives urging the complete and permanent erasure of the Japanese Canadian community from the province. Once Japanese Canadians were uprooted – and even sometimes before – neighbours rushed into their homes, stealing everything of value and often destroying much of the rest. After officials seized the assets, thousands bid on Japanese Canadian–owned real estate and clamoured for deals at auctions of their personal effects. These acts of complicity have been shrouded in silence; scholarship and public discussion has largely avoided the widely shared responsibility for Japanese Canadian losses.[10]

Despite the avarice and, indeed, evil evident in the dispossession, the policy was also governed, in part, by the recognition that Japanese Canadians were rights-holding citizens whose property deserved protection.[11] Indeed, the seizure of property was initially enacted as a protective trust.[12] Even in the midst of betraying this promise, central figures at the time – people who attended high-level policy meetings, wrote orders-in-council, and oversaw the administration of law – appear to have taken seriously the government's protective role. Ephraim H. Coleman, wartime undersecretary of state, to whom the Vancouver Office of the Custodian reported, wrote a colleague in 1942, "I do not think it was ever contemplated by the Government that they would deprive the Japanese owners of their property or the proceeds thereof."[13] In March 1942, he helped to specify, in law, that the government held Japanese Canadian–owned property as a trustee acting in their benefit. John Erskine Read also participated in making internment law (he wrote Order in Council 1665, authorizing the uprooting and internment, and worked closely throughout the period with the prime minister). While he felt that internment was justified, Read also believed, at least in 1942, that the Canadian government was required by law and common decency to hold their property in "benevolent trusteeship."[14] To understand the dispossession, we must comprehend not only the naked racism of a figure like Mackenzie but also the motives and actions of those like Read and Coleman: why did they remain in the room, playing crucial law-making and administrative roles, even as trusteeship was so badly betrayed?[15]

The hypocrisy of a state (and officials) purportedly committed to principles of equal citizenship and fair play, on one hand, and perpetrating blatant racist injustice, on the other, incensed many Japanese Canadians when they learned of their dispossession. Few expressed this tension with more explicit anger than Aya Suzuki, who wrote twice from internment in Slocan City after she received notice that her property had been sold in early 1944. Suzuki's family had purchased burial plots in Vancouver, she told officials: "isn't that enough to assure you that our hopes are to grow with Canada and die on her soil?"[16] She reminded them that at the time of her uprooting "your men had told us" that the Custodian's control of property "was to protect us ... But now you say ... this land has been sold":

> You have gone against our wishes, also without even consulting us, as any citizen of Canada would have the privilege of giving assent or refusal ... I feel before God that we have the right to contest it. After all what are we (Canada) fighting for? Not that same treatment the Nazi's [*sic*] gave the Jews be practiced here in our own country! But that Canadian citizens be free to exercise their rights and to contribute to the betterment of this land of our birth.[17]

For Suzuki, the comparison seemed to play a double role. She suggests that Canadian policies resemble those of the Nazis and yet also that they cannot – that her birthright as Canadian is meaningful, even sacred. Japanese Canadians, therefore, cannot be the victims of the kinds of policies directed at German Jews.[18] The comparison shames policy-makers by drawing Canada into association with Nazi Germany while simultaneously demanding that they uphold the differences between the two. For Suzuki Canada was not merely a racist state, even if her experience suggested that it was very much that. The history of dispossession needs also to seek comprehension of the complex and varied Japanese Canadian responses to the harms perpetrated against them.

Unlike most edited collections in the field of history, this book arises from the sustained efforts of a single research collective and presents its integrated results. All of the chapters, except two, are coauthored by the Landscapes of Injustice Research Collective, denoting the changing cast of seventy-odd people that since 2014 has been working collaboratively to unearth and tell this history.[19] We collectively conceived this project, applied for funds to support it, developed and modified ongoing research activities, and debated the meaning of our findings and the language in which to express them. In accordance with its origins, the book has an unusual introduction. In addition to presenting the chapters that constitute this book, I seek to convey the foundations (laid in scores of meetings, some 200 research presentations, and more than thirty publications) that underlie this volume's summative articulation of our conclusions.[20]

As a partnership – comprised of academics from across Canada, museum and archival professionals, teachers, major Japanese Canadian organizations, and established and emerging community leaders – our project has fostered a specific way of knowing and sharing a history of injustice. It seems to me (as its architect and lead researcher) that our project has been characterized by diverse ways of knowing that, while sometimes in tension, enrich rather than contradict one another. This history is known to some members of our collective through the sheer force of an injustice directly experienced. We are perhaps the last large-scale project that will have the opportunity to work with people who lived through these harms and can recall them vividly: Art Miki as well as Tosh and Mary Kitagawa, in particular, brought the lived experience of the dispossession to our project. Their various responses, expressed in circumspect optimism, dark humour, and sheer outrage, have shaped our work and greatly enriched our understandings of this past. And yet, it is simultaneously the case that, until we began our work – research that recovered hundreds of thousands of relevant archival documents, digitized thousands of records of real estate sale, and recorded more than 100 interviews – very little was known about the dispossession. Japanese Canadians who lived with the loss of property understood its impacts upon their families but neither the most influential scholarly histories, such as Patricia Roy's *Triumph of Citizenship*, nor the most compelling community-based accounts, such as

Ken Adachi's *The Enemy That Never Was*, explained why or how the dispossession happened, detailed the range of responses to the policy, or analyzed its effects. In the pages that follow we convey a historical understanding that has emerged from collectively holding complex ways of knowing. Our research is motivated by both the starkness of an injustice experienced and the struggle to understand a complex historical record.

The stark injustice of the dispossession revealed itself especially when members of our collective, or indeed archival sources, conveyed the harms brought upon Japanese Canadians during the internment era. Mary Kitagawa (née Murakami), a member of our community council, conveyed to our collective her memories of her father's incarceration in 1942, when she was seven years of age:

> We were prepared because [a local official] had told us that we should be prepared to have my father taken away. So when the RCMP came my father lined us all up in our living room, in order of our birth, and, um, tap – you know, tapped us all on our head and said to my mum and the children, "now be strong, I'll be back soon." And, told us children to be good to mum and to help as much as we could. And then he went out and we followed him.
>
> And as he approached the truck … the RCMP officer told him to hurry up. And then, as my father was getting into the, truck, the RCMP officer shoved him on, and, and my father fell on his stomach … hit his face on the, the flatbed of the truck. But my father jumped right up. To reassure us that he was fine. And he kept smiling and saying, "I, I'm okay, I'm okay" … And so … as he … was being driven out of our property, the RCMP officer jerked the gears in the truck and my father almost fell again … the girls, the four of us, ran after the truck, you know, crying and waving, and saying … "Daddy, Daddy, come back." And as he was driven away and he disappeared … into a void.
>
> But in my … seven-year-old mind … as my father was being, taken, onto the truck, I saw the gun, in the holster of the RCMP officer, and … I thought for sure that he was being – because of the way that he was being manhandled – I thought for sure that my father was being taken away to be shot. And it was a terrifying, terrifying time.[21]

The rest of the Murakamis were soon uprooted as well, taken separately to the holding stalls in Vancouver's Hastings Park and then banished from the "protected area." They were reunited with Mary's father five months later in a shack in Alberta, where he – a wealthy proprietor before the war – accepted labour as a farmhand. Their dirt-floor shack, adjacent to the pigpen, was so blanketed with flies that its raw wood exterior appeared black in the summer. After begging leave to relocate to a mass internment site in British Columbia, the family moved to the Slocan Valley, where thousands of

Japanese Canadians inhabited makeshift camps. A family of wealth, comfort, and accomplishment before the war, the Murakamis never regained what they lost.

Listening, I felt the truth of Mary's account in the heat of my cheeks and the tightness of my throat. Her story filled me with shame. I felt simultaneously estranged from and uncomfortably connected with the perpetrators of this harm against a child who grew up close to my home, on a beautiful local island where I vacation with my own children. The revulsion that we feel at such accounts and the judgment that they inspire spring from truths indispensable in telling a history of injustice. Doing this work in partnership with community, as well as educators who will tell this history to museum-goers and school children, has kept the moral truths of this history plainly in view.[22] We need those lessons from these pasts.

At the same time, our project – one of the largest assemblages of academics and community members ever to collectively engage the Canadian past – sat with the historical materials. We pored through records of the state and those preserved by members of the community. We traced title on properties in four sites of study. We listened to the people who remember this history, including bystanders and witnesses, and to their children. The result of this work is new analysis that could only come from research. We linked, more exhaustively than any past scholars, the immigrant experiences of the Issei generation (first generation immigrants from Japan), conveyed in their own language and their own sources, with the history of the dispossession. We reckoned with the legal and administrative processes that made the forced sales possible. We sought to understand, on the basis of their own writings, what property – and the loss of home – meant to Japanese Canadians. We identified key officials responsible for the policies and analyzed their own understandings of their actions. We researched the material harms of dispossession. We laboured to convey the fruits of long and exhaustive research, in which truth is seldom searing in its clarity.

Contemplating a very different historical injustice, but in ways that are instructive in this case too, Ira Berlin reflects, "if the evil of slavery was unambiguous, the lives of the men and women – both black and white – who lived through the era were as complicated as any."[23] Berlin's integration of evil and complication in one elegant sentence should not obscure the real ongoing tension between different forms of historical truth. Political violence makes hard history and academic perspectives do not always integrate easily with knowledge held within the affected communities. Collectively and individually, members of the Landscapes of Injustice Research Collective had to learn to do this work together. We had to learn to trust that our collective efforts would amplify our diverse perspectives on this past rather than pitting them in competition. In the end, we did not seek to erase or somehow overcome differences in how this history is viewed and understood but rather to work creatively within the space that tension creates.[24] In the pages that follow I hope that readers similarly struggle to find their own balance within a history of injustice. Such pasts should be unsettling.

Revisiting a history well told

Given the gravity of this history, it is appropriate that we are not the first to give it sustained scrutiny or careful expression. Japanese Canadian artists, scholars, and activists have for decades drawn attention to the mistreatment of their community by the Canadian state.[25] At the same time, an interdisciplinary scholarship – beginning with sociological research in the 1940s – has conveyed the internment era as evidence of Canadian racism, an infringement of constitutional rights, a catalyst to postwar reconsiderations of Canadian pluralism, and a key episode within the memories, gendered and family histories, and political consciousness of Japanese Canadians.[26] Official state histories, too, have engaged the topic. In 1988, after almost two decades of research and activism by a mobilized Japanese Canadian community, the Canadian federal government followed its US counterpart by acknowledging its wrongdoing of the 1940s and issuing Canada's first political apology, characterizing the era as an exceptionally dark chapter of the Canadian past.[27]

The apology did not close the books on the internment era. Rather, the acknowledgment of wrongdoing and the larger "terrain of memory" from which the internment era is viewed have themselves become generative subjects of critical analysis.[28] Official and community-based histories have also continued, perhaps particularly in recent years as the political moment seems, once again, to draw logics of national security into increasingly explicit connection with the politics of race. The Canadian Museum of History, an impressive and authoritative exhibition of the nation's past, and the Nikkei National Museum, the most important Japanese Canadian heritage institution, both continue to tell the story of the internment era as an integral part of Canadian history. Spin-offs from the Landscapes of Injustice project have contributed as well: in 2019 a former postdoctoral fellow in our oral history cluster, Heather Read, initiated and led *Being Japanese Canadian: Reflections on a Broken World*, a Royal Ontario Museum exhibit that interrupts visitors' experiences of canonical Canadian art with an installation inspired by responses to internment and dispossession. Our project also initiated *Writing Wrongs*, a Virtual Museum of Canada project to tell the history of Japanese Canadian internment in connection with the present politics of migration. Meanwhile, Mark Sakamoto's *Forgiveness* won the CBC's annual Canada Reads contest in 2018, an award that will bring tens of thousands of new readers to his memoir on the legacies of internment. Finally, in March 2019, Jam 3, a design studio in Toronto, and the National Film Board of Canada launched *East of the Rockies*, an augmented reality iPhone application created collaboratively with Joy Kogawa, the internment era's iconic literary voice, that communicates this history in digital spectral form.

Whereas our research collective has focused on the dispossession of property, prior histories and memories of Japanese Canadians in the 1940s have tended to emphasize the uprooting and internment of people. And for good reason. On 4 March 1942, three pressured months after the bombing of Pearl Harbor and Canada's declaration of war on Japan, members of the federal cabinet passed Order in Council 1665, creating the British Columbia Security Commission. As its first and fundamental duty, the commission was instructed to "plan, supervise and direct" the mass uprooting of "all persons of the Japanese race" from the "protected areas" of British Columbia, which had previously been specified to extend one hundred miles inland from the Pacific coast, a geography home to almost 22,000 Japanese Canadians.[29] The commission, headed by business tycoon Austin Taylor, had the power to pass bylaws, to mandate the "time and order" of the uprooting of groups and individuals, to determine their mode of transport, and to oversee "housing, feeding, [and] care" at sites of internment. In the months that followed, under the authority of the commission, Canada began a seven-year mass internment of people, three quarters of them born or naturalized British subjects of Canada, on the basis of their purported racial character.

These provisions and their implementation constituted, a "tragedy of democracy" as conveyed in the title of historian Greg Robinson's book on the topic. Eschewing categories of citizenship and nationality, Order in Council 1665 is a striking example of racial law in Canada. This dimension of the policy, though well established in prior works (such as Sunahara's foundational book *The Politics of Racism*) and in public memory (including via the 1988 apology) merits ongoing engagement. Although there was ample precedent for racism in Canadian law – including, for example, the entire apparatus of "Indian" policy, exclusions in immigration law, and restrictions in labour, housing, public accommodation, schooling, and political participation – the internment of Japanese Canadians constituted a major reassertion of the priority of race.[30]

At the same time, the story of Japanese Canadians did not begin or end with the internment era nor should their experience be defined by it.[31] Japanese migrants began to arrive (many of them via Hawaii) en mass to the Indigenous territories comprising British Columbia near the close of the 1800s; their numbers reached a crescendo in the first decade of the twentieth century, with more than 11,000 arriving between 1906 and 1908.[32] These newcomers, like others during the first great wave of mass immigration to Canada, followed in the footsteps of founding figures who built economic opportunity in British Columbia in the decades prior while contributing to the displacement of Indigenous people.[33]

The first known Japanese migrant to Canada, Manzo Nagano, stayed ashore in New Westminster in 1877 when the ship on which he had arrived departed for Japan.[34] Borrowing a boat with an Italian partner, Nagano was likely the first Japanese fisher in the Fraser River and hence the forerunner of thousands in the half-century that followed (including over 1,300 who would have their fishing vessels confiscated and sold in 1942).[35] By the mid-1880s, a steady stream of migrants from Japan, mostly young men, arrived annually in Canada's colonizing west coast, where they found employment in the fishing, mining, lumber, and construction industries, in particular. Many among them envisioned only a temporary sojourn in North America. Economic opportunity in British Columbia allowed migrants to return to their home prefectures and towns with sufficient wealth to pursue dreams, often of land ownership, that would have been unattainable without their earnings in an international labour market.[36] Thousands, however, settled in the province.

In time, hubs of an immigrant community took shape within the burgeoning economy. In 1887, Shinkichi Tamura, who would become one of the magnates of the immigrant community before returning to Japan, opened a toy shop at the corner of Cordova and Carrall in Vancouver's East End, helping to lay the foundations for a Japanese Canadian neighbourhood that would be the largest in the country.[37] Part of a bustling and diverse immigrant section of the city, the Powell Street neighbourhood soon housed hundreds of Japanese Canadian businesses, lodging rooms, and residences. In 1910, a Hompa Buddhist Temple was erected on Cordova Street, a landmark of the deepening roots of the Japanese Canadian community.[38]

Temporary migrants and settlers weighed many factors in both understanding British Columbia and choosing their paths within it, but racism was an unavoidable consideration. Joining a settlement predicated on the displacement of Indigenous people and intended by its leaders as white and British, Japanese Canadians were never immune to its foundational racism. As one immigrant to Vancouver's Powell Street neighbourhood later reflected, "ever since the Japanese arrived in BC, they have had to endure persistent anti-Nikkei campaigns" in which "absurd rumours" coloured public sentiment and motivated exclusionary law at every level of government.[39] The arrival of the SS *Kumeric* to British Columbia in July 1907 marked a pivotal moment in this history. "Hundreds of Mikado's Subjects Reached Vancouver," ran a headline in the *Vancouver Province* on the day the ship anchored in Burrard Inlet. "The decks of the steamer," reported the paper, "literally swarmed with the little brown men." Speculating that the passengers (whose actual number included more than 1,100 Japanese migrants) represented "the advance guard of a host soon to locate British Columbia," the paper noted that the ship "attracted no little attention."[40] Indeed, sounding alarm at an impending "invasion" of the province, the Asiatic Exclusion League spent the next month preparing a major Vancouver demonstration to protest the Pacific arrivals. When it occurred, on 7 September 1907, the demonstration escalated into rioting, with exclusionists ransacking Chinese and Japanese Canadian businesses and homes in the East End of the city, causing thousands of dollars of damage and sparking international controversy.[41] In response to the riots, Canadian officials chose to accommodate racism by arranging with Japan for the restriction of Japanese emigration.

Scholars have traced white supremacy in British Columbia for almost a century prior to the internment of Japanese Canadians. Inequality – in housing and labour markets, schooling, political participation, and the application of law – made race a fault line of British Columbian society. The province was a key site of the "hemispheric Orientalism" that historian Erika Lee sees as definitive of North America's expansive gateway to the Pacific world, participating in the much larger processes by which "Asian migrants were racialized as dangerous and unassimilable foreigners around the world during the late nineteenth- and early twentieth-centuries."[42] And yet race was also a changing, uneven, and unpredictable historical experience. Sometimes, as historian Patricia Roy has charted, the "Oriental Question," was a centrepiece of public and political discussion while at other times race slipped from the spotlight and "British Columbians were preoccupied with other problems."[43] Further, the politics of the "Oriental Question" changed over time, sometimes reflecting class interests (when, for example, employers favoured Asian immigration and organized labour opposed it) and sometimes cutting across ostensible lines of economic self-interest. All the while, Japanese immigrants and their children routinely encountered and built relations with British Columbians of other origins. Japanese Canadians lived on diverse streets and laboured in mixed company; friendships and alliances crossed racial lines, and Japanese Canadian neighbourhoods and stores attracted visitors of all backgrounds, often seeking imported merchandise from East Asia.[44]

Renisa Mawani ascribes such complications to a "deep paradox" of economic and social relations in colonial British Columbia. Economic production not only tolerated heterogeneity and plurality but explicitly commodified and valourized it: canners hiring within racialized and gendered international markets for labour, for example, specifically sought the purportedly dexterous hands of Asian women for precise manual tasks. These interests collided with widely held (indeed even by canners themselves) expectations that British Columbia was being established as British, respectable, and white.[45] Timothy Stanley, tackling similar tensions from another perspective, has described British Columbia as built upon systems of racial dominance and yet characterized by daily circumventions of racism.[46]

Meanwhile, a Japanese Canadian community took shape, both in relation to the mainstream currents of British Columbia society and independently of them. Contributor Eiji Okawa demonstrates here (and previously) that the cultural lives of Japanese immigrants were defined both in relation to and despite racism: although constantly conscious of their place in British Columbian society, Japanese immigrants, members of the Issei generation, were connected by a traditional sense of common "Japaneseness." His and Audrey Kobayashi's chapters in this volume emphasize that migrants and their children – the Canadian-born Nisei – did not make their lives in isolation but rather as part of Japanese familial and communal structures of obligation and trust.

Even as these traditional cultural forms continued to exert influence, the community changed significantly. For two decades, the restriction of Japanese immigration did not apply to the wives and children of Japanese Canadians already residing in the country. Partly as a consequence of this policy, a settlement of male sojourners with strong connections to Japan became, in the course of three decades, a multigenerational Canadian community. By the time of their uprooting from the west coast, 60 per cent of Japanese Canadians were native to British Columbia. In a province awash with newcomers, they stood out among settlers as particularly rooted in place.[47] In the face of persistent discrimination in the labour market, including the campaign to reduce their access to fishing licences, Japanese Canadians diversified their lives and economic activities, transforming Fraser Valley land long regarded as nonarable into thriving berry farms, establishing a hub of commercial activity on Vancouver's Powell Street, and finding other niches in the economy and society of British Columbia.[48] By the 1930s, Japanese Canadians farmed the Okanagan, fished the west coast of Vancouver Island and the northern stretches of the mainland coast, and owned (and worked) lumberyards in the Comox Valley. They laboured in mines, cooked meals, ran groceries, gardened, cut hair, and owned small businesses in locales throughout coastal British Columbia.[49] In 1935, after an extensive survey of the Japanese Canadian population, UBC master's student Rigenda Sumida (a visiting student from Japan, one of the categories of entry then admissible) noted the diversity of Japanese Canadian lives. Their average standard of living was lower than the population as a whole, but they had nonetheless achieved considerable economic stability. Countering racist caricatures, Sumida reflected, "They are human beings ... as intelligent and progressive as any race on earth, and they are not content to simply exist, but ... desire the comforts of fine homes, automobiles, radios, and all the other articles or services which Western civilization provides."[50]

The tensions that emerged from sustained invitation to Japanese-immigrant labour and persistent discrimination against Japanese Canadians, from immigrants building a community on their own terms while simultaneously responding as British subjects to Canadian racism, constitute the social and political bedrock on which the dispossession occurred. On the eve of Canada's entry into the war in the Pacific, Japanese Canadians were conscious of both injustices they had suffered and the significant but fragile gains they had achieved. When Thomas Shoyama, the brilliant editor of the Japanese Canadian weekly *The New Canadian* urged his readers in June 1941 to purchase Victory Bonds in demonstration of their loyalty to Canada, he reminded his readers that "as a Japanese racial minority in British Columbia we recognize the shortcomings of our Canadian democracy." Nonetheless, he wrote:

> if we have not always enjoyed the full benefits of democratic freedom and equality in our native and adopted land, we have not come to believe thereby that these are only empty phrases ... even more than the average Canadian we realize that [they] are charged with concrete meaning and significance.[51]

Shoyama's readers would have understood the background to these thoughts. Japanese immigrants could, and did, naturalize as British subjects; those born in Canada were British at birth. The remaining quarter of the population, unnaturalized immigrants, nonetheless had rights in Canada, including of land ownership, denied to their counterparts in the United States. And yet all Japanese Canadians in British Columbia were barred from the franchise on the basis of race, all were subjected to myriad restrictions of their social, political, and economic participation. In this context, a delegation of Japanese Canadians could travel to Ottawa in 1936 to demand voting rights, be supported in their campaign by a distinguished lawyer in Vancouver, and be granted a formal audience with parliamentarians. But that same historical context also meant that politicians could defend the status quo on the basis of their views that "to cross an individual of the white race with an individual of a yellow race is to produce, in nine cases out of ten, a mongrel wastrel with the worst qualities of both races."[52] The division between full and second-class citizens as well as the readiness to legislate and police this division on the basis of race, remained in place in December of 1941.

The contribution of *Landscapes of Injustice*, within the many tellings of this past, has been to look at the decade that followed from a perspective that places the seizure and dispossession of property at the centre of the story. Most of the remaining introduction is dedicated to conveying the summative results of our approach, organized into the four parts of this book: (1) The Deliberate Killing of Home, (2) Dispossession Required Sustained Work, (3) Reasoning Wrong, and (4) Dispossession is Permanent. Seeing the internment era from this perspective forces reconsideration of its origins, unfolding, and legacies: in sum, of its history. Before turning to these claims, however, I sketch three contextual considerations that, to various extents, helped to set the stage for these integrative reflections of the Landscapes of Injustice Collective.

A layered historical context

The history of Japanese Canadians is not the only relevant context for the story of the dispossession. To begin, Canada interned other civilians during the 1940s; in addition to the 22,000 Japanese Canadians, a comparatively small number of people of Italian (632) and German (847) origins (some of them naturalized British subjects of Canada suspected, often on flimsy grounds, of sympathy for or connection with enemy powers) were interned, along with more than one hundred Communists.[53] However, as Kaitlin Findlay and Nicholas Blomley observe, the selective nature of these internments – the fact that they were not implemented en masse on the basis of race – meant that property could usually be entrusted to family and friends who remained free and no large-scale dispossession occurred.[54] As a result, rather than these most proximate internments, our collective was more influenced by discussion of three historical cases of large-scale displacement and property loss: settler colonialism, the incarceration of Japanese Americans, and the 1930s "Aryanization" of the German economy.[55]

The land that Japanese Canadians owned and occupied in coastal British Columbia was overrun in the "Great Land Rush" that, as illustrated by historian John Weaver (and earlier Cole Harris), transformed vast Indigenous territories into geographies of colonial property (a process that, in addition to colonial settlement and the demarcation of reserves, involved surveying, mapping, title registration, and the codification of property law). In producing "real property" in land, this process dispossessed, relying upon and reinforcing racialized categorical distinctions among people. As legal historian Brenna Bhandar puts it, "there cannot be a history of private property … that is not at the same time a history of land appropriation … property became the *sine qua non* of civilized life and society, an axiom sharpened at the expense of Indigenous peoples throughout the colonial world," including British Columbia.[56]

The imprint of colonialism is evident within the history of the dispossession of Japanese Canadians. The racial laws of the 1940s and the racist perspectives espoused by key politicians were legitimated and entrenched in a Canadian political system that had demarcated "Indians" as an area of jurisdiction in its 1867 constitution. Colonialism trained Canadian lawmakers and courts to regulate and adjudicate on the basis of race.[57]

At times, the records convey their colonial context in acute and explicit terms, as for example in the dispossession of farms in Matsqui, southeast of Vancouver, where competing visions of who could and should embody the colonial improvement of land overlay the ongoing displacement of Indigenous people.[58] Ivan Barnet, the district superintendent for the Soldier Settlement Board in British Columbia toured Japanese Canadian–owned farms in the area in the spring of 1942. Barnet, one of the board's most senior officials, was there to survey lands that he, along with Ian Mackenzie, hoped would soon be transferred to veterans returning from war. A year later, this scheme came to fruition in the conveyance of 769 Japanese Canadian–owned properties to the director of the Veterans' Land Act in a transaction deliberately and drastically below reasonable market value.[59] When Barnet toured the Matsqui area in May 1942, however, Japanese Canadian farmers continued to work their land. Federal law passed in March had already authorized their uprooting and internment, but it also stipulated that the farms would be protected for the duration of the war and then returned to their owners. Barnet had a different future in mind. "We would be making a big error," Barnet felt, "if we ever permit these people to establish themselves in Canada again." Instead, he believed that "we must maintain the Pacific Coast as a white man's country, and … educate the white man to realize that he can make a comfortable living" by working the land. Successful cultivation of land, he believed, would require "the white man" to change "his line of thinking" and to reclaim agricultural occupations, thereby foiling what, in Barnet's imagining, was the "Japanese" effort to "overrun the lands of other [i.e. white] Nations."[60]

One owner in Matsqui, Kisaku Nishimoto, had a very different view of the matter. Nishmoto's dealings with the Custodian of Enemy Property – which sold his farm without consent and denied him the funds to support his son, sick with tuberculosis in New Denver – demonstrate the profound harms of the dispossession. But they also convey the layered injustices of colonialism. Protesting its sale, Nishimoto argued that his farm had been,

> made productive in the highest degree from a wild, neglected land, where the water had covered [it] most of the year making it only fit for hunting ducks … It was really … sweat and blood that … made this land a highly productive one.[61]

Indeed, having purchased the property ten years prior, Nishimoto dug 10,000 feet of ditches to drain the property and render it arable.[62] The injustice that he felt stemmed in part from the breach of a colonial order in which he had been a rule-abiding participant. Having purchased and worked "wild" land, having invested his labour, time, and dreams for the future, he now protested the very real harms that resulted from the dispossession.

Neither Nishimoto nor officials in the Office of the Custodian were concerned, in this exchange, that the marshes of Matsqui, cleared in years of hard labour, had made possible, since time immemorial, the flourishing of *má:th*, a root vegetable that was associated with the people of the area, the Máthxwi, and that gave the locality its name. Neither were concerned that the marshes were also renowned, for far longer than the entire history of colonial settlement in North America, for the "easy portage" they provided through the region. Neither remarked that Japanese Canadians were dispossessors before they were disposed. Further, the displacement of the Máthxwi people was not an event of the distant past in 1944 but an ongoing reality. In 1867 the British Columbian colonial government unilaterally reduced Matsqui's original 6,000-acre Indian Reserve to a mere eighty, and at a 1913 royal commission, representatives of the Matsqui struggled (unsuccessfully) to have those lands returned. In the 1940s, the Coast Salish system of governance (the potlatch) as well as the sacred winter ceremonial dances (tamanawas) remained outlawed under the Indian Act. A 1927 amendment to the law forbid Indigenous people from raising funds to hire legal counsel to contest their dispossession in law. Decades after the internment of Japanese Canadians, the Matsqui continued to assert their rights to these lands upon which multiple, layered dispossessions had taken place.[63]

That Nishimoto overlooked the colonialism inherent in the clearing of the marshes is not surprising, nor does this reality in any way diminish the extent of the harms perpetrated against him and his family.[64] And yet, our collective has debated and learned from the colonial context of his ordeal. These discussions attuned our project to technologies – maps, market appraisals, and bureaucratic structures – shared by these two forms of dispossession. They attuned us to the importance of government promises, to the impacts of their betrayal, and to the uneven place of law in injustice. We have also recognized in the protests of Japanese Canadians in the 1940s their participation in a system of property that always distributed uneven benefit within a colonial society. At the same time, recognition of this context requires that we acknowledge the differences between the Japanese Canadian case and that of Indigenous people. The dispossession of the lands of Indigenous people was foundationally organized to destroy their political sovereignty and Indigenous systems of ownership. Japanese Canadians, by contrast, made their lives within the property regime of the Canadian state that would betray them in the 1940s.

Given its centrality to scholarly and public discussion in British Columbia (and across Canada) during the conduct of our project, settler colonialism drew particular attention from members of our collective.[65] But other historical intersections also shaped our work. The framing of the project reflected from the outset a largely implicit relation with the United States, where incarcerated Japanese Americans suffered significant economic losses, but no state-administered dispossession took place.

In the United States, the War Relocation Authority articulated in 1942 a policy of "maximum utilization of evacuee property in the national interests and protection and preservation of the interests and equity of the evacuees," a position close to the official line in Canada at the same time.[66] Americans appointed bureaucrats to implement this difficult administrative task, and they, like their Canadian counterparts, struggled against competing demands within the state and an opportunist public. However, the policy in the United States never transformed into a wholesale seizure and sale of all property on the basis of race. Rather, on 23 January 1943, just four days after Canada's federal government broke its promise of protection and declared its authority to sell the property of Japanese Canadians, the War Relocation Authority articulated a "basic policy" that officials in the United States would "serve not as substitute owner, director, or operator … but in an investigational, informational, and advisory capacity."[67] While many Japanese Americans lost property during their incarceration, others were able to return to their former homes or else to sell on their own terms.[68] Canadians are perhaps unaccustomed to seeing their own racist history cast into sharp relief by a somewhat less draconian approach south of the border.[69]

Recognition of the American counterexample attuned our researchers to the specific circumstances and processes that led to the dispossession in Canada and grounded our work in the reality that Canadian policy was not the inevitable result of war or the internment. It also oriented our research to the implications of the forced sale of property in particular, including those in policy (such as the duration of the internment to 1949 and the scale of Canada's deportation program in 1946, both of which flowed, in part, from the state-manufactured placelessness of Japanese Canadians) and those for individuals and families stripped permanently and against their will of their homes.

While consideration of the United States situates Canada's dispossession alongside policies that stopped short of the harms perpetrated here, the wider global politics of race in the same era pushes in a different direction. Aya Suzuki, shaming Canadian officials for their resemblance to National Socialists, gestured to a context that must be contemplated in the study of mass uprooting and internment on the basis of race in the 1940s. Suzuki's more specific claims, in protesting the sale of her property, find support in a generation of scholarship on "Aryanization," the removal of Jews from the economic life of Germany in the 1930s. While caution must be exercised in comparing genocide with a history in which the state sponsored not a single murder of a Japanese Canadian, analyses of the expropriation of Jewish property include striking parallels to what we found in Canadian archives. "Aryanization," like the dispossession of Japanese Canadians, was the work of the administrative state. It was a "social process" involving large numbers of beneficiaries and profiteers, including at local levels. There too, dispossession helped to fund a larger machine of injustice.[70] Such research also illustrates the ways in which, as Holocaust scholar Harold James argues, "stripping property was a way of stripping dignity and converting citizens into surplus people whose welfare and even existence could be a matter of passive indifference for the population at large."[71] For anyone long-immersed in studying the dispossession of Japanese Canadians, this reflection should ring chillingly true. It might have for Henry Forbes Angus, an assistant to the Canadian prime minister in 1943, who forcefully objected to the dispossession of the property of Japanese Canadians, arguing that it would "legalize acts of gross injustice and oppression" and encourage "seriously minded people" to compare Canadian policy to "the Nurnberg [*sic*] laws against the Jews."[72] Like Suzuki, Angus saw in Canada echoes of an archetype of state malfeasance as well as ideals of justice and equal citizenship that should have prevented the unnecessary harms that he observed.

In our discussions of settler colonialism, the incarceration of Japanese Americans, and the Aryanization of Germany, members of our collective debated what we might consider cousins to the dispossession of Japanese Canadians. As cousins they are not just comparators to the history we have studied but rather linked to it in their shared DNA. The various members of our collective, depending on the task at hand as well as their own scholarly and personal perspectives, have seen one or the other of these cousins as most relevant, most important, most closely related to their work. In the research claims that follow, and in the rest of the book, readers will find gestures to each of these cousins of the dispossession, places where each of them has influenced our thinking about the history we have studied together. Readers, will also, I imagine, contemplate other cousins to the history we tell, conceiving connections that we have not yet articulated or explored. As a collection, and in its four major research claims, this volume carefully renders the dispossession so that it can be understood and studied alongside such related and yet distinct historical injustices.

The Deliberate Killing of Home

A key argument – indeed the foundational argument – of our project is that the loss of home was a specific harm of the larger internment era, a harm to which Japanese Canadians made specific responses. This observation draws their experience into relation with an international scholarship on displaced people. Japanese Canadians were victims of "domicide," a term used by geographers Douglas Porteous and Sandra Smith to denote "the deliberate killing of home."[73] Porteous and Smith document a staggering range of examples (their book contains 200 cases drawn from seventy countries, including one passing mention of Japanese Canadians) in which victims have lost their homes as a result of deliberate human action, noting that "historical accounts often pass over domicide, with all its attendant misery, in a single phrase: the town was burned; three hundred villages were destroyed; the whole country was laid waste."[74] Accounts of Canada's internment era often include a gesture of this kind to the forced sale of property. But the domicide of Japanese Canadians demands more than a phrase; it is more than an example of the politics of racism and more than a chapter within a larger history.

Understanding the significance of domicide requires us to engage with the complexity and richness of home. Porteous and Smith conceive "home" broadly, not as a parcel of real estate but rather as the loose constellation of "familiar objects, structures, and environments" that constitute our sense of belonging in place and, to a significant extent, of self.[75] Kim Dovey argues that, "home is a notion universal to our species, not as place, house, or city, but as a principle for establishing a meaningful relationship with the environment." Home, on this account, "is a place that is loved or the place of loving." It is a place of "security from physical and psychological danger" and implies a degree of power or control over space, including the ability to "determine who shall enter." Home, for Dovey, is a familiar place where "pretentions are dropped." It is a "starting and finishing point to life's activities." It is, in sum, "a principle by which we order our existence in space."[76] Along similar lines, Matthew Desmond, conveying the harms of eviction, writes that the "home is the wellspring of personhood."[77]

In contemplating the violence of the dispossession, we need not substitute these idealizations of home for the imperfect places – houses, apartments, neighbourhoods, cities – where people actually live. If Dovey is right to suggest that the notion of home is universal to our species, we must nonetheless remain conscious that many people do not feel at home in the places they inhabit. Although we may all aspire to find "a place that is loved or the place of loving," we must nonetheless recall that actual households are not always such homes. Domestic spaces are, as well, sites of powerlessness and abuse.

Indeed, it is perhaps the uncertainty of home, its aspirational character, that comes across most clearly in the writings of Japanese Canadians in the 1940s. When they learned that their property had been sold without their consent, many Japanese Canadians described years of labour, sacrifice, and hardship that they had invested in the places where they lived.[78] Toshiye Hoshiko lamented the loss of her "home for over twenty years. It was the work and hard work of two decades of toiling. It was where my children were born and raised."[79] Rokusaburo Taniguchi lamented the loss of "more than thirty years of sweat and hard labour" on his farm, remarking that, "money can never buy my youthful days spent uselessly, now, on that wonderful farm."[80] H.K. Naruse demanded that officials consider the prospect of losing their own houses:

> How would you … like to be kicked out of your house which you have planned and built to your own specifications and satisfactions. Then soon after informed that your house and land has been sold. Yes, sold … and at a ridiculous amount. Perhaps you did not go through the pains and joys of building on your own property … after so many years of saving and planning.[81]

Home, for Japanese Canadian migrants in an often hostile British Columbia was not a taken-for-granted or universal experience. Establishing home, creating a sense of belonging, was a process often involving much, pain, labour, and sacrifice. Home is further complicated in a context of international migration: as some Japanese Canadians made plans for permanent settlement, others envisioned property in Canada as means to securing a home in Japan. The violence of the dispossession was felt not in the loss of a perfect ideal but rather the theft of real places within which Japanese Canadians struggled to achieve security and belonging and in the obliteration of the varied aspirations that they built through property.

To take seriously the notion of home and the significance of domicide requires that we avoid conflating home with home-ownership or indeed with house. Home means simultaneously more and less than such conflations would suggest. A rich conception of home makes clear that people experience (or "practice") home without owning a house and that, even for those who do own houses, the loss of home means much more than a loss of the economic value they have invested.

During the 1940s, Japanese Canadians also gave powerful expression to the particular harms of domicide as distinct from the hardship of the internment. In a letter to officials, Rikizo Yoneyama displaced from Haney British Columbia distilled the difference, for him, between temporary internment and the permanent destruction of home: "I realize that we are the victims of a war emergency and as such are quite willing to undergo … hardship … to help safeguard the shores of our homeland," wrote Yoneyama. "However," he continued, "I do urgently desire to return to my home … when the present emergency ends. May I plead your assistance in the sincere request for the return of that home?"[82] Yoneyama wrote during the summer of 1944, a year after the transfer of his farm, and hundreds of others, to the director of the Veterans' Land Act. He still hoped, however, that there might be some reversal: "I am now fifty eight years and feel I cannot start again from the bottom," he explained, "my health is failing … my desire after hostilities have terminated, was to return to my home at Haney and continue where I left off."[83] In the fall of the same year, Toshiye Hoshiko, quoted above, wrote to the Custodian's office from Montreal, where she lived in "a miserable one room on the third floor of a dark damp house." "Partially crippled by rheumatism," she had no choice but to accept the funds from the forced sale of her home in Surrey, British Columbia. She still hoped that some vestiges of that home could be saved: "among the chattels on the property, I wish you would set aside the violin and the music and send them express collect."[84] Instead, the Custodian sold the instrument at auction for $5.50, along with the rest of her personal belongings.[85]

Recognizing the ubiquity, gravity, and distinctiveness of the loss of home for displaced people today, scholars and activists have increasingly advocated for specific legal protections of home and encouraged their integration into international human rights codes and legal practice.[86] As Scott Leckie recently summarized in an introduction to the United Nation's Pinheiro Principles, "people displaced by forces beyond their control should never face the prospect of losing their housing, land or property rights … few displaced persons willingly renounce their rights to the places they called home before fleeing … Nor should they have to."[87]

Landscapes of Injustice has placed the loss of home at the centre of analysis, opening new vistas within the history of the internment era. Focus on the dispossession has encouraged histories of individual and collective place making that constituted British Columbia as home for Japanese Canadians and attention to the dispossession as a dismantling of multigenerational social and economic networks that sustained the Japanese Canadian community. Our collective has analyzed diverse Japanese Canadians' responses to domicide as they challenged the dispossession in court, protested individually and collectively, protected their families, navigated (and even acted in complicity with) the power of the state, and rebuilt spaces of security and belonging.[88]

In part 1 of this book, four chapters convey the meaning of home and the ramifications of dispossession. Audrey Kobayashi details the reforms of late nineteenth-century Japan and the family and village social structures that prompted and sustained migration to Canada. Focusing on the village of Kaideima, she demonstrates that property ownership was a key Japanese cultural value and the impetus for trans-Pacific migration. The loss of home in the mid-twentieth century can only be fully understood in the context of the long journeys (through both time and space) that made property ownership possible. Eric M. Adams analyzes the uncertain ground on which Japanese emigrants landed, using the deportation proceedings against Munetaka Samejima to convey both the racism of immigration, domicile, naturalization, and citizenship law in the first half of Canada's twentieth century and its gestures toward equality. Tracing the responses of Samejima and other Japanese Canadian litigants in the face of white supremacist (and yet not monolithic) law, Adams reminds readers of the Japanese Canadian struggle to achieve "home" in Canada.

The final two chapters in part 1 continue these themes, while also pointing toward the second major argument of the book, which situates the dispossession with the activity of the administrative state. Eiji Okawa's chapter follows two interconnected families from immigration to dispossession and beyond, focusing on the Ebisuzaki store in Vancouver's Powell Street neighbourhood. Using archival materials produced and curated by its owners, Okawa conveys the store as a hub of familial and communal life. The violence of the dispossession, he argues, was perpetrated in part through the imposition of the state's conception of property on the complex social institutions that organized and gave meaning to Japanese Canadian life. Finally, Nicholas Blomley and I analyze letters of protest written by hundreds of Japanese Canadians to state officials when they learned that their property was being sold without their consent. Their protests leave little doubt of the significance of property as a foundation for home, the impacts of the dispossession, or the force with which Japanese Canadians responded to its harms.

Dispossession required sustained work

The dispossession of Japanese Canadians cannot be understood as a single panicked decision in the "crisis of war" or as a moment of racist hysteria. Instead, it involved dozens, even hundreds of choices to sustain ongoing violations of human and constitutional rights, even long after the war had ended. Although dispossession involved more than federal administrative processes – property was lost to vandalism and theft even before federal officials seized control of it – the bureaucratic mechanisms of dispossession illustrate the point. Officials exerted control over Japanese Canadian–owned property from 1941, when they seized fishing vessels, firearms, radios, and other forms of property, to 1952, when they closed the Custodian's Vancouver office.[89] The Custodian of Enemy Property, vested with the homes and belongings of Japanese Canadians, rented a floor in Vancouver's Royal Bank Building, hired more than one hundred staff, and bought enough cabinets to house tens of thousands of files containing hundreds of thousands of pages documenting their activities. The Vancouver office divided their cases into two categories: the first, for so-called "enemy" property, comprised a small minority of the total, some 1,000 people officially suspected of connection with Japan or seen to have disruptively resisted the internment policies. The remaining files, for so-called "evacuee" property, contained information on the holdings of more than 15,000 property owners who had been uprooted from the coast merely because of their origins. Office staff worked to ascertain the extent of the property vested in them, assessed the condition and value of that property, established title, maintained insurance, paid miscellaneous expenses, and translated and typed a deluge of communications with Japanese Canadians and those interested in their property. They toured neighbourhoods and inspected houses. They warehoused chattels, organized appraisals and auctions, and oversaw the sale of real estate. Through their control of assets, they administered Japanese Canadian lives as well, deciding which requests could be accommodated, how much money would be released to whom, and on what conditions. Rather than a story of political flashpoints, the dispossession unfolded in the innumerable decisions of a decade of administrative work.

The administrative character of the dispossession is by no means unique or even exceptional: When the massive states of the mid-twentieth century undertook large-scale projects, they required doing by people.[90] As Eric Muller has observed of the American efforts to assess the loyalty of more than 100,000 Japanese Americans in the same era, that process involved the "mundane business" of the administrative state, "quotidian decisions and conflicts that pushed the government through months and years of systematized repression."[91]

The dispossession draws our attention to administrative processes in part because, despite its significance to Japanese Canadians, the policy never drew the popular or political attention of other aspects of the internment era, such as the uprooting in 1942 or exile in 1946. Once Japanese Canadians had been interned and incarcerated, their former residences and businesses – standing empty or (more often) occupied by tenants – and warehouses of their personal belongings clearly posed no security threat. No one ever argued that they did. By the time of most sales, the sense of military threat to the Canadian Pacific had long dissipated.[92] As a result, most political leaders showed little interest in the issue. Four key cabinet members – Ian Mackenzie (Pensions and National Health), Secretary of State Norman McLarty (by law the official custodian of Japanese Canadian–owned property), Thomas Crerar (Mines and Resources), and Humphrey Mitchell (Labour) – attended the crucial meeting on 11 January 1943 that decided that all Japanese Canadian–owned property would be sold. But authorship of the law was left to a bureaucrat, Glenn McPherson. There is no record of the cabinet as a whole discussing the decision. It was never debated in the Canadian Parliament. Prime Minister William Lyon Mackenzie King never mentioned the decision in his copious diary of political events.[93] Nor was there public outcry about the property that Japanese Canadians had left behind. Although they reported on the sale of property, British Columbia newspapers neither mounted nor documented a campaign for the forced sales.[94] Some of this silence was doubtlessly wilful. Newspapers would, for example, have reported on the widespread looting of Japanese Canadian homes had the victims of the crimes been positioned otherwise than as a reviled enemies. At the same time, the quiet violence of the dispossession is perhaps characteristic of the administrative state. Once major policies are set in motion, subsequent little-known decisions compound their harms.

In the case of dispossession, politicians were most engaged with its key precipitating cause – the internment itself. Once that policy had been decided, subsequent decisions, such as the dispossession fell largely to bureaucrats. Officials like McPherson, who advocated the forced sales and then wrote Order in Council 469 to legalize his managerial preference, made and implemented Canadian law and policy. Richard B. Hanson, the leader of the opposition in 1942, decried bureaucratic "masterminds who behind the scenes" formulated federal policy without being "answerable to anybody."[95] Hanson's accusation should not be taken to exonerate the ministers who oversaw policy. It did not at the time. Instead, the minister of finance James Lorimer Ilsley (whose ministry was the object of Hanson's harangue) stood in the House of Commons that day to respond: "I shall answer … myself."[96] And well he should have. Elected politicians (and their constituents) are answerable for the wrongs committed under their leadership.[97] For the dispossession of Japanese Canadians, Ministers Crerar, Mackenzie, McLarty, and Mitchell, as well as Prime Minister King, must be held to account. And indeed, much previous scholarship has done so.[98] Yet, the importance of more minor figures, lower-level administrators handling day-to-day tasks, also comes to light in the history of the dispossession. Anyone subjected to the power of twentieth-century states will have felt the impact of bureaucrats who operationalized the wills of their political masters.

Correspondingly, Japanese Canadians felt the intrusion of the state into their lives on an ongoing basis, not as a momentary event. The dispossession unfolded in daily life as Japanese Canadians sought to navigate the hardships it imposed by, for example, concealing contraband possessions, seeking permission from officials to access their own funds for such basic necessities as medical care, and relocating to places with some prospect of employment and education. Dispossession unfolded in the autumnal chill of Edmonton, where, as Ariel Merriam discusses, a mother of seven begged for funds to purchase winter coats for her children.[99] It unfolded in the infancies of 2,500 children born to families dispossessed of the homes into which they should have arrived.[100] In powerful but often subtle ways, Japanese Canadians struggled for a decade to retain or reclaim a sense of ownership and belonging in the context of dispossession.

The cumulative impact of years lived under unjust administration was evident in late March 1945 when Japanese Canadians questioned Tom Pickersgill, an official who visited internment camps in the employ of the Department of Labour. In a barrage of questions, Japanese Canadians sought to understand what their futures in Canada might hold. If they moved to Eastern Canada, would they be free? In response, Pickersgill endeavoured to encourage as many as possible to accept exile to Japan, a country that most had never before visited.[101] Even Pickersgill's summary of these exchanges – questions asked of him by internees and his answers – partially rendered here, conveys the heartbreaking uncertainty of administered lives:

> Q: Will relocees to Eastern Canada receive treatment as full fledged Canadian citizens?
> A: We have replied quite frankly to this question that there are some details on which there is still some uncertainty.
> Q: Will the relocees be given full rights to private enterprise, occupational freedom and a right to own and rent property, real and otherwise?
> A: We told them that a complete and satisfactory answer could not yet be given to this question.
> Q: Will freedom of travel and transfer of residence in any part of Eastern Canada be permitted during and after the war?
> A: We explained that so far as during the war is concerned, the same regulations concerning travel will apply … So far as regulations after the war were concerned, we explained that details of this still had to be decided.
> Q: What is the policy of the disposal of liquidated assets of Eastern relocees, now held in trust by the Custodian?
> A: We explained that the same rule would apply as at present … Japanese people permanently relocating outside BC, would be provided with the assets from the sale of their property, when such sales were made.
> Q: In the event of anti-racial violence and consequent damages sustained, will the Dominion Government hold themselves responsible for rectifications?
> A: The Japanese people will have the same rights to police protection as any other people … but the Dominion Government could not commit itself to paying for damages sustained.
> …
> Q: Will the Elementary and High School education of relocees be granted on an equal basis as all other residents of the Province?
> A: We pointed out that Education was the responsibility of the Provincial Government and not the Dominion Government, and we could not say definitively what would apply.[102]

Japanese Canadians asked questions that pointed to the sustained intrusion of the state into virtually every aspect of their lives. They inquired broadly about citizenship but also drilled down to the details. Years of internment had taught them to distrust state officials whose violations of them were both pervasive and specific. The government interfered in their employment and enterprise, their freedom of movement, and their property ownership. As important, it failed to take responsibility for damages against them or to adequately exert police authority as their vacated homes were ransacked. To the great frustration of Japanese Canadians, it denied their children educations, a failure that prompted heroic community-based efforts to provide schooling in sites of internment. Pickersgill answered with a cruel demonstration of power. He deliberately obfuscated, stoking the very understandable anxieties of Japanese Canadians who, despite the coming end of the war (Germany surrendered a month later, in September Japan would fall) saw no apparent intention on the part of the Canadian government to end the internment. As Japanese Americans prepared for freedom, Japanese Canadians were instead subjected to a deliberate effort to alienate them entirely from their own country. For many, the effort succeeded.[103]

Sustaining the work of dispossession required the ongoing complicity of thousands. While prior work on the internment has drawn attention to the remote locales where Japanese Canadians were forced to stay (the "ghost towns" and isolated mountain valleys of interior British Columbia, for example), the dispossession instead occurred in populated centres and in plain sight. For introductory purposes, two images may suffice to convey the point (see figures I.1 and I.2).

Contemplating the varied and widespread forms of complicity present in this history, we might benefit from Michael Rothberg's conception of "implicated subjects" which seeks to complicate histories of violence beyond the binary of victim and perpetrator: "*implication*," he writes, "draws attention to how we are *entwined with* … histories and situations that surpass our agency as individual subjects."[104] Urging a "relational" perspective on property, Nicholas Blomley similarly argues that, on one hand, dispossessed people remain entangled in systems of property (which are the conditions for dispossession) and, on the other hand, that a wide range of individuals and institutions are "implicated in and … derive differential benefits from [the] hierarchical property relation[s]" that marginalize others.[105] Many were implicated in the dispossession. Thousands flocked to auctions and sales of Japanese Canadian goods that occurred almost weekly in the lower mainland from 1943 to 1945. Hundreds bid on real estate put to tender. Many, like Mrs Mary Smith (figure I.1), benefited directly from the sales by "moving in" while others, like "Honest" Jim Lemen, a Chinese Canadian depicted in the same 1942 *Vancouver Sun* spread, sought to avoid the collateral harms of being mistaken for a target. Hundreds, like the employees of the Custodian of Enemy Property or the P.S. Ross and Sons accounting firm, worked to appraise, store, advertise, and sell the possessions of Japanese Canadians (figure I.2). Dispossession, more directly than the internment itself, draws into view these many "beneficiaries of a system that generates dispersed and uneven experiences of trauma and wellbeing simultaneously."[106]

TREND OF THE TIMES IN VANCOUVER

Without fuss or friction, a change that may have a significant bearing on British Columbia's future is taking place in Vancouver. The Japanese are moving out, and Canadians are moving in. There are new faces behind the counters in establishments formerly operated by Nipponese, and it is expected their number will increase as the exodus from the coast gathers momentum. One instance is the Busy Bee, West End neighborhood store at Robson and Thurlow. A few days ago it was owned by Japanese, but it has been taken over by Mrs. A. L. Colburne. In the picture, Mrs. Mary Smith is getting ready for customers.

Honest Jim (Jim Lemen) has been taken for a Japanese so often he has now put up this sign at his stall in Blackburn's market.

Curfew to Restrict Movements of Japs In B.C. Coast Area

By B. T. RICHARDSON
Vancouver Sun Ottawa Bureau

OTTAWA, Feb. 26.—Following a series of orders, disclosed Wednesday by Prime Minister King, dealing with the Japanese problem on the British Columbia coast, a curfew order is being issued restricting the movements of Japanese between certain hours. It will be enforced by the RCMP.

Orders in council tabled in Parliament, including two important documents dated February 24, were hailed with satisfaction by B.C. members, who have conducted a caucus of their

Figure I.1 and I.2 (following page) The dispossession unfolded in plain sight. It was covered in the press, as in this *Vancouver Sun* article of 26 February 1942, and widely advertised.

While this entire book conveys the work of the dispossession, the chapters of part 2 devote sustained attention to this topic. In our chapter, Will Archibald and I grapple with the discovery that Glenn McPherson, founding director of the Vancouver Office of the Custodian of Enemy Property, was secretly an agent of the British Security Coordination, issuing anonymous, inflammatory, and unfounded attacks on people of Japanese descent in Pacific Canada. Meanwhile, in his "day job" with the Custodian,

This business is being liquidated by P. S. Ross and Sons, Controllers pursuant to authority of the Secretary of State of Canada, acting in his capacity as Custodian.

Pre-Christmas Closing-Out Sale

$40,000 WORTH OF MERCHANDISE

MUST BE SOLD!

A LARGE ASSORTMENT of High-Class Merchandise including — Dry Goods, Men's Wear, Groceries, Hardware, Drugs, etc.—now being sold at Greatly Reduced Prices.

A Great Percentage of this Merchandise is PRE-WAR STOCK — and make ideal Christmas Gifts!

SALE STARTS THURSDAY, DEC. 16

This $40,000 stock of merchandise is offered to the public at greatly reduced prices, and contains a large assortment of standard lines, including men's underwear, hose, shirts and overalls, piece goods, notions, groceries, crockery, hardware and drugs. These goods will be sold down to the last article. The range is at present fairly complete—so shop early and often to avoid disappointment.

LADIES' COATS Reg. value from $11.50 to $55.00. Clearing at .... $7.75 to $25.50

LADIES' DRESSES In cotton, silks and wool fabrics. Regular value from $1.65 to $9.50. Clearance .... $1.39 to $8.15

DRESS MATERIALS In printed and plain silks. Regular value, per yd., $1.16. Clearance price, per yard $1.07

MEN'S SUITS In sizes from 32 to 36 only. Regular $21.50 to $45.00. Clearance .... $12.95 to $30.00

12/15/43.

YOU CAN SAVE MONEY AND TIME

T. MAIKAWA STORES LIMITED

369 POWELL ST., VANCOUVER, B.C.

A large quantity of merchandise now in short supply. All will be sold without reserve.

McPherson operated with ostensible regard for the rule of law, even when this brought him into conflict with other officials eager to grab Japanese Canadian–owned lands. Drawing him into focus, we convey the central bureaucratic organ of the dispossession, the Custodian, through the complex figure of its most consequential leader. Ariel Merriam's chapter focuses on the Nagata family, whose life in Vancouver was irrevocably disrupted by internment and dispossession. Without escaping the state's grip on their lives, the Nagatas subtly manoeuvred to reunite, reestablish their home, and build a future. Using their knowledge of the system that was oppressing them and cultivating relationships with the individual bureaucrats who controlled their funds, the Nagatas were able to negotiate some measure of freedom in pursuit of their long-term objectives. Merriam's case study details the circulation of power between officials of the administrative state and Japanese Canadians subjected to their rule. Finally, Kaitlin Findlay and Nicholas Blomley fill a lacuna in prior accounts of this history, detailing the Custodian's mismanagement of personal or moveable property (everything except real estate). Chattels posed particular administrative problems for officials and seemed to inspire particular temptation in an avaricious public, which ransacked Japanese Canadian homes and warehouses of their belongings in search of anything removable. Detailing the devaluation that occurred – devaluation of both property and people – the chapter tells a harrowing story of official incompetence and neglect as well as widespread complicity in the dispossession.

Reasoning wrong

Race was the foundational ideology of the dispossession, making viable the operational category of internment law: "persons of the Japanese race." Race had deep, indeed constitutional, origins in Canadian law and "Japanese" was repeatedly rearticulated as an enforceable legal category in the decades prior to the 1940s. As the federal government made decisions to uproot, intern, and dispossess Japanese Canadians, important policy makers unequivocally embraced a racialized understanding of the "Japanese problem." In February 1942, for example, Prime Minister King wrote in his diary that "no matter how honourable they might appear to be, or how long they may have been away from Japan, naturalized, or even those who were born in [Canada] ... everyone [*sic*] of them ... would be saboteurs and would help Japan when the moment came."[107] Ian Mackenzie, as we have already seen, took the same view still further. Racial ideology permeated the bureaucracy as well. Glenn McPherson, was of the "opinion ... that ... the Japanese have developed a high inferiority complex and realize, even those Canadian born, that the only way the Yellow Race can obtain their place in the Sun is by winning the war."[108] Ivan Barnet, responsible for the survey and appraisal of Japanese Canadian–owned farms, saw his task as a racial mission. In sum, key officials at every level of the process saw race as an essential truth by which to organize their understandings of the world and to justify their actions. Within Canadian officialdom, racial ideology was, as Hannah Arendt observed of the twentieth-century world more broadly, a "system" of thought "strong enough to attract and persuade a majority of people and broad enough to lead them through the various experiences and situations of an average modern life."[109]

Despite this basic truth about the dispossession (that without pervasive racism, "persons of the Japanese race" could never have lost so much), its ideological dimensions cannot be reduced, as some previous scholarship has tended to do, to racism alone. As an explanatory device in this history – in helping us to understand why people did what they did – racism has only limited purchase. Why did Canadian officials seize the property of people of Japanese descent, when their American counterparts did not? Why did officials promise in law to protect the property that they had seized, establish complex administrative systems to this end, and then abruptly reverse course and sell everything?[110] Why did they establish files for every individual property owner, crediting individual accounts with the proceeds of all sales? Why, despite this seeming concern for the property of individuals, did they fail so miserably to protect chattels and insist on tightly controlling Japanese Canadians' access to their own funds?[111] Although racism should never be forgotten in answering such questions, the policies cannot be explained by reference to racism alone.

Instead, other systems of thought – other schemes of understanding and rationalizing action – operated alongside and in relation to the racism of the dispossession.

It is crucial, as we contemplate these other rationalizations, to avoid seeing them as only or even primarily competing with racism. Sometimes they did so, as for example, when John Erskine Read excoriated the proposed exile of Japanese Canadians in December 1945, writing to his deputy minister, Norman Robertson:

> Any measure which takes a Canadian citizen, born in this country, and in respect of whom there is no proven disloyalty, and against his will deprives him of his status as a Canadian citizen, and deports him to a hostile foreign land, runs contrary to principles which I have always regarded as fundamental in our constitution.[112]

Sometimes, the bureaucracy was a site of competing ideologies, in which concepts like citizenship were brought to bear against racism, with (in the case of Japanese Canadians) very little success. The plan to deport went ahead. However, this was not the primary way in which systems of ideas intersected to create policies like the dispossession. Instead, they interwove with one another; officials folded ideas together and arranged them alongside one another to justify the harms they perpetrated.

The ideological complexity of the dispossession is revealed in the discussions leading to the government's decision to abandon the protection of Japanese Canadian–owned property and instead to force its sale. In the first year of the internment, officials in the Custodian's office understood their tasks as property preservation and management. As McPherson explained to a colleague, "the Custodian, according to the wording of the Order-in-Council, is supposed to protect the Japanese [Canadian] interests." Any decisions taken in respect to property, he warned, must be defensible as benefitting its owners.[113] A lawyer, McPherson was aware that the people whose property he controlled were rights-holding Canadians, likely to bring government actions to account. In order to sell the property, the government would need reason.

In the summer of 1942, a key rationalization for the forced sales emerged from an unlikely precinct: the Vancouver Town Planning Commission initiated discussions that ultimately enabled officials to cast all Japanese Canadian–owned assets as perishable.[114] Even prior to the shift to wholesale dispossession, the Office of the Custodian authorized the sale of perishable property, that is, assets deemed likely to deteriorate in value over time, such as grocery stock. Such sales could be justified as serving the interests of their owners. But property with value that endured or increased over time (in particular real estate) could not be similarly discarded.[115] Town planners in Vancouver, meanwhile, were immersed in local and international conversations about the prospect of urban renewal to alleviate the ills of "blighted" and "slum" neighbourhoods, areas that were envisioned as festering and worsening wounds on the body of the city.[116] As elsewhere, Vancouver planners encountered significant obstacles to this aim: for slum clearance to be viable, the state had to be pushed into an active role in local real estate markets, and the inhabitants of the slum had to be relocated elsewhere.[117]

Planners quickly realized that Vancouver met these conditions in the summer of 1942. They had already earmarked the Powell Street area for redevelopment, noting three years prior that "the housing conditions of the Japanese must be bettered, not only in their own interests but in those of the community as a whole, since the health of a city is determined by the well-being of all of its parts."[118] The uprooting of Japanese Canadians meant that an area considered a "slum" by housing reformers was being emptied, its property vested in the federal government. At their July 1942 meeting, planners expressed their concern that "Japanese-owned houses, containing inadequate plumbing facilities, and being in a generally run-down condition, were being rented to newcomers to the city" as well as their hope that the "government might condemn the housing in certain central areas, and rebuild workers' dwellings on the sites."[119] They called for city council to create a special committee to address the issue.[120] Alderman George Buscombe, the city council's representative on the Planning Commission and an open racist, pledged to carry the proposal forward.[121] Within days, the city created a committee "to investigate the condition of premises in Jap Town, Powell Street, discuss this question with the Custodian of Enemy Property, and report."[122] The committee included Buscombe, as well as the corporate counsel, the building inspector, the medical health officer, and the city electrician. They proved a capable team.

By the early fall, officials of the Custodian in Vancouver reported pressure from "various Departments" of the municipality "relative to the condition of properties" vested in the federal government.[123] The electrical department threatened court action over the rental of substandard units. The chief sanitary inspector identified several buildings "badly infested with cockroaches," and the health department commenced boarding up structures that it deemed unsuitable for "human habitation."[124] "We do not wish to add to your problems and are willing to co-operate," explained a building inspector, "but remember Coroner's Juries are embarrassing."[125] Employees of the Custodian took these thinly veiled threats seriously, and their responses transformed federal policy.

Through the activities of the special committee, the Town Planning Commission gained traction with federal policy makers. But from there, the process eluded its control. Federal officials absorbed the message that the Powell Street area should be considered substandard and deteriorating but from there took matters in their own direction. Powell Street was not demolished or reinvented.[126] Nonetheless, the planners had given considerable impetus to the dispossession of Japanese Canadians. The activities of local officials encouraged federal bureaucrats, and in particular McPherson, to focus disproportionate attention on a small number of buildings in the Powell Street neighbourhood supposedly declining in value.[127] Synthesizing this issue with concurrent claims about the deterioration of farms and chattels, McPherson built a powerful argument that all property should be sold in the interests of its owners, even against their will.[128] In December 1942, he advised Coleman, "it is obvious, both in the city and country, that the Japanese property is going to deteriorate rapidly." The government's policy, "should be one of liquidation and this policy should eventually include all chattels." Despite "the danger of such a policy insofar as it might cause dissatisfaction among the evacuees," McPherson argued, "the deterioration of real property and the loss of chattels will soon liquidate the capital investment."[129]

These arguments rapidly ascended the federal chain of command. Upon reading McPherson's reports, Ephraim H. Coleman informed his superior, Secretary of State Norman McLarty:

> In respect to urban property, the principal problem is in relation to the Japanese business district in Vancouver centering around Powell Street … The Health authorities and the Engineering authorities of the City of Vancouver have, I think very properly, condemned many of these properties … I consider it doubtful whether … the premises can be made fit for … white people … Any comprehensive steps which may be taken to remedy the situation would almost amount to what might be described as a slum clearance.[130]

Ideas about property and the city interwove easily with racism, and the initiative of the City of Vancouver reached the ear of the secretary of state. McLarty forwarded Coleman's memo to Ian Mackenzie.[131] "If we endeavour to deal immediately with the urban property situation," McLarty editorialized, "it is tantamount to saying that [Japanese Canadians] will never be returned to Vancouver. This may of course be desirable, but I believe that careful consideration should be given before we finally deal with the question of property."[132] Mackenzie was quick to respond, pushing the boundaries of the discussion wider still. He confirmed that the Powell Street properties were "very much in the nature of definite slums," and expressed his support for the permanent exclusion of Japanese Canadians from the entire "coast of British Columbia."[133]

The logic of perishability managed to convince people who almost certainly had the best interests of Japanese Canadians in mind. Kishizo Kimura arrived in Canada from Japan's Tottori Prefecture in 1911 at the age of twelve and lived until the war in the Powell Street neighbourhood, where he achieved considerable economic success and social connection. He was one of two Japanese Canadians who agreed to serve on a pair of advisory committees overseeing the disposition of Japanese Canadian real estate in the spring of 1942. As its first order of business, Kimura's committee was entrusted to decide whether forced sales were warranted. Kimura thought that they were. With special permission to return to the coast for committee meetings, Kimura joined tours of his former neighbourhood in 1943 and concluded that real estate in the area was declining in value. "It seemed," Kimura later wrote, "that there were a considerable number of places that required large sums spent to comply with city bylaws."[134] The city's initiative had influenced his views. However, Kimura also described specific causes of further deterioration: Japanese Canadian–owned real estate, he worried, was unprotected against "theft and break-ins." Encouraged by "Anti-Nikkei agitators" who "took this opportunity to proclaim, maliciously, that all property belonging to Japanese Canadians should be disposed of to prevent their return to the west coast" as well as "the general public" that "turned a blind eye to the vandalism of empty houses," criminals grew "increasingly bold."[135] Given an atmosphere of widespread extremism and complicity, "it was easy to see that damages were increasing daily."[136] Six days after witnessing widespread destruction of Japanese Canadian–owned homes and businesses, Kimura joined the other advisory committee members in approving property dispossession.[137]

Claims about the perishability of property were false.[138] The sales did not serve the interests of Japanese Canadians; although vandalism and theft were indeed widespread, government incompetence and neglect should not have served as a justification for the further violation of property rights.[139] But the point here is not that the arguments were well founded or typically advanced in good faith. The forced sales cannot be understood in absence of racism. However, it was not palatable within the federal government to simply pronounce that, on the basis of race, all of the property would be sold. The specter of legal accountability, the knowledge and participation of Japanese Canadians, and the presence within the political process of officials uneasy with naked racism complicated the ideological terrain of the dispossession. Even the most openly racist participants in the process were forced to contemplate and justify their own actions in terms of property values, justice, "British fair play," administrative efficiency, political advantage, the rule of law, and the law of war. Particularly as the decade reached its midpoint, the war came to a close, and explicitly racist state policy came increasingly under criticism (and yet the internment and dispossession continued) these other ideas were required to keep the workers of state injustice on task.

A conceptual tool in untangling this thicket might be "permeability," which Michael Freeden uses to convey the reality that "ideologies are not mutually exclusive in their ideas, concepts, and conceptions. Rather, they intersect with one another at multiple points of contact."[140] Somewhat similarly, Freeden describes ideologies – systems of organized ideas – as "like a set of modular units of furniture that can be assembled in many ways … Through diverse arrangements of the furniture we can create very different rooms, even by using the same units."[141] Arranged in a room with a stove and a sink, chairs and tables mean one thing; situated alongside a whiteboard and flipcharts, they mean another. Correspondingly, the rule of law, the law of markets, property, and citizenship come to mean very particular things when arranged in a room with racism. From such places the dispossession emanated.

The two chapters in part 3 of this book explore the rationalities underlying the dispossession. They do so by focusing on moments of this history that previous scholarship has tended merely to gesture toward as symbols of a larger politics of racism. Eric M. Adams and I examine the government's spring 1942 promise, specified in law and broadcast in public, that it would preserve and protect the property of Japanese Canadians for the duration of the war and then return it to them. Until now, the promise has largely been remembered for its betrayal: Japanese Canadians who entrusted their homes and belongings to the Canadian government never saw them again. In her chapter, Kaitlin Findlay delves into the hearings of the Bird Commission, a postwar government inquiry into the economic losses of Japanese Canadians. The commission, whose constrained terms of reference precluded any possibility that it would deliver justice to Japanese Canadians, has also been remembered for its inadequacy, as a cynical and failed attempt by officials to close the books on the injustice they had perpetrated. Accepting such critiques – the promise was in important senses meaningless, the commission in essence a sham – our chapters nonetheless find important histories to tell. In these events we find countervailing conceptions of justice, unfulfilled opportunities for alternative action, and key figures who wanted more. Japanese Canadians spoke within both processes, shaping, in the limited ways available to them, the promise to protect and the postwar feint toward compensation. Injustice, these chapters argue, emerged not from the blunt instrumentalization of racism alone but rather through its generative intersection with alternative visions, ideals, and possibilities.

Dispossession is permanent

Canada's internment era was long. When Americans disbanded their camps in 1945, Canadian officials declined to follow suit. Instead, as Robinson writes, Canadians administered the "renewal and reinforcement" of the internment.[142] Full Japanese Canadian freedom of movement would not be restored until 1949. The Custodian of Enemy Property maintained its Vancouver office into the early 1950s. The internment era in Canada was not a wartime measure but, rather, the policy of more than a decade, most of it occurring beyond the end of the war.

Recognition of the unjust protraction of the internment still fails to convey adequately the duration of its harms. Once the government had seized and sold all of the possessions of Japanese Canadians, once it had administered domicide, it had done something that could not be reversed. Part 4 of this book conveys the permanence of the dispossession by exploring the massive aggregate losses (and benefits) of the dispossession of real estate, the memories still carried by Japanese Canadians of this history, and the legacy of activism that endures today. By way of introducing this theme,

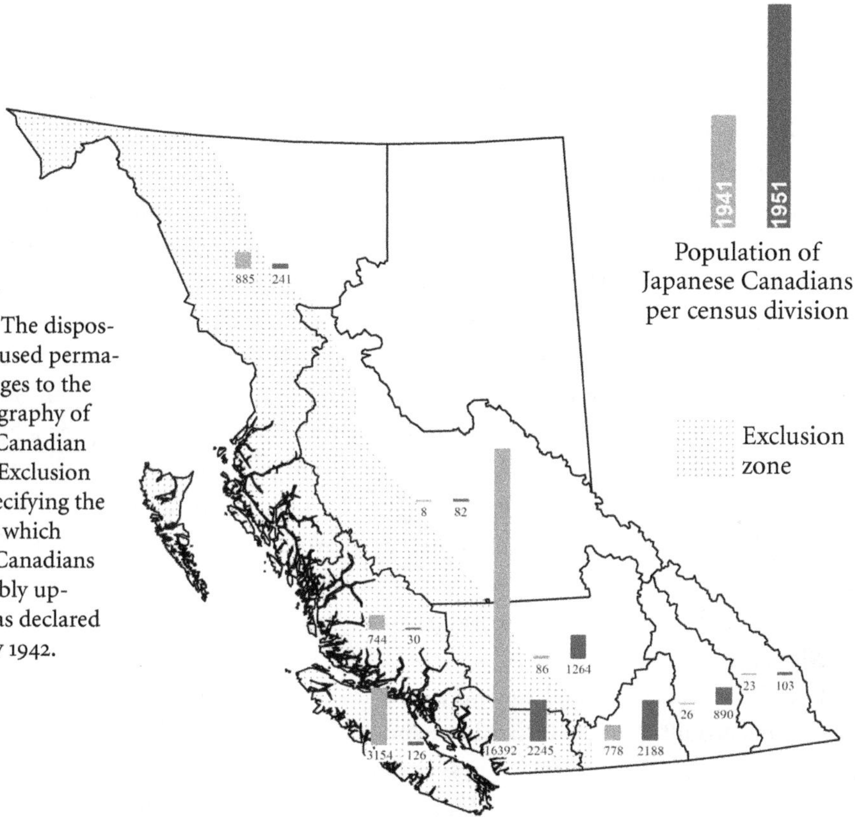

Figure I.3 The dispossession caused permanent changes to the social geography of Japanese Canadian life. The "Exclusion Zone," specifying the area from which Japanese Canadians were forcibly uprooted, was declared in January 1942.

and bringing to a close these wider reflections, perhaps several sketches will suffice.

The dispossession leaves enduring legacies of loss. Eikichi Kagetsu, among the wealthiest Japanese Canadians on the eve of Canada's entry into the Pacific War, lost nearly everything.[143] He had arrived in British Columbia in June of 1906 at the age of twenty-three, the oldest of eleven children from a poor household in Wakayama Prefecture. Beginning as a labourer in mines and sawmills, he saved and planned, managing to acquire rights to 160 acres in 1908, the first of many purchases. His story over the subsequent decades is not one of simple ascent but rather of the struggle and the uncertainty of success in British Columbia's lumber industry. Often threatened with insolvency and once bankrupted, Kagetsu managed to maintain and build his business into an enterprise producing tens of thousands of feet of lumber every day. Like other Japanese Canadians, he lived with racism, having to comply, for example, with such indignities as a law that barred him from operating his own steam-powered equipment. And yet he was a renowned success. In 1936 he joined a delegation of prominent Canadians at the unveiling of the Vimy Ridge memorial, visiting while there the graves of Japanese Canadian soldiers and taking tea with the British Royal Family.

The dispossession dismantled Kagetsu's accomplishments. In March of 1942, with an astonishing 2.5 million feet of timber felled on his lands and ready for shipment, Kagetsu was denied permission to retain employees for long enough to bring this mountain of logs to market. In April, he was forbidden from travelling to his business properties to wrap up his affairs. Then came the uprooting of his family. On 28 May, after a month of preparation, they boarded an overnight train to Minto City, in a remote canyon in the interior of British Columbia. In the years that followed, Kagetsu's lands and operation were sold to H.R. MacMillan Export Company, helping to expand a business that would become MacMillan Bloedel, one of the world's great forestry companies in the postwar period. Kagetsu never consented and was never adequately compensated. At the postwar royal commission inquiry into Japanese Canadian economic losses, he presented a claim for more than $460,000 (approximately $6,500,000 in 2020). After lengthy consideration by the commission, he was awarded a little more than a tenth of this amount.[144] Arriving in Toronto in 1945 at the age of sixty-two, he attempted, over the next decade, to start again, making forays into import and dry cleaning businesses with the limited capital that he retained. These enterprises were not successful. Kagetsu was seventy-three years of age when the last of his business ventures failed, and his only remaining asset when he died was the house he inhabited on Montview Avenue, Toronto.

The dispossession is also, however, a story of resilience and perseverance. Japanese Canadians rebuilt their materials lives and their communities against the headwinds of dispossession. Betty Toyota was seventeen years old in 1942 when her family was uprooted from Vancouver; in 2016, shortly before her death, she told her story to Landscapes of Injustice researchers. Unflinching in her portrayal of hardship, Toyota described arriving to the cold autumn of the Slocan Valley where her family's shack was not yet built, so they shivered in a tent awaiting its completion. The paltry infrastructure in the camp meant that internees were forced, throughout the winter, to draw water from an open well that was inevitably, given the conditions, surrounded by ice. One day, filling two pails, she slipped and fell, "And … I just swore my head off … I don't know where the words came from. I just swore and I thought, 'What did I do to deserve this?'"

Yet, Betty – like many confined to the camps – more often recalls the rebuilding of her community. Her future husband, Tak Toyota, was distinctive in the Slocan because he had managed to acquire an "old Jalopy," a Model A Ford, in which he moved about the multiple internment sites in the region. It was in the car that he would "come and court me." As he approached, "you could hear this chitty chitty bang bang, toot toot toot coming up the hill." Around this rare possession, stories were told:

> [Tak] always stopped and gave everybody a ride. Especially the older women, right? He would always give them a ride. And I remember mom and Mrs Shimizu; she lived with us in the same house. They used to walk downtown to buy stuff. And they used to go and buy tofu. There was this Japanese man that made tofu in downtown … So mom told me one day she went down to buy tofu

> and they put it in a cardboard container full of water … And they were walking home and Tak came, "Mr Toyota, Toyota-san stopped and gave us a ride." Mom didn't know Tak that well; it was Toyota-san then … Every time you see Tak's car go by he's full of giggling old women … and she said by the time they got out of the car in front of their avenue most of the water was gone from shaking.[145]

The car was a notable possession, a source of community, and a mechanism for mobility. Rather than conceiving of such stories on a continuum of positive to negative, they are most usefully understood as accounts of how Japanese Canadians remade a sense of home. They rebuilt material lives by opening tofu shops, jostling down rural roads in an old car, and laughing and living together. Their achievements in rebuilding community and home laid foundations for remarkable successes in subsequent generations, including that of Betty and Tak's son, Ron Toyota, who, when Betty gave her interview, was serving his third term as mayor of Creston, British Columbia.

The chapters in part 4 explore the permanence of dispossession from a variety of perspectives. My analysis of real estate exchange traces in economic terms the enduring benefits and losses of the forced sale of land. I argue that Japanese Canadian losses of autonomy – of the choice to sell or retain their property and also the opportunity to freely reinvest – had quantifiable impacts. We most clearly understand the economic harms that Japanese Canadians suffered and the gains reaped by others when we situate the forced sales in history, comprehending them as legacies. Drawing upon oral interviews of Japanese Canadians, Kaitlin Findlay, Heather Read, and I describe legacies of a very different sort. Our chapter, written as a conversation amongst its authors, provides a glimpse into how this history is remembered today, finding that stories about property are most often also about human relationships, that Japanese Canadian families strove for generations to rebuild a sense of ownership and belonging, and that returns to sites of dispossession – both conceptual and physical – carried enduring significance.

The final three chapters of the book focus on the postwar period and the lessons that we might still learn today. Ian Baird describes recent political controversies in Port Alberni concerning a street and a school named for Alan Webster Neill, a virulently racist midcentury politician notorious for his efforts to exclude Japanese Canadians from the fishing industry and his advocacy of their internment in the 1940s. The landscapes of British Columbia, Baird demonstrates, as elsewhere, bear the imprints of past injustices in the names that they carry and the histories they invoke. The names of our public places, he reminds us, convey our present values. In their chapter, Art Miki and Audrey Kobayashi, both part of the team that secured in 1988 an acknowledgment of wrongdoing on the part of the Canadian federal government, a redress settlement for the surviving victims of the policy, and the country's first political apology, remember the negotiations leading to that monumental event. A transcript of a presentation to a gathering of the Landscapes of Injustice Research Collective, it is both heartening and illuminating. What Audrey jokingly describes as "just … two seniors getting together to reminisce" is also a lesson about the hard work of activism in the wake of injustice, the contingency and possibility of political change, and the remarkable achievement of both a small group of people and the larger Japanese Canadian community. In the book's final chapter, Matt James and I argue that the 1988 settlement and apology continue to have vital democratic potential today. Interrogating in depth the question of responsibility for wrongdoing – a topic largely avoided in the state's original admission – we argue that ongoing critical engagement with political apology can spur individual and collective learning that is crucial to vindicating the basic democratic presumption that political communities can improve on their past choices.

***

A final legacy story. At a dinner party several years ago, a discussion of this research was interrupted by my host, who suddenly stood in excitement. She had to show me something and disappeared into her basement. Minutes later she reemerged with a brown box, about a foot squared. Opening the lid, she began unwrapping the fine china within, handing it, piece by piece, to me. Her parents' neighbours, she explained, had left it in their care in 1942 but never returned to collect. It had been passed, since then, in her family. She mused idly about what it might take to find the original owners. Standing in her kitchen, I held the dispossession in my hands. Had the property of Japanese Canadians not been confiscated, I would never have touched this teacup, that delicate plate. Had the dispossession never occurred, I would not have fascinated my dinner companions in its telling or written these words for you. There is scarcely a longstanding family in British Columbia not implicated, in one fashion or another, in this history. Dispossession is not a chapter that closes or a period that neatly ends. It leaves enduring legacies of benefit and harm, shame and silence, resilience and activism. We walk atop its sediment, unevenly layered over in subsequent years. We are heirs to landscapes of injustice.

NOTES

Parts of this introduction have previously appeared in various publications of Jordan Stanger-Ross and the Landscapes of Injustice research collective, including: "Introduction," in *Witness to Loss: Race, Culpability and Memory in the Dispossession of Japanese Canadians*, ed. Jordan Stanger-Ross and Pamela Sugiman (Montreal & Kingston: McGill-Queen's University Press, 2017), xxi–lx. Many thanks to readers, including Eric M. Adams, Nicholas Blomley, Jason Colby, Penny Bryden, Doug Harris, Laura Ishiguro,

Matt James, Laura Madokoro, Eric Muller, Hildy Ross, Laura Saimoto, Eric Sager, Nicole Yakashiro, Henry Yu, and Michael Zuckerman as well as the entire Landscapes of Injustice Steering Committee. A big thanks to research assistants who supported the final preparation of this manuscript: Natsuki Abe, Lindy Marks, and Jennifer Landrey.

Although I wrote the introduction alone, its intellectual development was collective and particularly reflects the work of participants in the research integration meetings of the spring of 2018 led by Kaitlin Findlay, the project's research coordinator, and me. Participants in our weekly sessions over the summer of 2018 read some twenty publications and drew them into a summative document. Kaitlin Findlay in particular assisted me in honing the four claims that became the skeleton of this book and that structure the introduction. Thanks also to Rosemary Ommer, Chad Gaffield, Eric Sager, and Henry Yu for emphasizing research integration.

1 A note on terminology: Landscapes of Injustice is a community-engaged project committed to working with Japanese Canadians, the people most affected by the dispossession, in the telling of this history. As part of the harms directed against Japanese Canadians in the 1940s, government officials and others developed euphemisms to obscure the real intent and impacts of their actions. These euphemisms have sometimes persisted in discussion of these events. We have worked with our community council to develop recommendations for the use of language within our project. I use the phrase "internment era" to refer to the period beginning in December 1941, when the government first uprooted Japanese Canadians from coastal British Columbia, and ending in April 1949, when the government finally lifted the prohibition on their return to the coast. In this context, "internment" refers not only to the sites of concentration in British Columbia but also and more broadly to the varied circumstances of Japanese Canadian life during this period. This usage follows the Oxford English Dictionary definition of the verb "to intern" as the act of confining people "within the limits of a country, area, or other place, esp. for political or military reasons; spec. (originally) to oblige (a person) to reside within prescribed limits." In addition, our research collective recommends that the following terms be avoided: (1) "evacuation," used by government officials to describe the forced *uprooting*, *internment*, and *incarceration* of Japanese Canadians; (2) "Japanese," when referring to *Japanese Canadians*, *Canadians of Japanese ancestry*, or *Nikkei*, who should not be confused with the country of Japan or its residents (at the time of their uprooting, 75 per cent of Nikkei in coastal British Columbia were born or naturalized Canadians); (3) "repatriation," sometimes used to refer to the *exile* of Japanese Canadians to Japan in 1946: this term falsely implies that the *exiles* originated in Japan. Our project is also committed to clarity of language with respect to the property losses. We therefore recommend the following terms: *Dispossession*, referring to the range of processes that led to the loss of property, including theft, vandalism, neglect, and forced sales; *Forced sales*, referring to the government policy of selling the property of Japanese Canadians without their consent. See also Roy Miki, *Redress: Inside the Japanese Canadian Call for Justice* (Vancouver: Raincoast Books, 2004), especially chapter 2; and Roger Daniels, "Words Do Matter: A Note on Inappropriate Terminology and the Incarceration of Japanese Americans," in *Nikkei in the Pacific Northwest: Japanese Americans & Japanese Canadians in the Twentieth Century*, ed. Gail M. Nomura and Louis Fiset (Seattle: University of Washington Press, 2005), 190–214.

2 Ken Adachi, *The Enemy That Never Was: A History of the Japanese Canadians* (Toronto:

McClelland and Stewart, 1976), 261. Interdepartmental Committee on Enemy Interests in Canada and Canadian Interests in Enemy Occupied Territories [June 1943], file 23-1-11-1, pt. 1, Japanese Property and Custodian of Enemy Property, vol. 655, RG 27, LAC.

3 "A Statement Is in Order," *The New Canadian*, 20 February 1943, 2.

4 "Would Ban Oriental from Living Here," *The Daily Colonist*, 22 November 1922, 7. See also "New Resolution on Oriental Question," *The Daily Colonist*, 17 November 1922, 9; Patricia E. Roy, *The Oriental Question: Consolidating a White Man's Province, 1914–41* (Vancouver: UBC Press, 2003), 116.

5 1944 speech quoted in Patricia E. Roy, *The Triumph of Citizenship: The Japanese and Chinese in Canada, 1941–1967* (Vancouver: UBC Press, 2007), 125.

6 Ian Mackenzie to T.A. Crerar, 14 April 1942, file V-8-10, pt. 1, Farm Properties, vol. 403, RG 38, LAC.

7 PC 1942-5523 (1942), file 2591G, vol. 1764, RG 2-A-1-a, LAC.

8 Ian Mackenzie to John Godwin, 7 December 1942, file 70-25(3), vol. 25, MG 27 III-B5, LAC.

9 Ian Mackenzie is a key figure in the most influential account of this history to date, Ann Sunahara's *The Politics of Racism: The Uprooting of Japanese Canadians during the Second World War* (Toronto: James Lorimer and Co, 1981), http://www.japanesecanadianhistory.ca/Politics_of_Racism.pdf.

10 A member of our collective has begun work on the silences in this history of complicity: Pamela Sugiman, "Acts of Kindness and Complicity" (speech, Victoria, BC, 28 January 2018).

11 Formally there was no Canadian citizenship until 1947. Rather, 75 per cent of Japanese Canadians, were "British subjects of Canada," either born or naturalized as such. However, people, including lawmakers, commonly used the language of citizenship before its formal enactment in law. Order in Council 288-1942, for example, described people of Japanese descent as "Canadian citizens whose productive power, by virtue of this ownership, contributed significantly to the fishing industry" (Order in Council PC 1942-288, file 2484, vol. 1744, RG 2 A-1-a, LAC).

12 Chapter 8.

13 Ephraim H. Coleman to Norman Robertson, 16 March 1942, file 4606-c-13-40, vol. 3121, RG 25, LAC.

14 John Erskine Read, Note for Undersecretary of State for External Affairs, 2 March 1942, file 3464-q-40, vol. 3005, RG 25, LAC.

15 To view this question as important does not require that we understand Coleman or Read as acting entirely in good faith. Coleman directly approved Glenn MacPherson's dual role as the director of the Custodian's office in Vancouver and, simultaneously, a covert operative reporting on Japanese Canadians to British security (see chapter 5). Read helped to devise the policy whereby Japanese Canadians were required to use the funds realized in the sale of their property to pay for their own internment (Interdepartmental Committee on Enemy Interests in Canada and Canadian Interests in Enemy Occupied Territories [June 1943], file 23-1-11-1, pt. 1, Japanese Property and Custodian of Enemy Property, vol. 655, RG 27, LAC). Neither emerged from the 1940s with clean hands. At the same time, neither were the rabid racists to whom the dispossession has often been attributed.

16 Aya Suzuki to P.H. Russell, 23 September 1944, image 1334, microfilm reel C9476, Office of the Custodian of Enemy Property, Vancouver Office: Office Files, Héritage (hereafter cited as C9476, Héritage).

17 Aya Suzuki to P.H. Russell, 18 January 1944, image 1334, C9476, Héritage.

18 See Stanger-Ross and Landscapes of Injustice Research Collective, "Naziism in Canada? The Internment of Japanese Canadians and the History of Comparison," in *After the Holocaust: Human Rights and Genocide Education in the Approaching Post-Witness Era*, eds. Charlotte Schaillé, Helga Thorson, and Andrea Van Noord (Regina, SK: University of Regina Press, forthcoming).

19 Some turnover of personnel is inevitable in a project of this size and duration. Student research assistants graduated. Changes also occurred due to retirements and transitions of staff at partner museums and archives. The complement of academic researchers, by contrast, has remained comparatively stable over time.

20 Selected prior works connected with the research collective include Jordan Stanger-Ross and Pamela Sugiman eds., *Witness to Loss: Race, Culpability, and Memory in the Dispossession of Japanese Canadians* (Montreal & Kingston: McGill-Queen's University Press, 2017); Tadashi Jack Kagestu, *The Tree Trunk Can Be My Pillow: A Biography of an Outstanding Japanese Canadian* (Victoria, BC: University of Victoria Publishing, 2017); Jordan Stanger-Ross, ed., "Landscapes of Injustice: Unearthing the Dispossession of Japanese Canadians, 1940s," special issue, *Journal of American Ethnic History* 37, no. 4 (Summer 2018); Eric Adams, "Constitutional Stories: Japanese Canadians and the Constitution of Canada," *Australasian Canadian Studies* 35 (forthcoming); Martin Holmes, "Algorithmic Determination of Japanese Ethnic Identity Based on Name," *Journal of the Japanese Association for Digital Humanities* 3, no. 1 (2018): 73–97; Matt James and Jordan Stanger-Ross, "Impermanent Apologies: On the Dynamics of Timing and Public Knowledge in Political Apology," *Human Rights Review* 19, no. 3 (September 2018): 289–311; Eric Adams and Jordan Stanger-Ross, "Promises of Law: The Unlawful Dispossession of Japanese Canadians," *Osgoode Hall Law Journal* 53, no. 4 (Spring 2017): 687–739; Jordan Stanger-Ross and Nicholas Blomley, "My Land Is Worth a Million Dollars: How Japanese Canadians Contested their Dispossession in the 1940s," *Law and History Review* 35, no.3 (August 2017): 711–51; Heather Read, "The Legacy of a Hidden Camera: Acts of Making in Japanese-Canadian Internment Camps during the Second World War, as Depicted in Tom Matsui's Photograph Collection," *Material Culture Review* 84 (Fall 2016): 26–47; Jordan Stanger-Ross, "Suspect Properties: The Vancouver Origins of the Forced Sale of Japanese-Canadian-Owned Property, WWII," *Journal of Planning History* 15, no. 4 (2016): 271–89; Jim Thatcher et al, "Revisiting Critical GIS," *Environment and Planning A* 48, no. 5 (2016): 815–24; Eiji Okawa, "Community Records and the Human Experiences of the Uprooting of Japanese Canadians," *Geppo-The Bulletin: A Journal of Japanese Canadian Community, History, and Culture* (October 2016); Ariel Merriam, "'Our Appreciation for All Your Goodness and Kindness': Power, Rhetoric, and Property Relations in the Dispossession of Japanese Canadians" (Landscapes of Injustice Working Paper, April 2016), accessed 18 September 2019, https://www.landscapesofinjustice.com/wp-content/uploads/2016/05/Ariel-Merriam-Thesis.pdf; Mike Perry-Whittingham, "Negotiating Space: Public Education and the Dispossession of Japanese Canadians" (Landscapes of Injustice Working Paper, October 2016), accessed 18 September 2019, https://www.landscapesofinjustice.com/wp-content/uploads/2016/02/TR_Working-Paper-2_Negotiating-Space_Mike-PW.pdf; Laura Ishiguro, Nicole Yakashiro, and Will Archibald, "Settler Colonialism and Japanese Canadian History" (Landscapes of Injustice Working Paper, September 2017), accessed 18 September 2019, https://www.landscapesofinjustice.com/wp-content/uploads/2018/02/Working-

Paper-3-Settler-Colonialism-and-Japanese-Canadian-History.pdf; Nicole Yakashiro, "Record Group: The Veterans Land Act" (Landscapes of Injustice Working Paper, January 2018), accessed 18 September 2019, https://www.landscapesofinjustice.com/wp-content/uploads/2018/02/Working-Paper-4-Veterans-Land-Act.pdf; John Lutz, Jordan Stanger-Ross, Kaitlin Findlay, and Tsugio Kurushima, "Island Voices: Teahouse Plan Offers a Vision for Esquimalt," *Times Colonist*, 24 April 2019; Jordan Stanger-Ross, Eric Adams, and Laura Madokoro, "Lessons from the Japanese Canadian Internments: Policies Built on Fear Won't Make Us Safer," *Globe and Mail*, 19 January 2016.

21 Keiko Mary Kitagawa, interview by Rebeca Salas, 17 June 2017, Tsawwassen, British Columbia, LOIOH.

22 Observation of the powerful moral truth contained in such testimony does not mean that listening to it is straightforward or that the actions that should follow from it are obvious. "Transformational listening," as Paige Raibmon has argued, is complicated and fraught (see "Introduction" in Elsie Paul, Paige Raibmon, and Harmony Johnson, *Written as I Remember It: Teachings (ʔəms taʔaw) from the Life of a Sliammon Elder* (Vancouver: UBC Press, 2015).

23 Ira Berlin, "Coming to Terms with Slavery in Twenty-First Century America," in *Slavery and Public History: The Tough Stuff of American Memory*, eds. James Oliver Horton and Lois E. Horton (New York and London: New Press , 2006 [distributed by Norton]), 3–4.

24 Our project benefits from partnership with major Japanese Canadian organizations – the Japanese Canadian Cultural Centre, the National Association of Japanese Canadians, the NNM, and the Vancouver Japanese Language School & Japanese Hall – created its own community council, comprised of leaders from across Canada, and included key individual Japanese Canadian researchers and educators. By the midpoint of the project, Japanese Canadian individuals and representatives of Japanese Canadian organizations constituted majorities on our major committees. However, not all Japanese Canadians support Landscapes of Injustice or research on these topics in general. On ambivalence within the community with respect to research on the internment, see Pamela Sugiman, "I Can Hear Lois Now: Corrections to My Story of the Internment of Japanese Canadians – 'For the Record,'" in *Oral History off the Record: Toward an Ethnography of Practice*, eds. Anna Sheftel and Stacey Zembrzycki (New York: Palgrave, 2013), 149–67. On some of the complications of engaging this history across differences of origin and experience, see Kirsten Emiko McAllister, *Terrain of Memory: A Japanese Canadian Memorial Project* (Vancouver: UBC Press, 2010), particularly chapter 6.

25 Japanese Canadians have created a vast cultural legacy. Some relevant books include Joy Kogawa, *Obasan* (Toronto: Penguin Books, 1983); Toyo Takata, *Nikkei Legacy: The Story of Japanese Canadians from Settlement to Today* (Toronto: NC Press, 1983); Muriel Kitagawa, *This Is My Own: Letters to Wes and Other Writings on Japanese Canadians, 1941–1948* (Vancouver: Talon Books, 1985); Roy Miki, *Surrender* (Toronto: The Mercury Press, 2001); Henry Shimizu, *Images of Internment: A Bittersweet Memoir in Words and Images* (Victoria: Ti-Jean Press, 2008); Takeo Ujo Nakano, *Within the Barbed Wire Fence: A Japanese Man's Account of his Internment in Canada* (Toronto: Lorimer, 2012); Mark Sakamoto, *Forgiveness* (Toronto: Harper Collins, 2014); Sally Ito, *The Emperor's Orphans* (Winnipeg: Turnstone Press, 2018). For a resource conveying Japanese Canadians in a wide variety of cultural fields, see http://japanesecanadianartists.com/.

26 Mona Oikawa, *Cartographies of Violence: Japanese Canadian Women, Memory, and the Subjects of the Internment* (Toronto: University of Toronto Press, 2012); McAllister,

Terrain of Memory; Masako Fukawa and Stan Fukawa, *Spirit of the Nikkei Fleet: BC's Japanese Canadian Fishermen* (Vancouver: Harbour Publishing, 2009); Greg Robinson, *A Tragedy of Democracy: Japanese Confinement in North America* (New York: Columbia University Press, 2009); Pam Sugiman, "'Life Is Sweet': Vulnerability and Composure in the Wartime Narratives of Japanese Canadians," *Journal of Canadian Studies* 43, no. 1 (2009): 186–218; Stephanie D. Bangarth, *Voices Raised in Protest: Defending Citizens of Japanese Ancestry in North America, 1942–49* (Vancouver: UBC Press, 2008); Roy, *The Triumph of Citizenship*; Ross Lambertson, *Repression and Resistance: Canadian Human Rights Activists, 1930–1960* (Toronto: University of Toronto Press, 2005); Roy Miki, *Redress: Inside the Japanese Canadian Call for Justice* (Vancouver: Raincoast Books, 2004); Audrey Kobayashi, "The Japanese-Canadian Redress Settlement and Its Implications for 'Race Relations,'" *Canadian Ethnic Studies* 24, no. 1 (February 1992): 1–20; Audrey Kobayashi, "The Uprooting of the Japanese Canadians after 1941," *Tribune* 5, no. 1 (1987): 28–35; Sunahara, *The Politics of Racism*; W. Peter Ward, *White Canada Forever: Popular Attitudes and Public Policy Toward Orientals in British Columbia* (Montreal & Kingston: McGill-Queen's University Press, 1978); Adachi, *The Enemy That Never Was*; Forrest La Violette, *The Canadian Japanese and World War II: A Sociological and Psychological Account* (Toronto: University of Toronto Press, 1948).

27 In chapter 14 of this book, Matt James and I challenge the "dark chapter" framing of this history.

28 Matt James, Jordan Stanger-Ross, and the Landscapes of Injustice Research Collective, "Impermanent Apologies: On the Dynamics of Timing and Knowledge in Public Apology," *Human Rights Review* 19, no. 3 (2018): 289–311; Stanger-Ross and Sugiman, *Witness to Loss*; Karen M. Inouye, *The Long Afterlife of Nikkei Wartime Incarceration* (Stanford: Stanford University Press, 2016); Oikawa, *Cartographies of Violence*; McAllister, *Terrain of Memory*; Sugiman, "'Life Is Sweet'"; Miki, *Redress*.

29 At the end of October 1942, the Canadian government reporting having interned and incarcerated 21,460 Japanese Canadians. They constituted more than 90 per cent of the total Japanese Canadian population (Adachi, *The Enemy That Never Was*, 415, 413).

30 Eric M. Adams, "Errors of Fact and Law: Race, Space, and Hockey in Christie v. York," *University of Toronto Law Journal* 62, no. 4 (2012): 462–97; Constance Backhouse, *Colour-Coded: A Legal History of Racism in Canada, 1900–1950* (Toronto: University of Toronto Press, 1999); James W. St G. Waker *"Race," Rights and the Law in the Supreme Court of Canada: Historical Case Studies* (Waterloo: Wilfrid Laurier University Press, 1997). The internment of German and Italian nationals in the same era brought its own injustices but, as we discuss in chapter 14, it was never contemplated for the government to uproot and intern all "persons of the Teutonic race" or the Italian race. Those internments operated within the categories of nationality and loyalty, rather than race.

31 The portrait that follows draws significantly on a similar sketch of the community in the introduction to Stanger-Ross and Sugiman, eds., *Witness to Loss*.

32 Rigenda Sumida, "The Japanese in British Columbia" (MA thesis, UBC, 1935), 28; John Douglas Belshaw, *Becoming British Columbia: A Population History* (Vancouver: UBC Press, 2009), 32. Although the overall population (and economy) was booming in this period, it also marked a period of demographic catastrophe for First Nations People (ibid., 72–90). On the political and geographic changes to British Columbia that accompanied these demographic shifts, Cole Harris, *Making Native Space: Colonialism, Resistance, and Reserves in British Columbia* (Vancouver: UBC Press, 2002).

33 John Lutz, *Makúk: A New History of Aboriginal–White Relations* (Vancouver: UBC Press, 2009).

34 Adachi, *The Enemy That Never Was*, 9–13. On Japanese migration to Canada in this era, see Yukari Takai, "Navigating Transpacific Passages: Steamship Companies, State Regulators, and Transshipment of Japanese in the Early-Twentieth-Century Pacific Northwest," *Journal of American Ethnic History* 30, no. 1 (Spring 2011): 7–34; Andrea Geiger, *Subverting Exclusion: Transpacific Encounters with Race, Caste, and Borders, 1885–1928* (New Haven: Yale University Press, 2011).

35 Sumida, "The Japanese in British Columbia," 23.

36 Audrey Kobayashi, "Emigration from Kaideima, Japan, 1885–1950: An Analysis of Community and Landscape Change" (PhD diss., UCLA, 1983); Adachi, *Enemy That Never Was*, 17. On circular migration more broadly, see Ewa Morawska, "From Myth to Reality: America in the Eyes of Eastern European Peasant Migrant Laborers," in *Distant Magnets: Expectations and Realities in the Immigrant Experience, 1840–1930*, eds. Dirk Hoerder and Horst Rossler (New York: Holmes & Meier, 1993), 241–63.

37 Adachi, *The Enemy That Never Was*, 51. The Tamura family lost an equivalent of more than $800,000 (2020 dollars) in the forced sale of a single property that they owned in the Powell Street neighbourhood. This figure is based on the author's calculations and the Landscapes of Injustice real estate database.

38 Adachi, *The Enemy that Never Was*, 112. A Methodist church had served the spiritual needs of Japanese Canadian Christians in the neighbourhood since 1906, (ibid., 111).

39 Kishizo Kimura, "Memoir," in *Witness to Loss*, eds. Stanger-Ross and Sugiman, 87.

40 "Dominion Policy in Favor of Influx," *Vancouver Daily Province*, 25 July 1907, 1.

41 Adachi, *The Enemy That Never Was*, 63–87; Patricia Roy, *A White Man's Province*, 185–228; Julie F. Gilmour, *Trouble on Main Street: Mackenzie King, Reason, Race, and the 1907 Vancouver Riots* (Toronto: Allan Lane, 2014); David Atkinson, "Out of One Borderland, Many: The 1907 Anti-Asia Riots and the Spatial Dimensions of Race and Migration in the Canada–US Pacific Borderlands," in *Entangled Migration History: Borderlands and Transnationalism in the United States and Canada*, eds. Benjamin Bryce and Alexander Freund (Gainesville: Florida University Press, 2015), 120–40.

42 Erika Lee, "Orientalism in the Americas: A Hemispheric Approach to Asian American History," *Journal of Asian American Studies* 8, no. 3 (2005), 237, 238. See also Kornel Chang, *Pacific Connections: The Making of the US–Canadian Borderlands* (Berkeley: University of California Press, 2012).

43 Roy, *The Oriental Question*, 5; Roy, *A White Man's Province*.

44 Patrick Dunae et al., "Making the Inscrutable, Scrutable: Race and Space in Victoria's Chinatown, 1891," *BC Studies* 169 (Spring 2011), 7–49; Renisa Mawani, *Colonial Proximities: Crossracial Encounters and Juridical Truths in British Columbia, 1871–1921* (Vancouver and Toronto: UBC Press, 2009); Timothy John Stanley, *Contesting White Supremacy: School Segregation, Anti-Racism, and the Making of Chinese Canadians* (Vancouver: UBC Press, 2011); Roy, *The Triumph of Citizenship*; Kay Anderson, *Vancouver's Chinatown: Racial Discourse in Canada, 1875–1980* (Montreal & Kingston: McGill-Queen's University Press, 1991); Roy, *White Man's Province*; David Chuenyan Lai, *Chinatowns: Towns within Cities in Canada* (Vancouver: UBC Press, 1988); Sunahara, *The Politics of Racism*; Ward, *White Canada Forever*; Adachi, *The Enemy That Never Was*.

45 Mawani, *Colonial Proximities*, 37.

46 Timothy Stanley, "Kishizo Kimura and the Articulations of a Society Structured in Dominance," in *Witness to Loss*, eds. Stanger-Ross and Sugiman, 123–45.
47 Belshaw, *Becoming British Columbia*, 57.
48 Adachi, *The Enemy That Never Was*, 142–53.
49 Sumida, "Japanese in British Columbia," 102–3, 419; Ann-Lee Switzer, *Gateway to Promise: Canada's First Japanese Community* (Victoria, BC: Ti-Jean Press, 2012); Fukawa and Fukawa, *Spirit of the Nikkei Fleet*; Michiko Midge Ayukawa, *Hiroshima Immigrants in Canada, 1891–1941* (Vancouver: UBC Press, 2008); Takata, *Nikkei Legacy*; Adachi, *The Enemy That Never Was.*
50 Sumida, "Japanese in British Columbia," 218–19.
51 "It's Up to Us," *New Canadian*, 5 June 1941, 2.
52 A.W. Neill, quoted in Adachi, *The Enemy That Never Was*, 163.
53 See Norman Hillmer, Bohdan Kordan, and Lubomyr Luciuk eds., *On Guard for Thee: War, Ethnicity, and the Canadian State, 1939–1945* (Ottawa: Government of Canada, 1988), 63. For a short time, Canada also interned refugees of enemy nationality, including German Jews. See Paula Jean Draper, "Fragmented Loyalties: Canadian Jewry, the King Government, and the Refugee Dilemma," ibid., 151–78.
54 See page 216 in this volume. Canada's First World War internments seem to offer closer parallel to the Japanese Canadian case. With more than 8,000 interned during that war, the Canadian government assumed control of significant property. See Bohdan S. Kordan and Craig Mahovsky, *Bare and Impolitic Right: Internment and Ukrainian-Canadian Redress* (Montreal & Kingston: McGill-Queen's University Press, 2004), 34–9.
55 With our focus on property came a shift in the contexts we regarded as relevant. Such corresponding reorientations should be expected. Philosopher of history Arthur Danto doubted that even the barest historical fact (e.g. the date of an event) could be established without connection to other historical events: historical explanation is the work of connection. Danto, who is regrettably overlooked in the profession's rush to Hayden White, memorably conveyed the link between focus and context in (for example) imagining an informant asked to "tell all" about the unfolding of a court trial. "I should be dismayed if," Danto observed, "he were to tell me how many flies were in the courtroom, and show me a complicated map of the precise orbit in which they flew, a vast tangle of epicycles" (*Narration and Knowledge* [New York: Columbia University Press: 1985], 131). The flight of a fly could only be relevant detail in connection with other events of significance: the witness displayed a strange phobia, an attorney made brilliant use of its presence to illustrate a point, a piece of evidence was ruined in an effort to shoo it away. Context and focus are interwoven to constitute narrative.
56 John C. Weaver, *The Great Land Rush and the Making of the Modern World, 1650–1900* (Montreal & Kingston: McGill-Queen's University Press, 2003); Brenna Bhandar, *Colonial Lives of Property Law, Land, and Racial Regimes of Ownership* (Durham, NC: Duke University Press, 2018), 3–4. See also Tracey Banivanua-Mar and Penelope Edmonds, eds., *Making Settler Colonial Space: Perspectives on Race, Place and Identity* (New York: Palgrave Macmillan, 2010); Cole Harris, "How Did Colonialism Dispossess? Comments from an Edge of Empire," *Annals of the Association of American Geographers* 94, no. 1 (March 2004): 165–82; Harris, *Making Native Space*; Sherene Razack, *Race, Space, and the Law: Unmapping a White Settler Society* (Toronto: Between the Lines, 2002); Hamar

Foster, "'Letting Go the Bone': The Idea of Indian Title in British Columbia, 1849–1927," in *Essays in the History of Canadian Law: British Columbia and the Yukon*, ed. Foster and John McLaren (Toronto: University of Toronto Press, 1995), 28–86.

57 See, for example, Backhouse, *Colour Coded*, chapters 2 and 4.

58 The following paragraphs draw significantly upon Ishiguro et al., "Settler Colonialism and Japanese Canadian History." See also Nicole Yakashiro, "Daffodils as Property: Settler Colonial Renewal and the Dispossession of Nikkei Farmers in the 1940s" (MA thesis, UBC, 2019).

59 Chapter 10.

60 Ivan Barnet to Gordon Murchison, 2 June 1944, file V-8-10, pt. I, vol. 403, RG 38, LAC.

61 Kisaku Nishimoto to F.G. Shears, 9 August 1944, image 1629, C9476, Héritage.

62 Case file 1035, Kisaku Nishimoto (Toronto), vol. 52, RG 33-69, LAC.

63 Keith Thor Carlson et al., "'For we are the real owners of the land from time immemorial as god create us Indians in this territory': Historical Land Use, Territory, and Aboriginal Title of the Matsqui People," hearing order OH-001-2014, 26 May 2015, https://apps.neb-one.gc.ca/REGDOCS/Item/View/2785415. Thanks to Keith Carlson for comments on this paragraph.

64 The toxicity of colonialism and racism also gave occasion for Indigenous people to abet discrimination against Japanese Canadians, as for example when some Aboriginal leaders supported their exclusion in testimony before the 1902 Report of the Royal Commission on Chinese and Japanese Immigration (Ottawa: 1902), 345, https://archive.org/details/cu31924023463965/page/n365.

65 Will Archibald, Laura Ishiguro, Laura Madokoro, and Nicole Yakashiro deserve particular credit for raising this topic for discussion within the research collective. Members of our project have sometimes debated the extent to which the Japanese Canadian experience was exceptional within the history of Canada or, conversely, typical of the foundational injustice of a colonial state. For my own part, I find both perspectives compelling but neither entirely so. In this respect I am reminded of the argument of Emil Fackenheim (a survivor of both a German concentration camp and an internment camp in Canada, where he and other German Jewish refugees were held as "enemy aliens"), for whom the terms "unique" and "universal" both failed to describe the Nazi Holocaust of the Jews ("Concerning Authentic and Unauthentic Responses to the Holocaust," *Holocaust and Genocide Studies* 1 [1986]: 101–20). The first threatens to reduce it to "a single aberration in an otherwise respectable history, which … may therefore be simply resumed" (104); the second risks overlooking the enormity of the event, "making it merely a case of the species 'persecution-in-general'" (104), a position that leaves room for neither history nor healing. See Stanger-Ross "Naziism in Canada?"

66 J.A. Krug, *The Wartime Handling of Evacuee Property* (Washington: US Government Print Office), 52, https://www.hathitrust.org/. Thanks to Eric Muller for sharing this source and his reflections on it.

67 Krug, *Wartime Handling of Evacuee Property*, 71.

68 The historiography in the United States does not yet include an accounting of property losses comparable with the work of Landscapes of Injustice. Thus, extensive primary research would be required to comprehensively assess the material impacts of the divergent policies.

69 On the American policy, see Greg Robinson, *By Order of the President: FDR and the Internment of Japanese Americans* (Cambridge, MA: Harvard University Press, 2001), 134–

46. More broadly on the economic impacts of the American incarceration, see Leonard Broom and Ruth Riemer, *Removal and Return: The Socio-Economic Effects of the War on Japanese Americans* (Berkeley: University of California Press, 1973 [1949]); Frank S. Arnold, Michael C. Barth, and Gilah Langer, *Economic Losses of Ethnic Japanese as a Result of Exclusion and Detention, 1942–1946* (Washington, DC: ICF Incorporated, 1983); Sandra C Taylor "Evacuation and Economic Loss: Questions and Perspectives," and Gary Y. Okihiro and David Drummond, "The Concentration Camps and Japanese Economic Losses in California Agriculture, 1900–1942," in *Japanese Americans: From Relocation to Redress*, ed. Roger Daniels et al. (Seattle: University of Washington Press, 1992), 163–75; Natasha Varner, "Sold, Damaged, Stolen, Gone, Japanese American Property Losses during WWII," Densho Blog, 4 April 2014, https://densho.org/sold-damaged-stolen-gone-japanese-american-property-loss-wwii/.

70 Frank Bajohr, "Expropriation and Expulsion," in *The Historiography of the Holocaust*, ed. Dan Stone (New York: Palgrave MacMillan, 2004), 59.

71 Harold James, *The Deutsche Bank and the Nazi Economic War Against the Jews: The Expropriation of Jewish-Owned Property* (Cambridge: Cambridge University Press, 2004), 4.

72 Memorandum by Henry Forbes Angus for Norman Robertson, 15 March 1943, file c-4606-13-40, vol. 3121, RG 25, LAC.

73 Douglas Porteous and Sandra Eileen Smith, *Domicide: The Global Destruction of Home* (Montreal & Kingston: McGill-Queen's University Press, 2001), 12.

74 Porteous and Smith, *Domicide*, 20, 7–8. Japanese Canadians are mentioned on 199.

75 Porteous and Smith, *Domicide*, 6.

76 Kim Dovey, "Home: An Ordering Principle in Space," *Landscape* 22, no. 2 (1978): 27–8.

77 Matthew Desmond, *Evicted: Poverty and Profit in the American City* (New York: Crown Publishers, 2016), 293.

78 The letters below are analyzed and contextualized in chapter 4.

79 Toshiye Hoshiko to Office of the Custodian, 22 October 1944, image 1524, C9476, Héritage.

80 Rokusaburo and Mitsuye Taniguchi, 31 July 1944, image 1445–1446, image 1424, C9476, Héritage.

81 H.K. Naruse to The Custodian'[*sic*] Office, 26 July 1947, image 1782, C9476, Héritage.

82 Rikizo Yoneyama to Minister of Justice, 31 July 1944, image 1448–1449, C9476, Héritage.

83 Rikizo Yoneyama to Minister of Justice, 31 July 1944, image 1448–1449, C9476, Héritage.

84 Toshiye Hoshiko to Office of the Custodian, 22 October 1944, image 1524, C9476, Héritage.

85 Toshiye Hoshiko, file 1336, vol. 67, RG 33-69, LAC.

86 Lorna Fox O'Mahony and James Sweeney, "The Idea of Home in Law: Displacement and Dispossession," in *The Idea of Home in Law: Displacement and Dispossession*, eds. O'Mahony and Sweeny (London: Routledge, 2010), 7–8; O'Mahony, "The meaning of home: from theory to practice," *International Journal of Law in the Built Environment* 5, no. 2 (2013), 161; Sarah Nield, "Article 8 Respect for the Home," *King's Law Journal* 24, no. 2 (2013), 147–71.

87 Scott Leckie, "An Introduction to 'The Pinheiro Principles,' in *The Pinheiro Principles: United Nations Principles on Housing and Property Restitution for Refugees and Displaced People* (Geneva: Centre on Housing Rights and Evictions, 2005), http://2001-2009.state.gov/documents/organization/99774.pdf, quoted in Anneke Smit, *The Property Rights of Refugees and Internally Displaced People* (London: Routledge, 2013), 14.

88 On complicity see Stanger-Ross and Sugiman, *Witness to Loss.*

89 Individual Japanese Canadians continued to pursue property claims for longer, especially Torazo Iwasaki, whose claim against the government was settled in the Supreme Court, against him, in 1969. This case is discussed at 284–5 and 356–9 in this volume. See also Brian Smallshaw "The Dispossession of Japanese Canadians on Saltspring Island" (MA Thesis, University of Victoria, 2017).

90 On such projects, see James C. Scott, *Seeing Like a State: How Certain Schemes to Improve the Human Condition Have Failed* (New Haven: Yale University Press, 1999). Similar observations could be made of the internment as well, which had its own ongoing administrative processes and challenges that have been underexamined within a Canadian historiography that has favoured political and cultural analyses. Rather than drawing a theoretical distinction between internment and dispossession, this work should invite critical inquiry into the administration of the internment.

91 Eric L. Muller, *American Inquisition: The Hunt for Japanese American Disloyalty in World War II* (Chapel Hill: University of North Carolina Press, 2007), 2.

92 Gerhard L. Weinberg, *A World at Arms: A Global History of World War II* (Cambridge, UK: Cambridge University Press, 1994), 310–65; Jack L. Granatstein, *Canada's War: The Politics of the Mackenzie King Government, 1939–1945* (Toronto: Oxford University Press, 1975), 211–12, 249–50. The contrast between the political contexts of the uprooting and the dispossession of property is apparent in William Lyon Mackenzie King's diaries. See "Diaries of William Lyon Mackenzie King," February 1942, December 1942, and January 1943, LAC, http://www.bac-lac.gc.ca/eng/discover/politics-government/prime-ministers/william-lyon-mackenzie-king/.

93 The journals of the provincial legislature in British Columbia similarly contain no direct discussion of the dispossession of Japanese Canadians in the period leading to Order in Council 469. In contrast, the war cabinet, King's diary, and the records of provincial government all touch upon uprooting and internment. The federal House of Commons engaged in heated discussion of the uprooting of Japanese Canadians, particularly in the summer of 1942. When Parliament resumed in January 1943, the forced sales had already been ordered. See Canada, House of Commons, Debates, 19th Parl., 3rd and 4th sessions, accessed 18 September 2019, http://parl.canadiana.ca/browse?show=eng_c_debates_19.

94 This claim is based on a reading of the *Vancouver Daily Province* and the *Vancouver Sun* in the summer and fall of 1942. The newspapers regularly published stories related to Japanese Canadians, including news of property sales, but they followed, rather than led, the Custodian in this respect.

95 Canada, House of Commons Debates, 30 June 1942, 19th Parl., 3rd sess., vol. 4, 3795, accessed 18 September 2019, http://parl.canadiana.ca/view/oop.debates_HOC1903_04/496?r=0&s=1 (quoted in Granatstein, *Ottawa Men*, 263).

96 Canada, House of Commons Debates, 30 June 1942, 19th Parl., 3rd sess., vol. 4, 3795, accessed 18 September 2019, http://parl.canadiana.ca/view/oop.debates_HOC1903_04/496?r=0&s=1.

97 See chapter 14.

98 Sunahara, *The Politics of Racism*; Roy, *The Triumph of Citizenship*; Miki, *Redress.*

99 See chapter 6.

100 Oikawa, *Cartographies of Violence*, 132.

101 As discussed in chapter 14, the mass exile of Japanese Canadians – officials sought to deport more than 10,000 people, almost 50 per cent of the prewar coastal population – was the nadir of a cascade of policies, perhaps most importantly the dispossession of all of their property, that created Japanese Canadian placelessness.
102 Memorandum to Arthur. MacNamara, 28 March 1945, file 104, pt. 2.1, vol. 5761, RG 25, LAC. In this summary I have included the first sentence of most of Pickersgill's reported answers. The fully recorded exchange also includes a great deal more detailed questions by Japanese Canadians.
103 Tatsuo Kage, *Uprooted Again: Japanese Canadians Move to Japan After World War II* (Vancouver: Ti-Jean Press, 2012).
104 Michael Rothberg, "Trauma Theory, Implicated Subjects, and the Question of Israel/Palestine," *Profession* (MLA 2014), https://profession.mla.org/trauma-theory-implicated-subjects-and-the-question-of-israel-palestine/ and *The Implicated Subject: Beyond Victims and Perpetrators* (Stanford: Stanford University Press, 2019).
105 Nicholas Blomley, "Precarious Relationality: Property law and the social order," *Antipode* (forthcoming).
106 Michael Rothberg, "Beyond Tancred and Clorinda – Trauma Studies for Implicated Subjects," in *The Future of Trauma Theory: Contemporary Literary and Cultural Criticism*, eds. Gert Buelens, Sam Durrant, and Robert Eaglestone (New York: Routledge, 2014), xv.
107 William Lyon Mackenzie King, *Diaries*, 28 February 1942, LAC.
108 Memorandum Re Japanese, 18 December 1941, file 16, vol. 2, RG 117, LAC.
109 Hannah Arendt, "Race-Thinking Before Racism," *Review of Politics* 6 (1944), 38.
110 Chapter 8.
111 Chapters 5 and 7.
112 John Erskine Read to Norman Robertson, 6 December 1945, file 104(s) part 2.2, vol. 5761, RG 25, LAC.
113 Glenn McPherson to Ephraim H. Coleman, 27 October 1942, file V-8-10, pt. 2, Japanese and Their Farm Properties, vol. 403, RG 38, LAC.
114 Much of the discussion that follows appeared previously as Jordan Stanger-Ross, "Suspect Properties." See also chapter 5.
115 Much of Japanese Canadian–owned real estate, particularly rural property, was increasing in value during this period. See chapter 10.
116 "Housing – A World Problem: A Report of the Vancouver TPC," January 1941, file 14, Housing (1937–1950), box 61-C-6, Town Planning Commission Fonds, CVA; "A Handbook on Urban Redevelopment for Cities in the United States" (Washington, DC: Federal Housing Administration, 1941), 53, file 4, box 15, Buck Fonds; Minutes, 2 July 1942, box 77-A-2, 1942–1943, CVA.
117 Housing in Vancouver, August, 1939, file 6, box 12, Buck Fonds.
118 Ibid.
119 Town Planning Commission Minutes, 2 July 1942, box 77-A-2, 1942–1943, CVA.
120 Ibid.
121 Town Planning Commission Minutes, 6 August 1942, box 77-A-2, 1942–1943, CVA. Buscombe was one of council's most outspoken racists. In September 1942 he moved a motion to council positing that the "assimilation of … [Japanese Canadians] is impossible" and calling upon the federal government to deport the entire population to Japan (City Council Minutes, 9 September 1942, vol. 43, MCR-1-43, CVA).

122 Minutes, Vancouver City Council, 17 August 1942, vol. 44, MCR-1-44, CVA.
123 Memorandum by K.W. Wright to Glenn McPherson, 16 October 1942, file 59008, pt. 1.1, vol. 2536, RG 117, LAC.
124 Ibid.
125 Ibid.
126 The TPC's loss of control might seem to confirm the view that city planning had little influence in Vancouver until after the Second World War (Will Langford, "Is Sutton Brown God?," *BC Studies* 173 [Spring 2012]: 13, 15). However, people outside the TPC used planning ideas to exert powerful influence, particularly over the city's most marginalized residents. On this theme, see also Jordan Stanger-Ross, "Municipal Colonialism in Vancouver: City Planning and the Conflict over Indian Reserves, 1928–1950s," *Canadian Historical Review* 89, no. 4 (December 1, 2008): 541–80.
127 Glenn McPherson to F.G. Shears, 12 January 1943, folder 2, box 2, F.G. Shears Papers, Thomas Fisher Rare Book Library, University of Toronto (hereafter Shears Papers).
128 Chapter 5.
129 Glenn McPherson to Ephraim H. Coleman, 12 December 1942, file V-8-10, pt. 2, Japanese and Their Farm Properties, vol. 403, RG 38, LAC.
130 Memorandum by Ephraim H. Coleman re: Real Estate owned by persons of the Japanese race evacuated from the Defence Area of British Columbia, December 1942, file 70-25c: Liquidating Lands in the Fraser Valley that are Jap Owned, vol. 25, MG 27 III-B5, LAC.
131 Sunahara places Mackenzie at the centre of the property dispossession, whereas I argue that he joined arguments already developed by others. See Sunahara, *The Politics of Racism*, chapter 5.
132 Norman McLarty to Ian Mackenzie, 21 December 1942, file 70-25c, Liquidating Lands in the Fraser Valley that are Jap Owned, vol. 25, MG 27 III-B5, LAC.
133 Ian Mackenzie to Norman McLarty, 23 December 1942, file 70-25c, Liquidating Lands in the Fraser Valley that are Jap Owned, vol. 25, MG 27 III-B5, LAC.
134 Kimura "Memoir," in *Witness to Loss*, eds. Stanger-Ross and Sugiman, 67.
135 Ibid., 98, 67.
136 Ibid., 67.
137 Ibid., 70.
138 See chapter 10.
139 See Stanger-Ross, "Suspect Properties," as well as chapters 5 and 7.
140 Michael Freeden, *Ideology: A Very Short Introduction* (Oxford: Oxford University Press, 2003), 63.
141 Ibid., 52.
142 Robinson, *Tragedy of Democracy*, 263. Stephanie Bangarth, in another comparative volume, notes that the policies in Canada and the United States began to "diverge dramatically" at this point (*Voices Raised in Protest*, 33).
143 The following portrait is drawn from Jordan Stanger-Ross, "Introduction," in Kagetsu, *The Tree Trunk Can Be My Pillow*.
144 Bird Commission Report, 24 March 1950, box 8, file 8, Shears Papers.
145 Betty Toyota and Joy Trapnell, interview by Kyla Fitzgerald and Mike Abe, 12 October 2016, Duncan, British Columbia, LOIOH.

PART ONE

The Deliberate Killing of Home

CHAPTER 1

Property and Its Transformation for Issei during the Meiji and Taisho Periods

Audrey Kobayashi

As we begin our analysis of property in the 1940s uprooting and dispossession of Japanese Canadians, the question arises: What did property mean in a Japanese Canadian community context? Property can be counted and assessed – and has been – in various ways, but what are the cultural considerations that can help us to understand its meaning for the ordinary people who were wrenched from their land holdings during the 1940s? Property represented their labours, their hopes for themselves and their descendants, and their status in a community built on common cultural principles and definitions of belonging in the world. In this chapter, I cast back to the political economy of the late nineteenth and early twentieth centuries, the later Meiji and Taisho periods, when the first generation of emigrants, the Issei, travelled to Canada to find labour that would allow them to purchase property. Some of the returned to Japan to purchase property, and others chose to purchase property in Canada. In either case, property ownership, which played a very explicit role in Japanese society, was the impetus for labour migration.

In his recent "reinterpretation" of Japan and of the various "modernization" theories to which that country has been subjected, Patrick Smith claims that both Japan and the "West" have undergone a series of reimaginings of what Japan is all about.[1] Smith's theme is that there is a long-standing contradiction between the big and small, between the sometimes excessive extremes of a national government that since the institution of the Meiji period in 1868 had lurched from one to another major political/economic/military reform to another, and the ordinary experiences of Japanese people, whose lives often but not always intersect with the exigencies of the state. Western scholars, Smith claims, have romanticized, Orientalized, misinterpreted, and misrepresented Japan in myriad ways in the name both of justifying perplexing and seemingly contradictory traits and, he claims, of trying to make them fit a Western scholarly world view. The Meiji period was rife with contradictions between the small lives of ordinary citizens and the big actions of an emerging nation-state. International emigration, the background for the formation of a Japanese Canadian community, was a series of small actions on the part of individuals attempting to make lives for themselves in the so-called "modernization" of Japan that the Meiji period represented.

The contradictions of the Meiji period

In keeping with Smith's point, my task here is to shed light on the conditions that were faced by ordinary Japanese people who by the turn of the twentieth century faced a contradictory situation. Since the Meiji restoration in 1868, they had undergone a fundamental shift in the meaning of citizenship as those who were previously commoners were given statutory rights, including the right to private ownership of property. Property ownership was welded onto a centuries-old tradition in which social life revolved around the hereditary household, or *dozoku*, which was run according to what are often called "Confucian" values of patriarchal obligation but that were in any case deeply rooted in patrilineal primogeniture. Eldest sons and their eldest sons inherited and passed on the responsibility to care for the household and the inhabitants who passed through the household from generation to generation. When the Meiji regime established the possibility of individual land ownership, replacing in principle the centuries-old tradition of vassalage, along with it came a strengthening of the ancient concept of the *dozoku* and a loosening of the relationship with the nobility that had marked the Tokugawa period but also an entirely new relationship with the modern nation-state in the form of taxation. It was an excellent fulfillment of the old adage that the government giveth and taketh.

The Meiji state acted very quickly to dismantle national institutions, especially those of fealty and isolationism, which had become an ossified set of structures under the Tokugawa, but the transformation of common society was a much more drawn out affair. It could be said that by building upon common traditions, and even elevating ideals and aspirations that had formerly been the reserve of the nobility (what some writers have called the "samuraization" of Japanese society), in a revolution from above, the new Japanese state established a hegemonic relationship with its citizens, preempting the widespread social disorganization that might have occurred. The Meiji measures of 1) entering a global capitalist economy; 2) establishing a powerful military; 3) developing massive infrastructure in the form of transportation and communication; and 4) creating a new political system of central control were all carried out autocratically.

A number of scholars have shown that notwithstanding the transformation of ordinary life through education and the revamping of the notion of citizenship, the local effects were actually quite disastrous.[2] The overall strategy was to maintain the agrarian economy until internal industrial production increased, without incurring a large foreign debt. The Land Revision Tax of 1873 set the terms of taxation, under which taxes were exacted for the first time in cash rather than in kind and standardized according to land holdings rather than the size of the crop.

The threat to agrarian life was of course a fundamental threat to life in general. No account was taken of the vagaries of natural conditions that caused drastic fluctuation in the farmers' yearly incomes, as agrarian households survived by a narrower and narrower margin.[3] When crops were damaged or destroyed either by drought in summer or by flooding caused by typhoons during the harvest season, people died. By the 1880s, when deflationary policies were introduced to offset the loss of specie in a globalizing economy, farming as a much-vaunted way of life was doubly threatened, at the same time that the government sang the virtues of the farmer.[4]

By lifting the Tokugawa ban on private sales of property, the government raised expectations of people with a newly forged sense of citizenship, while in reality consolidation of property in the hands of wealthy landlords was occurring rapidly. By the end of the 1880s, vassalage had been ended, but the proportion of land under tenant versus owner cultivation had risen drastically and dispossession rates increased. Bowen cites that the loss of agrarian land to tenants was huge: "the value of the land lost was twenty-seven times greater than the value of the average debt that each person owed in taxes."[5] There resulted mass migration (mainly to industrializing cities) and in some cases imprisonment and suicides. Added to taxation was a massive burden of conscription. By forcing the collapse of previously unassailable social classes, the Meiji government actually brought about a poverty of equality.[6] That is, ordinary people now had the rights but also the demands of full citizenship, including taxation and conscription, and the loss of whatever obligation former landlords may have had to feed them in difficult times. At the household level, one of the most powerful impacts of the Meiji measures was a transformation of the labour system. In the countryside the increases in taxes, along with the decline of traditional rural handicraft industries in favour of industrialization, suited the demand for low-paid industrial labour and created a massive blue-collar population over a few decades, beginning in the 1880s. There developed a widespread practice of *dekasegi* (meaning to "go out to work") that involved the mass movement of men and women from the countryside to the cities. Although this topic is beyond the scope of the chapter, working conditions were terrible on the whole, especially for women, and the difficulties of shifting to an industrial workforce only made greater the appeal of remaining in the rural areas as part of the valued and respected agrarian class. The *dozuko* system provided strong incentive and encouragement for those who were first-born sons to continue the household but also – and ironically – to use temporary industrial migration, *dekasegi*, to stabilize the financial conditions of the *dozuko*. Participation in the modern economy was necessary in order to preserve the traditional economy. For those who did not inherit, mainly second and third sons, or first sons of the poorest families, the options were to be adopted into a son-less farming family, to earn enough to establish a new household (very rare), or to migrate permanently. Few of those non-successor sons who undertook *dekasegi* ever returned to their villages, however, not only because the economic goals were unreachable but also because the rural economy could support only a limited population. As the philosopher Jean-Paul Sartre reminds us, scarcity (inflected with cultural definition) is often what drives both the individual and the community to reorganize their lives.[7]

The Canadian historian Herbert Norman's attempt to clarify the conditions under which Japanese "modernization" occurred remains remarkably apt. On the one hand, he claimed, the combined effects of the Meiji measures inscribed national loyalty, an antipathy to foreign ways, and national unity; on the other, it emphasized democracy, liberalism, universal suffrage, and the rights and dignity of the (land-owning) household.[8] By forcing the populace to become involved in activities heretofore outside the realm of their understanding, such as shifting from in-kind tariffs to taxes, and shifting from agrarian to industrial work, the government was matching its rhetoric with action in order to create – on the backs of the agrarian classes – a modern political economy while at the same time, Norman emphasizes, elevating principles of obligation and filial piety that had been at the centre of their understanding for centuries.

International migration as *dekasegi*

Overseas migration, which began in the 1880s, should be viewed as a form of *dekasegi* labour. People migrated for employment, whether to Honolulu, San Francisco, Vancouver, or closer to home in Osaka or Tokyo. International migration had been made possible in 1868 when the Tokugawa ban on travel was lifted, but it was not practical for some time. The first large migration was in the form of contract labour to Hawaii, where some 30,000 began to work in the 1880s.[9] Contract labour occurred as a result of recruitment from specific parts of the county, mainly in the western half, and like much of the *dekasegi* practice occurred through established lines of patronage.[10] Wakatsuki claimed that the key to understanding emigration lay not only in the ways in which *dekasegi* possibilities were communicated but also in the ways in which it fit regional patterns of social formation.[11] For one thing, the degree to which the industrial economy penetrated the countryside was uneven, as was the impact of modernization upon things such as taxation, crop yields, and connection to urban areas. There was regional variation not only in numbers but also in rates of remittances (to maintain households in the villages of origin) and in rates of return migration (especially for first sons to take up their hereditary duties).[12] These points are very important for understanding how emigration to Canada occurred.

The first labour immigration from Japan to Canada is believed to have commenced in 1877 (not counting diplomats, business people, scholars, clergy, etc.). A Japanese Canadian presence was established in the Vancouver sawmill industry in the 1880s and in the fishing and mining industries by the 1890s.[13] Early migrants were disproportionately from two prefectures, Shiga and Wakayama, and almost exclusively male, reflecting both the lines of patriarchy through which *dekasegi* was organized – as one migrant sponsored another, and he another, and so on – and specific regional economic systems.[14] The emigrants from Shiga Prefecture made up the largest group of workers in the sawmill industry, centred in but not exclusive to Vancouver; while those from Wakayama were the largest group in the fishing industry, centred in but not exclusive to Steveston.

For those Issei whose origins were in traditional agrarian areas of Japan, the desire to earn money to invest in a traditional Japanese life was very high. Put simply, emigration was considered a necessity if the agrarian household was to continue. Those migrants had a singular goal of earning enough to escape tenancy and to elevate their social status by acquiring property. Property acquisition was both the desire and the responsibility of first-born sons, who would continue the family line. The first emigrants, therefore, were usually household heads, many of who travelled back and forth across the Pacific in order to fulfill filial obligations. Second and subsequent sons were often sponsored by the original immigrants and it was these nonsuccessors who became the permanent immigrants and made up Japanese Canadian society. For second and subsequent sons, the objective remained that of establishing ideal conditions for a family.

By 1907–08, when labour migration was well established but the Canadian government had restricted immigration to those already in Canada and their immediate relatives, the "picture bride" system (*shashin-kekkon*) was developed in order to ensure that household formation could occur across the Pacific. In reality, of course, this system was merely an extension of the arranged marriage system through which household continuation was assured in the village. It was after 1908, therefore, that the community began to grow substantially, as the Issei settled in the two largest centres, the Powell Street area of Vancouver and Steveston, a fishing village on the Fraser River. These communities included infrastructure such as temples/churches, schools, newspapers, and commercial enterprises.

Property ownership was a very important part of the growing community. For some, especially from coastal fishing villages in Japan, it meant the purchase of a fishing boat as a means of livelihood. For some, it was commercial and residential property in Vancouver, as a means not only of livelihood but of community status as well. For many, especially second and subsequent sons for whom there was little or no prospect of returning to agrarian life in Japan, it meant the purchase of agricultural land, especially in the Fraser River Valley, on some of the islands in the Gulf of Georgia, or in the Okanagan Valley in the BC interior. There too, agriculture represented not only a livelihood but also a way of establishing a household in the traditional Japanese manner. Agrarian life remained a vaunted status, but it was one facet of the fiercely independent approach taken by the Issei.[15]

Rates of return to Japan also varied. They were very high for Shiga and low for Wakayama. It is widely speculated that the differences occurred because the Shiga emigrants originated from the Koto Plain, south of Hikone City, one of the most fertile and productive parts of the country, whereas those from Wakayama came from a coastal region where there was less room for productive agriculture. This deterministic explanation needs to be taken with scepticism and certainly needs development and complication, but we can recognize at the outset that many of the Wakayama emigrants had a background in fishing, an occupation they also followed in Canada, and almost all of the Shiga emigrants came from agricultural areas – albeit at the time of the greatest migration from the 1890s until World War I, the majority were landless tenants. I present here one case study of a small village in Shiga, which had one of the highest rates of emigration and one of the highest rates of return to purchase agricultural land in the original village. This case study allows us to understand the important role of agrarian property in traditional Japanese society, but it also sheds light on the ways in which Issei immigrants sorted themselves into those who returned to Japan and those who remained in Canada to form a permanent Japanese Canadian society in which property also played a major role.

Kaideima, Shiga prefecture: A case study

A casual visitor to the village of Kaideima today would likely marvel at the architectural splendour of the houses that line its extremely tidy streets. The majority of the homes in this compact settlement were built during the Taisho period (1912–26). They are substantial wooden structures that depict traditional craftsmanship: central post construction, elaborate entryways (*genkan*), floors covered in tatami mats. Inside, pride of place is held by an elaborate *butsudan* (Buddhist altar) made of lacquered wood and covered in gold leaf. Many of the houses are fronted by traditional gardens that evoke the centuries-old Buddhist values according to which they were constructed. The houses look very much like those of prosperous agricultural land owners/landlords of the Meiji period. But there is something amiss: In the Meiji period, there would have been one or two major landholders in a village this size. The majority of the population would have lived in a cluster of small straw-roofed houses and would have rented their fields from those who lived in the big houses. Indeed, local economic conditions and the sheer lack of sufficient agricultural land to support so many landowners would have made this village impossible. Key to understanding this peculiar village landscape is *dekasegi* migration to Canada and the role that migration played in allowing Kaideima households to maintain and enhance their traditional status. Kaideima is an excellent example of the paradox of embracing tradition through modernization.

A political economy of the village would identify it as an *imin-mura*, an "emigrant village," for which successful international *dekasegi* made return to the village possible at a time when the rural countryside – as discussed above – was being depopulated as the majority of the Japanese population transitioned to industrial occupations and urban life. Kaideima is one of a few dozen villages scattered throughout Japan that tell a different *dekasegi* story. Although many left the village for industrial work, the majority of households continued (to the present), in large part because international migration enriched the village sufficiently to allow the purchase of both residential and agricultural land.

The village of Kaideima comprises approximately 135 households along the Inugami River, just southwest of the city of Hikone, on what is known as the Koto Plain, an extensive alluvial area adjacent to Lake Biwa. This case study presents previously unpublished results from my PhD dissertation, which examined the impact of emigration upon the acquisition of both housing and agricultural property during the period 1885–1950, when the majority of households (107 out of 135) sent *dekasegi* emigrants to Canada, the majority to become part of the sawmill industry in Vancouver.[16] Kaideima's fascinating story shows the ways in which the villagers were caught up in all the compulsions of the Meiji period, used *dekasegi* as a means of improving economic conditions, especially by purchasing property and building houses, in the process extending and strengthening the traditional meaning of the *dozoku*, reinforcing patriarchal ties, and facilitating a conservative and traditional way of life based on agrarian social and religious practices. All but thirty nuclear families returned to Kaideima by 1946.[17] Emigration surpassed its economic motivation to become a way of life organized around traditional structures of kinship, patronage, friendship, and religion. The experience for any individual was conditioned by family position (especially birth order of sons), socioeconomic status (household property holdings), and length of tenure in Canada.

The study involved a detailed analysis of all demographic events (births, marriages, migrations, deaths, and, in some cases, adoptions from one household to another), matched to records of all property transactions (domestic and agricultural) over the period 1885 to 1950.[18] This timeframe extends past the emigration period to include events and transactions during the years following return migration, including the postwar national land reform redistribution.[19] Within the patriarchal system of primogeniture, the records provide information on hereditary male household heads (usually first sons but, in absence of a son, the inheritor may be an adopted son for whom marriage to a daughter was often arranged), as well as second and occasionally subsequent sons who established new branch households, a practice that was relatively rare in traditional Japan except for households of considerable means.[20] Data from historical records were augmented by in-person interviews and a written survey (conducted in 1981–82) with current household members, some of whom had been born in Canada during the 1920s and 1930s.[21]

The first international *dekasegi* from the village is believed to have occurred in the mid-1880s, but the individual who is credited with having established opportunities to immigrate to Canada left in 1895. He opened the first store on Powell Street to sell household goods imported from Japan and established labour possibilities for the villagers by becoming a contractor to the sawmills that formed Vancouver's original economic base. Such contractors were referred to as "bosses," who sponsored new immigrants, found them work, provided accommodation in the boarding houses on Powell Street (which they owned), and even provided translation services and transmission of remittances to Japan. Over the next several years, a group of twenty men left the village; they were the establishment of the village, men active in decision-making, known and respected, and for the most part household heads and already small landholders.[22] Emigration represented a significant investment, and therefore it was the household heads and their successors in whom the precious cash for an ocean passage was invested in the hope that they would earn funds to reinvest in the village households. These individuals travelled back and forth between Japan and Canada, and their remittances consolidated their place in the village by allowing them to increase agricultural holdings and to build substantial houses after a few years. The number of migrants increased, extending to lesser landholders and in many cases second and subsequent sons. The 1908 "Gentlemen's Agreement" between Canada and Japan limited further immigration to direct relatives of those already in Canada, including spouses, but by that time the number of households sending emigrants had already been established.[23]

It was possible to create a profile of each household in the village by combining all the data sources. In 1890, the majority of the land surrounding the village was held by landlords, the largest of whom was nonresident. Over the study period, 537 individual migrants from 140 family units were involved in migration to Canada: 125 male household heads and their successors; 117 male nonsuccessors; 115 women; and 190 second generation (Nisei) born in Canada, of whom forty-one were male successors.[24] Among the 125 household heads and successors, 118 returned to and remained in Kaideima, and seven remained in Canada after the 1940s. Among nonsuccessors, twenty-eight returned to and remained in Kaideima (a very high proportion compared to the rest of Japan), sixty-six eventually moved to other parts of Japan (a very low proportion), and twenty-three remained in Canada (two subsequently moved to the United States). Astonishingly, none of the emigrant household heads and successor sons who returned to the village subsequently moved to other parts of Japan; this pattern is completely at odds with Japanese population trends for the twentieth century, during which urbanization increased for most rural areas.

The majority of the Shiga emigrants lived in the Powell Street district of Vancouver, and most worked in the sawmills. They lived initially in boarding houses, which were built above and behind the commercial enterprises along Powell Street, and were owned by the "bosses" who acted as sponsors. There was a very strong reconstitution of traditional village and familial ties centred on boarding house culture. A significant number of the men moved from sawmill work to commercial enterprises, especially after women began arriving after 1908 and could contribute to family businesses. The families of Kaideima thus played a major role in the early Issei community.

Emigration was also a major economic stimulus that allowed landless families to purchase both houses and fields, and allowed those who already held land to hang onto it during periods of economic hardship and to build houses, in some cases for the families of more than one son. Up until the mid-twentieth century, socioeconomic status was defined in rural Japan almost entirely according to property ownership. At the beginning of the study period, more than two thirds of the households did not own any land (residential or agricultural), and more than 80 per cent were tenant farmers. By the end of the study, more than 80 per cent were landowners, and non-resident land owning had been eliminated.[25] The history of land purchases indicates that remittances were used first to build a house, thus securing a place in the village for current and future generations, and only after to buy agricultural property. Over the sixty-year study period, 3,000 agricultural and residential lots that make up the village changed hands an average of 3.3 times each, resulting in 10,000 transactions. It was the agrarian way of life, however, that was most cherished, rather than the actual income from the fields. Some households purchased as little as a couple of cho (about three square metres) of rice fields (*padi*) which, given the sacred esteem in which rice is held in traditional Japan, allowed them to take on the symbolic trappings of the vaunted agrarian way of life without necessarily having adequate income to sustain that life. In any case, in such families, it was possible to live through remittances from Canada before the 1940s, and after the War, most breadwinners lived in the village and travelled by automobile or public transportation to jobs in a nearby city. Among this group were thirty-four households headed by nonsuccessor sons, for whom remittances purchased residential land but no agricultural land.

It was among the poorer families that emigration had the greatest impact because in the normal course such families would not have had the resources to remain in the village beyond the turn of the twentieth century. Overall, the number of landholders doubled over a period when the national trend was for concentration under the control of wealthy landlords. Furthermore, there were generous, and very public, donations to the village shrine and temple, indications both of a certain degree of disposable income and of the importance of emigration in establishing civic pride (the names of donors are written conspicuously on plaques and statues within the shrine and temple).

The relatively high earnings attributed to emigration occurred not only because wages were higher in Canada than in Japan but also because of the strong patronage system that organized everything from purchasing tickets/passports, to obtaining labour contracts, to arranging marriages. This organization occurred through centuries-old social networks that defined village life and that were both modified and strengthened in the process of migration. The patronage system (known in Japanese as *oyakata–kokata*, literally parent–child, but referring to a relationship of sponsor and sponsored) operated at its full capacity, strengthened relationships, and was further consolidated in the built environment of the postmigration village in the form of houses, fields, shrines and temples, representing the domestic, the agrarian, and the religious landscapes that sheltered life. The meaning of those landscape elements, no matter their monetary value, cannot be understood simply as property. They represent not only the possibility but the sociocultural and ethical value of the agrarian village way of life, a way of life that borrowed much from the nobility's (*samurai*) values of the Tokugawa period but that was transformed into a set of common civil values during the Meiji period. Obligations to nation, to patrons, to family, and, crucially, to land and all that land represented, were bound up in the village landscape.

Dekasegi emigration can be understood as a modification of socioeconomic conditions in order to preserve or to enhance valued cultural traditions. In Kaideima, emigration allowed returned migrants to remain permanently in the village, decreasing economic gaps between wealthy and poor, establishing almost all of the returned migrants as land owners (even if owners of very small parcels of land), and creating a physical environment, a landscape, in which community and household could be continued according to a shared ideology. Traditional houses, plots of agricultural (rice-producing) land, and improved religious landscapes provide shared visual and symbolic representation of the relationship among these three elements according to the agrarian ideals of the Meiji period. In the postwar years, the material landscape has become a setting to reinforce traditional ideals, even as a changing national economy and changing transportation access (both rail and automobile) as well as improved education and professionalization for the descendants of emigrants, have effectively made the village a suburb from which most people commute daily to nearby Hikone and other regional cities, albeit a suburb that still looks like, and in many ways functions as, an entire village of Meiji/Taisho-period landowners.

The significance of property in Meiji Japan and Canada

The story of Kaideima should not be taken as strictly typical of all emigrant villages in Japan. Indeed, as demonstrated elsewhere, the patterns of emigration varied significantly according to regional circumstances and there is a considerable literature in Japanese that shows that such differences are related to many variables that range from local topography (hence potential to support an agrarian population), to religious differences, and social structures.[26] This story illustrates, however, some important points about the meaning of property in traditional Japan that should be borne in mind in relation to the meaning of property and its dispossession for Japanese Canadians.

First, property should be understood – in the Japanese case but indeed in almost any context – as more than a piece of land demarcated by ownership. In Meiji Japan it represented a fundamental alteration of the terms of citizenship, both formal and informal, that included the concept of civic equality (at least for men, and especially for male successors), human rights, and independence from the tyrannies of vassalage and tenancy. Economic conditions, especially through the introduction of taxes based on property holdings, made achieving the terms of property citizenship extremely difficult but all the more valuable because it presented not only economic livelihood but status within an agrarian social system that was bound up in patronage and patriarchy, fundamental forms of human connection. Property represented hope for both economic and sociocultural continuity.

Second, the majority of the Issei (first generation) who migrated to Canada considered themselves sojourners, working in sawmills or other labouring positions until such time as they had earned enough to secure their household property in Japan. Not all, of course, were as successful – for a variety of reasons – as those from Kaideima, and the process of deciding to remain in Canada was highly variable and involved individual household circumstances. We do not have the kinds of complete demographic data for other villages that we have for Kaideima, but what we know is strongly suggestive that the majority of the Japanese Canadian permanent population was made up of households headed by nonsuccessor sons. Successor status, more than any other factor, distinguishes those Issei who eventually returned to Japan from those who made permanent homes in Canada.[27] The study from Kaideima suggests that whereas it was most desirable for second sons to return to Japan to set up independent, property holding branch households, the second option was to stay in Canada and to set up households there.

We can only infer with great caution, of course, that the property purchased by those nonsuccessor Issei in Canada had meanings similar to those found in Japan. Certainly the individual circumstances of all Issei who purchased Canadian property varied greatly, and there would at the least have been a significant difference between urban and rural properties. In autobiographical accounts of Issei farm owners, virutally all mention the importance of owning property and the significance of the agrarian lifestyle for raising a family.[28] Much more detailed research is needed, but it is not too great an inference to think that property ownership in Canada was also associated with the Meiji values of independence, allegiance, and family/household continuity, especially in terms of providing for and nurturing offspring. There would also be major differences: we have no evidence to suggest that property in Canada had any national or religious meaning such as found in Japan. Nor was there necessarily any allegiance to ancestors or duty to parents – both traits that in any case would not have been carried by nonsuccessors – most of whom left their villages anyway – in Japan.

The ties to land were definitely cut by nonsuccessor sons – or cut for them by the lack of any filial rights or responsibilities – but they still maintained a set of values that linked property and a certain type of citizenship.

The final point is that in order to understand the meaning and impact of the dispossession of property from the Issei during the 1940s, it is necessary to understand that the land they owned had meaning for them in a specific and critical cultural context. The dispossession represented monetary loss to be sure, but it also represented a crucial loss of cultural identity that had been shaped and fashioned over decades to be different from that of Japan but with key traditional elements that were forged in the reformation of citizenship during the Meiji period. To understand this point helps us to understand the full magnitude and effect of the dispossession.

NOTES

1 Patrick Smith, *Japan: A Reinterpretation* (New York: Knopf, 2011).
2 See E.H. Norman, *Japan's Emergence as a Modern State: Political and Economic Problems of the Meiji Period* (New York: International Secretariat of the Institute of Pacific Relations, 1940); W.W. Lockwood. *The Economic Development of Japan: Growth and Structural Change* (Princeton, NJ: Princeton University Press, 1968).
3 Norman, *Japan's Emergence*, 144.
4 George Cyril Allen, *A Short Economic History of Modern Japan, 1867–1937* (London: George Allen and Unwin, 1972).
5 Roger Bowen, *Rebellion and Democracy in Meiji Japan: A Study of Commoners in the Popular Rights Movement* (Los Angeles: University of California Press, 1980), 96.
6 Thomas C. Smith, *Political Change and Industrial Development in Japan: Government enterprise, 1865–1880* (Stanford: Stanford University Press, 1955).
7 Jean-Paul Sartre, *Critique of Dialectical Reason*, trans. Alan Sheridan-Smith, ed. Jonathan Ree (London: New Left Books, 1976).
8 Norman, *Japan's Emergence*, 46–7. See also Herbert H. Norman, *Soldier and Peasant in Japan: The Origins of Conscription* (New York: International Secretariat of the Institute of Pacific Relations, 1940).
9 Hilary Conroy, *The Japanese Frontier in Hawaii, 1868–1898* (University of California: Berkeley and Los Angeles, 1953).
10 Alan Takeo Moriyama, "Imingaisha: Japanese Emigration Companies and Hawaii, 1894–1908" (PhD diss., UCLA, 1982).
11 Yasuo Wakatsuki, "Amerika imin tashutsu chiku no yooin bunseki" (An analysis of primary factors in the regions with high emigration levels to the United States), Tamagawa University, *Tamagawa Daigaku Nogakuo Kenkyuu Hookoku*, 19.
12 See Eishogo Ukita, "Imin no shiikiteki kendkuu" (A regional study of emigration), Okayama University, *Hoobun Gakubu Gakujutsu* Koyoo 4, 90–124.
13 Ken Adachi, *The Enemy That Never Was: A History of Japanese Canadians* (Toronto: McClelland and Stewart, 1976).
14 Audrey Kobayashi, Reuben Rose-Redwood, Sonja Aagesen, and the Landscapes of Injustice Research Collective, "Exile: Mapping the Migratory Patterns of Japanese

Canadians Exiled to Japan in 1946," *Journal of American Ethnic History* 37, no. 4 (Summer 2018): 73–89.

15 Adachi, *The Enemy That Never Was.* Audrey Kobayashi, "Emigration from Kaideima, Japan, 1885–1950: An Analysis of Community and Landscape Change" (PhD diss., UCLA, 1983).

16 Kobayashi, "Emigration from Kaideima." For an autobiographical account, see Masao Matsumiya, *Kaideima-Monogatari* (The Story of Kaideima) (Hikone: Hikone City Emigration Society, 1984).

17 Some of the villagers were on the "exile ships" that sent some 4,000 Japanese Canadians to Japan following the closure of internment camps in British Columbia. See Kobayashi et al., "Exile." But there were approximately thirty nuclear families (headed by nonsuccessor sons) remaining in Canada.

18 The demographic data were obtained from the *koseki*, the population registry, which is held at the City Hall in the City of Hikone. It is extremely rare for a researcher to be given access to population records. Property transactions are recorded in the *Tochi Dai-cho* (land records), which is held at the land records office of the City of Hikone. Over the study period, there were approximately 15,000 property transactions, measured in cho, a traditional plot comprising 1.53 square metres. Two additional sources of migration data were the records of the Gaimusho (Department of Foreign Affairs) stored in Tokyo (which recorded passports from 1897 to 1912) and various local and government records in Canada. All sources were handwritten original materials. The original village records were supplemented by data from the Shiga Prefecture *Tokei-shu* (prefectural statistics, which provide county-level surveys of all manner of things, including resident and overseas population).

19 See Toshihiko Kawagoe, "Agricultural land Reform in Postwar Japan: Experiences and Issues" (World Bank Policy Research Working Paper, 1999), http://documents.worldbank.org/curated/en/469971468771280762/Agricultural-land-reform-in-post war-Japan-experiences-and-issues.

20 In a traditional system of primogeniture, all emphasis is placed on the first son and his ability to maintain and continue the household. In households where there was no son, a suitable heir (usually a nonsuccessor son of another – often related – household) would be "adopted." Resources were too few to "waste" on setting up a second son in a branch household. In the case of Kaideima, however, international migration provided the means for a small number of nonsuccessors to return to the village to set up branch households, thereby starting a new line of primogeniture.

21 Ninety-five of 138 households surveyed responded; however, the quality and detail of information gained varied a great deal. A few provided in-depth stories and others were only vaguely aware of the role played by emigration in the village.

22 Kobayashi, "Emigration from Kaideima," 202.

23 The most comprehensive history of immigration from Japan to Canada is Adachi, *The Enemy That Never Was.*

24 The number of household heads exceeds the number of family units because in many cases there was more than one family unit per household. Note that the number of households varied over time as result of the creation of branch households, from 124 initially to 140 by midcentury, and about 150 today.

25 These figures include about twenty households that had previously been landless but received land in the postwar reforms between 1949 and 1950. During land reform,

9.4 hectares or 12 per cent of the total agricultural land shifted, but that figure represents a small proportion and nearly all of those who received such land were from nonmigrant households, since most of the migrant households had already purchased land.

26 Kobayashi et al., "Exile," provides a summary of the literature in Japanese.

27 I have read many biographical accounts in both Japanese and English, and it is extremely rare to find information regarding first sons. There are occasional references to someone being a first son of a very poor, landless family, but by far the majority claim to be second or younger sons. To cite one example, Gordon Nakayama interviewed thirty-nine Issei. Not all of those interviewed provided their birth order, but a considerable number mentioned being second or younger sons, while none mentioned being an eldest son or successor. Gordon Nakayama, *Issei* (Toronto: Britannia Printers, 1983). For a much more extensive but similar treatment, see Kazuo Ito, *Issei: A History of Japanese Immigrants in North America* (Seattle: Japanese Community Service, 1973). Ito also includes hundreds of examples of poetry, many of which celebrate agrarianism and the importance of family roots.

28 Juzo Suzuki, *Kanada Nihonjin nogyo hatten go*. (*The Development and History of Japanese Agriculture in Canada*) (Tokyo: Toyo Insatsu Kabushiki Gaisha, 1930).

CHAPTER 2

"Equally Applicable to Scotsmen": Racism, Equality, and Habeas Corpus in the Legal History of Japanese Canadians

Eric M. Adams and the Landscapes of Injustice Research Collective

Introduction

On 28 April 1931, a British Columbia provincial peace officer and immigration officer arrived at one of the lumber mills outside of Chemainus, British Columbia, with a warrant for the arrest of one of its workers, twenty-seven-year-old Munetaka Samejima. Summoned to the manager's office, a nervous Samejima faced a series of pointed questions about his immigration to Canada three years earlier. The immigration officer told Samejima that he would be taken to Victoria for further interrogation. What followed entangled Samejima in a multiyear odyssey of illegal detention, threatened deportation, and multiple judicial appeals invoking the ancient writ of habeas corpus. Ultimately reaching the Supreme Court of Canada, Samejima's case tells a story of the law's complicated interactions with migration, belonging, and equality and the uncertain relationship between courts and Canada's expanding administrative state in the early twentieth century. Exemplifying the racist disregard for the basic rights of Japanese Canadians in the everyday decisions of Canadian officials, Samejima's story also serves as a harbinger of the bureaucratic callousness that would cause so much harm in the internment, incarceration, dispossession, and exile to come.

Public displays of racism towards Japanese Canadians were common occurrences in the first half of the twentieth century. Whether in the declarations of politicians, labour leaders, or newspaper editorials, codified in legislation or orders in council, or practiced at the level of harassment, intimidation, and violence on the street, Canadian law enabled, enacted, and tolerated discrimination against Japanese Canadians and Asian Canadians more broadly.[1] Although distinct in various ways, Canada's repressive treatment of Japanese Canadians was part of a larger transnational trade in white supremacist ideas, policies, laws, and practices circulating across the British Commonwealth and United States.[2] The racist strands in Canada's immigration and citizenship law, in common with others across white settler societies, were premised on a fallacy central to the ideology of settler colonialism: that the land and its governance were exclusively for whites. At the same time, an expanding resource extraction economy and settler society demanded the skills, labour, and presence of migrants from around the world. "[W]hite supremacy on the periphery of European and American settlement," David Atkinson writes, "was fragile, apprehensive, and insecure" beset an ideological contradiction that the white race could simultaneously be supreme over others and yet under great threat. That the realities of British Columbia – the expanse and diversity of its Indigenous nations and territories, the settled presence of generations of successful migrants from Asia owning land and businesses while often becoming naturalized British subjects of Canada – undermined the fantasy of white exclusivity, only intensified the fervour of its staunchest proponents.[3] Overcoming the discriminatory features embedded within Canadian law and the prejudice of some of their neighbours, migrants from Japan continued to rely on networks of family and work to settle, participate in the economy, put down roots, and build lives and community in British Columbia.

This chapter is about the interplay between the constraining and liberating features in Canadian immigration and citizenship law. The power of law manifested in its control of bodies and shaping of destinies, in the demarcation of the contours of belonging in the political community. Law, as we shall see, formally subjected Japanese Canadians to differential treatment, but more often discrimination took shape in the discretion of the individuals, officials and police officers, lawyers and judges, wielding law's authority. While the formal status of British subject and Canadian citizenship appeared open to all, racism indelibly marked and directed the *experience* of immigration, residency, and citizenship for Japanese Canadians. Yet Samejima and his lawyers continued a tradition in the Japanese Canadian community of also calling upon the liberating features of law and broader appeals to constitutional equality and legality to challenge the unjust aspects of the racialized legal system they faced. Confronting law as a system of power, Japanese Canadians demanded that law also serve ideals of justice. If most judges opted to ignore or countenance the racist context, Samejima's case is notable for the chief justice of Canada's willingness to express unease at the discrimination at work in the everyday decisions of the Canadian state and to insist on a judicial role in scrutinizing administrative fairness. In these respects, *Samejima v Canada*[4] represents an important early equality rights case, even if still rooted in a racialized worldview. Justice is built not only in abstractions of virtue but in a crucible of adversity. It is built in our legal history.

This chapter begins with an overview of immigration, naturalization, and citizenship law as it pertained to Japanese Canadians before the Second World War. It was a system suffused with notions of racial hierarchy and animosity, the exercise of discretionary state power, and the construction of racialized notions of belonging and citizenship. In formal and informal ways, Japanese Canadians resisted that legal order by drawing on the latent features of equality, liberty, and legality of Canada's unwritten constitution. Part II returns to Samejima's immigration to Canada in 1928, a period of intensifying racial restrictions on migration and targeted deportations of Japanese Canadians. Samejima breaks a silence in the law by challenging his deportation in an era when Canada removed thousands of its residents mostly unseen and unheard within the historical record. Part III connects Samejima's legal entanglements to the history of Canadian habeas corpus litigation and dilemmas on the role of courts in supervising state action, especially in the context of racial discrimination. Part IV details Samejima's contribution to Canada's early jurisprudence of judicial review. Placing Samejima's case in historical context reveals the discriminatory power of opaque state administration, reminds us of the tradition of legal resistance employed by Japanese Canadians, and demonstrates the persistent tensions in law's competing capacities to harm and liberate.

I. Japanese Canadian citizenship: "Always remains a Japanese"

Before the Canadian Citizenship Act definitively created the statutory category of Canadian citizenship in 1946, one could become a British subject, and therefore in effect a Canadian citizen, by being born in Canada (a natural-born British subject) or by becoming a naturalized British subject according to the requirements laid out in federal naturalization legislation.[5] The precise legal consequences that flowed from status as a British subject were murky; individuals invoked its status symbolically as much as legally, often to appeal to historic rights and liberties nowhere specifically prescribed. As Peter Price explains, "[t]he term 'British subject' was remarkably capricious, a semantic shape shifter conditioned by context and person."[6] Nonetheless, status as a British subject did clearly delineate Canadians from "aliens" under the law and provide important protections of entry, as well as procedural protections in cases of threatened deportation in Canadian immigration law.[7] For most others, status as a British subject also enabled the ability to vote in federal, provincial, and municipal elections, although electoral law would specifically deny that privilege to Japanese Canadians. Beyond the formal law, qualifying as a British subject of Canada also played an important symbolic role in establishing belonging and membership in the political community of the nation state.

The ability to become a British subject was, in theory, open to all. In the first years after Confederation, immigrants from anywhere in the world could become a naturalized British subject of Canada simply upon swearing an oath of three years residence in Canada with an intention to settle and swearing an oath of allegiance to the sovereign.[8] The formal racial equality of Canada's naturalization law reflected the idea "that national allegiance was not an intractable inheritance, but a political relationship created and defined by law": a practical and sensible ethos in a nation building itself by the immigration of newcomers.[9] Nonetheless, racial equality was a mirage. Canada's new Constitution in 1867 asserted that Indigenous peoples – "Indians, and Lands reserved for the Indians" – were the subjects, not equal partners, of legislative sovereignty, wards of the state to be acted upon without their participation or consent.[10] Chinese Canadians joined Indigenous peoples as targets of legalized discrimination. In 1871, the British Columbia legislature disqualified "Chinese or Indians" from voting in provincial elections, a list expanded to include Japanese Canadians in 1895.[11] British Columbia enacted more than one hundred pieces of legislation in the ensuing decades imposing racist restrictions on mobility, additional taxes, and work prohibitions on Indigenous peoples, Chinese Canadians, Japanese Canadians, and an undefined larger category of Asians alongside them.[12] The federal government disallowed a number of these laws as unconstitutionally invading the federal government's exclusive jurisdiction over "Naturalization and Aliens," and courts struck down several others as either contrary to the division of powers or in conflict with existing federal law.[13] "Judicial interpretation," Bruce Ryder points out, "prevent[ed] the provinces from enacting legislation that interfered with the rights of Asians to reside in the province and work as wage labourers, but otherwise, with minor exceptions, left discriminatory legislation intact."[14] For its part, the federal government prohibited Asians from voting in federal elections in 1885, the same year in which it enacted a head tax on Chinese migrants, legislation that would persist for nearly four decades before giving way to an outright ban on immigration from China in 1923.[15] In combination, the array of racial restrictions imposed by law crafted hierarchies of belonging, marked nonwhites as unworthy of full citizenship, and created a form of "alien citizens" defined by invented mythologies of racial difference propagated and imposed by whites.[16]

International politics, however, complicated the racialized targeting of Japanese Canadians. The 1894 Treaty of Commerce and Navigation between Britain and Japan, renewed in 1905 and 1911, guaranteed the "full liberty" of both British and Japanese subjects to "enter, travel, or reside in any part of the dominions or possessions of the other [nation]" as well as the "full and perfect protection of their persons and property."[17] While the treaty was not initially binding on Canada, mindful of the strengthening relationship between Britain and Japan and of Japan's rising status as a Pacific power, the federal government attempted to steer a balance between racist intentions and diplomatic appearances. As Prime Minister Wilfrid Laurier's biographer explained, "while convinced that Asiatic immigration must be rigorously restricted, [Laurier] was scrupulously careful to avoid compromising imperial interests by an extreme policy or offensive means."[18] In the short term, that meant no head tax on Japanese migrants. Between 1897 and 1901 some 15,000 Japanese emigrants arrived in British Columbia, some to settle, others to work and return to Japan, and the majority on route to their ultimate destination in the United States. Amendments to Canada's Naturalization Act in 1881 confirmed that aliens could own and dispose of real and personal property, and Issei (first generation immigrants from Japan) did, working productively in a number of sectors in the British Columbia economy, especially lumbering, fishing, agriculture, and small business.[19] By the turn of the century the Japanese Canadian population neared 5,000 with British Columbia emerging as "a critical juncture in the networks of commerce and migration that connected Tokyo, Yokohama, Honolulu, Vancouver, Seattle, and San Francisco."[20] British Columbia had become an important site within the Pacific World.

Nonetheless, Japanese Canadians settling in British Columbia had to navigate an increasingly hostile domestic politics and innumerable legal obstacles erected by the British Columbia legislature, especially laws foreclosing fields of work. In 1900, the federal government formed a Royal Commission to address the provincial government's concern that "the province is flooded with an undesirable class of people non-assimilative and most detrimental to the wage-earning classes of the people of the province, and that this extensive immigration of orientals is also a menace to the health of the community."[21] Directed to investigate "whether or not [the Japanese] present the same objectionable characteristics as were alleged against the Chinese," commissioners held hearings along the West Coast in the spring of 1901 asking witnesses to address questions such as "How has Chinese and Japanese immigration affected white immigration?" and "Do Chinese or Japanese immigrants take any interest in our laws and institutions?"[22] The commission's final report in 1902 brimmed with racist invective, pernicious stereotypes, and flights of illogic. Its findings that Japanese migrants could not and would not assimilate and routinely sought fraudulent naturalization became the foundation of much destructive law and politics in the years to follow.[23] As the lawyer representing British Columbia testified, "the average Japanese remains what he always was, a Japanese, and notwithstanding the fact that he may take out a certificate of naturalization in this country, he never becomes, in truth and in fact, a Canadian, but always remains a Japanese."[24]

From the outset, Japanese Canadians turned to constitutional law and ideals of equality to resist the racist ascriptions of lesser citizenship. In 1897, identifying himself as a "loyal citizen of Canada," K.T. Takahashi published a remarkable pamphlet challenging the persistent accusations that Japanese Canadians were filing fraudulent naturalization claims.[25] Although employing his own harmful stereotypes in attempting to distance Japanese Canadians from the "low living" habits of migrants from China, Takahashi argued that attempts to diminish the citizenship of Japanese Canadians were themselves unconstitutional. "I ... declare most emphatically," Takahashi wrote, "that we are lawfully and legally the citizens of Canada, and that we shall consider any law which may be passed to vitiate this our sacred status, as both unjust, tyrannical and unconstitutional."[26] In 1900, Tomekichi Homma, with the support and coordination of the growing community of naturalized Canadians of Japanese origin, legally challenged British Columbia's election laws that prohibited Japanese Canadians from voting.[27] Initially victorious, Homma ultimately lost his case at Canada's then highest court, Britain's Judicial Committee of the Privy Council. The prohibition on voting had nothing to do with exclusive federal jurisdiction over naturalization, the Privy Council reasoned, since "[a] child of Japanese parentage born in Vancouver City … would be equally excluded from the possession of the franchise."[28] British Columbia's prohibition on voting fell within provincial jurisdiction, in other words, because the law lawfully discriminated on the basis of race, not by immigration or citizenship status.

Rumours of fraudulent naturalization claims by Japanese Canadians persisted. Responding to the Royal Commission, in 1903 Parliament amended the Naturalization Act to add procedural hurdles to the acquisition of naturalization and provide a venue for white settlers to vent their antagonisms directly at Japanese Canadian applicants. The Act now required "the names, residences, and occupations" of all individuals applying for certificates of naturalization to be posted in court for three weeks to allow members of the public to raise objections. Resolution in such cases would fall to a judge to determine the appropriate outcome.[29] Defending the wisdom of the amendment in the House of Commons, Robert George Macpherson noted that "[a] man who is himself a British subject is the best judge of the men who are likely to make good British subjects." To make the subtext plain, Macpherson added, "we cannot hope to make out of these orientals anything like the British subjects that we would like to get."[30] For Macpherson and others, citizenship carried an invisible racial barrier that must be maintained.

In 1908, Edward Alexander Lucas took up the call to challenge the veracity of the naturalization claims of Japanese Canadians. In a Vancouver court room, Lucas argued that the twelve Japanese Canadian applicants, as subjects of the Emperor of Japan, could never properly swear true allegiance to a Canadian sovereign, had no conception of the nature of an oath in any event, and did not intend to reside permanently in Canada.[31] Swatting away the arguments of "the aliens" that previous cases established that a court could not question the legality of certificates of naturalization once issued, Justice Grant observed that Parliament intended the new naturalization procedures to address "the gross irregularities as to the granting of naturalization papers" to Japanese Canadians highlighted in the 1902 Royal Commission Report.[32] Accordingly, Justice Grant ordered that the applicants return to court to face "cross-examination on their oaths of residence and allegiance."[33] Justice Grant was not finished. A year later, citing the "spirit and intention" of the Naturalization Act, he now went beyond the Act's wording to require that applicants for naturalization produce "evidence of at least 2 credible natural-born Canadian subjects" verifying their residency, intentions, and good character.[34] How many certificates of naturalization Justice Grant illegally denied or deterred on this basis, it is impossible to know.

We do know that claims that Japanese Canadians were improper, if not illegal citizens, could lead to violence. Against the backdrop of "anti-Asian riots rippl[ing] up and down the Pacific coasts," on 7 September 1907 thousands gathered at Vancouver City Hall, ostensibly to protest rumours of the arrival of ships carrying thousands of new immigrants from Asia.[35] Incendiary speeches calling the assembled to "stand for a White Canada," gave way as darkness fell to violence as the angry crowd moved through the city smashing the windows of the homes and businesses of Chinese Canadians and Japanese Canadians.[36] Through the cacophony of inarticulate yells, stomping boots, and shattering glass, Vancouver's chief of police recalled the message of one of the rioters, James McLaren, with clarity: "He said he was a God dam good British subject, and he would stay there if he wanted to, and he was pounding his breast."[37] A riot could speak in the languages of belonging and citizenship, too, and inflict the violent consequences of their denial.

Vancouver's riot highlighted the growing divide between international and domestic politics in relation to Japanese migration to Canada. Prior to the riot, Parliament enacted the Japanese Treaty Act, 1906, extending the terms of Britain and Japan's Treaty of Commerce and Navigation to Canada.[38] The "1894 treaty's guarantee to Japanese subjects of full liberty to enter, travel and reside in Canada," an observer notes, "was now federal law."[39] Law or not, following the riot, Prime Minister Laurier dispatched Minister of Labour Rodolphe Lemieux to Tokyo to negotiate with Tadasu Hayashi, Japan's foreign minister, to find a solution to placate racist tensions in Canada. More than a month of negotiations produced what became known as the Gentlemen's Agreement, the centrepiece of which was Japan's willingness to limit emigration to Canada to 400 persons per year, with admission restricted to immigrants previously domiciled in Canada, the wives and children of Canadian residents, domestic servants or farm labourers with arrangements to work for Japanese Canadians, or others specifically approved by the Canadian government.[40] Canada followed the restrictions on Japanese migration with a series of amendments to its immigration law designed to further restrict immigration by race. In 1908, the "continuous journey" provisions required immigrants to come to Canada directly from their country of origin as a means of ending immigration from the Indian subcontinent. In 1910, Parliament prohibited the immigration of any individual, by race or otherwise, deemed "unsuitable" to the climate or "other conditions … of Canada or because immigrants are deemed undesirable owing to their peculiar customs, habits, modes of life and methods of holdings of property," or simply because of an "inability to become readily assimilated or to assume the duties and responsibilities of Canadian citizenship."[41] Canada's immigration system now operated with implicit and explicit racial restrictions largely enforced at the discretion of immigration officials. Japanese migration to Canada fell to a few hundred individuals per year.

The Lemieux-Hayashi Agreement remained in place until 1928 when pressure from Canada resulted in Japan agreeing to further reduce Japanese emigrants to Canada to 150 per year with the same restricted categories.[42] In the intervening years, small numbers of Issei continued to settle in British Columbia, while earlier generations of Japanese Canadians expanded families, and built lives, businesses, and communities. The fight for full citizenship rights did not stop. More than two hundred

Japanese Canadian volunteered to serve in the First World War, often enlisting in Alberta to evade the racist objections of recruitment officers in British Columbia. Potential recruits hoped that military service for Canada would help Canada abroad and Japanese Canadians at home. "Until now," Iku Kumagawa stated, "Japanese Canadians have not been treated well here. But this [volunteering] will put future provincial governments in a position where they cannot deny Japanese their rights. As we look to the future as Japanese are establishing their place in Canada, we have no choice but to rise and meet the challenge."[43] After the war, Japanese Canadian veterans began a decade-long campaign pressing for the right to vote. They achieved a partial success when British Columbia extended the provincial franchise to Japanese Canadian veterans in 1931, a legal change that provided the right to vote to a few but reinforced the idea that race remained the presumptive category under which Japanese Canadians would be defined.

While the diplomatic understanding between Japan and Canada allowed a small and select number of Japanese migrants to settle in Canada, it also created a new spectre of concern for Canadian immigration officials: the *illegal* Japanese immigrant. Government officials now actively worried about Japanese migrants slipping across the border undetected or misrepresenting their intentions at the border in order to fit the agreement's restrictive categories. In October 1930, the Department of Immigration initiated a campaign to investigate every Japanese immigrant admitted between September 1928 and August 1929.[44] "A check-up of this kind," an official admitted, "takes considerable time and means a great deal of work, but is, I think worthwhile, as it will enable us to establish just what is transpiring."[45] Initial surveillance suggested that several of the individuals granted entry to Canada during the period were no longer working in their authorized work arrangements. The minister ordered that the offenders be tracked down and brought before boards of inquiry established under the Immigration Act in order to deport them from Canada. With an order of arrest signed by William J. Egan, the deputy minister of immigration, a provincial police officer and immigration officer went in search of Munetaka Samejima.

II. Migration and deportation in racist Canada

Munetaka was born in 1904 near Kagoshima City on western Kyushu, the southernmost of Japan's four main islands.[46] Raised in a merchant family of modest means, Samejima's uncle, cousin, and brother had all immigrated to British Columbia. Samejima wanted to join them. The bureaucratic hurdles to qualify for one of the few available Japanese passports available under the terms of the Lemieux-Hayashi Agreement were considerable, but in 1926, Samejima's uncle Kiichi Aiboshi wrote him with a promising lead. Aiboshi knew of a successful small store owner in Nanaimo, British Columbia, Jentaro Ueno, able to hire a domestic servant. The opportunity initiated nearly two years of required paperwork. Samejima secured a certificate from the mayor of Kagoshima of "good conduct," a medical certificate of "good health," and a certificate establishing his "family record" and forwarded them to his uncle in Canada to pass along to Ueno. In Canada, Ueno used Samejima's documents to apply to the Vancouver's Japanese Consulate for permission to hire a domestic servant. The permission granted and sent back to Japan, Samejima now applied to Japan's minister of foreign affairs for a passport and approval from the British consular general at Kobe. His emigration finally authorized in the fall of 1928, Samejima and his uncle Aiboshi, who had paid for his ticket, boarded the *Empress of Asia* at Yokohoma bound for Vancouver. At twenty-four-years old, Samejima arrived in Canada on 29 September 1928, his pockets carrying $250.00 and his hopes for a new life.[47]

Disappointment found him first. After landing in British Columbia, Samejima headed to Nanaimo to discover that his prospective employment had disappeared. Life had been difficult for Ueno during the lengthy period awaiting Samejima's passport. His wife's illness caused Ueno to return to Japan and leave his business selling fancy goods, fish, tobacco, and candy in the hands of a friend during his absence. Ueno returned to Nanaimo in September 1928 to discover that, during his time away, his business "had failed" and assets had been sold.[48] After discovering that Ueno could no longer employ him, Samejima returned to Vancouver to stay with a cousin to figure out what to do next. Unsuccessful at finding any work as a domestic servant in Vancouver, Samejima used connections within the Japanese Canadian community to find work in lumber mills in Woodfibre and Hillcrest, followed by a brief stint with a shoemaking business with his cousin in Duncan. When that venture failed to support him, Samejima took up a job in one of the busy mills in Chemainus. "I had to take any work I could get," he later said.[49] In doing so, Samejima like so many Japanese Canadian migrants turned to networks of family and the diaspora community to navigate economic hardship. Constrained by the formal and informal employment restrictions facing Japanese Canadians, the Japanese Canadian community evaded the economic dislocation of immigration by connecting new immigrants like Samejima with work opportunities among the few industries open to them. It was this story of evading economic hardship that Samejima told the police officer and immigration official in the manager's office of his workplace on 28 April 1931. Unmoved, the officers arrested Samejima and transported him to Victoria's infamous immigration "shed," a bleak two-story fortress constructed with "racially-segregated wards" to ensure that "white people … shall not comingle with the Orientals at any stage of their stay."[50]

After a night in detention, Samejima appeared before a three-member board of inquiry at the facility facing deportation. He appeared with no lawyer. He called no evidence. He did not, until the moment of the hearing itself, know or understand the case against him or appreciate its consequences. The in camera hearing lasted mere minutes. The chair of the board, J.A. Anderson, commenced by perfunctorily informing

Samejima that he had a right to a lawyer. "I am not going to have a lawyer," Samejima replied.[51] Anderson then noted that Samejima faced charges under section 33(7) of the Immigration Act, specifically: "Any person … who enters Canada by misrepresentation … shall be guilty of an offence under this Act." The provision provided for penalties of fine or imprisonment or, if an alien, deportation if ordered by a board of inquiry.[52] A series of rapid questions ensued: "How old are you?" "Of what race are you?" "Of what country do you claim citizenship?" Anderson next confirmed that Samejima had arrived to work for Ueno as a domestic servant. Pressed for details, Samejima explained: "After arriving at Vancouver I went to Nanaimo and I find no employer there because Mr Uyeno's [*sic*] store was closed." After ascertaining the rest of Samejima's work history in short order, the hearing turned adversarial, for the board of inquiry was structured to both prosecute and decide the case before them:

> Q: After you arrived you made no attempt to be a domestic servant.
> A: I tried several times to have domestic work in Vancouver but could not find any.
> Q: You have never been in domestic servant work in Canada?
> A: No, I have not.
> Q: Then you realize that you have entered Canada by misrepresentation do you?
> A: No, I don't know that. Because I try to get work but I could not help it.
> Q: But the fact that you have not taken domestic work shows you entered Canada by misrepresentation?
> A: I don't know.

"Mr Samejima," the chair concluded, "a motion has been duly moved and seconded and I declare it carried unanimously that you be deported." The last word went to Samejima: "I am going to appeal."[53]

Relying on networks within Victoria's Japanese Canadian community, Samejima secured the legal services of William Moresby, one of the city's lawyers known for his willingness to represent Asian Canadians.[54] Within a week, Samejima exercised the only right of appeal open to him under the Immigration Act, a written appeal to the minister of immigration.[55] Moresby's materials to the minister contained affidavits from Samejima, Ueno, and character references for them both from Kikujiro Ishii, a respected community leader and head of the Victoria Japanese Association.[56] Emphasizing the honour at stake for Issei in telling the truth and finding productive work, Ishii pointed out that if Samejima had really been intent on deceit he would have simply arranged a sham domestic service arrangement.[57] In appealing to the importance of honour, Ishii attempted to translate Issei values to officials who were not listening.[58] Samejima's thickening departmental file, labelled simply "Undesirable," collected the letters and memos of departmental officials declaring Samejima's story implausible.[59]

"[T]he statements made by the appellant's Counsel in this case looks like a very carefully engineered plan to effect the entry of a man who apparently was not and never intended to be a bona fide domestic," an official confidently asserted in a note to the deputy minister. "It would not appear that he is entitled to any consideration and I would recommend that deportation be effected." The deputy minister agreed.[60] On 4 June 1931, the department wrote to Moresby that Samejima's appeal had been denied and that arrangements "for the return of this man to Japan" were underway.[61]

The Department of Immigration's relentless and costly pursuit of Samejima's deportation can only be understood in the wider context of the changing politics of Canadian immigration in the early 1930s. The intensity of the racist attention fixed upon Japanese Canadians by legislators and the labour and nativist movements waxed and waned somewhat over the years and decades of the early twentieth century, but it never disappeared and was easily roused to action. As the Depression began to take hold, economic conditions deteriorated, and military suspicions escalated between Japan and the Commonwealth, political focus on Japanese Canadians sharpened. At the same time, the Department of Immigration was in the midst of a broader shift in priorities. By the spring of 1931, the new Conservative government of R.B. Bennett, having campaigned on greater immigration restrictions, foreclosed almost all legal immigration into Canada by order in council.[62] Long consumed with shaping what it considered the character of Canada by exercising discretion in its power of entry, the Department of Immigration now turned increasing attention to the deportation of individuals deemed unworthy, especially the unemployed or infirm, suspected communists, or individuals convicted of criminal offences.[63] The number of deportations escalated sharply in the early 1930s reaching more than seven thousand deportations in 1933.[64] "Canada's deportation practices were among the most arbitrary in the Commonwealth," Barbara Roberts writes, as "bureaucrats carried out a clandestine and illegal immigrant selection process, and deported immigrants according to their own informal and extralegal system of justice."[65] Targeting supposedly fraudulent Japanese Canadian immigrants for deportation fit within a long history of viewing Japanese migrants as unworthy, untrustworthy, and unwanted, but it also aligned with the department's new focus on sending "undesirable" people out, in addition to stopping people from getting in.

The Department of Immigration's increasingly intensive investigations of Japanese Canadian immigration eventually exposed an underground migration network designed to assist Japanese migrants to evade the limits of the Gentlemen's Agreement and earn a profit for its organizers and insiders. "Japanese migrants, careful students of exclusionary law and policy," Andrea Geiger notes, "found ways to challenge or avoid the growing web of legal constraints," and often those ways involved the necessity of money for bribes and fake documents.[66] In 1931, the RCMP's focus fixed on Fred Yoshi, a federal civil servant serving as the Japanese interpreter in Vancouver for the

Department of Immigration.[67] The RCMP arrested Yoshi on 3 July 1931 after discovering evidence that, possibly for years, he had helped an unknown number of migrants secure false naturalization certificates. The story became front-page news, as did Yoshi's conviction on 25 September 1931, and gave rise to further government campaigns to investigate and harass Japanese Canadians and treat them as suspect by race.[68] In the wake of Yoshi's case, in the House of Commons, Liberal member of Parliament Thomas Reid returned to his familiar theme of the necessity of racial exclusions. "I am not particularly interested … in the immigration of Anglo Saxon or European people," he needlessly prefaced; "I am concerned with the immigration of Asiatics into British Columbia." Declaring that, "over 40 per cent of the Japanese in British Columbia had entered illegally," Reid demanded to know what the government intended to do about it and how many deportations would follow.[69]

As the political focus on deporting Japanese Canadians intensified, Samejima hired Cornelius Hawkins (Neil) O'Halloran to take over from Moresby in bringing a writ of habeas corpus seeking his release. The ancient writ of habeas corpus, among the sacrosanct of English civil liberties, required that the state demonstrate to a court the legality of its detention of an individual. O'Halloran was the right lawyer for the case. Like Moresby, O'Halloran had previously represented Chinese Canadians and had specific experience in immigration and deportation matters.[70] Moreover, O'Halloran believed strongly in law's essential equality and in the capacity of habeas corpus proceedings to instantiate those legal values. At the end of the decade, the Liberals would appoint O'Halloran directly from practice to serve on the British Columbia Court of Appeal. In his most famous decision, O'Halloran dissented in a case upholding a tavern's right to refuse service to a black man arguing that "all British subjects have the same rights and privileges under common law – it makes no difference whether white or coloured; or of what class, race or religion."[71] O'Halloran brought a similar mindset to Samejima's case. With local Victoria lawyer John L. Clay, retained by the Department of Immigration to demand Samejima's immediate deportation, the parties appeared before Justice Alexander Ingram Fisher on 29 June 1931 to interrogate the lawfulness of Samejima's detention and determine the future course of his life.

In his decision released just over a week later, Justice Fisher first examined the order of deportation produced by the board of inquiry. "In the present case," Justice Fisher noted, "the only reason given" for the deportation order is that Samejima "is in Canada contrary to the provisions of the Immigration Act and effected entry contrary to the provisions of section 33, subsection 7 of the said Act."[72] Noting, however, that subsection 7 conveyed "several quite distinct offences," Justice Fisher held that the order of deportation was legally deficient since it only baldly and generally stated without particulars the specific factual and legal grounds upon which it rested. Justice Fisher held, without saying so explicitly, that the rule of law and administrative fairness required substantive *reasons* rather than simply blanket assertions of state power.[73] Quoting earlier cases, Fisher noted that given the serious consequences of "the liberty of the person ... when a person is ordered deported out of the country, the reasons for the deportation should be clearly stated in the order."[74] Justice Fisher also had to grapple with the Immigration Act's privative clause. Section 23 of the Act stipulated:

> No court, and no judge or officer thereof, shall have jurisdiction to review, quash reverse, restrain or otherwise interfere with any proceeding, decision or order of ... any Board of Inquiry ... relating to the ... deportation of any rejected immigrant ... unless such person is a Canadian citizen or has Canadian domicile.[75]

As we shall see, section 23 had produced widely divergent approaches among judges. Justice Fisher preferred the line of decisions holding that the Act could not displace the rights of habeas corpus if the Act itself had not been followed. "[I]t would, indeed, be strange," Justice Fisher quoted approvingly, "to find that the doors of the Court were shut against any person of any nationality, no matter what the act complained of might be."[76] Justice Fisher's decision opened more than just the doors of the court; in demanding a baseline of substantive legality in deportation matters, it set Samejima free.

Unhappy with the outcome, government officials devised a new strategy.[77] The most senior lawyer in the civil service, William Stewart Edwards, deputy minister of justice, now turned his mind and experience to the case and advised the Department of Immigration to instruct the board of inquiry to simply amend its deportation order to provide reasons.[78] Although Clay doubted the legality of the procedure, the department did exactly that. With an amended order from the board setting out more fully Samejima's alleged misrepresentation, officials rearrested Samejima on 23 September 1931 and ordered him deported.[79] Again. In response, O'Halloran brought a second application for habeas corpus, this time before Justice Denis Murphy. The case did not go well. In a short, two paragraph judgment delivered on 30 October 1931, Justice Murphy dismissed Samejima's application. There was no reason, he held, that a board of inquiry could not correct a procedural error and supply a new lawful order of deportation.[80] Samejima instructed O'Halloran to appeal, and the parties returned to court, now for a third time, to try and convince the British Columbia Court of Appeal.

On 29 January 1932, the Court of Appeal dismissed Samejima's appeal after the conclusion of three days of argument.[81] Although the panel divided 2–2 on the merits of the case, by tradition, a split decision could not overturn a lower court ruling. The dissenters, Justice Martin and MacDonald, would have held in Samejima's favour that a board of inquiry could not simply amend a deportation order previously quashed by a judge.[82] Professing shock at "such a mischarge of justice," Justice Martin bluntly declared that Samejima had been denied "the 'essential requirements of justice'" of "a full and proper hearing before being deported."[83] Chief Justice MacDonald disagreed, oddly devoting his reasons to the purported errors of Justice Fisher, a decision not under appeal. Justice Fisher was wrong, the chief justice held, because courts could not question any aspect of the decisions or orders of boards of inquiry given the protective shield enacted by section 23 of the Act. Since Justice Fisher's prior decision was "a nullity," the government had legal authority to deport Samejima under the original board of inquiry's deportation order at any time, he reasoned.[84] Justice McPhillips, whom O'Halloran knew best, having served as his former articling student, focused instead on what he viewed as the conclusive evidence marshalled against Samejima. If O'Halloran had been hoping for favourable treatment from his former mentor, he did not receive it. Agreeing that a court could not interfere with the process or decisions of a board of inquiry, Justice McPhillips emphasized that Samejima's testimony was "false, and has been proved to be false." Drawing repeated attention to Samejima's status as a noncitizen, Justice McPhillips concluded that Samejima "had a fair hearing, a proper inquiry, [and] every opportunity was afforded to make out his case."[85] Again facing deportation, Samejima's only option was to appeal to the Supreme Court of Canada.

At this point in the narrative, it is worth pausing to note how little Samejima's own story seemed to matter in his litigation. The British Columbia court decisions deciding his fate and Samejima's weighty Department of Immigration file, hundreds of pages thick, convey almost no details of the man, his labours, and the numerous bonds forged during his years in Canada. Stripped of personhood and rootedness to place, work, and family, Samejima was an abstraction, an alien in the eyes of the law, several judges, and the government seeking to deport him. Notably, there is no departmental correspondence even considering whether Samejima might be telling the truth. There are no memos deliberating on whether Samejima's circumstances might warrant discretion in his favour. The files never weigh whether the case against him warranted the costs. The single letter running against this grain was sent to the minister from the Japanese Public Justice Association just prior to Samejima's Court of Appeal hearing. After restating the "peculiar circumstances" and "unfortunate" facts of Samejima's work situation on arrival to Canada, the authors stress that Samejima "is now in this country well over three years and it is his intention to remain here permanently; moreover, he hopes … to apply for naturalization as a British subject." More to the point, Samejima "is a peaceful, law-abiding, steady young man," compelled to legal action only as a last resort.[86] The reply from a departmental official was brief: noting that little could be said given that the matter was before the courts, an official explained that "the circumstances surrounding the admission of the alien named are such that, in the event of the Courts dismissing the appeal, it is the intention of this Department to effect his deportation."[87] The last impediment to doing so was Samejima's appeal to the Supreme Court of Canada.

III. "If you had been seized": Race and equality in the law of habeas corpus

Every Canadian lawyer and judge in the 1920s would have been familiar with A.V. Dicey's famous assertion that the British constitutional tradition of the rule of law provided for "equality before the law, or the equal subjection of all classes to the ordinary law of the land administered by the ordinary Law Courts."[88] Japanese Canadians would have been more sceptical of how broadly that claim described Canada, but that did not mean that they were not prepared to defend or advance their interests in legal proceedings and draw upon the ideal, if not always the practice, of constitutional equality. As we would expect, Japanese Canadians sometimes found themselves in court like anyone else. The reported cases of the first decades of the twentieth century often reveal Japanese Canadians appearing in court in the unremarkable ways of everyday life: defending themselves or advancing their interests in cases of petty or serious criminality, contract squabbles, and property disputes. Other cases provide glimpses of the racism embedded throughout the legal system: a liquor licence application refused on racial grounds, a factum that labelled the Japanese Canadian plaintiff "a foreigner of bad character."[89] Of course, Japanese Canadians could only have appeared in court as litigants or witnesses not lawyers or judges since British Columbia's Law Society barred Asian Canadians from the legal profession.[90] In this respect, courts of law were never equal domains or full sites of justice for Japanese Canadians.

Significant scholarly attention has already been paid to the most prominent aspects of Asian Canadian litigation history before the Second World War: Tomekichi Homma's unsuccessful fight for the franchise for Japanese Canadians, and the extensive constitutional litigation spanning the 1880s to 1920s, largely fought between Canada and British Columbia, over the constitutional limits of British Columbia's authority to enact racist restrictions against Asian Canadians.[91] These cases illuminate the racist legislative landscape confronting Asian Canadians and tell us just how little equality rights appeared to matter in conceptions and arguments of Canadian constitutional law during the period. By contrast, the habeas corpus cases of the era, perhaps because they also engaged fundamental questions about the relationship between judicial and parliamentary power, more readily confronted questions of the constitutionality of discrimination. In perhaps surprising ways, a good portion of Canada's earliest equality jurisprudence can be found in the law of habeas corpus.

The language of habeas corpus began to appear in the law of England as early as the thirteenth century, initially as a demand of civil procedure to ensure an individual was present in court for a legal proceeding.[92] Over the centuries, habeas corpus signified considerably more as it morphed, perhaps more in rhetoric than reality, as "the Great Writ of Liberty" by which a prisoner could insist on appearing in court and requiring the state to defend the legality of the detention.[93] Yet fundamental aspects of its character remained uncertain into the twentieth century. Could habeas corpus be suspended? Did a privative clause – such as that contained in section 23 of the Immigration Act – displace the court's jurisdiction to consider habeas corpus applications? What form of administrative procedures or discrimination in the conduct of them would constitute illegality sufficient to warrant judicial intervention and lead to an individual's release? In the early twentieth century, Canadian courts produced inconsistent results on such questions yielding a wide array of theories on the nature of the constitutional relationship between courts and legislatures, and discrimination and administrative fairness when the liberty of the subject was at stake.

A number of those decisions warrant closer scrutiny. On 31 October 1905, four Japanese migrants landed at Vancouver via Yokohama. Detained by immigration officials to ascertain their medical status, three were diagnosed with a contagious eye infection and subsequently ordered deported.[94] Bringing an application for habeas corpus, the litigants produced evidence that they were free of disease. Justice Morrison agreed and ordered them released. The appeal before a full panel of the British Columbia Supreme Court turned on the question of whether a judge could ever question the factual findings of an official under the Immigration Act. During the hearing, Justice Gordon Hunter posed a question that would sporadically reoccur throughout such cases: "What have you to say," Justice Hunter asked Canada's lawyers, "as to the application of this provision to British subjects returning to Canada?" Justice Hunter's decision did not pursue that line of reasoning, but he rejected the claim that the Act removed the jurisdiction of courts to decide such questions of fact; indeed, in his view, an application of habeas corpus "bound" courts "to examine into the matter."[95] "As the decision in this case concerns the liberty of the subject," Justice Irving concurred, "I wish to add a few words … The object of the writ of habeas corpus," he stated, "is the protection of the liberty of the subject by affording a practical means of effecting the release of persons illegally detained." Only facts could make deportation legal, Justice Clement added, not simply the declarations of facts by "some particular official."[96]

A year later, two Japanese migrants again employed habeas corpus to test the limits of racialized treatment. Arriving at the Canadian border by rail travelling from Portland, Oregon, Nakane and Okazake refused to take the English language test imposed on them under British Columbia's intentionally exclusionary, British Columbia Immigration Act (Natal Act).[97] When the migrants refused to return to the United States, officials placed them in detention and an application for habeas corpus followed. Noting that the Canadian Immigration Act did not prohibit entry on racial grounds, Chief Justice Hunter found that British Columbia's purported immigration law conflicted with the free liberty of movement guaranteed to Japanese subjects under the federal Japanese Treaty Act and was therefore inoperative. Ordering Nakane's and Okazake's release, Chief Justice Hunter turned his mind to the potentially broader impact of the law. Questioned by counsel about the propriety of awarding costs to the applicants as would normally be routine, the Chief Justice responded, "Why should these people be deprived of their costs? They have been illegally detained. Are they not as much entitled to it as you would be if you had been seized?"[98] A Supreme Court panel of three judges dismissed the province's appeal with Justice Clement lamenting that British Columbia's case was so "hopeless ... that it should ever have been thought proper to attempt to enforce the British Columbia Immigration Act, 1908, as against these respondents."[99] The decisions in *Ikezoya* and *Nakane and Okazake* signalled a recurring undercurrent in the cases: judicial appetites for intervention in deportation matters was often linked to concern about the impact of unaccountable state power on groups beyond Japanese migrants, perhaps especially white British subjects.

The most infamous habeas corpus case of the period arose from the arrival of the Japanese steamship, the SS *Komagata Maru*. Carrying 376 passengers, mostly adult Sikh men from the Punjab, the vessel had voyaged from Hong Kong to Shanghai, Moji to Yokohama, and across the Pacific to Vancouver. The subject of a rich historical literature, Canada's refusal to allow the ship to port, its de facto imprisonment of the passengers onboard for two months, and ultimate deportation of its prospective immigrants to face violence overseas, stands as another chapter in the story of harms caused by racialized immigration practices and white supremacist ideology in twentieth-century Canada, just as it also tells of "the disruptive and subversive force of Indian anticolonialism" in challenging conceptions of racial hierarchy.[100] "I can only surmise that the instructions from the department at Ottawa to the immigration authorities," Joseph Edward Bird, one of the lawyers for the passengers would argue, "was to delay matters ... until such time as these people were starved back to their original port from whence they came ... There are no set of anarchists in Canada like the immigration officials who defy all law and order."[101] Represented by K.C. Cassidy and Bird, the passengers on board the moored *Komagata Maru* agreed to put forward the habeas corpus application of one of the passengers to serve as a test case binding all. Munshi Singh, like most on board, was a British subject, intending to immigrate to Canada. A board of inquiry had ordered all of the detained passengers deported for various infractions including the requirement that migrants arrive by "continuous journey" from their country of residence. Singh's lawyers argued that the Immigration Act was unconstitutional insofar as it authorized the deportation of British subjects, since only *aliens* fell within federal jurisdiction, that the discriminatory orders in council "of great and far-reaching consequence" lay beyond the powers the Act had granted, and that the board had no evidence upon which to make its findings that Singh was an "unskilled labourer."[102] None of the arguments succeeded.

"By terms of the British North America Act the Parliament of Canada is clothed with sovereign power in matters relating to immigration into any parts of the Dominion," Chief Justice Macdonald held. "Canada's authority to admit immigrants of any or every race or nationality, on any terms she pleases, is complete."[103] Moreover, the chief justice held, although the Immigration Act was not always clearly drafted, there was no doubt that its provisions intended to enable regulations that discriminated on the basis of race. As to questioning the factual findings of a board of inquiry, no court could do so, the chief justice held, unless the Act was unconstitutional or a board of inquiry acted without jurisdiction over the matter. "There is a complete chain of authority," Justice Irving added in summary "from the Sovereign, with the assent of the Imperial Parliament, down to the Board of Inquiry, and the proceedings are, on their face, regular in every respect."[104] Indeed, Justice Martin observed, the whole point of the legislative scheme was that "certain questions … relating to immigrants should be speedily and summarily decided, on the spot, so to speak, by the specified officers of the Crown."[105] Besides, he reasoned, "[d]emeanour is often all-important in such cases" and the board of inquiry was specially placed to determine the "intelligence, position, and character" of the potential immigrants to Canada.[106] "The Parliament of Canada," Justice McPhillips concluded

> may be well said to be safe-guarding the people of Canada from an influx, which it is no chimera to conjure up might annihilate the nation and change its whole potential complexity, introduce Oriental ways as against European ways, Eastern civilization for Western civilization, and all the dire results that would naturally flow therefrom.[107]

Singh's appeals to the Magna Carta, unfair discrimination, civil liberties, and the equality of British subjects, did little in the face of Justice McPhillips's logics of the laws of race. Implicitly or explicitly, all of the judges accepted that discrimination and racial protection served as the natural, valid, and fully constitutional object of Canadian immigration law.

The Supreme Court of Canada confronted a still unsettled jurisprudence when they heard Samejima's case in April of 1932. Alongside the competing strands of habeas corpus jurisprudence issuing from different courts, MPs in the House of Commons had long staked positions on either side of the debate. For the lawyer Rodolphe Lemieux, speaking in Parliament in 1914, habeas corpus was "an inherent right of every British subject … the palladium of British liberty" and accordingly the necessary domain of judicial oversight.[108] The former judge and newly minted minister of justice in Robert Borden's Conservative government, Charles Joseph Doherty disagreed. Quoting the former Liberal minister of the interior Frank Oliver back to Lemieux, Doherty declared Parliament supreme in its "control over our own immigration laws" and the issue of "who shall and who shall not come to Canada."[109] More to the point, habeas corpus had been fully displaced by the express terms of the Immigration Act, so much so that government officials, he counselled, should consider refusing to abide by orders from courts to produce detainees.[110] That may scandalize the "average lawyer" or render "hysterical" those worried about "danger to our liberty," but, he pointed out by way of solace, questions of entry and deportation in immigration matters bore "no application to the citizens of Canada." The minister of immigration, he concluded, "shall stand at the door and … shall say whether the people who knock shall be permitted to enter, and the courts shall not have anything to say about it."[111] In the series of lower court judgments concerning Samejima's deportation, judges had evenly divided on whether Lemieux or Doherty was correct. Was habeas corpus "one of the most precious privileges which the British Constitution guarantees to the subject of the kingdom" or had it been displaced by the firm parliamentary intent shielding immigration officials from all judicial scrutiny?[112] Did discrimination by race have any bearing on the fairness of the process? What was the place of equality, administrative fairness, and judicial review in Canadian constitutional law? Finally, as to the most immediate question before the court, did Canada have the lawful authority to deport Samejima? With written materials citing the various conflicting strands of authority on habeas corpus, and articulating fundamentally differing conceptions of the relationship between the judiciary and executive, lawyers headed to Ottawa to argue Samejima's case.

IV. Samejima at the Supreme Court of Canada

The Supreme Court of Canada had not previously demonstrated an interest in finding principles of racial equality at the foundation of Canadian law. In *Quong-Wing v The King*, some two decades earlier, the court upheld Saskatchewan's racist legislation forbidding white women from working in any business owned by a Chinese Canadian. Following the precedent which had upheld the constitutionality of the legislation denying Homma's right to vote, the court found that Saskatchewan was free to legislate racial discriminations, "however harshly it may bear upon Chinamen, naturalized or not."[113] Perhaps with this in mind, O'Halloran's legal argument attempted to keep the court's focus on the procedural anomalies in Samejima's case, especially as they related to the administrative disregard for Justice Fisher's decision quashing the original Order of Deportation.[114] The case might be won, O'Halloran surely surmised, if he could capture judicial attention with the disrespect displayed by officials towards the ruling of a fellow judge, rather than towards Samejima himself. Further, he hoped he might find judicial appetite at the Supreme Court to affirm a robust judicial role in assessing facts determined by boards of inquiry and in reviewing applications for habeas corpus broadly, particularly in this case given the "violation of justice and abuse of power" on display. "Even in the performance of a judicial duty," O'Halloran argued, "the Court will compel an officer or public body to act judicially and will not accept for the exercise of a discretion, reasons given which are nugatory or illusory, for that would be no exercise of discretion."[115] In an inspired manner, O'Halloran insisted that a spirit of legality informed by reason and expressed in reasons necessarily underlay the discretionary authority of boards of inquiry. In the absence of either, judges must intervene.

In finding a lawyer to respond to Samejima's appeal, Canada spared no expense. Replacing Victoria lawyer, John Clay, at the Supreme Court was the familiar stern face of William Norman Tilley, KC, treasurer of the Law Society of Upper Canada and one of Canada's leading lawyers. Tilley had argued before the Supreme Court on dozens of previous occasions and was known for a singular devotion to his legal practice, a gruff forceful manner, and high fees. "If we visualize a counsel as a hammer driving in a nail," a contemporary recalled, "then Tilley would qualify as a sledgehammer. He not only rode roughshod over other counsel, but also over most judges."[116] Drawing the court's attention to the British Columbia Court of Appeal's decision in *Re Munshi Singh*, Tilley reminded the court that, "no Court had jurisdiction to review or reverse any decision of any Board of Inquiry unless the immigrant possessed Canadian citizenship or domicile."[117] In any event, Tilley pointed out, the factual findings of the board of inquiry were undoubtedly true: Samejima had entered Canada by fraud. At the conclusion of Tilley's submissions, the five justices hearing the appeal – Chief Justice Francis Alexander Anglin and Justices Lyman Poore Duff, John Henderson Lamont, Robert Smith and Lawrence Arthur Cannon – reserved judgment and retired to consider Samejima's fate.

On 15 June 1932, the court delivered its answer. Samejima won. Like several of the judges in the British Columbia courts, however, Chief Justice Anglin (joined by Justice Smith) found "[n]o injustice whatsoever" on the facts, unless "the crossing of every 't' and dotting of every 'i' in all the proceedings taken in this matter is essential."[118] Continuing the tradition of accusing Japanese Canadians of deceit, the chief justice maintained that for Samejima "[t]o say that he had no notice" of the accusations against him, "to put it mildly, strikes me as dishonest."[119] In any event, the original sin was surely Justice Fisher's, Chief Justice Anglin held, since he had no jurisdiction to question the board of inquiry in the first place.

A majority of three judges disagreed. After recounting the facts and procedural twists of the case in some detail, Justice Lamont (joined by Justice Cannon) raised a new objection not aired in the courts below. He found that section 42 of the Immigration Act required that a hearing of a board of inquiry prior to deportation must be initiated by "a complaint."[120] "Parliament has not authorized the exercise of this jurisdiction on the complaint of an unknown person who might be an enemy or competitor or business rival of the immigrant, desirous of harassing him,"[121] he pointed out. Without a proper complaint, the whole process was void, Justice Lamont concluded. In any event, the board's Order of Deportation could not stand since it conveyed no reasons to support it. Since the Order was fundamentally improper, by definition it could not have been made under the proper authority of the Act; accordingly, he reasoned, no other section of the Act could deprive the courts of its jurisdiction to review. As to the board's power to amend a deficient Order, Justice Lamont ruled that after it has "been quashed by a court having jurisdiction, it cannot be amended for there is nothing to amend. The order of the Board no longer exists – it is a thing of naught."[122] Although Justice Lamont noted that Samejima could simply have been rearrested and placed before a new board of inquiry, the rest of his reasons do something no previous decision had done: he appeared to take Samejima at his word, finding his answers "straightforward" and the corroborating affidavits of Ueno and Ishii compelling, a subtle rejoinder, perhaps, to the chief justice's lingering accusation of dishonesty.[123]

The most remarkable of the decisions belonged to Justice Duff, the court's only member from British Columbia, just a year away from becoming chief justice.[124] In four short paragraphs, Justice Duff concurred with Justice Lamont's decision, agreeing that the board's Deportation Order lacked legality but went on to directly address the impact of section 23 on the judicial role. "The jurisdiction of the Board," he held is limited by the "spirit, as well as the frame, of the whole statute." It was a spirit, Justice Duff argued, that implied and required "intelligibility of allegation. Indeed, unless the person concerned is to have a reasonable opportunity of knowing the nature of the allegations, what is the purpose of requiring his presence?"[125] He followed that observation with a novel and notable passage in Canadian jurisprudence. "I gravely fear," he wrote,

> that too often the fact that these enactments are, in practice, most frequently brought to bear upon Orientals of a certain class, has led to the generation of an atmosphere which has obscured their true effect. They are, it is needless to say, equally applicable to Scotsmen. I admit I am horrified at the thought that the personal liberty of a British subject should be exposed to the hugger-nugger [*sic*] which under the name of legal proceedings is exemplified by some of the records that have incidentally been brought to our attention.[126]

More than twenty years before Justice Rand would famously do so in *Roncarelli v Duplessis*, Justice Duff agreed with O'Halloran's argument that a spirit of legality – requiring intelligibility, reasons, and fair process – animated the interpretation of legislation and bound its legal use.[127] More notably still, his reasons signalled the uncomfortable reality of gaps between formal law and its application. Justice Duff named what had theretofore been unsaid in Canadian jurisprudence: the law took different shape and meaning and carried different consequences when applied to different kinds of people on the basis of race and class. The rule of law was an ideal, but it was not, Justice Duff conceded, always a legal reality.

About explicitly racist law – legislation targeting particular groups on racial grounds to deny a benefit or impose a burden – Justice Duff had little legal concern, as his decision in *Quong-Wing* had illustrated. Nor is there much evidence the Justice Duff was particularly concerned by racist treatment of Japanese Canadians. A decade earlier, Justice Duff described British Columbia's attempts to discriminate against Japanese Canadian employment as the laudable exercise of its jurisdiction to ensure the "settlement by a suitable population," i.e, "settlers of a class who are likely to become permanently (themselves and their families) residents of the province."[128] What disturbed Justice Duff in *Samejima* was a law neutral on its face that, in the hands of potentially unreviewable government officials, could discriminate against Anglo Saxons, British subjects, Scotsmen. That was the "true effect" that gravely alarmed him: the threat of an administration capable of exposing whites to the vicissitudes of capricious state power. For better or worse, conceptions of legal equality tend to take root when judicial minds are capable of seeing themselves standing in the place of the vulnerable litigant. Doing so suddenly makes irrational state power appear not only personal but also constitutional in scope – a latent danger in the law to be exposed and torn out. If *Samejima* is among Canada's earliest equality rights cases for identifying the discrimination hidden in the application of Canada's immigration law and administration, its status is ambivalent owing to Justice Duff's instinct to see the real issue of concern through a prism of whiteness. Finally, one gains the impression that Justice Duff and the majority were waging war on another front entirely. In claiming continuing legal authority over and above the discretionary activities of officials, in spite of whatever intent Parliament may have had in keeping judicial meddling at bay, the court struck back against the perceived excesses of power reposing in the growing administrative state – a topic that was beginning to animate an increasing number of scholarly and judicial debates across the common law world.[129]

None of which likely mattered very much to Samejima, finally free after years of arrest, detention, legal appeals, and uncertainty. Government officials, as one might expect, greeted the decision with disappointment. Still, they decided to forgo an appeal to the Judicial Committee of the Privy Council and the prospect of rearresting Samejima and attempting to deport him all over again, thus conclusively ending his legal ordeal. An immigration official in Ottawa did want it impressed upon the original board of inquiry that their "error has resulted in a great deal of expense to the Department."[130] In its day, some lawyers welcomed the *Samejima* decision as a significant signal of judicial willingness to supervise the administrative state; a development others like John Willis worried deeply about.[131] While *Samejima* did insist on the presence of a certain bare minimum of protections within the procedures of boards of inquiry, and confirm the availability of habeas corpus for violations of certain of those procedures, the case did little to change Canadian immigration law in the short term. Boards of inquiry were certain to pay greater attention to providing substantive reasons in

Figure 2.1 Munetaka Samejima [Sameshima] in 1942. Left to right: Munetaka, Sukeo Sameshima, and unknown. Shoe repair shop, Hastings Park, Vancouver, BC, 1942.

their Orders of Deportation in the years that followed, but, beyond that, the only other lesson the Department of Immigration took away was to try and deport immigrants before they had the opportunity to make contact with lawyers.[132] Indeed, the number of deportations increased the year after Samejima's case.[133] The decision in *Samejima* did not ultimately settle much in the way of Canadian administrative law either. Although it signalled a willingness to judicially supervise some forms of administration, in what circumstances and to what degree remained unclear. It would take almost fifty more years for administrative law to abandon its "formal and conceptual" era focusing on jurisdictional error with a more sensible regime premised on deference to the expertise of administration and insistence on the reasonability of their decisions.[134] Although "famous" for a few years after its release, *Samejima* slipped from legal relevance and attention in the decades that followed, just as the man who gave the case his name slipped back into a life he fought so hard to live.

Conclusions

In the only image I have seen of Munetaka Samejima was taken a decade or so after he won his case. At that point, his last name had changed to Sameshima, perhaps to separate himself from a judicial record he wanted to live apart from. He stands in what looks like a shoe repair shop, his hands gripping tools, his eyes on the camera, his immediate world filled with mounds of exhausted black shoes. The shop is rudimentary: its shelving and walls bare planks of wood, the light overhead a naked bulb hanging from an unseen ceiling. The faces – Sameshima's and two others, a fellow worker and perhaps a customer – appear focused on the tasks at hand. Like all of history, context illuminates the snapshot. The 1942 photo was taken in the makeshift shoe repair shop in Vancouver's Hastings Park, the temporary clearinghouse for thousands of Japanese Canadians forcibly uprooted from their homes prior to removal to more distant sites of internment and incarceration. Fixing shoes – the resourcefulness of making do with what little one had – was an important task in a community deprived of what they owned and forced away from home. Sameshima would continue to fix shoes at Lemon Creek, later Bay Farm, and Slocan City for the duration of his internment. Not for the first time in his life, Sameshima found himself unlawfully detained by the Government of Canada. This time, the law did not come to his aid.

The last page in Sameshima's Department of Immigration file is a letter to the Registrar of Canadian Citizenship written in 1949. The Department of Immigration confirmed the date and circumstances of Sameshima's immigration to Canada. "We might mention," the Immigration commissioner felt compelled to add, "that Munetaka Samejima did not engage in domestic employment after his arrival and his deportation was ordered in 1931." He avoided deportation, the official wrote, "on a technicality." Nonetheless, the department conceded that his time in Canada now qualified him for "permanent immigration status."[135] Canadian citizenship arrived for Sameshima, despite the peevish tone of the letter, at an auspicious moment in Canadian legal history. In 1949, the federal government removed the final orders restricting the movement and liberty of Japanese Canadians; British Columbia removed its prohibition on voting. His citizenship in hand, in 1951 Sameshima moved to Toronto, perhaps, like so many other Japanese Canadians, because the law had helped to destroy what once had been his hard-earned home.

The law for Japanese Canadians in the first half of the twentieth century was defined by crosscurrents: the hopes of equality offset by the law's capacity to discriminate and inflict violence and cause harm. Law exists at the borders of these intersections between the ideals of justice and the mechanics of dispensing power. Japanese migrants operated within an immigration system that simultaneously legalized their entry and discriminated against them by diplomatic agreement and, less visibly, by administrative discretion. While many in the community insisted upon their rights as Canadians, everywhere around them law attempted to limit their mobility, restrict their economic opportunities, and deny their full participation in the political life of Canada. Understandably, much of the legal history of Japanese Canadians has focused on the most overt aspects of that legacy: the racist legislative debates and statutes, and the ideologies that fuelled them. This chapter has focused on Sameshima's story to highlight the less visible realms of legal life for Japanese Canadians, to see the ways in which racism, resistance, and claims to equality and fair treatment also typified encounters with the officials of government and judges alike. The jurisprudence created by such encounters stand as significant markers of Canadian constitutionalism in their uneasy grappling with equality and discrimination and uncertainty about the appropriate role of judicial review of the administrative state. The law emerges from this story, like the individuals that wielded its power, both culpable and virtuous, idealistic and petty, coercive and liberating. Sameshima experienced detention and freedom alike in the tension of those paradoxes.

"*Habeas corpus*," Justice Oliver Wendell Holmes Jr observed, "cuts through all forms and goes to the very tissue of the structure."[136] Perhaps above all other legal domains in the early twentieth century, the administration of immigration law and the jurisprudence of habeas corpus reveal the colliding structural logics of race and equality, exclusion and inclusion, in the makings of Canadian constitutional law. It was not a simple story of enlightened judges curbing the authority of bad faith officials. Japanese Canadians confronted racist aspersions, obdurate suspicions, and assumptions of unbelonging at the hands of border officials and judges alike. But in linking their claims to control their personal liberty to the judicial role in supervising state powers, especially as it may relate to others, Japanese Canadian litigants sometimes found a legal strategy that could succeed. The nature of those legal victories sheds light on the further puzzle of why habeas corpus was not used to challenge the legality of the laws of internment, as was the case in the United States.[137] In their stark racial targeting and explicit discrimination, Canada's laws of confinement and dispossession were never applicable to Scotsmen. By contrast, before the internment era, habeas corpus "provided a way for lawyers and nonlawyers alike to talk about the moral ends they hoped to achieve through law."[138] For Japanese Canadians those moral ends included equality and fairness. For a slim majority of judges, the law of habeas corpus was a route to finding a footing for their supervisory role in Canada's constitutional order. Those projects found common cause in the liberating potential of the writ of habeas corpus and insistence on stricter attention to the procedural forms, if not always the substance, of administrative fairness. The spirit of legality litigants and judges drew upon in doing so did not prevent the violence and harms of the internment, dispossession, and domicide to come. True constitutional equality, *Samejima* reminds us, can only succeed as a shared project of ideals encompassing judges and administrative officials, lawyers and litigants, citizens and residents. In times of real, perceived, or concocted emergency that project can break down in the moment when we need it most. The vulnerability of constitutional law is an enduring reminder from legal history we forget at our peril.

NOTES

This chapter benefitted from the assistance of *Landscapes of Injustice* research assistants and, in particular, the work of Monique Ulysses, Lauren Chalaturnyk, Manjot Parhar, Rachel Weary, Gordon Lyall, Connell Parish, and Kaitlin Findlay.

1 Ken Adachi, *The Enemy That Never Was: A History of the Japanese Canadians* (Toronto: McClelland and Stewart, 1976); W. Peter Ward, *White Canada Forever: Popular Attitudes and Public Policy towards Orientals in British Columbia*, 3rd ed. (Montreal & Kingston: McGill-Queen's University Press, 2002); Patricia Roy, *A White Man's Province: British Columbia Politicians and Chinese and Japanese Immigrants, 1858–1914* (Vancouver: UBC Press, 1989), and *The Oriental Question: Consolidating a White Man's Province, 1914–41* (Vancouver: UBC Press, 2004). See generally, Constance Backhouse: *Colour-Coded: A Legal History of Racism in Canada* (Toronto: University of Toronto Press, 1999).

2 Marilyn Lake and Henry Reynolds, *Drawing the Global Colour Line: White Men's Countries and the International Challenge of Racial Equality* (Cambridge: Cambridge University Press, 2008); David Scott FitzGerald and David Cook-Martin, *Culling the Masses: The Democratic Origins of Racist Immigration Policy in the Americas* (Cambridge, MA: Harvard University Press, 2014); David C Atkinson, *The Burden of White Supremacy: Containing Asian Migration in the British Empire and the United States* (Chapel Hill, NC: University of North Carolina Press, 2016).

3 Atkinson, *The Burden of White Supremacy*, 11. On the complexity and multiplicity of cross-racial encounters in colonial British Columbia, see Renisa Mawani, *Colonial Proximities: Crossracial Encounters and Juridicial Truths in British Columbia* (Vancouver: UBC Press, 2009).

4 *Samejima v. Canada*, [1932] S.C.R. 640.

5 See generally George T. Tamaki, "Canadian Citizenship Act, 1946," *University of Toronto Law Journal* 7, no. 1 (1947): 68–97.

6 Peter Price, "Naturalising Subjects, Creating Citizens: Naturalisation Law and the Conditioning of 'Citizenship' in Canada, 1881–1914," *Journal of Imperial and Commonwealth History* 45, no. 1 (2017): 15.

7 Immigration Act, R.S.C. 1927, c. 93.

8 An Act Respecting Aliens and Naturalization, S.C. 1868, c. 66, s. 3. Although facially neutral on questions of race, the act continued deeply entrenched gendered notions of citizenship: women could gain or lose their status as naturalized depending on the status of their husbands.

9 Price, "Naturalising Subjects," 8.

10 Constitution Act, 1867, s. 91 (27).

11 The Qualification and Registration of Voters Act, 1871, S.B.C 1872, c. 39, s. 13, as amended by Provincial Voters Amendment Act, 1895, S.B.C. 1895, c. 20, s 2. See Patricia E. Roy, "Citizens Without Votes: East Asians in British Columbia, 1872–1947," in *Ethnicity, Power and Politics in Canada*, eds. Jorgen Dahlie and Tissa Fernando (Toronto: Methuen Publications, 1981), 152. As Henry Yu points out, the removal of voting rights from Asians and Indigenous peoples served more than a symbolic function. The exile of Asian Canadians and Indigenous peoples from the political community enabled further repressive discriminatory measures without any political accountability to the targeted groups. Henry Yu, "A Provocation: Anti-Asian Exclusion and the Making and Unmaking of White Supremacy in Canada," in *Dominion of Race: Rethinking Canada's*

International History, eds. Laura Madokoro, Francine McKenzie, and David Meren (Vancouver: UBC Press, 2017), 31.

12 See the list compiled by the Government of British Columbia of racially discriminatory laws passed between 1872 and 1948: https://www2.gov.bc.ca/assets/gov/british-columbians-our-governments/our-history/historic-places/documents/heritage/chinese-legacy/discriminatory_legislation_in_bc_1872_1948.pdf. See generally, H.F. Angus, "The Legal Status in British Columbia of Residents of Oriental Race and Their Descendants," *Canadian Bar Review* 9, no. 1 (1931): 1–12.

13 Union Colliery Co v. Bryden, [1899] A.C. 580 (J.C.P.C.); Re Nakane and Okazake (1908) 13 B.C.R. 370; In re Employment of Aliens, [1922] 63 S.C.R. 293. A holdover from the constitutional model of preconfederation imperial oversight of the colonies, section 90 of the Constitution Act, 1867 enabled the governor general to disallow provincial legislation, in practice, based on ministerial advice from the federal executive. Ryder reports that between 1884 and 1908 the federal government disallowed virtually all of the near annual legislative attempts by the British Columbia legislature to prohibit immigration into the province from Asian migrants either by express prohibition or the imposition of a mandatory English language test. See Bruce Ryder, "Racism and the Constitution: The Constitutional Fate of British Columbia Anti-Asian Immigration Legislation, 1884–1909," *Osgoode Hall Law Journal* 29, no. 3 (Fall 1991): 619–76.

14 Ryder, "Racism and the Constitution," 623.

15 Electoral Franchise Act, S.C. 1885, c. 40, s. 2; Act to Restrict and Regulate Chinese Immigration into Canada, S.C. 1885, c. 71. On its history and legacy see David Dyzenhaus and Mayo Moran, *Calling Power to Account: Law, Reparations, and the Chinese Canadian Head Tax* (Toronto: University of Toronto Press, 2005).

16 "[A]lien citizenship," Mae Ngai argues, "spoke to a condition of racial otherness, a badge of foreignness that could not be shed" (*Impossible Subjects: Illegal Aliens and the Making of Modern America* [Princeton: Princeton University Press, 2004], 8).

17 "Treaty of Commerce and Navigation between Great Britain and Japan, signed at London, 16 July 1894," in *The Consolidated Treaty Series: Vol 180*, ed. Clive Perry (Dobbs Ferry, NY: Oceana Publications, 1979), 259. As Ryder elaborates, although a British treaty with China, the *Treaty of Nanking* of 1842, provided similar assurances, "diplomatically [China and Japan] were worlds apart. Japan was a rising international power; China a subjugated state. As a result, Canadian authorities paid little heed to the Chinese treaties, while they treated Japanese treaty rights very seriously, even before they were enacted into domestic law in 1907" ("Racism and the Constitution," 636).

18 Oscar Douglas Skelton, *Life and Letters of Sir Wilfrid Laurier: Volume II* (Toronto: Oxford University Press, 1921), 348.

19 The Naturalization Act, R.S.C. 1886, c. 113, s. 3. See Audrey Kobayashi and Peter Jackson, "Japanese Canadians and the Racialization of Labour in the British Columbia Sawmill Industry," *BC Studies 103* (1994), 39–45.

20 Atkinson, *The Burden of White Supremacy*, 83. On the role of steamship companies in fostering such circuits, see Yukari Takai, "Navigating Transpacific Passages: Steamship Companies, State Regulators, and Transhipment of Japanese in the Early-Twentieth-Century Pacific Northwest," *Journal of American Ethnic History* 30, 3 (Spring 2011): 7–34. See generally, Lon Kurashige, *Two Faces of Exclusion: The Untold History of Anti-Asian Racism in the United States* (Chapel Hill: University of North Carolina Press, 2016).

21 *Report of the Royal Commission on Chinese and Japanese Immigration* (Ottawa: King's Printer, 1902), xiii.

22 *Report of the Royal Commission*, xiii, 4–5.

23 Ibid., xiii, 337, 351, 356.

24 Ibid., 283.

25 K.T. Takahashi, *The Anti-Japanese Petition: Appeal in Protest against a Threatened Prosecution* (Montreal: Gazette Printing, 1897), 3.

26 Ibid.

27 Andrea Geiger-Adams, "Writing Racial Barriers into Law: Upholding BC's Denial of the Vote to Its Japanese Canadian Citizens, *Homma v Cunningham*, 1902," in *Nikkei in the Pacific Northwest: Japanese Americans and Japanese Canadians in the Twentieth Century*, eds. Gail M Nomura and Louis Fiset (Seattle: University of Washington Press, 2005), 21. Relying on the Privy Council's recent decision in *Union Colliery Co v Bryden*, [1899] A.C. 580 (P.C.), Homma argued that British Columbia lacked the jurisdiction to deny the franchise to immigrants because it interfered with exclusive federal jurisdiction over s. 91(5), Naturalization and Aliens.

28 *Cunningham v. Tomey Homma*, [1903] A.C. 151 (P.C.). "No Japanese Need Apply to Be Voters," the *Vancouver Daily Province* informed readers, quoted in Geiger-Adams, "Writing Racial Barriers into Law," 31.

29 Naturalization Act, R.S.C. 1906, c. 77.

30 Quoted in Price "Naturalizing Subjects," 10.

31 *In re Saddjiro Malsufuro*, (1908) 13 B.C.R. 417 (C.C.), 417-18.

32 Ibid., 420.

33 Ibid., 421.

34 *Re Fukuichi Aho*, [1909] 9 W.L.R. 652 (C.C.), para 9.

35 Erika Lee, "Hemispheric Orientalism and the 1907 Pacific Coast Race Riots," *Amerasia Journal* 33, no. 2 (2007), 9.

36 Atkinson, *The Burden of White Supremacy*, 101–3. On the damages to the approximately sixty Japanese Canadian businesses ransacked during the riot see W.L. Mackenzie King, *Report of W.L. Mackenzie King … Commissioner Appointed to Investigate into the Losses Sustained by the Japanese Population of Vancouver, BC on the Occasion of the Riots in that City in September 1907* (Ottawa: Dawson, 1908).

37 *R v. McLaren*, group 0149, box 122, file 085, BCA.

38 Japan Treaty Act, 1906, S.C. 1906, c. 50. When Britain renewed its treaty relationship with Japan in 1911 Canada enacted new legislation adopting its terms, although, again, violating the spirit of its terms. See the Japanese Treaty Act, S.C. 1913, c. 27.

39 Gib van Ert, "A Suitable Population: British Columbia's Japanese Treaty Act Litigation, 1920–1923," *Canadian Journal of Comparative and Contemporary Law* 3, no. 1 (2017): 139.

40 Atkinson, *The Burden of White Supremacy*, 104. In the view of Oscar Skelton – later to become one of Mackenzie King's most trusted advisors – Laurier's "brilliant" solution saved both "Japan's pride and Canada's racial integrity." Skelton, *Life and Letters of Sir Wilfrid Laurier*, 350.

41 Immigration Act, R.S.C. 1927 c. 93, s. 38(a), (c). The provisions began as an order in council and were formally added the Act in 1910.

42 H.F. Angus, "Canadian Immigration: The Law and Its Administration" *American Journal of International Law* 28, no. 1 (1934): 84.

43 Quoted in Lyle Dick, "Sergeant Masumi Mitsui and the Japanese Canadian War Memorial: Intersections of National, Cultural, and Personal Memory," *Canadian Historical Review* 91, no. 3 (2010): 444. Dick writes: "if we refer to the reported words of the recruits … Kumagawa and Ishihara asserted that while the strengthening of Canada's war efforts was the 'primary aim,' they hoped that prospective military service would gain them recognition as Canadians and 'help lessen discrimination against future Japanese,'" (444). See also Roy Ito, *We Went to War: The Story of the Japanese Canadians Who Served during the First and Second World Wars* (Stittsville, ON: Canada's Wings, 1984).

44 A.E. Skinner to Division Commissioner, 12 January 1931, file 491970, vol. 368, RG 76, Immigration Branch, LAC.

45 Memorandum by A.E.J., 19 January 1931, file 491970, vol. 368, RG 76, Immigration Branch, LAC.

46 Much of the emigration from Japan to Canada was concentrated among a few prefectures, Kagoshima among them. Andrea Geiger, *Subverting Exclusion: Transpacific Encounters with Race, Case, and Borders, 1885–1928* (New Haven: Yale University Press, 2011), 16.

47 "Certificate of Landing," file 491970, vol. 368, RG 76, Immigration Branch, LAC; Munetaka Samejima, affidavit, 25 September 1931, S.C.C., file6000-6007, vol. 631, RG 125, LAC.

48 "In the Matter of the 'Immigration Act', Declaration of Jentaro Ueno," 5 May 1931, file 491970, vol. 368, RG 76, Immigration Branch, LAC. It is possible, of course, that Samejima's agreement to work for Ueno as a domestic servant had been negotiated as a cover for entry and was never intended to actually supply work. For what it is worth, reading Samejima's testimony, affidavit, and those of Ueno strongly lead me to accept their recounting at face value.

49 Munetaka Samejima, affidavit, 25 September 1931, S.C.C. file 6000-6007, vol. 631, RG-125, LAC.

50 Steve Schwinghamer, "Canadian Immigration Facilities at Victoria, BC" (Research Paper, Canadian Museum of Immigration at Pier 21), https://pier21.ca/research/immigration-history/canadian-immigration-facilities-at-victoria-bc.

51 A full transcript of the hearing is in Samejima's Appeal Book, S.C.C. file 6000-6007, vol. 631, RG-125, LAC.

52 Immigration Act, R.S.C. 1927, c. 93, s. 33(7).

53 Appeal Book, S.C.C. file 6000-6007, vol. 631, RG-125, LAC.

54 See, for example, Moresby's representation of the Chinese Canadian defendant in *R v. Sam*, [1930] 53 C.C.C. 252 (B.C.C.A.).

55 Immigration Act, R.S.C. 1927, c. 93, s.s. 19, 23. "In the case of the appeal being dismissed by the Minister," the section provided, "the appellant shall forthwith be deported."

56 William Moresby to Minister of Immigration, 11 May 1931, file 491970, vol. 368, RG 76, Immigration Branch, LAC.

57 "As Head of the Victoria Japanese Community," Ishii wrote, "I am desirous that the Japanese in British Columbia and any Japanese entering British Columbia from Japan shall conduct themselves in such a way as to preserve the good relations prevailing between Canada and Japan."

58 As Eiji Okawa has argued, like other migrant communities, in significant ways the Issei continued to draw deeply on cultural ideas, traditions, and concepts from their

homeland to navigate and make sense of migration and settlement. Eiji Okawa and the Landscapes of Injustice Research Collective, "Japaneseness in Racist Canada: Immigrant Imaginaries during the First Half of the Twentieth Century," *Journal of American Ethnic History* 37, no. 4 (2018): 10–39. Geiger makes a similar point in *Subverting Exclusion*.

59 "Cover Page: Immigration and Colonization: File No. 491970," file 491970, vol. 368, RG 76, Immigration Branch, LAC.

60 Memorandum by A.L. Joliffe to W.J. Egan, 1 June 1931, file 491970, vol. 368, RG 76, Immigration Branch, LAC. See also Memorandum by A.E. Skinner, 9 May 1931, file 491970, vol. 368, RG 76, Immigration Branch, LAC.

61 A.E. Skinner to W.C. Moresby, 4 June 1931, file 491970, vol. 368, RG 76, Immigration Branch, LAC.

62 See Orders in Council 2115 (16 September 1930) and 695 (21 March 1931). H.F. Angus writes: "In recent years there has been a very rapid transition from regarding Canada as a country which requires … immigration on a very large scale, to thinking of immigration as constituting an economic peril to the present population" ("Canadian Immigration," 75).

63 On persecution of Communists in particular see Dennis G Molinaro, *An Exceptional Law: Section 98 and the Emergency State, 1919–1936* (Toronto: University of Toronto Press, 2017). See generally Shin Imai, "Deportation in the Depression," *Queen's Law Journal* 7, no. 1 (1981): 66–94.

64 Barbara Roberts, *Whence They Came: Deportation from Canada 1900–1935* (Ottawa: University of Ottawa Press, 1988), 35–8.

65 Ibid., 3.

66 Geiger, *Subverting Exclusion*, 99.

67 See James D. Cameron, "Canada's Struggle with Illegal Entry on Its West Coast: *The Case of Fred Yoshy and Japanese Migrants before the Second World War*," *BC Studies* 146 (2005): 37–62.

68 "Deportation Threatens Hundreds of Japanese," *Ottawa Citizen*, 6 July 1931; "Mounted Police Net Closes on Alien Suspects," *The Daily Province*, 5 July 1931; "New Evidence at Yoshi Trial," *The Daily Province*, 24 September 1931; "Japanese Smuggling Charge Before Jury," *The Daily Province*, 23 September 1931; "Yoshy Convicted on Second Charge," *The Daily Province*, 26 September 1931.

69 Canada, House of Commons, Debates, 22 April 1932, 17th Parl., 3rd sess., vol. 2, 2278, accessed 18 September 2019, http://parl.canadiana.ca/view/oop.debates_HOC1703_02/1160?r=0&s=1.

70 Ex p Chin Shack, [1928] 1 D.L.R. 779 (B.C.C.A.).

71 *Rogers v. Clarence Hotel*, [1940] 2 W.W.R. 545 (B.C.C.A.). See Christopher Moore, *The British Columbia Court of Appeal: The First Hundred Years* (Vancouver: UBC Press, 2010), 51–2; Ross Lambertson, "The BC Court of Appeal and Civil Liberties," *BC Studies* 162 (2009): 88–9.

72 Samejima, B.C.S.C.; Section 33(7) of the Immigration Act, R.S.C. 1927, c. 93 prohibits the entry of Canada by misrepresentation, among other misdeeds.

73 The Supreme Court of Canada would return to the issue of the necessity of reasons and fairness in the immigration context nearly sixty years later in *Baker v. Canada*, [1999] 2 S.C.R. 817.

74 Justice Fisher quoting *R v. Lantalum: ex parte Offman* [1921] 62 D.L.R. 225, 238.
75 Immigration Act, R.S.C. 1927, c.
76 Justice Fisher quoting Hunter, CJBC in *Narain Singh*, [1913] 18 B.C. 506, 511.
77 An annoyed Egan complained to the minister of justice that he failed to see why the Order for Deportation should be "of such vital importance in the matter." Letter, DM to Edwards, 29 July 1931, LAC, Immigration Branch, RG 76, Vol 368, File 491970.
78 Edwards to Egan, 4 September 1931, LAC. For his part, John Clay advised against the strategy, recommending instead that Samejima be rearrested and an entirely new Board of Inquiry constituted to determine the appropriate outcome. Clay to R. Roff, 3 August 1931, file 491970, vol. 368, RG 76, Immigration Branch, LAC.
79 Deputy Minister to A.E. Skinner, 18 September 1931, file 491970, vol. 368, RG 76, Immigration Branch, LAC.
80 Samejima, Justice Murphy decision, file 491970, vol. 368, RG 76, Immigration Branch, LAC.
81 The ethnic diversity of the four-member panel is conveyed by the names of the judges hearing the appeal: Chief Justice James Alexander Macdonald, Justices Archer Martin, Justice Albert Edward McPhillips, and, for good measure, a second Justice Macdonald, this one named Malcolm Archibald.
82 *Canada v. Samejima*, [1932] 3 W.W.R. 201, para. 15, pers. Martin, J [Court of Appeal].
83 Samejima, Court of Appeal, para. 16, 21, pers. Martin, J.
84 Samejima, Court of Appeal, para. 5, pers. Macdonald, CJBC.
85 Samejima, Court of Appeal, paras 23, 27, 34, 36 per McPhillips, J. Section 16 of the *Immigration Act* provided, "In all such cases, a Board of Inquiry may at the hearing, receive and base its decision upon any evidence considered credible or trustworthy by such Board in the circumstances of each case; and in all questions where the question of the right to enter or land in Canada under this Act is raised the burden of proof shall rest upon the immigrant, passenger or other person claiming such right."
86 Japanese Public Association to The Honourable Minister of Immigration and Colonization, 3 December 1931, file 491970, vol. 368, RG 76, Immigration Branch, LAC.
87 Commissioner to Japanese Public Justice Association, 16 December 1931, file 491970, vol. 368,RG 76, Immigration Branch, LAC.
88 A.V. Dicey, *Introduction to the Study of the Law of the Constitution*, 8th ed. (London: Macmillan, 1915), 189, 198.
89 Re Kanamura, [1904] 10 B.C.R. 354 (B.C.S.C.); Dominion Fire Insurance Co v. Nakata, [1915] 52 S.C.R. 294, 295.
90 Joan Brockman, "Exclusionary Tactics: The History of Women and Visible Minorities in the Legal Profession in British Columbia" in *Essays in the History of Canadian Law: British Columbia and the Yukon*, eds. Hamar Foster and John McLaren (Toronto: University of Toronto Press, 1995).
91 Geiger-Adams, "Writing Racial Barriers into Law"; Ryder, "Racism and the Constitution; van Ert, "A Suitable Population"; John P.S. McLaren, "The Burdens of Empire and the Legalization of White Supremacy in Canada, 1860–1910," in *Legal History in the Making: Proceedings of the Ninth British Legal History Conference, Glasgow 1989*, eds. W.M. Gordon and T.D. Fergus (London: Hambledon Press, 1991), 187–202; McLaren, "The Early British Columbia Supreme Court and the 'Chinese Question': Echoes of the Rule of Law," *Manitoba Law Journal* 20, no. 1 (1991): 107–47; Elder C. Marques, "What

the Law Does Not Allow: The Boundaries of Canadian Constitutionalism and the British Columbia Supreme Court, 1878–88" *Queen's Law Journal* 30, no. 1 (2004–2005): 35–78.

92 Judith Farbey and R.J. Sharpe, with Simon Atrill, *The Law of Habeas Corpus*, 3rd ed (Oxford: Oxford University Press, 2011), 2.

93 On its history see Paul D. Halliday, *Habeas Corpus: From England to Empire* (Cambridge, MA: Harvard University Press, 2010), 2. The English law of habeas corpus as codified in statutes in 1679 and 1816 passed into Canadian law at reception. D.A. Cameron, *The Law of Habeas Corpus in Canada* (Toronto: Butterworths, 1974) at 2. In British Columbia, specifically, see The English Law Act, R.S.B.C. 1911, c. 75, s. 2.

94 *Ikezoya v. Canadian Pacific Railway*, [1907] 12 B.C.R. 454 (B.C.S.C.).

95 Ibid., para. 6.

96 Ibid., para. 14.

97 re Nakane and Okazake, [1908] 13 B.C.R. 370 (B.C.S.C.).

98 Ibid., 373.

99 "We live under a Federal system of government," Justice Clement held. "With regard to certain matters the Canadian people speak as a unit, while as to other matters we speak separately, and, if we choose, diversely by Provinces. The system was brought to birth after long travail. The minds of our best men were long occupied in fixing upon the proper line of diversion between matters of general Canadian concern and matters of more immediately local or provincial concern, and the result of their labours as embodied in the British North America Act should be loyally recognized and respected." In re Nakane and Okazake, 376–7.

100 Renisa Mawani, *Oceans of Law: The Komagata Maru and Jurisdiction in the Time of Empire* (Durham, NC: Duke University Press, 2018), 6. See also Hugh J.M. Johnston, *The Voyage of the* Komagata Maru*: The Sikh Challenge to Canada's Colour Bar* (Vancouver: UBC Press, 2014).

101 Quoted in Michael Bird, "Behind the *Komagata Maru*'s Fight to Open Canada's Border," *Globe and Mail*, 24 May 2014.

102 Re Munshi Singh [1914], 20 B.C.R. 243, 252 (C.A.).

103 Re Munshi Singh, 255, 259. "Canada has a right … to make laws for the exclusion and expulsion from Canada of British subjects whether of Asiatic race or of European race, irrespective of whether they come from Calcutta or London," Justice Irving agreed.

104 Ibid., 261.

105 Ibid., 271.

106 Ibid., 271, quoting the Privy Council in *Khoo Sit Iloh v. Lim Thean Tong*, [1912] A.C. 323 (J.C.P.C.) at 325.

107 Ibid., 291. For a reading of the intersections of the decision's racialized thinking with colonial ideologies see Renisa Mawani, "Specters of Indigeneity in British-Indian Migration, 1914," *Law and Society Review* 46, no. 2 (2012): 369–403.

108 Canada, House of Commons, Debates, 2 March 1914, 12th Parl., 3rd sess., vol. 2, 1230, accessed 18 September 2019, http://parl.canadiana.ca/view/oop.debates_HOC1203_02/220?r=0&s=1.

109 Ibid., 1256.

110 Ibid., 1261.

111 Ibid., 1262.

112 Contrast *Re Harry K. Thaw (No 3)* [1913], 13 D.L.R. 715 at 718 (Qc KB) and *Lancet v. O'Connell* [1923], 61 C.S. 9 at 20 (Qc Sup Ct).

113 *Quong-Wing v. The King*, [1914] 49 S.C.R. 440 at 447, per Davies J. Even Justice Iddington's powerful dissent rested on the concern of the legislation's discriminatory treatment of British subjects, not on racial grounds per se.

114 Appellant's Factum, Appeal Book, S.C.C., file 6000-6007 vol. 631RG-125, LAC.

115 Ibid.

116 David Ricardo Williams, *Just Lawyers: Seven Portraits* (Toronto: University of Toronto Press, 1995), 60.

117 Respondent's Factum, S.C.C., file 6000-6007, vol. 631, RG-125, LAC.

118 Samejima, S.C.C., 651, 654.

119 Ibid., 654.

120 Immigration Act, R.S.C. 1927, c. 93, s. 42.

121 Ibid., 645.

122 Ibid., 647.

123 Ibid., 649.

124 See David Ricardo Williams, *Duff: A Life in the Law* (Vancouver: UBC Press, 1984).

125 Samejima, S.C.C., 642.

126 Ibid. at 642. The archaic expression "hugger mugger" denotes a concealment or a disorderly muddle, both of which might apply here. The passage bears enough similarity to aspects of the famous dissents in *Fong Yue Ting v. United States*, 149 US 698 (1893) to suggest that Justice Duff may have read and been influenced by them. In dissent in that case involving the habeas corpus proceedings of Chinese Americans failing to take out certificates of residency, Justice Field asked, "Is it possible that Congress can, at its pleasure, in disregard of the guaranties of the Constitution, expel at any time the Irish, German, French, and English who may have taken up their residence here?" In turn, it is possible that Justice Duff's formulation influenced a similar turn of phrase in Justice Rand's reasons in *Reference re Persons of the Japanese Race*, [1946] S.C.R. 248.

127 *Roncarelli v. Duplessis*, [1959] S.C.R. 121. See Eric M. Adams, "Building a Law of Human Rights: *Roncarelli v Duplessis* in Canadian Constitutional Culture," *McGill Law Journal* 55, no. 3 (2010): 437–60.

128 Re Employment of Aliens, [1922] 63 S.C.R. 293 at 326.

129 Michael Taggart, "Prolegomenon to an Intellectual History of Administrative Law in the Twentieth Century: The Case of John Willis and Canadian Administrative Law," *Osgoode Hall Law Journal* 43, no. 3 (2005): 223–67.

130 Commissioner to Acting Division Commissioner of Immigration, Vancouver, 25 June 1932, file 491970, vol. 368, RG 76, Immigration Branch, LAC.

131 Moffat Hancock, "Discharge of Deportees on Habeas Corpus," *Canadian Bar Review* 14, 2 (1936): 116–36; John Willis, "Statutory Interpretation in a Nutshell," *Canadian Bar Review* 16, no. 1 (1938): 1–27.

132 Hancock, "Discharge of Deportees," 132. C.F. Fraser, "Administrative Control Over Aliens in Canada," *George Washington Law Review* 7, no. 3 (1939): 458. The American experience was similar in this regard. In the Pacific Northwest immigration officials complained of having to deal with the burdens imposed by habeas corpus. An official urged that deportation proceedings be "kept quiet" so that "habeas corpus proceedings may be avoided" (Hidetaka Hirota, "Exclusion on the Ground: Racism, Official Discretion,

and the Quotidian Enforcement of General Immigration Law in the Pacific Northwest Borderland," *American Quarterly* 69, no. 2 [2017]: 356).

133 Roberts, *When They Came*, 38. Of the twenty habeas corpus proceedings launched against deportations from Canada in 1932, only one succeeded. Imai, "Deportation in the Depression," 70. On the continuing vulnerabilities faced by noncitizens across the Commonwealth, see Rayner Thwaites, *The Liberty of Non-citizens: Indefinite Detention in Commonwealth Countries* (London: Hart, 2014).

134 See Matthew Lewans, *Administrative Law and Judicial Deference* (Oxford: Hart, 2016), 138–56.

135 Commissioner to Registrar of Canadian Citizenship, 6 May 1949, file 491970, vol. 368, RG 76, Immigration Branch, LAC.

136 J. Holmes, in *Frank v. Mangum*, 237 US 309 (1915) at 346.

137 On the importance of habeas corpus in the legal history of Japanese Americans during the Second World War see Amanda Tyler, *Habeas Corpus: From the Tower of London to Guantanamo Bay* (Oxford: Oxford University Press, 2017), 211–43.

138 Paul D. Halliday, *Habeas Corpus: From England to Empire* (Cambridge, MA: Harvard University Press, 2010), 8.

CHAPTER 3

The Wealth of My Home: A Story of a Japanese Canadian Family

Eiji Okawa and the Landscapes of Injustice Research Collective

The Wealth of My Home
My house is merely ten tsubo [approx. 300 square metres, read small]
The garden is no more than three
Some say it's so small, that it's very cramped.
The house may be cramped, but it's enough to fit my legs.
The garden might be small, but it's enough for me to gaze upon the vast, azurean sky,
to take a few steps and think of eternity.
The divine moon and sun shine upon this space, and the four seasons come here, too.
Wind, rain, snow, and fog all come and go, one at a time.
The joy the place brings is not slight.
Butterflies come and dance, cicadas come to sing, birds come to play and in the fall,
fireflies come and chirp.
When I perceive things quietly, I come to know that much of the wealth of the
universe is right here in my tiny garden.[1]

One spring day in the mountain-surrounded internment camp of Lemon Creek in British Columbia, Teiji Morishita penned this poem. His handwriting is as elegant as the poem is evocative. The poem is not his creation. The writer Tokutomi Roka composed it and featured it in his book *Nature and Life* (*Shizen to jinsei*) published in Japan in 1900. It must have resonated with Teiji. He copied the verses three times each. Perhaps he wanted to remember it by heart and gaze at his yard to contemplate the meanings of the space that surrounded him. Perhaps he wanted to borrow from it during a poetry meeting with his friends and associates.

The context of Teiji's writing demands attention. On 11 March Shōwa 21, or 1946, he sat to write out the poem after long and agonizing years of loss. As one of approximately 21,000 people of Japanese heritage who were evicted from their homes in coastal Canada by the government, he lost his home and business in Vancouver. His house was seized and sold without his knowledge or approval. His business on Powell Street, the heart of a Japanese Canadian neighbourhood, was shuttered and its outstanding accounts were being sorted out by officials and accountants whom he had never met. Losing his livelihood, Teiji and his family faced economic hardship and uncertainty. In fact, on the same day, he spent eight hours chopping wood, a job for which his career in business did not prepare him.[2] The meagre income from menial jobs ran short of supporting the six children he had with Sawa, his wife.

Teiji's text casts light on Japanese Canadian history as well as the history of a systematic dispossession of Japanese Canadians by a state policy. This chapter contributes to the first research claim articulated in the introduction of this book: that the dispossession entailed the very specific harms of the loss of home. It also speaks to the second research claim: that the dispossession required ongoing administrative work and that Japanese Canadians suffered specific harms as a result of and formulated specific responses to the enduring intrusions of the administrative state. To understand the losses of Japanese Canadians during the 1940s we must comprehend what their property meant to them, and its significance is best understood through their own sources. Using the records of one family, supplemented by state records, this chapter asks how Japanese Canadians related to their material resources. Taking cues from Nicholas Blomley's analyses of relationality and spatiality of property, this study examines the socioeconomic interactions that shaped social life before, during, and after the rupture of the 1940s.[3] Property is an institutionalized form of relation to a place or thing as well as to other people and the state. As Eduardo Pañelvar puts it, "each parcel of land in a city would be unique, in a sense, because of the relationship it bears with the web of human interactions, within which it is situated."[4] However, relations are not woven on bare land but on developed land, in cities, via institutions like businesses, schools, homes, or streets. These are subject to rights as defined by the law and support and foster relations among individuals and groups in multifaceted and dynamic ways.

What roles did property play in the family and communal lives of Japanese Canadians in the prewar period? How was the dispossession carried out, and how did it affect social networks and relational practices developed and sustained through property? Delving into these questions, I focus on Teiji's family business in Vancouver, the Ebisuzaki store (known in the community as Ebisuzaki shōten, meaning store, and officially as M. Ebisuzaki Company) located on Powell Street. A store, as property, is integrated into society differently from a home. This store was run by a family and catered mostly to members of the Japanese Canadian community. The discussion to follow is based on my analysis of two types of source materials. The core materials are the textual records of the store and the family, originally preserved by Teiji, and archived today at the Nikkei National Museum in Burnaby, British Columbia, as the *Morishita Family Collection*. The collection includes records of prewar business activities, photographs, correspondence with family members and associates, the family's response to the dispossession, among others; it was donated by Teiji's eldest daughter, Nancy Morishita. My understanding of the family's history owes much to Nancy's memory, shared with me in our conversations.[5] In addition to these "voices" of the family, I use records of the Custodian of Enemy Property, pertaining to its handling of the family's property over the course of the dispossession.

This chapter reconstructs how members of a Japanese Canadian family organized their lives and positioned themselves in social space, then situates the rupture of the 1940s within the longer history of their relational practices. Engaging with the experience of dispossession through the texts they produced for themselves, it explores their structural relation with the institution of property and recovers the tension between, on the one hand, their mode of economic organization and, on the other, the formalized property relations which shaped the execution of the dispossession. Examining administrative processes and ground-level interactions, I suggest that the history of dispossession offers a wealth of empirical data not only on racist injustice but also the nature and boundaries of the property regime in mid-twentieth-century Canada, a system of order that was taken for granted by officials implementing the policy.

Family, store, and wealth

The history of the Ebisuzaki store is the story of an extended family and their community. Founded by Masatarō Ebisuzaki in 1909, the store sold diverse goods and merchandise: clothes and apparel, food and household wares, gifts and ceremonial items like dolls. Its location at 337 Powell Street placed it at the centre of the largest Japanese Canadian neighbourhood.[6] A few lots away, the Maikawa merchant family ran their department store. Across the street, the grand Tamura building stood high, its ornate rooftop feature recalling a Shinto shrine and projecting the cultural heritage of the community, while the Japan-Canada bank on the ground floor enabled the transpacific flow of capital that characterized migrants' economic lives. A 1921 record shows a remarkable 117 Japanese Canadian businesses and associations in the 300 block of Powell Street alone, including bathhouses, a pharmacy, restaurants, a midwifery clinic, an insurance company, and a fish monger.[7] The owners of the Ebisuzaki store lived in the next block on East Cordova Street, no more than a five-minute walk away, along Oppenheimer Park, home field of the now-legendary ball club the Vancouver Asahis, whose tactical displays the family could watch from the window of their own home.[8]

As a family business, the Ebisuzaki store was owned, managed, and staffed by a network of close relatives. Like her husband, Hide Ebisuzaki (Masatarō's wife) was an immigrant from the Fukuoka Prefecture in southern Japan.[9] She was a crucial figure in the ownership and operation of the business. In 1920, her brothers Teiji and Jiichir crossed together from Japan, to join their sister in the family store.[10] Hide and Teiji managed affairs on the store front, while Masatarō, closely involved with the Fukuoka prefectural association, handled purchasing, including imports from Japan, and diversified the family's enterprise by investing in a shingle plant.

When Sawa Hamada married Teiji in 1929, she quit her job at the post office in the town of Moji, also in Fukuoka, to join Teiji in Vancouver. The house was shared with Teiji's sister Hide and brother-in law Masatarō, and their two sons Kentarō and Kōjirō. The children went to Japan for schooling but returned to Canada in their teens in 1930. Kentarō, elder of the two, studied at a commercial school in Vancouver and helped his mother manage matters related to the store. Kōjirō worked as a driver delivering goods to customers who lived on Vancouver Island. In addition to these "blood" relatives, young women from Japanese Canadian agrarian communities in the Fraser Valley lived in the house while they apprenticed at the store to gain work experience. Sawa took charge of work on the domestic front, enabling the others to focus on business matters. In addition to rearing her children (who numbered five before the family was uprooted), Sawa cooked for everyone and performed daily household chores. Sometimes, Masatarō came home late in the evening, after socializing with associates and making business deals, and Sawa would prepare hot meals for him. She would often get no more than three hours of sleep a day. Sometime in the 1930s, Masatarō went to Japan. He never returned, becoming ill and dying there in 1943.

Let me return to Teiji's poem cited at the start. The poem of course is about the wealth of a home, and the form of wealth evoked is intangible, experienced through a subjective identification of the self with the riches of the universe manifesting in the physical terrains of home and garden. More relevant to the current analysis is the metaphor of the wealth of a home in a material sense. Wealth, or *tomi* in Japanese, refers to the conventional economic usage of the term. Teiji surely was painfully aware of the need for money to support himself and his family, having lost all of his. A month earlier, he had asked staff of the Custodian of Enemy Property to send him cash from his account, which contained funds from the sale of his home. He needed it to buy warm winter clothes because a severe cold snap had hit Lemon Creek and the Slocan. All the clothes they had brought from the coast for their children had become worn out, and they were going to schools and kindergartens wearing "old rags" that were "beyond patching."[11] The Custodian declined the request.[12]

Teiji wrote out the poem after having his request turned down. As in the case of Japanese Canadians whose experiences of the dispossession are conveyed in other chapters of this book, this state decision caused harm to him and his immediate family. But in Teiji's case, the richness of his family's records allows us to see the harms of the era from a broader perspective. The dispossession not only alienated Teiji from his personal funds and individual well-being but also disrupted the broader family and communal networks of the Ebisuzaki store. The "wealth" that he lost was multifaceted: social and individual, communal, familial, and personal. Here, normative ideas about property or proprietorship may cloud our vision. We need to peel back a layer and look at social organization that developed around material resources.

Given the labour of the Morishita and Ebisuzaki family members that went into the running of their store, family life and business operation coalesced without a sharp divide, calling to mind the idea of household as "the social unit that effectively over long periods of time enables individuals, of varying ages of both sexes, to pool income from multiple sources in order to ensure their individual and collective reproduction and well-being," to borrow from Emanuel Wallerstein and Joan Smith.[13] As they point out, households can be broader than a nuclear family, and nonwage labourers on the domestic front play a crucial role in sustaining the unit against the economic pressures of the capitalist world. This model fits with our two families, who lived together to form a single household. Their life together was not a given but a mode of organized life emerging from the joint project of running the business. Sawa's domestic work was critical to direct the other labour of the household toward the store, the cheap or free labour of children and family was indispensable to the success of the business. The store was a part of the household economy and the production and management of wealth inseparable from familial and domestic arrangements.

Store and community

Emerging from the household, the Ebisuzaki store served as the hub of a much wider social network. Boasting an impressive selection of merchandise including clothing and accessories, such as handmade children's overcoats with puffy collar attachments, lady's silk robes, and velvet baby dresses, and a wide selection of groceries and dry goods, it was a versatile general retailer, the type that declined with the proliferation of super markets and mega-retailers.[14] Pedestrians strolling Powell Street would see clothes and household wares, stacked and shelved tightly in the front section of the store. On festive occasions like the Girls Day (3 March) and Boys Day (5 May) Japanese dolls were displayed for immigrant parents wishing to celebrate the growth of their children in a traditional fashion. Making their way into the inner section of the store, perhaps through the displays of ceramic wares that were imported from Japan, shoppers would reach the grocery area. Carrying rice, miso, soy sauce, dried bonito, tea, noodles (including "Italian *udon*"), pickles, fish, eggplants packed in *karashi*-mustard, sardines, kelp for making dashi stock, and lard, the Ebisuzaki store catered to the needs of its clientele who preferred to eat Japanese (and sometimes Italian) meals as they carried on with their diverse lives.

The store was linked with consumers and suppliers dispersed well beyond the city. In April 1941, C. Nishimura, a resident of a small fishing village on the Pacific coast of Vancouver Island, wrote the store to propose a trade: "We have started making tempura kyanzume now so I wonder if you could buy some from us as we want to get some goods from you. We will be looking forward to get an order sometime soon."[15] Nishimura, a fisher or cannery worker with a creative mind, came up with a potentially marketable product and sought ways to sell it through barter if not for cash. Whether or not they made this deal is uncertain, but the store was part of a wider socioeconomic network. Another telling example is one of the store's flyers, likely from the early 1930s:

> No Empty Raffle Ticket during Our Collaborative Great Sale with Prizes
> · · · ·(from December 1 to 30th)· · · ·
>
> Anyone who buys anything from our over-thirty-thousand-item inventory with over-$6000 in value will receive a raffle ticket. There are other prizes, up to $100 in value!
>
> To thank you for your continued patronage, we are covering the postage for your mail orders. You can stay home and shop as though you were in the store, at no additional cost!
>
> The rice polishing department features the Marutsuru-brand Japanese rice at a special bargain price: $4.30/100 kin (approx. 60 kgs). Additional saving of 35 cents for cash purchases!
>
> Befitting the emblem of the crane [*tsuru*], the Marutsuru rice is a true classic. You will not find better rice for the price. Our motto as always is "thin profit and thick trust." Come and try the rice; you will want to place your order.
>
> Incessant as you are in improving your lives, with Christmas and New Year around the corner, it is time of the year to send gifts to repay your debts and to sustain trustful relations. With kindness and quality service as our utmost priority, our store features fine goods at low rate. We wait on patronage from each and every one of you.[16]

The self-styling of the store as "everyone's loyal servant" (*minasama no chūboku*) gives a glimpse of the marketing culture of the day, as does the emphasis on the debts (*on*), which refers not to debts in a financial sense but a sense of moral obligation and gratitude toward persons who have helped and supported you. *Oseibo*, or year-end gifting, was an established social custom based on the notion that these moral debts must be repaid at regular intervals to express gratitude with gifts and sustain ethically sound social relations. The custom was a business opportunity for the store, which tried to expand sales by enticing its clientele to do their annual *oseibo* shopping, as well as Christmas shopping, at Ebisuzaki. To ease the hassle of *oseibo* shoppers, the store also provided packing and wrapping services, complete with "beautiful boxes and appropriate decorations." As just one of many retailers in the Japanese Canadian niche, the store also used raffle tickets and prizes to lure patrons during the prime shopping season.

At the same time, Ebisuzaki customers could "stay home and shop as though you were in the store, at no additional cost!" Just when the store began to offer mail order sales is uncertain. The practice surely served to boost sales and linked the retailer with Japanese Canadians far beyond the neighbourhood itself. At first, the store seems to have outsourced delivery, utilizing a third-party carrier. By the late-1930s, it managed its deliveries in-house by investing in automobiles. There were three main delivery regions: (1) Vancouver Island, (2) the northern area of the Fraser Valley including Haney, Mission, and Port Hammond, and (3) southern Fraser Valley localities such as Langley, Coghlan, and Clayburn each serviced by a designated driver, one of whom was Teiji.

Teiji kept some records of the delivery runs. Listing names by region with dates, the records show dollar values next to each name, likely representing the amount sold to each client.[17] Surviving sources show delivery to nineteen communities on Vancouver Island and in the Fraser Valley. Below is an example of the record pertaining to Royston, a logging community on Vancouver Island, dated 9 June 1941:

Royston Buddhist Association, youths division	$1.95
Royston Buddhist Association (bukkyōkai)	28.95
Kawaguchi Shigeo	2.75
Fujioka	2.00
Asaka-sensei	7.80
Doi Kenichirō	21.29
Deguchi Tatsugorō	6.40
Deguchi Genichi	1.00
Iwaasa Tadao	7.21
Kobayashi Motoo	63.36
Kimura Kōsaku	6.05
Katō Guntarō	16.26
Kobayakawa Masao	3.50[18]

This is likely from a delivery run made by Kōjirō, Teiji's nephew responsible for deliveries on the island. In addition to Royston, the same text suggests he delivered to nine other communities on the island, the total sales amounting to $1,851. According to Nancy, deliveries were made on a monthly basis, and it took several days for the store's three drivers to reach all customers.[19] En route they would stay at homes of their customers, as interpersonal networks overlapped with paths of economic exchange.

The Ebisuzaki network spanned the southern coastal region of British Columbia. Generating wealth for the store and the proprietors, the network constituted precious social capital built through rigorous efforts. The importance of regulars to this network is demonstrated by the year-end *oseibo* the store sent them. Following Masatarō's practice, Hide and Teiji continued to send gifts to their loyal clients and business

Figure 3.1 *Right* Sawa and the Morishita children on the front steps of their home on Cordova Street, Vancouver. Date and photographer unknown.

Figure 3.2 *Opposite* Morishita children [Nancy and Teruo?] along with workers of the Ebisuzaki store on a beach outing in Vancouver. Date and photographer unknown.

associates until the time of the uprooting. A 1941 record indicates the store gave $634 worth of personalized *oseibo*.[20] The 1936 list of gifts includes a woman's shirt to H. Kubo and socks to T. Kubo; two boxes of bonito flakes and one box of cigarettes to Eguchi Jukichi; two kinds of ladies' scarves and a necktie to the Toyodas in Duncan; a package of superior tea to the Abes in Chemainus; toys to the Shimozawas in Nanaimo; a white ladies' shirt, a rain coat; five towels to Y. Suzuki, and one box of candies to the Nakatsus.[21]

The savvy business practice was the flipside of the hard reality of running a business. To stay afloat and preserve its good reputation, the store had to innovate, keep up with the latest fashions, and ensure customer satisfaction. As we will see, like any other enterprise, the store had mortgages and debts. It was probably not an exaggeration when they stated, in their flyer for Girls Day dolls, that the management was "making strenuous efforts without rest" to deliver top quality products and services. Fortunately, their efforts paid off. Not only did the household own a house, they had four cars.[22] The children had fancy clothes, Nancy took dance lessons, and Kōjirō went skiing. They collected vinyl records and dolls, enjoyed picnics, and remodelled their basement to fit a Japanese-style bath. They were part of Canada's rising middle class.

Like many Japanese Canadians, Teiji and his family lost virtually everything in the 1940s. For Teiji, prewar life in Vancouver may have seemed like a dream when he wrote on 11 September 1946: "We lost everything … Late Mr Ebisuzaki started this business and took all our twenty best years of our lives to build it up. Our living was simply

cut off on that afternoon of April 28, 1942."[23] As Hide recounts, on that day a carpenter suddenly showed up and began installing a new door lock on the store. He was dispatched by the Custodian of Enemy Property, which administered the seizure, management, and forced sale of Japanese Canadian–owned property in coastal British Columbia. Much to Hide's surprise, the carpenter forced her to pay for his work, then she and Kentarō were kicked out of the store.[24]

Dispossession

State interference with the Ebisuzaki store began on 11 December 1941 when Glenn W. McPherson, who directed the Custodian's activity in Vancouver, ordered the business to provide a report of its ownership structure. In reply, Teiji stated that it was a partnership enterprise run by Masatarō, Hide, and Teiji, with Hide entitled to half of the profits and the other two splitting the rest.[25] Soon, accountants working for the Custodian found that the arrangement was established by a partnership agreement dated 30 July 1936.[26] In December, dispossession was not yet state policy, but officials were already taking stock of the property of Japanese Canadians and codifying its formal organization for their records.

Property, as Henry Smith asserts, is a "right to a thing good against the world." It organizes "this world into lumpy packages of legal relations."[27] You cannot hold property without the force of law. Officials dealt constantly with law and codified

Figure 3.3 Teiji and his children on the sofa in their Vancouver home. Date and photographer unknown.

rights in property as they administered and then forced the sale of the property of Japanese Canadians. The dispossession was not simply the selling of property but also the undoing of rights: it involved the removal of Japanese Canadians from the property regime.

Five months after determining the ownership status of M. Ebisuzaki Company, the Custodian decided to "wind up" the business. The rationale for this, as McPherson put it, was "that the Company's management was affected because of the evacuation of the party having fifty percent interest."[29] This referred to the fact that only Hide remained in the city. Masatarō was in Japan and Teiji had moved with his family to Alberta, outside of the "protected area." Obviously, it was only a matter of time before Hide, too, would be forced from the coast. The Custodian ordered the liquidation of the store without consulting the proprietors, yet this was to be, in official terms, a "voluntary" liquidation. The mechanism for this was created by McPherson in his "Certificate" dated 27 April 1942, which conferred:

> upon FREDERICK FIELD … a representative of P.S. ROSS AND SONS, such powers as are exercisable by a liquidator in a voluntary winding-up of a company, including the power in the name of Masataro Ebisuzaki, Mrs Hide Ebisuzaki and

> Teiji Morishita carrying on business as M. EBISUZAKI AND COMPANY or in his own name and by deed or otherwise to convey or transfer any property and power to apply to the court having power to appoint a receiver or liquidator or to grant a winding-up order, or a judge thereof to determine any question arising in the carrying out of this order.[29]

Issued "under and by virtue of authority given to him [the secretary of state] by Regulation 8 of the Consolidated Regulations Respecting Trading with the Enemy (1939)," this order annulled the proprietors' control over their own company. Accountant Field alone represented it, with full and unconditional discretion over the store after physically ripping it from its owners.

The accounting work that followed demonstrates the mundane nature of the dispossession. P.S. Ross and Sons was tasked with the investigation of the store's financial standing. Accountants identified twenty creditors and fifty debtors.[30] Eight creditors had Anglo names, one was a Chinese Canadian company, and eleven were Japanese Canadians. By contrast, all debtors had Japanese names, and each owed only a small amount; they were probably former customers who had purchased on accounts. P.S. Ross and Sons found that the store owed more than it stood to collect, and in September 1942 the Custodian declared the store "insolvent" and proceeded to pay the creditors by selling assets, managing to pay only fifty cents on the dollar.[31] As for the monies owed to the store, the accountants did contact debtors but managed to collect less than half of what was owed. The challenge in collecting followed from the conditions of the internment itself: the debtors were all uprooted and dispersed, their capacity to repay undermined by the internment. Some could pay only a portion of what they owed. Others, impoverished by state action, claimed to have no funds at all. Another did not recognize his debt, while one said he had already paid it. After 1946, some were in Japan as a result of the government's so-called "repatriation" program.[32]

The Custodian also administered the store's building and the land on which it stood. Officials conducted a title search, revealing that the real estate was owned by Masatarō individually and separately from the business and was encumbered by two mortgages.[33] In May 1943, the Custodian advertised the property for sale by tender, while contacting mortgagee Ruth Leverson for her input.[34] After three months on the market, the property had not sold. Leverson, much disappointed with the significant devaluation of the real estate as a result of the uprooting and internment of the store's clientele, applied through a solicitor for a "quit claim" to transfer the property in her favour.[35] The Custodian eventually processed the request, issuing a certificate vacating its managerial control of the property and transferring it to Leverson.[36]

In 1945 Hide learned of the Custodian's accounting and was shocked by the figures presented to her. "This can not be true," she wrote in response, "I wish to know to whom the company owes so much."[37] The accountant's grasp of the store's finances may be questioned but "insolvency" was a fact. It resulted directly from the closure of the store, which brought its economic activity to a standstill. The business no longer generated income, while the debts remained. The merchandise was auctioned to a market from which its loyal customers had been forcibly excluded.[38] With the store closed, the building and land became vulnerable to seizure by a mortgage holder.[39] Further, the vesting of the property by the Custodian itself created unsupportable expenses, including accountants' fees for liquidating the company. A total of $2,918 was deducted for processing transactions totalling $11,477.[40] Insolvency was a reality with which administrators struggled, but their records show no realization that state intervention itself had bankrupted the store. Officials and bookkeepers devoted themselves to sorting out the numbers in arrears, rather than accounting the larger injustice.

All this put the family in an excruciating position. Their crippled household economy was being dismantled. When funds from the store ran out, accountants turned to the personal assets of the proprietors ("partners"), held separate from their business ("partnership"), to meet the creditors' demands. Neither Hide nor Masatarō had assets under the Custodian's purview, but Teiji did: the family house on Cordova Street, or rather the money realized through its forced sale, which remained in Teiji's account held by the Custodian. Field, as the liquidator of M. Ebisuzaki and Company, requested that the money in Teiji's account be allocated to the store's creditors.

Here the activities of the Custodian ran up against legal uncertainty. Even as it perpetrated injustice, the Custodian sought to act (or at least appear to act) as a "public authority," standing above private interests to protect and enforce rights and obligations deemed universal by law.[41] Notably, for example, it recognized the rights of Japanese Canadians as creditors, seeking to collect on debts owed to them. Similarly, officials hesitated to use the sale of Teiji's house to pay the store's debts. To do so would require using equity from the sale of a property belonging to one legal entity (Teiji) to pay the debts of another (his business). Frank Shears, the director of the Custodian's office in Vancouver, sought the advice of K.W. Wright, counsel to the Custodian in Ottawa, who responded "[b]efore taking any further action in this matter, you should ask Mr Sheppard [of a private Vancouver law firm] to cause the usual search to be made in connection with the Partnership Agreement and obtain his opinion as to Morishita's liability under the British Columbia Law."[42] Sheppard examined the documents and advised that Teiji's funds could be used: property belonging to individual partners "would be applied first in payment of the separate debts of that partner, and any surplus could then be incorporated into the partnership assets for payment to the partnership creditors."[43] As of 15 December 1947, the outstanding liabilities of the business totalled $4,499, while cash assets stood at $78. Teiji's personal account showed a balance of $1,132.[44] The cruel machination was about to consume the wealth of the household to the last cent and leave them in debt.

Throughout this process, the state focused on individuals. Hide, Teiji, and Masatarō were recognized as "partners" in their capacity as atomized individuals, not members of a family working together. That they were related had nothing to do with how their rights to property were institutionalized; the family was outside of the formal purview of property. Yet, how could the store be separate from the family that owned and ran it? Herein lies the structural tension between property relations recognized in officialdom, on the one hand, and socioeconomic interactions intricate to property on the ground level, on the other. But this cold accounting of individuals and their property did not go unchallenged.

Negotiation

The household counteracted the force of deprivation on at least two occasions. The Ebisuzaki-Morishita as a cohabiting collective came to an end in the spring of 1942. On 4 March 1942 Teiji went to a government office to ask permission to move to Alberta. At that time, men were already being forced from their homes to road camps in the interior, a measure that split families. Teiji figured it better to move with his own funds out of the "protected area" and to stay with his family. One of his clients lived in Raymond, Alberta, and Teiji reached out to him for help finding home and work. He went alone on 5 March, moved into a rental home in Raymond, and began work on a sugar-beet farm. On 26 April, Sawa and their children, along with Teiji's older brother Jiichirō, packed their bags and left for Raymond. Meanwhile, the Ebisuzakis stayed in Vancouver. In her 21 May letter, Hide described the anxiety and confusion of Japanese Canadians in the city where thousands of people, including families crammed into the make-shift "manning pool" set up in Hastings Park, were uncertain as to where they were headed. She thought that it was matter of time until they would lose the store and that officials would take it all and do as they pleased.[45] In September, the Ebisuzaki relocated to the internment camp in Lemon Creek, eventually moving to Toronto early in 1946, while the Morishitas stayed in British Columbia.[46] They negotiated with creditors and officials after their physical split across the continent.

The family first contested their dispossession by filing a claim with the royal commission established by the federal government to offer some compensation for the property losses of Japanese Canadians, incurred as a result of the Custodian's sale below the "market value."[47] Teiji, filing on behalf of M. Ebisuzaki and Company, worked with Vancouver solicitor R.J. McMaster.[48] Aware of the financial standing of the business, McMaster proposed to negotiate the sharing of any "award," as it was called, attained from the commission with the creditors. They figured that the award at the most would yield $3,500 to $4,000 but that would fall short of covering all the debts, and so unless some terms of sharing with the creditors was established, it would all be lost to them. McMaster was especially hopeful that because "of the $4499.46 owing creditors, something over $3,000.00 is owing Japanese creditors. We feel certain that these creditors would be interested in an arrangement whereby they might split the award 50-50 with you."[49]

Teiji agreed, and McMaster pursued this plan. He did so in consultation with Shears at the Custodian's office, who felt that the proposal was "equitable." Shears also advised McMaster that Japanese Canadian creditors exiled to Japan "might be contacted for their consent in the same manner as other creditors"[50] because, as he told McMaster, "they returned 'voluntarily' and accordingly, the Custodian while he has control of their assets, has no power to compromise a debt on their behalf."[51]

Sadly, the plan failed. According to McMaster, while "most of the larger occidental [white] creditors have agreed … [he was] having difficulty getting agreement from a number of the Japanese creditors."[52] At least in part, this derived from the fact that they could not effectively communicate with the creditors in Japan. The process churned on, and on 19 August the Custodian sent Teiji an ultimatum, stating "that unless we hear from you before September 1, 1948, we will, on that date, pay over to the Controller the funds standing to your credit in this office."[53]

This was the context of the family's second attempt to preserve some of their wealth. On 28 August Teiji sent a bold telegram to the Custodian, "DO NOT PAY MY FUNDS TO CONTROLLER STOP LETTER FOLLOWING."[54] His letter explained:

> After I bought my house, at 466 East Cordova St, Vancouver, BC, I had to do a great deal of repair. This cost me quite a sum of money. I asked my nephew, Mr Kentaro Ebisuzaki, for loan at three occasions, the total of $1,000.00. Without his help, I would not have been able to make that house liveable … I always did and still do consider him as part-owner of my house, since I can not pay him. I want to pay him back out of my funds you hold but you do not release it to me. Now you say you must pay the amount to the Controller … it is very cruel for you, as a branch of our Government, to prosecute us to this extent. Now you are trying to meet my creditors of my business with my personal money. Before you do this, I want you to pay my personal debts.[55]

As we see, Teiji evoked the creditor's right, albeit to the home and not the business, to ward off the creditors' demand for Teiji's money. He used the rationale that his personal debt came before that of his company's insofar as the distribution of his personal money was concerned. The scheme, which depended upon the state official's commitment to apply the laws of property on an impartial basis, exemplifies the ingenuity on the part of the family; it was their desperate attempt to fight back under suffocating circumstances. Not surprisingly, officials were alarmed by the late and sudden surfacing of the loan and demanded proof of the debt. And here, the family erred. Kentarō sent as the proof a typed note signed and dated 15 September 1936, which was written on the same paper as the one he had used in his 1948 correspondence with the Custodian.[56] Questioned about this, Kentarō explained that he translated the original into English and had his uncle sign it, then destroyed the original thinking that it was useless. Doubting the authenticity of the loan, the Custodian consulted their legal advisor for an opinion:

> Circumstances under which these claims are now being made lead us to believe that these Japanese may be attempting to claim the money for themselves rather than allow it to be used to settle the liabilities of the partnership.[57]

For the officials, it was ultimately a matter of the formality of documentary process. Following the instructions of K.W. Wright in Ottawa, Shears wrote to Teiji, telling him that "evidence before us is insufficient and … if the facts are as have been previously indicated by yourself and Mr Kentaro Ebisuzaki, that an affidavit disclosing all the details concerning this loan should be made by yourself, and a further affidavit from Mr Kentaro Ebisuzaki in support of this claim."[58] The family complied. Receiving appropriate documents from Teiji and Kentarō, the accountants followed Sheppard's advice that "[w]hile the transaction is still suspicious yet it is of a type that could occur between Orientals and in the same family"[59] and transferred the money to the nephew.

The ambiguity of the loan is worth unpacking. As "creditor" and "debtor," the two men became separate legal entities competing with one another; first and foremost they were autonomous individuals who bore universalized rights. Their rights, moreover, were exclusive, not shared, in contradiction to the household principle of sharing. This logic is consistent with the titular arrangement of property. As far as the records went, Teiji held the title to the house, hence the right to the money realized by selling it. Now, Kentarō entered the same domain of rights to lay claim to Teiji's money. On this account, the existence of a shared household is out of the picture. And yet, the claim clearly emerged from the shared resources of a family, which even Sheppard recognized as common among Japanese immigrants. This tension is illuminated by Teiji's argument that he considered Kentarō "part-owner" of the house. Kentarō, too, emphasized the same idea in his statutory declaration: "while I speak of 'my uncle's home' it is merely for convenience's sake because, while it was registered in my uncle's name, I was a co-owner with him of the same."[60] Fascinatingly, however, this statement has been crossed out in the text filed by the Custodian.

The initial L.C.K written in the same blue ink as the lines crossing out the passage is that of Kentarō's solicitor in Toronto, Lucien C. Kurata. Why did he scratch it out and submit the document with such a visual distraction? Perhaps he believed that such a claim was irrelevant to the formal rights to property (title) and that it would have no bearing on the case at hand. The declaration, after all, confirmed Kentarō's status as "creditor," not coowner. As a practitioner of law, perhaps he thought this revision, however inelegant, would streamline his client's negotiation with the state.

The mutation of identity that accompanied the claim can be considered in light of Hegel's seminal insight that "civil society tears the individual from his family ties, estranges the members of the family from one another, and recognizes them as self-subsistent persons."[61] In this case, the family's strategy evaded in complicated ways a state process that prioritized individual creditors.[62] Surely, the loan did not signify the disintegration of the household, but rather it was a household strategy. Teiji and Kentarō obscured their familial connections in order to make them powerful in law. By representing their family bonds as the relations of creditor and debtor they rendered ties of obligation and reciprocity enforceable in law, even as officials recognized that this was precisely what they were doing.

Indeed, the loan signifies the convergence of seemingly incongruous spaces – each supported by distinctive logics of societal formation – under the exceptional circumstance of the dispossession. By alienating people from their property, officials devoted their working hours to the neutralizing formal rights to property; paradoxically they also found themselves constrained by the principle of the rule of law amid the injustice they perpetuated. Despite its complexity, this tension considers merely one aspect of actual social relations. There was the other space of the family and community. Practices of that domain were marginalized if not ignored in the hegemonic space of officialdom. As we have seen, it was not just that officials acted upon narrow legal norms within which familial and communal bonds had no standing, but Japanese Canadians, too, were compelled to downplay the practices of their lived experience in their negotiation with the state. Needless to say, the power differential between the two spaces was insurmountable. Yet the plasticity of status evinced by the loan suggests the two were linked. Of course, the loan was not the first time for this family to anchor their relations in the official arena. They were already there, as a result of the original registration of their properties. Had that not been the case, the dispossession would have entailed an entirely different process.

The officials' condescending imposition of their categories is a caution for us historians and analysts, who, too, could fall in a similar trap and alienate historical actors from their contexts. There is a rich social terrain to be recovered. By examining its dynamics on their own terms, we may gain a fuller understanding of the wider implications of the dispossession. A key task to that end might be to relax the hold of such ideas as the individual, right, and property and instead focus on ground-level interactions and norms concerning the use of resources and assets. With that in mind, let us turn to correspondence among the household members in the early postwar period.

Shared economy

While officials used individual right as the red thread to navigate the chaos they confronted, the concept has little salience in records of the community. The crux of the matter is the configuration of the individual in society. Elsewhere, I have deliberated on the disjuncture between the idea of the individual and notions of the self as expressed by migrants of Teiji's generation (the Issei) in Japanese-language prints.[63] When articulating the self, they emphasized the mind-heart (*kokoro*), which expressed emotions and spirits in the civic sense and had little legal connotation. Subjectivity was asserted by situating the self in collectives through ethical principles, not asserting independence and apartness. Individualism (*kojin shugi*) was despised, while individuality (*kosei*) was celebrated, in so far as it integrated the self in collectives.[64] In short, their identity and sense of belonging operated on a Japanese cultural logic. The records of the dispossession offer another vantage point on the same issue and suggest the intricacy of Japanese immigrant relational identity and economic life.

Letters from the wartime and the early postwar era among the members of the Ebisuzaki and Morishita families reveal a strong sense of shared economy, that is, a pattern of economic organization in which resources as well as obligations were held not individually but by the family. For example, on paper the property at 337 Powell Street was Masatarō's individually, as were his debts. But in practice the lot and mortgage were household property. This can be inferred from the fact that mortgage payments continued to be made by Hide and Teiji after Masatarō's departure to Japan.[65] In a sense, the family or household was the basic unit of social organization, and this was not opposed to the logic of individual rights but rather complemented and augmented it.

This is not to suggest that all things were held in a common, but sketching the full contours of the family's complicated economic relations, including what they owned individually, is beyond my scope. In what follows, the focus is limited to specific instances when their relational practices come to the fore in the existing records. The family's letters are fragments of the past, emerging from specific moments and speaking to objective conditions as well as values and emotions that animated social experiences. Reading them, we can reconstruct some of the richness of the family's social and economic interrelations.

The sense of shared economic obligation to the store extended beyond the Ebisuzaki-Morishita household. For example, one family, the Ikedas, eventually repaid a debt to the store despite extraordinary disruption of their lives. Specifics of this family are uncertain; they are only described in a letter Hide wrote to Teiji, undated but likely between 1948 and the early 50s. From that letter, we know the Ikedas were exiled to Japan in 1946, but before that, the family head (father) left word with Hide that he would make his eldest son repay the debt. In the years that followed, Hide exchanged several letters with his heirs in her attempt to collect. In one letter, she emphasized that their relation was "not so cold as relations of legal this and that" (*hōritsu toka nantoka iu tsumetai tsukiai*). But all she could do was wait. Just when she had nearly given up, a registered mail from Japan arrived with a $300 cheque. It was from the Ikedas, enclosed with a letter confessing they had wanted to but could not repay sooner. The Ikedas do not appear in the list of creditors used by the Custodian, and perhaps there was no formal record of the debt. But evidently, the two families were bonded by a concept of trust embraided into their economic relations, and though it nearly terminated with internment and displacement, the family eventually lived up to their obligation.

A similar sense of collective debt is expressed – indeed taken for granted – by Teiji's older brother Jiichirō, who had a rice store on Hastings Street in Vancouver before the war. In 1952, he wrote Teiji with advice on rebuilding his career in the new era. His letter appears to have been a reply to Teiji's seeking advice on a plan to borrow money to set up a business. At this time, Teiji was in Slocan city in the interior of British Columbia, and his eldest daughter Nancy had moved back to Vancouver to attend a nursing school.[66] She was staying at the home of a Mr Jameson, who was an entrepreneur. He had a logging mill in Prince Rupert, staffed before the war by Japanese migrant workers. The Ebisuzaki store used to send food items to the mill, and this connection helped when it came time to find a place for Nancy in Vancouver. At Jameson's, Nancy stayed as a "school girl," helping with household chores while attending school during the day. Teiji also saw him as a potential source of credit. "When I think of your livelihood," Jiichirō wrote,

> what course of action you should be taking, given that from now until May next year [you won't have a job], you are going beyond temporary unemployment; I think it would be difficult for you to find a decent job as a hired worker in Vancouver, but to start an independent business requires considerable amount of capital, and you ought to be very cautious before getting into fields that you have no experience for ... I think you should write to the hakujin [white] Jameson. Tell him that you are unemployed but want to start a small hotel or a rooming house. Ask him if he can loan you funds. If he can, you should buy a plot of land with a building on it. If he won't agree to it, you would have to pursue a different path, but you won't know unless you ask. I say that you write him and tell him you want to buy a small hotel or a rooming house, with land, for up to about fifty-thousand dollars. Ask him if he would be willing to cover the costs and assure him that you and your siblings as well as relatives as a whole would be devoted to paying it back.[67]

The loan imagined by Jiichirō is informal where the creditor covers the cost temporarily (*tatekae*) to enable Teiji to make an investment and start a business. The borrower would be Teiji, but a collective vaguely articulated as "your siblings as well as relatives as a whole" is implicated in the arrangement. The debtor is not really Teiji alone but the family as a whole. Implicit is the idea of the household as an enterprise whose members are woven into its economic fabric. Though not explicitly stated, we can surmise he envisioned the business would be supported by the labour of the family, including of course Sawa and perhaps their children. Jiichirō, who worked for a time at a hotel, may have envisioned the possibility of him getting involved in the business as well. The greatest concern was survival of the family, and property was a means to that end. In their minds, the boundary between individual and family holdings was fuzzy and porous.

Consider Jiichirō's situation. His wife and children had been in Japan since 1939, and the war and the consequences of the dispossession prevented the family from reuniting. When he wrote the letter, he was in Vancouver working menial day jobs and waiting for the day to board the ship to Japan to rejoin his family. He missed them dearly, especially his children and mother. A letter had arrived after the war's end, telling him that his beloved son had died, not in combat but from illness and exhaustion from overwork. One can only imagine the pain that pierced his heart when he read that his son called for "papa" on his deathbed.[68] His family wanted him to come back as soon he could, and it bewildered them that he had not returned with other migrants in neighbouring villages who went back in 1946 with the "repatriation" program of the Canadian government. Jiichirō was deeply conflicted. Of course, he wanted to go back to Japan and join his family much sooner, and the family had a pressing reason to demand his immediate return. The Allied Occupation of Japan implemented reforms to redistribute land from landlords to tenant farmers, in order to dismantle exploitive landlordism and the hardship it caused for tenant farmers.[69] The policy targeted absentee landlords. The family had a plot of farmland registered under Jiichirō's name but really bequeathed to his generation from the ancestors. A county office notified the family that unless they provided documentation showing Jiichirō's "naturalized" status in Canada, the land would be subject to the reform.[70] Naturalized he was not.

No doubt, Jiichirō was conflicted. He knew about the land situation, as well as the dismay of his family at his choice to remain in Canada. All the same, he was determined he should not leave unfinished business on the continent. He had borrowed $2,000 from a Seattle financer with a branch in Yokohama and used a Japanese bank account (which he had purchased from his associate) as a collateral.[71] With the shattered economy after the war, the value of Japanese currency plummeted and Jiichirō had no cash to make up for the deficit. One option was to go back to Japan and work, but with the economy in shambles and inflation rampant, he believed he would not be able to pay back the debt. Inevitably, the land would be seized by the creditor, which would be much worse than him returning a few years later after having settled the debt by working in Canada. But compounding the situation was the winding up of his rice business, which, like the Ebisuzaki store, involved the settling of outstanding accounts. He figured he had to wait for the Custodian to liquidate the store to declare bankruptcy.

At the same time, economic prospects were somewhat better in Canada – even for former internees – than in Japan. Jiichirō did not want to go back penniless and without items (*shinamono*), for life there was going to be tough. Due to inflation, the family in Japan could not even afford to buy a kimono for Kiyoko, his wife, which she needed to work, and the family asked Jiichirō and Teiji to procure for them in Canada such items as a sewing machine, fabric, and a rear car tire, all of which were selling at exorbitant rates on the Japanese black market. So Jiichirō slowly obtained items and sent them to Japan.[72] He also sent them what money he could every month. Eventually he purchased his ticket to Japan with *senbetsu* or gift of parting from family and associates.[73]

Bearing the brunt of dispossession, Jiichirō understood the importance of property in the capitalist world and made strategic decisions. However, we must also recognize the subjective dimension of his relational identity and his sense of belonging in the collective, his duty as father, husband, son, and so on. Without accounting for that, we would be reducing and dehumanizing his history to the sheer materiality of economics. The records of dispossession cut to the core of how we think of ourselves, relate to one another, and confront challenges.

The intricacy of mentality and materiality in the household collective is expressed evocatively in a letter by Kōjirō, Teiji's nephew and the Ebisuzaki store driver, to the Morishitas in the New Year, likely of 1946. In the spring of 1942 he had been incarcerated in the Prisoner of War Camp in Angler, Ontario for protesting the government's relocation plans. Prior to that unfortunate event, he had driven four vehicles owned by the household into the impoundment lot at Hastings Park in Vancouver. At the time, he was presented forms that required him to sign as the "owner" as he left the vehicles under the care of the Royal Canadian Mounted Police.[74] Kōjirō was the driver, not the owner, but the forms could not accommodate even this minor complication, so he had to sign. Several years later when he wrote his uncle the letter, he was starting his life anew with his wife Yaeko in Hamilton, Ontario. The Morishitas, for their part, were debating exile to Japan. Initially, Teiji signed to be "repatriated" because his wife refused to move east of the Rockies as required by government officials, but he reconsidered as his daughter Nancy did not want to relocate to a country she had never before even visited. They were impoverished, and the imminent closure of the internment camp must have been a major cause for uncertainty. Aware of the Morishita's dilemma, Kōjirō wrote:

> Happy New Year. Please forgive me for not writing for so long. I was shocked to see Kuniko' letter. It's all my fault. I am very sorry about that. As for me, I finally recovered and I have been working at a press shop since just before Christmas. I should be getting about thirty to forty dollars a week starting this month. If you are going to stay in Canada for three or four years, why don't you come over here? The housing situation should improve by spring. It's just the two of us here and – you might laugh at this – we can look after two or three of your kids. My brother and his family are still in the camp, but they should be coming over here in spring. Today, my wife Yaeko went to a local branch of Security Commission to ask them about my brother, and they gave an okay. The war is over now, so there is no reason for them not to be allowed to move out here … We don't have money but I want to send you a little each week, so please let me do that … As for the money to go to Japan, I will save it up for you in a couple of years, so don't worry about that.[75]

Barely settled in the city himself, Kōjirō was willing to go at lengths to help his uncle's family. On the one hand, his offer of support reflects Kōjirō's own generous character. At the same time, his statements ought to be contextualized within the pooling structure of the household. It should be recalled that he had lived with them in the Vancouver home, where Sawa cooked for him and he drove the truck to deliver goods for the store. For Kōjirō, the thirty to forty dollars a week that he was now earning was not his alone but filled a coffer dispensable toward the collective's needs. He was offering not only mone, but his and his wife Yaeko's labour; together they could care for a couple of the Morishita's children should they move to Hamilton as he suggested. Yaeko's voice is absent from the surviving records, but we can establish that, in Kōjirō's mind, he and Yaeko formed a socioeconomic unit still linked with the larger Ebisuzaki-Morishita household.

These records point to attitudinal norms and societal expectations entwined with economic relations. Wealth, property, or obligations tied individuals to household collectives, which in turn situated them in community and society. Contexts changed, relations evolved, and the pooling practice responded to shifting circumstances, but kin relations figured prominently in economic life. These glimpses of the lived arena demonstrate a pattern of social organization that defies the rigid ordering of rights in the formal arena. Rigid conceptions of rights and entitlements fall short of conveying the interactions and sentiments characteristic of family and community experience. Indeed, our understanding of the significance of having and losing property is much enhanced by accounting for idiosyncratic relations developed around property and wealth, and situating the loss in the longer span of social history.

Conclusion

The liquidation of the store began on 27 April 1942 and ended on 18 October 1950.[76] The time it took the Custodian to complete the task is a testament to the complexity of the dispossession. But the foregoing suggests that it would be more accurate to say that property was complex, hence the dispossession convoluted and frustrating even for those carrying it out. Needless to say, the store posed no security threat and the war was long finished as the dispossession lingered on. The process carried on until the business was laid to rest at last.

The dissonance between state records and family records can be explained at least partly by James Scott's notion of "state simplification." According to Scott, the state's grasp of society "did not successfully represent the actual activity of the society they depicted, nor were they intended to; they represented only that slice of it that interested the official observer."[77] In contrast, the actual "social hieroglyph," shaped as it is by "a host of informal practices and improvisations … could never be codified."[78] This is valid in our case, insofar as titular arrangements processed by officials were formulaic entitlements abstracted from the community. But a simple dualism obscures the interface of power and social processes. As Teiji put it, his relations to the state was like a "rotten karma" (*kusare en*), a tenacious tie that one cannot rid.[79] The maxim may have resonated with the officials. For they could not end their business with the dispossessed before completing years' worth of stultifying paperwork.

The wealth of records on the dispossession enable us to shed light on the diverse strands of ideas and practices stitched into a thick historical brocade. Whereas state records depict a world where the individual is the protagonist of social formation, the world portrayed in family and community records is defined by porous or undistinguished boundaries of individual and household property as well as obligations. In the official register, M. Ebisuzaki and Company was owned and operated by individualized "partners," but as a living business it was sustained by and in turn sustained a tight-knit household that shared a home, wealth, and resources. It fostered a dense web of its own, giving rise to a vibrant regional sphere of civil interactions where relational practices were imbricated less with laws than notions of trust, obligations, and the sway of the family and collectives. This space was a part of the uneven social collage of twentieth-century Canada developed upon the mantle of proprietary rights.

When the dispossession dislodged Japanese immigrants (and the wider Japanese Canadian community) from the Canadian system of rights, it is not surprising that they turned to household practice to mitigate loss, navigate the destruction, and rebuild their lives for the new era. From the norms of this day and age when economic independence is extolled, their household economy and relational practices may seem strange, archaic, constraining, or perhaps an antidote to social dislocation of modernity. But we should really appreciate them as part and parcel of their struggle for survival, security, and prosperity as well as the pursuit of order in the volatile world. Speaking evocatively to heartfelt human conditions of the past, their records encourage us to contextualize their experiences with the norms of their organized lives and diversify and enrich our engagement with history. Lastly, for the Morishita-Ebisuzaki household, solidarity as well as the mentality of shared wealth persisted well into the postwar era. Below is Kentarō's letter to Teiji, written in 1965 more than two decades after the families had been forced from their shared Vancouver home and business. Teiji, in Vancouver, had wired money to Kentarō in Toronto without being asked, to help with his son Toyonobu's trip to Japan.

> To everyone [of the Morishita family]:
> Thank you so much for sending $200 for Toyonobu. He is a lucky boy. Five years ago, he was given the opportunity to go to Europe and now he's going to Japan … He took the night train at eleven pm, and as he left he told us how excited he was to visit Japan where his *bāchan* [grandmother] was born. Teruo [Morishita] has gotten well and is now working. We're all happy about that. The money that you sent us for Toyonobu is just too much. I talked about it with mother [Hide] and Kinuko [wife], and we decided to take $50 and wire the rest back to you. Even that is too much. Thanks to you, we were able to let Toyonobu take some money with him. We're very grateful for your kindness, and please don't feel bad that we're sending some of the money back to you.
>
> We received Kimie's postcard from Winnipeg. She must be just about reaching Banff by now. We also received a letter from Misako [Morishita]. As I said over the phone, she is planning to arrive in Toronto on August 24th. Her itinerary sounds very good, and we think it would be great if Sawa-san joins her to come out east for sightseeing. If she comes together with Setsuko [Morishita] and Misako, she would not have anything to worry about. Mother and Kinuko, too, are saying that she should definitely come … We're not trying to reject your favour, so please don't be offended. I'm sure that we'll always be relying on your guidance and care. It's going to get hot as we get into summer, so please take good care … P.S. We have lots of space here, so don't worry and just come. We won't make you sleep on the floor.[80]

NOTES

1 Teiji Morishita's personal notes, folder 2, MS 91, Morishita Family Collection, NNM, Accession 2011.79.3.3 (hereafter Morishita Collection).

2 Teiji preserved detailed records and logs of his work during the internment era and beyond, including pay stubs. Teiji Morishita Ledgers, 1942–1955, folder 1, MS90, Morishita Collection, Accession 2011.79.1.1.4a.

3 Nicholas Blomley, "The Boundaries of Property: Complexity, Relationality, and Spatiality," *Law & Society Review* 50, no. 1 (2016): 224–55; "Property, Law and Space," *Property Law Review* 229 (2014): 229–35.

4 Eduardo M. Peñalver, "Land Virtues," *Cornell Law Review* 94, no. 4 (2009): 829.

5 Much of her stories that I am using in this study were conveyed to me in our conversation in Vancouver on 18 September 2016.

6 According to a 1921 Japanese-language magnum opus on the migrant community in Canada, Masatarō first opened a general store at 254 Powell Street and in 1916 moved the store to 337 Powell Street. Jinshirō Nakayama, *Kanada Dōhō Hatten Taikan* (Tokyo: Japan Taimusu, 1921), 476–7.

7 This draws on an analysis by Toshiji Sasaki and Yūki Shimomura of Japanese Canadian businesses in prewar Vancouver. The 1921 source is Nakayama's book cited above. Sasaki and Shimomura, "Shiryō: Senzen bankūbā ni okeru nihonjin-gai no hatten to henyō," *Kōbe kokusai daigaku kiyō* 47 (1995).

8 Author's conversation with Nancy Morishita, 18 September 2016.

9 It is uncertain when Hide migrated to Canada, but by 1921 she was married to Masatarō and had their two children. Nakayama, *Kanada Dōhō Hatten Taikan*, 476–7.

10 Jiichirō may have worked at the store at first, but later he opened his own rice shop on Hastings Street. The family called him the "rice merchant" (*kome-ya san*). Author's conversation with Nancy Morishita, 18 September 2016.

11 Teiji Morishita to B.R. Dusenbury, 11 February 1946, folder 3, MS 88, Morishita Collection, Accession 2011.1.1.2g.

12 B.R. Dusenbury to Teiji Morishita, 25 February 1946, folder 3, MS88, Morishita Collection, Accession 2011.1.1.2g.

13 Immanuel Wallerstein and Joan Smith, "Households as an Institution of the World-Economy," in *Creating and Transforming Households: The Constraints of the World-Economy*, eds. Immanuel Wallerstein, Joan Smith, et al (Cambridge: Cambridge University Press, 1992), 13.

14 Drafts of advertisements of the store for prewar Japanese-language print media, Morishita Collection, folder 9, MS90; folder 2, MS91, Accessions 2011.79.3.2 (1/2) and 2011.79.3.3.

15 Nishimura to Ebisuzaki, 5 April 1941, folder 2, MS 91, Morishita Collection, Accession 2011.79.3.3.

16 Ebisuzaki store flyer, undated, folder 9, MS 90, Morishita Collection, Accession 2011.79.3.2 (1/2).

17 Untitled list, 9 June 1941, folder 1, MS 91, Morishita Collection, Accession 2011.79.3.2 (2/2).

18 Ibid.

19 Author's conversation with Nancy Morishita, 18 September 2016.

20 Ebisuzaki store's oseibo list, 1941, folder 9, MS 90, Morishita Collection, Accession 2011.79.3.2 (1/2).

21 Ebisuzaki store's oseibo list, 1936, folder 9, MS 90, Morishita Collection, Accession 2011.79.3.2 (1/2).

22 Including three delivery trucks (a 1933 Chevrolet panel, 1937 Chevrolet, 1940 Dodge panel) and a new 1941 Dodge sedan. Royal Canadian Mounted Police Exhibit Reports, 9–10 March 1942, file 56177, pt. 2-2, Ebisuzaki, M and Co., Case Files series, vol. 2479, RG117, LAC.

23 Teiji Morishita to R.J. McMaster, folder 5, MS88, Morishita Collection, Accession 2011.79.1.1.2i.

24 Hide Ebisuzaki to Teiji and Sawa Morishita, undated [1952?], folder 5, MS85, Morishita Collection, 2011.79.1.1.2i.

25 Teiji Morishita to G.W. McPerson [*sic*], 20 December 1941, file 56177, pt.2-2, Ebisuzaki, M and Co., vol. 2479, Case Files series, RG 117, LAC.

26 P.S. Ross & Sons to the Custodian's office in Vancouver, 5 January 1942, file 56177, pt.2-2, Ebisuzaki, M and Co, vol. 2479, Case Files series, RG 117, LAC.

27 Henry E. Smith, "Property as the Law of Things," *Harvard Law Review* 125, no. 7 (2012): 1693, 1706.

28 Memorandum, G.W. McPherson, 26 August 1942, file 56177, pt.2-1 Ebisuzaki, M and Co., vol. 2479, Case Files series, RG 117, LAC.

29 G.W. McPherson Certificate, 27 April 1942, file 56177, pt.2-2, Ebisuzaki, M and Co., vol. 2479, Case Files series, RG 117, LAC.

30 Statement of collection and disbursement, enclosed with letter from C.H. Reed to Hide Ebisuzaki, 28 November 1950, file 56177, pt.2-1, Ebisuzaki, M and Co., vol. 2479, Case Files series, RG 117, LAC.

31 W. Nielly and E.W. Thomas to Custodian, Vancouver, 11 February 1943, file 56177, pt. 2-2, Ebisuzaki, M and Co., vol.2479, Case Files series, RG 117, LAC; W.J. Johnston to Hide Ebisuzaki, 10 October 1945, file 56177, pt.2-1, Ebisuzaki, M and Co., vol. 2479, Case Files series, RG 117, LAC.

32 Correspondence regarding these receivables are found in file 56177, pt. 2-1, Ebisuzaki, M and Co., vol. 2479, Case Files series, RG 117, LAC.

33 Confirmation of ownership, 4 February 1943, file 56177, pt.2-2, Ebisuzaki, M and Co., vol. 2479, Case Files series, RG 117, LAC.

34 The advertisement was first posted on 20 May 1943, on the *Vancouver Sun*. Advertised as follows, file 56177, pt.2-1, Ebisuzaki, M and Co., vol. 2479, Case Files series, RG 117, LAC; K.W. Wright to Maitland, Maitland & Hutcheson, 26 May 1943, file 56177, pt.2-1, Ebisuzaki, M and Co., vol. 2479, Case Files series, RG 117, LAC.

35 In the words of her solicitor, she "had looked upon this property as reasonable security for her loan." Maitland, Maitland & Hutcheson to Office of the Custodian, 24 June 1943, file 56177, pt.2-1, Ebisuzaki, M and Co., vol. 2479, Case Files series, RG 117, LAC. The two mortgages taken out in 1923 and 1924 totalled $10,250, but in 1943, legal advisor to the Custodian K.W. Wright suggested the office accept "an offer that will net the Custodian the sum of $2500.00 … [even though] the assessment value is as follows: Land: $3500.00 Improvements: $2700.00" (K.W. Wright to Pemberton, 1 September 1943, file 56177, pt. 2-1, Ebisuzaki, M and Co., vol. 2479, Case Files series, RG 117, LAC). Accountants who were tasked with the liquidation believed that the property had the assessed value of $6,600, but the realtor firm Pemberton appraised it at $2,500 in April 1943. Shocked by this low amount, the accountants asked the Custodian for assessment from a different realtor (Ross & Sons to the Office of the Custodian, Vancouver, 27 April 1943, file 56177, pt. 2-1, Ebisuzaki, M and Co., vol. 2479, Case Files series, RG 117, LAC) to which it complied, but the other realtor appraised no different (Johnson and Reeve to the Custodian's Office, Vancouver, 29 April 1943, file 56177, pt. 2-1, Ebisuzaki, M and Co., vol. 2479, Case Files series, RG 117, LAC). The Custodian, realtors, and accountants all realized the value of the property was greater than what the market at the time would have it. Pemberton, for instance, reported that, "At present time these premises

would likely only have a sale value of about $2,500.00. The building itself should be insured for about $3,000.00. If it were not for the fact that these premises are situated in the surroundings that they are, they would likely sell for about $3,800.00" (Pemberton to K.W. Wright, 20 April 1943, file 56177, pt. 2-1, Ebisuzaki, M and Co., vol. 2479, Case Files series, RG 117, LAC; K.W. Wright to P.S. Ross & Sons, 17 August 1943, file 56177, pt.2-1, Ebisuzaki, M and Co., vol. 2479, Case Files series, RG 117, LAC).

36 K.W. Wright to Maitland, Maitland & Hutcheson, 17 September 1943, file 56177, pt.2-1, Ebisuzaki, M and Co. vol. 2479, Case Files series, RG 117, LAC. Evidently, the "vesting" of the property in the Custodian had to be rescinded via a formal certificate lest it would compromise the right of the mortgagee to the property. For 337 Powell Street, "Certificate vacating certificate of vesting" was issued on 5 October 1943. File 56177, pt.2-1, Ebisuzaki, M and Co., vol. 2479, Case Files series, RG 117, LAC.

37 Hide Ebisuzaki to Custodian's office in Vancouver, 19 November 1945, file 56177, pt.2-2, Ebisuzaki, M and Co., vol. 2479, Case Files series, RG 117, LAC.

38 Auction notice, file 56177, pt.2-2, Ebisuzaki, M and Co., vol. 2479, Case Files series, RG 117, LAC.

39 See note 35.

40 M. Ebisuzaki Company, undated, file 56177, pt.2-1. Ebisuzaki, M and Co., vol. 2479, Case Files series, RG 117, LAC.

41 T.M. Knox (trans.), *Hegel's Philosophy of Right* (Oxford: Clarendon Press, 1952), para., 219.

42 Wright to Shears, 2 January 1948, file 56177, pt. 2-1, Ebisuzaki, M and Co., vol. 2479, Case Files series, RG 117, LAC.

43 Shears to Locke, et al, 25 September 1950, file 56177, pt. 2-1, Ebisuzaki, M and Co., vol. 2479, Case Files series, RG 117, LAC.

44 F. Shears to K.W. Wright, 15 December 1947, file 56177, pt. 2-1, Ebisuzaki, M and Co., vol. 2479, Case Files series, RG 117, LAC.

45 Hide Ebisuzaki to Morishita, 21 May 1942, folder 3, MS85, Morishita Collection, Accession 2011.79.1.1.1c.

46 Kentarō and the Ebisuzaki family arrived in the Slocan area in the interior of British Columbia, one of the six major sites of Japanese Canadian internment, just before 14 September 1942. Kentarō Ebisuzaki to Teiji Morishita, 14 September 1942, file 3, MS 85, Morishita Collection, Accession 2011.79.1.1.1c.

47 Chapters 9 and 10.

48 It has to be pointed out that McMaster's law firm, Campbell, Brazier, Fisher & McMaster, was located in the same Royal Bank building on Hastings Street in downtown Vancouver as the Vancouver Custodian's office and the accountant firm P.S. Ross & Sons that was charged with the liquidation of M. Ebisuzaki Company.

49 A.E. Cobus to Teiji Morishita, 11 May 1949, folder 6, MS88, Morishita Collection, Accession 2011.79.1.1.2j.

50 Shears Memorandum, 4 November 1949, file 56177, pt.2-1, Ebisuzaki, M and Co., vol. 2479, Case Files series, RG 117, LAC.

51 McMaster stated as thus, of his conversations with Shears. R.J. McMaster to Teiji Morishita, 29 November 1949, folder 6, MS88, Morishita Collection, Accession 2011.79.1.1.2j.

52 R.J. McMaster to Teiji Morishita, 29 November 1949, folder 6, MS88, Morishita Collection, Accession 2011.79.1.1.2j.

53 B. Good to Teiji Morishita, 19 August 1948, file 56177, pt. 2-1, Ebisuzaki, M and Co., vol. 2479, Case Files series, RG 117, LAC.

54 Teiji Morishita to B. Good, 28 August 1948, file 56177, pt. 2-1, Ebisuzaki, M and Co., vol. 2479, Case Files series, RG 117, LAC.

55 Ibid.

56 As stated, for instance, in item 6 of Kentarō Ebisuzaki's Statutory Declaration, 23 September 1950, excerpt of which is featured below. The Custodian's office immediately inquired Kentarō about this documentary "flaw." Frank Shear's correspondence with Kentarō in regards to this matter is reproduced in Shears to K.W. Wright, 10 July 1950, file 56177, pt. 1. M. Ebisuzaki Company In, vol. 2479, Case Files series, RG 117, LAC.

57 B. Good to Locke, Guild, Lane, Sheppard & Yule, 28 September 1948, file 56177, pt. 2-1, Ebisuzaki, M and Co., vol. 2479, Case Files series, RG 117, LAC.

58 Frank Shears to Teiji Morishita, 31 August 1950, folder 7, MS88, Morishita Collection. See also Shears to Locke, Guild, Lane, Sheppard & Yule, 25 September 1950, file 56177, pt. 1. M. Ebisuzaki Company In, vol. 2479, Case Files series, RG 117, LAC.

59 Locke, Guild, Lane, Sheppard & Yule to the Office of the Custodian in Vancouver (copy), 30 September 1950, file 56177, pt. 2-1, Ebisuzaki, M and Co., vol. 2479, Case Files series, RG 117, LAC.

60 Kentarō Ebisuzaki Statutory Declaration, 23 September 1950, file 56177, pt. 1. M. Ebisuzaki Company In, vol. 2479, Case Files series, RG 117, LAC. Note that Kentarō and Teiji submitted Statutory Declarations, not of affidavits, because the Custodian accepted a gentle suggestion by Kentarō's solicitor, Lucien Kurata, that "statutory declarations is normal in these circumstances, and is of the same force and affect as an affidavit by the virtue of the Canada Evidence Act." Lucien C. Kurata to the Office of the Custodian, Vancouver, 7 September 1950, file 56177, pt. 2-1. Ebisuzaki, M and Co., vol. 2479, Case Files series, RG 117, LAC.

61 Knox, *Hegel's Philosophy*, para. 238 and 188. Hegel's German is translated here as "civil society" but, according to the translator Knox, it was the norm for eighteenth-century thinkers to use the expression civil society "in contexts where we would now normally speak of 'the state,'" x. It was Marx who established a firm conceptual divide between the state and civil society, and that view likely holds sway in contemporary social analysis. Neera Chandhoke, *State and Civil Society: Explorations in Political Theory* (New Delhi, Thousand Oaks, CA, and London: Sage Publications, 195), 129, 135–8. Jürgen Habermas, *The Structural Transformation of the Public Sphere*, trans. Thomas Burger (Cambridge, MA: The MIT Press, 1989), 122–3.

62 The claims process reflected Naoki Sakai's broader observation that the "liberal notion of individualism is, in the final analysis, no more than a symbolic expression of the commodified human relationships in capitalist societies." See Naoki Sakai, "From Relational Identity to Specific Identity: On Equality and Nationality," in *Values, Identity, and Equality in Eighteenth- and Nineteenth-Century Japan*, eds. Peter Nosco et al. (Leiden and Boston: Brill, 2015), 303.

63 Eiji Okawa and the Landscapes of Injustice Research Collective, "Japaneseness in Racist Canada: Immigrant Imaginaries during the First Half of the Twentieth Century," *Journal of American Ethnic History* 37, no. 4 (2018): 10–39.

64 For a discussion of individuality in early modern Japan, see Peter Nosco, "The Early Modern Co-Emergence of Individuality and Collective Identity," in Nosco, *Values, Identity, and Equality*, 113–33.

65 According to Hide, the last payment of one of the mortgages, not to Leverson, was made "just before the Company was closed." Hide Ebisuzaki to Custodian, 49 November 1945, file 56177, pt. 2-2, Ebisuzaki, M and Co., vol. 2479, Case Files series, RG 117, LAC.

66 Author's conversation with Nancy Morishita, Vancouver, 18 September 2016.

67 Jiichirō Morishita to Teiji Morishita, 28 November 1952, folder 5, MS 85, Morishita Collection, Accession 2011.79.1.1.1e.

68 Jiichirō Morishita to Teiji and Sawa Morishita, 11 April c.1945–52, folder 3, MS85, Morishita Collection, Accession 2011.79.1.1.1c.

69 For a classic study of this policy in English, see R.P. Dore, *Land Reform in Japan* (London: The Athlone Press, 1959).

70 This is mentioned in several documents in the Morishita Family Collection, including a notice that was sent to the Morishita family in Japan by a committee that appears to have been involved with the implementation of the reform on the local level. Notice from the Agrarian Land Committee of Yatsuta village (Yatsuta-mura nōchi iinkai), 8 October 1948, folder 2, MS88, Morishita Collection, Accession 2011.79.1.1.2f. See also Relative in Fukuoka, Japan to Teiji Morishita, 9 October [1948?], folder 5, MS85, Morishita Collection, Accession 2011.79.1.1.1e.

71 Jiichirō Morishita to Teiji and Sawa Morishita, 2 June c.1945–52, folder 4, MS88, Morishita Collection, Accession 2011.79.1.1.1d.

72 Jiichirō Morishita to "everyone" [minna, that is, of Teiji's family], 17 March c.1945–52, folder 4, MS85, Morishita Collection, Accession 2011.79.1.1.1d.

73 Jiichirō Morishita to Teiji and Sawa Morishita, 1 February c.1945–52, folder 5, MS85, Morishita Collection, Accession 2011.79.1.1.1e.

74 The records show that he took in four vehicles on 9 and 10 March. Royal Canadian Mounted Police Exhibit Report, 9–10 March 1942, file 56177, pt.2-2, Ebisuzaki, M and Co., vol. 2479, Case Files series, RG 117, LAC.

75 Kōjirō Ebisuzaki to the Morishita family, 7 January [1946?], folder 4, MS85, Morishita Collection, Accession 2011.79.1.1.1d.

76 F.G. Shears to K.W. Wright, 21 October 1950, file 56177, pt.1, Ebisuzaki Company In, vol.2479, Case Files series, RG 117, LAC.

77 James C. Scott, *Seeing Like a State: How Certain Schemes to Improve the Human Condition Have Failed* (New Haven: Yale University Press, 1998), 3.

78 Ibid., 6.

79 Carbon copy of Teiji Morishita's handwritten letter, 4 February 1948(?), folder 8, MS 88, Morishita Collection, Accession 2011.79.1.1.2l. He evoked this concept to describe his entrenched relation with the British Columbia Security Commission, which managed the forced relocation and internment of Japanese Canadians, when he thought it finally ended. While the commission restricted the freedom and movement of his family, Teiji also found work with the commission, including driving a truck to clean up the site after the residents had left upon the closure of the facility. It is uncertain to whom the letter was addressed, but with the addressee's name left blank, it appears to have been a template of a letter that addressed numerous persons with whom he and his family were acquainted.

80 Kentarō to Teiji, 27 June 1965, folder 4, MS84, Morishita Collection, Accession 2011.79.1.1.1d.

CHAPTER 4

"My Land Is Worth a Million Dollars": How Japanese Canadians Contested Their Dispossession in the 1940s

Jordan Stanger-Ross, Nicholas Blomley, and the Landscapes of Injustice Research Collective

It is a mistake to try to reduce values to a single metric such as wealth, utility, well-being, or liberty … [T]he more nuanced language of values allows us to think more deeply about the scope of property rights and the nature and obligations of ownership.[1]

Introduction

On 31 July 1944 Rikizo Yoneyama, a former resident of Haney, British Columbia, an agricultural area east of Vancouver, wrote to the Canadian minister of justice to protest the sale of his property. Two years earlier, when he and his family had packed their belongings for their forced expulsion from coastal British Columbia, they could take with them only what they could carry and, like other displaced people, they left much behind. "I realize that we are the victims of a war emergency and as such are quite willing to undergo … hardship … to help safeguard the shores of our homeland," wrote Yoneyama, "however, I do urgently desire to return to my home … when the present emergency ends. May I plead your assistance in the sincere request for the return of that home?"[2] When letters like his did receive a response from the federal government (there is no record that he did so in this case) it came in the form of standard letter, acknowledging that "the disposal of … property will be a matter of personal concern" but informing Japanese Canadians that, in conformity with a new federal law, everything, including their homes, would be sold.[3]

Along with Yoneyama, hundreds of Japanese Canadians immediately objected. This chapter engages 292 letters written by Japanese Canadians who protested the sale of their property between 1943 and 1947, providing a window into the perspectives of property-owning Japanese Canadians articulating the value of their lands and belongings and the harms of the policies that dispossessed them. Hundreds of Japanese Canadians shared Yoneyama's assessment of the time: "It does not seem just," he wrote, "that as Canadians my family should be deprived of a home."[4]

To understand the meaning of the destruction of Japanese Canadian homes, the voices of ordinary property owners protesting their losses must be heard. The scholarship on the federal policies directed at Japanese Canadians has often taken as self-evident the injustice of property loss, analyzing the dispossession primarily through the prism of state racism.[5] Close attention to the letters of protest allows us to place property – as a relation among people and with the state – at the core of this history.[6] The protests of Japanese Canadians illuminate the specific and complex harms of property loss, even in the context of a larger injustice. As Japanese Canadians articulated their attachments to property, they explained how its loss, in some senses above and beyond their uprooting and internment, threatened a permanent rupture in their sense of belonging and their faith in the state. As such, they reveal the fundamental injustices wrought by the policy. The injustice of the dispossession, the letters tell us, centre on what Japanese Canadians lost, how they lost it, and what that loss signified.

At the same time, the protests demonstrate that Japanese Canadians still sufficiently identified with their country to write to officials in condemnation of this act. Many believed that the state, on some level, could be reasoned with when it came to property. They clung to the notion that basic rules – especially those concerning the value of property and the terms of its exchange – might still hold fast, even for people ripped from their homes and interned on the basis of race. The letters of protest convey the courage of Japanese Canadians in confronting their losses of home and property, losses that were specific within the larger injustices of the era and complex in their own right.

This chapter conveys the harms of the forced sale of property as distinctive within the larger injustices of the internment era. Informed that they would lose their homes and all of the personal and landed property that they had been forced to leave in coastal British Columbia, Japanese Canadians wrote powerful letters, many of them conveying the experiences that link people to their belongings. Toyo Takahashi, for example, wrote the Custodian in April 1944 to argue that the forced sale of her home at 42 Gorge Road in Victoria was "against your promises, and my wishes, furthermore … utterly undeserved." Over a decade of work, she and her husband had painstakingly and lovingly cultivated a garden outside their home that was the site of rare and exotic plants and the recipient of a horticultural award. In 1937 it had merited royal recognition: "We treasure the memory of seeing Her Majesty turn her head to see our garden," she wrote. "This property is our home," she summarized near the end of her letter, "the reward for long years of toil and anticipation, a source of recreation, a stake in the future of Victoria, and an insurance for our later welfare."[7]

Takahashi's connection to property was expressed in a story that combined many different grounds for objecting to the government's policy. Other letters derived their power from simplicity. Tomio and Akira Yokoyama, for example, stated, "enclosed [are] the two cheques which we are returning to you as we are not satisfied with the sale."[8] Their letter conveys the futility of seeking to reason with an unreasonable state. In general, however, such letters were rare. Japanese Canadians sought to explain their objections to federal policy and they did so in complex and plural ways.

These letters had been read before, by federal officials. Frank Shears, who oversaw the daily operations of the Vancouver Office of the Custodian, instructed staffers to type and forward to him "all letters from Evacuees protesting to the sale of their properties," which he filed together with carbon copies of official responses, largely form letters explaining that the property sales were made on the basis of appraised values and in accordance with federal law.[9] In February 1947, following a similar initiative in the United States, momentum built toward a federal inquiry into the dispossession of Japanese Canadians, so Shears reviewed the letters for the legal representatives of the Custodian. He quoted twenty-three separate phrases that, in his view, gave "a fair representation" of the protests. Among them:

> The price is ridiculously low ... The qualified Appraisers must have been unfair ... This is my formal protest against the sale ... I am awaiting the judgment of the Court for the legality of the Orders-in-Council concerning the sale of real property . . .You must remember you are not dealing with animals ... We have nothing to do with this war ... To say that I am shocked is putting it mildly ... I have receipts showing what this property was bought for which will show that you have gyped me ... You have taken a step which is reminiscent of Nazi Germany ... I think you are just like the Fascists confiscating people's property and chasing them out of their homes ... I think the selling of property is unjust and a digression of Canadian fair play.[10]

Some of the quotes, including references to Nazis, were rare among the letters. Shears may have selected them because they seemed to articulate the anger simmering in almost all of the protests. Other grounds of protest, including the contestation of the sale price and emphasis of consent, were common. Shears recognized in the letters monetary claims but also sentiments that went beyond pecuniary harm. "I think it can be said," he summarized, "that all claims would fall broadly into two classes which perhaps might be called 'Tangible' and 'Intangible.'" In response to plural property claims, he suggested, the Custodian's response "should lie strictly with the tangible and specific."[11] Shear's distinction – between claims that could be assessed in monetary terms (tangible) and those that made broader claims of injustice or harm (intangible) – will be disputed in the pages that follow. Monetary losses in this case cannot be separated from the larger injustice of the uprooting; for Japanese Canadians, the harms to their livelihoods were inextricably tied to the broader assault on their lives. However, many officials would follow Shears in contemplating the loss of property from the narrow perspective of market value, notwithstanding their knowledge that losses went far beyond this calculus.[12]

Property's complexity and pluralism

Shears's reductive account of the property loss experienced by Japanese Canadians, in which the dispossession and forced sale of chattels, land, and housing can be resolved through cash payments, echoes a wider tendency to regard property as a straightforward matter. As Alexander and Peñalver note, a pervasive utilitarianism judges property arrangements in terms of the degree to which they advance maximal utility, which in contemporary scholarship tends to be understood in terms of preference satisfaction.[13] From this perspective, goods are always substitutable – the challenge lies in determining the proper rate of market exchange. In the context of the dispossession of Japanese Canadians, discussions of exchange rates can have significant material implications. As we assess the prices for which the state sold Japanese Canadian–owned assets, should the benchmark be market value at the moment of the transactions? Should sale prices instead be juxtaposed against values in 1949, when Japanese Canadians were permitted to return to British Columbia? Could an argument be made for an exchange rate based on the values of property in British Columbia today?[14] Such questions arise in a discussion of the dispossession that focuses primarily on the exchange value of property. The answers given – especially in a context of rapid increase in the value of property in postwar British Columbia – have significant consequences.

Nonetheless, any discussion based on exchange alone makes the erroneous assumption that the value that people attach to property can be reduced to its value in a market.[15] Psychologists and behavioural economists have long recognized that owners' actual valuations of their possessions diverge from metrics that presume a uniform and rational market and have sought to explain such "anomalies" in psychological terms (finding "endowment effects," "status quo biases," and "aversions" to loss).[16] Although their experiments have largely explored cases of choice – comparing what people would choose to pay for a given good against what they would be willing to accept for its loss – the lessons they impart are crucial here as well: namely that people value property in the context of lived experiences that involve attachment over time, emotional meaning, and painful losses.

Legal theorists excavating the social and political foundations of property have arrived at similar conclusions. For Alexander and Peñalver, property "is simply too complex and heterogeneous to be explicable by reference to a single, all-encompassing moral value."[17] In a similar vein Singer articulates the plural meanings of property:

> Property gives us freedom and stability, provides a source of wealth and well-being, the bases for creating work and useful investment. Property provides a place to create a family life, to nurture friendships, to rest, and to have fun. Property allows us to be good neighbors and good citizens, and it promotes various

> human values, including privacy, the freedom to associate with others, religious liberty, tranquility, and peace of mind.[18]

Among many forms of ownership and exchange, property relations in land stand out as particularly complex because they serve as a basis for human sociability: "Each parcel of land ... will be unique, in a sense, because of the relationship it bears to the web of human interactions within which it is situated."[19] Also, land has "memory," Peñalver points out, materializing ongoing human engagements and interactions. People foster a sense of identity that depends on memories of the past and expectations of the future. Memory, particularly in the case of the loss of property, is a powerful and "normatively ambiguous" phenomenon, extending beyond a monetary calculus to include questions of cultural identity, status, and intergenerational transmission.[20] Radin draws from Hegel to ground the intricacy of property relations in core principles of human self-development.[21] To be a person requires some control over resources in the external environment. She argues that most people "possess certain objects they feel are almost part of themselves. Those objects are closely bound-up with personhood because they are part of the way we constitute ourselves as continuing personal entities in the world."[22] Such forms of "personal" property, as she puts it, can be distinguished from "fungible" property (i.e. property that can be substituted). In this sense, people may experience and value some assets in ways that defy simple substitution. People form connections with particular pieces of property such that the property becomes inextricably bound up with their pursuit of the well lived life.

Analysis of letters

With these insights in mind, we return to the letters that Japanese Canadians wrote to protest the sales of their property. To do so, we must recognize their specificity. Federal authorities collected letters of protest beginning in 1943, when Japanese Canadians wrote to them, usually in response to letters notifying owners that their property had been sold and specifying the sale price. It is not surprising, therefore, that many focus on the sale itself, expressing surprise, anguish, and protest. As we would expect, questions of property value, financial or otherwise, are central to many responses. Further, the actions of the state in regards to property rights also figure centrally. Many Japanese Canadian owners seek to contest the terms of sale or the very act itself. They plead, petition, cajole, and threaten. As such, we can assume that they also seek to present their case in terms that they imagine will resonate with the authorities. In part, therefore, we can understand the letters as strategic acts of claim making, generated for many by a sudden traumatic moment of state force and oppression. However, as time wore on, it was clear that their letters had little prospect of changing policy. Japanese Canadians continued to write even after the government had been selling without consent for years, giving no indication that protest would stop them (including protest in the form of a formal legal challenge that went to a federal court in the same period).[23] Japanese Canadians knew this was the case (as one author, Risa Ono, wrote, "Although my protest will have very little weight in the matter, I am informing you that it was very much against my wishes to have the property sold").[24] Some saw practical advantage, nonetheless, in writing to create an official record of their objections, in hopes that this might serve future legal utility. Indeed, some make explicit reference to the advice of lawyers and a small number sent form letters that reflect legal advice. The vast majority, however, wrote in their own words and their letters convey their feelings. The letters were strategic, but it is difficult to read them without concluding that owners also wrote to express the depth of their losses and to give heartfelt expression of the meanings of their property to them.

The 292 letters filed by the Vancouver Office of the Custodian as letters of protest convey the voices of 247 separate authors.[25] Many more Japanese Canadians wrote in protest; their letters are dispersed across tens of thousands of government files. For example, Takateru Takarabe was informed in October 1948 that his house and property in Crofton had been sold; he was one of many Japanese Canadians who suffered the particular indignity of losing their home long after the end of the war. Outraged, he wrote the next day to protest: "I have written time and again that, I didn't want my house and properties sold," he explained, "I wanted them to be taken care of … Therefore I am returning this cheque and will not accept it at all."[26] Takarabe received the standard official reply, but his protest was not filed along with the others, perhaps because the Bird Commission had already commenced and the Custodian had already formulated its self-defence. The letters analyzed here, in short, reflect the voices of Japanese Canadians but also the priorities and decisions of officials who assembled the file to document their protests. A full account of Japanese Canadian protest lies outside the scope of this chapter and would constitute its own very worthy research endeavour.

The sentiments expressed in letters likely also convey the perspectives and feelings of many who never wrote. Japanese Canadian letter writers undertook considerable risk given the very real insecurity of their positions during the 1940s; earlier Japanese Canadian resistance to the uprooting, and to the breakup of families in its first months, had been punished with incarceration in prisoner-of-war camps in Ontario.[27] Further, federal responses to the letters deliberately offered no indication that they might change policy. In his tabulation of letters in 1947, Shears warned, "It must not be thought … that other Japanese [Canadians] are satisfied." Rather the Custodian's responses had been so discouraging that many others, he surmised, "thought it would be useless to complain knowing the type of answer they would be given."[28] In the immediate postwar period, even though their internment had not yet ended, more than 1,400 Japanese Canadian property owners presented claims to the royal commission investigating their losses.[29] This figure also surely underrepresented the number who felt grounds for protest, given that the appeal process cost money, held little promise of significant remuneration, and was conducted by a government still in the midst of undermining their citizenship. The protesters were unrepresentative in undertaking the risks of voicing their dissent directly to a government in which they could place little trust.

Nonetheless, the authors of the protest letters collected together by federal officials constituted a reasonable cross-section of Japanese Canadian society in the internment era. Most authors were men, but at least forty-three letters included a female signatory.[30] They originated from key sites of settlement, with the greatest numbers displaced from Vancouver, which housed the largest Japanese Canadian urban neighbourhood before the war, the fishing centre of Steveston, and the rich agricultural areas of the lower mainland, where Japanese Canadians had built large multigenerational communities. Authors came also from the remote settlements – Ucluelet, Port Essington, Prince Rupert – where smaller numbers had made their lives before the internment (figure 4.1). Having been uprooted and displaced, the authors wrote from the varied sites of internment that housed Japanese Canadians during the war. The largest number, though less than a majority, wrote from the camps and ghost towns in British Columbia – Greenwood, Lemon Creek, New Denver, Slocan, Tashme – where Japanese Canadians were interned en masse. Fifty wrote from the small Alberta towns, like Picture Butte and Raymond, where they laboured. Forty-five wrote from Ontario, almost half of these from Toronto, which, especially after 1944, became a magnet for Japanese Canadian resettlement. In all, the protests came from six provinces and almost one hundred localities, reflecting the extent of Japanese Canadian displacement and dispersal during the decade (figure 4.2).[31]

Sources as complex and multivocal as these invite a wide range of analytic approaches. Analysis might emphasize their heterogeneity, examining the role of gender, geography, or types of property (real estate versus personal property, urban versus rural, for example) in Japanese Canadians' expressions of loss. In this volume, our colleagues have linked similar letters to other available sources to tell stories that unfold over longer chronologies, documenting Japanese Canadian acquisitions of property, their experiences of loss in the 1940s, and then the remarkable achievements of so many in rebuilding their lives thereafter.[32] Given the dissonance between property owners and officials over what kind of loss counted, it might also be useful to isolate for analysis those types of harms – the emotional, personal, or even political – that government officials denied but Japanese Canadians asserted. The letters, overlooked for decades, are now (thanks to the canadiana.ca project) freely available online; we hope that this chapter will encourage others to read these remarkable sources and to pursue some of these lines of inquiry.[33]

Our analysis aimed from the outset to understand the protests of Japanese Canadians in a comprehensive and inductive fashion. We found, in taking this approach,

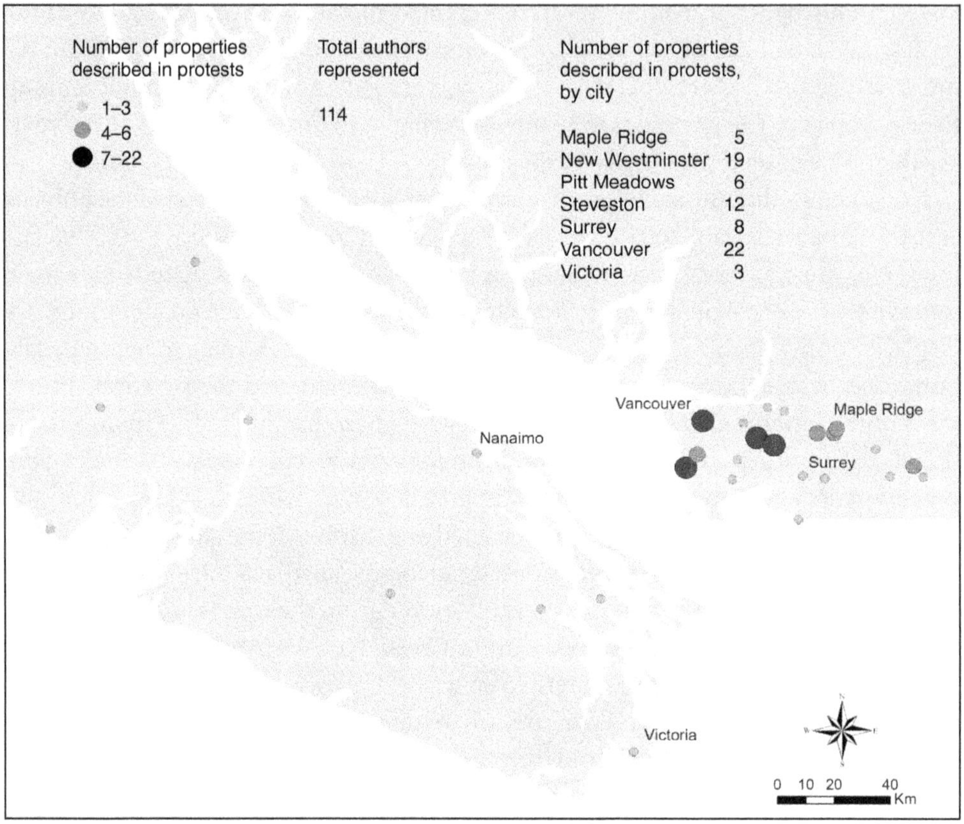

Figure 4.1 *Above* British Columbia origins of letter writers.
Figure 4.2 *Opposite* Locations of authors when they wrote protest letters.

that it was also invocatory of key facets of property theory. Although the letters are powerful and individual (speaking to personal experiences that we do not intend to overlook in the reflections that follow), we seek to be comprehensive. That is, our analysis is guided by patterns of argument within the entire collection of letters. We situate individual claims within the context of hundreds that were written in protest. To achieve this kind of analysis, we first coded all 292 letters, identifying their most common argumentative themes.[34] Perhaps the most striking aspect of the collection is the plurality of grounds of protest expressed. Japanese Canadians contested market values ascribed by appraisers and described competing (and higher) offers for their lands and belongings. They talked about the money, time, and labour that they had invested in improving their lands. They described their needs. They emphasized an owner's right to consent, or at least to be consulted, in the sale of their property. They invoked law as well as justice, fairness, and trust. They spoke about the significance

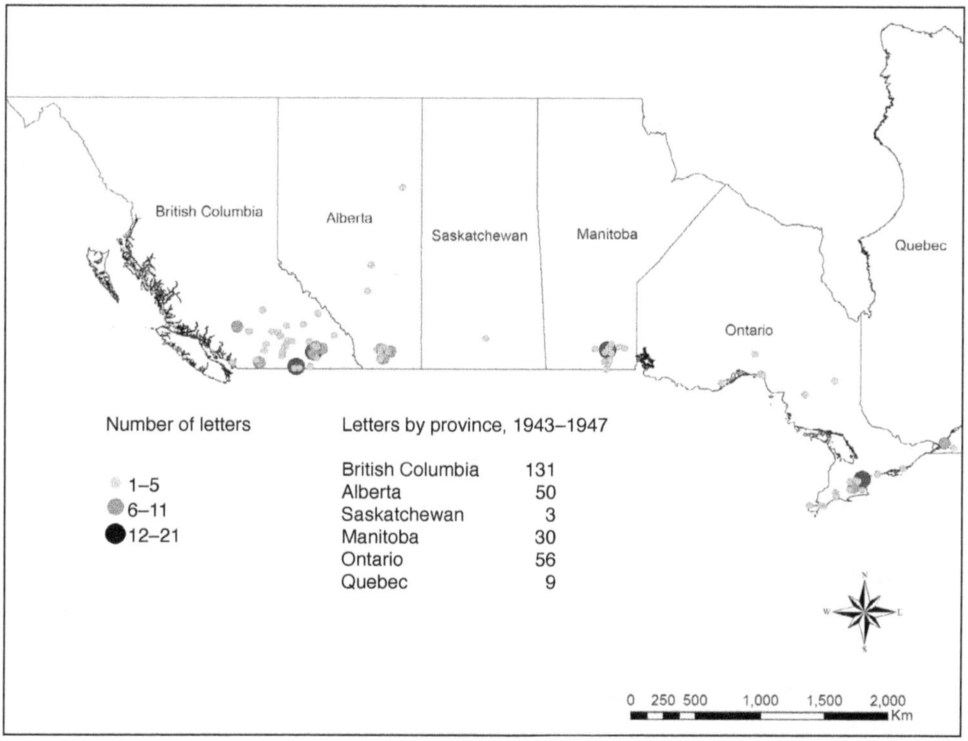

of citizenship, democracy, and rights. They appealed to the service they had given their country and described the benefits they still hoped to reap from their possessions. Japanese Canadians, in short, articulated many grounds of protest.

In the pages below, we focus analysis on the two most common arguments made by Japanese Canadian property owners. First, almost 70 per cent of authors explicitly contested property exchanges on the basis of price. In these letters, authors used terms such as ridiculous, absurd, or shocking to describe sale prices, cited a higher amount that should have been realized in the sale of their property, described government appraisers as biased or unfair, and stated, plainly, that the price was too low. These authors were concerned about monetary value. They felt their property worth more, sometimes far more, than the amount credited to them by federal officials. Second, just over half of the authors invoked the principle of consent in contesting the sale of their property, making this the second most common ground for protest. Letters indicating that the owner did not wish to sell, did not give permission for the sale, or refused the sale were coded in this category. Notably, letters invoking both the principles of exchange price and consent were underrepresented, and when authors protested on complex and plural grounds, those focusing on exchange tended to draw upon somewhat different complementary arguments than those emphasizing consent.[35]

We found that patterns within the collection of letters echoed the observations of some property theorists. Alexander, for example, draws a distinction between a property's "commodity" function, in which property serves market-oriented ends, and its association with "propriety," in which property arrangements are organized so as to shape and establish the proper social order.[36] From this latter perspective, personal security means not security against material losses, "but against political-ethical loss, that is, loss of the self-respect that is the basis for proper citizenship and, ultimately, the proper social order."[37] Rose also notes an important distinction between a "preference-satisfying" understanding of property, and a proprietarian conception, in which property serves to maintain appropriate relations in the commonwealth or body politic.[38] Such perspectives, over and above the distinctions they draw, are also useful in pointing us to the pluralism of values that property serves.

In the two sections that follow, we unpack some of the meanings conveyed in letters in the two main clusters within the collection. Then, in a final section, we consider letters that address both exchange value and consent. In the first two sections, we argue that exchange and consent are both internally complex and powerful grounds of protest and that they are in important ways conceptually distinct from one another. Further, we argue that exchange and consent are inextricably enmeshed with expressions of emotion, identity, dignity, and outrage; these very personal responses of Japanese Canadians to their losses cannot be separated from their appeals to conventionally articulable values or legal principles. In the final section of our analysis, we explore letters that integrate both exchange and consent to convey the multiple and tangled meanings of property loss.

Exchange value

The sale of their property for less than its worth had material consequences for the economic well-being of Japanese Canadians but also protests about exchange were grounded in wide-ranging claims about the injustice of the dispossession. When Japanese Canadians contested the prices for which their property sold, they did not do so by reference to an impersonal market of exchange. Owners did not appeal to prevailing real estate markets or price trends, they did not convey the worth of their lands and belongings by explicit comparison with other sales. Rather, Japanese Canadians protested because their own, very personal investments – of money, time, labour, emotion – were not repaid in sales by the Custodian. In this regard, the letter writers anticipated property scholar Debbie Becher's recent observations about the multiple and deeply felt investments of owners in their property. Owners, she writes, "sacrifice" value of many kinds "money, time, labour, love or relationships – in the hope of future benefits."[39] "We know that people put all kinds of value into real property," she explains:

> They use money to buy, rent and improve their properties, and they also use time, skill and physical effort for improvements. They take advantage of social networks for support and advice about their properties, and they put furnishings and building materials into their properties. Finally, they put emotion into the decisions they make and into the time they spend with their properties. And as they sacrifice all these types of value, they expect to enjoy various types of value in the future.[40]

Japanese Canadians protested the prices for which their properties sold on the basis of such plural and personal investments. The plurality of their claims can be verified numerically: only a small number of authors (14 percent) objected to the sale price without also invoking at least one additional ground for protest. The majority (55 percent) combined their indictment of exchange values with at least two other grounds. However, the importance of their investments in their property, and the relation of these investments to the injustice of forced property sales, can only be understood by attending more carefully to what Japanese Canadians actually wrote.

As they contested sale prices, Japanese Canadians sought to convey to officials how much of themselves they had put into their lands and belongings. A. Masuhara, for example, argued that his property in Vancouver was "sold by the Custodian at [a] price far below [its] actual worth." Justifying this claim, he explained that when the family moved in, it was a "broken down small building … [T]he garden was stone and garbage and full of brush. After I bought the place had the whole place changed." Masuhara offered significant detail: "floors, partitions, doors, walls, and [the] ceiling" were "renewed & painted." New structures were built to accommodate both commercial and residential uses, and the back yard was "cleared … and made lovely garden with lovely many flowers and bulbs by gardener. I have spent lots [and] lots of money for the place." Labour, time, and monetary investments interwove to create Masuhara's sense of the value of his lands. He had invested thought and vision into remaking the property. The "absurdly low" figure for which the Custodian sold was, in Masuhara's letter, measured against a very personal sense of property's real worth.[41]

Similar investments are expressed in letter after letter in the collection. Sakae Takenaka, for example, protested the "unbelievably low price" ($1,020) for which the government sold her farm, property that her family had purchased years earlier for $1,800. In the intervening time, she argued, the value of the property had increased. "Every chicken house on the farm," she wrote, "was built by us" and had been constructed with "flooring two inches thick instead of the usual one inch." In addition to their labour, these improvements had cost the Takenakas $760 in cash. An independent valuation of the farm in 1942, she continued, had assessed its value at $5,000, a price that reflected the reality that "any chicken farmer would be able to make two or three thousand dollars a year" on the farm.[42] The family's prior interaction with a "real estate valuator" suggests that they may have previously considered selling. Even so, the letter invoked not an impersonal market of exchange but rather the very specific value of this very specific farm, value created by hand by the Takenakas themselves.

Many authors, like Takenaka, expected to see their labour in land repaid in the sale of their property. References to toil and time abound. One correspondent noted that "the labour in clearing that wild land, the trees planted … [and] buildings have entirely been overlooked," with another protesting that "$200.00 is just giving the land free after all the time and labour I put in."[43] Yoichi Okuma itemized the multiple buildings he built on his farm, the labour entailed in clearing the bush, and the many crops that he planted: "You don't realize the hard labour, money and time it has taken me to build up to what I have. Thirty years of hard work and building up one by one has gone to ruins. What is the idea making such an unreasonable transaction?"[44]

References to the labour invested are so widespread that they deserve more careful attention. These claims have monetary basis: an investment of energy and time, they argue, should be recognized in the sale price. Market equity should match sweat equity. As Shig Kato complained, "Don't you think yourself that the selling price was but a mockery to all hard working people? Even more to a[n] old man who worked hard, put everything he had into his bit of land."[45] Given his investment of labour, Yoichi Okuma felt "You are taking too much advantage of me. The price for which you made the sale is most disappointing." Estimating the value of his house at $5,000.00, he nonetheless concluded his letter with a gesture to an unimaginable financial sum – "this land is worth one million dollars."[46] His letter thus simultaneously invokes a language of market valuation while also exploding its very applicability to the depth of his investments in his land. Others contested price while also protesting the very notion that the market could repay their investments. Rokusaburo Taniguchi's letter stated his dissatisfaction "with the amount for which you disposed of the property." Valuing his farm at $8,000, Taniguchi had received "several good offers for the property," contributing to his outrage at its sale for less than $3,000. This was, then, a transaction with serious economic repercussions for the family. But it was also more than that:

> I had no desire to exchange my property, which represents more than thirty years of sweat and hard labour, and the place where I spent the best years of my life, for a small handful of paper money. Money can never buy my youthful days spent uselessly, now, on that wonderful farm.[47]

Toshiye Hoshiko similarly described investments that defied market valuation while simultaneously contesting a specific sale price:

> It was my home for over twenty years. It was the work and hard work of two decades of toiling. It was where my children were born and raised. And now

> you tell me that the property was sold and that the balance of my credit at your office is only a mere $1340.11 and on top of that you subtract $50.00 for "legal expenses."[48]

Such protests clearly speak to the financial value of an asset but also exceed it. Cash value needs to be recognized, claimants argue, but it is also entangled in other values that monetization, at least in the form of the Custodian's sales, fails to capture.

Perhaps such accounts of the multiple investments associated with the improvement of property rely on a prevailing view, echoed by Locke, of property as a reward for useful labour. Not only do they itemize financial investments, in other words, they also serve to inscribe entitlement in the land. To sell my property below the price that I ascribe to it, some writers seem to say, is to efface the right I have in the land, marked not only in the formal title that I hold but also through the manner in which I have performed ownership through my actions. If so, the authors articulate private property within a particular cultural register perhaps especially salient in settler colonial societies. Property can usefully be thought of as a series of enactments and practices.[49] Clearing land, growing gardens, "improving" and making land productive are all means by which property can be performed. The sale of property below its value not only causes monetary harm but also undoes these important acts of ownership.

Following this thread, the Custodian's sales can be understood as undermining important forms of communication. Their letters suggest that many Japanese Canadians believed that, through their many investments in property, they had communicated their status as good owners, as people committed to the places they lived, as people who belonged. Sales markedly below value served abrupt notice, even in the context of the larger uprooting, that such acts of communication, often performed over decades of hard work, were to be ignored. As Carol Rose notes, "persuasion … is what makes property available to action."[50] Property – both in law and every day practice – relies upon communicative acts and compelling stories through which we persuade ourselves and others of our entitlements. As "persuasion tells a story," so some Japanese Canadians narrated the extraction of their land from a state of "wilderness."[51] C. Kobara notes, "I labored and cleared six acres in ten years to see the fruits of my work" and as such "I cannot bear to see it go at such a rediculous [*sic*] amount"[52] Similarly, Kisaku Nishimoto explained that ten years of hard labour had made his farm "productive in the highest degree from a wild, neglected land, where the water had covered most of the year."[53] Given the meaning of these acts, the ownership that they ought to have communicated, Nishimoto was "simply appalled at seeing such insulting figures" for the sale of his farm.[54] Claimants frequently narrated their investment, documenting how they came to the land, improving it and investing in it. To sever that relationship is to destroy a personal history and geography. For H.K. Naruse, expressing a sentiment later echoed in scholarship by Radin, the entanglement between personhood and property is palpable:

> How would you … like to be kicked out of your house which you have planned and built to your own specifications and satisfactions. Then soon after informed that your house and land has been sold. Yes, sold … and at a ridiculous amount. Perhaps you did not go through the pains and joys of building on your own property … after so many years of saving and planning.[55]

Ownership of the kind created through the investments of planning, labour, and time is, in this formulation, fuller than that which follows from a mere acquisition of title. Only some owners – and Naruse speculates perhaps not his correspondent at the Office of the Custodian – have performed and experienced this deeper and more personal kind of proprietorship.

Time is central to such investments. This occurs not only in terms of the time already spent but also, crucially, in terms of a set of expectations regarding future benefits.[56] Masahiro Sakamoto wrote of his hopes to return to his farm after the war ended. "It is here in this district," he wrote,

> that I grew up and had my schooling. The school that I went to from grade 1 to High School is only about a block away from the farm and I am hoping that my children will be able to go to it also. It was with this in mind that I bought that farm … If I may start once again in the district of my childhood I would be very happy.[57]

Another writer remembered his parents "both deceased" who had "worked so hard to leave something of Canada for us, their offsprings." "Personally," he continued, "I would consider disposing of my property, but when you state the sale price as a fair one, I can only say that it is adding insult to injury."[58] Another author, who returned the cheque sent to him by the Custodian, explaining that it was "below my valuation," noted that, "it has always been my wish and intention that my son take over my property for his own use."[59] Writing for the members of the South Fraser Farmer's Union, President T. Maruno implied similar plans for the future: "our children were born on, and loves [*sic*] these farms. I realize that you will understand that it will be hard for these second generations to trade their birthplace for money or any other thing."[60]

For others, land secured not only a future in terms of familial commitments but also acted as a buffer against an uncertain world. C. Kobara noted that without the six acres cleared in ten years of hard labour, he saw "no security or future ahead."[61] Takahashi, on a similar theme, argued, "After all our efforts in good citizenship we do not deserve to have our retirement jeopardized by the liquidation of our properties."[62] Overlapping themes of security and familial succession, Shig Kato evocatively referred to his property as land that he had "looked upon as a child who had at last grown up to a stage where it was ready to help."[63]

Japanese Canadians who contested the price for which their property sold argued that their plural and temporal investments failed to register in the state's narrow logic of valuation. They echoed Becher's observation that legitimate compensation for property loss is "an act of recognition – specifically, government's recognition of someone's investment."[64] Thus Naruse, who described the "pains and joys" of building property caustically rejected the Custodian's "'qualified' appraiser who was guilty of such a moronic valuation."[65] For Kane Tanaka, whose home in Vancouver boasted a "beautiful and valuable landscaped garden," the property valuation was an "obvious case of misfeasance attributable to unsympathetic and very careless handling … No Canadian property owner in his right mind would willingly consent to the sale of his property based on such a valuation standard."[66] Such personalized investments cannot register in the dispassionate calculus of the state, notes another claimant: "After twenty (20) odd years of hardship I believe that others should have more consideration and figure out for themselves, the greater value of my properties."[67] For Tsurukichi Mishima, "you will never no [*sic*] what energy and sweat I have put in it to make it produce as it does now … I am sure that any scale by which you have sold lands … will not be satisfactory for us."[68] It is clear, then, that claimants do not evaluate the cash derived from forced sales as a dispassionate substitution of the assets. Judging by the letters, many respond with anger, disbelief, sadness, and surprise at the sale, the low valuation, and the failure to recognize the depth of their ties to property and the value of their investments.

Consent

Half of the letter writers protested on the grounds that they had not consented to the sales. In these letters, the writers often also articulate their protests in terms of the relationship between the state and property owners. For many authors, property's value turns less on its commodity form than the manner in which in encodes a set of foundational political relations. Letters focusing on consent, in particular, reinforce Singer's observation that "the legal structure of property reflects norms and values that are not fully expressed by reference to the market value of property rights"; instead, property also must be understood as a "constitutional problem."[69] Property rules organize and structure relationships according to a set of democratic principles predicated on respect and personal dignity; property "builds the floor on which we stand; it is the foundation that lets us live our lives in conditions of human decency." As such "property law defines things that we would *like to take for granted*; it does so by setting the boundaries of just social relationship."[70]

The taken-for-grantedness of property offers an explanation of the common and enduring conviction of many protestors that they retained the right to veto the sale of their property. Shichitaro Odagaki, upon being informed that his property was to be sold, replied, "I have thought over this matter very seriously and come to the conclusion that I will not sell my property … I will appreciate very much if you would inform this buyer that my property is not for sale."[71] He was joined in this sentiment by dozens of others who expressed the view that they had the power to deny the sales, for example:

> I am thoroughly disgusted with the absurd transaction so cancel this sale immediately … I would like you to know that I will not sell my property no matter how many times you write … I am not selling the land … Please be informed that I definitely *do not* wish to have my property sold … please put our names on your list of people, who do *not* wish their property to be sold … I have no intention to sell my property, whatever the Government policy is.[72]

These letters assume and assert a view of property as a foundational relationship between owner and state. Taking for granted that an owner's intentions with his or her property should be enforced, these letters reaffirm foundational norms that the forced sales threaten to shatter. Owners will pay taxes, abide by government regulations, and generate and derive benefits from their property. Government will secure property and protect over time the diverse forms of value that owners hold in their property.[73] By refusing sales that they have been told will occur (or have occurred) Japanese Canadians repudiated state action that would allow their property to be taken away and transferred to others against their will. These letters imply a contract with the state that was violated by the dispossession.[74]

Other protestors made property's place in the political order explicit in their frank outrage at the government policy. Tatsuo Onotera responded to a letter regarding the sale of his and his brother's property:

> It was a shock and surprise as I had no previous notice or correspondence on the matter. I knew different properties were being sold of former coast Japanese, but I didn't think for a moment that such a thing was possible. I feel as a Canadian citizen born and raised here that I could have at least been notified[.] I have been brought up as any one of your other citizens believing this a fair and Democratic country, but the way we are being treated I have my doubts.[75]

If, as Singer argues, "[o]ur regulations … shape the house that we live in," here it is both Onotera's house and a set of presumptions regarding the legal norms that make this house his that have been violated.[76] Rather than leaving these norms implied, authors like Onotera articulated their expectations of a political society that upheld property:

> You have gone against our wishes, also without even consulting us, as any citizen of Canada would have the privilege of giving assent or refusal … I want to know from who did you get permission to sell my property … I thought the Custodian suppose [*sic*] to look after the land and responsible for everything, not sell it … I will, with all my efforts, let the Canadian Public know what form of injustice is carried on in spite of the true form of government and policy which Democracy stands for in Canada … To my thinking the Canadian Government should make some kind of restitution on properties … and help us get back on our own so that we may live as … true Canadian Citizens.[77]

In affirming their Canadian citizenship, such writers both articulated the contractual implications of democratic governance and pushed back against the widespread tendency in the 1940s for policy makers and the wider public to misconstrue them as foreigners. As Isamu Kai wrote, "During the war I was forced to evacuate from New Westminster where I was born and classed as an enemy alien."[78] The effort to be regarded as Canadian was conjoined with an affirmation of the legal and normative meanings that should attach to political belonging.

A number of authors affirmed the notion of political contract by emphasizing their ongoing performance of the obligations of citizenship. Some did so by noting their efforts to remain financially self-sufficient despite the disruption of the uprooting and internment. Thus, Sajiro Wakita wrote, "I and my family are not dependent on the government maintenance, therefore, you should not need to sell my property which I altogether refuse in selling."[79] Similarly, Chieno Kuroyama asked officials to recognize "how great my shock and disappointment would be, to be informed that my last remaining possession, my house, had been sold … Especially when you know that we have done our utmost not to be a burden on the Canadian Government by being self supporting."[80] James Hasegawa objected to the sale of property belonging to his father ("a naturalized citizen of Canada since 1913"), in part on the grounds that "He has given us a liberal education by sending us to Universities so that we in turn could become useful citizens instead of a burden upon the government."[81] Takeo Yoshida argued in 1946, almost two years after Japanese Canadians were given the opportunity to enlist in the Canadian military, that "many friend and persons of our minority have joined the services of Canada for right, justice, and fairness, for everything that the war stood for," an effort that he described as "a dead cause when there is injustice of liquidating personal assets and belonging[s] without the approval of its rightful owners."[82] Aya Suzuki wrote with a warning:

> that property is one place I do not want to see sold as most of us were born there … Mother's heart & soul is in to get back to that house yet I am trying to wean

> her away from the re-location centre to go east for awhile. Yet you still insist it is Ottawa's Orders and take a dictatorial hand not a *democratic* way. Please do not try us any further.[83]

In her view, the cooperation of Japanese Canadians with federal directives, including their relocation to destinations east of British Columbia, was contingent on the government's fulfillment of its obligations. Violations of that contract, she implied, could bring unforeseen and undesired consequences for officials.

In such cases, one may expect an individualized and rights-based defence of private property given the prevailing view of property as a bulwark that protects the individual from the state. By seizing and forcibly liquidating assets, the state has violated the liberty and autonomy of the individual liberal subject. Indeed claims about rights did cluster (in a statistically significant fashion) in letters that focused on consent; however, more striking in the letters is the limited use of such rights-based normative claims. Only thirty-three letters (10 per cent) invoke rights explicitly, and almost half of these are form letters that accompanied the court challenge to the forced sales launched by Japanese Canadians in 1943. These letters are crafted to allow Japanese Canadians to accept funds realized in the sale of their properties while at the same time registering their objections: "I wish to make it clear that [funds] are only being accepted under protest and without prejudice to any rights which I have or may have arising out of what I consider the wrongful sale and disposition of my property."[84] In scattered other instances, Japanese Canadians "reserve the right to take legal action" or invoke the owner's "right to appeal for fair sale price" under conditions of expropriation, but such examples are notable for their scarcity.[85] Far more frequent are the appeals to broad norms of contractual citizenship, which themselves could sometimes be expressed in terms of rights, as for example, when Aya Suzuki wrote that "Canadian citizens" should be "free to exercise their rights and to contribute to the betterment of this land of our birth."[86]

The language of consent, rather than one of rights, is worth noting. Rather than an absolutist conception of property as a zone from which the state is excluded, by right, consent here implies a structured and predictable relationship between state and owner, ideally governed by norms of mutuality, equality, respect, and dignity. While it presumptively privileges the interest of the owner, it does not rule out the interests of the state. As such, it rests on a set of relationships between owner and state, rather than a simple opposition.

Interweaving exchange and consent

While the isolation of exchange from consent has conceptual advantages (allowing us to delve deeply into each theme) and follows a statistically significant trend within the collection of letters (whereby they were used in combination less often than we would have expected and tended to overlap with different supplementary themes), this division nonetheless overlooks another important aspect of Japanese Canadian protests to the government policy: a large number of authors invoked both exchange and consent. Indeed, although statistically underrepresented, the majority (more than 60 per cent) of writers who objected to the failure of the government to secure their consent also protested the monetary value of the exchanges. From the opposite perspective, among the 70 per cent of writers who objected to the price for which their property was sold, almost half also mentioned the failure of the government to obtain their consent. Further, these letters exemplify the complexity and power of the entire collection and the reality that Japanese Canadians had many interwoven grounds to protest the forced sale of their property.

Among these is the letter of Rikizo Yoneyama, which gracefully and painfully expressed the layered significance of the ownership violated by the dispossession. Yoneyama wrote about monetary value: "During May of this year," he explained, "I received notification that my property … had been sold for the sum of $1,406.98." This amount fell far below his estimate of the worth of his estate: "My property there consisted of seventeen and a half acres of land and other household goods … which I valued at the total sum of $4,500."[87] Like most Japanese Canadian protesters, Yoneyama emphasized the exchange value of his property: the price for which the government had sold was less than the property's rightful market value. But Yoneyama wrote to protest much more than this.

He explained that after years of labour, he had transformed his land into a productive farm that played an essential role in his family's success in Canada. Years of "hard work," he wrote, had built the farm "up to a point of security for my wife and my children." An annual income of some $3,500 (more than twice the sale price) had enabled him to "put two of my children through university as doctor and dentist respectively." These lines could scarcely convey the remarkable personal journey that lay behind them. Born in 1887 in the Kanagawa Prefecture, southwest of Tokyo, Yoneyama traversed the Pacific at the age of twenty. In the first decade after his immigration, during which he married and fathered two daughters, Yoneyama worked in a sawmill and then a pharmacy, saving enough money to purchase land, seven and a half acres in Haney, where he dug a well by hand so that he could raise chickens and pigs and cultivate berries, apples, pears, plums, and cherries as well as a variety of vegetables. There, two more children were born. Supplementing the income of this farm with additional wage labour, Yoneyama was able in 1935 to purchase additional land, where he built a two-storey chicken coop and an enlarged family home. As his letter indicated, by 1942, his children had already begun their entry into Canadian professional life; when his family packed their bags for Edmonton, Alberta they went to join his two oldest daughters where they were training.[88] Yoneyama sought to convey to federal

Figure 4.3 Rikizo Yoneyama (sunglasses) and family. Harold Yoneyama in bowtie.

officials the extent to which his property was woven into the story of his personal and family history. The farm was invested with his labour and a container of his memory; it was tied with his identity as a father, husband, and provider.[89]

In these respects, the farm was also essential in Yoneyama's aspirations for the future. He had planned, after the war, to return to Haney and to resume his work, so that his "two remaining children, who are dependent upon me, receive the same privilege as their two older sisters." His third daughter, he hoped, might become an optometrist, while the youngest, "my only son," aspired to be an electrical engineer. "I am now fifty eight years and feel I cannot start again from the bottom," he wrote "my heath is failing … my desire after hostilities have terminated, was to return to my home at Haney and continue where I left off."[90]

Yoneyama's land was also part of the story of his citizenship, a status inseparable from the larger narrative of his family. "I came to Canada in 1907," he wrote, "and was allowed the privilege of Canadian Citizenship on December 22, 1914." "This was to me," he wrote, "the most gracious opportunity given by the country of my adoption. Through it, I realized an ambition I had desired since landing on this continent, that of being able to raise a family of Canadian sons and daughters." The story of his migration and citizenship and that of his role as a father entangled with his property, "which to us meant more than just a home. It was to us, the foundation of security and freedom as Canadian citizens."[91] Here Yoneyama seems to suggest, as Adachi would later argue, that Japanese Canadian property ownership constituted a refuge from and a response to decades of racism and exclusion in British Columbia, providing the "economic and emotional security around which they organized their tightly-knit family and community life."[92]

It is in this context, then, that Yoneyama expressed indignation at the violation of his right to refuse the sale of his property: "The Custodian has not at any time requested my sanction [to] dispose of my property and had he done so, I would have been most reluctant to sell." Yoneyama's protest extended beyond the $3,000 in losses that he estimated, beyond the future economic benefit that he had anticipated: irrespective of the price obtained or the value acknowledged, he should, in this view, have had the right to choose.[93] If conceptually distinct, these values were not separate in his experience. His investment in property over time was also a history of choices that he had made; the monetary losses that he suffered were also a violation of his ability to provide as a father and to act as a citizen.

Tsurukichi Takemoto's family was not consulted before the forced sale of their personal belongings, including "Japanese dishes, trays, etc.," which were important family heirlooms. "These things are very valuable to us" she wrote, they "are not what you think they are." The use of this powerful phrase to describe personal property reminds us that the investments of Japanese Canadians were not limited to real estate.[94] Among the letters, 118 specified personal property lost, often enumerating it in addition to their real estate and emphasizing its value. Many, like Takemoto felt that officials badly underestimated the value of their moveable property; she wrote, "The total cost of the property we had in the premises," which the government had sold for $325, "is about $3500.00. What do you think about that!" Her loss, she affirmed, was significant in monetary terms alone. But her words suggest something more, namely that officials had no understanding of the meaning of these items, which were, as she wrote, were "very valuable *to us*" (our emphasis). As Csikszentmihalyi and Rochberg-Halton observe, cherished personal objects are valued for their craft and physical characteristics but also for the ways in which they represent their owners' senses of self and accomplishment, their relations to kin and friends, their connection with wider communities, and their investments of time and memory.[95] The complex losses suffered by Japanese Canadians were not merely the losses of the lands and buildings where Japanese Canadians had lived but also of the countless objects that constituted them as homes.

For Takemoto, this loss of investment, taken in the context of the wider policies directed at Japanese Canadians, signalled a profound rupture of the Canadian political order. "I did not answer [the government's notification of sale] until now," she wrote, "because your letter just made me mad enough not to answer."

> Why did you sell without even consulting us. Isn't the method you're using like the Nazis? Do you think it is democratic? No! I certainly think you're just like the Fascists confiscating people's property, chasing them out of their homes, sending them out to a kind of a concentration camp, special registration cards, permits for travelling. Don't you think this is the method used in dictatorship countries. Democracy means no racial discrimination, or it the very opposite.[96]

Here, as in dozens of other cases, the full weight of the two main grounds of protest landed in forceful condemnation of Canadian policy. Like Yoneyama, Takemoto conveys the dispossession of property as materially significant: the sale of her family's treasured belongings at a fraction of their value was an emotional affront and a devastating economic blow. More broadly, the forced sales – along with neglect, theft, and vandalism – cost Japanese Canadians dearly. These acts significantly compromised their material well-being and letter writers protested strenuously against this reality. At the same time, the forced sale was a political act, a violation of the basic rules of democratic society. These two dimensions of the forced sales can be analyzed separately (and many letter writers used them independently) but they were nonetheless knotted together. Here no distinction between exchange and consent will hold. They were each of them complex and inseparably entangled.

Conclusions

The letters reveal the multiple injustices of the forced sale of Japanese Canadian–owned property. With no plausible connection to the security of coastal British Columbia, the forced sales seemed to Japanese Canadians at the time, and ever since, to reflect a malice that extended beyond the exigencies of war. It reflected the desire, among some in British Columbia's racist political establishment, to see that Japanese Canadians never again returned to the province.[97] The dispossession of Japanese Canadians was part of the "politics of racism" of this era. This collection of letters demonstrates that Japanese Canadians immediately perceived the wrong of forced property loss and responded emphatically.

The dispossession was distinctive as a state act perpetrated against property owners. In their letters to the federal government, Japanese Canadians expressed the specific harms of this violation; they conveyed what their property meant to them. Their protests confirm the pluralism and complexity of ownership. Japanese Canadians, like other owners, had made multiple and deeply felt investments in their homes, lands, businesses, and belongings. The harms of property dispossession had to do with monetary sacrifices and rewards but also with much broader and deeper investments of time, labour, love, pride, and connection. The loss of their property without their consent or even their knowledge, the violation of foundational norms of civic and social relations in a society of private property ownership, constituted a particular kind of injustice, which stood distinct from (even as it was connected with) the wider array of policies that overturned the lives of Japanese Canadians in the 1940s.

Violations of property are deceptively hard to repair. Attempts to redress the harms of Japanese Canadian property losses – the royal commission created by the federal government in the immediate postwar (a rather half-hearted attempt) but also initiatives of the Japanese Canadian community (such as the Price Waterhouse estimation of material losses by Japanese Canadians) – have taken their cue from the market. Because transactions of property do occur, wherein the complex investments that owners make in their property are reduced to a single exchange value, it has been repeatedly imagined that the harms of forced dispossession might be repaired by monetary compensation. The letters of Japanese Canadians do suggest that money needed to be part of any discussion of redress. And yet, they also suggest the extent to which any monetary resolution of these harms will always be inadequate.

Owners valued their land and assets in ways that could not always be compensated by cash payouts. Property was not an easily alienated commodity but had become incorporated into life plans. Real and personal property materialized memory, recorded lives of hard work, and signalled security. Farms, businesses, and homes were entangled in local networks of meaning, belonging and association, echoing Alexander and Peñalver's comments:

> Once a person (or a community) has sufficiently incorporated a piece of land into her life plans, exchanging that land for some other good (even a good of very great economic value) or for some other piece of land can hinder, in some cases, irreparably, her ability to flourish. Losing the land can short-circuit long-term plans, deeply held commitments, and carefully constructed identities in ways that resist compensation.[98]

Such valuations of property's worth do not easily align with the state's calculations. Firstly, the amount of the cash derived from a forced sale is unlikely to adequately align with the multiple "investments" made by owners, in which the land is worth "a million dollars," as one correspondent put it. Secondly, a cash payment is itself inherently constrained, squeezing the multiple and diverse attachments that people have with land and assets into a monetized calculus. Such assets are not simply substitutable, as the state presumed. To assume otherwise is to engage in an invidious form of reductivism.

Here the work of Becher, upon which we have already drawn above, may be especially instructive.[99] She notes that officials tend to find satisfactory arrangements (from both their own perspectives and those of property owners) for expropriation when the property in question was "vacant, dangerous, unsafe, and practically unsellable on the market."[100] Although officials sometimes attempted to make such arguments of Japanese Canadian–owned property, almost all of it instead contained carefully built and deeply valued investments. The expropriation of such property, even for much better reason, generates conflict and protest.[101] Compensation for takings of this kind, Becher argues, should "recognize the years that owners and residents have spent with their property … [as well as] expectations of future benefits from properties" by supplementing market-based compensation with rules that take into account longevity of ownership and include "mechanisms for sharing the profits" derived from expropriate properties.[102] Writing of the very different context of rural development in South Africa, Ndabe Zibuqu pushes toward a similar point, asking, "unless claims are settled in a manner which gives a real sense of redress to the claimant group and which takes into account loss of history, livelihood, dignity and time as well as a loss of a stake in the property market – can it really be called restitution?"[103]

Today, Japanese Canadians are divided about the advisability of further negotiation that might directly, and more comprehensively, address property loss. For example, after the recent revelation that the City of Vancouver bore an important share of the responsibility for the dispossession of property, some members of the community saw this information as supporting a broad project of antiracist education, while others instead saw an opportunity to press for restitution by the city.[104] More generally, Japanese Canadians vary in their memories of and perspectives upon their history with the Canadian state and its efforts at acknowledgment and repair.[105] It is not the purpose or the place of the present analysis to intervene in such discussions, which instead involve the Japanese Canadian community and, at times, their elected representatives. However, if a process of restitution were to be undertaken, it seems likely that the perspective advocated by Becher, with its emphasis on the complexity of investment, would be most likely to yield results that respond to the protests voiced decades ago by the Japanese Canadians who lost their homes and belongings.

The letters of Japanese Canadians to the Canadian state bring into sharp focus a historical reality of societies organized around private property. While scholars have been right to critique private, individual proprietorship as only one form of ownership, of tenure in land as only one way of belonging in place, it has nonetheless been a tremendously powerful and motivating force. Japanese Canadians built lives around private property ownership; owning land, in particular, was a goal that had motivated the migration of first-generation emigrants from Japan.[106] For Rikizo Yoneyama, among many others, property ownership was essential to a multigenerational plan, core to a project that defined his life. Thus he could endure a temporary (although nonetheless unjustified) internment while he retained the promise of returning to his property and continuing where he left off. Deprived of this too, he despaired but also tried to use his own story to fight back. In important respects, he failed. His property was never restored. In 2005, his son, Yutaka Harold Yoneyama returned with his children and grandchildren to Haney, hoping to show them the farmhouse in which he had been born. "Unfortunately," he found, "the farmhouse was razed and the farmland has been developed into single family mansions and townhouses."[107] Indeed, all of the landmarks of his youth had been erased in redevelopment. Still, Rikizo's project had also succeeded. His son indeed became an engineer, his youngest daughter an optometrist. His letter of protest and the hundreds of others written by Japanese Canadians offer a powerful testament to the human importance of such aspirations, the harms of their forced compromise, and the courage of everyday people contesting injustice.

NOTES

A longer version of this chapter appeared as an article in the *Law and History Review* 35, no. 3, under the same title.

1 Joseph Singer, "Democratic Estates: Property Law in a Free and Democratic Society," *Cornell Law Review* 94, no. 4 (2009): 1054.

2 Rikizo Yoneyama to Minister of Justice, 31 July 1944, image 1448–1449, microfilm reel C9476, Office of the Custodian of Enemy Property, Vancouver Office: Office Files, Héritage, (hereafter C9476, Héritage).

3 See for example a letter that Yoneyama received to an earlier inquiry: W.E. Anderson to Rikizo Yoneyama, 4 July 1944, image 1452, C9476, Héritage.

4 Rikizo Yoneyama to Minister of Justice, 31 July 1944, image 1448–1449, C9476, Héritage.

5 Ann Gomer Sunahara, *The Politics of Racism: The Uprooting of Japanese Canadians during the Second World War* (Toronto: J. Lorimer, 1981), chapter 8. See also Jordan Stanger-Ross, "Suspect Properties: The Vancouver Origins of the Forced Sale of Japanese-Canadian-Owned Property, WWII," *Journal of Planning History* 15, no.4 (2016): 271–89; and Jordan Stanger-Ross, "Telling a Difficult Past: Kishizo Kimura's Memoir of Entanglement in Racist Policy," *BC Studies* 181 (9 April 2014): 39–62.

6 Our work can be compared to recent scholarship in a wide variety of national settings that explores attachments to property and homes in the face of displacement and dispossession and that has sought to place "the lived experiences of the displaced or dispossessed people at the centre of the discussion" (Lorna Fox O'Mahony and James A. Sweeney, "Re-thinking Responses to Displacement and Dispossession," in *The Idea of Home in Law: Displacement and Dispossession*, eds. O'Mahony and Sweeny (Farnham, UK: Ashgate, 2011), 1–12. Sarah Nield, "Article 8 Respect for the Home: A Human Property Right?," *King's Law Journal* 24, no. 2 (2013): 147–71; Anneke Smit, *The Property Rights of Refugees and Internally Displaced Persons: Beyond Restitution* (New York: Routledge, 2012); Martin Dean, Constantin Goshler, and Philipp Ther, eds., *Robbery and Restitution: The Conflict over Jewish Property in Europe* (New York: Berghahn Books, 2007); Scott Leckie ed., *Returning Home: Housing and Property Restitution Rights of Refugees and Displaced Persons* (New York: Transnational Publishers, 2003); Douglas Porteous and Sandra Eileen Smith, *Domicide: The Global Destruction of Home* (Montreal & Kingston: McGill-Queen's University Press, 2001). While it is essential to recognize the specificity under which dispossession occurs, this literature is useful in alerting

us to the significance, complexity, and pluralism of people's attachment to land and assets, echoing that of Japanese Canadians.

7 Toyo Takahashi to the Department of the Secretary of State, 12 April 1944, image 1339–1440, C9476, Héritage.

8 Tomio and Akira Yokoyama to the Department of the Secretary of State, 2 March 1947, image 1713, C9476, Héritage.

9 P. Douet to F.G. Shears, 11 September 1944, image 1492, microfilm reel C9476, Héritage. This means, of course, that the staff of the Custodian of Enemy Property curated the collection of letters that we analyze and discuss; it includes only letters that they recognized as protests. The collection is thus implicitly dialogical, reflecting the claims of Japanese Canadians that were found meaningful by bureaucrats. See chapters 4 and 6.

10 F.G. Shears to K.W. Wright, 27 February 1947, file 55908, pt. 2.2, RG 117, LAC (1st of two letters of that day).

11 F.G. Shears to K.W. Wright, 27 February 1947, file 55908, pt. 2.2, RG 117, LAC (2nd of two letters of that day).

12 Chapters 9 and 10.

13 Gregory Alexander and Eduardo Peñalver, *An Introduction to Property Theory* (Cambridge: Cambridge University Press, 2012). In 1991, Daniel Kahneman, Jack L. Knetsch, and Richard H. Thaler described the fungability of property as "one of the first lessons in microeconomics," a view that has been somewhat unsettled by their own research ("Anomalies: The Endowment Effect, Loss Aversion, and Status Quo Bias," *The Journal of Economic Perspectives* 5, no. 1 [Winter 1991]: 196).

14 See chapter 10.

15 In the discussion that follows, we interpret the claims of Japanese Canadians in the context of a body of property theory rooted in Europe and North America, although often applied outside of these contexts. This approach seems to us appropriate, given that most Japanese Canadian immigrant property owners had been in Canada for at least three decades prior to the uprooting and that 60 per cent of the uprooted population was born in Canada. Further, as we shall see, the statements of Japanese Canadians about their property closely align with these theoretical insights. However, Japanese cultural values surrounding property are also critical for understanding the dispossession. See chapters 1 and 3.

16 Kahneman, Knetsch, and Thaler, "Anomalies."

17 Alexander and Peñalver, *An Introduction to Property Theory*, 211.

18 Singer, "Democratic Estates," 1054.

19 Eduardo Peñalver, "Land Virtues," *Cornell Law Review* 94, no. 4 (2009): 829.

20 Eduardo Peñalver, "Property's Memories," *Fordham Law Review* 80 (2011): 1072. See also Ann Grubbstrøm, "Emotional Bonds as Obstacles to Land Sale – Attitudes to Land Among Local and Absentee Landowners in Northwest Estonia," *Landscape and Urban Planning* 99, no. 1 (2011): 31–9; Frode Flemsaeter and Gunhild Setten "Holding Property in Trust: Kinship, Law, and Property Enactment on Norwegian Smallholdings," *Environment and Planning A* 41, no. 9 (2009): 2267–84.

21 Margaret Jane Radin, "Property and Personhood," *Stanford Law Review* 34, no. 5 (1982): 957–1015.

22 Radin, "Property and Personhood," 959.

23 Chapter 8.

24 Risa Ono to George Peters, 4 August 1944, image 1458, C9476, Héritage.

25 Because some authors wrote more than once, the number of authors is lower than the number of letters. These numbers are based on 292 letters that we were able to read/code. There were several illegible letters. A small number of letters (twenty-six) included second authors, some of whom had separately authored letters themselves. Second authors have not been included in the total count of 247.
26 Takateru Takarabe to Mr Bell, 12 October 1948, file 58591, vol. 2515, RG 117, LAC.
27 Ken Adachi, *The Enemy That Never Was: A History of the Japanese Canadians* (Toronto: McClelland & Stewart, 1976), 242–3.
28 F.G. Shears to K.W. Wright, 27 February 1947, file 55908, pt. 2.2, RG 117, LAC (1st of two letters of that day).
29 Chapter 9.
30 The gender of letter writers could be determined for 193 letters.
31 Oikawa (*Cartographies of Violence*) analyzes the importance of the multiplicity of internment sites and experiences._
32 Chapters 3, 6, and 11.
33 See Héritage, microfilm reel C9476, starting from image 1329.
34 Three researchers working closely together did this coding. We began with thematic categories rooted in our reading of the scholarship on Japanese Canadian experiences (thus, for example, (1) racism, (2) citizenship, and (3) betrayal of trust were themes that we looked for), our reading of property scholarship (thus, for example, (1) exchange value and (2) sacrifice were themes) and a preliminary reading of the letters (thus, for example (1) consent and (2) consult were themes). Our initial process was for all three researchers to read the same fifty letters and to code them according to our draft codebook. Thereafter we met to check accuracy (coding was identical in more than 90 per cent of cases) and to discuss adjustments to the codes and categories that should be added. Thereafter the researchers each coded one third of the letters. Accuracy was checked again on a sample of letters afterward and remained high (meaning that our researchers were all coding in the same fashion). Our analysis is based on twelve themes that appeared in at least 5 per cent of the letters.
35 In almost 40 per cent of "consent" letters, the authors made no mention of sale price, a figure that significantly exceeds, from a statistical perspective, the number we would expect. These claims follow from thematic coding and statistical analysis of the letters. For a full explanation, see our article version of this material: "My Land Is Worth a Million Dollars: How Japanese Canadians Contested their Dispossession in the 1940s," *Law and History Review* 35, 3 (2017).
36 Gregory Alexander, *Commodity and Propriety: Competing Visions of Property in American Legal Thought, 1776–1970* (Chicago: University of Chicago Press, 1997).
37 Gregory Alexander "Property as Propriety," *Nebraska Law Review* 77, no. 4 (1998): 698.
38 Carol Rose, "Property as Wealth, Property as Propriety," *Nomos* 33 (1991): 223–47.
39 Debbie Becher, *Private Property and Public Power: Eminent Domain in Philadelphia* (New York: Oxford University Press, 2014), 8.
40 Becher, *Private Property and Public Power*, 18.
41 A. Masuhara to Office of the Custodian, 9 March 1947, image 1717, C9476, Héritage.
42 Sakae Takenaka to Custodian's Office, 12 May 1944, image 1372, C9476, Héritage. Takenaka also invoked democratic principles in her letter, a topic that we address below. "We have suffered enough injustices and for a country that has boasted of its democratic principles I think this sale was very unfair," she wrote.

43 Asa Amemori to F.G. Shears, 21 April 1944, image 1348 and Yoichi Okuma to Office of the Custodian, 3 July 1944, image 1425, C9476, Héritage.

44 Yoichi Okuma to Office of the Custodian, 3 July 1944, image 1424, C9476, Héritage.

45 Shig Kato to Custodians Office, 4 December 1946, image 1677, C9476, Héritage.

46 Yoichi Okuma to Office of the Custodian, 3 July 1944, image 1424, C9476, Héritage.

47 Rokusaburo and Mitsuye Taniguchi, 31 July 1944, image 1445–1446, image 1424, C9476, Héritage.

48 Mrs Toshiye Hoshiko to Office of the Custodian, 22 October 1944, image 1524, C9476, Héritage.

49 Nicholas Blomley, "Performing Property, Making the World," *Canadian Journal of Law and Jurisprudence* 27, no. 1 (2013): 23–48; Patricia Seed, *Ceremonies of Possession in Europe's Conquest of the New World, 1492–1640* (Cambridge: Cambridge University Press, 1995).

50 Carol Rose, *Property and Persuasion: Essays on the History, Theory and Rhetoric of Ownership* (Boulder: Westview Press, 1994), 296.

51 Rose, *Property and Persuasion*, 285.

52 C. Kobara to Department of the Secretary of State, January 1947, image 1683, C9476, Héritage.

53 Kisaku Nishimoto to F.G. Shears, 9 August 1944, image 1629, C9476, Héritage.

54 Ibid.

55 H.K. Naruse to The Custodian' [*sic*] Office, 26 July 1947, image 1782, C9476, Héritage. See Radin, "Property and Personhood." Naruse also decried the sale of his land without his consent. We will examine more closely letters that combined these two grounds of protest in our section below on interweaving consent and exchange.

56 See Becher, *Private Property and Public Power*.

57 Masahiro Sakamoto, 25 August 1944, image 1478, C9476, Héritage. This letter was not, strictly speaking, the protest of a sale as Sakamoto was uncertain whether his property had yet been sold or not. However, the Custodian filed it with the protest letters, perhaps anticipating that the investments it expressed were not recognized in the forced sale.

58 Toshio Oki to F.G. Shears, 12 August 1944, image 1461–1462, C9476, Héritage. This letter also protested the sale of the land without his consent. See the section below.

59 Yoshi Nikaido to Department of the Secretary of State, 17 September 1947, image 1798, C9476, Héritage. On similar themes see Flemsaeter and Setten "Holding Property in Trust." This letter also protested the sale of the land without his consent. See the section below.

60 T. Maruno and K. Kinoshita to the Custodian of Enemy Property, 13 June 1943, image 1330, C9476, Héritage.

61 C. Kobara to Department of the Secretary of State, January 1947, image 1683, C9476, Héritage.

62 Toyo Takahashi to the Department of the Secretary of State, 12 April 1944, image 1339–1440, C9476, Héritage.

63 Shig Kato to Custodians Office, 4 December 1946, image 1677, C9476, Héritage.

64 Becher, *Private Property and Public Power*, 202.

65 H.K. Naruse to The Custodian' [*sic*] Office, 26 July 1947, image 1782 and H.K. Naruse to The Custodian, 21 June 1944, image 1414, C9476, Héritage.

66 Mrs Kane Tanaka to Office of the Custodian, 18 July 1947, image 1778, C9476, Héritage.

67 Yaozo Nomura to Office of the Custodian, 21 June 1944, image 1416, C9476, Héritage.
68 Tsurukichi Mishima, 19 August 1944, image 1474, C9476, Héritage.
69 Joseph Singer, "Democratic Estates," 1010; Joseph Singer, "Property as the Law of Democracy," *Duke Law Journal* 63, no. 6 (2014): 1299.
70 Singer, "Democratic Estates," 1062, our emphasis.
71 Shichitaro Odagaki to Office of the Custodian, 24 November 1944, image 1533, C9476, Héritage.
72 Matsujiro Ryujin to Department of the Secretary of State, 8 May 1944, image 1360, Suejiro Mori, 9 May 1944, image 1366; Otomatsu Mukai, 6 June 1944, image 1396, Kashiro Akai to Department of the Secretary of State, 25 July 1944, image 1439, Haruo Maeda to Custodian, undated (circa September 1944), image 1489, and Ryukichi Miyake to Office of the Custodian, 25 October 1944, image 1526, C9476, Héritage.
73 See Becher, *Private Property and Public Power*, 8.
74 Singer, "Property as the Law of Democracy."
75 Tatsuo Onotera to F.G. Shears, 10 July 1944, image 1429, C9476, Héritage.
76 Joseph Singer, "Things That We Would Like to Take for Granted: Minimum Standards for the Legal Framework of a Free and Democratic Society," *Harvard Law and Policy Review* 2, no. 1 (2008): 141.
77 Aya Suzuki to P.H. Russell, 18 January 1944, image 1334, Kazue Kasubuchi, 8 May 1944, image 1362, Y. Okita for Gihachi Ito to The Custodian's Office, 20 May 1944, image 1382, Takeo Yoshida to P. Douet, 12 February 1946, image 1596–1597, and Isamu Kai to The Custodian's Office, 27 February 1947, image 1708, C9476, Héritage.
78 Isamu Kai to The Custodian's Office, 27 February 1947, image 1708, C9476, Héritage.
79 Sajiro Wakita to George Peters, 12 July 1944, image 1431, C9476, Héritage.
80 Chieno Kuroyama to Dept. of the Secretary of State, 14 May 1945, image 1578, C9476, Héritage.
81 James Hasegawa to George Peters, 12 February 1945, image 1558, C9476, Héritage.
82 Takeo Yoshida to P. Douet, 12 February 1946, image 1596–1597, C9476, Héritage.
83 Aya Suzuki to George Peters, 23 September 1944, image 1499, C9476, Héritage.
84 See images 1468, 1470, 1472, 1484, 1494, 1497, 1516, 1555, 1562, 1573, 1574, 1576, and 1584, C9476, Héritage.
85 Ryushi Koyanagi, 5 August 1944, image 1460, Tokuji Hirose to Dept. of the Secretary of State, 22 April 1944, image 1350, C9476, Héritage.
86 Aya Suzuki to P.H. Russell, 18 January 1944, image 1334, C9476, Héritage.
87 Rikizo Yoneyama to Minister of Justice, 31 July 1944, image 1448-1449, C9476, Héritage.
88 Yutaka Harold Yoneyama, *An Evacuee's Memoir* (Toronto: Pro Familia Publishing, 2008), 3–30.
89 Rikizo Yoneyama to Minister of Justice, 31 July 1944, image 1448–1449, C9476, Héritage.
90 Ibid.
91 Ibid.
92 Adachi, *The Enemy That Never Was*, 319.
93 Rikizo Yoneyama to Minister of Justice, 31 July 1944, image 1448–1449, C9476, Héritage.
94 See chapter 7. While some 1,700 parcels of real estate were sold, virtually all Japanese Canadians lost some property in the context of their uprooting. Indeed the Custodian of Enemy Property itself had more than 15,000 property files, which means that chattels were a more significant aspect of its business – the business of dispossession – than real estate itself.

95 Mihaly Csikszentmihalyi and Eugene Rochber-Halton, *The Meaning of Things: Domestic Symbols and the Self* (Cambridge: Cambridge University Press, 1981), 55–89.

96 Tsurukichi Takemoto to H.F. Green, 5 September 1946, image 1634, C9476, Héritage.

97 Ann Gomer Sunahara, *The Politics of Racism: The Uprooting Japanese during the Second World War* (Toronto: Lorimer, 1981), chapter 8.

98 Alexander and Peñalver, *An Introduction to Property Theory*, 32–3.

99 It is with caution that we can compare the policy and experience of dispossession in this case with that of the state expropriation of property, particularly through what would be termed the exercise of "eminent domain" in the United States. There are valuable points of comparison in the manner in which such losses are evaluated. (See Anneke Smit "Making up for the loss of 'home': compensation in residential property expropriation" in *Public Interest, Private Property: Law and Planning Policy in Canada*, eds. Anneke Smit and Marcia Valiante [Vancouver: UBC Press, 2016]; Becher, *Private Property and Public*.) Indeed, some of the actions of the Canadian state in this case (notably financial compensation) seem to echo expropriation procedures. However, it should be noted that Canadian expropriation practice is quite distinct from the United States. For example, there is no constitutional protection of private property nor is there a "public use" justification in statute (Anneke Smit, "Expropriation and the Socio-economic Status of Neighbourhoods in Canada: Equal Sharing of the Public Interest Burden," *Oñati Socio-Legal* Series 5, no. 1 [2015]: 258–79) while the basis for compensation is ambiguous (Paul A. Warchuk, "Rethinking Compensation for Expropriation," UBC *Law Review* 48, no. 2 [2015]: 655–92). Further, we would argue that the process whereby Japanese Canadians were dispossessed cannot be thought of as a form of "expropriation." First, the development of the policy itself was clearly distinctive, as detailed above, shaped by the fiduciary relationship of the Custodian to owners. The subsequent shift toward dispossession also had a distinctive logic. Second, the clearly racialized character of the policy, the lack of any clear public good, and the territorialized manner in which it was exercised marks it as distinctive. As is evident here, the experience of owners, who were not only dispossessed but also uprooted and interned, cannot easily be compared to that of the disgruntled owner experiencing eminent domain.

100 Becher, *Private Property and Public Power*, 225.

101 Stanger-Ross and Landscapes of Injustice, "Suspect Properties."

102 Becher, *Private Property and Public Power*, 230–1.

103 Ndabe Ziqubu, "What do Claimants Get Out of Restitution?," AFRA *News* 61 (December 2006), 8–11, quoted in Smit, *The Property Rights of Refugees and Internally Displaced People*, 193.

104 For the former perspective, see CBC *Vancouver Television News*, aired 16 January 2016, available online at http://www.cbc.ca/player/play/2682083326/. For a sense of historical divides over this issue within the Japanese Canadian Community, see Miki, *Redress*.

105 See Pamela Sugiman, "I Can Hear Lois Now: Corrections to My Story of the Internment of Japanese Canadians – 'For the Record,'" in *Oral History off the Record: Toward an Ethnography of Practice*, eds. Anna Sheftel and Stacey Zembrzycki (New York: Palgrave, 2013), 149–67.

106 Chapter 1.

107 Yoneyama, *An Evacuee's Memoir*, 189.

PART TWO

Dispossession Required Sustained Work

CHAPTER 5

The Unfaithful Custodian: Glenn McPherson and the Dispossession of Japanese Canadians

Jordan Stanger-Ross, Will Archibald, and the Landscapes of Injustice Research Collective

The individual most directly responsible for the forced sale of Japanese Canadian–owned property was Glenn Willoughby McPherson, the executive assistant to the Custodian of Enemy Property. McPherson, like many in the wartime federal bureaucracy, was young, only thirty-two years of age in 1943, when the Canadian government authorized the forced sales.[1] Despite his relative youth, he had experienced a rapid ascendancy through the ranks of the Canadian bureaucracy and in the fall of 1942 emerged as a powerful advocate of forced sales.[2] His memos on the topic circulated to the highest reaches of the federal government, including to the cabinet ministers who made the final decision. He attended the meeting in which ministers resolved to dispose of all of the assets of Japanese Canadians. McPherson was then given the responsibility of writing the first draft of the order in council, quite literally serving as the author of the "liquidation order." Once it passed, McPherson oversaw its implementation and, for the rest of his life, continued to defend the policy.[3] McPherson was not an unknowing cog in the inscrutable gears of state power: he was an important Canadian policy maker. Yet he is a virtually unknown historical figure.

Many accounts of the dispossession have overlooked McPherson because they have focused on political actors, most notably Prime Minister King, cabinet minister Ian Mackenzie, and vocal British Columbia politicians such as Thomas Reid. McPherson frequently appears by name only in footnotes, his correspondence mined for evidence of a faceless malevolent state or the agendas of his political masters. Roy Miki is perhaps the only scholar to have apportioned significant responsibility to McPherson, identifying him in passing as "likely the one most responsible for Order-in-Council [P.C. 1943-469]."[4] Yet most scholars have followed Ann Sunahara in describing the policy as "an accomplishment of Ian Mackenzie," for who the forced sales were key to a larger campaign "to obliterate what he called the Japanese menace."[5] The dispossession thus epitomized the larger "politics of racism" documented in Sunahara's book; forced sales were, for figures like Mackenzie, the culmination of decades of public and politically opportunist racism.

Sunahara and the scholars who have followed this interpretation have good reason. In the decades prior to the forced sale of Japanese Canadian–owned property, racist legal structures and social practices in Canada discriminated in immigration and employment, segregated schools and neighbourhoods, restricted the right to vote, encouraged rioting in Vancouver in 1907, and, most immediately, enabled the uprooting of the Japanese Canadian population.[6] Key federal politicians absorbed and espoused racist caricatures and failed Japanese Canadians.

In 1940s Canada, however, bureaucrats had enormous power.[7] People like McPherson determined the fates of ordinary Canadians, particularly when it came to matters like the property of Japanese Canadians, which were not priorities for most political leaders. Roy Miki has argued that government staff, "translate[d] the inherent racism" of Canadian policies "into the language of bureaucratic efficiency."[8] But bureaucrats did far more than craft euphemisms. Under the authority of the War Measures Act, the federal cabinet had the power to pass law without parliamentary review. The sheer number of regulations, however, made it impossible for the twenty-one politicians who comprised the cabinet to scrutinize all of them.[9] Issued on 19 January 1943, the authorization to dispossess Japanese Canadians was the 469th order in council to pass that year, so the clerk of the Privy Council had signed into law an average of more than thirty-six orders per weekday since the start of January.[10] This work was accomplished in batches: the report to council that included P.C. 469 comprised 165 separate laws. While the dispossession order was only three pages, many others were longer (for example, the 1,665th order in council of 1942, passed 4 March, took eight pages to specify the administrative mechanisms of the uprooting and internment).[11] With tens of thousands of orders passed during the war, cabinet ministers could hardly be expected to read them all, much less assess them with care. This made bureaucratic labour crucial to the operation of the wartime state. Officials like McPherson steered policy, wrote laws, and oversaw their implementation. To understand the dispossession of Japanese Canadians, and to make its author answerable, at least to historical scrutiny, we must draw back the curtain of the state to reveal his role.

When McPherson has come (fleetingly) into the account of the policy, he has been portrayed as an embodiment of larger structures of racism.[12] Closer attention reveals McPherson as a more complicated figure. He shared the views of many of his contemporaries, imagining innate racial differences that he tied closely to loyalty. But he was no politician. His career was not one of public race baiting, but rather of quiet bureaucratic activity, of solving the practical problems of statecraft in expeditious, economical, and legally defensible ways. In Second World War Canada, McPherson was the bureaucratic expert on so-called enemy property, redirecting government policy in this area even before he became embroiled in Canada's mishandling of Japanese Canadian–owned assets.

Troublingly, McPherson was also an intelligence agent, working during the war to collect information for the British Security Coordination, an apparatus based out of New York and tasked with protecting British interests in the Western Hemisphere.[13] With the approval of the undersecretary of state, Ephraim H. Coleman, McPherson merged this work with his responsibility for the property of Japanese Canadians, reporting to Stephenson the security situation on Canada's West Coast. In this role, he authored secret and unsubstantiated claims against Japanese Canadians, both collectively and individually, arguing that they were indisposed, as a matter of racial character, to remain loyal to Canada. Entrusted to protect the property of Japanese Canadians, McPherson was damningly compromised in this task.

In the pages that follow, we situate these entanglements in the context of McPherson's personal and professional background, using previously untapped archives to understand the author of the dispossession of Japanese Canadians. Our reading of this record has convinced us that, as an individual, McPherson mattered. Few, in his place, might have halted the forced sale of property, which had powerful political support outside of his office. But McPherson, of his own initiative, developed the logics to justify the forced sales, wrote the policy into law, and installed the administrative processes of sale. McPherson acted as an unfaithful Custodian: his intelligence activities against Japanese Canadians compromised his task of protecting their property. No Japanese Canadian, knowing his dual role, would have entrusted property to him. Nonetheless, we argue that the politics of racism only partially explains the policy that he devised and that analysis painting him as a simple agent of ideology substitutes a one-dimensional caricature in place of a complex reality. The practical problems of governance in a context of legal accountability shaped McPherson's handling of property. The forced sales emerged, in part, from the challenges of property management that followed from the uprooting of Japanese Canadians. McPherson attempted to solve these problems (and to advance a white supremacist agenda – this is not a case of either but rather of both) in compliance with law, even when this position brought him into conflict with other officials seeking to benefit from the maltreatment of Japanese Canadians. Drawing McPherson into focus, we have found the policy both easier and harder to understand: easier because the records of his life and work detail the process by which this consequential policy emerged within the wider context of the internment but harder because, unlike political actors whose animosity toward Japanese Canadians in this era was often plain and public, McPherson's motives are more obscure, his actions more secretive.

Born 29 April 1910 in Portage La Prairie, Manitoba, Glenn McPherson was the third son of Ewan McPherson, lawyer and eventual chief justice of Manitoba, and his wife Winnie. Blessed with a privileged childhood, his path was eased by the elder McPherson's eminence and robust political networks. As the younger McPherson was graduating from Portage Collegiate in 1927 and boasting a Governor General's medal for academic excellence, his father was serving a term on the Liberal backbenches in Ottawa, having defeated former Prime Minister Arthur Meighan for the Portage La Prairie seat in 1926.[14] McPherson seemed destined to follow in his father's footsteps as he commenced law school at the University of Manitoba in 1929.[15]

Figure 5.1 Glenn McPherson (with pipe) pictured in 1942 with Under Secretary of State Ephraim Coleman (with cigarette), to whom he reported directly in the 1930s and 1940s. Frank Delaute (phone) was not involved in the forced sale of Japanese Canadian–owned property.

During his training, Glenn McPherson sought out connections that would sustain a successful career. Even as his father (along with many in the Liberal government) was defeated in the 1930 election, McPherson joined and became the secretary of the Young Liberal organization at his university. He became friends with Young Liberal branch president and aspiring barrister Osbourne "Ozzie" Sorflaten. He also caught the eye of the dean of the law school, Ephraim Herbert Coleman, a future undersecretary of state, perhaps in no small part due to Ewan McPherson's 1932 appointment as provincial treasurer in John Bracken's Liberal-Progressive cabinet. In 1935, Glenn McPherson graduated, passed the bar, and began a promising legal career.[16]

There is no evidence that McPherson aspired in this period to a role in federal politics or policy. Instead, his attention was occupied by the routine personal and professional aspirations of a privileged young man. In September of 1936 he proposed to his girlfriend of three years, Peggy McQuarrie, a stenographer with the Canadian Pacific Railway.[17] His legal practice was flourishing as well, and he relished the opportunity to battle his university friend and colleague Ozzie from opposing sides of the courtroom. Only twenty-six, McPherson was established in Winnipeg with a promising career and a tightly knit group of friends. Yet, less than a year later, this young, newly engaged lawyer from Portage La Prairie found his life irrevocably changed.[18]

"Two Winnipeg Citizens, Hurt in US Mishap, Die: O.M. Sorflaten and Peggy McQuarrie Succumb to Injuries from Highway Crash,"[19] read the headline on a 2 September 1937 article in the *Winnipeg Evening Tribune*. A catastrophic car accident four days earlier near Hoople, North Dakota, had fatally injured both McPherson's best friend and his fiancée. McPherson, a passenger in the vehicle, reportedly "escaped with cuts on the face and sprained muscles in the neck and back."[20] Although he walked away from the scene of the accident, its emotional impact was profound. "I wanted to get away from everything that would remind me of Peggy and … Ozzie," he recalled over forty years later, but "everything reminded me of the accident."[21]

Slipping into a deep malaise, McPherson withdrew from family and work, his former life now insufferable. What happened next was, in McPherson's words, "almost a miracle"; an opportunity arose for him to start anew.[22] A few months after the accident, in November 1937, McPherson's father had been rewarded for decades of political service and loyalty to the Liberal party when Prime Minister Mackenzie King appointed him chief justice of the court of King's Bench in Manitoba.[23] Ephraim Coleman, meanwhile, had left the University of Manitoba in 1933 to take up a post as the federal undersecretary of state. Learning of the horrific car accident and the toll it had taken on the younger McPherson, Coleman phoned the newly minted chief justice with a proposal: his son would come to Ottawa for six months, escape daily reminders of the tragedy, and use his legal training to help resolve a decades-old bureaucratic quagmire in the Office of the Custodian of Enemy Property.[24]

The Office of the Custodian of Enemy Property had been established by the Canadian government after the First World War to deal with property owned by nationals of enemy and occupied countries.[25] Working under Coleman's supervision as the counsel for the Custodian of Enemy Property, McPherson cut all contact with his old life, moved to Ottawa, and threw himself into his work.[26] His job, as outlined by the secretary of state, was to resolve all remaining disputed claims and close the Office of the Custodian in only six months.[27] The Canadian government's seizure of property designated as belonging to "enemies" during the war had left behind a towering mound of claims, as the Custodian was unable, in many cases, to prove that the property had actually been "enemy-owned."[28] The staff of the Custodian had, for eighteen years, attempted to close disputed claims remotely – the sluggish ebb and flow of investigating and negotiating by mail led to large swaths of paper and very little practical result.[29] McPherson's hiring was precipitated by the Amsterdam Stock Exchange's ban on trading Canadian bonds and securities, which followed from claims that Canada had unfairly seized CPR shares belonging to Dutch citizens during World War I.[30] With the snail's pace of the Custodian's business now affecting Canada's stature on the worldwide financial stage, there was an urgent need to accelerate the resolution of claims.

Through his investigations into disputed ownership and international treaties, McPherson was immersed into a particular conception of ownership and property and became an expert on the intricate regulations governing the Office of the Custodian. Alone in Ottawa, still under the shadow of the car accident that brought him there, McPherson eschewed most interpersonal relationships, spending nearly all of his waking hours absorbed in his work. Solving the complex puzzle of the Custodian's leftover business, he later recalled, became his escape from his own past.[31] As the enormous scope of the task at hand came into focus, McPherson's initial six-month appointment was extended indefinitely.

During his early years with the Custodian, McPherson had one constant in his life – Ephraim Coleman, "a man of few words who would sit and smoke and read and never speak to you."[32] A silent, stoic travelling companion, Coleman was guarded, a perfectionist, and a workaholic – qualities that resonated deeply with McPherson as he sought mentorship for a new chapter of his life. With the urgency for swift resolution of Canadian entanglements heightened by the escalation of tension in Europe, McPherson spent much of 1938 and 1939 alongside Coleman on the continent.[33] For much of those two years, Coleman and McPherson travelled around Europe, visiting various stock exchanges and negotiating the settlement of old cases in person. Meanwhile, the storm clouds over Europe suggested that new files would soon be opened.

As Canada's entry into the war drew closer in the summer of 1939, federal officials prepared to designate new groups of "enemy aliens," renewing the importance of the Office of Custodian. In this context, McPherson's detailed knowledge of the inner workings of the office became a vital asset. Working around the clock, he spent much of August 1939 drafting new Trading with the Enemy Regulations, leaving a pronounced mark upon the new legislation.[34] In reviewing the work of the Custodian during the First World War, McPherson "had found that the great weakness of the Canadian position was that we had to make a … case that any vesting orders we applied for were based on some fact that would indicate an enemy interest."[35] He "felt that this was wrong, that in wartime the whole English rule that you are innocent until proven guilty should be waived."[36] Despite acknowledging that "this was a real departure from British jurisprudence" and that "some of the Cabinet would probably object," McPherson added a clause that automatically vested all "German owned assets in Canada" upon the declaration of war.[37] A separate provision in the regulations, also inked by McPherson, shifted the burden of proof with respect to enemy interest to the accused rather than the accuser – if the Custodian determined assets to be enemy-owned, the burden fell to the owner to prove otherwise.[38] In the following year, he travelled across Canada building the capacity to implement the new policies, establishing partnerships in major cities and educating various chartered accounting firms as to the precise regulations and powers of the Custodian. Also responsible for locating German assets at home and abroad, as well as the imposition of blacklists and contraband control measures, McPherson made numerous trips in the first years of the war to a branch office of the Ministry of Economic Warfare located in the British Embassy in New York.[39]

"Fighting the economic war," as McPherson put it, was not the only thing that occupied his attention; he had a second, far more secretive role in the war effort.[40] In 1940, while working for the Custodian, he was called into a meeting with Coleman and "Mr Coit" – a representative of William Stephenson's British Security Coordination. With Coleman's blessing, McPherson began to perform odd jobs for Stephenson's organization, leveraging the privileged information and connections of his position with the Custodian to provide British agents with easy access to foreign currency, equipment, and sensitive data about "enemy" companies.[41] His involvement with the British Security Coordination steadily increased over time, and in September 1941 Coleman loaned McPherson to Stephenson on a semipermanent basis. In New York, McPherson found himself working as a kind of "personal assistant" to Stephenson, serving as a recruiter for "trustworthy" agents and administrators and continuing his work investigating "enemy" company interests.[42] Stephenson trusted McPherson so much that, for the duration of the war, he granted him power of attorney in the case of death or incapacitation and named him the executor of his will.[43]

In the aftermath of the Japanese attack on Pearl Harbor, McPherson's dual roles – as an officer of the Custodian of Enemy Property and an agent of the British Security Coordination – intersected with the fate of Japanese Canadians. The British Security Coordination's intelligence assets on Canada's West Coast were meagre at best, and Stephenson decided to deploy a trusted agent.[44] Meanwhile, the responsibilities of the Office of the Custodian in British Columbia increased exponentially with the outbreak of the war in the Pacific. McPherson was chosen for both tasks.

The fate of Japanese Canadians had not yet been decided, but it was clear that the Custodian would have an important role to play in Vancouver. The declaration of war against Japan suddenly transmuted large amounts of previously "neutral" assets into "enemy" holdings.[45] McPherson spent much of December 1941 setting up the groundwork for the Vancouver Office of the Custodian, reporting daily to Coleman about his "official" activities.[46] During this period, the Office of the Custodian devoted itself exclusively to the control and management of "enemy property," that is the property of "all persons regardless of their nationality who reside in enemy or enemy occupied territory" as well as the property of "all persons who are detained under the Defense of Canada regulations."[47] Very little Japanese Canadian–owned property fit this description. As McPherson publicly announced on 12 December 1941, the activities of the Custodian did "not affect the property of persons of the Japanese Race who are conducting themselves in a proper manner and who have not been detained."[48]

At the outset, the Custodian remained primarily an agency of international affairs, not domestic control. As McPherson oversaw this process, he continued his clandestine intelligence work.

Judging from what he reported to Coleman, McPherson's dossier for Stephenson would have painted a threatening picture of the coast. "Police Intelligence are grossly understaffed," he wrote on 18 December 1941, a criticism of the RCMP's handling of Japanese Canadians that he would later repeat many times over.[49] He offered "my own opinion ... that ... the Japanese have developed a high inferiority complex and realize, even those Canadian born, that the only way the Yellow Race can obtain their place in the Sun is by winning the war."[50] In the case of an invasion by Japan, "we [would] find hundreds of the Japanese, regardless of the nationality helping the invader – as I would do myself in Japan."[51] Predicting the uprooting of Japanese Canadians, he envisioned that political support for internment might be motivated by "the influential packers, and by letters to the Press demanding action."[52] On 19 December, he provocatively invoked the idea of a deeply ingrained racially derived spirituality, stating that "the Japanese are basically religious fanatics and their fanaticism interferes with their loyalty if there is a conflict with the Mikado."[53] Despite such rhetoric, McPherson nonetheless saw himself as a rational, moderate party in an otherwise emotionally charged context. Tellingly, he reported his admiration for an informant he saw as providing a "balanced" perspective – Mr Sydney Rosenberg, who knew "something of the danger in intolerance and generalization of a race of people."[54] Rosenberg did "not talk like the representatives of the other packers who would cut the Jap's throats to further their own business," although he did assert that "the Japanese in this Province constitute a dangerous menace."[55]

The internment of Japanese Canadians soon commenced. In early 1942, cabinet undertook the uprooting of Japanese Canadians. Order in Council 1486 of 24 February authorized the federal government to require "any or all persons" to leave coastal British Columbia. Eight days later, Order in Council 1665 created the British Columbia Security Commission, entrusted to apply this power to "all persons of the Japanese race."[56] Forced to leave coastal British Columbia, Japanese Canadians were able to take only tokens of their materials lives with them: homes, farms, businesses, fishing vessels, automobiles, and the great bulk of their personal belongings were left behind, entrusted to the protection of McPherson, in his capacity with the Custodian of Enemy Property.

The responsibility to protect and preserve the property of more than twenty thousand people, most of them Canadian, brought novel and awkward challenges to an agency created to manage the assets of a small number of "enemy aliens."[57] Its resources were rapidly overwhelmed, and officials scrambled to devise a strategy and to hire staff to deal with a range of difficulties: ascertaining the extent of the property vested in them, assessing the condition and value of that property, establishing title,

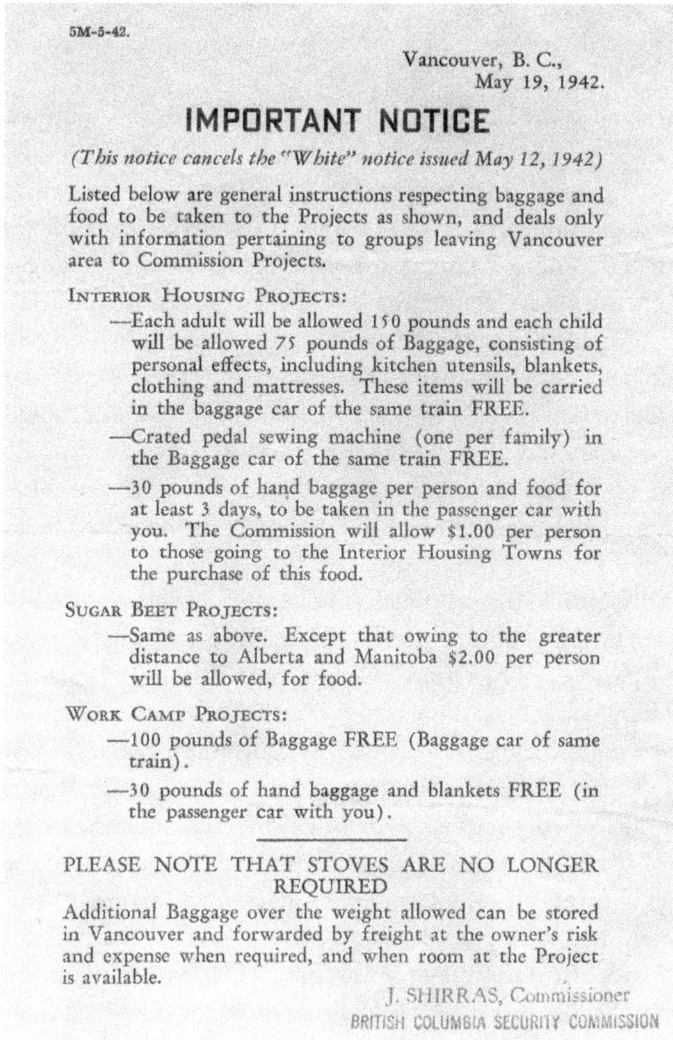
5M-5-42.

Vancouver, B. C.,
May 19, 1942.

IMPORTANT NOTICE

(This notice cancels the "White" notice issued May 12, 1942)

Listed below are general instructions respecting baggage and food to be taken to the Projects as shown, and deals only with information pertaining to groups leaving Vancouver area to Commission Projects.

INTERIOR HOUSING PROJECTS:

—Each adult will be allowed 150 pounds and each child will be allowed 75 pounds of Baggage, consisting of personal effects, including kitchen utensils, blankets, clothing and mattresses. These items will be carried in the baggage car of the same train FREE.

—Crated pedal sewing machine (one per family) in the Baggage car of the same train FREE.

—30 pounds of hand baggage per person and food for at least 3 days, to be taken in the passenger car with you. The Commission will allow $1.00 per person to those going to the Interior Housing Towns for the purchase of this food.

SUGAR BEET PROJECTS:

—Same as above. Except that owing to the greater distance to Alberta and Manitoba $2.00 per person will be allowed, for food.

WORK CAMP PROJECTS:

—100 pounds of Baggage FREE (Baggage car of same train).

—30 pounds of hand baggage and blankets FREE (in the passenger car with you).

PLEASE NOTE THAT STOVES ARE NO LONGER REQUIRED

Additional Baggage over the weight allowed can be stored in Vancouver and forwarded by freight at the owner's risk and expense when required, and when room at the Project is available.

J. SHIRRAS, Commissioner
BRITISH COLUMBIA SECURITY COMMISSION

Figure 5.2 Strict limits on the goods that Japanese Canadians could carry to internment ensured that they would be forced to leave much behind.

maintaining insurance, paying miscellaneous expenses, and translating and typing communications with Japanese Canadian property owners. Even as they came to grips with the range of the property in their hands, officials were inundated by over ten thousand claims by creditors against that property. As one official remarked, "before there was any organization set up to handle it the work had already begun."[58]

Coleman enlisted McPherson to oversee the Vancouver Office of the Custodian and to ensure it could meet these considerable administrative challenges.[59] McPherson agreed to work full time for the Custodian, while continuing to provide information and support to the British Security Coordination where possible. Acting as both a mid-level bureaucrat and intelligence agent, McPherson took a central part in the trusteeship and later forced sale of Japanese Canadian–owned property.[60] As the Custodian's authorized deputy, McPherson was the effective head of the Vancouver office for the next year. Responsible for "all question[s] of policy,"[61] he was given control of the funds of the Vancouver office and acted as the Custodian's liaison with the British Columbia Security Commission.[62]

In the first months after the uprooting, McPherson established structures that were equipped to preserve most of the property of Japanese Canadians. The policies of the Custodian distinguished "enemy" Japanese Canadians from so-called evacuees.[63] The category of "enemies" was defined narrowly, including only property owners residing in Japan or Japanese-occupied territory, as well as those who had been incarcerated under the Defence of Canada Regulations; in total, these comprised less than 10 per cent of the Custodian's property files.[64] The vast majority of uprooted Japanese Canadians were categorized as "evacuees," individuals forced away from the coast merely because they were "of the Japanese race."[65] The large majority of these were Canadian-born or naturalized subjects, and the Custodian distinguished them from "enemies."

Accordingly, McPherson established two administrative "sections": one for "enemy" property and the other for the property of "evacuees." The "evacuee" section organized to manage and maintain property. Earnings from "evacuee" properties, derived in the first months after the uprooting for the most part from rents collected on real estate, were credited to individual Japanese Canadian owners, whereas funds realized from "enemy" properties were to be part of diplomatic negotiations at the cessation of hostilities. Further, "the cost of the work of the Evacuation Section, by reason of the wording of the order-in-council," was not charged against the property, in contrast to the costs of administering "enemy" property. Thus, under McPherson's direction in 1942, "evacuee" property was positioned to be preserved and managed rather than sold. It had its own administrative processes, and the expenses incurred in its guardianship by public officials (though not those owed to private firms hired for property management) were to be paid from government coffers.[66]

Even in these first months of the uprooting, however, McPherson also began sales without the consent of so-called evacuee owners. From the outset of the uprooting, the Custodian sold anything classed as "perishable"; assets such as grocery stock were sold without consultation with Japanese Canadian owners, on the assumption that this course of action served their interests, and the funds were credited to accounts held with the Custodian.[67] Outside of McPherson's purview, a similar logic was applied to fishing vessels owned by Japanese Canadians, when the committee entrusted to oversee the vessels concluded that the federal government could not maintain them in sites of impoundment without the vessels suffering significant damages.[68] McPherson applied the same argument when he spearheaded the forced sale of Japanese Canadian–owned automobiles in the summer of 1942, arguing that the deteriorating condition and value of the cars sitting unused in government lots left no other option.[69] Eventually, in the fall and winter of 1942, McPherson would argue that all Japanese Canadian–owned assets were perishable, including real estate, and his arguments to this effect would steer policy toward the forced sale of everything that Japanese Canadians had been compelled to leave behind. But in the spring and summer of 1942, the logic of perishability was applied selectively and the offices of the Custodian organized to preserve the rest.

Meanwhile, McPherson continued to investigate Japanese Canadians and to promulgate doubt of their loyalty to Canada. While only a small selection of his confidential correspondence is accessible in the archives today, McPherson the secret agent reads very differently from the bureaucrat who crafted the logic of perishability to justify forced sales. His tone shifts markedly from his carefully guarded language as deputy Custodian, referring to the British Columbia Security Commission's handling of the uprooting as a "farce" and making copious reference to "Japs" and "henchmen."[70] His confidential letters take on an almost pulpy quality, as if he were playing out his own personal spy drama. Dripping with suspicion and distrusting the RCMP's handling of what he saw as a credible threat from Japanese Canadians, McPherson informed Stephenson in the spring of 1942 that he was "convinced that [British Columbia] is full of fifth columnists who could be split wide open if a proper intelligence system were established."[71] In McPherson's view, "the Mikado was controlling Powell Street [the largest Japanese Canadian neighbourhood in Vancouver] right up to the time they left."[72] McPherson submitted dossiers and memoranda to the Security Coordination casting aspersions toward prominent Japanese Canadian businessmen such as Charles (Chosuke) Nakamura and Eikichi Kagetsu. In a January 1942 memorandum, written before the Canadian government made the decision to uproot and incarcerate Japanese Canadians, McPherson lamented to his masters that "it doesn't appear that we can get the RCMP to do anything about Kagetsu."[73] He made similar complaints about Nakamura.[74] As the Custodian took control of all Japanese Canadian–owned property, records evidence slippage between McPherson's roles as bureaucrat and intelligence agent. Indeed, in a 19 May 1942 memorandum to the British Security Coordination, McPherson proudly reported that he had wielded his position and authority as the deputy Custodian to block Kagetsu's petition for the release of his cars, which Kagetsu had hoped to use to inspect his significant timber holdings, imperilled by the government take over. "After getting the letter" proposing that Kagetsu make this trip, "I called the Secretary of the Commission and began by saying I presumed the man [Kagetsu] was crazy, putting the Secretary on the spot, he having to say he was and there was nothing in it."[75]

In June 1942, the British Security Coordination submitted a 161-page anonymously authored report to the RCMP, launching provocative accusations of disloyalty and sedition at numerous prominent members of the Japanese Canadian community.[76] With only a skeleton apparatus of agents in Canada, this report must have drawn heavily from McPherson as Stephenson's primary man on the ground. Entries on individual Japanese Canadians such as Kagetsu, Nakamura, Teigo Noritake, and Etsuji

Morii closely match McPherson's surviving intelligence memoranda. The report also contains numerous references to debts owed and property owned, information McPherson would have had close at hand in his day job. The report identified thirty-five "Class A" suspects to be "arrested immediately and simultaneously" and "interrogated individually by those acquainted with the Japanese mentality."[77] According to the report, "in view of the multifarious ramifications of the Japanese network, information of vital importance to the whole defence of the Western Hemisphere may be forthcoming."[78] It also described 173 "Class B" suspects and seventy-four "Class C" suspects deemed dangerous to public safety, accusing people such as school principal Sadayoshi Aoki of thinking "the Mikado is a Divine Power and should be worshipped,"[79] and claimed that one Japanese Canadian sex worker was "the type of person the Japanese would use as an agent."[80] In *Stories of My People*, Roy Ito evocatively summarizes the tenor of the security report:

> The [British Security Coordination] report leaves one laughing and crying. The British agent must have talked to men like Wilson, Reid, McNeill, and the woolly characters who wrote rambling letters to their favourite anti-Japanese politicians. The tears would be for the disillusionment with the British Intelligence Service long reputed to be directed by thinking men with sound judgement and the bitter realization that most BC citizens perceived the situations as depicted … One wonders who was this "talented" agent sent by Stephenson to British Columbia to assess the Japanese situation.[81]

One wonders indeed.

The impact of the report in shaping state policy is hard to assess – for the RCMP's part, Commissioner S.T. Wood and Pacific Intelligence Section Head J.K. Barnes offered a thinly veiled rebuke on 5 August 1942: "We have had no evidence of espionage or sabotage among the Japanese in British Columbia. The situation has changed considerably since the report was written, and most of these people are now in isolated areas."[82] Hinting at layers of correspondence and conversation absented from the official record, McPherson penned a response to Stephenson on 29 August 1942 stating that "basically the report is correct and the arguments put up by Barnes weaken rather than strengthen his case."[83] Regardless of the British Security Coordination's degree of influence over Canadian national security issues, the report offers a window into the worldview that McPherson brought to his work with the Custodian.

As the summer of 1942 came to a close, McPherson's intelligence work began to spin down. He nevertheless continued to criticize the RCMP. On 29 July, amid rumours of Japanese Canadians returning to the coast and individuals requesting their cars and radios from the Custodian's office, McPherson declared to Stephenson that, "from a standpoint of security the situation is heartbreaking."[84] The stresses of his dual roles

Figure 5.3 In the summer of 1942, McPherson sold Japanese Canadian–owned automobiles on the grounds that they would deteriorate in value over time. That fall, he applied the same argument to everything Japanese Canadians owned.

were taking their toll, as he complained that "my time is taken up completely ... and I have very little time to do this work."[85] On 29 August, he reported on the progress of the uprooting and ruminated on a common rumour regarding the perceived proximity of Japanese Canadian–owned property to points of strategic importance: "as to the Japs being in the important points, before they became important, this is a matter that will require investigation of Land Titles ... I am following this up."[86] Nothing exists in the surviving records to suggest he found anything he could imagine as a smoking gun. By the end of September 1942, the near-complete removal of Japanese Canadians from the coast left little room to imagine an imminent threat to public safety; with McPherson's concerns about security diminished in urgency, his once-divided attention turned wholly to the administration of Japanese Canadian–owned property.

In this period McPherson shifted away from the position of the federal government the previous spring and began to advocate the forced sale of all Japanese Canadian–owned property. By late 1942 he believed that all of it could be classified as perishable. His arguments in this respect synthesized claims coming from three separate precincts. During the summer of 1942, the city government of Vancouver initiated inspections and condemnations of Japanese Canadian–owned real estate that had been vacated by its owners, attempting to demonstrate that their homes, particularly those in the large Japanese Canadian neighbourhood in the East End of the city, were "in a generally run-down condition," and therefore unfit for "human habitation."[87] City officials wanted to see the homes demolished, rather than rented for the duration of the war. Meanwhile, assessors working with the federal Soldier Settlement Board had been authorized to inspect Japanese Canadian–owned farms, with an eye to accommodating returning soldiers on lands from which the owners had been uprooted. In the fall of 1942, the director of that agency echoed claims of Vancouver officials, describing the "great difficulty" of maintaining farms "in reasonable repair and productiveness, due to the scarcity of skilled tenants," a situation that purportedly caused the "inevitable deterioration of Japanese farm properties."[88] Finally, staffers of the Custodian, under McPherson's supervision, reported the "rapid deterioration" of the personal belongings of Japanese Canadians; stored in warehouses, all manner of property was alleged to be losing value due to "dampness and vermin" as well as "the prevalence of theft."[89]

These separate lines of discussion converged in McPherson, who drew them together into a single argument for the forced sale of all of the belongings of Japanese Canadians. In December 1942, he advised Coleman, "it is obvious, both in the city and country, that the Japanese property is going to deteriorate rapidly." The government's policy, he counselled, "should be one of liquidation and this policy should eventually include all chattels that are not required in the Japanese evacuees' new home." McPherson claimed to understand "the danger of such a policy insofar as it might cause dissatisfaction among the evacuees, but the deterioration of real property and the loss of chattels will soon liquidate the capital investment."[90] Coleman repeated such arguments in communication with Norman McLarty, the secretary of state; McPherson's memos also circulated to Thomas A. Crerar, the minister of mines and resources, and Ian Mackenzie.[91] The alleged deterioration of Japanese Canadian–owned real estate was the first agenda item on 11 January 1943, when the ministers, along with McPherson and other key staffers, met to discuss Japanese Canadian–owned property. Writing to a colleague the next day, McPherson reported that, "the decisions of the committee as to policy are far better than I had hoped to obtain."[92] Federal politicians had embraced the logic of perishability, affirming the powers of the Custodian to sell all Japanese Canadian–owned property. McPherson, as the initial advocate of the policy and expert in the intricacies of the Custodian's legal frameworks, was tasked with drafting an amending order in council to authorize the comprehensive forced sale of real and personal property.[93] That draft would become P.C. 469, under which the government executed the wholesale dispossession of Japanese Canadians.

The full record of these events demonstrates that the logic of perishability, as we have called it, should not have been applied to all chattels and real estate. In the context of the war effort, relatively minor federal expenditure would have sufficed to hire full-time security staff and to improve the standards of the warehouses of the personal belongings of Japanese Canadians. Neither measure was taken. It was simply untrue, in early 1944, for federal officials to claim that "every possible precaution" had been taken in "the matter of protection" of chattels.[94] Meanwhile, Japanese Canadian–owned real estate, on the whole, was not deteriorating in the ways described. In Vancouver, city officials condemned only a small minority of Japanese Canadian–owned properties. The vast majority, some 90 per cent, was leased by the start of 1943.[95] Even in the Powell Street neighbourhood, the cash ledgers of the Custodian showed healthy income on Japanese Canadian–owned properties, with rental incomes exceeding costs.[96] Urban real estate could have been maintained. With respect to rural properties, officials of the Soldier Settlement Board conceded in their private communications that high wartime wages encouraged "a general increase in the value of the lands" that, coupled with "speculative" investment, more than offset the alleged "deterioration" of Japanese Canadian–owned farms.[97] Indeed, after the 1943 decision that Japanese Canadian–owned lands would be sold, officials of the Soldier Settlement Board pressed for a transfer of lands to their branch as quickly as possible: if the sale was delayed, worried one official, "I can tell you I do not look forward with any pleasure to the prices that will have to be paid to acquire lands in any volume."[98] Despite McPherson's claims to the contrary, a government faithfully committed to the interests of owners would have held these properties, not sold them.

These records, together with McPherson's role in gathering intelligence on Japanese Canadians at the same time as he was purportedly working in their interest, support Miki's contention that the bureaucracy served to "whitewash" racism.[99] McPherson's communications with the Soldier Settlement Board (SSB), in particular, suggest that he was concealing his true intentions. In the summer of 1942, SSB officials hoped to survey and gain authority over the rural holdings of Japanese Canadians, which they planned to distribute for the benefit of returning soldiers. According to Coleman, McPherson cautioned against revealing these intentions while the uprooting of Japanese Canadians remained incomplete: "While from the from the point of view of the Custodian's Office we have no objection to the proposed policy," he wrote, "McPherson told me that the situation with respect to the evacuation is critical and that any further Orders made at Ottawa and promulgated in British Columbia might have serious repercussions until the process of evacuation is further advanced."[100] This is among the most direct evidence on record that the Custodian's early stance to protect Japanese Canadian–owned property was a ruse, intended to misguide Japanese Canadian owners until their uprooting had been completed in an orderly fashion. In September of 1942, McPherson visited the Vancouver City Council offering similar advice: namely, that their designs on the East End neighbourhood should be "held in abeyance until the evacuation has been completed."[101] Was McPherson nothing more than a racist working to conceal the real motives of Canadian policy? Were the initial promises to protect

Japanese Canadian–owned assets and subsequent claims about the necessity of sales nothing more than deliberate obfuscation?[102]

Surprisingly, McPherson's relations with the SSB, which supply the most damaging perspective on his actions, also provide the strongest evidence that he (and by extension the Custodian) did at times seek to protect the economic interests of Japanese Canadians. McPherson's relations with the SSB were contentious. He clashed with SSB officials primarily over a technical matter – the legitimacy of clauses inserted by some Japanese Canadians into leases of their farms to non-Japanese Canadian tenants – but this disagreement brought to the fore broader conflict over the government's obligations. The controversial clauses obligated tenants to sell their produce to the Pacific Co-operative Union, which was owned in the majority by Japanese Canadian shareholders (largely the farmers themselves). Because of these clauses, Japanese Canadian farmers/shareholders were able to receive cash advances from the co-operative based on the promise of subsequent yields, providing them with essential funds as they responded to the exigencies of their uprooting. The director of the SSB, Gordon Murchison, objected: "It seems to me that we would be going pretty far on behalf of the smooth Japanese if we [enforce leases] … which will force white men to pull the Japanese chestnuts out of the fire."[103] McPherson, however, consistently defended the leases. The board's lead agent in British Columbia, Ivan Barnet, complained that, "Mr McPherson attaches primary importance to the welfare of the Pacific Co-Operative Union rather than the good will of the [white] tenants."[104] "Apparently," Barnet explained to his supervisor in Ottawa, "Mr McPherson thinks that his Department and you are working at cross purposes: in other words, that they are out to get the best they can out of these holdings for the Japanese, and to maintain fruit production, whereas we want the properties for other purposes. I declined to be drawn into an argument of this nature."

McPherson articulated his position in correspondence with Coleman, arguing, "the Custodian, according to the wording of the Order-in-Council, is supposed to protect the Japanese interests." Despite the difficulty facing some tenants, he cautioned, "it does not necessarily follow that the Custodian should wipe out the covenant given by the white tenant to the Japanese owner to deliver his crop to [the Pacific Co-Operative Union]. If the Custodian ignores this covenant … [he] will have no logical answer at a reparation hearing as to why he did change the provisions of the lease to this extent."[105]

McPherson maintained this position in 1943, even after the policy of forced sales had been adopted and rural properties seemed likely to be sold for the purposes of settling soldiers. Speaking to the advisory committee charged with overseeing the disposition of the rural holdings of Japanese Canadians, he advised that "in considering the desirability of adopting a policy of a bulk sale to the Soldier Settlement," members of the committee "should keep in mind the fact that the Custodian as Trustee for the

Japanese evacuees is not primarily concerned with any supposed rights of white people to purchase their land."[106] Such quotes make it difficult to arrive at a simple account of McPherson's intentions and, more broadly, the role of the bureaucracy that he oversaw in the forced sale of property.

There is also evidence to dissociate McPherson's position on property from his views about Japanese Canadians. By 1939, well prior to his involvement in the Japanese Canadian file, McPherson had developed strong, indeed perhaps extreme, views about federal prerogative over property during wartime. His application of these ideas with respect to citizens of Canada reflected his racialized worldview – surely he would not have advocated a similar approach to all Canadians of German descent – but he did arrive at the Vancouver Office of the Custodian already an advocate of unfettered federal power, and this view did not owe its origins to his antipathy for Japanese Canadians.

Further, McPherson explicitly articulated the view that the decision to force the sale of property could not be made on the basis of race. Defining "evacuee" property owners for the advisory committee tasked to review the policy of forced sale before placing Vancouver properties on the market, McPherson emphasized, "The question of whether ... a person is or is not an enemy does not depend on his nationality, but primarily the question of whether or not he is under the control of the enemy such as residing in enemy territory." With the exception of the small minority of Japanese Canadians incarcerated in Ontario, he advised, "it is ... not correct to say that Japanese subjects residing in Canada who have been evacuated from the protected areas ... are enemies." A contrasting hypothetical drove the point home: "it is correct to say that a British subject residing in enemy territory is an enemy."[107] Race, in this view, could not formally govern the handling of property. Rather, the categorization of property owners followed geopolitical lines: owners likely to be under the sway of the Japanese government were "enemies." Other Japanese Canadians could not be deemed "enemies" simply because of their purported racial origin.[108]

It seems likely that McPherson's primary concern, in making such arguments, was the legal position of the government rather than genuine apprehension about the economic interests of Japanese Canadians. Anticipating a postwar "reparation hearing" (which did in fact take place, with the establishment of the Bird Commission in 1947), McPherson crafted an official record of the forced sales that focused on legally defensible rationales. On this reading of the documents, we might say that McPherson sought to obey what historian Tina Loo has called the "rules of legal rhetoric." Within the constraints of legal argumentation, important matters ("larger social, political, and economic" concerns) are often omitted, such that law is, in significant ways, decontextualized.[109] Although racism was an essential context for the dispossession, McPherson left it outside the official discussion of the forced sales. He shared the larger social, political, and economic concerns of figures like Mackenzie, but he believed that such concerns should be excluded from the official, and legally defensible, rationales governing the administration of Japanese Canadian–owned property. Hence, the logic of perishability became critical to the arguments about a policy that was, in fact, motivated by other concerns. These rationales were more than just a veneer to disguise racism (although they were also that): they were arguments that could move state power in a context of legal accountability. The work of people like McPherson was crucial to making unjust state action legal.

Stepping back from McPherson as a bureaucrat, and returning to the young man who fled his home in the wake of a tragic accident, other, more personal, motives for the forced sale of property come into view. According to members of the SSB, McPherson struggled with the task put to him in the summer of 1942. In July, Barnet remarked, "it is apparent that [McPherson] is becoming exhausted. He frankly admits he will have to get away from the problem for a time or go to pieces."[110] In late August, Barnet elaborated: "From [McPherson's] personal appearance it is evident that the load being carried is more than he can stand up under over an extended period. If he is getting out I don't blame him. I know he feels that sooner or later there will be a royal commission appointed to investigate this whole Japanese problem from start to finish."[111]

Barnet reaffirms the impression that McPherson was concerned about legal accountability, linking this observation with his failing personal well-being. Corroboration of this perspective comes from a very different source; McPherson's daughter Marilyn later recalled that in the decades after the war her father talked "a great deal" about his role in Canada's handling of Japanese Canadians. Conveyed in these recollections, too, was the stress of the situation: "It's amazing [his] being 31 years old … when he had all this responsibility and huge job and secretive job and nobody to talk to out here in the sense that he couldn't tell them what he was doing … outside the very small group." Guarding the secret of his work from his father was, according to Marilyn, particularly isolating:

> He was very, very close to his father who was the Chief Justice of Manitoba and he was a lawyer and a judge and his father was very upright and [a] real man of integrity and my dad just loved him, adored him and they talked they had always been able to talk about jobs and what to do now and he was always consulting my grandfather for advice but here he couldn't talk to anyone about it so he agonized over it, you known, the decisions that had to be made.[112]

Still very much a young man scarred by his personal trauma, McPherson had spent the previous half-decade on the move, relocating across North America and spending itinerant years in Europe. He had, for much of two years, served two masters (as bureaucrat and intelligence agent), in roles that were often at cross-purposes. The office of which he was director possessed little experience or capacity to accomplish its job. Isolated and overburdened, McPherson lacked the guidance of a father, judge, and "real man of integrity" who, he anticipated, would see these actions weighed on postwar scales of justice. When McPherson acquiesced to the designs of the SSB and the City of Vancouver, perhaps he had run out of steam. Perhaps he was attracted to the forced sales because, by appointing advisory committees to sell the property and then moving funds from his department to the accounts of the British Columbia Security Commission, McPherson absolved himself of onerous responsibilities.

The second life that McPherson led working for the British Security Coordination sheds further light on the contours of dispossession. Detached from the main office of the Security Coordination, unable to speak of this work to friends and family, McPherson stewed in isolation, fighting what he framed as a lonely crusade to protect British Columbia from a rampant fifth column. The two worlds collided on a regular basis, with McPherson using his position as deputy Custodian to procure information, control access by Japanese Canadians to their property, and advocate for particular security policies. The shift in his language between his custodial role and his intelligence correspondence is telling – a man who emphasized, and even fought for, clear distinctions between "enemy" and "evacuee" property penned screeds about disloyal "Japs" and offered the paranoid whisperings of a handful of informants as fact. There is a strange sense of freedom to how he writes those letters to Stephenson and the Security Coordination, unshackled from a need to put up appearances. Yet the collision between McPherson's overtly racist intelligence reports and his dispassionate justifications for dispossession suggest more than just McPherson crafting a convenient, legally defensible euphemism. His story, and the intertwined story of this policy, points towards a fusion of race, state power, and the law that allows the imagining of property owned by racialized subjects as disposable, unsettling, even threatening to the security of the state.

Despite its troubling (and exceptional) details, our analysis of McPherson converges with longstanding scholarly analyses of modern states. Introducing a collection of classic and recent contributions to the "anthropology of the state," Aradhana Sharma and Akhil Gupta emphasize, as have many others, the legitimacy created by the "*routine* and *repetitive* procedures of the state."[113] McPherson was a key bureaucratic administrator in this respect. By establishing rules and procedures for handling "enemy" property in wartime Canada, offices that filled and filed forms, and standardized assessment and appraisal processes, he routinized state force. Such work is also a matter of representation: the state must convey itself in specific ways to audiences.[114] McPherson sought to communicate the dispossession as both justified and legal. His audiences included Japanese Canadians, other state officials with conflicting interests, the politicians who could sign his designs into law, future courts in which his actions might be judged, and, perhaps, his own father. This final point draws attention to an additional observation: because the state depends upon the ongoing activity of the "people who comprise it," its operation is "not as smooth and inevitable a process as it sometimes appears to be."[115] McPherson's involvement in this history was contingent and problematic. The dispossession resulted from the work of a real person.

Historians should not take for granted the perspectives and motives of figures like McPherson. Considerable work – an article and now a book – has explored the origins and motives of Kishizo Kimura, a Japanese Canadian who participated in the dispossession of his own community.[116] Kimura's actions seem to call forward the topic of where individuals stand in history, of how their experiences and decisions are connected with their origins. We feel compelled to ask, and to ask deeply, how Kimura could serve on government committees that oversaw the forced sale of Japanese Canadian–owned property because he himself was Japanese Canadian. The participation on those same committees by Vancouver City Alderman Charles Jones or Chairman Justice Sidney Smith, or, indeed, McPherson's role in creating such committees (in the spring of 1943) seem, at first glance, to raise fewer questions because of where they came from. This imbalance is in some respects justified: none were as affected by this history as Japanese Canadians, and the larger story of which this is a part cannot be told without careful consideration of their perspectives. And yet, this imbalance is also an extension of a history of racism and inequality. The reification of categories of origin into assumptions about thought and behaviour was a root cause of the dispossession. McPherson is far more culpable for the dispossession of Japanese Canadians than Kimura and should be held to account just as much as he. His participation in the forced sale of property, if more likely, was no more inevitable than Kimura's. McPherson's story, too, offers important lessons on the complex intersection of origins with circumstances and with choice.

NOTES

A previous version of this chapter appeared under the same title in the *Journal of American Ethnic History* 37, no. 4 (2018).

1 Undated transcript, file 7-09: "Draft manuscripts, British Columbia Railway annual report," box 7, McPherson Fonds, UBC RBSC (hereafter McPherson transcript). The interview transcripts in this collection are not always dated, sometimes have been cut into multiple pieces, and do not include any of the questions or prompts used. The "McPherson transcript" is not dated, but the tapes appear to have been recorded around 1980 as McPherson refers to the fall of Joe Clark's minority government as a recent event. On the ages of key bureaucrats in this era, see J.L. Granatstein, *The Ottawa Men: The Civil Service Mandarins, 1935–1957* (Toronto: Oxford University Press, 1982).

2 McPherson transcript, RBSC.

3 "Japanese Canadians Suffered Loss of Freedom and Property during WWII Internment," *The Fifth Estate*, 15 October 1985, Canadian Broadcasting Corporation. Available online at the CBC Digital Archives.

4 Roy Miki, *Redress: Inside the Japanese Canadian Call for Justice* (Vancouver: Raincoast Books, 2004), 143. Miki incorrectly refers to the order in council as "PC 465."

5 Ann Gomer Sunahara, *The Politics of Racism: The Uprooting of Japanese Canadians during the Second World War* (Toronto: James Lorimer, 1981), 101.

6 Introduction and chapter 2.

7 Granatstein, *The Ottawa Men*. Within the scholarship on the internment of Japanese Canadians, Granatstein is best known for his defence of the internment. While we oppose his perspective on that topic, his important analysis of the Canadian civil service "Mandarins" of the midcentury points to their influence and shares much (in its biographical approach) with our treatment of McPherson.

8 Miki, *Redress*, 51.

9 Government of Canada, Privy Council Office Guide to Canadian Ministries, 16th Ministry, http://www.pco-bcp.gc.ca/mgm/dtail.asp?lang=eng&mstyid=16&mbtpid=1.

10 This calculation includes Friday, 1 January 1943 as a workday.

11 PC 1942-1665, March 4,1942, file 2516G, vol. 1750, RG2-A-1-a, LAC.

12 See, for example Sunahara, *The Politics of Racism*, 91–3.

13 Bill Macdonald, *The True Intrepid: Sir William Stephenson and the Unknown Agents* (Vancouver: Raincoast Books, 2001); H. Montgomery Hyde, *The Quiet Canadian: The Secret Service Story of Sir William Stephenson* (1962; London: Constable, 1989); William Samuel Stephenson, *British Security Coordination: The Secret History of British Intelligence in the Americas, 1940-1945* (New York: Fromm International, 1999).

14 Glenn McPherson, interview by Kay Alsop, undated transcript, file 5-5: "Outlines, draft manuscripts, newspaper clippings, notes, interviews, 1943–1945, 1993–1998," box 5, McPherson Fonds, RBSC (hereafter Alsop Papers, file 5-05).

15 McPherson transcript, RBSC.

16 Ibid.

17 "Two Winnipeg Citizens, Hurt in US Mishap, Die: O.M. Sorflaten and Peggy McQuarrie Succumb to Injuries from Highway Crash," *Winnipeg Evening Tribune*, 2 September 1937, 3.

18 McPherson transcript, RBSC.

19 "Two Winnipeg Citizens, Hurt in US Mishap, Die."

20 Ibid.

21 McPherson transcript, RBSC.

22 Ibid.

23 Dale Brawn, *The Court of Queen's Bench of Manitoba, 1870–1950: A Biographical History* (Toronto: University of Toronto Press, 2006), 309.

24 Glenn McPherson, interview by Kay Alsop, telephone transcript, 3 October 1994, Alsop Papers, file 5-05, RBSC; Glenn McPherson, interview by Kay Alsop, undated transcript, Alsop Papers, file 5-05, RBSC.

25 Judith Roberts-Moore, "The Office of the Custodian of Enemy Property: An Overview of the Office and Its Records, 1920–1952," *Archivaria* 22 (1986): 95–106.

26 Glenn McPherson, interview by Kay Alsop, undated transcript, Alsop Papers, file 5-05, RBSC.

27 Glenn McPherson, interview by Kay Alsop, transcript, 27 September 1994, Alsop Papers, file 5-05, RBSC.

28 Glenn McPherson, interview by Kay Alsop, transcript, undated, Alsop Papers, file 5-05.

29 Ibid.

30 Ibid.

31 Glenn McPherson, interview by Kay Alsop, transcript, 27 September 1994, Alsop Papers, file 5-05.

32 Untitled manuscript, file 7-10: "Draft manuscript," box 7, McPherson Fonds, RBSC.

33 Undated interview, file 5-5, McPherson Fonds, RBSC; Interview with McPherson, 3 October 1994, file 5-5 McPherson Fonds, RBSC.

34 Untitled manuscript, file 7-10: "Draft manuscript," box 7, McPherson Fonds, RBSC.

35 Ibid.

36 Ibid.

37 Ibid.

38 Ibid.

39 Ibid.; Glenn McPherson, interview by Kay Alsop, transcript, October 1994, file 6-07: "Interviews, newspaper clippings," box 6, McPherson Fonds, RBSC; Glenn McPherson, interview by Kay Alsop, transcript, 18 May 1994, file 6-06: "Correspondence, newspaper clippings, notes, drafts, memorandums, interviews," box 6, McPherson Fonds, RBSC.

40 Untitled manuscript, file 7-10: "Draft manuscript," box 7, McPherson Fonds, RBSC.

41 Ibid; Glenn McPherson, interview by Kay Alsop, transcript, undated, Alsop Papers, file 5-05.

42 Letter to Glenn McPherson from William Stephenson, 8 May 1945, file 1-04: "War Years 1937–1948," box 1, McPherson Fonds, RBSC; Untitled manuscript, file 7-10: "Draft manuscript," box 7, McPherson Fonds, RBSC.

43 File 3-2: "Correspondence, memorandums, newspaper clippings, 1941–1948, 1984–1994," box 3, McPherson Fonds, RBSC.

44 On British Security Coordination activities in Canada, see also file: "Report on Japanese Activities in British Columbia," vol. 3569, RG 18, LAC.

45 Untitled manuscript, file 7-10: "Draft manuscript," box 7, McPherson Fonds, RBSC.

46 Memoranda from 10 December 1941 to 20 December 1941, file 16: "Communications," vol. 2, RG 117, LAC.

47 *Consolidated Regulations Respecting Trading with the Enemy* (1939), s. 24, file 1948G-1953G, vol. 1653, RG 2, LAC.

48 Notice, newspaper clipping, 12 December 1941, file 10, vol. 1, LAC.

49 Memorandum Re Japanese, 18 December 1941, file 16: "Communications," vol. 2, RG 117, LAC.

50 Ibid.

51 Ibid.

52 Ibid.

53 Memorandum Re Japanese, 19 December 1941, file 16: "Communications," vol. 2, RG 117, LAC.

54 Ibid.

55 Ibid.

56 PC 1942-1486, 24 February 1942, the Canada Gazette, vol. 75, no. 212 (Ottawa: King's Printer, 27 February 1942); PC 1942-1665, March 4, 1942, file 2516G, vol. 1750, RG 2-A-1-a, LAC.

57 Report to the Under Secretary of State Regarding the Japanese Evacuation Section of the Office of the Custodian at Vancouver, BC, 26 June 1942, vol. 2, RG 117, LAC.

58 Ibid. See also Report to McLarty by Shears, 28 January 1944, file 16, vol. 2, RG 117, LAC.

59 Report to the Under Secretary of State Regarding the Japanese Evacuation Section of the Office of the Custodian at Vancouver, BC, 26 June 1942, vol. 2, RG 117, LAC.

60 Letter to Glenn McPherson from William Stephenson, 8 May 1945, file 1-04: "War Years 1937–1948," box 1, McPherson Fonds, RBSC.
61 Memorandum Re Japanese Section, January 1942, file 10, vol. 1, RG 117, LAC.
62 Ibid.
63 Patricia Roy, *The Triumph of Citizenship: The Japanese and Chinese in Canada, 1941–67* (Vancouver: UBC Press, 2007), 36–7. See also Letter from H.L. Keenleyside to Ian MacKenzie, 26 January 1942, Reel T-10137, RG 27, LAC.
64 In January 1944, the Custodian reported 15,500 files on "evacuee" property, as against 1,418 files for property belonging to "enemies." Report to McLarty by Shears, 28 January 1944, file 16, vol. 2, RG 117, LAC.
65 Memo to Ireland from McPherson, 28 July 1944, file 16, vol. 2, RG 117, LAC.
66 This clean distinction in theory was muddied somewhat by the reality that individual families often included both "enemies" and "evacuees" and the former were sometimes reclassified and released from prison after their initial incarceration.
67 Report to McLarty by Shears, 28 January 1944, file 16, vol. 2, RG 117, LAC; Address delivered to the Vancouver Junior Board of Trade, 23 July 1942, file 6-06: "Correspondence, newspaper clippings, notes, drafts, memorandums, interviews," box 6, McPherson Fonds, RBSC.
68 Jordan Stanger-Ross, "Telling a Difficult Past: Kishizo Kimura's Memoir of Entanglement in Racist Policy," *BC Studies* 181 (2014): 39–62. Jordan Stanger-Ross and Pamela Sugiman, eds., *Witness to Loss: Race, Culpability, and Memory in the Dispossession of Japanese Canadians* (Montreal & Kingston: McGill-Queen's University Press, 2017).
69 Glenn McPherson, interview by Kay Alsop, transcript, 15 September 1994, file 6-05: "Correspondence, newspaper clippings, notes, interviews, photocopies," box 6, McPherson Fonds, RBSC.
70 Memorandum, 29 July 1942, file 6-06: "Correspondence, newspaper clippings, notes, drafts, memorandums, interviews," box 6, McPherson Fonds, RBSC.
71 Untitled manuscript, file 7-10: "Draft manuscript," box 7, McPherson Fonds, RBSC.
72 Memorandum, 19 May 1942, file 6-06: "Correspondence, newspaper clippings, notes, drafts, memorandums, interviews," box 6, McPherson Fonds, RBSC.
73 Memorandum, 24 January 1942, file 6-06: "Correspondence, newspaper clippings, notes, drafts, memorandums, interviews," box 6, McPherson Fonds, RBSC.
74 Ibid.
75 Memorandum Re: Kagetsu, 19 May 1942, file 6-06: "Correspondence, newspaper clippings, notes, drafts, memorandums, interviews," box 6, McPherson Fonds, RBSC; Tadashi Jack Kagetsu, *The Tree Trunk Can Be My Pillow: The Biography of an Outstanding Japanese Canadian* (Victoria: University of Victoria Press, 2017).
76 "Report on Japanese Activities in British Columbia. June, 1942," file: "Report on Japanese Activities in British Columbia," vol. 3569, RG 18, LAC.
77 Ibid., 15.
78 Ibid.
79 Ibid., 114.
80 Ibid., 111.
81 Roy Ito, *Stories of My People: A Japanese Canadian Journal* (Hamilton, ON: S-20 and Nisei Veterans Association, 1994), 207–8.
82 Letter from S.T. Wood to William Stephenson, 5 August 1942, vol. 3569, RG 18, LAC.

83 Memorandum Re: Report, 29 August 1942, file 6-06: "Correspondence, newspaper clippings, notes, drafts, memorandums, interviews," box 6, McPherson Fonds, RBSC.
84 Memorandum, 29 July 1942, file 6-06: "Correspondence, newspaper clippings, notes, drafts, memorandums, interviews," box 6, McPherson Fonds, RBSC.
85 Ibid.
86 Memorandum, 29 August 1942, file 6-06: "Correspondence, newspaper clippings, notes, drafts, memorandums, interviews," box 6, McPherson Fonds, RBSC.
87 Minutes, Town Planning Commission, 2 July 1942, box 77-A-2, 1942-1943, CVA; Memo to McPherson from Wright, 16 October 1942, file 59008 pt 1.1, vol. 2536, RG 117, LAC; Jordan Stanger-Ross and the Landscapes of Injustice Research Collective, "Suspect Properties: The Vancouver Origins of the Forced Sale of Japanese-Canadian-Owned Property, WWII," *Journal of Planning History* 15, no. 4 (2016): 271–89.
88 Letter from Gordon Murchison to T.A. Crerar, 30 November 1942, file V-8-10, pt 2: "Japanese and Their Farm Properties," vol. 403, RG 38, LAC.
89 F.G. Shears, *Annual Report*, 28 January 1944, image 229, microfilm reel C9469, Office of the Custodian of Enemy Property, Vancouver Office Files, Héritage.
90 Letter, McPherson to Coleman, 12 December 1942, file V-8-10 pt 2: Japanese and Their Farm Properties, vol. 403, RG 38, LAC.
91 Memo by Coleman re: real estate owned by persons of the Japanese race evacuated from the Defence Area of British Columbia, December 1942, file: 70-25c: "Liquidating Lands in the Fraser Valley that are Jap Owned," vol. 25, Mackenzie Fonds, LAC; Letter to Mackenzie from McLarty, 21 December 1942, file: 70-25c: "Liquidating Lands in the Fraser Valley That Are Jap Owned," vol. 25, Mackenzie Fonds; Letter to McLarty from Mackenzie, 23 December 1942, file: 70-25c: "Liquidating Lands in the Fraser Valley That Are Jap Owned," vol. 25, Mackenzie Fonds; Letter from Hamilton to Senior, 7 January 1943, file 67-25(4): "Vancouver Centre Japanese in BC 1942–1944," vol. 24, Mackenzie Fonds.
92 Letter to Frank Shears from Glenn McPherson, 12 January 1943, folder 2: "Private and Confidential, 1942–1946," box 2, F.G. Shears Papers, Thomas Fisher Rare Book Library, University of Toronto.
93 Ibid.
94 F.G. Shears, *Annual Report*, 28 January 1944, image 229, microfilm reel C9469, Office of the Custodian of Enemy Property, Vancouver Office Files, Héritage.
95 Telegram to McPherson, 4 January 1943, file 59008 pt 1.1, vol. 2536, RG 117, LAC.
96 Real Estate Agents Cash Journal, December 1942, vol. 69, RG 117, LAC.
97 Letter from Murchison to McKay, 28 January 1943, file V-8-10, pt 2: "Japanese and Their Farm Properties," vol. 403, RG 38, LAC.
98 Letter to Gordon Murchison from Ivan T. Barnet ("Barney"), 28 March 1943, file V-8-10 pt 3: "Japanese and Their Farm Properties," vol. 403, RG 38, LAC.
99 This term is attributed to bureaucratic activity by Miki, *Redress*, 51.
100 Letter from Coleman to Murchison, 21 May 1942, file V-8-10, pt 1: "Japanese and Their Farm Properties," vol. 403, RG 38, LAC.
101 City Council Minutes, 1 September 1942, box 23-D, series 31, [CVA].
102 Chapter 8.
103 Memorandum, Gordon Murchison, 30 October 1942, file V-8-10, pt 2: "Japanese and Their Farm Properties," vol. 403, RG 38, LAC.

104 Letter to Gordon Murchison from Ivan Barnet, 10 October 1942, file V-8-10, pt 2: "Japanese and Their Farm Properties," vol, 403, RG 38, LAC.
105 Letter from Glenn McPherson to Ephraim Coleman, 27 October 1942, file V-8-10, pt 2: "Japanese and Their Farm Properties," vol. 403, RG 38, LAC.
106 Minutes of the Second Meeting of the Advisory Committee on Rural Properties, 18 March 1943, image 1875, microfilm reel C9469, Office of the Custodian of Enemy Property, Vancouver Office Files, Héritage; Adams et al., "Promises of Law."
107 Letter to Smith from McPherson, 21 March 1943, file 5, fonds AM199-Advisory Committee on Japanese Properties in Greater Vancouver, City, box 513-E-2, CVA.
108 Note that the advisory committee included a Japanese Canadian member. See Stanger-Ross, "Telling a Difficult Past"; Stanger-Ross and Sugiman eds., *Witness to Loss.*
109 Tina Loo, "Dan Cranmer's Potlatch: Law as Coercion, Symbol, and Rhetoric in British Columbia, 1884–1951," *Canadian Historical Review* 73, no. 2 (June 1, 1992): 134–5.
110 Letter to Gordon Murchison from Ivan Barnet, 28 July 1942, file V-8-10, pt 1: "Japanese and Their Farm Properties," vol. 403, RG 38, LAC.
111 Letter to Gordon Murchison from Ivan Barnet, 27 August 1942, file V-8-10, pt 1: "Japanese and Their Farm Properties," vol. 403, RG 38, LAC.
112 Marilyn Overland, interview with Pamela Sugiman, 25 April 2015, Vancouver.
113 Aradhana Sharma and Akhil Gupta, *The Anthropology of the State: A Reader* (Malden, MA: Blackwell Publishing, 2006), 11. Original emphasis.
114 Sharma and Gupta, *The Anthropology of the State*, 18–19.
115 Alison Mountz, *Seeking Asylum: Human Smuggling and Bureaucracy at the Border* (Minneapolis: University of Minnesota Press, 2010), xxxiv; Sharma and Gupta, *The Anthropology of the State*, 14.
116 Stanger-Ross, "Telling a Difficult Past"; Stanger-Ross and Sugiman, eds., *Witness to Loss.*

CHAPTER 6

"Our Deep and Sincere Appreciation … for Your Kindness to Us": A Japanese Canadian Family and the Administrative State

Ariel Merriam and the Landscapes of Injustice Research Collective

Introduction

Shinko Nagata was nineteen years old when a knock on the door of her childhood home in Vancouver changed her life forever. She answered the door to find two RCMP officers standing outside. They asked to speak to her father, a respected businessman, who agreed to go with the officers for questioning. Shinko, a student at the University of British Columbia, wanted to ask why her father was leaving, where he was going, and what time he would be coming back. She would not see him again as a free man for more than a year. The date was 7 December 1941.

Nearly seventy years later, the image of her father being led away from their home between two police officers that evening remained etched into her memory, a painful reminder of injustice that was only just beginning for her family:

> [T]hat moment is something that I had closed [off] for a long, long time. I was not able to talk about it … [b]ecause I had to understand what happened to me at that time, when I saw my father taken away between two police officers … [My father was] respectable … honest, hardworking, and [he] knew the Canadian ways. And then here is a man being whisked away without any question. I was afraid. I was supposed to be respectful. I was supposed to understand that this is the Canadian way, where you're allowed to be questioned. At that moment I could see my mother crying, wondering, and my stomach was upside-down. I was anxious, frightened. I couldn't say I was angry. There was no room for me to be angry. I didn't have time to be angry … And for years, I closed my mind to the image of my father walking between the two men. He didn't protest. He was quiet [and] obedient.[1]

Shinko's father, Shichitaro Nagata, was born in 1886 in Japan. In 1907, at the age of twenty-one, he moved to Canada and found work in Vancouver.[2] During his earliest business trips to Canada, he attended night school to learn spoken and written English. He was employed by the Queen Charlotte Timber Holding Company, of which he became treasurer and office manager. The company offered him good wages and provided him with a home at 2330 Wall Street in East Vancouver, where he and his wife Naka raised their seven Canadian-born children. The couple's two eldest children, daughters Shinko Mary and Fusako Ruth, were born in 1922 and 1923, respectively. The sisters remembered their childhood in that home with great fondness. There was a garden out back, where pear and cherry trees grew, and a green park down the road. Just across the street were picturesque views of Burrard Inlet and the North Shore Mountains, and a terminal dock where the children would swim. The family lived in a quiet, predominantly white neighbourhood. Despite prevailing attitudes of racism and exclusion in Vancouver at the time, the sisters remembered finding acceptance from their neighbours:

> Where we lived we had wonderful neighbours ... Mostly Caucasian ... [W]e got to exchange ideas of their cooking, exchange recipes ... We had fun with the neighbours' children. My mother ... invited all of the neighbours' children [to play] with us ... All together – Japanese and Canadians together. And it was possible because we were in a quiet section. We had close connections with our neighbours.[3]

The Nagata family was close knit. Whenever he had time outside his busy work schedule, Shichitaro would pile his seven children into the family car and take them on trips around Vancouver – to Kitsilano, Point Grey, and the Capilano Suspension Bridge. "He didn't have hobbies," Fusako reflected. "It was family." Their mother, Naka, was "the matriarch of the family," remembered as a strict but loving woman who ensured that their home served as the centre of their cohesive and organized family. The sisters reflected with pride on their family's blending of Japanese and Canadian customs. Although her children attended an English school, Naka ensured they were raised with an understanding of Japanese traditions and customs and taught them the Japanese language after school every day. "We had a touch of non-Japanese culture," Shinko stated, "and at the same time we were absorbing Japanese customs."

The same was also true with regard to religion. Naka was Anglican. Shichitaro, a Buddhist, converted to Christianity when they married. Their children were baptized and raised in the Anglican faith but also had an understanding and appreciation for Buddhism. "He was both," Shinko said of her father. "We had the privilege of knowing both." Being able to communicate with others, to foster understanding across such barriers of difference, was important to the family. As Shinko put it, "My mother ... knew we had to understand other people."

Although Shinko's neighbours at home were accepting of difference, school was a different story. She recalled facing exclusion and name calling from her classmates in primary school and the comfort she found in the advice of her parents:

> My parents were very strong in that we must have a good education. We must go to school regardless … I was always an outsider. [And] there was a lot of name-calling. So … I used to tell my mother and father, and their [response] was "Never mind. You must do your best. You must be the very best, and it will all come right in the end." And so it did.[4]

When she finished high school, Shinko spent time volunteering with the Canadian Red Cross before enrolling in classes at the University of British Columbia in the fall of 1940. Being accepted to university was a proud achievement for Shinko, which she saw as the fulfillment of her parents' most important goal: for their children to receive a good education. Shinko's time at UBC also marked her first real exposure to other Nisei – the Canadian-born children of immigrants from Japan. She was delighted to discover and to join a Japanese Students Club on campus.[5]

The idyllic childhood of Shinko's memories ground to a sudden halt that December evening, watching as her father was taken from their home by two police officers. In that moment, the unity of her family was shattered, the security of her own home violated, and her trust in Canadian values and institutions shaken to the core. Her father was one of thirty-eight Japanese Canadians deemed a threat to national security and arrested the evening of the attack on Pearl Harbor.[6] All were men and nationals of Japan. Along with the others, Shichitaro was subsequently incarcerated at Petawawa, Ontario and later Internment Camp 101 at Angler, Ontario – both prisoner of war camps.[7] He was not released until a year later, in December 1942. He would never return to his family's home in Vancouver. In the intervening months, along with many thousands of others, the members of the Nagata family were forced to give up their education, leave behind their beloved house, endure banishment from the city they called home, and face a choice between internment in an interior town camp and exile from British Columbia. Over the course of the next three years, the family journeyed across Canada, uprooted first to Edmonton and then later to Toronto. They lost control of their property, finances, and freedom of movement. At every step along the way, they found themselves separated from one another, in dire financial circumstances, and confronted with the racist attitudes of administrators, employers, and neighbours.

As individuals and as historians, we tend to make sense of the past by organizing it into a sequence of important moments that had a clear and measurable impact on the course of history. For Shinko, the events of 7 December 1941 marked a distinct end to her childhood and changed her life in every possible way. In her own words, "everything happened on December 7. Everything is related to December 7, for me."[8] Similarly, the history of Japanese Canadians in the mid-twentieth century is often understood by way of highly visible moments of government action and subsequent reaction by Japanese Canadians: First, the attack on Pearl Harbor provided "an opportunity to achieve the ultimate objective of ridding the province – and Canada – entirely of its Japanese minority."[9] Then, in March 1942, Order in Council P.C. 1665 provided the mechanism for achieving this goal by directing and empowering the British Columbia Security Commission to displace Japanese Canadians from their homes and catalyzing the mass exile of Japanese Canadians from coastal British Columbia.[10] Finally, in January 1943, Order in Council P.C. 469 set in motion the forced sale of all Japanese Canadian–owned real and personal property remaining under the control of the Custodian of Enemy Property.[11] Key moments such as these are often used to explain the process of displacement and dispossession.

While there is clearly value in understanding this history in terms of moments of state action that altered the lives of Japanese Canadians dramatically and permanently, attention is less often paid to the daily processes of administration that unfolded during the seven-year period in which displacement and dispossession were enacted. The records of the Office of the Custodian of Enemy Property offer a rich avenue for such an exploration, documenting the daily correspondences of individual Japanese Canadian families with representatives of the Custodian's office during the 1940s.[12] The Nagata family had a particularly long and detailed correspondence with the Custodian's office, approximately 250 pages of which are documented within the records, mostly between 1942 and 1944. The letters Shichitaro, Naka, and Shinko exchanged with various representatives of the Custodian offer a detailed account of where the family went, how they understood their relationship to the Custodian and to their property, and the numerous setbacks and hardships they endured along the way. The case file details a complex and shifting administrative process in which those subject to administration had direct communication with administrators, knew them personally as individuals, and could leverage these connections to strategically negotiate access to their property and some degree of movement despite the oppressive constraints placed on them. The letters reveal that the processes of displacement and dispossession did not occur under the purview of a unified administrative state but within the context of ongoing interactions between various individuals, administrators, and administrative bodies, each of whom could influence the others, and whose interests and priorities could exist in harmony or in tension with one another. They show us that the mechanisms of dispossession were not monolithic but highly contextual, varying over time and across circumstances. This perspective offers a more complex and nuanced reading of how the dispossession unfolded on a daily basis during the 1940s.

This chapter draws on a Foucauldian interpretation of power in its analysis of relations between the Nagata family and representatives of the Custodian's office. It understands power not as something possessed by one group or class and to which others are subjected but as imminent and decentred. Even in contexts of stark domination and oppression, such as the administration of displacement and dispossession, power circulates.[13] In focusing on individual people within the wider articulation of power, this chapter also draws on Giddens, who, somewhat in contrast to Foucault, emphasizes the ability of individual agents to use their inherent knowledgeability about the structures and relations of power in which they are embedded in order to intervene in processes and produce effects in the world.[14] It also takes inspiration from Loo and White, who have gestured to the shared rhetorical culture of legal argument as a mechanism through which power can be strategically exercised by those familiar with its language, even those in marginalized positions.[15] This chapter suggests that the day-to-day interactions between the Nagata family and representatives of the Custodian's office occurred within a shared social and cultural context. The Nagatas' knowledge of this context equipped them to communicate persuasively with the individual administrators controlling their assets and movements in small but meaningful ways.

Over the course of the Nagatas' correspondence with their administrators, they consistently used patterns of argument designed to appeal to government officials. They often began letters by acknowledging the concerns of the Custodian's office and even by apologizing. They routinely conveyed their experiences in organized and strategic ways, appealing to moral and economic sensibilities that the administrators would find compelling in order to justify their actions and requests.[16] In some cases they made emotional appeals that implied personal relationships with individual bureaucrats. In their attempts to alleviate some of the constraints placed on them, the family demonstrated their knowledgeability of the views and inclinations of both the Custodian's office in general and individual administrators in particular.[17] At once complex and captivating, the Nagata correspondences cast a new light on the day-to-day interactions of the internment era. In doing so, they help us understand with greater depth and detail how power relations unfolded in the context of displacement and dispossession.

In its analysis of the daily processes of the dispossession, this chapter also draws on notions of property as socially constructed and relational. Blomley suggests that property ownership is not inherently stable but requires continual performative enactment through narrativizing in order to be understood and legitimated by others.[18] On more than one occasion, members of the Nagata family enacted ownership of their property despite its dispossession by telling stories about its history, explaining their relationship to it, and asserting their property rights over others. Furthermore, this chapter understands property not only in terms of monetary value and ownership but, following Radin, as fundamental to the constitution of individual personhood.[19] In the letters and recollections of the Nagata family, we see clearly that the violation of property rights during the dispossession was not just a matter of tangible or financial loss but constituted an acute and continuous threat to the family's ongoing development and sense of identity. Although the Nagatas never owned their house in Vancouver in the sense of possessing the land title, it is evident from Shinko's later reflection on the meaning of her childhood home that it was nonetheless deeply important to who they were as a family or, in Radin's words, "the scene of [their] history and future, [their] life and growth."[20] The correspondences between representatives of the Custodian's office and the Nagata family reveal tensions between fungible and personal interpretations of property as the Nagatas attempted to express the meaning of their property in the context of dispossession. From the Nagata letters, we can understand the dispossession not as a single moment of forced sale but as a process that unfolded in the context of ongoing interactions between administrators and those subjected to administration.

It is important to clarify that, despite the ability of the Nagata family to manoeuvre within the oppressive context of the dispossession in personally meaningful ways, this chapter does not imply that the harms of displacement and dispossession were in any way undone. The circulation of power remained fundamentally uneven. The Nagatas could participate effectively in the rhetorical culture to which they and the representatives of the Custodian belonged, but they could not alter its terms. Arguments that members of the family put forward to regain their property, purchase real property elsewhere, or return to British Columbia were all thwarted unilaterally. The small but significant victories the Nagata family did achieve – such as securing permission to move from Edmonton to Toronto in 1943 – were somewhat exceptional. As a highly literate middle-class family able to communicate their needs in ways that representatives of the Custodian's office could find compelling, the Nagatas were privileged in a way that many other Japanese Canadians were not. This became apparent to Shinko in the weeks following her father's arrest:

> I went several times to look for my father. And one of the greatest awakenings to me [happened] when I went to the detention place where I thought my father was. The women, the men from the fishing boat villages were all in the detention room, all speaking Japanese, crying in Japanese, and the officers trying to give orders didn't understand [their] English. And I thought, "This is not right" … They couldn't express how they were feeling because they didn't understand what was going on. They weren't able to communicate.[21]

The Nagata family represents a minority of the 23,000 Japanese Canadians who called British Columbia home in 1941, most of whom could not afford to move their families and belongings and support themselves outside the interior camps of British Columbia, and many of whom struggled to communicate effectively with an administrative state that had little interest in meeting them on their own terms.

The complexities of daily administration during the dispossession revealed by the Nagata correspondences also shows us that they cannot be understood as helpless victims of actions and policies perpetuated by an omnipotent and oppressive state.

Rather, the Nagatas – and all Japanese Canadians who endured displacement, dispossession, and exile – must be acknowledged and honoured for their determination and their will to continue in spite of the oppressive and unjust circumstances inflicted upon them. The Nagata case exemplifies one of many ways Japanese Canadians dared to withstand and challenge the injustices to which they were subjected during the 1940s: some through outright protest, others through more strategic communication. All attempted to continue living their lives as normally as possible. It illustrates the remarkable tenacity and determination shown by Japanese Canadians during the internment era, most of whose stories are not documented in this level of detail. The story of the Nagata family is most importantly one of perseverance.

Vancouver: Winter 1941–spring 1942

Shinko's life changed in many ways the night her father was taken away. In his absence, with her mother not fluent in English and unable to take care of the family alone, it fell to Shinko to become a family leader. She stopped attending classes at UBC and spent the following months trying to find out where her father was detained and communicating with officials on her family's behalf. As a result of Shichitaro's business managing a number of companies based in Japan, the Nagatas' assets were immediately seized and placed under the control of the Custodian of Enemy Property. Decades later, Shinko reflected on the difficult and paralyzing situation this inflicted on her family: "All assets were frozen. You can imagine: you're stuck."[22] She credited her mother with keeping the family from falling apart at the time, a level-headed presence focused on ensuring her family could move forward: "'Don't look back. Proceed.' That was her motto. That's what kept us together during the evacuation."[23] In the early months, under her mother's guidance, Shinko assumed responsibility for looking after her family and their future.

Early correspondences between the Nagata family and state representatives demonstrate the family's skill in composing arguments that would resonate at the Custodian's office. One of the first instances of communication between Shinko and the Custodian's office involved the seizure and sale of the family's two vehicles. On 19 December 1941, following Shichitaro's interrogation, the RCMP went to the Nagata home and seized the family's 1940 Model 10 Austin coach.[24] While there, they also found a 1940 Pontiac coupe, which Naka claimed she had paid for, although the registration was in her husband's name. As a result, the Custodian's office requested that she provide a written explanation of her claim to the vehicle.[25] This provided Shinko with a chance to narrate her family's relationship to the car and make a case against its dispossession on her mother's behalf. The resulting letter provides a needs-based justification for their ownership of the vehicle and a clear expression of its importance to the family.

Shinko opened the letter in the same way that many of the family's correspondences would begin over the next two years: with an apology. "We all knew it was very extravagant to possess two cars," she wrote contritely to Frederick Field, the Custodian representative in charge of administering the family's property, on 4 February 1942.[26] After establishing her own economic sensibility as the basis for her argument, she proceeded to organize the family's needs and motivations in a way that represented the decision as rational, practical, and frugal. She explained that although the Austin coach was an economical model that "cut gasoline consumption in half," its engine was not powerful enough to "climb the hill when the family were all in." She emphasized that her mother had purchased the Pontiac from a friend at a low cost. Clarifying that the car had been paid for in full and would incur no additional expenses for the family, Shinko requested that the car not be sold "if it is possible." Indeed, retaining the car "would be more economical to operate this car than to pay for all the taxi fares as there are seven of us with mother." She thereby framed her family's ownership of the two vehicles as rational, based on frugality and the practical needs of her large family.

Shinko also made a second, implicit argument: that the vehicles were important to her family's identity and continued well-being. "My sister and I, were, after we had learned to drive, to use the car to go to school," she explained. The car was not simply a piece of property, but a vessel within which her future hopes and plans were bound. Shinko also made a personal argument near the end of her letter, stating that "Mother is not very strong and thus she always resorts to the car instead of the street car." By explaining that her mother's health led her to rely on the car to get around, Shinko linked ownership of the vehicle with the family's well-being and ability to function in the world. This letter offers a sense of how the Nagatas understood their relationship to their property, of how its seizure and sale impacted their family, and of the arguments that they thought officials would find persuasive.

Shinko's appeal was unsuccessful. The car was seized on 10 February 1942 and subsequently sold.[27] This is unsurprising given that the general order for the forced displacement of Japanese Canadians from the coast would be issued in early March.[28] Nevertheless, this letter represents an early example of the appeals the Nagatas would use throughout their communications with the Custodian, in which they paired apologies with strong claims to economic and practical principles seeking access to their property.

One episode in particular from the family's time in Vancouver speaks clearly to the complexity and contextuality of the process of administration, showing how the family articulated their relationship not only to their property but also to the individual administrators responsible for their dispossession. On 5 March 1942, one day after Order in Council P.C. 1665 empowered the BC Security Commission to displace all

Japanese Canadians from the coast, Naka delivered a radio to the house of Frederick Field as a personal gift to him.[29] Along with the radio was a note signed by Naka, explaining that the gift was intended to represent "a very small symbol of our deep and sincere appreciation … for your kindness to us."[30] The note explained that while the family had received several offers for the radio, they felt that they "would not be able to accept the money, as it would represent my father's hobby, his great love for radios and books." The author expressed certainty "that if my father were here he would also give the radio to you."[31] Naka thus positioned the radio as a meaningful family heirloom with strong connections to their memories and family identity and for which no monetary price would be acceptable.

The giving of this gift adds new layers of complexity to our understanding of the relationship between the Nagatas and the administrative state. It points to the unusual situation of the Nagatas as a family whose assets had been taken over by the Custodian's office prior to the mass displacement as a result of Shichitaro's classification as a supposed security risk. Being in the same city as the agent in charge of their property prior to their exile, the Nagatas knew him personally, even to the point of knowing his home address. This small detail adds a new dimension to the sphere of interaction in which the dispossession took place – that of the intimate and personal. It is impossible to draw firm conclusions about the meanings and motives behind the gift. The information on record is limited to the files kept by the Custodian's office. We have no documentation of the personal meetings between them nor is there any record of Field's written replies to Naka. These interactions are gone, and their meaning is lost to time.

However, what remains of their correspondence gestures to a fascinating complexity of two-sided relationships unfolding within the context of the administrative state, and the possibilities that it suggests are worth considering. Perhaps the gift should be taken as a heartfelt gesture of thanks to an agent who had shown kindness and sympathy to the family in a period of desperate insecurity. The possibility of rapport between Field and the family is supported by a 1943 letter from Naka to Field, following the transfer of control of the family's property from Field to another agent, in which she explained that she had continued to communicate with him directly because "I feel that I can express the matter to you more easily."[32] Perhaps the radio was of such personal value to the family that they could not bear to see it sold to a stranger but wished it to be kept safe by someone they knew and trusted. Presumably, however, they could have more easily entrusted the radio to a neighbour if this was the case. There is also the possibility that the gift was intended as an attempt to leverage preferential treatment from an administrator with power over the family's possessions and finances in the uncertain context of their impending exile from British Columbia. These possibilities are not mutually exclusive, and each opens up new avenues of complexity in the relationship between the Nagata family and administrators in the process of their dispossession.

Each possibility also begs the question: who was Frederick Field and how did he interpret the gift? The letters give little indication. On 2 April 1942, nearly a month after the radio was delivered to his house, Field informed the head of the Custodian's office that he had told Naka he would "hold [the radio] for her account."[33] However, it was not until several months later, in October 1942, that he finally removed the radio from his house and delivered it into the care of the Custodian's office, where it would later be sold.[34] The length of time between the delivery of the radio to his house, his disclosure of the gift to his superiors, and its delivery to the Custodian's office is suspect, but its meaning is unclear. Field never disclosed his personal feelings on the matter, and we can only speculate as to what they were. Did he contemplate keeping the radio? What was his relationship to the Nagatas, not as a government administrator but as an individual? Was he a friend? A sympathetic advisor? An opportunist willing to accept a bribe from a family whose property and future were in his hands? In attempting to gift their property rather than letting it be seized, the Nagata family perhaps expressed the sentiment found in much of the correspondence of the dispossession era, in which Japanese Canadians often rejected the economic valuation of their property by the state and elaborated at length on its personal value and the harms they experienced when it was sold without their consent.[35] Whatever the meaning of the interaction, each possibility suggests new dimensions of complexity in the processes of the dispossession, which occurred not as a single moment of state acting upon marginalized group, but as a process unfolding in contextual and relational ways. In the case of the Nagata family, it seems that such relationships were particularly complex and multidimensional.

The family's actions prior to leaving Vancouver also demonstrate some of the legal and administrative complexities of the dispossession. The Nagatas did not own or pay rent for their home on Wall Street; the property belonged to the Queen Charlotte Timber Holding Company, which had provided it to them as a work benefit before the company and its assets were seized by the Custodian. Nonetheless, the family took steps to claim the property as their own, first by securing a tenant independent of the Custodian's influence and later by seeking to have the Custodian act as property agents on their behalf. In June 1942, an agent of the P.C. Gibbens & Co. real estate office contacted the Custodian's office, informing them that he had found a tenant for the property at Naka's request, who would pay rent of $25 monthly to the Nagatas after their departure from Vancouver.[36] By positioning themselves as landlords entitled to receive rent, the Nagatas enacted a claim of ownership on the property despite their lack of legal title. Nearly a year later, faced with the impending forced sale of the house, Naka again claimed the property by attempting to raise the rent and evict the tenant, Mr

Tudor Jones. In a letter to Field, she stated flatly, "We do not wish this house to be sold."[37] She further asserted her right to the property by advocating the eviction of the tenant living there. In renting the property out, in seeking to evict tenants, and in expressing views about its future disposition, Naka expressed ownership.

As Canada's internment policies were being specified in early 1942, Naka came to feel that she and her children could not safely remain in British Columbia. Her husband's arrest and incarceration and the erosion of the family's property rights were accompanied in March 1942 by the order for the forced removal of all Japanese Canadians from the coast. The coming wave of racist and exclusionary policy put the family's present well-being and future aspirations under threat. Faced with the prospect of an uncertain future in the internment camps of the interior, Naka made a decision. She and her family would leave the province entirely and move to Edmonton.

Edmonton: Summer 1942–summer 1943

Sometime in the spring of 1942, Shinko boarded a train and travelled to Edmonton alone, ahead of the rest of her family.[38] It was the first time she had ever been outside British Columbia. Her task was to find a place in Edmonton for her family to live and to enrol herself and her sister at the University of Alberta. Prior to leaving Vancouver, she had petitioned the British Columbia Security Commission on behalf of her family, proposing that they could support themselves financially if they were allowed to move to Edmonton. The Security Commission, responsible for displacing Japanese Canadians from the coast to sites of internment, had decided that if families could prove they had sufficient resources to support themselves and made their own travel arrangements, they would be allowed to leave the province under their own agency.[39]

Meanwhile, the rest of the family faced the task of packing what belongings they could and leaving their home behind, uncertain of when they would be allowed to return. Decades later, Shinko's younger sister Fusako remembered the anxiety and confusion that characterized that time:

> My mother and myself and [the five younger children] had to figure out what to do with the house, what to take … with us on the train and what to leave behind. We even had to leave our dog – a collie dog … It was just anxiety and turmoil in [my] mind. But my mother kept saying to me, "Look. We've got things to do. We have to sort it out." I remember I never knew how to tie knots in my life, but we had to get boxes to [pack] books and papers. We could only take a certain amount of things … I don't know how we did it, how we managed … [T]he six of us went on a train and got to Edmonton.[40]

It is likely that the Nagatas received outside support for their move. The Edmonton City Council was resistant to admitting any Japanese Canadians into the city and banned their admission altogether in June of 1942, ostensibly due to a housing shortage.[41] Earlier that year, however, nine families – perhaps the Nagatas among them – had petitioned the city council for permission to enter the city and find homes.[42] These applications were supported by Reverend J.T. Stephens, who had testified that all the applicants were both Christians and "patriotic Canadians."[43]

Despite having managed to avoid the isolated internment sites of the British Columbia interior, the Nagatas continued to face hardship, partly as a result of strict state control of their resources. Like other Japanese Canadians whose finances were controlled by the Custodian, the Nagata family could withdraw a maximum of $100 per month to support themselves.[44] Although most families who moved east of the Rocky Mountains were entitled to receive full control of their finances, this was not the case for the Nagata family since Shichitaro remained incarcerated in a prison camp.[45] As a result, the eight Nagatas were forced to subsist in the fall of 1942 on a monthly allowance of just $100, with a further $50 provided to pay their rent.[46] The family's exchanges with Custodian representatives during this period demonstrate the personal and financial harms inflicted upon them by displacement and dispossession and reveal the complex ways in which these unfolded in the context of the administrative state.

In Edmonton, the family continued to use the strategies that they had developed prior to their departure from Vancouver, adapting them to their new circumstances. On 15 November 1942, Naka penned a lengthy letter to Field expressing the hardship faced by her family and requesting that their meagre allowance be increased. In the same way Shinko had done months earlier, she began with an apology: "I too was in a way shocked at the expenditure of the last eight months ... I must apologize and more than apologize for these expenses."[47] Apologizing for this transgression and thereby appealing to the bureaucrats' concern for frugality, she proceeded to provide specific and extensive justifications for the family's expenses, which represented them as necessary rather than wasteful. She explained that the family's allowance from the Custodian sufficed to cover rent and routine bills but that extra expenses had been incurred during the move to Edmonton. In order to emphasize her frugality, Naka detailed the kinds of "luxuries and non-essentials" that she avoided altogether, including "unnecessaries such as shows, clothes, and others." Nonetheless, the allowance simply could not sustain her large family for a month, and although she had "tried very hard for the last few months," she always ran out. She requested that their allowance be increased, promising again that, "I do not use any [money] on luxuries and non-essentials." By detailing these expenditures and her own self-restraint, she succeeded in appealing to the Custodian's sensibilities and secured a one-time payment of extra funds for winter clothing and subsistence.[48] The family's recurring allowance, however, remained at $100 per month.

The deeply apologetic, despondent tone of the letter attests to the state of anxiety and uncertainty that displacement and dispossession had forced upon the Nagata family. In the letter, Naka characterized their financial situation as "both difficult and embarrassing," attesting to the anxiety induced by the loss of control over her family's finances. The stakes were high. If she could not support her family on her own and the family's accounts were drained, she and her children would be forced to relocate to an internment camp in British Columbia. However, she emphasized her determination to avoid that outcome at all costs, explaining to Field that, "my husband and I are fully prepared that all our accounts will disappear." Despite having known that moving to Edmonton would drain the family's resources, she expressed no regrets, since "I wanted the children to get an education." Her determination to move to Alberta despite the personal and financial stress it would cause is a testament to her strength and perseverance and speaks to the sacrifices the family was prepared to make in order to secure a future for their children.

Finances were not the only source of concern for the Nagatas in Edmonton. The loss of certainty and stability that accompanied exile and dispossession is also evident in discussions of the family's unpreparedness for the harsh winter climate in Edmonton. Also in November 1942, Naka requested extra money to buy winter clothing for her children, making reference to the fact that Edmonton was "really cold with quite deep snow" and bitter wind, for which the family was "not at all prepared." In the same month, Fusako wrote to Field requesting money to buy winter clothing for herself and her sister Shinko after they realized they would have to walk through heavy snow every day to get to the university.[49] The family's difficulty with the harsh weather in Edmonton, to which they attributed much anxiety, discomfort, and ill health, and their trouble in accessing the resources it demanded of them, shows how the loss of control over their personal property and finances caused profound and daily hardship.

The following month, on 14 December 1942, the family received an unexpected telegram: Shichitaro had been released from incarceration and was on his way to Edmonton.[50] He arrived home that evening and was reunited with his family for the first time in a year. The circumstances of his release are unclear but may be connected to a letter he wrote to Canadian Minister of Justice Louis St Laurent from Camp 101 at Angler on 7 November 1942, in which he appealed for release. Shichitaro emphasized that, since his arrival to Canada more than three decades earlier, he had been "an ardent admirer and believer" in Canadian institutions and ways of life. He provided as evidence his seven, Canadian-born children, who had been raised as Anglicans and "earnest supporters of Christian faith." He also asserted that he had always conducted his business as a manager and shareholder in several Japanese holding companies in the spirit of forging "a better and closer understanding between the two countries." Nagata concluded his appeal by vowing that, if released, he would continue to support Canada's war efforts and cooperate fully with its wartime regulations regarding Japanese Canadians.[51]

Whether or not the letter to St Laurent was directly connected with Shichitaro's release is unclear. However, his argument, like those of the rest of his family, was carefully crafted. His expression of Christian faith, economic contribution, and loyal citizenship demonstrates an understanding of the kinds of moral and economic rhetoric that might influence government officials to make decisions in his favour. The appeal was also well timed. An incident at the Petawawa internment camp in Ontario that July, where guards had opened fire on Nisei inmates who were disciplining a fellow inmate, had sparked discussion among officials about the unique and ambiguous status of incarcerated Japanese Canadians not as "enemy aliens," but as "Canadians 'detained at the pleasure of the Minister of Justice.'"[52] Shichitaro was undoubtedly aware of the incident as a prisoner at the camp, and it is likely he was also aware of the surrounding reconsideration of his status as a Japanese Canadian. He may have made his appeal for release on this basis. In any case, the context in which his release occurred suggests that such administrative decisions were often contextual and could be negotiated in certain circumstances.

Shinko would later describe her father's return as the start of a "new life" for the family, undoubtedly an important step in reconstituting their identity and plans.[53] However, the family's hardship did not come to an end with Shichitaro's return. During his year of incarceration in the prisoner-of-war camps at Petawawa and Angler, his life would have been strictly scheduled and regulated, his days dominated by work, parades, and inspections, with only a few hours in the evenings for free time.[54] Although he never spoke of what had happened during that year of separation, Shichitaro bore scars from his incarceration, as his daughters Shinko and Fusako later recalled: "He was not the same … you could see it from his eyes. They changed him."[55] Shichitaro was also in poor physical health after his return, plagued with a heart condition and other illnesses that prevented him from working.[56] Meanwhile, other members of the family also fell ill. Double pneumonia forced Shinko to leave her job at the Oliver Mental Hospital in 1943. Naka too was in poor health and required Fusako to remain home to care for her. Even when the adult members of the family were well enough to work, they found it extremely difficult to find lucrative employment, perhaps due to the prevalence of racism in Edmonton.[57]

Financial circumstances grew increasingly dire. The family's monthly allowance remained at $100, and they had to negotiate access to more funds whenever extra expenses came up. Ad hoc requests worked at first, but as their finances dwindled officials grew unwilling to allow the family access to their own accounts. In April 1943, Field cautioned Naka that if the family was unable to secure employment and stabilize their financial situation, the Security Commission would insist on their relocation to an internment camp in British Columbia.[58] Faced once more with this threat, the family made the decision to attempt to move again, this time to Toronto.

Toronto: Summer 1943–present

According to Shinko and Fusako, the family's contacts in the Anglican Church in Edmonton encouraged them to relocate to Toronto because "there were good schools [there]."[59] Since the spring of 1942, entry to Toronto had been denied to Japanese Canadians by city officials, who expressed concern about the need to protect the war industry. However, throughout 1943 enforcement became less absolute, and an estimated 700 Japanese Canadians were permitted entry by the end of that year.[60] In fact, despite local opposition, the Security Commission encouraged families to relocate to Toronto, where they would be dispersed farther across the country and where their concentration in enclaves would be discouraged.[61] By August 1943, the Nagata family had formulated a plan to solve their financial and personal troubles by moving to Toronto. To do so, however, they had to contend with administrative obstacles at multiple levels: obtaining travel permits from the Security Commission, securing money from the Custodian's office to finance the move, and facing racism and exclusion at the local level.

The circumstances surrounding the family's move to Toronto once again show the complexity and multiplicity of the administrative state. In order to move, the Nagatas had to contend with both the Custodian's office and the Security Commission. Although these federal agencies both formed part of the same exclusionary state, their priorities differed in significant ways. While the Custodian was responsible for administering Japanese Canadian–owned property and ensuring families like the Nagatas remained self-supporting, the Security Commission was in charge of displacing Japanese Canadians eastward and overseeing their movements and activities. In 1943, the Security Commission was encouraging young Japanese Canadians to move to Toronto ahead of the rest of their families in order to disperse the population more widely across Canada.[62] In the Nagatas' interactions with the Security Commission and the Custodian's office during this time, they demonstrated an ability to manoeuvre within the complexities of this multifaceted administrative state.

Although the full correspondence between the Nagata family and representatives of the Security Commission – if it remains in existence – has not been unearthed in the archival research for this chapter, enough evidence has been found in the Custodian of Enemy Property files to outline its contours. Fusako reached out to the Security Commission in Lethbridge on 15 August 1943, expressing her and Shinko's desire to "proceed to Toronto for the purpose of continuing University education."[63] The Security Commission responded on 17 August that it would consider approving their transfer to Toronto for the purpose of attending university if the sisters could demonstrate "evidence of [their] ability to maintain [themselves] in the City of Toronto." From this brief note we can infer that the Nagatas were forthcoming with the Security Commission about their main reason for moving to Toronto, and that the commission raised no objection to Shinko and Fusako enrolling at the University of Toronto. However, the family's financial situation was extremely precarious, and they now faced the difficult task of convincing the Custodian's office to write to the Security Commission in their support.

To this end, the family made subtly different claims to the Custodian's office. On 24 August 1943, Naka made a detailed case for why the family should be allowed to move to Toronto, appealing first and foremost to the economic concerns of the Custodian's office. She began with her customary expression of regret, explaining: "Since our departure from Vancouver it had been my sincere wish to have my family secure employment of some form … But unfortunately neither my husband nor my daughters could find suitable work with the situation as at present."[64] She then provided a detailed justification for this turn of events based on two sets of circumstances. The first was the illnesses that had plagued the family over the past year, which she attributed to the harsh climate in Edmonton: "Unfortunately the severe climate particularly in winter has not been suitable for the health of my children, my husband and myself and we have encountered numerous medical bills during the past year." She also alluded to the prevalence of racism in Edmonton as a factor in the family's difficulty finding employment and contrasted this with Toronto, where she claimed that even "Japanese nationals have been successful without difficulty to find employment." Naka then outlined in financial terms why Toronto was the best option for the family suggesting that the costs of living would be the same as those in Edmonton, the family's health would improve, and her husband and daughters would be able to find employment easily as a result of more tolerant attitudes. Naka appealed to the Custodian's financial priorities, proposing a plan by which the family might become indefinitely self-supporting.

Later in the letter, Naka hinted at the family's intent to send Shinko and Fusako to university in Toronto for the fall term and requested that the Custodian's office write to the Security Commission in support of the move. This was important for the well-being of her family, she wrote, as confinement to a camp in British Columbia would be "contrary to my main purpose – to educate all my children in Canadian ways and customs." This appeal to assimilationist sensibilities may also have been persuasive to Custodian representatives reading her letter. However, these came second to her financial justifications for the move.

Naka was successful in persuading the Custodian to support her daughters' move to Toronto. Shinko and Fusako received travel permits from the RCMP on 16 September 1943 and boarded a train bound for Toronto that night. In a letter to the Custodian's office earlier that day, Shinko echoed her mother's assimilationist appeal and expressed that work was also a priority for both her and her sister: "At Toronto we shall do our best in our studies [and] be loyal Canadians. We shall endeavor to work for our next school fees in our summer holidays."[65] She expressed hope that the rest of her family would obtain travel permits and leave for Toronto by the end of the week.

Despite the Nagatas' clear communication of their goals and plans, Custodian representatives had evidently misunderstood their intentions at some point. In late September, Naka wrote to the Custodian's office to request money for her daughters' entrance fees at the University of Toronto. K.W. Wright, a representative of the Custodian's office, contacted the Security Commission and expressed confusion, explaining his belief "that the removal to Toronto was so that Mr Nagata and the two older daughters could secure lucrative employment."[66] His confusion suggests that he would have withheld permission for the move if he had known that only Shinko and Fusako would be moving for the purpose of attending school, with the rest of the family to follow later. There is no way of determining whether the Nagatas deliberately misled the Custodian's office on this point. Perhaps Wright had simply been lazy or hurried in his reading of previous letters, glancing only at what he perceived as the most salient points before approving their request. In any case, the tilt of their argument toward the financial benefits of moving to Toronto reflects their understanding of the Custodian's desires and motivations.

Shinko was apologetic when she received word of Wright's consternation: "I … am also sorry that I had not perhaps written, as I had thought, clearly, to you as to the continuation of university here in Toronto for my sister and myself and our wish to work in our summer vacation."[67] The unfolding of events during the time of the family's move to Toronto suggests much about the nature of administrative regulation during the dispossession. It shows that the Nagatas were knowledgeable about the administrative system in control of their lives and capable of manoeuvring through it to advance their goals and better their circumstances. It also reveals the tensions inherent in the multiplicitous nature of the administrative state, which was not unified but made up of multiple agencies containing many individual agents with whom Japanese Canadians interacted. This conglomeration of imperfectly aligned understandings, interests, priorities, and powers created a context in which areas of uncertainty and negotiation existed – areas that the Nagatas navigated with proficiency.

Although the two oldest girls arrived in Toronto in mid-September 1943, the rest of the family continued to face setbacks. Significant delays in obtaining travel permits from the Security Commission combined with the rapid deterioration of their finances to place the Nagatas in a position of particular uncertainty and instability for several months. On 10 September Naka wrote to Wright emphasizing the need for haste in obtaining permits, as schools in Toronto were beginning classes and her younger children were at risk of falling behind.[68] Four days later, she wrote again requesting a total of more than $800 for the move and explaining that they expected to receive permits to leave Edmonton by the end of the week.[69] The following day, Wright replied that the balance of the family's finances had been reduced to $380 and the Custodian would withhold most of these funds until the family could demonstrate that it was in a better financial position.[70] However, continued delays in securing travel permits meant that their funds continued to dwindle, since bills and expenses in Edmonton had to be paid as long as the family lived there.[71] By 26 September, the children had been delayed starting school, many of the family's clothes and belongings had been packed for shipment, and they faced the prospect of having to pay rent for October. Trapped in a situation of personal and financial instability, Naka pleaded with Wright that they be allowed to move before the end of the month.[72] On 30 September she reiterated that the move to Toronto was necessary in order for her husband and daughters to be able to find work and support the family.[73]

Meanwhile, a shortage of housing combined with discriminatory attitudes in Toronto and the family's poor financial situation had made it difficult for Shinko and Fusako to find a home in the city. They spent most of September living at the YWCA, attending classes at the University of Toronto, and attempting to find a house for their family. Shinko recalled those weeks as a difficult and stressful time, during which homeowners refused to rent to them upon discovering that they were Japanese Canadians:

> I spent all of September – every day – looking for a house to rent … I spent 29 days being refused. Each door we went [to], the door was closed, or the house was [already] rented, or [owners said] "there are too many children," because I had three brothers and three sisters.[74]

The sisters had to navigate these difficulties in constant negotiation with an obstructionist state. Although poor market conditions favoured the purchase of a home over rental, they were informed by a representative of the Custodian that it was "contrary to the regulations for persons of the Japanese race to acquire land during the continuation of the state of war."[75] When the sisters did find a house to rent near the end of September, at a cost of $90 per month, officials in the Custodian's office argued that the rent was "out of line with the financial position of the family," implying that they would withhold the necessary funds.[76] Fortunately, however, when the sisters visited the house they discovered that the rent was actually $75 – still a high number but within the range that the Custodian's officials would permit. The Nagatas' search for housing involved negotiation of both racism on the ground and the paternalist interventions of state officials.

Almost seven decades later, sitting in the living room of the very home that she rented in 1943, at 22 Dunbar Street in Toronto, Shinko reflected on finding that house as a significant moment in her life. At the end of September 1943, she found the advertisement in the back of a newspaper. Her long and fruitless search for housing in Toronto had left her anxious and half-certain she would be turned away at the door again:

> When I got on the phone [with the owner], I said, "I would like to rent the house. However, before I come, I would like to let you know that we are a Japanese family. I have three brothers and three sisters." He said, "Come right away." I came here, to this house. He opened the door. I was frightened. "Will he shut the door on me?"[77]

However, when the owner, Mr Henderson, opened the door, he greeted her not with hostility but with a warm welcome poignantly remembered for the rest of her life:

> [He was a] perfect gentleman. [He] opened the door [and said] "Come in. Welcome. Come in and we'll talk." … To think, [a] Japanese Canadian: refused for 30 days, refused so many places in Alberta, kicked out of Vancouver. But this man said, "Come in, sit down, be comfortable and we'll have a chat." It was beyond my expectations, beyond what I had anticipated… [He was] a magnificent person.[78]

In the context of the displacement, dispossession, and discrimination she had experienced across Canada, Henderson's gesture of kindness and acceptance meant a great deal, as did the house that would become the family's permanent home:

> I was so, so happy, so thankful because I wanted a house for my father. I hadn't seen my father for all those years, and I needed a home for my father and my mother … This house, to me, represents understanding [and] compromise … And my parents and my brothers and sisters have been here since.[79]

The house they rented in Toronto took on a great deal of significance for the family, representing a refuge from the layers of obstruction and repeated displacement they experienced in the world just outside their front door.

Yet, the family's hardship continued as the fall of 1943 progressed. On 8 October 1943, shortly after arranging a one-year lease for the house on Dunbar Street, Shinko received a letter from the Security Commission office in Toronto explaining that a municipal ban had been implemented "on further admission of Japanese males to Toronto."[80] This notice came less than a month after the family had been informed by the Security Commission in Lethbridge that they would receive permission to move to Toronto as soon as they had secured a place to live.[81] As previously mentioned, the Security Commission was eager to see Japanese Canadians dispersed ever farther eastward. However, city officials in Toronto, increasingly concerned about the arrival of Japanese Canadians, objected to their presence in the city. Two elected city controllers ordered an investigation into the situation, following which several media outlets reported that Japanese Canadians were "running around Toronto."[82] Soon after, Toronto ceased permitting entry to Japanese Canadians except in special "compassionate cases."[83] One such special circumstance provided for the reunion of families, which appears to have been a consideration in the case of the Nagata family.[84] Shinko sought "special reconsideration" of her family's case from the Security Commission, and Shichitaro requested that the Custodian's office contact the commission in support of the family in light of the fact that they had already applied for travel permits and arranged a one-year lease for the house in Toronto.[85] Eventually, the rest of the family was able to secure permission to enter the city, but their arrival was delayed until mid-November, months after they had planned to begin their life there. The family's move to Toronto was characterized by obstruction at multiple levels, which resulted in an arduous, confusing, and often contradictory experience. The hardship inflicted by exclusionary policy was compounded by its administrative processes.

In Toronto, the family's personal and financial situation remained precarious. Although Shichitaro had been a successful and experienced businessman in Vancouver, Japanese Canadians in Toronto at that time were most often relegated to poorly paid industrial labour and service jobs.[86] His health also remained poor, which made finding steady work even more difficult. As such, the family had to strategize new ways to stabilize their finances to ensure that their children could continue their education and the family would not be forced into internment in British Columbia.

In 1944, Shichitaro developed a new strategy to provide for his family. He sought to use the power of the Custodian's office to leverage claims against his former employer, the Queen Charlotte Timber Holding Company, which was then an "enemy" asset under control of the Custodian. Shichitaro detailed his claim against the company in early 1944, explaining that he felt he was entitled to unpaid bonuses from the company for the years 1931 to 1941, as well as his salary from December 1941, which amounted to a total claim of $6,020.[87] Shichitaro represented these as reasonable requests for repayment of hard work rendered to the company, indicating that he had sacrificed his bonuses in anticipation of a time when the company would be in a better financial situation. He also emphasized the importance of the claim to his family's well-being, self-sufficiency, and ability to live as responsible Canadians:

> I would stress again the necessity of its approval in any case for the support of my family of nine. Fortunately Toronto is the type of place we had been looking for as a centre of education and it is my wish therefore to send the children to school as far as it is possible for obtaining a good Canadian education.[88]

He therefore linked his claim implicitly with the Custodian's financial concerns as well as assimilationist values, which he reinforced by announcing his intent to find work as soon as his health permitted.

Shichitaro's claim received external support. In April 1944, the Custodian's office contacted the company's former director, James H. Lawson, who confirmed that Shichitaro had "devoted a large part of his time to the affairs of this Company" and suggested that his claim was reasonable.[89] Based on this supporting evidence, the Custodian accepted Shichitaro's claim, contacting him in May 1944 to inform him that it would credit the funds to his account.[90] This success was made possible by his position within a hierarchy established by the Custodian, in which the property rights of the Queen Charlotte Timber Holding Company as an "enemy" entity were compromised to a greater degree than Shichitaro's own property rights. In addition, the Custodian prioritized the claims of creditors, including Japanese Canadian creditors, in its management of business enterprises.[91] By positioning himself as a creditor – and confirmed as such by a seemingly disinterested party – Shichitaro gained significant advantage. In this framework, he was situated by the Custodian in a position of power with respect to his former employer, whose property rights had been irreparably revoked, and he was able to exercise power on this basis. Wright informed him that he would be forwarded a monthly cheque of $200 from the balance, to be used specifically "for maintenance of [himself] and [his] family."[92] Despite his ability to position himself above his former employer within the administrative process, his power with respect to the Custodian's office did not change. The funds he received from his claim were tightly controlled, and he continued to face significant and paternalistic constraints on its use.

The outcomes of the Nagata family's move to Toronto can be considered a success in many ways. The family was able to manoeuvre within the oppressive constraints of administrative structures in order to evade the interior internment camps in British Columbia and achieve their goal of sending their children to university, despite the sacrifices they made to get there. As Naka wrote to Field in April 1944:

> I realize perhaps we would have made a greater saving following the plan of others by going to an interior settlement plan. Yet, I believe that expensive [as] everything may have been, my wish in educating my children as far as possible has proved worthwhile – my daughters graduating within a year or so and them able to carry on the support of the family.[93]

The move to Toronto is a testament to the family's success in advancing their goals, yet it also shows the hardship they were forced to endure at every step: their months-long battle to obtain travel permits and the right to enter Toronto, their ongoing struggle to access their own funds, and their efforts to find housing and employment once they arrived. It is in their endurance and perseverance through this hardship – by enrolling two of their children at the University of Toronto, finding a place to live, and making successful claims to improve their financial situation – that we can see how the family was able to move within oppressive circumstances and mitigate some of the harms done to them.

Conclusion

The Nagata case offers insight into the operation of the administrative state and particularly the human experience of being administered over the course of years of dispossession. The letters contained in the file expose the enduring harms of the uprooting and dispossession and reveal the complex contexts of their processes. They demonstrate that the administrative state was not a unitary entity but an amalgamation of various agencies that could work in cohesion or in tension with one another. Furthermore, the state was comprised of individuals with various perspectives on their roles, some of whom the Nagatas knew personally and perhaps even well. These factors created the potential for negotiation between Japanese Canadians and state officials. Using strategic appeals to assimilationist cultural values and bottom-line economic concerns, the Nagata family was able to anchor their interests within the operational logics of the Custodian's office and appeal to the interests and priorities of individual officials. By doing so, they were able to bend the constraints of Custodian policy in order to safeguard their well-being and advance their goals as a family. In some cases, they could even leverage the state against other entities, although in doing so they remained positioned within a hierarchy of power and property rights established by the Custodian. The exchanges that unfolded between the Nagata family and representatives of the Custodian over the course of their displacement and dispossession reveal that dynamics of power, although certainly unequal and oppressive, were nonetheless complex and relational, and yielded opportunities through which Japanese Canadians could affect their circumstances in meaningful ways.

However, it also shows the limits of such possibility. Although the Nagatas were skilled and active negotiators, the grounds on which they argued were vastly uneven, and some terrain was impossible to shift. Between 1948 and 1949, Shichitaro made several attempts to resume business with the Queen Charlotte Timber Holding Company. He used a variety of appeals involving his loyalty to Canada, his previous efforts to support the war effort during the 1930s, and his position as stakeholder in the company to assert his right to continue business in British Columbia on behalf of the company's former owners in Japan. However, his attempts to obtain information from the Custodian regarding the state of the business were continually rebuffed. The final letter on the matter from the Custodian's office, in March 1949, stated briefly that, "all the assets of the company, including the timber licenses, have been liquidated and the company wound up."[94] It is clear that the dispossession resulted in many permanent harms that no amount of argument could mitigate. The Nagatas would never be able to return to their home in Vancouver or resume the life they had lived there.

To fail to honour the family's small but significant successes, however, would do a great disservice to the sacrifices they made in order to achieve them and to the perseverance they exhibited. Although they endured ongoing disruption and trauma in which their lives were fractured and upended – Shichitaro's arrest and year-long incarceration, their exile from British Columbia and subsequent displacement to Edmonton and then Toronto – these are not the defining characteristics of the family's story. Rather, the processes unfolding between and within these moments – in which the Nagatas demonstrated on a daily basis dedication to continually reconstitute themselves as a family, strength and skill to assert their interests, and determination to continue to pursue their goals despite unjust circumstances – tell us who this family was. These sources allow us to move beyond a discussion of action, reaction, and resistance and toward a more nuanced analysis of how Japanese Canadians interacted with the Canadian state.

When Shinko reflected back on her family's experiences during those difficult years, she credited her family's survival to her mother. "If she could hear me today," Shinko declared tearfully, "I would say that if it wasn't for her toughness, for her dedication, none of us would be here today."[95] She frequently described her mother as the embodiment of *shoganai* (translatable as "it cannot be helped"), a Japanese cultural and philosophical value which holds that while some events cannot be controlled, they must be proceeded through with strength and dignity. There were several moments following her father's arrest when Shinko felt afraid and alienated, questioning the values of the country in which she had been born. In these moments, such as her train journey alone from Vancouver to Edmonton, her mother's philosophy gave her the strength to carry on: "[T]hings happen. We must accept it and proceed. And with that courage – I guess that's what kept me going until today." This perspective produced real-world effects. The survival and success of the Nagata family – and of so many other Japanese Canadians in the face of a government that betrayed them – stand as its living testament and enduring legacy.

NOTES

1 Shinko Mary Nagata (Kato), "An Interview with a UBC Japanese Canadian Student of 1942," UBC Japanese Canadian Students of 1942 Project, Vancouver, University of British Columbia Library, 2012 [Nagata (Kato), "An Interview"], accessed 18 September

2019, https://open.library.ubc.ca/cIRcle/collections/ubclibraryandarchives/43377/items/1.0107967.

2 Shichitaro Nagata to Louis St Laurent, 7 November 1942, in Office of the Custodian of Enemy Property. Vancouver Office: Office Files. Obtained from LAC via ATIP request.

3 Nagata (Kato), "An Interview."

4 Ibid.

5 The Japanese Students Club at UBC was founded in 1932. Its purpose was to discuss issues facing Nisei students at the university and promote mutual understanding and respect between students on campus. By the beginning of 1942, membership had risen to seventy students. All seventy-six Japanese Canadian students at the university were forced to leave their studies and exiled from the coast in 1942. In 2012, the university conferred honorary degrees to students whose studies had been interrupted by the displacement, Shinko Nagata among them. For more information, see https://japanese-canadian-student-tribute.ubc.ca/.

6 Ken Adachi, *The Enemy That Never Was: A History of the Japanese Canadians* (Toronto: McClelland and Stewart, 1976), 199.

7 Ann Gomer Sunahara, *The Politics of Racism* (Ottawa: Ann Gomer Sunahara, 2000), 86, http://www.japanesecanadianhistory.ca/Politics_of_Racism.pdf.

8 Nagata (Kato), "An Interview."

9 Adachi, *The Enemy That Never Was*, 201.

10 Ibid., 217.

11 Ibid., 321.

12 The records of the Office of the Custodian of Enemy Property contain more than 250,000 pages of correspondence belonging to 15,000 individual case files. Many of these records have been digitized and are available online at http://heritage.canadiana.ca.

13 Michel Foucault, *Power/Knowledge: Selected Interviews and Other Writings, 1972–1977* (New York: Pantheon Books, 1980), 98.

14 Anthony Giddens, *The Constitution of Society: Outline of the Theory of Structuration* (Cambridge: Polity Press, 1984), 14, 179, 257–8, 290, 318.

15 Tina Loo, "Dan Cranmer's Potlatch: Law as Coercion, Symbol, and Rhetoric in British Columbia, 1884–1951," *Canadian Historical Review* 73, no. 2 (1992), 165; James Boyd White, *Heracles' Bow: Essays on the Rhetoric and Poetics of Law* (Madison, WI: University of Wisconsin Press, 1985), 98.

16 Loo, "Dan Cranmer's Potlatch," 133–4.

17 Giddens, *The Constitution of Society*, 179, 290.

18 Nicholas Blomley, "'Acts,' 'Deeds,' and the Violences of Property," *Historical Geography* 28 (2000), 86. Chapter 4.

19 Margaret Jane Radin, "Property and Personhood," *Reinterpreting Property* (Chicago: University of Chicago Press, 1993), 35–6.

20 Ibid., 57.

21 Nagata (Kato), "An Interview."

22 Ibid.

23 Ibid.

24 H.F. Price and C.H. Hill, Re: Shichitaro Nagata, (Jap) Alien Enemy, Vancouver, BC, 19 December 1941, image 2817, microfilm reel C9304, Office of the Custodian of Enemy Property, Vancouver Office: Office Files, Héritage.

25 P.S. Ross & Sons to G.W. McPherson, 5 February 1942, image 2819, microfilm reel C9304, Office of the Custodian of Enemy Property, Vancouver Office Files, Héritage.
26 Shinko Nagata to Frederick Field, 4 February 1942, image 2820, microfilm reel C9304, Office of the Custodian of Enemy Property, Vancouver Office Files, Héritage.
27 Shinko Nagata to Frederick Field, 10 February 1942, image 2822, microfilm reel C9304, Office of the Custodian of Enemy Property, Vancouver Office Files, Héritage.
28 Adachi, *The Enemy That Never Was*, 216–17.
29 Frederick Field to G.W. McPherson, 2 April 1942, image 2841, microfilm reel C9304, Office of the Custodian of Enemy Property, Vancouver Office Files, Héritage.
30 Naka Nagata to Frederick Field, 5 March 1942, image 2842, microfilm reel C9304, Office of the Custodian of Enemy Property, Vancouver Office Files, Héritage.
31 Although Naka Nagata signed the note, this reference suggests Shinko or Fusako may have been its actual author. Given that Naka was not completely fluent in English, it seems likely she had some level of help from her children in composing correspondences. The extent to which letters signed by Naka were influenced by her daughters – whether they acted as scribes, translators, or authors – is unclear. However, it suggests that Shinko may have had a larger presence in the family's correspondences than is outwardly indicated. Depending on the actual division of authorship between family members, it is possible that Shinko bore the largest share of responsibility for the family's strategic communication with representatives of the Custodian. Or, she could have been writing under the direct instruction of her mother. The truth most likely lies somewhere in between.
32 Naka Nagata to Frederick Field, 1 May 1943, image 2913–14, microfilm reel C9304, Office of the Custodian of Enemy Property, Vancouver Office Files, Héritage.
33 Frederick Field to G.W. McPherson, 2 April 1942, image 2841, microfilm reel C9304, Office of the Custodian of Enemy Property, Vancouver Office Files, Héritage.
34 P.S. Ross & Sons to the Custodian, 20 October 1942, image 2857, microfilm reel C9304, Office of the Custodian of Enemy Property, Vancouver Office Files, Héritage.
35 See chapter 4.
36 P.C. Gibbens & Co. Ltd. to Office of the Custodian, 8 June 1942, image 2844, microfilm reel C9304, Office of the Custodian of Enemy Property, Vancouver Office Files, Héritage.
37 Naka Nagata to Frederick Field, 1 May 1943, image 2314 microfilm reel C9304, Office of the Custodian of Enemy Property, Vancouver Office Files, Héritage.
38 Nagata (Kato), "An Interview."
39 P.S. Ross & Sons to Office of the Custodian, 1 May 1942, image 2845, microfilm reel C9304, Office of the Custodian of Enemy Property, Vancouver Office Files, Héritage.
40 Nagata (Kato), "An Interview."
41 Patricia Roy, *The Triumph of Citizenship: The Japanese and Chinese in Canada, 1941–67* (Vancouver: UBC Press, 2007), 87.
42 Ibid., 86.
43 Ibid.
44 Sunahara, *The Politics of Racism*, 96.
45 Ibid.
46 P.S. Ross & Sons to Office of the Custodian, 27 November 1942, image 2870, microfilm reel C9304, Office of the Custodian of Enemy Property, Vancouver Office Files, Héritage.

47 Naka Nagata to Frederick Field, 15 November 1942, image 2866–7, microfilm reel C9304, Office of the Custodian of Enemy Property, Vancouver Office Files, Héritage.
48 Naka Nagata to Frederick Field, 2 December 1942, image 2873–4, microfilm reel C9304, Office of the Custodian of Enemy Property, Vancouver Office Files, Héritage.
49 Fusako Nagata to Frederick Field, 17 November 1942, image 2868, microfilm reel C9304, Office of the Custodian of Enemy Property, Vancouver Office Files, Héritage.
50 Shinko Nagata to Frederick Field, 18 December 1942, image 2881, microfilm reel C9304, Office of the Custodian of Enemy Property, Vancouver Office Files, Héritage.
51 Shichitaro Nagata to Louis St Laurent, 7 November 1942, Office of the Custodian of Enemy Property, Vancouver Office Files. Obtained from LAC.
52 Sunahara, *The Politics of Racism*, 78.
53 Nagata (Kato), "An Interview."
54 Sunahara, *The Politics of Racism*, 77.
55 Nagata (Kato), "An Interview."
56 Naka Nagata to K.W. Wright, 24 August 1943, image 2929, microfilm reel C9304, Office of the Custodian of Enemy Property, Vancouver Office Files, Héritage.
57 Sunahara, *The Politics of Racism*, 74–5.
58 P.S. Ross & Sons to Naka Nagata, 17 April 1943, image 2915, microfilm reel C9304, Office of the Custodian of Enemy Property, Vancouver Office Files, Héritage.
59 Nagata (Kato), "An Interview."
60 Adachi, *The Enemy That Never Was*, 287.
61 Roy, *The Triumph of Citizenship*, 78.
62 Ibid.
63 BC Security Commission to Fusako Nagata, 17 August 1943, image 2932, microfilm reel C9304, Office of the Custodian of Enemy Property, Vancouver Office Files, Héritage.
64 Naka Nagata to K.W. Wright, 24 August 1943, image 2929, microfilm reel C9304, Office of the Custodian of Enemy Property, Vancouver Office Files, Héritage.
65 Shinko Nagata to K.W. Wright, 16 September 1943, images 2946–7, microfilm reel C9304, Office of the Custodian of Enemy Property, Vancouver Office Files, Héritage.
66 K.[W.] Wright to BC Security Commission, 28 September 1943, image 2955, microfilm reel C9304, Office of the Custodian of Enemy Property, Vancouver Office Files, Héritage.
67 Shinko Mary Nagata to K.W. Wright, 30 September 1943, images 2959–64, microfilm reel C9304, Office of the Custodian of Enemy Property, Vancouver Office Files, Héritage.
68 Naka Nagata to K.W. Wright, 10 September 1943, image 2941, microfilm reel C9304, Office of the Custodian of Enemy Property, Vancouver Office Files, Héritage.
69 Naka Nagata to K.W. Wright, 14 September 1943, images 2942–3, microfilm reel C9304, Office of the Custodian of Enemy Property, Vancouver Office Files, Héritage.
70 K.W. Wright to Naka Nagata, 15 September 1943, image 2944, microfilm reel C9304, Office of the Custodian of Enemy Property, Vancouver Office Files, Héritage.
71 Naka Nagata to K.W. Wright, 21 September 1943, images 2949–50, microfilm reel C9304, Office of the Custodian of Enemy Property, Vancouver Office Files, Héritage.
72 Naka Nagata to K.W. Wright, 26 September 1943, image 2954, microfilm reel C9304, Office of the Custodian of Enemy Property, Vancouver Office Files, Héritage.
73 Naka Nagata to K.W. Wright, 30 September 1942, images 2957–8, microfilm reel C9304, Office of the Custodian of Enemy Property, Vancouver Office Files, Héritage.

74 Nagata (Kato), "An Interview."
75 Ibid.; K.W. Wright to F.H. Cosgrave, 5 October 1943, image 2971, microfilm reel C9304, Office of the Custodian of Enemy Property, Vancouver Office Files, Héritage.
76 K. Wright to BC Security Commission, 28 September 1943, image 2955, microfilm reel C9304, Office of the Custodian of Enemy Property, Vancouver Office Files, Héritage.
77 Nagata (Kato), "An Interview."
78 Ibid.
79 Ibid.
80 Trueman to Shinko Nagata, 8 October 1943, image 2977, microfilm reel C9304, Office of the Custodian of Enemy Property, Vancouver Office Files, Héritage.
81 A.E. Russell to Shichitaro Nagata, 17 September 1943, image 2978, microfilm reel C9304, Office of the Custodian of Enemy Property, Vancouver Office Files, Héritage.
82 Roy, *The Triumph of Citizenship*, 78.
83 Adachi, *The Enemy That Never Was*, 287.
84 Ibid.
85 Shichitaro Nagata to K.W. Wright, 13 October 1943, image 2976, microfilm reel C9304, Office of the Custodian of Enemy Property, Vancouver Office Files, Héritage.
86 Roy, *The Triumph of Citizenship*, 78.
87 Shichitaro Nagata to Frederick Field, 1944, images 2992 and 3002, microfilm reel C9304, Office of the Custodian of Enemy Property, Vancouver Office Files, Héritage.
88 Shichitaro Nagata to Frederick Field, 1944, images 2992 and 3002, microfilm reel C9304, Office of the Custodian of Enemy Property, Vancouver Office Files, Héritage.
89 James Lawson to P. Ross, 25 April 1944, Office of the Custodian of Enemy Property, Vancouver Office Files. Obtained from LAC via ATIP request.
90 K.W. Wright to Shichitaro Nagata, 2 May 1944, Office of the Custodian of Enemy Property, Vancouver Office Files. Obtained from LAC via ATIP request.
91 See chapter 3.
92 K.W. Wright to Shichitaro Nagata, 2 May 1944, Office of the Custodian of Enemy Property. Vancouver Office Files. Obtained from LAC via ATIP request.
93 Naka Nagata to Frederick Field, 6 April 1944, images 3007–8, microfilm reel C9304, Office of the Custodian of Enemy Property, Vancouver Office Files, Héritage.
94 F.G. Shears to Shichitaro Nagata, 14 March 1949, Office of the Custodian of Enemy Property, Vancouver Office Files. Obtained from LAC via ATIP request.
95 Nagata (Kato), "An Interview."

CHAPTER 7

(De)valuation: The State Mismanagement of Japanese Canadian Personal Property in the 1940s

Kaitlin Findlay, Nicholas Blomley, and the Landscapes of Injustice Research Collective

Personal property.
Generally referred to – ominous word "*Chattels*"
Movable property ... Indeed so – Elusive
Parody
They seek them here ... there
Custodian seeks them everywhere
Are they in Storage?
Have they *disappeared*
Those – elusive Personals.[1]

From the notes of Frank Shears, Office of the Custodian of Enemy Property, 1947

Introduction

At the auctions, Japanese Canadians' belongings sold well. Lined up on tables arranged along walls, items were inspected by bidders before the sales began.[2] No doubt, there were particularities about the stock. "We handled dozens and dozens of old cupboards," an auctioneer recounted, "every Jap seemed to have built nine cupboards in his life."[3] And some items generated little interest altogether. "There ... was a great big steam cooker of Japanese origin, and this machine was badly damaged," the same auctioneer explained, "and everyone was scared of it and it was not sold."[4] Overall, however, the belongings sold well. Every two weeks, for nearly three years, hundreds of people attended the auction of Japanese Canadians' belongings in the Fraser Valley. Each week, the Canadian state held two auctions in Vancouver.[5] Elsewhere in the province, the public had intermittent opportunity to purchase Japanese Canadians' belongings. In total, there were more than 250 auctions, selling up to 400 items each, between 1943 and 1947. The auctions were so well attended and so competitive, the auctioneers later reported, that the sales were not necessarily bargains.[6] The competitive bidding, they suggested, was proof of the fairness of the auctions and the fairness of the state process. The federal government later upheld these sales, recorded in the fastidiously issued receipts, as the best way to protect Japanese Canadians' economic interests.[7]

This chapter tells the story of the dispossession of Japanese Canadians' personal belongings. To do so, we must be attentive to the auctions as well as the dispossession of Japanese Canadians by others means. Many of Japanese Canadians' belongings never made it to auction. Before the first bidding started, on 15 September 1943, the federal government had already lost an unknowable amount of property. Thieves were part of the problem. Likewise, were vandals. Government officials, in their attempts to manage Japanese Canadians' property, hemorrhaged belongings. Attention to the Canadian state's mismanagement of Japanese Canadians' personal belongings reveals its fundamental and sustained devaluation of Japanese Canadians and their belongings. It also reveals the manner in which mismanagement became a justification for forced sale, and the administrative challenges of dispossession were blamed upon the dispossessed.

(De)valuation

The forced sale of personal, or moveable, property remains a little-understood process within the broader history of the dispossession of Japanese Canadians. Even the accounts that are most attentive to property dispossession privilege the processes affecting real estate and fishing vessels, touching on the policies affecting personal belongings only briefly.[8] This chapter brings personal property to the fore.[9] The dispossession of Japanese Canadians' belongings ensured the permanent eradication of their homes, whether owned or rented. It severed any material ties to their prewar lives. Further, the story of personal belongings offers lessons beyond its pernicious effects. The haphazard and fateful decisions of state officials in the management of Japanese Canadians' belongings also allow us to trace the sustained, everyday work of dispossession. As the introduction to this collection reminds us, quiet, persistent labour, played a crucial role in enacting state policy. Most of this labour, we shall note, entailed state officials, who were obliged to negotiate the messy and often contradictory work of racialized politics. But dispossession required the complicity of nonstate actors as well, and this chapter documents the active collusion of those who avidly snapped up Japanese Canadian possessions in auctions or, more malevolently, broke into their homes and temples, and vandalized or seized goods. This history, too, needs to be acknowledged and reckoned with.

The public and state record of the dispossession of personal belongings is disparate and disorganized, encouraging historians to neglect personal property. Unlike Japanese Canadians' real estate or fishing vessels, officials never knew the extent of chattels that it held in state protection, never compiling a centralized list of the objects vested in their care. Barring a single file titled "Chattels (Japanese)" that reflects higher-level policy decisions, documentation of the dispossession of Japanese Canadians' personal belongings is spread across thousands of records. Only with the recent public availability of more than 15,000 Office of the Custodian case files has it become possible to glimpse the fuller story of what happened to personal belongings. It is shocking to realize that nearly each case file contains details of a unique instance of ransacking, theft, or looting; to read how officials obfuscated in their communications with Japanese Canadians, downplaying the damage; and to grasp the significance of these files when taken together. The state's seizure, management, and sale of Japanese Canadians' personal belongings was a massive undertaking that touched thousands of British Columbians and unfolded publicly over the course of years. Never in the state's interest to admit the extent of its miscarriage of process, its records remain dispersed throughout the archive and memory, experienced by individuals but never accounted for in total.

Our goal in this chapter, most immediately, is to document this understudied but vital story. Our focus is not on the experience of loss: that is explored elsewhere. Rather, we investigate the everyday, administrative work of the state, concerning ourselves with the state actors and officials charged with the job of administering and ultimately selling the personal property of thousands of Japanese Canadians. The challenges associated with the management of the personal effects of the "evacuees," as they were misleadingly designated, were problems of the state's own creation. These "elusive Personals," as Frank Shears described them, had to be made visible to the state, when they were often concealed, stolen, and dispersed. They had to be made knowable, through forms of registration, when they were often jumbled. In some cases, they had to be returned to the owner, yet were hard to retrieve and expensive to ship. They were "property," vested in the state and legally held in trust; they had to be protected.

The governance of personal property was a highly improvised one.[10] It relied on an infrastructure that took many forms, including nonstate actors. Central to the process of governance, we shall argue, was the process of valuation. Valuation is "any social practice where the value or values of something is established, assessed, negotiated, provoked, maintained, constructed and/or contested."[11] Valuation, and its logical corollary, devaluation, was central to the everyday work of the state.

Valuation is a pervasive human practice: "Countries, restaurants, schoolchildren, damages, pets, waste and indeed academics, appear all to be subject to a wide variety of valuations to assess such things as creditworthiness, performance, aesthetics, or return on investment."[12] As John Dewey argues, valuation is a complex social practice, ranging from individualized expressions to complex cultural assessments.[13] Valuation necessarily entails some intersubjective forms of appraisal and it also produces social relations: "The performance[s] of valuations are thus not only ubiquitous; their outcomes participate in the ordering of society."[14] The continued valuation of Japanese

Canadians and their belongings, and their attendant devaluation, was both foundational to, and instrumental in, a massive state policy of forced uprooting and permanent displacement. The sections that follow describe processes that began sequentially but, once begun, unfolded concurrently, revealing the manner in which both Japanese Canadians and their personal property were valued and devalued by state officials and neighbouring British Columbian residents.

Vesting and precedents

There was little precedent for the policy that placed the personal property of virtually every Japanese Canadian in the hands of federal officials. Federal law made the internment of all "persons of the Japanese race" the responsibility of the British Columbia Security Commission (BCSC) and vested all of their belongings in the Custodian of Enemy Property.[15] By contrast, when Canada declared war against Germany and Italy, the federal government issued orders to intern nationals from those countries. Along with individuals that the RCMP deemed suspicious, these "enemy aliens" were incarcerated in Canada.[16] For the duration of their confinement, the Office of the Custodian oversaw the internees' property. In these cases, the office would ensure that the internees' family members could reasonably care for their property and, if not, would take a more active hand.[17] Real estate remained in the internees' names and their belongings remained in their homes. In the case of businesses, the Office of the Custodian worked with prestigious accounting firm P.S. Ross & Sons to liquidate the perishable items and attribute the proceeds of the sale to their owners accordingly.[18] Importantly, the precedent for managing the property of non-Japanese Canadian internees was based on citizenship status and an interference-if-necessary basis.

Crucially, the policies affecting Japanese Canadians diverge at their foundation: rather than nationality, or what we would today call citizenship, the policies enacted against Japanese Canadians hinged on race. This had pivotal implications for the management of Japanese Canadians' personal property. Having uprooted communities in their entirety, the Office of the Custodian could not follow the same processes as for Italian or German internees. Rather than relying on family and community members to oversee the property of internees on the ground (even if final responsibility lay with the state), the internment of the entire population meant that the government became caretakers to everything that Japanese Canadians owned. Immediately following Order 1665, the state relayed the responsibility of the Office of the Custodian to Japanese Canadians: "persons of the Japanese race are urged to report their property immediately instead of waiting until their evacuation as this will enable the Custodian to take prompt action to protect and administer the same."[19] The total uprooting of Japanese Canadians from the "protected area" and their internment meant not only that the Canadian state became responsible for an unprecedented number of personal properties, but also marked a notable departure from established policy.

The internment of Japanese Canadians brought with it a fundamental and deeply racist process of devaluation. Valuation of objects entailed the valuation of subjects, echoing Dewey's recognition of the double meaning of the verb "to value," signifying both the practice of prizing, or holding something (or someone) as precious and laudable, and that of appraisal, or the act of assigning relative value.[20] At its very outset, then, the state's policy of vesting rested on a profound devaluation of supposedly prized property rights to manage and control personal property – vital sticks in the rights basket – on the basis of a crude racist calculus.[21]

The problem of chattels

Protection

The inherent qualities of Japanese Canadians' moveable property challenged the Canadian state. Moveable property lacks a formal registry of ownership, is seldom marked or labelled by its owners, and is easily relocated. Unlike land, personal property can be lost, hidden, or stolen. It can be prone to damage or decay, especially when moved or stored en masse. Carelessly handled, chattels can quickly become difficult to identify with their owners.

To state the obvious, personal property mattered to its owners. Although only a proportion of Japanese Canadians owned real estate (some 1,700 parcels of real estate were forcibly sold), nearly each of the 22,000 Japanese Canadians had some sort of personal property to their name. Every Japanese Canadian had a bed that they slept in, clothing that they wore, and a kitchen table where they shared meals with family and friends. Each likely had cherished mementos. Many had pets. Japanese Canadians owned tools required to make a living: saws, fishing nets, and sewing machines. Merchandise lined the shelves of their businesses and farm equipment filled their sheds. Many families honoured ancestors at Buddhist altars, or preserved prized kimonos or tea sets. Japanese Canadians valued their personal property in diverse and personal ways. Some objects were fungible assets or resources used to achieve economic ends. Some were quotidian, everyday objects, like tables and plates. Others communicated cultural and religious meanings, like family shrines or were forms of "memory in property," in which objects of property store individual and collective memories.[22] In all its variety and abundance, the moveable property of Japanese Canadians fell under the control of the Office of the Custodian in the spring of 1942.

The physical uprooting of all Japanese Canadians began in earnest when the Canadian state assumed control of the buildings at Hastings Park on 11 March 1942. Within a week, families began to arrive in the centre's livestock barns and exhibition halls.

Figures 7.1–7.6 (opposite, above, and following page) These photographs suggest how personal belongings were woven into the individual, collective, familial, functional, and economic lives of Japanese Canadians. The Office of the Custodian used the legal term "chattels" to describe the diverse possessions of Japanese Canadians.

The first arrivals, and the thousands that followed, passed through this processing centre to sites of internment in the interior and across the prairies. The uprooting process lasted nine months, the final residents leaving the "protected area" in late October.[23] As they locked their homes behind them, Japanese Canadians could only trust that the government would protect the belongings they left there.

The pretence of urgent uprooting shaped the BCSC's policies regarding Japanese Canadians' belongings. As the Office of the Custodian assured Japanese Canadians that their property would be protected in their absence, the BCSC instructed them to bring only what was immediately necessary upon their arrival in the sites of internment. Prioritizing the speedy shipment of people over their things, the BCSC limited what Japanese Canadians could bring with them according to weight. Japanese Canadians could bring 150 pounds of personal effects per adult and 75 pounds per child, to a maximum of 1,000 pounds per family. The BCSC urged Japanese Canadians to take small cookstoves (to be crated and shipped by freight), sewing machines, "as well as provisions for 3 or 4 days time."[24] In early May, the BCSC firmly warned Japanese Canadians that baggage exceeding these limits "would have to be left at the station."[25] A few weeks later, *The New Canadian*, the sole Japanese Canadian newspaper permitted to publish (under the surveillance of the BCSC) during internment, relayed a "special communique from Nisei baggagemen in the ghost towns." Reaffirming the BCSC's need for restrictions, it warned: "And don't take too much, since space is very limited and accommodation is crowded!"[26]

The BCSC acknowledged that Japanese Canadians might want other belongings in the sites of internment. Officials assured Japanese Canadians that "additional baggage" could be stored in Vancouver and "forwarded by freight at the owner's risk and expense when required."[27] Meanwhile, the Office of the Custodian arranged storage in Hastings Park that soon expanded to sites across the province. In October 1942, the BCSC announced that, provided that they could pay all expenses, Japanese Canadians could "order all personal effects, furniture and other goods left behind them" to be delivered to their site of internment.[28] A year later, however, Glenn McPherson (at the time the director of the Vancouver Office of the Custodian) reflected on these arrangements with perverse and wilful ignorance. "The Custodian's work would have been greatly facilitated if the Japanese had taken their chattels with them," he wrote in October 1943, "but this was neither predictable nor desirable at the time of evacuation. All the Custodian could do, therefore, was to store the chattels and endeavor to protect them."[29]

The task of storage and protection fell to the rapidly expanding Office of the Custodian, headquartered at the Royal Bank Building in Vancouver's business district. In the first weeks of April 1942, the office hired personnel to register Japanese Canadians and their property before they left the province. Making Japanese Canadians' personal property legible to the state required improvised creativity.[30] A system of forms, numerical coding, and manila folders soon emerged under the supervision of Alma McArthur, manager of the newly minted Property Administration Department.[31] The Office of the Custodian urged Japanese Canadians to complete a four-page registration form detailing their property before they departed from the coast.[32] The form solicited details on real estate holdings, financial investments, occupancy and leases, livestock and pets, insurance policies, and the location of pertinent documents. In the six lines provided, it also asked Japanese Canadians for a brief description and the location of "furniture, fixtures, equipment and machinery, stock and trade, and personal effects."[33] Receiving these forms in Vancouver, McArthur created files for each Japanese Canadian adult.[34] In addition to the registration forms, the files would soon hold any correspondence and documentation relating to the management of that owners' property. As the forms came in, these thousands of files became a system for monitoring and surveying Japanese Canadians' property.

Displaced from their homes, Japanese Canadians were forced to make cruel decisions about the management of their personal property. In the uncertain time available before uprooting – warning ranged from twenty-four hours to several months – Japanese Canadians made arrangements for their absence. Their decisions reflected their judgements of the state and their neighbours. They packed their belongings and stored them away, placed property under the care of friends or, even, left their homes with belongings in-place, as if they were simply departing for a weekend. Some sold their businesses and homes, while others, reticent to see heirlooms in the hands of the

Figure 7.7 Japanese Canadians registering with the Custodian of Enemy Property.

state or vandals, buried and even destroyed the items that they valued most.[35] As a result of these wide-ranging strategies, when the Vancouver Office of the Custodian took responsibility for Japanese Canadians' belongings it inherited hundreds of thousands of items in countless locations, some in plain view and others hidden. Thousands of meaningful objects, all of them left behind in ways laden with the significance of displacement and internment, became a bureaucratic problem for the Canadian state.

In practice, then, the vesting of personal property in the state was a messy, chaotic process. An exit report from a lower-level staffer in the Protection Department, G.B. Spain, vividly portrays the simultaneous events that frustrated the Office of the Custodian's administrative process. Describing the initial work of the Protection Department in 1942, Spain documents the challenges of accessing and identifying often concealed property, while contending with thieves:

> The Department of Labour … adopted a very arbitrary practice of giving the Japanese an evacuation date notice without giving us similar advance notice of such intentions. The first notice we received of such evacuation was a day or two after the evacuation had been made, and this necessitated quick action by our field staff to reach the former homes of the Japanese before the thieves moved in. In many cases we reached the scene too late and the thieves had arrived first, or the Japanese had already sold many of their chattels between the date of registration and the date of evacuation. The Protection Department regarded themselves

Figures 7.8–7.9 Photographs of the baggage room at Hastings Park and Japanese Canadians arriving in the Popoff internment camp show the role of personal effects in the internment process.

> as fortunate men when they found the remains of the bacon and eggs on the still warm breakfast dishes. It only meant cleaning the dishes. Then there were gas or electric stoves and water fixtures to be disconnected. The walls, basements and attics had to be examined with the eye of a detective for panels that sounded hollow to the touch or showed signs of recent wall papering which might conceal personal property. It was probably a harrowing experience to the Japanese and I saw plenty of evidence of mental disturbance ... Many Japanese women believed that their friends would not be evacuated; that the war would be finished soon; that they would be back themselves; etc., and left their chattels strewn around the country in anyone's charge. This did not help the Protection Department in identifying chattels.[36]

Over the subsequent months, similarly contradictory impulses – of Japanese Canadians to protect and manage their own property, of thieves to steal, of vandals to destroy – frustrated the state's administrative process. Undermined by its own mishandling, and despite its attempts at registration and inventories, the Canadian state failed to effectively control and manage Japanese Canadians' belongings.

The realities of Japanese Canadian homeownership and renting forced the Office of the Custodian to make quick decisions about storage. In spring 1942, the Office of the Custodian was obliged to remove Japanese Canadians' belongings from rental properties to make way for new tenants.[37] Officials settled on centralized storage, eventually establishing at least forty major storage sites across the province: nine in Vancouver, ten in Steveston, four in New Westminster, five in the Fraser Valley, and twelve "upcountry" (from Salt Spring Island to Ucluelet to Prince Rupert).[38] This approach had advantages for the state. First, it offered the Administration Department an opportunity to compensate for partial reporting. Finding that Japanese Canadians completed their forms in general terms, officials became responsible for creating itemized lists of their property.[39] These inventories were crucial to locating and identifying Japanese Canadians' belongings. Soon officials began to relocate belongings from homes that Japanese Canadians owned, not merely those that they rented. This process facilitated inventory making but also addressed a second problem: by emptying Japanese Canadian homes of their belongings and renting them to tenants, officials felt they could better protect real estate, as vandals were much less likely to rampage through a house rented to white tenants than an empty Japanese Canadian–owned property.[40] In the process of "handling, moving and stor[ing]" Japanese Canadians' belongings, officials entered homes across the province, rearranging the property of the former occupants in their absence.[41]

If the storage centres solved immediate pressures related to renting and vandalism, however, they also created problems. As low-level officials relocated Japanese Canadians' belongings to storage centres, they made judgements about value that disrupted the owners' original organization of their belongings. W.E. Anderson, an Office of the Custodian official, described these decisions when he testified at the Bird Commission in 1948:

> [Anderson] A: [The field men] were to inventory the articles of value as was declared by the Japanese or if they found anything additional, to inventory this, and to give a rough description of the property, and how it was looked after, whether the place was boarded up, who the tenant was, and things like that.
>
> ...
>
> [Solicitor] Q: You mentioned they were to inventory the things which they thought worthwhile inventorying, or valuable?
>
> A: Yes; the majority of the Japanese registered the articles they considered of value, and others just said "household furniture, farm implements"; they did not list anything, so *the men were instructed to use their discretion as to what articles were considered to be of value*. They did not inventory junk and broken stuff [our emphasis].[42]

These incremental decisions could have disastrous consequences for Japanese Canadians if they later requested that the BCSC ship their property to sites of internment.[43] Placed in storage and separated from their physical context (a particular room or building, and other related items), individual objects often held little obvious trace of ownership.

Similarly, "haphazard" practices of storing compromised the Office of the Custodian's ability to administer Japanese Canadians' belongings.[44] Protection Department staffer G.B. Spain recalled that, at the Custodian's largest storage site in Vancouver, the Crone Storage Company "would do the moving into the warehouse during the days and leave the stacking, swamping and listing until nightfall" which, given the faulty lighting in the warehouse, "made careful work irresponsible." Their lists, the official wrote, "were just so much illegible scribble."[45] Spain wrote a report that pushed the office to hire a new moving company but, if the new company's services were "satisfactory and much more economical," their "documentary method left much to be desired."[46] Insufficient inventories rendered Japanese Canadians' belongings misplaced and mislaid. Once the officials removed Japanese Canadians' belongings from their original contexts, their management (and protection) became increasingly complicated. No longer able to infer ownership from location, the state became reliant on its own practice to manage Japanese Canadians' belongings. Dependent on the integrity of third-party agents across the province, the Office of the Custodian's grasp of Japanese Canadians' belongings was tenuous at best.

Haphazard and incomplete, the measures the Office of the Custodian adopted in the spring and summer of 1942 were nevertheless its most faithful attempts to protect

Figure 7.10 The Crone Storage Company was initially the primary service working with the Vancouver Office of the Custodian.

the property of Japanese Canadians. Forms, manila folders, and inventories were the tools by which officials sought to fulfill the promise of protection. Recognition of these efforts of the Office of the Custodian, however, does not alleviate its culpability for mismanagement. Instead, it highlights how the contradictory impulses within policy manifested in practice. Despite officials' efforts to fulfill a promise to protect Japanese Canadians' property, they did not fully comprehend, much less compensate for, the various forms of devaluation that they caused. Even as the Office of the Custodian attempted to make legible Japanese Canadian's belongings, the broader circumstance created by the federal policy of total uprooting frustrated this project. The total uprooting of Japanese Canadians as a racial category made it impossible for the Custodian to replicate its approach in other contexts, namely of entrusting property to free kin and community. Japanese Canadians, responding to their mass internment, sold, hid, and relocated their own belongings, never fully complying with the state's aspiration to transparent records. Thieves stole and vandals destroyed untold amounts of property. And the Custodian's own field men, in negligence and arbitrary decisions, mishandled their tasks. "Movable property" was a thorny problem in the chaotic climate of mass uprooting.

If relocation and storage created challenges in the management of Japanese Canadians' personal property, the immediate alternative was often worse. In their owners' absence, Japanese Canadians' *in situ* property risked destruction or theft.[47] The extent and severity of this destruction is often elided in the Office of the Custodian's summary records.[48] It emerges, instead, in the daily reporting of the administrative state. Officials describe the property damage euphemistically (as "pilfering" or as "petty thefts") and explicitly (as "ransacking," "looting," or "wanton destruction").[49] Taken together, the reports of low-level bureaucrats build a shocking portrait of pervasive and targeted theft and destruction.[50] Throughout the province, vandals and thieves knocked in panels, smashed glass, broke locks, wedged apart iron grills, burrowed tunnels, and tore holes in roofs to access the belongings of Japanese Canadians.[51] In Steveston, an official reported, "[a]lmost every building formerly owned by Japanese … has been entered at one time or another."[52] In Maple Ridge and Pitt Meadows, another echoed that the "homes and chattels of the Japanese … [had] in the majority of cases been broken into." The houses had been stripped. The report continued:

> Doors have been smashed, windows broken, and in some instances so many chattels stolen, that anything which has been left is of no or very little value. Many stoves and heaters appear to have been removed, also dishes, farm implements and carpenter tools. In many cases when ransacking the houses, it appears to be just the love of destruction which has made the thieves go through the buildings[.][53]

The destruction of Japanese Canadians' material lives occurred in both nefarious and overt ways. In countless cases, neighbours quietly took belongings from Japanese Canadians' homes. In other moments, local British Columbians enacted targeted, riotous violence on the property of Japanese Canadians. The vandalism and desecration of Buddhist temples is perhaps especially illustrative. Between November 1942 and November 1945, the Kitsilano Buddhist Mission was ransacked five times.[54] In Steveston, destruction began in November 1942, just after the last Japanese Canadians had been forced from the coast. Vandals reduced the temple to "shambles" (the "articles used in the church service … broken and mutilated") before an agent for the Custodian removed what remained to storage for protection.[55] He overlooked, however, critical items.[56] In March 1943, vandals returned. The destruction was sufficient to offend the sensibilities of the *Marpole-Richmond Review*, which reported that "vandalism [had] probably its miserable peak within the substantial walls of the commodious Buddhist Temple":

> the written records of the temple – marriage licenses, birth certificates, financial records, cancelled checks, books and papers of all kinds, have been ruthlessly thrown over the floor, torn and trampled upon.

> More gruesome, numbers of cans in which have been deposited the white ashes of cremated former citizens of Steveston, have had their seals broken and their contents scattered over the floor, seats and shrine.[57]

It was not the only incident in which such sacred property was desecrated.[58] The reporting on the Buddhist Temple highlights the specific harms entwined with religious or other symbolically sacred property. Attacks on the objects of property were clearly assaults on their owners.[59] Along the coast, religious sites and objects became some of the countless artifacts of Japanese Canadian life targeted and destroyed.

The state responded by disavowing responsibility.[60] Sometimes, derelictions of the duty to protect were minimized through characterizations of these assaults as forms of "pilfering" (literally, minor thefts of items of little value), diminishing the scope and intensity of the actions. Little or no effort was made to identify or apprehend suspects, most often referred to generically as youths.[61] Discussing break-ins in the Powell Street neighbourhood, officials sometimes displaced the specific harms of targeted theft and vandalism by referring broadly to the supposed general character of the area. On two separate occasions, Spain wrote that the Powell Street district was the "hang-out corner of the worst element in Vancouver," and was a "bad neighbourhood," being a "favourite rendezvous of Vancouver's Zoot Suiters."[62] Obscuring the circumstances of the thefts, another official attributed the violations to the "wave of crime" in Vancouver.[63] A summary report from Steveston conveyed another explanation used by contemporaries: "continual house-breaking at Steveston," explained one official, was "blamed by the white population on the influx of Indians who took the place of the Japanese." In fact, he argued, "the white population appear to have been at least equally to blame."[64]

Apprehending vandals fell to the responsibility of local police who, in turn, made few convictions.[65] This was at least partly because police could expect little assistance from the Office of the Custodian. A rare instance where a culprit was identified, serves mostly to reveal why so little was done. At the shipyards of Whonnock, a Mr Peter Rempel was identified by local authorities as a key vandal. Despite sufficient evidence to proceed, the Office of the Custodian demurred. As one official explained, the Custodian had been "more or less forced to shut our eyes" to such "petty thefts." The reason was twofold. First, there was the "difficulty of identification" and, second, "the fact that if any charges were laid it would be a Japanese versus a white man." He explained that

> positive identification was impossible without going to the expense of bringing the actual Japanese involved back to the Protected Area, and as all the chattels could only be considered as used goods, there was little likelihood of positive

> identification being made anyway, and that the Custodian [sic] office would therefore not place any actions.

The problem of identification referred not to the vandal (Mr Rempel) but to the challenge of identifying ownership of the items stolen or vandalized. To do so required the owner's testimony, an arrangement that seemed implausible. The Custodian's office saw the pursuit of such charges as a waste of resources, particularly given the likely futility of a claim from a Japanese Canadian against a white man. Ultimately, the Office of the Custodian convinced local authorities not to report Rempel.[66] Similarly, in another case of an apprehended man, Edward Knowlan, in possession of Japanese Canadians' belongings, the Office of the Custodian "did not prefer a charge against him."[67] The office did not pursue criminal proceedings.

The break-ins and ransacking were ruinous even for the property that vandals left behind. Shears summarized this concern in the 1944 Vancouver Office of the Custodian annual report, writing that the "worst feature" of the break-ins was "not so much the amount stolen, but the throwing of the contents of boxes on the floor in search for values makes it difficult or impossible to identify the goods belonging to various owners."[68] This further problem of identification was prevalent throughout the protection department. Officials reported belongings so scattered "that it [was] quite impossible to repack them," ransacking causing "confusion over the floor" making it "often impossible to identify the ownership of many things," and the contents of boxes scattered and piled "in a state of utter confusion, making shipment impossible."[69] Though these items remained in the state's possession, the break-ins severed belongings from their real owners and impeded the Office of the Custodian's ability to ship Japanese Canadians their belongings or even maintain that the properties were protected.

The Office of the Custodian's portrayals of the vandalism as "senseless" is clearly disingenuous. From the officials' reports, it is clear that deliberate destruction took place. The officials' reports that "[a]lmost every building formerly owned by Japanese … has been entered at one time or another" suggests a widespread, acquisitive motivation for breaking into Japanese Canadians' homes and storage sites across the province.[70] Many facing scarcity themselves likely took the opportunity to improve their circumstances. Further, the reports of destruction suggest what sociologist Stanley Cohen describes as "vindictive" motivation. In this conception, property destruction offers a solution to a range of problems (spite, revenge, or a grudge). For someone with these motivations, vandalism is both "emotionally satisfying" and safe: "detection is unlikely," Cohen writes, "and one is far less likely to be hurt than if personal violence is resorted to."[71] In such cases, the identity of the owners matter; both they themselves and their status as owners are the targets of destruction.[72] Cohen's conception brings into view what state officials rarely mentioned: that the continued and repeated ransacking targeted the belongings of Japanese Canadians. The theft of belongings may have devalued Japanese Canadians' rights as property owners, but their total destruction – the smearing of ashes at the Steveston Buddhist Temple, the smashing of shrines – was a violent devaluing of the people that objects represented.

Racist animus, old rivalries, and blunt greed surely motivated thieves and vandals. Yet the state was also clearly complicit in this racialized violence. By downplaying the severity of vandalism in annual reports, failing to pay for effective security, and deciding against the pursuit of perpetrators, the state created a climate wherein thieves and vandals knew they had little to fear. Focusing on youths, officials trivialized the matter. More fundamentally, the original act of forcibly relocating and detaining thousands of British Columbians and seizing their property on racial grounds, sent a powerful message regarding their relative worth.[73] Rather than a protected population, they become potentially injurable. Rather than property-owning citizens, they become disinvested enemies.

State protection of Japanese Canadians' belongings was deeply flawed. The management of Japanese Canadians' possessions required improvised solutions to practical problems: what would the state do with the belongings of renters as new tenants arrived to replace them? How should the belongings of real estate owners be protected, given widespread theft and vandalism? Where would belongings be stored once removed? How would it respond to the challenge of warehousing the belongings of thousands of people? The Office of the Custodian implemented solutions that never fully accounted for the magnitude of their responsibility or met the compounding challenges of their task. Property was mislaid, mishandled, and misjudged. Vandals and thieves ran free. Further, the very nature of personal property (that it was moveable, that ownership was obscure) dictated that critical moments of protection lay in the value judgements of dozens of individuals (whether field men, storage workers, or watchmen), whose haphazard judgements were fundamentally disconnected from the owners' notions of worth. Between 1942 and 1947, Japanese Canadians lost personal belongings due to state negligence and pervasive animosity.

Shipping and objects of value

Evidently, storing personal property in unsecured homes or poorly managed state depots raised considerable challenges for state officials. In late 1942, the problem of chattels became one of the several rationales federal officials used to shift policy towards total sale.[74] Order in Council PC 469, passed on 19 January 1943, enacted this aspiration in law. Ironically, the policy makers argued, sale was a necessary measure to fulfill the Office of the Custodian's promise to protect Japanese Canadians' interest in their property. Japanese Canadians protested; within two months of Order 469, a network of property owners launched a legal challenge.[75] Despite this resistance, July saw the mass forced sales of real estate and September the first auction of personal belongings. Auction would be the state's method of extinguishing responsibility over Japanese Canadians' chattels. As we shall suggest, the reductive logic of the state that saw the cash proceeds of sale as a legitimate expression of the multiple values that Japanese Canadians derived from their personal property constituted an important dimension of this injustice.

Immediately following PC 469, however, some government officials questioned the indiscriminate sale of Japanese Canadians' possessions. At the very moment the Office of the Custodian gained unrestricted purview to sell (and solve its administrative problems), the Department of Labour, which oversaw the BCSC and the administration of the internment, insisted that the Custodian of Enemy Property recognize some of the personal values Japanese Canadians attributed to their belongings. Concerned with maintaining Japanese Canadians' cooperation in the camps, officials in the Department of Labour pushed their counterparts in the Office of the Custodian to sell only selected personal belongings and to preserve what Japanese Canadians held most dear. In the compromise that ensued, federal officials articulated, and then failed to meaningfully implement, a process to respect (at least partially) the property rights of Japanese Canadians.

Conflict emerged from overlapping authority over the belongings of Japanese Canadians. During the forced uprooting, the BCSC had assured Japanese Canadians that the Department of Labour would ship their possessions to sites of internment at their request.[76] Given the complications of locating and identifying property, however, the Office of the Custodian resented this promise, considering it an unjustifiable resource drain. The issue of shipping thus became an indicator of the departments' sincerity in respecting the property rights of Japanese Canadians and the values they attached to their personal possessions.

The divergent positions first surfaced in late summer 1942. In the midst of the chaotic management of Japanese Canadians' property, McPherson appealed to the BCSC to postpone shipping any further "personal effects." "The Custodian's Agents are continuing to do this special work," he explained, "which takes up considerable time, and in many cases appears to be unjustified under the present situation." He included a request for shipment from Tori Tamoto and the relevant documentation as "an example of the difficulties experienced in complying with requests received." As soon as the Custodian's protection department received the request, McPherson explained, they checked the house and found that it had been "broken into." He pointed to three divergent inventory lists from Tamoto's file (Tamoto's declared property, the agent's inventory, and Tamoto's requests for property) believing that the challenge that ensued from these discrepancies was self-evident. The categories of Tamoto's initial declaration were clear but general, the Custodian's agents' inventory selectively itemized, and Tamoto's request was specific. As before, a problem created by the state was reframed by McPherson as a problem created by the dispossessed:

> I do not know what your personal opinion is as to the Custodian's Agent wasting his time finding the property disclosed on this form, but it seems to me that we are going to the extreme to co-operate with these Japanese, and much unnecessary work is being placed on the Custodians' Agents at a time when they can be more usefully used in other work.

McPherson requested that shipment be halted until the "evacuation is completed and the particular individual or family [is] in their new home."[77] The Office of the Custodian's administration was failing and staff members were unable to return Japanese Canadians their belongings.

The tension between the Department of Labour and the Custodian reemerged after Order in Council PC 469 purported to expand the Custodian's power to sell Japanese Canadians' belongings, a power that had the potential to eliminate the burdensome management of chattels. In the weeks that followed, McPherson reshaped the Vancouver Office of the Custodian's approach to chattels to fit the new ethos. In conformity with the arguments that rationalized the forced sales, McPherson emphasized the potential deterioration of moveable property and diminished to irrelevance the question of consent on the part of owners. He instructed that all "stock ... likely to deteriorate or disappear" could "be considered as perishable" and should be sold.[78] Just as he had in advocating the new policy, McPherson stretched the notion of perishability in its implementation to encompass property that might be vandalized, stolen, or lost. The logic is wilfully circular. Personal property "perished" as a direct and predictable consequence of the state's own policy. Yet the state's very failure to protect Japanese Canadians' belongings now became a justification for forced sale.

Order in Council PC 469 had implications for interdepartmental policy. In early March, McPherson met with George Collins, commissioner of the BCSC, to discuss the change. The two conceived of advisory committees that would oversee the sale of real estate and made arrangements for the anticipated income that would soon flow into Japanese Canadians' accounts.[79] A sticking point, however, was sale of all personal property. Having completed its initial task of forcibly uprooting Japanese Canadians, the BCSC had reoriented towards a new policy objective: the permanent dispersal of Japanese Canadians from British Columbia. Chattels figured into their plans. On one hand, it was in the Department of Labour's interest for Japanese Canadians to have as few belongings as possible, to facilitate their imminent relocation. To McPherson, Collins described the "considerable amount of furniture which" Japanese Canadians "already [had] in their possession" and which the BCSC was encouraging them to sell

Figure 7.11 The belongings that Japanese Canadians accumulated in internment camps created procedural challenges for the Office of the Custodian and the British Columbia Security Commission.

"before they move east. "I realize that by moving a lot of cheap kitchen chairs, tables, etc.," he wrote, "we are simply cluttering up the Railways and these articles can be sold here and replaced with the equivalent sum of cash on their arrival in Manitoba, or eastern Canada."[80] On the other hand, however, Collins recognized the emotional significance of personal property and the ill will that might arise if all of it was sold without consent. As deputy minister of labour Arthur MacNamara later agreed: "The matter of selling household and personal chattels of the Japanese is a delicate one, and if approached in the wrong way it may arouse a storm of protest."[81]

Conceding to McPherson's push for sale, the Department of Labour insisted on two stipulations. First, MacNamara requested that the government (and specifically the Office of the Custodian) pay for shipment of Japanese Canadians' belongings. MacNamara explained that it was "preferable" to charge fees associated with the shipment of Japanese Canadians' goods "to the Government of Canada as a service to the

Evacuees, who were removed from their homes by Government Order as a war measure." After all, the department was "endeavouring to persuade these people to move east into productive employment, and therefore, desire to avoid arousing resentment which may hamper such movement at this time."[82] Additional fees resulting from a hardship already outside Japanese Canadians' control were not likely to garner goodwill toward the Canadian state. Thus, the Department of Labour proposed offering shipment as a service, free-of-cost, to Japanese Canadians.

Initially, the Office of the Custodian conceded to this request. Shipments would continue, but (rather than the Office of the Custodian) it would be the BCSC that absorbed the costs and responsibility. The Office of the Custodian's field men continued to locate belongings, "acting as agents for the British Columbia Security Commission."[83] Reticence continued about the costs of the program. Oblivious to the values that Japanese Canadians may derive from their personal property, officials in the Custodian's office persistently questioned whether the belongings were worth the cost of shipping, and in spring of 1944 the process was discontinued.[84] At this point (recall that internment continued until 1949), the BCSC and the Department of Labour accepted the Custodian's logic. Moveable property still in storage was at risk of devaluation and should be sold. As of May 1944, McPherson described his office as having "a free hand to proceed with the liquidation."[85]

The Department of Labour's second stipulation, that certain possessions be protected from forced sales, proved more enduring. This measure was also intended to encourage goodwill on the part of interned Japanese Canadians. "The Japanese as a group will not express strenuous opposition to their chattels being disposed of," Collins surmised, so long as "personal effects of a sentimental nature or religious nature which will not deteriorate with storage will be centralized and stored in safekeeping and withheld from sale or other disposition for the time being."[86] More forcefully, MacNamara proposed what appeared to be a radical departure from the standard operating procedures of the Office of the Custodians: consultation with owners. He wrote:

> I would advise asking each head of a Japanese family to draw up a list of articles of a sentimental or religious nature which he wishes to keep either with him or in storage, on the understanding that he thereby gives consent for the sale of the rest of his Chattels by the Custodian at as high a price as can be obtained.[87]

For the Department of Labour, then, the management of Japanese Canadians' personal possessions was closely entwined with the success of their future dispersal policy, that is, their management of people. To accomplish the forced dispersal, Collins and MacNamara were partially willing to recognize and respect the variegated values Japanese Canadians ascribed to their belongings.

In response to this request, the Custodian of Enemy Property agreed to preserve property of "sentimental value and religious nature." This remained the policy throughout the auctions and until 1949. Critically, however, the policy proceeded without consultation. Although the origins of the category lay in a recognition of the personal significance of the belongings – that the forced sale of certain objects, over others, could arouse "resentment" – it was implemented in disregard of the preferences of owners. MacNamara's recommendation to have Japanese Canadians identify items of "religious or sentimental value" was never initiated. This left critical valuation decisions about belongings in the hands of the very same low-level officials who had already misplaced and mishandled much of what Japanese Canadians owned. Perhaps they feared, as Collins did in April 1943, that "if we were to ask the Japanese to indicate articles which had a sentimental value, they would include everything that they own."[88]

Taking it upon themselves to ascribe meaning to the possessions of others, officials had choices to make. Although officials frequently referred to "personal effects of a purely religious or sentimental nature" in their internal reporting, they rarely elaborated on what this designation entailed.[89] In April 1943, however, when Collins confirmed that the policy would continue, he described the category through contrast, saying that that the Custodian

> might decide to dispose of furniture and miscellaneous items such as washtubs, dishes, etc. However, trunks, pictures, ceremonial regalia, etc., which would be considered to have a sentimental value would not be disposed of and would be stored by the Custodian for return to the Japanese at some future date.[90]

Nearly a year later, Coleman described the same category in terms of religious significance:

> The chattels, as a general rule, were not of any considerable value. Care had to be exercised also in respect of other chattels of little tangible value but which, it was suggested, were invested with some degree of religious significance under the religious beliefs of some of these people.[91]

If the policy emerged out of a recognition of the varied meanings of the belongings of "these people" (and the implicated harm of sale), it was difficult to put into practice on the ground. Office of the Custodian staff relied on largely arbitrary judgements about value as they transferred the possessions from storage centres to auction houses. Take, for instance, Shears' consideration of Japanese festival dolls: "Their intrinsic value is very small and judged by European standards is only a very cheap doll and in normal times could be very easily replaced." He admitted that in "some upper class

Japanese families the dresses on these dolls are quite elaborate and are supposed to be meticulous as to period" but suggested that the officials "clean up what [was] left" (in other words, dispose of what remained in the storehouses). Anticipating criticism of his decision, Shears wrote that, if they had any religious significance, it was minor: "Both Mr Bell and Mr Spain assure me that they are of no religious significance but were brought out for display once a year at one festival in March."[92] Without consulting Japanese Canadian owners, officials made arbitrary decisions about the value of Japanese Canadians' belongings, in which racist ignorance masquerading as expertise devalued their religious and cultural meanings (many important holidays only occur once a year).

Yet more prosaically, the category of objects of sentimental value denotes objects without fungible value, objects that the state could not sell (even if it tried). From the perspective of the state, these were objects of no market value, comparable to what it devalued as "junk" or "rubbish." In September 1945, Shears travelled to the Steveston storage centre to investigate what remained after two years of auction. What remained was a "large number of trunks, cartons, and parcels, many of them broken and containing a lot of stuff which can only be described as junk." He and the accompanying staff "dumped out a number of trunks and a number of packages and found that much of the contents could only be considered as rags and worthless material and in many cases pure rubbish." Reporting to the Rural Advisory Committee, he explained that there "remained to be dealt with … some items which are saleable but largely comprising clothing, rags, paper books as well as such items as photographs, small shrines and personal correspondence and items of a purely personal nature." The committee settled on a five-pronged valuation practice. They advised the Custodian to sell what it could, donate old clothing and fabrics to rag or old clothes dealers, discard or destroy what was "entirely valueless" and keep a record of their actions. All the while, they would "set aside purely personal items which could not be replaced."[93] In practice the policy, designed to preserve a measure of Japanese Canadians' belongings, came to indicate those things, like "rubbish," that could not be sold.

The interdepartmental negotiations over the management of Japanese Canadians' personal belongings undermine the Office of the Custodians' claims that they made the most of a difficult circumstance.[94] Although strategic in intention, the Department of Labour's willingness to consider the complex values of property – and to advocate consultation with owners – accentuates the reluctant approach taken by the Office of the Custodian. Officials could have consulted with Japanese Canadians about which belongings to sell and what to preserve. Instead, the Office of the Custodian remained committed to a process that could not and would not accommodate Japanese Canadians' valuations. At a critical juncture, before Japanese Canadians' personal property became available for sale, the officials decided against pursuing a policy of consultation or consent.

Auctions

The Office of the Custodian decided that given the range of the goods in its purview, their "perishability," and the challenges involved in their shipment and storage, auctions were the most feasible approach. The sale of merchandise was not foreign to the Office of the Custodian: the office had already sold by tender merchandise and property deemed perishable. In early 1943, however, Shears argued that, in the case of all Japanese Canadians' property, the diversity of the holdings (if it were to be sold by lot according to owner) would deter customers. "In Public Auction those interested are likely to be larger," Shears explained, "some people requiring one article and some another."[95] The office chose this route. Forced sale at auction entailed a pervasive yet very powerful form of valuation known as commensuration: the presumption that "all value is relative and that the value of something can be expressed only in terms of its relation to something else. This valuing denies the possibility of intrinsic value."[96] One example of commensuration is that of attributing monetary values to things. Fourcade notes the prevalence of an economic logic of evaluation for assessments of worth relevant to the liquidation process: "first, money is a good enough metric for the 'utility' we get from commodities; second, consumer behavior, for example, what people are willing to pay [e.g. at auctions], is a good enough indicator of the value of things."[97]

Insofar as the state was concerned, auctions allowed the straightforward conversion of the values that Japanese Canadians had in their personal property into its commensurate cash value. This assumes either a value monism that gives one value, such as utility, overriding significance or the presence of substitutability, whereby multiple values, if they exist, are commensurate: all that matters is determining the appropriate rate of exchange.

Commensuration imagines that justice could be served by realizing the best cash value of assets and ensuring its transfer to the former owner. Yet singular and substitutable forms of valuation, while bureaucratically appealing, do not easily align with lived forms of valuation. People experience and value assets in ways that defy simple substitution. People "possess certain objects they feel are almost part of themselves. Those objects are closely bound up with personhood because they are part of the way we constitute ourselves as continuing personal entities in the world."[98] The multiple and diverse values that Japanese Canadians derived from their objects are surely not always commensurable or reducible to singular cash values.[99] More fundamentally, the very act of sale negated the value that owners attached to holding on to these objects.[100]

Seeing no such problems of valuation, the Custodian made auctions a regular public event across coastal British Columbia. The first was held on 15 September at the Fuji Chop Suey restaurant on Powell Street, almost nine months to the day after Order 469.[101] Between 1943 and 1945, the 250 auctions across British Columbia sold roughly

Figure 7.12 The Vancouver Office of the Custodian enlisted private auctioneers across the province to sell Japanese Canadians' belongings.

90,000 individual items and grouped lots for $245,583.89.[102] After deducting costs of advertising, handling, and the auctioneer's 10 per cent commission, the Office of the Custodian deposited the proceeds into the accounts of individual Japanese Canadians. Often unaware that their property had been up for sale, Japanese Canadians received notice in the form of type written receipts that recorded the details of such transactions. In Vancouver, officials kept duplicates of the receipts for their own files, creating a bureaucratic record of the state's (ostensibly) accountable management of property.

Despite the meagre sums that Japanese Canadians received, the auctioneers reported lucrative sales, attributing the success of the auctions to a scarcity of goods during the war, compounded by an influx of people to coastal BC. One described a "terrific shortage of goods at that particular time," when, for instance, "all furniture stores were completely devoid of chesterfields. Stoves, dining room suites – good stoves were practically impossible to obtain at that time, kitchen ranges."[103] Also citing "scarcity," another auctioneer described the auctions as "very much better" than ordinary sales "for the reason that there were so many people demanding goods at that time … so many people coming to the city and there were good pay rolls and they had lots of money."[104] A third attributed their success to the influx of wealth owing to the war: "more people had money then," he explained, "the soldiers left the wives their money, and they bid vigorously where previously … they were not in a position to do so."[105] In all, auctioneers described over-crowded auction halls with brisk and competitive bidding and high demand.[106] They cited their own benefit (making a percentage on each sale) and the dealers' dismay (at the high prices) as evidence of competitive rates.[107]

The frequent, well-attended auctions were widely known. Advertisements for auctions, sometimes mentioning the names of the former owners, circulated both in local newspapers and featured on public signage.[108] Robust attendance drove competitive bidding and sale prices. One auctioneer recalled that he "got a better price from the Japanese sales than we got on our own [regular sales]," explaining that

> I think the reason was it was something out of the ordinary; and we got ladies from the towns that would never bother to go to an agricultural market, but they were going to see what there was cheap at the sale, and the result was they were a little bit more wealthy than my general run of people, and the prices were considerably higher.[109]

Likewise, another auctioneer explained that the volume of goods attracted interested crowds (in search of bargains), while the crowds, in turn, drove up the prices. Compared to auctions "for other people," auctions for Japanese Canadians' belongings "were very good, because there was a larger quantity of goods and a larger variety offered and more curiosity expressed over it and more people would attend the sale there."[110] This very "variety," of course, was the result of thousands of people, of varying means and occupations, forced to sell all that they owned. At the same time that Japanese Canadians' property was a target for vandalism and theft, auctions allowed former neighbours to acquire the seized property legally. Purchasing Japanese Canadians' property, thousands of ordinary people became complicit in the dispossession process.

Impressive prices at auction, however, still diverged profoundly from an owners' valuation of their own belongings. Part of the explanation of this dissonance – in which auctioneers saw great prices and owners the opposite – resulted from a commercial valuation process, in which objects were appraised by auctioneers. Though

Figure 7.13 The Vancouver Office of the Custodian enlisted private auctioneers across the province to sell Japanese Canadians' belongings.

auctioneers sold machinery, radios, refrigerators, and washing machines (items for which market value could be easily discerned), these items were in the minority. More commonly, they sold many goods that would likely have never made it onto the market in any other circumstances.[111] The testimony of Gowing Frost, an auctioneer from Abbotsford, illuminates the valuation of these items. In his municipality, which was rural and agricultural, there were "two rather outstanding Japanese who had very[,] very nice stuff, but the majority were peasant Japanese people, who would rather make anything than pay out cash, and as the result, it was a lot of home-made stuff that they had[.]" Another auctioneer described a surplus of handmade cupboards. Never intended to be sold on the market, these homemade belongings nevertheless comprised the households and lives of many Japanese Canadians. In the eyes of state officials, obtaining any monetary return for such homemade and "low-class stuff" was a success.[112] As Shears, pleased after the first auction, claimed that, "Mr Thompson, the Auctioneer, considered the prices obtained for all items of any importance to be satisfactory and we were also able to dispose of items of no real intrinsic value at very fair prices."[113]

After the final auctions in 1947, the Office of the Custodian cleared out and reorganized its storage houses. Only fragments of Japanese Canadians' material lives remained. In Vancouver, dozens of photograph albums, kotos, and family shrines filled storage units. In Haney, the storage house held more disparate items, clearly things that did not sell at the auctions, including many "unidentified belongings," which were similarly personal but could not be reunited with their owners.[114] The rest of Japanese Canadians' belongings were thoroughly dispersed throughout the province. They had sold in public and well-advertised ways. Auctions had offered the Canadian state a way to escape its failing measures to protect Japanese Canadians' moveable property. Commensuration, in this case converting the values that Japanese Canadians attributed to their property to cash value, offered the economic logic for the sales. Thousands of British Columbians bid vigorously at the auctions, seizing the opportunity they presented. Disregarding the wishes of the Japanese Canadian owners, the state eliminated their material ties to their prewar lives. With its meticulous records and receipts, the Office of the Custodian claimed that due process had been honoured.

Conclusion

Between October 1942 and April 1949, very few Japanese Canadians obtained permission to return to their homes, even to visit. If they had, they would likely have been aghast. They might have caught state officials carting away their packed belongings, former neighbours stealing their farm equipment, or crowds bidding on their kitchenware. They would have seen much to counter the Office of the Custodian and BCSC's claims of protection. Yet the chaos that they might have seen – what Shears dubbed as both a "parody" and "tragedy" – was called protection by the state.[115] There is much more to be said regarding the state's mismanagement of Japanese Canadian personal property during the 1940s. In this preliminary foray, we have tried, at minimum, to carefully document the crucial steps through which this process passed – vesting, challenges of management and storage, failure to protect property from widespread theft, destruction and vandalism, debates over consent, and the crucial decision to force sale via auctions. Attention to the management of Japanese Canadians' personal belongings offers a unique pathway to understanding the everyday racism and complicity of state officials and bystanders in Canada's internment era. The records of personal property portray a chaotic, haphazard, and grievously neglectful set of state practices.

Further, the management of chattels offers a robust opportunity to study how divergent impulses within federal policy play out in practice. Ostensibly concerned with protection and accountability, the Office of the Custodian (led by McPherson) made firm decisions about the limits of the state's responsibility to Japanese Canadians. This is, by any measure, a story of profound and enduring injustice, at multiple levels, including the racialized grounds for vesting, the lack of stewardship shown in storage and protection, and the reductive logic of the auction house. Devaluation – of a community of people, of their property rights, of the values they attached to their possessions, and the places in which they were grounded – made this policy possible and suffused the way in which it unfolded.

Focusing on the everyday bureaucratic processes through which this occurred is vital, allowing us to see its messy, contradictory, and often ugly rationalities. This is also useful in reminding us that dispossession was experienced in multiple and manifold encounters between state officials, ordinary British Columbians, and Japanese Canadians, particularly when personal property was at stake. The archive reveals that the encounters of dispossession were not isolated moments but were experienced through repeated acts of devaluation. The message of personal property is that there was no moment of dispossession, as such. Rather, there were ongoing experiences of dispossession, involving countless people (children, fishers, renters, field men, auctioneers, vandals), regarding multiple objects (wardrobes, clothing, pets, religious artefacts, tools), and entailing iterative acts of state violence, devaluation, and misvaluation. We conclude, therefore, with just one such story, that of Kaoru Atagi, at least insofar as it appears in the state archive, and the manner in which it illustrates the broader account above.

Kaoru Atagi was an unmarried boat builder, who owned property in Steveston with his brother. His father had started the Atagi Boat Works in 1900, acquiring title to the land in 1925, dying in 1944, after the family were interned on 21 May 1942, when Kaoru was twenty-nine years old. Kaoru had turned the keys over to a white neighbour, Christen Bredersen, on the understanding that the Custodian had charge over his property, with the expectation that he would return after his "evacuation." His personal property, reported in his official form, included both domestic items – such as a gramophone, a "Japanese bath," a carpet sweeper – and many work items, essential to his trade – two crosscut saws, an air drill, and two sledgehammers, for example. In mid-August, Bredersen reported to the BCSC that the house had been broken into and the place burgled. He noted that he had reported the entry to the police "who came out but could do nothing." The local agent, C.C. Robinson, removed the remainder of the chattels but reported that, "my opinion is that a lot of furniture and utensils and clothing had been stolen and removed before we arrived. It took us 3 days and even then we noticed pilfering over night … This is a very bad case of pilfering."[116]

The value of all that Atagi lost was at issue six years later when Atagi submitted a claim to the Bird Commission. Atagi estimated the actual cash value of his lost land and chattels, some of which he had concealed in a hidden compartment when he was uprooted, as nearly three times the amount he had actually received from the forced sales.[117] The commissioner asked Atagi to calculate the value of the goods in the concealed compartment. "This is very hard to do," Atagi confessed. Perhaps his difficulty reflects not only the challenges of commensuration (how much is the cash value of a shrine, for example?) but also the broader challenge of collapsing the presumably multiple familial, cultural, spiritual values of these items into a narrowly framed cash calculus. The commissioner became increasingly frustrated as Atagi tried to itemize the value of the materials in the compartment, grumbling that "with a thousand claims to be heard, I can't stop here to have you go over all the minute details of your household goods," echoing the state's broader frustrations with the diversity and multiplicity of the personal possessions that it became obliged to manage.[118] Indeed, as is clear from our broader account, the "minute details" matter a very great deal, both for Atagi and for the thousands of other Japanese Canadians who found the complex values and meanings they attached to their personal property denied, ignored, misread, and abbreviated.

NOTES

Sincere thanks to Eric M. Adams, Jordan Stanger-Ross, Gord Lyall, and Trevor Wideman for their helpful comments on an earlier draft of this chapter.

1 Excerpt from Frank Gould Shears's notes in preparation for his testimony at the Royal Commission on Japanese Claims. [F.G. Shears?], typed notes, [1941?], file 10, box 11, series four, "Office Documents," F.G. Shears Papers, Thomas Fisher Rare Book Library, University of Toronto (hereafter Shears Papers).

2 Testimony of William Eric Anderson, 29 September 1948, file "General Evidence (Sept. 24–30, 1948)," vol. 76, RG 33-69, LAC, 670.

3 Testimony of William Graydon Willard, 6 December 1948, file "General Evidence (Dec. 1–6 1948)," vol. 76, RG 33-69, LAC, 627–8.

4 Ibid., 621. Particular thanks to Nicole Yakashiro for highlighting this exemplary articulation of exoticization of objects ("People In-Between," Landscapes of Injustice Working Paper, March 2018), accessed 18 September 2019, https://www.landscapesofinjustice.com/wp-content/uploads/2019/09/Working-Paper-5-People-In-Between_-Yakashiro-Nicole_March-2018.pdf.

5 Testimony of Francis Edward Binnington, 6 December 1948, file "General Evidence (Dec. 1–6 1948)," vol. 76, RG 33-69, LAC, 592.

6 Testimony of Charles Spencer Pallot, 28 September 1948, file "General Evidence (Sept. 24–30, 1948)," vol. 76, RG 33-69, LAC, 606; Testimony of Gowing Frost, 29 September 1948, file "General Evidence (Sept. 24–30)," vol. 79, RG 33-69, LAC, 653.

7 Henry Irving Bird, "Report Upon The Investigation Into Claims of Persons of The Japanese Race Pursuant to Terms of Order-in-Council PC 1810, July 18, 1947, as amended," [3 April?], 1950, file 2, "Bird, Henry Irvine, Report upon the investigation into claims of persons of the Japanese race pursuant to terms of order-in-council PC 1810. [copy 2], [1950]," box 5, series 2, "Reports," Shears Papers, 56–7.

8 Scholars have granted the state's management and sale of Japanese Canadians' personal belongings only passing attention. Jordan Stanger-Ross is most attentive to the process on the ground in his introduction to *Witness to Loss* where he momentarily considers the process and aptly describes it as "unprepared" and abysmal. Though brief, his astute observation that the state's solution to the "problem of chattels" was sale informs this chapter. Jordan Stanger-Ross and Pamela Sugiman eds., *Witness to Loss: Race, Culpability, and Memory in the Dispossession of Japanese Canadians* (Montreal & Kingston: McGill-Queen's University Press, 2017), xviii–xix. The foundational scholars of the internment era noted the sale of Japanese Canadians' belongings, yet a reliance on oral histories and public-facing government inquiries and reports (specifically the 1947 Standing Committee on Public Accounts hearings and the Bird Commission) produced only partial accounts in which chattels are overshadowed by real estate sales. Ann Gomer Sunahara, *The Politics of Racism: The Uprooting of Japanese Canadians during the Second World War* (Toronto: J. Lorimer, 1981), 96, 141; Ken Adachi, *The Enemy That Never Was: A History of the Japanese Canadians* (Toronto: McClelland and Stewart, 1976), 322, 330–1. Mona Oikawa drew on Nisei women's oral histories to convey the loss of personal belongings. In her study, narrators describe the dispossession in relation to specific belongings, whether cherished items, "family things," furniture, or pets (*Cartographies of Violence: Japanese Canadian Women, Memory, and the Subjects of the Internment* [Toronto: University of Toronto Press, 2012], 106–12).

9 To the officials of the Office of the Custodian of Enemy Property, chattels excluded automobiles, radios, cameras, fishing vessels, fishing nets, and firearms. Albeit not real property, these types of moveable property were subject to distinct policies of seizure and sale.

10 Alex Jeffrey, *The Improvised State: Sovereignty, Performance and Agency in Dayton Bosnia* (West Sussex: John Wiley & Sons, 2012).

11 https://valuationstudies.liu.se.

12 Claes-Fredrik Helgesson and Fabian Muniesa, "For What It's Worth: An Introduction to Valuation Studies," *Valuation Studies* 1, no. 1 (2013): 2.

13 John Dewey, *Theory of Valuation* (Chicago, IL: The University of Chicago Press, 1939).

14 Helgesson and Muniesa, "For What It's Worth," 3; Michèle Lamont, "Toward a Comparative Sociology of Valuation and Evaluation," *Annual Review of Sociology* 38, no. 1 (2012): 201–21.

15 PC 1942-1665, 4 March 1942, file 2516G, vol. 1750, RG 2-A-1-a, LAC.

16 Reg Whitaker and Greg Kealey write that the total number of internees of German and Italian descent, combined with communists and Canadian Nazis, was just over 1,200 in 1940. It was under the same laws that the RCMP arrested and interned thirty-eight Japanese Canadians immediately after Canada declared war against Japan in December 1941. Reg Whitaker and Greg Kealey, "A War on Ethnicity? The RCMP and Internment," in *Enemies Within: Italian and Other Internees in Canada and Abroad*, eds. Franca Iacovetta, Roberto Perin, and Angelo Principe (Toronto: University of Toronto Press, 2000), 129; Adachi, *The Enemy That Never Was*, 199. As noted in the introduction, the

closest precedent in Canada may have been the World War I internment of Ukrainians (lxi, note 53).

17 Memorandum from McPherson to P.S. Ross & Sons, Re: Internees' Assets, 20 December 1941, file 16: "Vancouver Office – Reports, Correspondence, memoranda re administration and operations of the Vancouver Office. 1941/12-1950/01," vol. 2, RG 117-C-1, LAC.

18 Ross later became absorbed by the global accountancy firm Deloitte (http://cbhf.ca/philip-s-ross).

19 "Note to Persons of The Japanese Race," *The New Canadian*, 12 March 1942, 4.

20 Dewey, *Theory of Valuation*, 194–5; John Dewey, Jo Ann Boydston, and Larry A Hickman, *The Collected Works of John Dewey, 1882–1953 (2nd release). Electronic Edition. The Later Works of John Dewey, 1925–1953. Volume 13: 1938–1939, Essays, Experience and Education, Freedom and Culture, and Theory of Valuation* (Charlottesville, VA: InteLex Corporation, 2009), http://VH7QX3XE2P.search.serialssolutions.com/?V=1.0&L=VH7QX3XE2P&S=JCs&C=TC0001862262&T=marc&tab=BOOKS.

21 Maureen E. Brady notes that since at least the eighteenth century chattel property has been characterized by three rights: (1) the ability to exclude others, (2) the ability to transfer the object, and (3) control over its use. Use, transfer, and control were all negated by the state ("The Lost Effects of the Fourth Amendment: Giving Personal Property Due Protection," *Yale Law Journal* 125, no. 4 [2016]: 946–1017).

22 Eduardo M. Penalver, "Property's Memories," *Fordham Law Review* 80, 3 (2011): 1071–88; Rebeca Salas, "Spatial Narratives of Property Loss: Social Memory and the Dispossession of Japanese Canadian-Owned Property in British Columbia" (MA thesis, Simon Fraser University, 2018).

23 "Report on Administration of Japanese Affairs in Canada, 1942–1944," file 147715: "Labour – Report On Administration Of Japanese Affairs In Canada. 1944/10/10," vol. 2116, RG 13, LAC.

24 "First Group Leaves Steveston Sat., Men Back from Camps to Prairies," *The New Canadian* 25 April 1942.

25 The article reported that, "in a number of cases the provisions for free baggage were being grossly abused." The article also referenced future reimbursement for the "families who were evacuated in great haste from up-coast points" who paid for their own shipping. "May Get Effects from Up-Coast Points," *The New Canadian*, 2 May 1942.

26 *The New Canadian* was the sole Japanese Canadian newspaper permitted to continue publication during internment. As Eric M. Adams and Jordan Stanger-Ross note, however, at this time, the British Columbia Security Commission had assumed full editorial control of the paper. Eric M. Adams, Jordan Stanger-Ross, and the Landscapes of Injustice Research Collective, "Promises of Law: The Unlawful Dispossession of Japanese Canadians," *Osgoode Hall Law Journal* 54, no. 3 (Spring 2017): 708.

27 This appeared in notices and *The New Canadian*. "Important Notice, May 19 1942," personal archives of Masako Fukawa (see figure 5.2, chapter 5); "New Baggage Regulations Issued," *The New Canadian*, 23 May 1942. For a more detailed discussion, see chapter 7. In early 1942, the Office of the Custodian and BCSC planned to eventually ship Japanese Canadians their belongings by "car lot." Letter from Glenn McPherson to Mr Fisher (BCSC), 28 August 1942, file 10: "Vancouver Office – General Correspondence, memoranda and clippings. 1941/04-1947/10," vol. 1, RG 117-C-1, LAC.

28 "Will Ship Stored Goods Only at Owner's Expense," *The New Canadian*, 9 September 1942; "Supervisor's Okay, Send for Goods in Storage," *The New Canadian*, 7 October 1942.

29 Letter from McPherson to MacNamara, 14 October 1943, file 59010: "Chattels (Japanese)," vol. 2826, RG 117-A-3, LAC.

30 Here we take inspiration from James C. Scott's discussion of "legibility." Scott offers the term to describe the process whereby officials take "exceptionally complex … and local social practices … and [create] a standard grid" whereby their subject of interest can be "centrally recorded and monitored." This "narrowing of vision," Scott explained, renders an "overall, aggregate, synoptic view of a selective reality" that aims to facilitate (ideally) "a high degree of schematic knowledge, control, and manipulation." James C. Scott, *Seeing Like a State: How Certain Schemes to Improve the Human Condition Have Failed* (New Haven: Yale University Press, 1998), 3, 11.

31 "Property Administration, Supervisor – Mrs A.G. McArthur," [F.G. Shears ?], Overview of the support structure, responsibilities and operations of the Vancouver branch of the Custodian of Enemy Property, [1942?], file 1, box 11, series 4: "Office documents," Shears Papers.

32 "Make Application, Custodian to Take Control of Property of Evacuees," *The New Canadian*, 12 March 1942; "Custodian To Act For Evacuated People," *The New Canadian*, 6 April 1942; "All Information at These Offices," *The New Canadian*, 25 April 1942.

33 Few Japanese Canadians wrote an itemized list of their possessions (though some did attach inventories of their stock and trade). Perhaps they believed that listing the location of their possessions was enough and that their house or farm would be protected as an entity, each item a component of the whole.

34 "Property Administration, Supervisor – Mrs A.G. McArthur," report, file 1, box 11, series 4, Shears Papers. See also "Vancouver Office of the Custodian Annual Report, 1944," image 360, microfilm reel C9469, RG 117-C-1, LAC, 15.

35 Oral histories tell us a range of stories of personal property that eluded the government's records. See chapter 11.

36 Memorandum from G.B. Spain to F.G. Shears, 29 October 1946, file 7: "Green, H.F. [Protection Dept., Office of the Custodian], Thefts and Vandalism, 1942–1947," box 4, series 2: "Reports," Shears Papers. Spain's comments about gender are important. In January, the state had ordered all men between ages eighteen and forty-five to work in road camps outside of the restricted area. As a result, women were often forced to do the painful triage, deciding what to bring to internment and what to leave behind.

37 For premises owned by Japanese Canadians, Shears later explained, the issue was "not quite so urgent as in many cases storage was arranged in a room in the house" or was included in a rental arrangement. "Vancouver Office of the Custodian Annual Report, 1944," image 263, microfilm reel C9469, RG 117-C-1, LAC, 18.

38 "Vancouver Office of the Custodian Annual Report, 1944," image 265, microfilm reel C9469, RG 117-C-1, LAC, 20.

39 Ibid.

40 Ibid.

41 "Vancouver Office of the Custodian Annual Report, 1944," image 263, microfilm reel C9469, RG 117-C-1, LAC, 18.

42 Testimony of W.E. Anderson, file: "General Evidence 24 Sept–30 Sept, 1948, vol. 76, RG 33-69, LAC; file 7: "Green, H.F. [Protection Dept., Office of the Custodian], Thefts and Vandalism, 1942–1947," box 4, series 2: "Reports," Shears Papers.

43 The issue arose in Steveston, for instance, where the Office of the Custodian agent C.C.

Robinson had selectively removed Japanese Canadians' belongings from their homes. Memorandum by F.G. Green, 28 March 1944, file 7, box 4, series 2, Shears Papers.

44 Memorandum from G.B. Spain to F.G. Shears, 29 October 1946, file 7, box 4, series 2, Shears Papers.

45 Ibid.

46 Ibid.

47 Letter from F.G. Shears to K.W. Wright, 8 March 1946, file 7, box 4, series 2, Shears Papers.

48 Vancouver Office of the Custodian Annual Reports, images 218–620, microfilm reel C9469, RG 117-C-1, LAC.

49 Letter from F.G. Shears to K.W. Wright, 8 March, 1946, file 7: "Green, H.F. [Protection Dept., Office of the Custodian], Thefts and Vandalism, 1942–1947," box 4, series 2: "Reports," Shears Papers; "Vancouver Office of the Custodian Annual Report, 1946," image 365, microfilm reel C9469, RG 117-C-1, LAC, 25; Memorandum from W.E. Anderson to Shears, "Re: Chattel Thefts," 19 February 1945, file 7, box 4, series 2, Shears Papers; Letter from G.B. Spain to H.F. Green, 24 July 1943, file 7, box 4, series 2, Shears Papers; Memorandum from F.G. Shears to G.B. Spain, 23 July 1946, ibid.; Memorandum from F.G. Shears to Green, 20 November 1943, ibid.; Shears to Green, 5 September 1944, ibid.

50 The prevalence of theft emerges when one reads the case files for each individual Japanese Canadian, as forced entries are mentioned explicitly in officials' reports. Meanwhile, significant personal property also disappeared without report (perhaps as a result of theft by officials or without forced entry), a phenomenon revealed by contrasting inventories of Japanese Canadians' property over time. See, for instance, the Bird Commission case files for Kaoru Atagi (case file #59), Sakiye Takasaki (case file #429), or Fusamatsu Tamaki (case file #819).

51 Letter from Wm. Wills to Spain, "Re: Buddhist Temple, 604 Cordova Street," 28 June 1943, file 7, box 4, series 2, Shears Papers; G.B. Spain to H.F. Green, 23 July 1943, "Re: 992 Powell Street", ibid.; Letter from E.W. Forward to Custodian, 3 July 1942, file "General exhibits 1-63," vol. 78, RG 33-69, LAC; Memorandum from George Peters to F.G. Shears, "Re: Thefts & Vandalism at Steveston, Steveston Japanese Association," 19 March 1946, ibid.

52 Memorandum from Green to Shears, 20 November 1943, file 7, box 4, series 2, Shears Papers.

53 Report on General Conditions of Japanese Property and Chattels in the Districts of Maple Ridge and Pitt Meadows, BC, 19 November 1942, file: "General exhibits 1-63," vol. 78, RG 33-69, LAC.

54 Memorandum from G.B. Spain to F.G. Shears, 23 July 1946, file 7, box 4, series 2, Shears Papers.

55 Letter from C.C. Robinson to P.H. Russell, "Re: Buddhist Temple," 18 March 1943, file 7, box 4, series 2, Shears Papers.

56 Ibid.

57 "Vandals Overrun Steveston Temple," 17 March 1943, *Marpole–Richmond Review*, file 7, box 4, series 2, Shears Papers.

58 Memorandum, "Re: Kitsilano Buddhist Mission," 2 August 1945, file 7, box 4, series 2, Shears Papers.

59 Thereby connecting to grave desecrations in Cumberland, Chemainus, and Victoria.

See Eric Adams, "Constitutional Stories: Japanese Canadians and the Constitution of Canada," *Australian Canadian Studies* (forthcoming).

60 Scott Veitch, *Law and Irresponsibility: On the Legitimation of Human Suffering* (London: Routledge-Cavendish, 2007). A particularly egregious case of state mismanagement and disavowal of responsibility is that of C.C. Robinson, the Office of the Custodian official stationed in Steveston. Under Robinson's watch, fishing nets rotted, a third went missing, and countless belongings disappeared unaccounted for. In a rare instance of punitive measures within the office, Shears reduced Robinson's pay by a third. Robinson would use this reduction to justify his further misconduct. Letter from Shears to McPherson, 29 August 1944, file 1 pt 1: "Correspondence Relating to Various Staff Members, Vancouver Office," vol. 1, RG 117-C-1, LAC; Letter from Shears to McPherson, 31 January 1945, ibid; Vancouver Office of the Custodian Annual Report, 1945," images 368–374, microfilm reel C9469, RG 117-C-1, LAC, 28–33; Letter from Shears to Wright, 29 October 1946, folder 7, box 4, Shears Papers.

61 Letter from G.B. Spain to Chief Constable MacKay, 9 September 1943 file 7, box 4, series 2, Shears Papers; Letter from Green to Shears, 20 November 1943, ibid; Green to Shears, 2 April 1945, ibid; Spain to Green, 15 May 1945, ibid; Chief Constable D. MacKay to Custodian of Alien Property, 25 May 1945, ibid; Letter from George Peters to Shears, 5 January 1946, ibid; Memorandum from Peters to Shears, 19 March 1946, ibid.

62 Memorandum by G.B. Spain, 12 August 1943, ibid.; Letter from Spain to Green, 15 March 1945, file 7, box 4, series 2, Shears Papers.

63 Letter from Green to Alexander, 27 July 1943, file 7, box 4, series 2, Shears Papers. Spain's comments fit into the general discourse of social deviancy and crime in Vancouver of the time. Diane Purvey and John Douglas Belshaw, *Vancouver Noir, 1930–1960* (Vancouver, BC: Anvil Press, 2011).

64 Memorandum by Green, "Re: Phoenix Cannery – Japanese Effects," 28 March 1944, file 7, box 4, series 2, Shears Papers.

65 Like the Office of the Custodian, municipal police departments were reluctant to allocate adequate resources to oversee the properties. As a result, the office hired private security services to oversee the storage sites. When, after two years of break-ins, the Vancouver office contracted Wilson's Night Patrol to routinely check on the city's largest storage site, 922 Powell, Shears wrote, "Why didn't we think of this before?" Handwritten note on Memorandum from Green to Shears, 22 January 1944, file 7, box 4, series 2, Shears Papers.

66 Anderson to Shears, "Re: Chattel thefts," 19 February 1945, file 7, box 4, Shears Papers. Cockrell's report first came to the Advisory Committee on Rural Properties. Meeting minutes, 1945, file 2: "Reports from the Advisory Committee on Rural Property," box 11, series 4: "Office Documents," Shears Papers.

67 Memorandum from Shears to Spain, "Re: Theft of Radios and Cameras from Custodian Warehouse, 992 Powell St.," 6 September 1945, file 7, box 4, series 2, Shears Papers.

68 "Vancouver Office of the Custodian Annual Report, 1943," image 228, microfilm reel C9469, RG 117-C-1, LAC, 9. See also: Letter from G.B. Spain to H.F. Green, "Re: Japanese Language School 154 West 5th Ave.," 24 July 1943, folder 7, box 4, Shears Papers.

69 Letter from Green to Alexander, "Re: 154 West 5th and 992 Powell," 27 July 1943; Memorandum from Green to Shears, 20 November 1943; Memorandum by G.B. Spain, 12

August 1943; Memorandum from Green to Shears, 20 November 1943; Memorandum from Green to Shears, "Re: Storage in Vancouver, "22 January 1944; and Letter from C.C. Robinson to F.H. Green, 4 February 1944, file 7, box 4, series 2, Shears Papers.

70 Memorandum from Green to Shears, 20 November 1943, ibid.

71 Stanley Cohen, "Property Destruction: Motives and Meanings," in *Vandalism*, ed. Colin Ward (London: Architectural Press, 1973), 42.

72 Ibid., 46.

73 Michele Emanatian and David Delaney, "What Message Does 'Send a Message' Send?," *Journal of Language & Politics* 7, no. 2 (September 2008): 290–320.

74 See introduction and chapter 5.

75 Chapter 8. See also "United Action of Evacuees Sought to Aid Test Case," *The New Canadian*, 10 April 1943, 1; "Test Case Receiving Support From Evacuees Across Canada," *The New Canadian*, 17 April 1943, 1; "Launch Fund Campaign – Ten Per Cent of Taxes Asked," *The New Canadian*, 1 May 1943, 1.

76 Correspondence between lower level officials contains explicit details indicating that the office was careful not to disclose the destruction of their property to the Japanese Canadian owners. Letter from F.G. Shears to K.W. Wright, 8 March 1946, folder 7, box 4, Shears Papers.

77 Letter from McPherson to Coleman, 28 August 1942, file 10: "Vancouver Office – General Correspondence, memoranda and clippings. 1941/04-1947/10," vol. 1, RG117-C-1, LAC.

78 Letter from Shears to McPherson, 19 February 1943, file 59010: "Chattels (Japanese)," vol. 2826, RG 117-A-3, LAC; Letter from McPherson to Shears, February 22 1943, file 59010, vol. 2826, RG 117-A-3, LAC.

79 Memorandum from Collins to McPherson, 16 March 1943, file 23-1-11-1, pt. 1: "Japanese Property and Custodian of Enemy Alien Property," vol. 655, RG 27 O-1, LAC.

80 Memorandum from Collins to MacNamara, 20 March 1943, file 23-1-11-1 pt. 1, vol. 655, RG 27 O-1, LAC.

81 Letter from MacNamara to Collins, 26 March 1943, file 23-1-11-1, pt. 1, vol. 655, RG 27 O-1, LAC.

82 Letter from MacNamara to Coleman, 26 March 1943, file 23-1-11-1, pt. 1, vol. 655, RG 27 O-1, LAC.

83 McPherson to MacNamara, 14 October 1943, file 59010, vol. 2826, RG 117-A-3, LAC.

84 Letter from MacNamara to McPherson, 6 October 1943, file 59010, vol. 2826, RG 117-A-3, LAC; Letter from McPherson to MacNamara, 14 October 1943, file 59010, vol. 2826, RG 117-A-3, LAC. See also Testimony of W.E. Anderson, 670, LAC, file: "General Evidence 24 Sept–30 Sept, 1948," vol. 76, RG 33-69, LAC.

85 Memorandum from McPherson to Coleman, Re: Vancouver Trip, 29 May 1944, file 16, vol. 2, RG 117-C-1, LAC.

86 Memorandum from Collins to McPherson, 16 March 1943, file 23-1-11-1 pt. 1, vol. 655, RG 27 O-1, LAC.

87 Somewhat surprisingly, the issue of consent remained part of these discussions over the course of spring 1943. As there was no formal reason to secure consent, it is hard not to read this as an improvised strategy in response to possible future challenges rather than a principled response to the concerns of owners (thanks to Eric M. Adams). Letter

from MacNamara to Collins, 26 March 1943, file 23-1-11-1 pt. 1, vol. 655, RG 27 O-1, LAC. MacNamara also described this approach to the Department of External Affairs: MacNamara to Scott, 26 March 1943, file 23-1-11-1 pt. 1, vol. 655, RG 27 O-1, LAC.

88 Letter from Collins to MacNamara, "Re: Disposal of effects by the Custodian," 15 April 1943, file 23-1-11-1 pt. 1, vol. 655, RG 27 O-1, LAC.

89 Memorandum by McPherson for Coleman, "Re: Vancouver Trip," 29 May 1944, file 16, vol. 2, RG 117-C-1, LAC.

90 Letter from Collins to MacNamara, "Re: Disposal of effects by the Custodian," 15 April 1943, file 23-1-11-1 pt. 1, vol. 655, RG 27 O-1, LAC.

91 Letter from Coleman to Neill, 23 February 1944, file 59010, vol. 2826, RG 117-A-3, LAC.

92 Memorandum from Shears to McPherson, "Re: Personal Effects," 7 April 1945, file 59010, vol. 2826, RG 117-A-3, LAC.

93 Extract from the Minutes of the Meeting of the Rural Advisory Committee, 5 October 1945, file 59010, vol. 2826, RG 117-A-3, LAC.

94 See chapters 9 and 10.

95 Letter from Shears to McPherson, 1 March 1943, file 59010, vol. 2826, RG 117-A-3, LAC. It is interesting to note that the state elected to use private auctions despite its seizure and management of personal property. This presumably was justified by the desire to get good sales using professional auctioneers. However, the effect, intentional or not, was to "privatize" state policies, allowing for a disavowal of state injustices, while also creating a familiar market "space" for ordinary British Columbians to become complicit in liquidation.

96 Wendy Nelson Espeland and Mitchell L. Stevens, "Commensuration as a Social Process," *Annual Review of Sociology* 24 (August 1998): 324.

97 Marion Fourcade, "Cents and Sensibility: Economic Valuation and the Nature of 'Nature,'" *American Journal of Sociology* 116, no. 6 (2011): 1721.

98 Margaret Jane Radin, "Property and Personhood," *Stanford Law Review* 34, no. 5 (1982): 959.

99 Gregory S. Alexander and Eduardo M. Peñalver, *An Introduction to Property Theory* (New York: Cambridge University Press, 2012), 211.

100 Alexander and Peñalver, *An Introduction*, 211. Even further, the one thing we know for certain about every owner of a thing is that the owner values the ownership of the tangible item *above* the monetary value of that item otherwise the owner would have sold the item.

101 In June and July, the Office of the Custodian warned Japanese Canadians in *The New Canadian* that, unless told to preserve items for shipment, sales would begin that fall. "Property Tender Ads Begin on Sat. June 19," *The New Canadian*, 1 June 1943, 1; "Believe Auction to Start with Goods Stored in Halls and Institutions," *The New Canadian*, 31 July 1943, 1.

102 $3,568,974.58 in 2018 Canadian dollars. "Vancouver Office of the Custodian Annual Report, 1946," image 405, microfilm reel C9469, RG 117-C-1, LAC, 65.

103 Testimony of William Graydon Willard, 6 December 1948, file: "General Evidence 1 Dec.–6 Dec. 1948," vol. 79, RG 33-69, LAC, 618.

104 Testimony of Francis Edward Binnington, 6 December 1948, file: "General Evidence 1 Dec.–6 Dec. 1948," vol. 79, RG 33-69, LAC, 586–7.

105 Testimony of Gowing Frost, 29 September 1948, file: "General Evidence (Sept. 24–30, 1948)," vol. 76, RG 33-49, LAC, 639.
106 Testimony of Douglas Phipps, 28 September 1948, file: "General Evidence (Sept. 24–30, 1948)," vol. 76, RG 33-49, LAC, 632; Testimony of Gowing Frost, 29 September 1948, file "General Evidence (Sept. 24–30, 1948)," vol. 76, RG 33-49, LAC, 638; Testimony of William Graydon Willard, 6 December 1948, file "General Evidence 1 Dec.–6 Dec. 1948," vol. 79, RG 33-69, LAC, 618; Testimony of Francis Edward Binnington, 6 December 1948, file "General Evidence 1 Dec.–6 Dec. 1948," vol. 79, RG 33-69, LAC, 586.
107 Testimony of Charles Spencer Pallot, 28 September 1948, 610, LAC, RG33-49, vol. 76, file "General Evidence (Sept. 24–30, 1948)."
108 Testimony of William Graydon Willard, 6 December 1948, file "General Evidence 1 Dec.–6 Dec. 1948," vol. 79, RG 33-69, LAC, 515."
109 Testimony of Gowing Frost, 29 September 1948, file: "General Evidence (Sept. 24–30, 1948)," vol. 76, RG 33-49, LAC, 639.
110 Testimony of Douglas Phipps, 28 September 1948, file: "General Evidence (Sept. 24–30, 1948)," vol. 76, RG 33-49, LAC, 627.
111 Arjun Appadurai's conception of "terminal" commodities – those commodities that "make only *one* journey from production to consumption" – is helpful here. Placed outside a "demarcated zone of commoditization," the items nevertheless register other forms of value. Poignantly, Appadurai addresses the divergence of commodities from their specified paths: it "is always a sign of creativity or crisis, whether aesthetic or economic," he writes, with one form of crisis being "warfare and the plunder that historically has accompanied it." "Theft," Appadurai continues, "condemned in most human societies, is the humblest form of diversion of commodities from preordained paths." In the presence of homemade, or "terminal," commodities on the market, we see such a divergence from preordained paths. Arjun Appadurai ed., *The Social Life of Things: Commodities in Cultural Perspective* (Cambridge: Cambridge University Press, 1988), 23. Thank you to Yasmin Railton for this recommendation.
112 Indeed, Frost explained that there were "plenty of white people" for whom these homemade goods held a certain value. Testimony of Gowing Frost, 29 September 1948, file "General Evidence (Sept. 24–30, 1948)," vol. 76, RG 33-49, LAC, 642, 646–7. Testimony of William Graydon Willard, 6 December 1948, file "General Evidence (Sept. 24–30, 1948)," vol. 76, RG 33-49, LAC, 627.
113 Letter from Shears to McPherson, 18 September 1943, file 59010, vol. 2826, RG 117-A-3, LAC.
114 Images 756–795, microfilm reel C12822, Japanese Canadian Citizens Association fonds, Héritage.
115 F.G. Shears [?], typed notes, 1941 [?], file 10, box 11, series 4: "Office Documents," Shears Papers.
116 Testimony of Kaoru Atagi, 10 February 1948, case file 59: "Atagi, Kaoru (Kamloops)," vol. 4, RG 33-69, LAC, 15. For a fuller account of the destruction and vandalism of Atagi's property (including "nightly raids by thieves"), see case file 8965: "Atagi, Kaoru," microfilm reel C9387, RG 117-C-3, LAC.
117 Atagi declared the value of the Boat Works and real estate to be $8,375 total: Testimony of Kaoru Atagi, 10 February 1948, case file 59: "Atagi, Kaoru (Kamloops)," vol. 4, RG 33-69,

LAC, 5–7, 15. Additionally, he claimed the value of his chattels, including machinery belting, to be $9,291.60: "Analysis of personal Property Claim" and "Recap of Claim," ibid. Importantly, this excludes another $2,438.19 that he claimed for accounts receivable and goodwill for his business.

118 Testimony of Kaoru Atagi, 10 February 1948, case file 59: "Atagi, Kaoru (Kamloops)," vol. 4, RG 33-69, 15, 30.

PART THREE

Reasoning Wrong

CHAPTER 8

Promises of Law: The Unlawful Dispossession of Japanese Canadians

Eric M. Adams, Jordan Stanger-Ross, and the Landscapes of Injustice Research Collective

On the evening of 28 May 1944, Eikichi Nakashima, Tadao Wakabayashi, Jitaro Tanaka, and their lawyer, J. Arthur MacLennan, entered the dining room at the Chateau Laurier in Ottawa. Given the anxiety over the ongoing war in the Pacific and the hotel's history of racial exclusion, the appearance of three Japanese Canadians in the Laurier's ornate dining room likely drew unwanted attention.[1] But Nakashima, Wakabayashi, and Tanaka had greater concerns than the prejudices of their fellow diners. In September 1942, government officials had forcibly removed them and their families from their Vancouver homes, seized control of their real and personal property, and interned them in crowded camps in the interior of British Columbia. They were, along with more than twenty-one thousand other Canadians of Japanese descent, "the enemy that never was,"[2] victims of a "politics of racism" that disregarded their basic human rights.[3] In the spring of 1944, Nakashima, Wakabayashi, and Tanaka came to Ottawa not to protest those injustices but to place their faith in the promise of law.

This chapter is a history of a largely forgotten legal promise. It is a story of law's capacity to carry multiple meanings – protection and coercion, trust and duplicity, justice and injustice – and to shift in meaning over time. The racist treatment of Japanese Canadians before, during, and after the Second World War has been the subject of important scholarship,[4] but legal historians have overlooked key aspects of these events, including the laws that dispossessed Japanese Canadians of everything they owned.

The sale of Japanese Canadian–owned property was consistent with other moments in Canadian history when promises lost meaning as government interests shifted, officials' memories (conveniently) faded, and new legal interpretations of those promises took their place. The events chronicled here echo the federal government's treaty promises to First Nations, which were backed by oral promises that officials later abandoned in favour of narrow legal interpretations – with devastating consequences for Indigenous peoples.[5] The dispossession of Japanese Canadians is another instance in which the Crown created circumstances of dispossession coupled with a paternalistic promise of protection that it did not keep. When the federal government seized the property of Japanese Canadians it made assurances in law, repeated by officials to

Japanese Canadians on the doorsteps of their homes, that the property would be held as a "protective measure only" and would someday be returned. This chapter excavates this legal promise to protect, examines its reception among property owners, and assesses the little-known legal case it initiated, *Nakashima v Canada*.[6] A full accounting of the power of law in twentieth-century Canada must wrestle equally with its dual capacity to impose and constrain power.

Given the eventual fate of Japanese Canadian–owned property, the dispossession can appear as a linear story in which widespread racist views always prevailed. One possibility is that the promise to protect was a ruse, a tool that encouraged Japanese Canadians to cooperate with their uprooting and internment but abandoned when that process was completed and the property could be acquired by whites and other non-Japanese Canadians.[7] The influence of racist leaders in the political process and the vehemence with which they expressed their discriminatory objectives, discussed in the introduction to this book, encourage this view. In addition, some evidence suggests that the laws protecting Japanese Canadian–owned property were meant from the outset to deceive. Before the war in the Pacific began, officials in the British Columbia government had their eyes on the property holdings of the Japanese Canadian community. A "quiet" government initiative compiled a list of "the names, addresses, and business of Japanese who hold trade licences in British Columbia" as part of a study into "the extent and character of oriental penetration in the economy of this Province."[8] After the war began, McPherson met with City of Vancouver officials on 1 September 1942, while Japanese Canadians were still being rounded up and sent inland, to discuss the city's interest in acquiring their property. McPherson advised city leaders to delay pursuing this plan, at least for the moment, "to avoid taking any action that would conflict with the steps now being taken" to remove Japanese Canadians.[9] McPherson may have hinted to city officials, however, that the Custodian's approach to Japanese Canadian–owned property would not always be one of protection.[10] In a similar vein, once the entire Japanese Canadian population of coastal British Columbia had been uprooted, George Collins, chairman of the British Columbia Security Commission told his staff that the organization would now shift its focus: "these people will be dispersed across Canada in small groups … *That is the undeclared policy of Ottawa*."[11] If an "undeclared" plan to permanently exile Japanese Canadians from the province existed from the start of Canada's war in the Pacific, then its blueprints could not have included Japanese Canadians maintaining their homes in coastal British Columbia.[12]

Direct evidence of the creation of the laws of dispossession, however, suggests that the ubiquity of racism and the government's ultimate violation of the promise should not obscure its full history. The promise to protect resulted from multi-vocal processes, conflicting pressures, and competing conceptions of citizenship, legality, and justice, rather than simple racist deceit and financial opportunism. Certainly, some of the officials responsible for drafting the laws of dispossession believed that promises to protect would facilitate the uprooting and internment. Yet those same officials – almost all of them lawyers – also saw the protection of property as a requirement of orderly governance, natural justice, and inchoate notions of citizenship and liberty. Lofty sentiments are more likely to find their way into official documentation than is a secretive plot to deceive. Archives have gaps, some of them deliberate.[13] Nonetheless, the records of law making, and the broader context in which they are embedded, demonstrate that officials also intended the promise of protection to carry legal significance and to create a trust, in both the legal and colloquial sense, in the government's treatment of seized property. From this perspective, we might conceive of the dispossession as fundamentally unlawful on its own terms, rather than as the regrettable culmination of legalized racism.

Part I of this chapter explains how and why the orders of dispossession took shape. It reveals a wartime bureaucracy of conflicting interests, intense pressures, and administrative constraints. From this context arose the promise to protect the property of Japanese Canadians. The story of that promise has been lost in large part because of the decision of Justice Thorson in *Nakashima v Canada*, the focus of part II. In *Nakashima*, the promise to protect disappeared under evasive legal argument, medieval conceptions of Crown liability, absolute deference to government decision making in times of war, and judicial sanction of racialized injustice. Contrary to the position adopted by Canada to win the *Nakashima* case, we argue that the promise to protect enacted a legal trust as the product of the interaction of text, intention, administrative action, and the interpretations of those subject to it. The risk in overlooking the promise to protect property is to cast Canada's wartime history as inexorable. Throughout this history, there were choices made, paths not taken, doubts supressed, and promises made. To focus only on promises broken or, worse yet, to ignore legal promises entirely, is to misrepresent the laws of dispossession and to silence Japanese Canadians and the federal officials who inscribed in law an obligation to protect.[14] The dispossession of Japanese Canadians was a complicated product of law – enabled by legal force, yet equally constrained by legal principle. Its neglected history sheds light on the nature of law and Canadian history in equal measure.

I. Creating a promise: The origins of the dispossession orders in council

The promise to protect property and its subsequent violation emerged out of the context of Canada at war. In the emergency federal cabinet meeting on 1 September 1939, following news that Germany had attacked Poland, Justice Minister and Acting Secretary of State Ernest Lapointe proclaimed an apprehended state of war and invoked the War Measures Act (WMA).[15] As in the First World War, the WMA transferred virtually unlimited legislative authority to the federal cabinet. In the broad words of the act, "[t]he Governor in Council may do and authorize such acts and things, and make from time to time such orders and regulations, as he may ... deem necessary or advisable for the security, defence, peace, order and welfare of Canada."[16] The act specifically placed "appropriation, control, forfeiture and disposition of property" within federal executive control.[17] In litigation arising out of the First World War, the Judicial Committee of the Privy Council upheld the constitutionality of WMA under the federal power to legislate for the "peace, order, and good government of Canada" in times of national crisis.[18] As one government committee summarized, the act granted "the Executive ample authority to take pretty well whatever action might be found to be necessary to meet the exigencies of war."[19]

Long before the war in the Pacific, Japanese Canadians had been the subject of racist treatment under the law.[20] In keeping with longstanding state hostility to Japanese Canadians, on 1 October 1940 the Cabinet War Committee established a "Special Committee on Orientals in British Columbia," to keep "the Government constantly informed ... as to the oriental situation in that Province."[21] Hundreds of orders in council restricting the liberty of Japanese Canadians followed. The eventual dispossession, internment, incarceration, exile, and prohibitions on returning to British Columbia were all products of law: orders in council drafted by a federal bureaucracy and approved by committees of cabinet.

Following Canada's declaration of war against Japan on 7 December 1941,[22] the legal focus on Japanese Canadians intensified. A series of orders in council over the ensuing months enabled the uprooting and dispossession of all those living within the "protected area" of British Columbia, an enormous area of land covering the coast to one hundred miles inland.[23] As a precursor to the internment, in late February 1942, Order 1486 empowered the government to "require any and all persons to leave such protected area."[24] On 4 March 1942, Order 1665 put the internment policy into legal effect. Citing the necessity of "the security and defence of Canada," the order established the British Columbia Security Commission (BCSC), headquartered in Vancouver, "to plan, supervise and direct the evacuation from the protected areas of British Columbia of all persons of the Japanese race."[25] The uprooting and internment of Japanese Canadians created an immediate problem of what to do with the empty properties and vulnerable possessions of Japanese Canadians forced from their homes. The solution was for the secretary of state, Norman McLarty, to take custody of seized property and promise its protection.

The Need to Promise

The role of the Custodian evolved rapidly during the eight days between 24 February 1942, when the government announced its authority to require "any and all persons" to leave the "protected area" of British Columbia and 4 March, when Order 1665 specified that this power would be applied to "all persons of the Japanese race." Prior to this crucial week, the Custodian managed only the property of "all persons regardless of their nationality who reside in enemy or enemy occupied territory" as well as the property of "all persons who are detained under the Defense of Canada regulations."[26] Before the uprooting of all Japanese Canadians from the one hundred-mile "protected area," very little of their property fell under this state authority. Indeed, McPherson had previously announced that his office had no purview over "the property of persons of the Japanese Race who are conducting themselves in a proper manner and who have not been detained."[27]

A late intervention in the planning of the internment transformed the Custodian's function.[28] The first drafts of Order 1665 overlooked the question of property and omitted the Custodian from the list of departments and agencies (RCMP, Departments of Transport, National Defense, Munitions and Supply, and Labour) whose involvement civil servants imagined necessary to the internment.[29] But what would become of the property of Japanese Canadians once interned? Austin C. Taylor, the man most responsible for overseeing the uprooting of Japanese Canadians in its first months, raised the question first. Taylor agreed to serve as the chairman of the BCSC and saw early drafts of Order 1665. A British Columbia mining magnate, reported to have invested $1 million in war bonds, Taylor was a man accustomed to thinking about property.[30] Seeing an oversight in the proposed law, Taylor wrote Cabinet Minister Ian Mackenzie on 28 February 1942 to inquire about a "Custodian for evacuated property."[31] Mackenzie responded quickly. By 1 March he had secured from Ephraim H. Coleman, the under secretary of state responsible for the operations of the Custodian of Enemy Property, agreement to appoint "additional Custodians … with a view to providing for the care" of the property of Japanese Canadians.[32] Officials failed to document the nature of the "care" envisioned (the exchange between Mackenzie and Coleman took place by phone), but, whatever its details, the order in council was revised by the Department of Justice and submitted to cabinet the following day.[33]

Under the heading "Custody of Japanese Property," Order 1665 provided as follows:

> 12.(1) As a protective measure only, all property situated in any protected area of British Columbia belonging to any person of the Japanese race resident in such area … shall be vested in and subject to the control and management of the Custodian as defined in the Regulations respecting Trading with the Enemy, 1939; provided, however, that no commission shall be charged by the Custodian in respect of such control and management.[34]

Section 12 concluded that the "property, rights and interests so vested in and subject to the control and management of the Custodian … shall be dealt with in such manner as the Governor in Council may direct."[35]

The cavalier treatment of property in Order 1665 met with immediate internal criticism. Among its most trenchant opponents was John Erskine Read, legal advisor for the Department of External Affairs and former dean of Dalhousie Law School.[36] Reviewing Order 1665, he expressed a professorial attentiveness and attachment to the common law of property and natural justice. Read had written the first drafts of the order, which had been silent on the question of property.[37] Having been assured on 1 March that his draft was "right in every way," he was shocked a day later to read a key change in the law: the proposed vesting of all Japanese Canadian–owned property in the hands of the Custodian.[38] As he interpreted the revisions, "all property of any sort in the protected areas is being taken away from the Japanese and handed over to the Custodian." In a memo to his supervisor, Under Secretary of State, External Affairs Norman Robertson Read excoriated the version that ultimately became law for "abandoning completely" the principle of "fairness."[39]

Emphasizing that Japanese Canadians were British subjects, Read saw Order 1665 as a betrayal of good governance and natural justice. "It strips them of every cent they may have in their pockets or in the banks," Read wrote, "it takes the clothes off their backs and removes the tools of their trade: fountain pens from their pockets, books from their libraries; and hands them all over to the tender mercies of the Custodian."[40] Read himself had drafted the provisions that would tear Japanese Canadians from their communities in coastal British Columbia. These, however, he justified as necessities of war. The confiscation of property, he noted by contrast, had "nothing whatever to do with security."[41] Read's advocacy for the property rights of Japanese Canadians also had a more instrumental rationale. Although he criticized government excess in relation to property, he accepted that "the scheme of evacuation," as he called it, "is based upon [the] ultimate absorption of at least a substantial part of [Japanese Canadians] … outside of the protected areas." Thus, he joined others like Ian Mackenzie, in intending that most Japanese Canadians would never return to British Columbia. In Read's view, recklessness with respect to property would "hamper absorption" because it deprived Japanese Canadians of the means to reestablish themselves east of the Rocky Mountains.

Instead, Read advocated measures similar to the law that governed Japanese Canadian–owned fishing vessels (a scheme he had created). With respect to fishing vessels, Read explained, "care was taken to establish a benevolent trusteeship … to protect the interests of British subjects whose fishing vessels were taken."[42] Indeed, Order 288, of January 1942, had explicitly acknowledged that the owners of the vessels "though being of Japanese origin, are Canadian citizens" and had emphasized that their dispossession should have "due regard to the equity of the *Japanese Canadian* owners."[43] The law created a committee, headed by a judge and including a Japanese Canadian member, whose explicit mandate was to "make it possible for the present owners of detained vessels to freely negotiate for charters, leases, or sales."[44] In practice, however, the freedom of owners was severely constrained from the outset by the circumstances of their uprooting, and, ultimately, the committee broke the law and forced the sale of vessels.[45] Still, in March 1942, Read criticized Order 1665 by pointing to a precedent offering more explicit property protection, in contrast to a law in which he saw "no element of trusteeship recognized, and no attempt to set up machinery that would enable the property of these British subjects to be sold so as to preserve and protect their interests."[46]

Japanese Canadians also closely scrutinized the laws that would upend their lives and threaten their property. The sole Japanese Canadian newspaper permitted to publish after the attack on Pearl Harbor, *The New Canadian*, diligently reported on and sometimes challenged federal policy, even as government censors oversaw the paper's operation.[47] Published under the editorial leadership of Thomas Shoyama, the paper was, in the words of one reader at the time, "intoxicating ... [i]t brought young kids like me to our first contact with the bright young Nisei minds. It filled us in with political background and news."[48] The paper's accomplishments were in significant measure attributable to Shoyama. Born in Kamloops in 1916 and a 1938 graduate of the University of British Columbia, Shoyama viewed *The New Canadian* as a "vehicle of our response" to government policy, an opportunity, "in spite of the bonds of wartime censorship ... to try to voice a right and forceful demand for democratic justice."[49]

Government officials allowed *The New Canadian* to continue in part because they regarded it as an effective propaganda tool, but Shoyama and his colleagues managed to preserve the integrity of the paper even in the context of government oversight. The editorial team continued to serve the community by carrying announcements and human interest stories, detailing the experiences of Japanese Americans, and selectively criticizing federal policies. Although editors could not prevent the federal government from inserting policy statements and notices directly into the paper, they found subtle ways to contextualize and criticize such official announcements. In the first months of Canada's war in the Pacific, *The New Canadian* usually carried government statements on its back pages. In many cases, the editors contrasted these back-page bulletins with front-page journalistic articles. These articles distinguished the federal announcements from journalism (government insertions were subjects of reportage, not acts of reporting) and allowed the editors to emphasize facets of policy and law that they saw as especially important. In doing so, they preserved the sense that the newspaper was more than a mouthpiece for the government. If reading the paper was an intoxicating experience, it was partly because of the opportunity to decode subtle, multivocal explanations of law.

In the first weeks of March 1942, *The New Canadian* conveyed the federal promise to protect Japanese Canadian–owned property, but at the same time it warned readers that Order 1665 should be regarded with caution. The 12 March 1942 edition was the first to report the order, running a "Notice to Persons of the Japanese Race," penned by McPherson, the deputy Custodian. Quoting the law, "[a]s a protective measure only," McPherson wrote, "all property situated in any protected area of British Columbia belonging to any person of the Japanese race" would be vested in the Custodian, who would charge "no commission" for services in the "control and management" of property. Japanese Canadians were "urged to report their property immediately instead of waiting until their evacuation as this will enable the Custodian to take prompt action to protect and administer the same."[50] McPherson's announcement repeatedly echoed the language of "protection," a term that he explained in private government communication as positioning the Custodian as a "Trustee."[51] "[I]nsofar as the property of Japanese Evacuees is concerned," McPherson would argue near the end of the war, "the Custodian is definitely holding such property, in trust, for the former Japanese owners, and will be held strictly accountable to them."[52]

Editors at *The New Canadian* expressed scepticism. A short front-page article undermined the government's official statement. McPherson's notice, the author explained, was "a paid newspaper announcement," not journalism. The article avoided use of the phrase "protective measure," emphasizing instead the wide discretionary power granted to the Custodian.[53] Five days later, another front-page article highlighted the relationship between the Custodian's activity and the disruption of Vancouver's Powell Street neighbourhood. The Custodian had established "miniature offices" in a previously bustling Japanese Canadian–owned restaurant, Fuji Chop Suey, where "booths formerly used for dining" were equipped with typewriters and staff ready "to assist those anxious to report their assets and liabilities" to the federal government. Once again, the newspaper eschewed the language of protection, explaining that "[u]nder [Order 1665], the Custodian has been authorized to take control of property," subjecting it "to the consolidated regulations on trading with the enemy" and authorizing its disposal at "the direction of the federal government."[54] The issue also reprinted a biting editorial from the non-Japanese Canadian press, a rarity at this juncture of the Pacific War, asking, "What is this anyway – Hitler's country or a democracy?"[55] An advertisement printed alongside this disconcerting comparison encouraged Japanese Canadians to seek alternatives to the federal government for the safekeeping of their property: "Your Household Goods Are Valuable," read an advertisement for Campbell's Storage Limited, "Have them carefully packed and stored or shipped by trained professionals at very reasonable rates."[56] For readers of *The New Canadian* in early March 1942, Campbell's Storage may well have seemed the more reliable promise of protection.

Federal officials knew that Japanese Canadians distrusted their policies, including the promise to protect property. Many feared that disbelief might encourage resistance to the internment process, a particular worry because public calm on Canada's Pacific coast was widely regarded as fragile.[57] On 4 March 1942, when Order 1665 created the

BCSC, Taylor wrote to Mackenzie discouraging actions or pronouncements that might further alienate Japanese Canadians. "[A]t [the] moment we believe we have cooperation of [the] Japanese community," he remarked. However, "if ... further restrictions be placed on [the] Japanese we will lose present cooperation and create an element of distrust and complete lack of confidence which will add tremendously to our present problem."[58] Quieting unrest among Japanese Canadians would remain a preoccupation for Taylor and the BCSC in the months that followed. In April, Taylor speculated that the unchecked circulation of "fears" and "rumour" among Japanese Canadians might eventually prompt sufficient defiance to require their mass imprisonment, a prospect far more difficult and expensive than their confinement in sites of internment.[59] Central among the "rumours" of concern to Japanese Canadians were hints that government policy might leave them destitute after the war. Such impressions, many officials worried, could have spiralling consequences.

Distrust of the government posed additional practical problems for federal officials. As a report by the Vancouver Office of the Custodian later reflected, "the Japanese were obviously distrustful of the whole machinery set up ... and it shortly became quite clear that they were taking little advantage of the facilities which were offered [to register their property]."[60] This failure to cooperate posed a problem for the office because the Custodian risked being "charged with the administration and control of large quantities of property of which he had no knowledge."[61] Ignorance of the property vesting in the Custodian obstructed officials scrambling to respond to their mandate under Order 1665. As they struggled to hire staff for a range of property management tasks – assessing the condition and value of property, maintaining insurance, making repairs, collecting rents, and paying creditors – they needed Japanese Canadians to help them understand the extent of the property concerned and, even better, to deliver property to government officials.[62] The government would soon extend a more robust promise to protect property in hopes of securing Japanese Canadian cooperation.

Strengthening the Promise

Facing internment, Japanese Canadians could see the precarious position of their property and they demanded its protection. Under Secretary of State Coleman realized that the promise of protection in Order 1665 was insufficient.[63] On 16 March he explained to the Departments of Justice and External Affairs that "leaders in [the Japanese Canadian] community" were "exercised" about the property situation and indicated that the BCSC regarded this as a matter of "importance and urgency."[64] He recommended an amendment to Order 1665, which included "dropping completely" the offending clause, 12(3). "I do not think," wrote Coleman, "it was ever contemplated by the Government that they would deprive the Japanese owners of their property or the proceeds thereof." The existing wording, however, left the law "susceptible of the interpretation that something in the nature of confiscation is taking place and I am sure," he repeated, "this was not the intention of this Government."[65] Citing the necessity to encourage Japanese Canadians to register their property with the Custodian, and the "very heavy responsibilities" placed upon the BCSC, Coleman proposed a rewording of the law.

The promise to protect emerged from a number of interests that, for the moment, intersected. One thread, most clearly expressed by Read, drew together a connection between the rights of British subjects, common law property rights, and rights of natural justice. Normative concerns for fairness were bolstered, however, by instrumental values that sought cooperation, administrative simplicity, and cost effectiveness in the implementation of the racialized internment and dispersal of Japanese Canadians. Coleman, for his part, made a pragmatic case. Japanese Canadians were "exercised" and their fears about the handling of their property jeopardized the activities of both the BCSC and the Custodian. His proposed amendments, which would take the form of Order 2483 on 27 March 1942, aimed to reassure Japanese Canadians and hence facilitate the work of the uprooting. And yet, his argument also conveyed something of Read's view that confiscation would violate core principles of property rights.[66] Coleman took for granted, at least rhetorically, that the government would not confiscate the property of British subjects. Almost a year later, Coleman and his supervisor, the secretary of state, described the forced sale of all Japanese Canadian–owned property as a significant shift away from the protection envisioned in Order 2483.[67]

Just over three weeks after Order 1665 became law, the cabinet amended it with Order 2483.[68] The preamble explained the reasons for the revisions, noting "that it is desirable to provide that any plan with regard to the placement of such persons *be limited* to making provision for the *temporary placement only* of such persons *during the continuation of the state of war* now existing." The preamble also cited recommendations by the BCSC that "*a greater degree of protective control* over persons of the Japanese race and the property of such persons be provided for." The substantive provisions stipulated the powers of the commission to include "the temporary placement only" of Japanese Canadians "during the continuation of the state of war now existing."[69] Additionally, section 12 was amended to add the following:

> 12 (2) The Custodian may, notwithstanding anything contained in this Regulation, order that all or any property whatsoever, situated in any protected area of British Columbia, belonging to any person of the Japanese race shall, *for the purpose of protecting the interests of the owner or any other person*, be vested in the Custodian, and the Custodian shall have full power to administer such property *for the benefit of all such interested persons*, and *shall release such property* upon being satisfied that the interests aforesaid will not be prejudiced thereby.[70]

The order continued to incorporate referentially the wide discretionary power of the Custodian in relation to the "control and management" of the property as found in the Regulations Respecting Trading with the Enemy.[71] On the basis of Orders 1665 and 2483, the Custodian seized control of hundreds of millions of dollars' worth of property belonging to Japanese Canadians.[72]

In the wake of Order 2483, the federal government once again addressed Japanese Canadians in *The New Canadian.* A lengthy statement by Austin Taylor on 6 April 1942 sought to allay concerns or, in his words, to counter "baseless rumours being bandied about."[73] Promising the "true facts," Taylor urged readers to "PAY ATTENTION TO THEM AND NOTHING ELSE," before beginning his explanation of multiple facets of government policy. With respect to property, he wrote,

> A Custodian of (Alien) property has been appointed by the Government and charged with the protection of all property placed voluntary [*sic*] under his control. This is not confiscation and the Custodian will administer the property in the interests of the people which should prevent them from disposing of their assets at a sacrifice or in an unfavourable market. We mention this because there seems to be a lack of under standing [*sic*] of the Custodian's position.
>
> We repeat that property delivered to the Custodian will be administered in the interests of the Japanese evacuated … and such property will not be disposed of at a sacrifice to pay … debts.
>
> We feel it is in the interest of those evacuated to place their property under the Custodian's control, and if this is not done before leaving the Protected Area, the Custodian cannot protect the property during the absence of any person evacuated.[74]

The statement mischaracterized the law on several points, both understating and overstating the promise to protect. The Custodian's responsibility for the property of Japanese Canadians was not limited to that property registered with its office nor was the vesting of property voluntary. The promise was more encompassing than advertised. On the other hand, the promise of protection did not prevent sales for the purpose of paying debts owed by Japanese Canadians. On the contrary, the equity of creditors was explicitly guaranteed in Order 2483. However, the notice did repeat three times that the Custodian served the interests of Japanese Canadian property owners. Taylor's statement unambiguously relayed the most substantive and important facet of the amended order in council: the position of the Custodian as a trustee.

As it had with Order 1665, *The New Canadian* contextualized Taylor's announcement with an article of its own. While the front-page story, "Custodian to Act for Evacuated People," carried Taylor's statement, the article that followed questioned the reliability of that assurance in the absence of specifics. Quoting the essential message of Order 2483 – "Property delivered to the Custodian will be administered in the interests of the Japanese Evacuated" – the article nonetheless articulated grounds for misgivings. "Confusion thus far has arisen over the fact that the administrative policy of the Custodian has not yet been defined," the article pointed out; "he is thus unable to answer many details which arise in the disposing of various kinds of property."[75] Shoyama and his colleagues knew, just as Read did, that the devil was in the details. On 15 April, *The New Canadian* announced that Japanese Canadian organizations would press the federal government for answers to "many questions of basic importance," including "losses and damage to property arising out of the evacuation program."[76] Responses would not be forthcoming. The federal government never took responsibility for such losses, later using them disingenuously to justify the forced sales of the property they had promised to protect and return.

As would become evident in the *Nakashima* case, the orders that constituted the dispossession created a cross weave of conflicting powers and responsibilities. Aspects of the orders suggest essentially unlimited governmental power over all Japanese Canadian–owned property, including the power to dispose of the property for any reason. Reference to the Regulations Respecting Trading with the Enemy also indicated a pervasive tendency to conflate Japanese Canadians with the country of Japan and to cast loyal Canadians of Japanese decent as enemies. But the wide powers of disposal and racist framing must be considered alongside provisions that created a legal trust. Beginning with the notion that property was being held in "custody," without charging administrative fees, the orders overlaid the vesting of Japanese Canadian–owned property in the Custodian with a legally significant purpose: "as a protective measure only." Order 2483 further stipulated that property was to be held for the "benefit" of "interested persons" (earlier defined as "the *owner* or any other person" – presumably family members and creditors without title). Moreover, given that the orders granted only the "temporary" power to remove and intern Japanese Canadians, the orders assumed that property would be returned to original owners at the conclusion of "the state of war now existing." Read together, and in sequence, the orders circumscribed the Custodian's powers over Japanese Canadian–owned property with deliberate limits. Without saying so expressly, Order 1665 as amended by Order 2483 created a legal trust.

Undermining the Promise

In the months that followed, property owners concerned about the implementation of the orders of dispossession would find no answers in the pages of *The New Canadian*. On 21 April 1942, the BCSC announced that it had taken control of the newspaper, which, they explained, was to convey only "the truth about measures being taken."[77] Rebranded as the "recognized organ for the dissemination of official information," the paper was to be distributed free to all Japanese Canadians. Commissioners hoped privately that these measures would dispel "fears being created ... by the spread of unfounded rumour."[78] In May and June 1942, the paper fell almost silent on the topic of property, even as significant assets were sold without the consent of their owners, including fishing vessels and automobiles.[79] In these months, the only hint that the property of Japanese Canadians still hung in the balance came in the form of classified advertisements from those seeking to benefit from Japanese Canadian losses: a "refined" elderly woman sought to rent a home in suburban Vancouver and hoped that a displaced Japanese Canadian might offer an affordable option, a store promised to pay "highest cash prices" for Japanese Canadian–owned furniture, and two clinics offered to painlessly "destroy" the household pets of Japanese Canadians forced to internment.[80]

In these crucial months of the uprooting, *The New Canadian* never questioned the government's policy. The promise of Order 2483 – to administer the property of Japanese Canadians in their interest and to return it – had been stated, but its mechanisms had never been adequately explained. When Shoyama and his editorial team reassumed control of the paper in early summer 1942, the question of property quickly returned to the headlines. However, by this time the promise of protection seemed perhaps a distant past as Japanese Canadians struggled to grapple with the uprooting of the entire population as well as the Custodian's neglect and, in some cases, sale of their property.[81]

During the summer and fall of 1942, federal officials began to contemplate a breach of the legal trust and a betrayal of the promise to protect. Officials in the Custodian's office faced mounting pressure to sell Japanese Canadian–owned farms (from staff of the Soldier Settlement Board, which wanted them for veterans) and urban properties (particularly in the City of Vancouver, where officials contemplated a redevelopment of the largest prewar Japanese Canadian neighbourhood).[82] As the Custodian's office considered these proposals, they began to discuss the sale of all Japanese Canadian–owned property, including real estate and personal belongings. These communications continued to focus on pragmatic concerns. McPherson in particular came to see sale as the most feasible solution to the problems of property management.[83] At the same time, the sales would allay concerns about costs of the internment, since the funds realized in the sale of the property would be credited to the Japanese Canadian property owners and put towards the costs of maintaining internment.[84] By leaving Japanese Canadians with virtually nothing in British Columbia, the forced sales also advanced the aim, shared by almost all officials (even advocates of robust trusteeship), to permanently disperse Japanese Canadians from the province. In a letter to the Minister of Justice Louis St Laurent, Secretary of State McLarty (a former lawyer as well) conveyed the policy consensus that "[t]he situation in British Columbia concerning both urban and farm properties of Japanese who have been evacuated is exceeding difficult." "[I]t was the unanimous view of the members of Council who looked into the problem," he wrote, "that it would probably be necessary to take steps to liquidate, with appropriate safeguards for the protection of the interests of the owners of the Japanese race."[85] The government decided that all Japanese Canadian–owned property remaining in the "protected area" would be sold.

On 19 January 1943, the government announced in Order 469 that, "the evacuation of persons of the Japanese race from the protected areas has now been substantially completed and that it is necessary to provide facilities for liquidation of property in appropriate cases."[86] "Wherever," Order 469 stated,

> under Orders in Council ... the Custodian has been vested with the power and responsibility of controlling and managing any property of persons of the Japanese race evacuated from the protected areas, such power and responsibility shall be deemed to include and to have included from the date of the vesting of such property in the Custodian, the power to liquidate, sell, or otherwise dispose of such property.[87]

Sales of the real property of Japanese Canadians began in the spring of 1943. Within the year, the Custodian had sold the majority of Japanese Canadian–owned real estate, although periodic sales continued for more than six years thereafter.[88]

Despite the fact that Order 469 reiterated that the Custodian's power of "management and control" included the authority to sell, that power had always been present as long as the Custodian acted according to the terms of the trust: namely, selling property only if such sales were for the protective benefit of Japanese Canadian owners, and if the property could not be returned at the conclusion of the war. The power to sell was always qualified by a legal promise to protect the owners' interest in their property. The government's promise to protect was all the more important since the government had created the conditions that made the protection necessary in the first place; it was the uprooting that emptied houses, abandoned vehicles in driveways, and left household possessions the target of looters and thieves.[89] It was the demands of Japanese Canadians, and the threats of their resistance, in addition to internal concerns about property rights and natural justice, that led to the promise to protect.

Even as officials settled on a policy of forced sales, the notion of government trusteeship lingered. They described the sales as benefitting Japanese Canadian owners, claiming that urban properties were amassing debts, farms were being mishandled by tenants, and chattels were going to waste in government warehouses. Under these conditions, officials argued that forced sales benefited owners: better to hold equity in cash, the argument went, than in diminishing assets. Few Japanese Canadians would agree, particularly given the prices for which the Custodian sold their property and the requirement that those living in government camps exhaust their equity in order to pay for their own incarceration. Further, the records of government contradict the argument that the sales served the interests of owners. Virtually all Japanese Canadian–owned urban properties were rented, generating sufficient income to cover the costs of their maintenance. The farm properties were in intense demand and rapidly increasing in value. The government could have done far more to protect chattels.[90] Nonetheless, even as officials turned toward the forced sale of everything that Japanese Canadians owned, they preserved the language of interest and the logic of trust, if disingenuously, that had been established by the promise to protect. Ironically, both the undermining and preservation of the trust combined to support the forced sales. The notion of a trust allowed officials to reason that it was in the best interests of Japanese Canadian owners for the Custodian to sell – a rationale enabled by the failure of the Custodian to honour the obligation to protect the property in the first place.

The editors of *The New Canadian* saw the forced sales as a breach of trust, a violation of basic civil norms, and a betrayal that would undermine the loyalty of Canadian citizens. A powerful editorial on 20 February 1943 portrayed the new powers as a direct threat to the promise to protect. Calling on the federal government to issue a clear statement to "bolster" Japanese Canadian "belief in a democratic government," the editors described Order 469 as a "great shock and disappointment" to property owners who "were content to leave control of their property to the Custodian, because of the implied assurance that the Federal Government was taking over 'as a protective measure only.'" Explicitly tying ownership in land to citizenship, the editors argued,

> [I]t is safe to declare here and now, that those who invested their earnings in assets as solid as good Canadian soil thereby gave notice of their wish and intention to remain in Canada as good Canadian citizens. There is assuredly no reason today why any policy needs to be carried out in a way that weakens, rather than strengthens that wish.[91]

"The common feeling among property-owners," they continued, "was ... that no matter how their cash and other assets might dwindle and vanish during the war, they were assured at least of a house or a piece of land which might see them through the uncertain period after the war." Now this security was lost and, as many Japanese Canadians correctly anticipated, their equity in real estate would "dwindle and vanish" along with the other cherished and quotidian assets of their lives.

In the same issue, *The New Canadian* reprinted an article from *The Vancouver Daily Province* attempting to reassure readers that the promise of protection had not been abandoned. Frank Shears, who managed the Vancouver Office of the Custodian, told the Vancouver paper, "A lot of people are assuming that because the property may be sold the Japanese will not come back." Despite allowing this possibility, he explained that, "it could also mean that the Dominion Government prefers to have the property held for them in cash."[92] While Shears equivocated on the intention of the policy, property, in his formulation was still "held for them" – the power to sell was commensurate with the duty of the federal government to hold property for the benefit of owners. Indeed, according to the *Daily Province*, "[s]hould the Japanese be allowed to return here it may be in the better interest of both the government and the Japanese to hand them a cash sum rather than return their property."[93] Japanese Canadians, according to the logic of the federal government, were best served by a policy of forced sale.

That argument failed to convince Japanese Canadians. It also failed to persuade Henry Forbes Angus, a prominent official in External Affairs. In a memo to Norman Robertson on 15 March 1943, Angus forcefully objected to the turn in policy, which, in his view, would "legalize acts of gross injustice and oppression." In complying with their internment, Angus argued, many citizens of "unimpeachable character" had already "been called on to make very great sacrifices in the interests of public security." These policies had brought grievous harm to the economic well-being of Japanese Canadians. "Through no fault of his own," Angus wrote, the Japanese Canadian citizen "has been deprived of the major part of his earning power, has been removed from his home, has seen his children's educational opportunities gravely impaired." The new policy would mean that "[he] finds himself in a position in which he may be substantially forced to use the proceeds of the enforced liquidation of his capital assets to meet what would for citizens of other races would be considered normal living expenses." Angus raised a number of legal objections to the policy: it exceeded the necessity of war, trespassed provincial jurisdiction, contravened the previous word of the prime minister in the House of Commons, and violated the Atlantic Charter. He portrayed it as a breach of "British tradition" that encouraged the "belief among responsible citizens that the Canadian Government is emulating the Nurnberg [*sic*] decrees."[94]

Japanese Canadians objected with even greater force and clarity.[95] Hundreds wrote in protest when notified of the sale of their property without consent. Many among them referenced the promise of protection that had been betrayed. When Hanjiro Yoshijima was informed in July 1943 that his property in New Westminster had been rented for what he viewed as an astonishingly low figure, he wrote the Office of the Custodian in "shock": "We had believed," he wrote, "that the Custodian was to protect and administer our property ... in a way in which the owner would have done himself and had trusted you to handle our affairs as sanely and as sensible as possible in our interest."[96] The language of protection and administration, of the "interest" of the owner, suggests that Yoshijima knew Order 2483 and saw it as committing the government to act in his interest. He was to be disappointed. Almost two years later, when officials sold his property without his consent, he wrote again, but without faith that the government could be held to its word: "Perhaps it is useless to inform you now, but, all the prices listed [for his property] are outrageous and believe me, there is not a single article that was sold for even a quarter of its real value."[97]

Others wrote the federal government to express similar views of a promise breached. "I never thought," wrote Tokujiro Takenaka, "that the trustworthy Custodian will dispose of my property at such a cheap price."[98] Aya Suzuki remembered, "before leaving Vancouver your men told us that this process was to protect us and in your assurance we had our businesses put into our local agents whom we trusted as you had promised ... [b]ut now you say according to Ottawa this land has been sold." She forcefully objected to this reversal, accusing authorities of an unforgivable breach of the rights of citizens.[99] Macer Okamoto wrote in disbelief that his family's belongings were slated for forced sale: "[S]urely," he wrote, "there must have be a terrible mistake somewhere! ... We had everyfaith [*sic*] that it was for our protection when we handed everything to the Custodian for safe keeping [*sic*]. Otherwise we would have sold some of the things on our own as many were doing."[100] Toyo Takahashi, in a letter protesting the sale of her home in Victoria, described it as "against your promises, and my wishes, furthermore it is utterly undeserved."[101] Many Japanese Canadians, seeing few other options, had placed their trust in the federal government's repeated promise to protect their property. When the federal government sold all Japanese Canadian–owned property under Order 469, letters of protest conveyed the bitterness, disappointment, and regret of a broken trust.

II. Litigating the promise: *Nakashima v Canada*

Between the passage of Order 469 and the start of property sales in the spring of 1943, leaders in the Japanese Canadian community repeatedly sought clarification and assurance from the federal government concerning the fate of their property. Tempering their outrage at the prospect of sale was a continuing faith in the Custodian's trusteeship and rumours that rented properties would not be sold.[102] By early April 1943, however, *The New Canadian* reported that the "[l]atest developments seem to dispel this impression"; all property would be sold regardless of rental status.[103] Still, the newspaper found cause for faint hope, noting that the government had emphasized that, "the whole purpose of the Custodian's taking over the property ... is in order that it may be properly protected."[104] Despite the dire circumstances in which they had been forced to live, Japanese Canadians organized to hold the government to its promise. In April 1943, *The New Canadian* announced that "[n]umbers of former residents of the coastal district in the Slocan, New Denver and Kaslo [sites of internment] have voiced their wish to organize as an amalgamated 'property-owners' association' in order to carry the fight to the courts of law." Calling for the establishment of local committees of concerned property owners, editors predicted "that the litigation is likely to be long, involved and costly."[105] They were right.

At Kaslo, under the chairmanship of Dr Kozo Shimotakahara, the "well known pioneer physician," the Amalgamated Property Owners' Association (APOA) began to organize its litigation strategy.[106] Seeking to challenge "the constitutional power of the government even in war time to order liquidation of evacuee-owned property," the committee called upon all "[r]eal property owners anxious to retain their interest in their homes, land and buildings" to defray the anticipated legal costs of $8,500.[107] "It is not known as yet," the article admitted, "whether goods, chattels, and personal property falls within the provisions of the order or the policy to be adopted by the Custodian," but, if so, all Japanese Canadians would be enmeshed "in an issue fundamental and basic to Canadian democracy as the right to hold property clearly is."[108] Subsequent articles suggested that all property owners should contribute to the legal fund, setting contributions at "ten per cent of the annual taxation paid upon their property,"[109] while reinforcing the argument that what was at stake involved "the safeguarding of fundamental" and "democratic rights."[110] By the end of May 1943, small amounts of money collected from Japanese Canadians, in mostly desperate circumstances enabled the APOA to retain the Vancouver law firm of Norris and MacLennan. The appearance of legal counsel setting out the route by which the orders might be legally challenged offered some solace from what was otherwise a week of bad news: McPherson had announced that the Custodian's office had prepared a catalogue of all Japanese Canadian–owned property for listing and that sales were imminent.[111]

Thomas Grantham Norris and J. Arthur MacLennan had joined as partners in legal practice in the late 1930s. Norris, the senior partner, had been called to the British Columbia Bar in 1919 after distinguished military service in the First World War.[112] Norris's legal career had included stints in Vernon and Kelowna and, for a short while, as solicitor for the Soldier Settlement Board. As a lawyer, Norris engaged in a wide-ranging practice and was regarded among his peers as a tough-minded, "openly declared law and order" lawyer.[113] It is unclear how Norris came to represent members of the Japanese Canadian community, although we know that by the mid-1930s Norris had begun to represent Eikichi Kagetsu, owner of a highly successful lumber business.[114] By the outbreak of war, Norris's firm was widely known for its advocacy on behalf of Japanese Canadians, "at a time when few would do anything for them."[115] In filling out their declarations of property in the lead up to the internment, many Japanese Canadians turned to Norris and MacLennan for assistance. Norris's firm was the obvious choice for the APOA, although not Norris himself. Having agreed to serve as deputy judge advocate general for the Twenty-First Army Group for the duration of the war, Norris had handed his practice over to his junior partner, Art MacLennan.[116] With Norris returning to military service in 1941, MacLennan found himself handling Norris's clients, including the challenge to the constitutionality of the sale of Japanese Canadian–owned property.

The case against the government on behalf of Japanese Canadian property owners posed a number of substantive and procedural difficulties. The first issue concerned the nature of the suit itself. Still protected by medieval theories of Crown immunity, the Crown could not be sued without its consent.[117] Likewise, the Trading with the Enemy Regulations stipulated that the Custodian could not be sued without his consent.[118] Finally, as MacLennan pointed out in an opinion letter to his clients, a reference case concerning the constitutionality of the orders of dispossession would require the cooperation of either the provincial or federal government.[119] In other words, either the Custodian or cabinet would be required to give consent before the lawsuit could even begin.

The case also raised a number of substantive obstacles. The Canadian judiciary had shown consistent deference to government action throughout the war, and the widespread racist animosity towards Japanese Canadians would not have inspired confidence about a different outcome in this particular case.[120] And yet, as some lawyers plainly saw, the injustice of the forced sale, the severity of its consequences, its affront to notions of fairness and citizenship, the absence of any logical security rationale, and, perhaps above all, the promises of protection in the form of a legal trust made this a case worth fighting. On 1 June 1943, the APOA instructed MacLennan to initiate a Petition of Right in the Exchequer Court of Canada seeking an injunction against property sales and challenging the constitutional validity of orders that "[cast] aside the rights of a citizen under conditions not related to the efficient prosecution of the war."[121] "In the past half century of our somewhat troubled life on the coast," editors of *The New Canadian* wrote,

> we have had numerous instances of test cases, in the highest courts, in the legislative buildings, in the local community halls. We cannot say that they met with success, but when we look back in the years to come, perhaps these cases will be the milestones that will mark our long and rocky road to citizenship.[122]

Vindication did not seem imminent. One week after the editorial, the Custodian listed hundreds of parcels of Japanese Canadian–owned real estate for sale.

MacLennan drafted three Petitions of Right dated 19 July 1943. They were filed with the Exchequer Court in October of the same year. To challenge the orders in their application to all Japanese Canadians, the APOA put forward three categories of litigants: Eikichi Nakashima, a naturalized British subject; Tadao Wakabayashi, a British subject by Canadian birth; and Jitaro and Takejiro Tanaka, Japanese nationals resident in Canada.[123] Before the internment, Nakashima had worked as a fish buyer for BC Packers Co. and lived in the Powell Street district of Vancouver (688 E Cordova Street) with his wife and eleven-year-old son, Shinji. Nakashima and his family had registered their property with the Custodian in April 1942, before the government interned them at Lemon Creek in September. Wakabayashi, a Nisei, had been born in Vancouver and had made his living as a truck driver. Along with his wife, Akiko, Tadao had lived at 2456 McGill Street in Vancouver before being forced from his home. In addition to his residential property, Tadao and Akiko listed "53 Pieces Japanese Dishes" and one "pair ice skates" among the extensive list of personal property seized by the Custodian. The third set of litigants comprised brothers born in Japan, Jitaro and Takejiro Tanaka. The brothers were joint tenants of 162 E 5th Street in Vancouver. A manager at the West Coast Trading Company before the internment, Takejiro lived with his wife Ayako and four children under the age of ten. Listing his possessions for the Custodian he included three five-dollar war savings certificates in the names of his children.[124]

Although the personal details in the opening paragraphs of each Petition of Right differed, the balance of the claim was common to all. Disputing the authority of the Custodian to "sell, liquidate or otherwise dispose of the said property against the wishes and desires of the Suppliant," the petition cited Orders 1665 and 2483 to assert that the Custodian acquired Japanese Canadian–owned property "upon Trust requiring him to hold same in Trust for the protection of the Suppliant and under his management and control upon a condition requiring the Custodian to return to the Suppliant the said property … upon expiration of the existing war."[125] In the alternative, the petition alleged that the orders, individually or collectively, were beyond the powers allocated by the WMA and therefore unconstitutional. As to a remedy, the petition sought a declaration of constitutional invalidity, a declaration that the Custodian was a trustee of the dispossessed Japanese Canadian property owners, and an injunction restraining the sale of the property of Japanese Canadians.[126] As the Custodian initiated property sales, the litigants, MacLennan, and the broader Japanese Canadian community waited for the government's permission to sue.

Permission of the secretary of state arrived in October 1943, triggering the Crown's duty to produce a Statement of Defence but introducing another procedural difficulty: the location of the trial. MacLennan explained to his clients that the trial could be held in Vancouver but that would require the government to send one of the two judges on the Ottawa-based Exchequer Court to hold a special session on the West Coast. Failing that, the case would have to be heard in Ottawa and, in that instance, not until the following September, at which point most of the property might have been sold.[127] MacLennan dispatched lawyer F. Drewe Pratt to Ottawa to inquire about expediting a hearing in Vancouver, while the APOA requested that the Custodian cease all property sales until the legal matter had been resolved. Neither effort succeeded.[128] Periodic reports in *The New Canadian* speculated about when the case might finally be heard. "Auctioning of goods and chattels has also been proceeding steadily," the paper reported "from warehouses, private homes and stores in which the goods were kept."[129]

Finally, word arrived that the case would be heard at the end of May 1944. "[T]he long delay," MacLennan explained, "had been caused by the pressure of duties of Department of Justice officials entrusted with the handling of the case."[130] Indeed, the litigation had attracted the attention of the highest officials in the Department of

Justice. The case would be defended by the deputy minister of justice himself, Frederick Percy Varcoe, along with David W. Mundell, who would go on to a famed career as a government constitutional lawyer in his own right. Varcoe began his career in the Department of Justice during the First World War as an expert in the operation of the Military Service Act.[131] Rising to the position of deputy minister in 1941, Varcoe knew each of the orders at issue having overviewed their drafting from his chair at the Department of Justice.

On the morning of 29 May 1944, after dining at the Chateau Laurier the night before, MacLennan along with Nakashima, Wakabayashi, and Tanaka (having received government permission to leave their sites of internment to attend their hearing), appeared in the grey stone gothic courthouse near Parliament Hill. Back in British Columbia, the editors at *The New Canadian* recognized that "delay has served to increase suspicion that Justice may be conveniently blinded to suit the purpose of the Government" but counselled all the same that "[w]e must pledge in this, our responsibility, every resource at our command, to defend rights which never before have been so violated in a democratic country."[132] Reporting for *The New Canadian* directly from the courthouse was Kunio Hidaka, a graduate student at Queen's University.[133]

Hidaka, the litigants, and the gowned lawyers – MacLennan, Varcoe, and Mundell – rose for the arrival in court of Justice Joseph Thorarinn Thorson. Varcoe knew the presiding judge well. Thorson had been dean at the Manitoba Law School before entering public life as a Liberal member of Parliament, first in Winnipeg and then in Selkirk, Manitoba. In 1941, Mackenzie King appointed Thorson minister of national war service.[134] As minister, Thorson coordinated domestic local volunteer groups in assisting the war campaign, as well as domestic censorship and propaganda.[135] His time in cabinet was short. A year later, on 6 October 1942, his cabinet colleague Louis St Laurent recommended Thorson's appointment as president of the Exchequer Court of Canada. As deputy minister, Varcoe would have supervised the mechanics of Thorson's judicial appointment. Two years into a judicial career that would stretch another twenty, Justice Thorson settled the courtroom and asked Varcoe to begin his arguments.

Varcoe's first argument was a sweeping one: "that the Custodian is not the Crown, and … that this is not a proper action against His Majesty because the Custodian is not His Majesty or the servant or agent of His Majesty."[136] The position had the advantage of dismissing the entirety of the claim and it found some favour in recent case law.[137] It was also purely strategic. Varcoe argued precisely the opposite a year later when confronted with a dispute between the Custodian and the Department of National Defence (DND) concerning thousands of dollars of damage that Canadian soldiers had caused to a Japanese language school while the DND had leased the premises from the Custodian during the war. When McPherson, acting for the Custodian, sought compensation for the damage, the DND sought Varcoe's support shielding it from liability.

Putting his argument in *Nakashima* out of mind, Varcoe bluntly informed the Custodian that since both the Custodian and DND operated as instruments of the Crown there could be no liability between them. This time, it was McPherson's turn to confront the legal contortions of his own government. Seeking remedy for the Custodian, he pointed out that such a position was directly at odds with Varcoe's argument in *Nakashima*. Varcoe coolly replied that the contexts were different.[138]

Varcoe also argued that the relevant orders created no trust. Stressing that Order 2483 contained two distinct methods by which property might become vested in the Custodian, Varcoe noted that section 12(1) concerned all property vested in the Custodian by virtue of being "situated in any protected area," "turned over to the Custodian," or otherwise left behind because of the internment.[139] Property which vested under this subsection, Varcoe argued, did not contain any of the additional protections outlined in section 12(2): namely, stipulations that the Custodian was to hold property "for the purpose of protecting the interests of the owner" and the promise to "release such property" at the conclusion of the war.[140] Section 12(2) and its protections, he argued, only pertained to property vested in the Custodian by "order" of the Custodian. All of the property at issue in this case, Varcoe declared, had vested under section 12(1).[141] Accordingly, Varcoe concluded, the Custodian remained unhindered by any trust and possessed full discretion to do whatever he liked with the property of Nakashima, Wakabayashi, and Tanaka, including the power to sell.

As to the constitutional validity of the orders at issue, Varcoe stressed that the question was beyond judicial competence to review. Relying on the Supreme Court of Canada's decision *Reference Re: Regulations in Relation to Chemicals*,[142] Varcoe averred that judges could not second-guess what the governor in council deemed "necessary or advisable for the security, defence, peace, order and welfare of Canada."[143] Certain passages of the *Chemicals Reference* bolstered Varcoe's interpretation of virtually absolute deference to government in executing its legislative capacities in times of war. Noting the "plenary discretion" afforded by the WMA, in the *Chemicals Reference*, Chief Justice Duff doubted "that it is competent to any court to canvass the considerations which have, or may have, led [the governor general in council] to deem such Regulations necessary or advisable for the transcendent objects set forth." "The authority and duty of passing on that question," Chief Justice Duff stated, "are committed to those who are responsible for the security of the country – the Executive Government itself."[144] In rhetoric, reasoning, and result, the *Chemicals Reference* followed the judicial trend of extending unfettered deference to government officials in the exercise of their wartime duties. Varcoe knew he was on sure footing, especially in making such arguments to a judge present at the cabinet table only two years prior.

In response, MacLennan challenged Varcoe's interpretation of the *Chemicals Reference*. Arguing that the WMA circumscribed the federal government's authority to legislate, MacLennan proposed that since "the liquidation of the properties has no conceivable relationship to the prosecution of the war," Order 469 was *ultra vires* the WMA and hence illegal.[145] Since the WMA was itself only constitutional insofar as it related to the emergency powers of peace, order, and good government (the constitutional regulation of property normally lying within provincial jurisdiction), any order passed under the WMA's authority must comply strictly with its conditions: "orders and regulations, as [the governor general in council] may by reason of the existence of real or apprehended war, invasion, insurrection deem necessary or advisable for the security, peace, order and welfare of Canada."[146] Without saying so explicitly, MacLennan impressed upon Justice Thorson the continuing constraints of the rule of law, notwithstanding the existence of war, which suggested that statutes could only lawfully empower state action in accordance with the purpose and conditions for which they had been enacted.

As the argument carried over to the following morning, Justice Thorson questioned whether a judge could ever second-guess government decisions during war. MacLennan argued that a careful reading of the *Chemicals Reference* reinforced the capacity of judicial review.[147] Despite a general tone of deference, MacLennan drew attention to Chief Justice Duff's concession that in some cases "the plain terms of the order-in-council itself" may indicate that the order was not deemed "necessary or advisable by reason of the existence of war."[148] MacLennan bolstered his argument with reliance on *Price Brothers*, a Supreme Court decision of the First World War in which a majority struck down a federal order setting the price of newsprint as bearing insufficient connection "to the perils actual or possible of real or apprehended war ... or ... to the prosecution of the war or the objects of it."[149] The powers of judicial review in relation to war matters were to be exercised with caution, but that did not mean they did not exist, MacLennan argued. Turning to the case before them, MacLennan concluded that the sale of property "does not add one iota to the object of winning the war or the security of Canada."[150] Without a necessary connection to wartime security, Order 469, insofar as it authorized the blanket sale of all property, was therefore unconstitutional.

As to the validity of the power of sale more broadly, MacLennan argued that, "sale might be justifiable if it is for the protection of the property, itself, or the Japanese because ... properties are to be held by the Custodian for the benefit of the owners, to be managed and controlled for their benefit."[151] MacLennan rejected Varcoe's theory that there were two methods of property vesting in section 12 of Order 2483, arguing instead that subsection 2 was merely an explanation of subsection 1.[152] As an alternative, he stressed that the protective language of subsection 1, as well as the notion of "management and control," similarly enacted a trusteeship premised on the promise that property would be protected and returned. In addition, he raised a handful of other less persuasive arguments on the basis of a contract formed between the Custodian and Japanese Canadians. The crux of his argument, however, lay in two overarching claims: Order 469 was *ultra vires* because sale promoted a policy objective divorced from either emergency or wartime security, and, if Order 469 was *intra vires* then the Custodian's power to sell under that order was constrained by the trust conditions imposed by Order 2483.

In reply, Varcoe argued that, even if a trustee, the Custodian was fully entitled to sell. It is worth quoting Varcoe at length to illustrate how the logic of trust became contorted to support white supremacist aims.

> Varcoe: Suppose … that the Custodian is compelled to sell parcels X, Y, Z, three blocks of property. Then, the next block is not in such a bad position. I have sold X, Y, Z to be inhabited by white persons. I could not sell to anyone else. I think it is undesirable, under those circumstances, that that next parcel should be held by or for Japanese and therefore I think it is time to sell this property …
> Justice Thorson: You mean that the evacuation may be a permanent thing.
> Varcoe: It may be that, yes, he does not know.
> Justice Thorson: In which case, you could not just leave the properties in a mere state of management and control, they would have to be sold. You may decide there is an area which has been inhabited by Japanese people, but you are not going to have any more Japanese in that district, that is going to be for white people or somebody else; therefore, you will sell all the houses in that particular block or area.
> Varcoe: Yes, some of which are in bad condition. They are in bad condition and I cannot remove them because they are held by Japanese, too. If I can go to the purchaser with some kind of assurance that this will be a white man's property, I can get a good price for it. Assuming everything in my friend's favour, these are the things the Custodian would be bound to take into account in determining whether or not he would continue to hold the property at this high rental or whether he would sell it.[153]

Here the presence of the trust took on a sinister character. Varcoe alleged that selling everything would be in the interests of Japanese Canadian owners since white purchasers would only pay a "good price" if they had assurance that adjacent properties would also be sold. Varcoe's theory that prospective purchasers would balk at ownership next to a Japanese Canadian was not supported by evidence – Japanese Canadians had long owned alongside neighbours of other backgrounds and, in rural areas, officials struggled in the face of excess demand for Japanese Canadian–owned farms, not the opposite.[154] Facts were not Varcoe's concern, however. Instead he gestured to a deeper perception: that fulfilling the terms of the trust required British Columbia to be "white man's property."[155]

Whether Justice Thorson followed this particular logic was unclear. His interjections pushed towards conceptualizing the permanent exclusion of Japanese Canadians as an act of emergency:

> Justice Thorson: So that the power of sale might have some relationship to the emergency that brought about the evacuation in the first place and it might be ancillary.
>
> ...
>
> Varcoe: I would say that I would doubt whether any greater emergency was created in the Dominion of Canada than was created by the Japanese situation and everything which was done in connection with it was ancillary to the emergency.
>
> Justice Thorson: Even sale, after the Custodian had obtained full control.
>
> Varcoe: Yes, that he had to have that wide power to dispose of these properties if, for nothing else, to satisfy public opinion in Vancouver.[156]

In his final gesture, Varcoe argued that racial anxiety in British Columbia was itself a sufficient emergency to authorize government action under the WMA. With that, two days of argument concluded. "I do not think anyone expects me to give judgment now," Justice Thorson said. "Judgement will be reserved."[157]

Three years passed with no decision in *Nakashima* from the Exchequer Court. During that time, the government completed the bulk of its sales (excluding the three properties at issue in the Nakashima case), the Second World War ended, and the government began to exile almost 4,000 Japanese Canadians to Japan.[158] "Inquiries in Ottawa as to why the decision has not been handed down," *The New Canadian* reported, "draw a blank."[159] The injustice of the delay in releasing the *Nakashima* decision began to attract wider attention. In the House of Commons, Angus MacInnis, the CCF member of Parliament for Vancouver East, asked the Liberal justice minister to explain how a decision could take three years to complete. "I regret that condition of affairs," the minister admitted, offering only that "[s]ome judges were slower than others ... and perhaps some took more pains than others."[160] With only two judges, both seemingly beset by procrastination, delay had become endemic at the Exchequer Court.[161] Justice Thorson finally released his decision on 28 August 1947. There was nothing in the relatively short judgment of twenty-one paragraphs that would even remotely account for the three years and three months it took him to decide the case. Nakashima, Wakabayashi, and Tanaka lost.

Perhaps in part because of the delay, Justice Thorson's decision largely slipped from legal and historical attention. Justice Thorson began his reasons noting the "Japanese origin[s]" of the "suppliants." Avoiding any personal details of the litigants, Justice Thorson explained that Nakashima "is a British subject by naturalization," Wakabayashi "a British subject by birth," and the Tanaka brothers, "Japanese nationals."[162] Such differences, he ruled, were immaterial – "the answer in any one case will be equally applicable in the others."[163] Justice Thorson devoted not another moment to the litigants themselves: their history, families, real estate, possessions, and lives. Instead, his necessary "sequence of events" detailed the orders creating the protected area of British Columbia, implementing the "evacuation," and dealing with property.[164] Turning to the issue of whether the legal claim had been properly initiated, he noted that the proceedings assumed that the Custodian held the property "as the servant of the Crown."[165] This, Justice Thorson maintained, was a fatal error. Emphasizing the Custodian's wide discretion in dealing with property and its independence from government, he held that the Custodian could neither be characterized as the Crown nor its servant.[166] The plaintiffs should have sued the Custodian and not the Crown, he concluded. The case ended before it began.

Despite declaring that, "this ends the matter" and expressing misgivings about even considering the broader issue of constitutional validity, Justice Thorson decided to address the issue in *obiter* "since it is of great importance."[167] "[T]he two conditions of jurisdiction prescribed by the War Measures Act have both been satisfied," he stated without explication. "It is, therefore, not open to the Court to question the validity of the order-in-council empowering the Custodian to sell the properties vested in him."[168] "The Court has no right," he continued, "to substitute its opinion of what is necessary or advisable for that of the Governor in Council or to question the validity of an order so made."[169] "The Custodian has," Justice Thorson concluded, "the lawful right to liquidate, sell, or otherwise dispose of the property vested in him."[170] As to the question of whether the Custodian was a trustee, he declared that since the Custodian was not a servant of the Crown the question need not be answered. There was only one final matter. Justice Thorson ordered Nakashima, Wakabayashi, and Tanaka to pay the government's legal costs.

In contrast to the attention *The New Canadian* gave the case at the outset, by the time of its release, the result in *Nakashima* was met with sparse coverage and only muted disappointment.[171] MacLennan informed his clients that he could see no grounds for appeal.[172] Probably Japanese Canadians had long reconciled themselves to the outcome. Certainly there would have been ample grounds to have lost faith in the judicial process. By the summer of 1947, more pressing legal matters preoccupied the Japanese Canadian community, including the Bird Commission's inquiry into the Custodian's sales and continuing orders restricting the movement and liberty of Japanese Canadians. Their wartime experiences had also caused Japanese Canadians to shift their attention towards the project of constitutional change. Just before the

Nakashima ruling, a meeting of Japanese Canadian organizations in Toronto called for "a national bill of rights for Canada – to define the fundamental and inalienable rights of citizenship."[173] "The Canadian emergency laws," *The New Canadian* editors agreed, "are too ready-made for a would-be dictator."[174] Legal change, Japanese Canadian community leaders would argue for the next half century, must come in the form of constitutional rights.

Its relative obscurity has meant that the reasoning in *Nakashima* has not received much scrutiny. Certainly, to modern eyes, the case and its reasoning raise a number of concerns. One might question, at the outset, whether Justice Thorson should have heard the case in the first place given his membership in the cabinet that produced several of the orders under review and his recent professional relationship with the Custodian. While the Exchequer Court only had two members in 1944, the case could have been assigned to a judge less implicated in government wartime policy. More pointedly, the delay in hearing and especially in deciding the case was inexcusable and unjust. Neither the government nor Justice Thorson dealt with the case with the expediency that the issue required and deserved. It is also difficult not to see the delay as motivated at least partly by a desire to dispose of Japanese Canadian–owned property before the legal issues in the case were determined. At the very least, Justice Thorson should have issued an injunction preventing sales until the legality of the Custodian's actions could be determined and possibly appealed. Time only sharpens the sense that bad faith lay at the heart of the government's handling of the case from the outset.

Justice Thorson was also wrong to uncritically accept the government's convenient distinction between the Custodian and Crown as a matter of law. Without question, the issue was complicated by a common law that effectively insulated government from legal proceedings. Change and rationalization of proceedings against the Crown would not arrive in Canada until the 1950s when Parliament and provincial legislatures enacted legislation that enabled legal claims against government.[175] Perhaps MacLennan should have attempted to sue the Custodian directly rather than pursuing the Crown via a Petition of Right. But as the Regulations Respecting Trading with the Enemy stipulated, the Custodian could not be sued without its consent either. Further, even if the Custodian had granted consent, the Regulations suggested a claim against the Custodian could only address a narrow range of issues and certainly not ones involving the constitutional validity of the orders themselves.[176] Given the Petition of Right's origins in equity, it was open to Justice Thorson to find that his court provided the only avenue for the petitioners to question the exercise of the Custodian's trusteeship and the constitutional validity of the orders. Nakashima, Wakabayashi, and Tanaka were defeated not only by the common law's hostility to Crown liability but also by Justice Thorson's narrow interpretation of civil procedure.

Justice Thorson also had questionable grounds for dismissing MacLennan's constitutional argument. Orders passed under the WMA were constitutional only insofar as they complied with the specific preconditions of the WMA itself: 1) *by reason* of war, invasion, or insurrection; 2) *deemed* necessary or advisable by the governor in council; and 3) *for the* security, defence, peace, order and welfare of Canada.[177] The governor in council may have favoured the forced sale of Japanese Canadian–owned property and the permanent exclusion of Japanese Canadians from British Columbia, but that policy did not have any connection to the war beyond timing and opportunity nor could it be justified as advancing the security, defence, peace, order, and welfare of Canada, notwithstanding racist prejudice and assumptions to the contrary. Selling Japanese Canadian–owned property promoted an altogether different long-standing objective: making British Columbia a "white man's province." As Justice Murphy of the United States Supreme Court famously held in dissent in *Korematsu*, the internment of Japanese Americans on racial grounds, "goes over 'the very brink of constitutional power' and falls squarely into the ugly abyss of racism."[178] That Justice Thorson was unwilling or incapable of seeing the forced sales as acts of racism rather than security does not change their unconstitutional nature.

MacLennan's strongest argument concerned the promise to protect. Justice Thorson ignored this argument entirely, but there was ample evidence that the Custodian controlled and managed the property of Japanese Canadians as a trustee, including the Custodian's interpretation of its own mandate. The history of Order 2483 makes the existence of a trust relationship clear. Read's critique of Order 1665 stemmed from his concerns that an insufficient trust relationship had been established in its drafts. Order 2483 replaced Order 1665 specifically to address that concern and said so in its preamble. McPherson, the policy architect behind the dispossession and the orders, did not hesitate to describe the Custodian as a trustee and he deliberately impressed the notion of trusteeship in communicating the dispossession to Japanese Canadians. The Japanese Canadian community, with justifiable suspicion of false motives, relied on the promise to protect in good faith.

Canadian trust law of the 1940s, as today, recognized that a trust could be created in a variety of ways, most typically by express words and intent.[179] "A trust," a leading text writer of the period explained, "is an equitable obligation, binding a person (who is called a trustee) to deal with property over which he has control (which is called the trust property), for the benefit of persons (who are called the beneficiaries)."[180] Whether a trust arises expressly by explicit intention or constructively by circumstances and conduct, the legal result is the same: an obligation on the part of the trustee to manage the property for the benefit of the beneficiary.[181] The circumstances, intentions, and language of Order 2483, and probably Order 1665 as well, created an express trust. The power to sell, stipulated from the outset in the Custodian's powers, was also fully consistent with the existence of a trust because it may be in the interests of the beneficiary for the trustee to sell a rapidly deteriorating asset. Significantly, Order 469 did not amend or repeal Order 2483; it simply confirmed a qualified power of sale that had always been present in the Custodian's powers. Content to weave a promise to protect property into law, to create a trust relationship, and to accept the cooperation of Japanese Canadians on that basis, Canada abandoned its legal promise at the moment it was needed most. The Custodian breached that trust in its negligent treatment of chattels and household goods, in its failure to police and protect vacant properties, and in its bad faith sales of all Japanese Canadian–owned property in promotion of racist policy objectives unconnected to the war. The Department of Justice further breached that trust in its bad faith litigation strategy and its warping of the trust to justify racist ends. In its inexcusable delay, its failure to recognize the harms suffered by the litigants and its sanction of racist policy, motive, and argument, Justice Thorson's decision in *Nakashima* betrayed that promise too.

III. Conclusions

This legal history has traced the life of a promise of law from its origin to its demise, chronicling its shifting meanings, interactions, and consequences for the people whose lives it forever altered. Reading the origins of the promise to protect alongside its defeat in court helps us to better understand and contextualize both. Multiple actors shape the life, death, and meaning of law: drafters and civil servants crafting government policy into words on a page; the subjects of law in their acts of interpretation, resistance, and compliance; and the officials, lawyers and judges enforcing, arguing, and interpreting law in retrospect. In litigation, government lawyers turned the trust against the interests of the people it was intended to protect. More brazenly, the government's legal objective was to write the promise to protect out of the law entirely. The history of the dispossession should not do the same.

The story of this legal promise is one of stark simplicity and tangled complexity. In important ways, the promise of law was meaningless. Eikichi Nakashima, Tadao Wakabayashi, Jitaro and Takejiro Tanaka, and thousands of other Japanese Canadians lost their homes and livelihoods; they lost their court case too. A long history of failing to see racialized minorities as full citizens, the unjust association of Japanese Canadians with an enemy country, administrative incompetence, and economic and territorial avarice motivated a commitment to white supremacy fuelled the dispossession policy. A combination of war, racism, and exclusionary citizenship gave the patina of legal licence to virtually all discriminatory actions taken against the Japanese Canadian community, even those that made no one safer. Many in British Columbia intended that Japanese Canadians never return from internment. The Custodian sold the property of Japanese Canadians without compunction or sanction. Varcoe, in defending the Custodian's actions, and Justice Thorson, in his inexcusably delayed ruling, ignored or looked past the legal trust that had been created. The promise of law failed to halt a single sale of property.

But the dispossession is also complicated by the presence of a promise. At earlier moments in the life of the laws of dispossession, figures like Read, Angus, and Coleman invoked legal principles that should have constrained government action. They did so in direct response to the actions of Japanese Canadians. McPherson believed, and rightly so, that the laws of dispossession imposed a trustee relationship between the Custodian and Japanese Canadians. MacLennan had a legal case to argue because the activism of Japanese Canadians carved a promise of protection into law. Acknowledging this complexity does not absolve the federal government of responsibility for the promise's ultimate breach. As Tina Loo has argued, "oppression is not automatic and the reproduction of relations of domination is not straightforward because the power of the law is not totalizing." History, by foregrounding people in their variety, ambiguity, and complexity, renders visible the "opportunities within the rule of law and the larger discourse from which it is derived" for alternative outcomes.[182] A different history would have been possible had promises been honoured. Remembering the dispossession only as a story of the power of sale runs the risk of perpetuating a narrative adopted by government actors in order to conceal the legal significance of the promise to protect. The laws of dispossession and *Nakashima* are a story not only of law's will to power but its will to promise as well. That those promises lay broken and abandoned with such injustice should not obscure the ways in which the law finds meaning not only in after-the-fact judicial interpretation but also in the good faith actions and interpretations of the people subject to its rule.

This chapter is also about the role of vulnerable citizens in making law and resisting state power, and the limits of the rule of law. Japanese Canadians demanded and placed their trust in the promise to protect, just as they prepared for it to be broken. Alert to the possibility that some British Columbians would attempt to use a temporary state of war to exile Japanese Canadians from the province, they interrogated state action and sought to hold officials to their own principles and legal promises. While Japanese Canadians were shocked by the betrayal of the promise, their legal challenge was also part of a vigilance to uphold the law and an expression of faith in legality. Disappointment in the *Nakashima* ruling did not end the community's engagement with legal promises. In the decades after the conclusion of their legal challenge, Japanese Canadians continued to remind the government in public testimony, royal commission hearings, the redress movement, and courts of law, of the legal significance of the broken promise.[183]

In 1968, *Nakashima* and the promise to protect returned briefly to the legal spotlight. Torazo Iwasaki sued the federal government, alleging that the Custodian had breached its trust obligations in selling his land on Salt Spring Island in 1945 without his consent.[184] Relying on Justice Thorson's reasoning in *Nakashima*, Justice Sheppard of the Exchequer Court held that "the discretionary powers of the Custodian are inconsistent with any trust."[185] Iwasaki's "complaint is without foundation," the judge declared,

> The complaint is that orders-in-council 1665 and 2483 set up a trust to return the lands to the suppliant, wherefore the lands vested in the Custodian as trustee under duty to manage and return, and that order-in-council 469 in authorizing a sale, was void. That was an error; there was no trust ... nor was there any breach of trust.[186]

After hearing Iwasaki's appeal, a unanimous Supreme Court of Canada issued its decision orally from the bench. "We are all of the opinion that the appeal fails," Justice Fauteux informed the courtroom. "The property in question in these proceedings became vested in the Custodian by legislative action. He had the power to sell and he did sell."[187] *Nakashima* has not been cited by a court of law since.

The rule of law project is a long one and legal history can play a key role within it by excavating lost promises and the people and stories behind them. The history of the dispossession revealed here suggests that the forced sales should be approached not simply as bad law but as the unlawful manipulation of the law. Ultimately, the promise of law encompasses more than the responsibilities encoded in any specific law. The rule of law is also a promise, perhaps especially necessary in times of emergency, to rule by a legal order of good faith, nondiscrimination, and rationality.[188] Telling the dispossession as a story of promises highlights the extent and tragedy of the government's breach but it also helps to reclaim a deeper set of principles of justice and the promises of legality that the law makes to all.

NOTES

A previous version of this chapter appeared under the same title in the *Osgoode Law Review* 54, Issue 3 (2017). Eric M. Adams, Jordan Stanger-Ross, and the Landscapes of Injustice Research Collective. This work was inspired by conversations with the Landscapes of Injustice Community Council, especially Keiko Mary Kitagawa, Tosh Kitagawa, Art Miki, and Vivian Wakabayashi Rygnestad. We are also deeply indebted to the exceptional research assistance of William Archibald, Lauren Chalaturnyk, Kaitlin Findlay, Adam Kostrich, Rachel Weary, and Monique Ulysses. Trevor Wideman played a particularly key role in identifying documents and formulating early analyses of this material. Thanks also to the journal's anonymous reviewers, Penny Bryden, Philip Girard, Malcolm Lavoie, Laura Madokoro, Jim Phillips, Hildy Ross, Jim Walker, and Bruce Ziff, who read and commented on earlier versions of this paper. This chapter benefited from presentations at the 2016 Landscapes of Injustice Spring Institute, York University's conference honouring Douglas Hay, and the Queen's Faculty of Law Speaker Series. We thank the organizers and audiences at those events.

1 The dinner was sufficiently memorable to appear in MacLennan's obituary. A.T.C., "Nos Disparus: J. Arthur MacLennan, Q.C.," *The Advocate* 55, no. 1 (1997), 124. For a sample of reporting detailing rumours of an imminent "enormous Pacific offensive" see "Tokyo's Next Bombing Very Close, US Is Told," *Toronto Daily Star*, 30 May 1944, 1. On racial exclusions of the period see, Eric M. Adams, "Errors of Fact and Law: Race, Space, and Hockey in Christie v. York," *University of Toronto Law Journal* 62, no. 4 (2012): 462–97. At the *Christie v York* trial one of the former waiters at the Chateau Laurier recalled, "If I remember rightly, at the Chateau Laurier we were told not to serve coloured people." *Christie v York Corporation* (1937), 75 RJQ 136 (Sup Ct) (Discovery Transcript), Bibliothèque et Archives nationals du Québec.

2 Ken Adachi, *The Enemy That Never Was: A History of the Japanese Canadians* (Toronto: McClelland & Stewart, 1976).

3 Ann Gomer Sunahara, *The Politics of Racism: The Uprooting of Japanese Canadians During the Second World War* (Ottawa: Ann Sunahara, 2000).

4 In addition to Adachi and Sunahara, see e.g., Mona Oikawa, *Cartographies of Violence: Japanese Canadian Women, Memory, and the Subjects of the Internment* (Toronto: University of Toronto Press, 2012); Pamela Sugiman, "'Life Is Sweet': Vulnerability and Composure in the Wartime Narratives of Japanese Canadians," *Journal of Canadian Studies* 43, no. 1 (2009): 186–218; Stephanie Bangarth, *Voices Raised in Protest: Defending Citizens of Japanese Ancestry in North America, 1942–49* (Vancouver: UBC Press, 2008); W. Peter Ward, *White Canada Forever: Popular Attitudes and Public Policy Towards Orientals in British Columbia* (Montreal & Kingston: McGill-Queen's University Press, 2002); Patricia Roy, *A White Man's Province: British Columbia Politicians and Chinese and Japanese Immigrants, 1858–1914* (Vancouver: UBC Press, 1989), *The Oriental Question: Consolidating a White Man's Province, 1914–41* (Vancouver: UBC Press, 2003), and *The Triumph of Citizenship: The Japanese and Chinese in Canada, 1941–67* (Vancouver: UBC Press, 2007).

5 See Arthur J. Ray, Jim Miller, and Frank Tough, *Bounty and Benevolence: A History of Saskatchewan Treaties* (Montreal & Kingston: McGill-Queen's University Press, 2000), 214; James Daschuk, *Clearing the Plains: Disease, Politics of Starvation, and the Loss of Aboriginal Life* (Regina: University of Regina Press, 2013), chapter 6–9. On remembering and forgetting Crown promises, see William Wicken, "'Heard It from Our Grandfathers': Mi'kmaq Treaty Tradition and the *Syliboy* Case of 1928," *University of New Brunswick Law Journal* 44 (1995): 145–62. See also Eric M. Adams, "Ghosts in Court: Jonathan Belcher and the Proclamation of 1762," *Dalhousie Law Journal* 27 (2004): 321–46.

6 [1947] Ex CR 486. The decision is much less well known (even among Canadians) than the American case law on the Japanese American internment. See e.g. *Hirabayashi v United States*, 320 US 81 (1943), 63 S Ct 1375; *Ex Parte Endo*, 323 US 283 (1944); *Korematsu v United States*, 323 US 214 (1944), 65 S Ct 193. On the American cases, see Eugene V. Rostow, "The Japanese American Cases – A Disaster," *Yale Law Journal* 54, no. 3 (1945): 489–533; Eric K. Yamamoto et al., *Race, Rights and Reparation: Law and the Japanese American Internment*, 2nd edition (New York: Wolters Kluwer, 2013).

7 This perspective is conveyed in the most widely cited source on the dispossession of Japanese Canadians, Sunahara, *The Politics of Racism.*

8 G. Neil Perry to Colonel E. Pepler, 10 August 1940, file 3, box 14, GR-0268, BCA, Victoria.

9 City Council Minutes, 1 September 1942, file 17: Japanese Property, Powell Street, box 27-E-6, series 27, City of Vancouver fonds.

10 Quoted the next day in the Japanese Canadian newspaper *The New Canadian*, Alderman George Buscombe, who had attended the meeting with McPherson, said "[w]e'll wait and see what happens after September 30," when he presumed the internment would be complete. "We don't want the Japanese to return here after the war," he continued, "[t]hey are going to outbreed the whites and eventually outnumber us" ("Custodian Not Selling Real Estate Left Behind by Evacuated Owners," *The New Canadian*, 2 September 1942, 1–2).

11 Minutes of the British Columbia Security Commission Conference, 6 March 1943, file 163, vol. 7, RG 36-27, LAC (emphasis added).

12 Note, however, that other federal officials, including Ephraim H. Coleman, under secretary of state, saw the decision to force the sale of the property of Japanese Canadians as a *change* in policy toward permanent exile from BC. Coleman did not understand this as the implicit approach from the outset. See Jordan Stanger-Ross and the Landscapes of Injustice Research Collective, "Suspect Properties: The Vancouver Origins of the Forced Sale of Japanese-Canadian-Owned Property, WWII," *Journal of Planning History* 15, no. 4 (2016): 271–89.

13 Edward Dunsworth, "Race, Exclusion, and Archival Silences in the Seasonal Migration of Tobacco Workers from the Southern United States to Ontario," *Canadian Historical Review* 99, no. 4 (2018): 563–93.

14 See generally Jim Phillips, "Why Legal History Matters," *Victoria University of Wellington Law Review* 41, no. 3 (2010): 293–316.

15 RSC 1927 (hereafter WMA), c 206. Despite being proclaimed on 1 September, the apprehended state of war was backdated to 25 August 1939 to capture certain military purchases that had already been made. For a history of the War Measures Act, see F. Murray Greenwood, "The Drafting and Passage of the War Measures Act in 1914 and 1927: Object Lessons in the Need for Vigilance" in *Canadian Perspectives on Law and Society: Issues in Legal History*, eds. W. Wesley Pue and Barry Wright (Ottawa: Carleton University Press, 1988). After passage of the WMA in 1914, orders in council were passed to register enemy aliens and then to intern more than 8,000 persons, the majority of whom were Ukrainian Canadians. See Bohdan S. Kordan, "'They Will Be Dangerous': Security and Control of Enemy Aliens in Canada, 1914," in *Canadian State Trials Volume IV: Security, Dissent and the Limits of Toleration in War and Peace, 1914–1939*, eds. Barry Wright, Eric Tucker, and Susan Binnie (Toronto: University of Toronto Pres, 2015), 45. See also Peter McDermott, "Enemy Aliens in the First World War: Legal and Constitutional Issues" in ibid, 77.

16 WMA, s 3. The language parallels President Roosevelt's Executive Order No 9066 of 19 February 1942, subsequently ratified by Congress, authorizing actions deemed "necessary or desirable to prescribe military areas … from which all persons may be excluded" (*Hirabayashi*, at 86).

17 WMA. This is contrary to the clear peacetime allocation of matters of "Property and Civil Rights" to provincial jurisdiction.

18 *Fort Frances Pulp and Paper Co v Manitoba Free Press Co*, [1923] 3 DLR 629 at 633, AC 695. [*Fort Frances*]. Fitzpatrick C.J. also commented on this, holding that "[i]t seems to me obvious that parliament intended, as the language used implies, to

clothe the executive with the widest powers in time of danger. Taken literally, the language of [section 3 of the WMA] contains unlimited powers" (*Re George Edwin Gray*, [1918] 57 SCR 150 at 158-59, 42 DLR 1 [*Re Gray*]).

19 Interdepartmental Committee on Emergency Legislation, *Report* (Ottawa: King's Printer, 1939).

20 See chapter 2; Bruce Ryder, "Racism and the Constitution: The Constitutional Fate of British Columbia Anti-Asian Immigration Legislation, 1884–1909," *Osgoode Hall Law Journal* 29, no. 3 (Fall 1991): 619–76; Andrea Geiger, "Writing Racial Barriers into Law: Upholding BC's Denial of the Vote to its Japanese Canadian Citizens, Homma v. Cunningham, 1902," in *Nikkei in the Pacific Northwest: Japanese Americans and Japanese Canadians in the Twentieth Century*, eds. Gail Nomura and Louis Fiset (Seattle: University of Washington Press, 2005): 20–43.

21 PC 1941-117, 7 January 1941, file 2247G, vol. 1701, RG 2-A-1-a, LAC. See also Adachi, *The Enemy That Never Was*, 190–1.

22 PC 1941-9592, 7 December 1941, file 2463G, vol. 1741, RG 2-A-1-a, LAC.

23 PC 1942-365, 16 January 1942, file 2487G, vol. 1744, RG 2-A-1-a, LAC. See Adachi, *The Enemy That Never Was*, 199–224.

24 PC 1942-1486, 24 February 1942, *The Canada Gazette*, vol. 75, no. 212 (Ottawa: King's Printer, 27 February 1942).

25 PC 1942-1665 (hereafter Order 1665), sec. 10(1), 4 March 1942, file 2516G, vol. 1750, RG2-A-1-a, LAC. In addition to powers to "require by order any person of the Japanese race, in any protected area in British Columbia … to leave his place of residence and proceed to any other place within or without the protected area," the order granted the commission the power to "make orders respecting the conduct, activities, and discipline of any person evacuated under the provisions of these Regulations." (ss 11(1), (2)).

26 *Consolidated Regulations Respecting Trading with the Enemy* (1939), s 1(b)(ii), (iv), file 11367, pt. 2, vol. 1550, RG 125, LAC.

27 Notice (newspaper clipping), 12 December 1941, file 10, vol. 1, RG 117. On property and the performance of citizenship see Gregory Alexander "Property as Propriety," *Nebraska Law Review* 77, no. 4 (1998): 667–702.

28 Before this time, the Custodian controlled the property of several hundred Japanese Canadians whose property was deemed "enemy" property. The new orders in council vested the Custodian with the property of more than 15,000 Japanese Canadians. See Glenn W. McPherson to Ephraim H. Coleman, 2 February 1942, file 10, vol. 1, RG 117, LAC. Report of the Vancouver Office of the Custodian, 25 February 1942, file 10, vol. 1, RG 117, LAC.

29 Draft to His Excellency the Governor General in Council, 28 February 1942, file 3464-q-40, vol. 3005, RG 25, LAC.

30 "Austin C. Taylor, Financier, Dead," *The New York Times*, 2 November 1965.

31 Telegraph from Austin C. Taylor to Ian Mackenzie, 28 February 1942, file 67-25(1), vol. 24, MG27 III-B5, LAC. On the origins of the Custodian of Enemy Property see, Judith Roberts-Moore, "The Office of the Custodian of Enemy Property: An Overview of the Office and its Records, 1920–1952," *Archivaria* 22 (1986): 95–106.

32 Ian Mackenzie to Prime Minister, 2 March 1942, file 67-25(1), vol. 24, MG27 III-B5, LAC.

33 Ian Mackenzie to John E. Read, 1 March 1942, file 67-25(1), vol. 24, MG27 III-B5, LAC.

34 Order 1665, s. 12(1).

35 Order 1665, s. 12(3). Punishment for breach of any aspect of the order or by-laws made

under it involved a five hundred dollar fine, up to twelve months of imprisonment, or both (s 15).

36 Read studied at Dalhousie, Columbia, and then Oxford as a Rhodes Scholar and briefly practised law before joining Dalhousie, where he specialized in property law. After the war, Read would go on to a distinguished judicial career on the International Court of Justice. On Read's deanship during Dalhousie's so-called "golden age," see John Willis, *A History of Dalhousie Law School* (Toronto: University of Toronto Press, 1979), 93, 96–9.

37 John E. Read to Ian Mackenzie (copied to Frederick P. Varcoe), 28 February 1942, file 3464-q-40, vol. 3005, RG 25, LAC.

38 Ian Mackenzie to John E. Read, 1 March 1942, file 3464-q-40, vol. 3005, RG 25, LAC; Note for the Under Secretary of State for External Affairs, 2 March 1942, file 3464-q-40, vol. 3005, RG 25, LAC (hereafter Note for Under Secretary). We believe that the promise of protection was inserted into the draft by the deputy minister of justice, Frederick Varcoe, or by someone working directly under his supervision in the Department of Justice. Unfortunately, the records of this process have been significantly withheld from research by LAC, in part on the basis of the view that the records contain "information the disclosure of which would reasonably be expected to be injurious to the conduct of international affairs, the defence of Canada … or the detection, prevention or suppression of subversive or hostile activities." Security rationales continue to play perplexing and disconcerting roles in this history.

39 Note for Under Secretary.

40 Ibid.

41 Ibid.

42 Ibid.

43 PC 1942-288, 13 January 1942, file 2484G, vol. 1744, RG 2 A-1-a, LAC (emphasis added) (hereafter Order 288). This may be one of the only instances in which the wartime government referred in law to "Japanese Canadians." Note for Under Secretary.

44 Order 288 (emphasis added).

45 The illegality of these sales was later acknowledged by the federal government. "In the Matter of the 'Inqueries Act,'" 13 February 1948, images 458–77, microfilm reel C9434, Office of the Custodian of Enemy Property, Vancouver Office Files, Héritage, accessed 15 September 2019, heritage.canadiana.ca/view/oocihm.lac_reel_c9434. See also Masako Fukawa and Stanley Fukawa, *Spirit of the Nikkei Fleet: BC's Japanese Canadian Fishermen* (Madeira Park, BC: Harbour, 2009), chapter 7; Sunahara, *The Politics of Racism*, chapter 2; Adachi, *The Enemy That Never Was*, 228–9; Jordan Stanger-Ross, "Telling a Difficult Past: Kishizo Kimura's Memoir of Entanglement in Racist Policy," *BC Studies* 181 (2014): 40.

46 Note for Under Secretary.

47 Except for a short time, when it was brought under full government control (21 April – 27 June 1942), the paper maintained a critical editorial perspective. Adachi, *The Enemy That Never Was*, 233.

48 Frank Moritsugu, "My Love Affairs with The New Canadian," *The New Canadian*, 31 May 1958, 8.

49 Shoyama went on to a distinguished postwar civil service career in the Saskatchewan and federal governments. Gregory Marchildon, "Shoyama, Thomas Kunito," in *The Encyclopedia of Saskatchewan*, 2007, online ed., accessed 15 September 2019, https://

esask.uregina.ca/entry/shoyama_thomas_kunito_1916-.jsp. See also, Tom Shoyama, "As I Remember a Bit of It," *The New Canadian*, 31 May 1958, 2. On the censorship process, see Frank Moritsugu, "My Love Affairs with the New Canadian," *The New Canadian*, 14 June 1958, 1.

50 Glenn W. McPherson, "Notice to Persons of the Japanese Race," *The New Canadian*, 12 March 1942, 4. This notice was also carried in mainstream Vancouver dailies. See e.g. *Vancouver News Herald*, 11 March 1942.

51 Glenn W. McPherson, "Appendix C, Memorandum by Counsel for the Custodian," 30 July 1941, file 52, vol. 8, MG 30-E148, LAC.

52 Glenn W. McPherson to DesRosiers, "Re: Japanese Language Association School," 14 July 1945, file 58998, vol. 2535, RG 117, LAC.

53 "Make Application: Custodian to Take Control of Property of Evacuees," *The New Canadian*, 12 March 1942, 1.

54 "Powell Offices Aid Report of Property to Custodian," *The New Canadian*, 17 March 1942, 1.

55 "A Country Editor Views Evacuation," *The New Canadian*, 17 March 1942, 2. On comparisons of Canada to Nazi Germany see Jordan Stanger-Ross and Landscapes of Injustice Research Collective, "Naziism in Canada? The Internment of Japanese Canadians and the History of Comparison," in *After the Holocaust: Human Rights and Genocide Education in the Approaching Post-Witness Era*, eds. Charlotte Schaillé, Helga Thorson, and Andrea Van Noord (University of Regina Press, forthcoming).

56 "Your Household Goods Are Valuable," *The New Canadian*, 17 March 1942, 2.

57 Roy, *Triumph of Citizenship*, chapter 1.

58 Austin C. Taylor to Ian Mackenzie, 4 March 1942, file 67-25(1), vol. 24, MG 27 III-B5, LAC.

59 Minutes of the British Columbia Security Commission, 23 April 1942, file 163, vol. 7, RG 36-27, LAC.

60 Report to the Undersecretary of State Regarding the Japanese Evacuation Section of the Office of the Custodian at Vancouver, BC, 26 June vol. 2, RG 117, LAC.

61 Ibid.

62 Ibid.

63 Having served as part-time dean of the Manitoba Law School, Coleman left legal practice in 1933 to take up a position in Ottawa. Considered an "urbane intellectual with a mania for reading," Coleman "was a quiet, cautious, rather formal man who put heavy emphasis on form, precedent, and tradition. He never gave a swift judgement and seldom made a quick decision." R. St J. Macdonald, "An Historical Introduction to the Teaching of International Law in Canada: Part III," *Canadian Yearbook of International Law* 14 (1976): 227, footnote 153; Hugh L. Keenleyside, *Memoirs of Hugh L Keenleyside: Volume 1: Hammer the Golden Day* (Toronto: McClelland & Stewart, 1981), 485. On Coleman's conservative views on legal education, see W. Wesley Pue, *Lawyer's Empire: Legal Professions and Cultural Authority, 1780–1950* (Vancouver: UBC Press, 2016), 159–60, 209.

64 Ephraim H. Coleman to Norman Robertson, 16 March 1942, file 4606-c-13-40, vol. 3121, RG 25.

65 Ibid.

66 Positioning the protection of property as a premise of discussion, Coleman seemed to ascribe to property the same foundational role explicated by Joseph Singer, who writes

"[p]roperty law defines things that we would like to take for granted; it does so by setting the boundaries of just social relationships" ("Democratic Estates: Property Law in a Free and Democratic Society," *Cornell Law Review* 94, no. 4 [2009]: 1062).

67 Ephraim H. Coleman, re: Real Estate owned by persons of the Japanese race evacuated from the Defence Area of British Columbia, December, 1942, file 70-25c, vol. 25, MG 27 III-B5, LAC.

68 PC 1942-2483, 27 March 1942, file 2531G, vol. 1752, RG2-A-1-a, LAC.

69 Ibid, s 2 (emphasis added).

70 Ibid, s 4 (emphasis added).

71 Regulations Respecting Trading with the Enemy. The regulations stipulated that, "The Custodian may, where he considers it advisable to do so, liquidate any enemy property vested in him" (s 38). See also sections 39 and 40(1) which allowed for any "notice, conveyance, transfer or release as he may think proper" and granted the authority to "dispose of any property, right or interest at such time and place and to such person or persons and upon such terms and in such manner, whether publicly or privately, as he in his discretion shall think proper."

72 Value expressed in current dollars.

73 Austin C. Taylor, "Roads, Ont Mills, Beet Fields, Interior Towns," *The New Canadian*, 6 April 1942, 3.

74 Ibid.

75 "Custodian to Act for Evacuated People," *The New Canadian*, 6 April 1942, 1.

76 "Ask Details of Custodian Policy," *The New Canadian*, 15 April 1942, 1.

77 "An Editorial Message from the BC Security Commission," *The New Canadian*, 21 April 1942, 2.

78 Ibid. Minutes of the British Columbia Security Commission, 23 April 1942, file 163, vol. 7, RG 36-27, LAC.

79 During this period, the Japanese Fishing Vessel Disposal Committee commenced forced sales and the Custodian transferred automobiles without consent to federal departments. See Adachi, *The Enemy That Never Was*, 229, 233; Stanger-Ross, "Kishizo Kimura," 39–42; "Army to Absorb Japanese Cars," *The Vancouver Province*, 2 June 1942.

80 "Classified Ads," *The New Canadian*, 6 May 1942, 2; "List your House for Rent," *The New Canadian*, 20 May 1942, 3; "Classified Ads," *The New Canadian*, 23 May 1942, 3; "Pets May Be Destroyed Painlessly at Clinic," *The New Canadian*, 27 May 1942, 3.

81 "Control Farm Land Sale, Lease," *The New Canadian*, 8 July 1942, 1; "Berry Crop One-Quarter of Normal; Weeds Over-run Many Farms," *The New Canadian*, 11 July 1942, 1; "Confiscated Cars Offered For Sale; Custodian to Credit Former Owners," *The New Canadian*, 18 July 1942, 1; "Fish Boat Committee to Wind Up July 31," *The New Canadian*, 22 July 1942, 1; "Custodian Not Selling Real Estate Left Behind by Evacuated Owners," *The New Canadian*, 2 September 1942, 1.

82 See introduction and chapter 5.

83 Chapter 7.

84 Stanger-Ross, "Suspect Properties," 272. See also Sunahara, *The Politics of Racism*, chapter 5.

85 Norman McLarty to Louis St Laurent, 15 January 1943, file 144935, vol. 2819, RG 13, LAC.

86 PC 1943-469, 19 January 1943, file 2710G, vol. 1789, RG 2-A-1-a, LAC.

87 Ibid.

88 The final sale of a parcel of real estate in Vancouver's Japanese Canadian neighbourhood

surrounding Powell Street occurred on 9 January 1950 (Landscapes of Injustice Real Estate Database).

89 In this sense the promise and its breach can be considered in comparison with other contexts in which the Canadian state placed people at great disadvantage while simultaneously and paternalistically purporting concern for their interests. See Sarah Carter, *Lost Harvests: Prairie Indian Reserve Farmers and Government Policy* (Montreal & Kingston: McGill-Queen's University Press, 1990). See also Tina Loo, "Africville and the Dynamics of State Power in Postwar Canada," *Acadiensis* 39, no. 2 (2010): 23–47.

90 Telegram to McPherson, 4 January 1943, file 59008, pt 1.1, vol. 2536, RG 11, LAC; Real Estate Agents Cash Journal, December, 1942, vol. 69, RG 117, LAC; Ivan Barnet to Gordon Murchison, 28 March 1943, file V-8-10, pt. 3, vol. 403, RG 38, LAC; "Annual Report of the Vancouver Office of the Custodian (1943)," 28 January 1944, images 219–42, microfilm reel C9469, Office of the Custodian of Enemy Property, Vancouver Office Files, Héritage, accessed 15 September 2019, heritage.canadiana.ca/view/oocihm.lac_reel_c9469.

91 "A Statement Is in Order," *The New Canadian*, 20 February 1943, 2.

92 "Government Prefers Money: Selling of Japanese Property Does Not Mean Japs Banned," *The Vancouver Daily Province*, 11 February 1943.

93 "Japanese Property Sale Does Not Mean Ban from BC after War," *The New Canadian*, 20 February 1943, 1.

94 Henry Angus to Robertson, 15 March 1943, file c-4606-13-40, vol. 3121, RG 25, LAC. The correct spelling in German would be "Nürnberg" or "Nuernberg." Angus, a long-time University of British Columbia sociology and political science professor, and a former member of the Rowell-Sirois Commission, served during the war as an assistant to the Canadian prime minister.

95 Chapter 4.

96 Héritage, "Hanjiro Yoshijima to Office of the Custodian," 21 July 1943, image 1332, microfilm reel C9476, Office of the Custodian of Enemy Property, Vancouver Office Files, Héritage, accessed September 15, 2019, http://heritage.canadiana.ca/view/oocihm.lac_reel_c9476/1332?r=0&s=4.

97 Ibid. at image 1594.

98 Ibid. at image 1333.

99 Ibid. at image 1334.

100 Ibid. at image 1335.

101 Ibid. at image 1339. For dozens of other letters expressing similar sentiments, see microfilm reel C9476, Office of the Custodian of Enemy Property, Vancouver Office Files, accessed 15 September 2019, heritage.canadiana.ca/view/oocihm.lac_reel_c9476. See also chapter 4.

102 "Legal Opinion Disposal Beyond Governm't Power," *The New Canadian*, 3 April 1943, 1.

103 Ibid.

104 Ibid.

105 Ibid.

106 "United Action of Evacuees Sought to Aid Test Case," *The New Canadian*, 10 April 1943, 1.

107 "Test Case Receiving Support from Evacuees across Canada," *The New Canadian*, 17 April 1943, 1.

108 Ibid.

109 "Launch Fund Campaign – Ten Per Cent of Taxes Asked," *The New Canadian*, 1 May 1943, 1.
110 "Property Sale Cases Studies by Dominion Wide Organizations Occidentals Send Contributions," *The New Canadian*, 8 May 1943, 1.
111 "Property Sale to Begin This Week Warns Custodian," *The New Canadian*, 29 May 1943, 1.
112 G.S. Cumming, "Nos Disparus: The Honourable Thomas Grantham Norris, MC, QC" *The Advocate* 35:1 (1977): 69. Norris would go on to serve as president of the Vancouver Bar Association, a bencher and then treasurer of the British Columbia Law Society, and, in 1959, on the bench of the Supreme Court of British Columbia.
113 Ibid.
114 Thomas Norris Fonds, file 13-1, box 13, and file 31-17, box 31, RBSC, University of British Columbia.
115 Cumming, "Nos Disparus," 70.
116 A.T.C., "Nos Disparus," 124.
117 Petition of Right Act 1876, SC 1876, c 27. See also Peter W, Hogg, Patrick J. Monahan, and Wade K. Wright, *Liability of the Crown*, 4th ed (Toronto: Carswell, 2011), 4–5, 8. As the authors explain, "the reason why the King could not be sued in the royal courts was the feudal principle that a lord could not be sued in his own court."
118 Consolidated Regulations Respecting Trading with the Enemy, s 27.
119 "Property Sale to Begin This Week Warns Custodian," *The New Canadian*, 29 May 1943, 1.
120 For wartime deference to government action under the DOCR, see *Yasny v Lapointe*, [1940] 48 Man R 56, 3 DLR 204 (Man CA); *R v Stewart*, [1940] OR 178, 1 DLR 689 (Ont CA); *R v Burt*, [1941] OR 35, 1 DLR 598 (Ont SC); *R v Ravenor* [1941] 1 WWR 191, 75 CCC 294 (BC Co Ct); *R v Cooper*, [1941] 2 WWR 206, 76 CCC 277 (BCSC). As the Ontario Supreme Court put it in *Ex parte Sullivan*, "[w]ar could not be carried on according to the principles of Magna Carta." [1941] OR 417 at para 16, 1 DLR 676 (Ont CA). See also Eric M. Adams, "The Idea of Constitutional Rights and the Transformation of Canadian Constitutional Law, 1930–1960" (PhD dissertation, University of Toronto, 2009), 76–136.
121 "Property Owners Give Go-Ahead Signal for Action," *The New Canadian*, 5 June 1943, 1.
122 "Our Fights for Justice," *The New Canadian*, 12 June 1943, 2.
123 At the start of the war, approximately 23,000 of the total population of 25,000 Japanese Canadians lived in British Columbia. Of British Columbia's population of Canadians of Japanese descent, approximately 7,200 were Japanese nationals, 2,400 were naturalized Canadians, and 13,400 were Canadian by birth. H.F. Angus, "The Effect of the War on Oriental Minorities in Canada," *Canadian Journal of Economics and Political Science* 7, no. 4 (1941): 506. Until the passage of the Canadian Citizenship Act created the legal status of Canadian citizenship in 1946, Canadians had status as British subjects and naturalized Canadians under the Naturalization Act, RSC 1927, c 138 and Canadian Nationals Act, RSC 1927, c 21.
124 *Nakashima* case file, file 20087, 20088, and 20089, vol. 2186, R 14188, LAC.
125 Petition of Right, filed 13 October 1943, ibid.
126 The *New Canadian* continued its coverage of the case, including quoting the legal arguments drawn from the Petitions of Right at length for its readers. See "Japanese

Property Bids Very Slow: Case Likely to Be Held in Vancouver September," *The New Canadian*, 31 July 1943, 1.

127 "Property Owners Win Right to Sue Ottawa in Exchequer Court," *The New Canadian*, 23 October 1943, 1.

128 "Visits Ottawa to Ask Haste in Property Case," *The New Canadian*, 27 November 1943, 1; "Property Owners Review Situation," *The New Canadian*, 18 December 1943, 1.

129 "No Official Word on Exchequer Case," *The New Canadian*, 8 April 1944, 1.

130 "Court to Rule If Sale of Property Is Constitutional," *The New Canadian*, 13 May 1944, 1.

131 "Frederick P. Varcoe: Lawyer Headed Department," *The Globe and Mail*, 16 October 1965, 46.

132 "To The Highest Court," *The New Canadian*, 20 May 1944, 2. See also "Broad Constitutional Rights at Stake In Court Battle Against Forced Sale," *The New Canadian*, 27 May 1944, 1.

133 Kunio Hidaka, "Pro and Con on Property Rights," *The New Canadian*, 10 June 1944, 7. Hidaka, a graduate of the University of British Columbia, was no stranger to legalized racism. At UBC he compiled a list of racist legislative instruments targeting Japanese Canadians. He would go on to play an important role in the redress movement. See Roy Miki, *Redress: Inside the Japanese Canadian Call for Justice* (Vancouver: Raincoast Books, 2004), 16–18.

134 Ian Bushnell, *The Federal Court of Canada: A History, 1875–1992* (Toronto: University of Toronto Press for the Osgoode Society for Canadian Legal History, 1997), 124–5. See also W. Kristjanson, "Hon Joseph Thorarinn Thorson," *The Icelandic Canadian* 37 (1978): 13. Thorson is best remembered for his contribution to the law of public interest standing. In the early 1970s, a retired Thorson launched a quixotic attack on the constitutionality of the Official Languages Act. In the Supreme Court of Canada decision granting him standing to pursue his claim, Justice Laskin held that "[t]he question of the constitutionality of legislation has in this country always been a justiciable question. Any attempt by Parliament or a Legislature to fix conditions precedent, as by way of requiring consent of some public officer or authority, to the determination of an issue of constitutionality of legislation cannot foreclose the Courts merely because the conditions remain unsatisfied." "It would be strange," Justice Laskin held, "and, indeed, alarming, if there was no way in which a question of alleged excess of legislative power … could be made the subject of adjudication." *Thorson v Canada*, [1975] 1 SCR 138 at 145, 151, 43 DLR (3d) 1. The result is deeply ironic when contrasted with Justice Thorson's judgment in *Nakashima*.

135 See The National Resources Mobilization Act, 1940, SC 1940, c 13, s 2. See generally, Jeffrey A. Keshen, *Saints, Sinners, and Soldiers: Canada's Second World War* (Vancouver: UBC Press, 2003), 27.

136 An incomplete transcript of the hearing is contained in the *Nakashima* case file, 8–9.

137 *Ritcher v Canada*, [1943] Ex CR 64.

138 Frederick Varcoe to Glenn W. McPherson, "Re Lease – Japanese Language Ass'sn," 10 May 1945, file 58998, vol. 2535, RG 117, LAC.

139 Section 4 amending Order 1665, s 12(1).

140 Section 4 amending Order 1665, s 12(2).

141 Varcoe's distinction between the various subsections of s 12 possesses a certain superficial logic but falls apart quickly on closer inspection. To begin, there was no property that would have vested independently under s 12(2), since s 12(1) covered "all property

situated in any protected area ... belonging to any person of the Japanese race resident in such area." Moreover, the drafting history of Order 2483 makes clear that s 12(2) was intended as an elaboration of the promise of protection outlined in s 12(1) and was conveyed as such to Japanese Canadians.

142 [1943] SCR 1 at 12, 1 DLR 248 [Chemicals Reference].

143 WMA, s 3.

144 Chemicals Reference, 12. The Canadian wartime jurisprudence never cited American cases from the period, but the points of convergence are striking. In upholding a similarly broad granting of discretion authorizing curfews imposed upon Japanese Americans in the "Military Area," the United States Court held that "[s]ince the Constitution commits to the Executive and to Congress the exercise of the war power in all the vicissitudes and conditions of warfare, it has necessarily given them wide scope for the exercise of judgement and discretion in determining the nature and extent of the threatened injury or danger and in the selection of the means for resisting it." *Hirabayashi*, 93.

145 Transcript, *Nakashima* case file, file 20087, 20088, and 20089, vol. 2186, R 14188, LAC, 97.

146 WMA, s 3. On the constitutionality of the WMA, see *Fort Frances*, 631. See also *Re Gray*, 150.

147 Chemicals Reference, 144.

148 Ibid., 13.

149 Re *Price Bros and The Board of Commerce of Canada*, [1920] 60 SCR 265 at 272, 54 DLR 286. Justice Duff (as he then was) also stated, "I think such orders are reviewable, in this sense that when in a proper proceeding the validity of them is called into question, it is the duty of a court of justice to consider and decide whether the conditions of jurisdiction are fulfilled and if they are not being fulfilled, to pronounce the sentence of the law upon the illegal order." On the economic theory animating the Court's decision, see Bernard J. Hibbitts, "A Bridle for Leviathan: The Supreme Court and The Board of Commerce," *Ottawa Law Review* 21, no. 1 (1989): 65–117.

150 Transcript, *Nakashima* case file, file 20087, 20088, and 20089, vol. 2186, R 14188, LAC, 113. "As a matter of fact," MacLennan elaborated, "you could ... say it is more of a war measure for him to maintain the property, to make sure it is being kept under government control, rather than in the hands of someone who might do some danger because once the Custodian sells it he has no more control over it."

151 Transcript, *Nakashima* case file, file 20087, 20088, and 20089, vol. 2186, R 14188, LAC, 106.

152 Ibid. at 143.

153 Transcript, *Nakashima* case file, file 20087, 20088, and 20089, vol. 2186, R 14188, LAC, 169–70.

154 Stanger-Ross, "Suspect Properties," 276; Ivan Barnet to Gordon Murchison, 19 May 1942, file V-8-10 Part 1: Japanese and their Farm Properties, Ottawa, LAC (vol. 403, RG 38).

155 See: Ward, *White Canada Forever* and Roy, *A White Man's Province.*

156 Transcript, *Nakashima* case file, file 20087, 20088, and 20089, vol. 2186, R 14188, LAC, 170.

157 Transcript, *Nakashima* case file, file 20087, 20088, and 20089, vol. 2186, R 14188, LAC, 171.

158 In the summer of 1944, Prime Minister King explained that after the war "loyal" Japanese Canadians would be permanently settled in central and eastern Canada, "disloyal" Japanese Canadians would be exiled to Japan, and any persons wishing to voluntarily return to Japan could do so at the government's expense. As the war neared

its end, government officials toured internment sites pressuring Japanese Canadians to sign forms indicating a "desire to relinquish my British nationality and to assume the status of a national of Japan" in order to "effect my repatriation to Japan." By the time of Japan's official surrender in September 1945, nearly ten thousand people had signed (or had signed on their behalf in the cases of wives and minors) repatriation forms. Canada, House of Commons, Debates, 19th Parl., 5th sess., vol. 6, 4 August 1944, 5916–17, accessed 15 September 2019, parl.canadiana.ca/view/oop.debates_HOC1905_06/482?r=0&s=1. In his speech, King also announced the cessation of all future Japanese immigration. Sunahara, *The Politics of Racism*, 117.

159 "One for the Lawyers," *The New Canadian*, 22 February 1947, 2.

160 Harvey Hickey, "Ilsley in Quandary as MP's Score Exchequer Court's Judgment Delays," *The Globe and Mail*, 2 July 1944, 10.

161 Most cases took more than a year to be decided, thirty per cent took more than two years, and seven per cent took more than three. Bushnell, *The Federal Court of Canada*, 135.

162 *Nakashima*, 488.

163 Ibid.

164 Ibid.

165 Ibid., 491.

166 Ibid., 492, 495, 498.

167 Ibid., 498.

168 Ibid., 502. "Parliament," Justice Thorson continued, "has left the decision as to the necessity or advisability of such an order for the security, defence, peace, order and welfare of Canada, not to the Court, but to the Governor in Council." The nonjusticiability of whether government decisions were necessary or advisable under the WMA had been "conclusively settled," Justice Thorson held, by Reference re Persons of Japanese Race, [1946] SCR 248, 3 DLR 321. Ibid. at 504.

169 Ibid., 504.

170 Ibid.

171 "Property Owners' Petitions Dismissed in Test Cases," *The New Canadian*, 20 September 1947, 1.

172 "Property Owners Asked to File Loss Claims by November 30," *The New Canadian*, 27 September 1947, 10.

173 "Ready-Made for Dictatorship," *The New Canadian*, 4 October 1947, 2.

174 Ibid.

175 Hogg, et al., *Liability of the Crown*, 8–9.

176 Consolidated Regulations Respecting Trading with the Enemy, s 27.

177 WMA, 21.

178 *Korematsu*, 233.

179 The existence of a trust remained largely a question of the common law, with some modifications of the duties of a trustee expressed by statute. See Trustee Act, RBSC 1936, c 292, s 2.

180 Sir Arthur Underhill assisted by Edward Bagshawe, *The Law Relating to Trusts and Trustees*, 9th ed. (London: Butterworth & Co, 1939), 3. See also *Attorney-General of Canada v CC Fields & Co*, [1943] OR 560, 1943 CanLII 97 (Ont CA).

181 Ibid., 8. The duties of the trustee include the duty to manage and treat the property with a reasonable standard of care. "A trustee is not called upon to be omniscient,"

Justice Middleton explained. "All that he is called upon to do is honestly to exercise his best judgment, to take the same care of the property as he would have taken if it had been his own." *Davies v Nelson*, [1928] 1 DLR 254 at 256, 1927 CanLII 452 (Ont CA).

182 Tina Loo, *Making Law, Order, and Authority in British Columbia, 1821–1871* (Toronto: University of Toronto Press, 1994), 162.

183 See the powerful testimony of the National Association of Japanese Canadians at the special parliamentary hearings prior to the enactment of the *Canadian Charter of Rights and Freedoms*, *Minutes of the Proceedings and Evidence of the Special Joint Committee of the Senate and House of Commons on the Constitution of Canada* (Government of Canada: Ottawa, 1980), 13:6.

184 Further, the agent of the Custodian, G.C. Mouat, sold Iwasaki's land to a company, Salt Spring Lands Ltd, in which Mouat held a 20 per cent interest. *Iwasaki v Canada*, [1969] 1 Ex CR 281 at para 35, 2 DLR (3d) 241.

185 Ibid., para. 21.

186 Ibid., para. 49.

187 *R v Iwasaki*, [1970] SCR 437 at 438, CanLII 191 (SCC).

188 "Surely," Lon Fuller wrote, "it is not only in the affairs of everyday life that we need clarity about the obligation of fidelity to law, but most particularly and urgently in times of trouble." Lon L. Fuller, "Positivism and Fidelity to Law – A Reply to Professor Hart," *Harvard Law Review* 17, no. 4 (1958): 634. See also David Dyzenhaus, *The Constitution of Law: Legality in a Time of Emergency* (Cambridge, UK: Cambridge University Press, 2006).

CHAPTER 9

Creating the Bird Commission: How the Canadian State Addressed Japanese Canadians' Calls for Fair Compensation

Kaitlin Findlay and the Landscapes of Injustice Research Collective

Somewhere in Vancouver on 31 July 1947 Robert McMaster passed Frank Gould Shears on the street. Shears was then the director of the Vancouver Office of the Custodian. McMaster was a local lawyer who, over the past year, had become deeply involved in the Japanese Canadian campaign to gain compensation for the losses they suffered under the internment policies. That spring, the issue of compensation had hit front-page news across the country, and McMaster became embroiled in a struggle with cabinet over the purview (or the terms of reference) of the royal commission appointed to investigate Japanese Canadians' claims. It was members from the Toronto branch of his affiliated civil liberties organization, the Co-Operative Committee on Japanese Canadians (CCJC), who aggressively pursued meetings with members of cabinet, but McMaster nonetheless followed the issue closely from Vancouver. Recognizing Shears on the sidewalk, McMaster boldly informed him that he could anticipate further "representations in Ottawa as the Terms of Reference were considered to be far from adequate."[1]

The encounter was likely uncomfortable for Shears but not entirely surprising. Since February he had known a commission was in the making.[2] Further, the Vancouver Office of the Custodian had always operated in anticipation of such an inquiry. "You will appreciate that there will be a day of accounting," a superior once warned him, "and that the Custodian must be in a good position to take account for all the property taken under his control, its administration and its disposition."[3] In 1947, it seemed that day had arrived. Yet if the government officials anticipated the commission, they could not control its course. Now, they faced the activism of hundreds of Japanese Canadians, backed by religious groups, civil liberties organizations, and mainstream media, who called for fair compensation for the losses resulting from the forced uprooting and dispossession.

The inquiry came to be known as the Bird Commission.[4] For three years, it consumed Japanese Canadian resources and activism for little yield. Announced on 18 July 1947, the commission opened in December before travelling through British Columbia and across Canada to hear Japanese Canadian claims. Before Commissioner Henry Irvine Bird submitted his final report in 1951, more than 1,400 Japanese Canadians testified to their losses and submitted evidence detailing the value of their

Figure 9.1 On 3 December 1947, the Bird Commission opened in the Vancouver courthouse (the low, columned building on the far right), two blocks south of the Vancouver Office of the Custodian.

homes, businesses, and belongings. Japanese Canadians had protested the forced sale of their property since 1943, including in federal court.[5] Four years later, Japanese Canadians once again organized collective representation. Individuals paid, with what remaining funds they had, legal fees to present their claims. Ultimately, the compensation Bird awarded failed miserably to address the losses resulting from forced uprooting, seven years of internment, and dispossession. Rather than focusing on this ending, however, this chapter follows the Bird Commission as it unfolded, guided by the often conflicting and sometimes concurring demands of its stakeholders, in the late 1940s. At its centre was the chance at financial reparation for Japanese Canadians who, impoverished by forced displacement and dispossession, needed immediate compensation. At stake more broadly, however, was how the Canadian state's dispossession of its own citizens would be understood and remembered in the postwar years.

This chapter examines the Bird Commission as an attempt at reparations in the wake of injustice. To do so, I attend to familiar and unfamiliar terrain. The familiar is the controversy surrounding the Bird Commission terms of reference. Here, I complicate existing accounts by emphasizing that the critical period of policy development began in December 1946. Most scholars earmark the evidence and testimony produced at the Standing Committee of Public Accounts (SCPA) examination of the Office of the Custodian in May and June 1947 as the watershed moment in the campaign for compensation.[6] The early development of the commission, however, reveals that, by the time the SCPA hearings began, the Cabinet Committee on Japanese Problems already had an approved order in council to announce a royal commission to investigate Japanese Canadians' claims for property loss. The SCPA examination cemented popular support for an investigation into the wartime management of Japanese Canadians' property. It also provided grounds for later amending the commission's initial terms of reference. But by the time of its first hearings, the fundamental shape of the Bird Commission was already established. Revisiting this familiar terrain of the commission's development brings into view the priorities and considerations that shaped its purview.

This early policy development reveals that government officials conceived of the commission as an effective tool to put accusations of discriminatory policy to rest. They recognized that the commission's findings would inform popular understandings of the dispossession and state accountability. In this regard, it is useful to view the Bird Commission from the perspective articulated by Jane Jensen, who views commissions as capable of presenting "a new view of the world in paradigmatic form."[7] According to Jensen, royal commissions may be involved in "generating new representations of history, of the present community and of available futures."[8] "The decision to establish an inquiry of this kind," Supreme Court Justice Gerald Le Dain likewise wrote in an influential essay on royal commissions, "is a decision not only to release an investigative technique but a form of social influence as well."[9] Thus, the decision to address Japanese Canadians' calls for compensation was *responsive* – responding to the shift in public opinion and campaigns by Japanese Canadians and their allies – but it was also meant to be *instructive*. By 1946, the deportation of and continued restrictions on Canadian citizens undermined a government that trumpeted the values of democracy, freedom, and liberalism. Saddled with the legacy of uncomfortable policies from the wartime era, cabinet used the issue of property compensation to define injustices against Japanese Canadians as matters of procedural error. By investigating the operations of the Office of the Custodian, the government sought to prove its own accountability and teach Canadians how to understand Japanese Canadians' claims against the Canadian state.

The Bird Commission hearings comprise this chapter's unfamiliar terrain. I attend to Japanese Canadians' sustained attempts to hold the Canadian state accountable for its wrongdoing. To do so, it is necessary to be attentive to the positioning of their legal team who tried to make an imperfect commission work in their clients' favour. Considerable scholarship exists on the CCJC as a foundational civil rights group and their leadership in the campaign against the deportation of Japanese Canadians in 1945 and 1946.[10] Regarding their role in the Bird Commission, however, the literature is sparse.

Scholars have critiqued their legal decisions and leadership without closely examining the hearings themselves.[11] In addressing the hearings, this chapter analyzes Japanese Canadians' allies as mediators within the Bird Commission process. It demonstrates how legal counsel, working in good faith, nonetheless became entwined in the state's priorities as they tried to work the Commission in Japanese Canadians' favour.

Closer attention to the dynamics of the hearing process reveals the degree to which Japanese Canadians' articulations of loss and injustice, and claims for fair compensation, were actively excluded from the Bird Commission hearings.[12] Understanding the constraints and dynamics within which Japanese Canadians' lawyers tried to attain justice for their clients, but became entangled in the state's priorities, allows us to more clearly understand the historical and political constraints to fair compensation.

As this chapter traverses these two terrains, familiar and unfamiliar, it also introduces a contest between two narratives. The first narrative is produced by the state, crafted by cabinet members, bureaucrats, policy makers, and the prime minister to distance the liberal government from the increasingly uncomfortable policies of the Second World War. In face of other proposals, officials designed a commission that would prove the state's accountability, rather than acknowledge injustice. If successful, the commission would counteract mounting criticisms of Canada's race-based policies and move the state into the postwar era. The second was articulated by Japanese Canadians and supported by their allies. Japanese Canadians demanded that the state recognize their rights as citizens and property owners. They challenged the government to adhere to a higher standard of accountability. They claimed loss and compensation in broader terms outside the hearings of the Bird Commission, while also adapting these claims to be recognized by the commission.

What emerges from this contest is a fuller portrayal of Japanese Canadians' relation to the state in the 1940s. It was one of unequal power, wherein the state determined the parameters of negotiation. For three years, Japanese Canadians and their allies organized to pursue state accountability and fair treatment under Canadian law. The Bird Commission, however, from its founding documents to the constraints imposed throughout its process, was a calculated response, designed to uphold the appearance of a progressive and just government.

Commissions of inquiry

A mainstay of the Canadian political process, royal commissions are temporary institutional sites designed to supplement regular government operations. They are appointed by an order in council "with a precise mandate as an *ad hoc* response to some previously legislated statute, usually an *Inquiries Act*."[13] With funding and staff devoted to a specific mandate, commissions solicit public input alongside expert advice. "They supplement the traditional machinery of government," Justice Thomas Berger writes, "by bringing to bear resources of time, objectivity, expertise, and by offering a forum for the expression of public opinion."[14] Scholars often delineate two categories of inquiries: those that deal with broad questions of public policy (such as medicare, free trade, or reproductive technologies) and those that look into specific allegations of wrongdoing or blameworthiness (arising out of claims of conflict of interest, aircraft going down, or mines collapsing). Despite these fundamental characteristics, commissions of inquiry take on vastly different forms. Across their varied forms and functions, commissions are commonly met with scepticism, often perceived as a tool to postpone an awkward decision, stave off public pressure, provide support for a government decision already made, or to cool an explosive issue.[15]

The Bird Commission is remembered for what it was not: that is, it was not a just resolution to the devastating material losses of the 1940s. Scholars and community members alike remember it as a predestined failure, with narrow terms of reference that only addressed a fraction of what was taken.[16] Historians have characterized it as a defensive mechanism, intended by the government to limit financial compensation and to avoid the admission of greater injustice.[17] Such criticisms have good reason. Yet the commission was also an important historical process: more than 1,400 Japanese Canadians testified at its hearings. We must contend with a past in which this limited commission heard their claims. It deserves scrutiny for what it was. Indeed, in understanding what it was we emerge with a clearer vision of what it was not.

The Liberal cabinet hoped the commission would influence public opinion, provide closure to the internment era, and mark the start of the postwar period. A constrained definition of loss was integral to this project. As Japanese Canadians sought to expand this definition to address their claims, the proceedings became a record of their contest over the meaning of property loss and the legacy of the dispossession. In submitting claims that intentionally and unintentionally pushed against the restricted terms of reference, Japanese Canadians and their solicitors participated in a broader struggle over the narrative of the forced uprooting and dispossession in a society seeking to distance itself from a legacy of racialized policy. This contest, captured in the commission proceedings, provides a pathway into the complex history of the postwar years as Canadians grappled with the racism of the Second World War, including Canada's own race-based policies, and looked towards new approaches to pluralism.[18]

Cabinet considers addressing injustices perpetrated against Japanese Canadians

On 24 January 1947, cabinet issued a press release from the prime minister's office meant to mark the end of Japanese Canadian policy. It announced that no further Japanese Canadians would be deported and promised compensation for any property sales made by the Custodian of Enemy Property for less than fair market value. "The decision of the government respecting certain orders in council," the statement read, "marks the substantial completion of a program contained in the statement I [Prime Minister King] made in the House of Commons on August 4, 1944." Regarding Japanese Canadians' property that the Custodian had sold,

> the government is of the opinion that the sales were made at a fair price. In all cases a complete appraisal was made before disposition. The total of the prices secured is greater in aggregate than the total appraisal value. To ensure, however, the fair treatment promised in 1944, the government is prepared in cases where it can be shown that a sale was made at less than a fair market value to remedy the injustice.[19]

The announcement appealed to public opinion; amongst Japanese Canadians it was met with "a sigh of relief" and cautious celebration.[20] In the previous year, criticism at the government's treatment of Japanese Canadians had emerged in force. While their forced uprooting and dispossession had been met with little public resistance in 1942, by 1946 Japanese Canadians had the support of various civil advocacy groups and prominent newspapers. Canadians increasingly recognized the deportation of citizens as a violation of civil rights and protested. Though the deportation orders were congruous with the laws enacted in the years prior (and affirmed by the highest courts), the Liberal government had lost both explicit and tacit support for its actions.[21] With this announcement, cabinet planned to distance the Liberal government from the increasingly uncomfortable internment policies and to shape how they would be remembered. Amidst this, the "property issue" would be a strategic tool to bring closure to the internment era.

The 24 January statement was critical to building a public narrative that would distance the government from the racism of the Second World War. It was the product of debates over the two months prior, when the Cabinet Committee on Japanese Problems met to review and strategize the future of "Japanese policy."[22] Public criticism made clear that a continuation of policies such as deportation would be politically injurious. Working through a list of the orders in council affecting Japanese Canadians, the cabinet committee decided which policies to rescind and which to extend.[23] In these discussions, the permanent dispersal of Japanese Canadians across Canada remained a fundamental aim of cabinet. Thus, while the cabinet committee repealed the deportation orders, they extended the restrictions on the movement of Japanese Canadians within the country (Japanese Canadians could not be permitted, from the perspective of lawmakers, to return to British Columbia or to otherwise concentrate in potentially problematic ways).

Amidst these debates, cabinet's strategy for dealing with the "the property issue" remained ambiguous.[24] In advance of their December policy discussions, Gordon

Figure 9.2 The 16th Canadian Ministry in 1945. Prime Minister William Lyon Mackenzie King sits front-row centre (in the light grey suit) and is accompanied by several members of the Cabinet Committee on Japanese Problems: Ian Mackenzie (front row, fourth from left), Colin W.G. Gibson (front row, second from right), and Humphrey Mitchell (front row, very right).

Robertson of the prime minister's office circulated a memorandum outlining "problems relating to the general Japanese question" to supplement the proposed agenda that focused on the deportation policies. It was primarily concerned with the internal restrictions on Japanese Canadians (like land purchase and fishing licences) and the complications of citizenship, but the third point was the "restitution for property disposed of." Robertson suggested that, "it might be worth consideration whether some sort of coalition should be established to hear claims and try to dispose of the matter."[25] The Cabinet Committee on Japanese Problems, however, dropped the suggestion. Instead, its members debated how to complete the dispossession, with the liquidation of the forty properties remaining in the Custodian of Enemy Property's holding. As the committee prepared for King's press release rescinding the deportation orders, property restitution remained "less urgent."[26]

Yet, for a brief time, the desire to "dispose" of the property issue prompted consideration of a direct and broad remedy to the material impacts of the forced uprooting, internment, dispossession, and dispersal. This possibility was expressed in the first draft of what became Prime Minister King's press release of 24 January 1947. Reflecting deep concern about the public perception of the internment policies, this earlier draft, dated 23 January, proposed a novel approach to alleviating public criticism: apology. "To ensure fair treatment," it explained, "the government has decided to authorize investigation of any claims that land, buildings, or other property ... had been sold at unduly low prices." It stated that the "government would be prepared to authorize compensation" where "less than a fair market value had been secured for the Japanese owner." Strikingly, this version continued,

> The Prime Minister states that he regretted the extent to which the exigencies of war, and the urgent necessities it has imposed in the domestic field had caused hardships and inconvenience for many persons of Japanese origin who had themselves been innocent.[27]

Furthermore, in this version, the government was "determined to do all it could to remove any sense of racial discrimination in Canada and to ensure equitable treatment of all." It concluded with a repetition of a similar press release from 1944, wherein King, despite the draconian policies he imposed, denounced "the hateful doctrine of racialism which was the basis of Nazism everywhere."[28] Three years later, in their first draft, King's speech writers situated the issue of property loss within a larger struggle against racism. To bring closure to the internment policies, cabinet considered recognizing the "hardships and inconvenience" endured by "innocent" Japanese Canadians. The proposal offered a route to build from King's 1944 denunciation of "racialism."

Statements of regret and condemnations of racism, however, together with a broader approach to remedy, would have been a difficult story for Canadians to hear and for the government to tell. Yet the drafting shows the possibility of debating this narrative in the immediate postwar years. In contrast to the government's public rhetoric, there were people pushing for this self-critical framing. The first draft recognized the hardships endured by innocent Japanese Canadians under the wartime policies. Likely penned by G. Robertson, it may have reflected an avenue that he considered possible after the "lengthy conversation" held in cabinet on 22 January, wherein the Cabinet Committee on Japanese Problems and the prime minister made the final decision to repeal the deportation policies.[29] Had Robertson's approach won out, there might well have been a very different postwar culture of memory around these events.[30] The experiences of Japanese Canadians and their families might have been, in some important ways, improved.[31] Instead, officials chose a different route.

Ultimately, cabinet decided that a narrative of procedural accountability would best address Japanese Canadians' claims and steer the government away from the internment era policies. Announcing that the repeal of the deportation orders marked the "substantial completion of the program," the final press release outlined the success of the dispersal policy. The promise for compensation remained intact.[32] The 24 January statement affirmed that Japanese Canadians' property was sold "at a fair price" through a complete appraisal process and that "the total prices secured is greater in aggregate than the total appraisal value."[33] The statement named the Custodian explicitly, narrowing the scope of state culpability. "[T]o ensure, however, the fair treatment promised in 1944," it continued, "the government is prepared in cases where it can be shown that a sale was made at less than a fair market value to remedy the injustice."[34] This was deliberately specific. By focusing on the Custodian's actions, emphasizing preexisting procedures to ensure market sales, and narrowing attention to one aspect of the dispossession (i.e. were the prices in keeping with other concurrent sales), the cabinet committee framed any questions of justice in terms of procedural accountability. Rather than addressing the government's imposition of "hardship" upon an "innocent" people, the statement placed the burden of proving loss on the shoulders of Japanese Canadians. This decision made the property issue one of procedural error rather than a matter of national regret for policies emerging from the domestic and international politics of race.

Emphasizing the possibility of procedural errors, cabinet could propose a narrative around the inevitable difficulty of major policy initiatives. Their willingness to investigate such errors, in this conception, only further affirmed the fairness of government action. This approach sought to demonstrate that injustice was a matter of *exceptions* to a generally just policy, obscuring the reality that the real injustice here was the policy as a whole, and the hardship inflicted by federal action on people who were innocent. Remarkably, the second story (one of profound injustice) was not just on the minds of Japanese Canadians, civil liberties groups, or even the press, but was also being articulated by high-level officials as a possible direction for the official narrative of these events. Instead of broader recognition, however, cabinet chose a route that would narrowly address Japanese Canadians' claims for property loss and, in doing so, seek to prove its accountability.

The Office of the Custodian directs the fundamental design of the proposed commission

With the promise of compensation announced, a stream of inquiries flooded the secretary of state and the prime minister's office. How would property loss be considered? When would this inquiry take place? Internally, the Cabinet Committee on Japanese Problems advised caution, wary that the "property issue" could be politically damning.[35] The prime minister's office turned to the bureaucrats responsible for an account of the dispossession.[36] Frank G. Shears, the director, was reluctant to have his office take the fall for what he saw as a larger issue of policy. Having managed the Vancouver Office since 1942, Shears worried that an investigative body would overlook the unique challenges of their task and portray the Office of the Custodian in an unfavourable light. He advised against any inquiry or at least that it should be postponed until he could provide sufficient evidence on the office's behalf. Reluctantly, Shears ordered preliminary research into the claims made by two Japanese Canadians. The reappraisal confirmed that the properties had been significantly undervalued in their forced sale.[37] In turn, Shears warned Kenneth W. Wright, the Office of the Custodian's legal advisor, that the government would have to "face the fact" that the appraisals of the Soldier Settlement Board, which had determined prices in the sale of hundreds of farms, were in most cases "below a value which might fairly have been placed upon these properties." He cautioned,

> If this is the result of a review made by such a person … who at least is not unfavourable to our administration, it is quite evident that a Solicitor, acting on behalf of a Japanese, would be able to produce evidence in support of his contention that the property was sold at less than fair market value.[38]

The administration of Japanese Canadians' property had been a chaotic, overwhelming task. Shears recognized investigation of the operations of the Office of the Custodian could be politically disastrous.

Uncomfortable with the prospect of the potential inquiry, Shears and Wright tried to shape it in their favour. Shears and Wright recommended appointing Judge Whiteside to sit on a three-judge commission. Since Whiteside had chaired the Rural Advisory Committee, in charge of selling Japanese Canadians' property outside the Vancouver area, the bureaucrats believed that he could balance the perspective that might be exposed by an outsider.[39] In another attempt to protect the department, Shears recommended that all claims be first submitted to his Vancouver office rather than directly to the commission. This, Shears explained, would allow the Custodian of Enemy Property to provide sufficient contextual information on the sale, saving the proposed commission valuable time.[40] If it came to an investigation, Shears hoped that the Office of the Custodian would be "in a position to present the overall picture."[41]

Cabinet also looked to the Office of the Custodian for an assessment of the claims that Japanese Canadians might bring to the commission. Wright assured the cabinet committee that those who were responsible for the administration were "confident that as, if and when an inquiry is made, an account of good stewardship will be presented."[42] Wright warned that Japanese Canadians' claims extended "far beyond" losses at the hand of the Custodian. First, Japanese Canadians claimed "economical losses caused by the evacuation," more broadly, rather, than just the sale of their property.[43] He advised that cabinet constrain the investigation to the terms laid out in the prime minister's announcement, otherwise claims would "far exceed those referred to in the

Figure 9.3 In February 1947, Shears sent appraisers to the Fraser Valley to assess the merit of Japanese Canadians' claims. They found entire buildings unaccounted for in the original appraisals. Here, CCJC delegates visit the property of the Nagai family to gather evidence for their claim.

statement." Second, Japanese Canadians claimed damages in connection with chattels (or personal property). Wright explained that, "there was a considerable amount of chattels left in the Protected Area which … the Custodian was not able to protect due to the speed with which evacuation proceeded." To avoid culpability for losses due to theft, vandalism, and spoilage, he recommended that the government take the position that the "Custodian had exercised all reasonable care" for the property that the office "actually disposed of" and could "not be accountable" for the chattels that had not passed through the office's management.[44] The alternative, Wright explained, was for the government to concede responsibility for any property left by Japanese Canadians in the protected area, and that claimants were entitled to receive "fair value for it." This alternative, he suggested, was impractical. If cabinet stuck with a narrower approach, the "period of time during which any commission might … sit would be greatly reduced."[45]

Similarly, Shears sought to exclude claims that Japanese Canadians' might make for economic damages that resulted from the forced uprooting. These included sales made by Japanese Canadians in haste and panic, as well as due to vandalism, theft, crop spoilage, and lost wages. In a letter summarizing Japanese Canadians' protests, Shears emphasized the breadth of Japanese Canadians' articulations of loss and calls for compensation.[46] Echoing Wright, he recommended that cabinet limit the commission to claims for "tangible and specific" property that the Custodian had been "charged to manage and then sell."[47] Shears sought to narrow the terms of the inquiry and preserve the reputation of his office.

Wright and Shears both emphasized that Japanese Canadians would overstate their losses. As he outlined the categories of Japanese Canadians' claims – real estate, equipment, and greenhouses, for instance – Shears portrayed a gap between the "Japanese idea of worth" and the real market value of property.[48] Wright warned that Japanese Canadians had "exaggerated ideas as to the value of their holdings, and unfortunately many members of the legal profession are all willing to support their demands."[49] The Office of the Custodian thus simultaneously reported that Japanese Canadians' claims were extensive and, at least partially, unfounded. Having conveyed the spectre of an unmanageable commission, the bureaucrats advised cabinet on how to restrict its purview.

Wright and Shears' reports became foundational documents for the creation of the order in council announcing the commission, Order 1810. The Cabinet Committee on Japanese Problems (renamed in April the Cabinet Committee on Japanese Questions) did not follow their recommendations completely, but they preserved two key elements of their perspectives.[50] First, the characterization of Japanese Canadians' claims as "grossly exaggerated" informed the initial meetings of policy development, likely encouraging fears of unpredictable claims and an unruly, expensive commission.[51] Second, Wright's standard of "reasonable care" became a recurring tool to limit the purview of inquiry. Familiar with Japanese Canadians' protests, the Office of the Custodian characterized their articulations of loss as potentially problematic for the government. They steered the government towards terms within which it could prove accountability and sidestep larger questions about the internment and dispossession.

Internally, the cabinet committee agreed on 24 March to appoint a royal commission to investigate Japanese Canadians' claims.[52] At the following meeting, they worked with a comprehensive list of potential claims, crafted by the Department of Justice, to define the specific purview of the commission.[53] Using this list, the cabinet committee eliminated categories of claims where fair compensation would be too hard to determine, where cabinet saw no culpability, or where (as in the case of claims for economic damages) they judged compensation too costly. The proposed commission would not consider the claims for vessels sold by the Japanese Fishing Vessel Disposal Committee (JFVDC) but would accept claims for the 200 vessels that were transferred to the Custodian once the JFVDC had been disbanded. It would not consider losses under the control of agents appointed by Japanese Canadians, only those under direct control of agents of the Custodian. Further, the commission would not consider claims for compensation for loss of revenue for the duration of internment.[54] On went the edits.[55] Over a series of meetings, the cabinet committee carefully restricted the purview of the proposed commission to claims that could be easily tied to the Office of the Custodian and addressed.

The proposed commission remained at a standstill for the next month as officials debated *how* to measure property loss. Officials agreed that the commission would recognize failures of custodial care. That is, losses arising out of property "lost, destroyed or stolen while in the possession or under the control of the Custodian."[56] But, the cabinet committee remained divided over another key term.[57] In late April, the committee members considered empowering the commission to investigate claims: "that the amount received ... for real and personal property was less than the market value thereof at the time of the evacuation of the owner."[58] The alternative inserted a further restriction: it proposed a commission to inquire into claims that, "*by reason of the failure of Custodial care* ... the amount received ... was less than the market value thereof at the time of the forced uprooting of the owner.[59] The first option, by measuring loss according to value at the time of "evacuation," followed the American precedent and followed the direction advised by civil liberties groups. The second version instead created a burden to prove failures of the Custodian's management and would reduce the likely compensation to be paid. At the meeting on 28 April, the committee agreed to follow the second option.[60]

As the Office of the Custodian tried to evade an embarrassing inquiry, cabinet members and policy writers designed the commission to uphold an appearance of state accountability. Deputy Minister of Justice Frederick P. Varcoe observed around that time: "The Custodian's office ... would like to be able to say to the Commissioner that what they did was fair and reasonable (even if it was not, I suppose)."[61] Commenting in relation to ongoing debates in the House of Commons over the continued "discriminatory regulations" that May, Gordon Robertson described the strategy behind the commission:

> If the Commission to handle compensation is reasonably successful, I think the government will have come out of an embarrassing and difficult problem as well as could have been expected.[62]

By mid-May, cabinet was satisfied with their proposed commission and, believing that it would quell the mounting calls for justice, was prepared to pass it as law. It would be a contained, manageable inquiry. The order in council was approved to investigate claims for property loss, defined as the difference between market value *at the time of uprooting* and the eventual sale price of Japanese Canadian property. Only losses that resulted from a failure by the Office of the Custodian to exercise *reasonable care* in the processes of sale would be considered. Justice, in these terms, would be a matter of procedural accountability. Before the order in council was formally passed, the Office of the Custodian, however, would have a final opportunity to narrow the terms.

Public and political criticism interrupts the planned announcement of cabinet

The debates over the proposed inquiry did not simply occur within bureaucratic memos and cabinet committee meetings. As cabinet designed the terms of reference, Japanese Canadians and their allied advocacy groups campaigned for an inquiry that would compensate their losses. This continued an organized campaign for compensation that began in 1942, when Japanese Canadians learned that their property was placed in the hands of the Office of the Custodian.[63] By late 1946, the CCJC was making a concerted effort to gather evidence of Japanese Canadians' property losses to press for compensation.[64] The specificity of King's 24 January statement alerted them to the possibility of a limited inquiry. They noticed that the statement tied any losses to the actions of the Office of the Custodian, a qualification that excluded substantial losses. The CCJC immediately called for clarification of "the type of machinery required to ensure that the promise of fair treatment is implemented."[65] The CCJC offered their existing research to inform the design of the proposed commission.[66] When Andrew Brewin (the CCJC's lead lawyer) met with Secretary of State Colin Gibson, in early March, he argued that the commission must follow the American precedent in addressing claims resulting from the forced uprooting, rather than limiting its purview to concrete breaches of custodial responsibility, to attain at least some measure of justice.[67] Letters from Japanese Canadians, allied organizations, church groups, and sympathetic individuals streamed into government offices throughout early 1947.[68] Japanese Canadians and their allies pressured cabinet to make good on the prime minister's promise of an inquiry.

The demands from the Co-operative Commonwealth Federation (CCF) in the House of Commons directly influenced the commission's terms. Beginning in January, they pressed for closer examination of the Liberal government's wartime proceedings. The CCF called for the repeal of Bill 22, the Revised Regulations respecting Trading with the Enemy. This sparked questions about the accountability and transparency of the Custodian's office. The debates that followed included sweeping criticism of the government's treatment of Japanese Canadians during the war. The pressure came to a head in April 1947.[69] The debates were fierce, emphasizing government accountability to Canadian citizens – regardless of race – and succeeded in bringing the Custodian's office under the examination of the Standing Committee on Public Accounts in late May.[70] Cabinet shelved the claims commission approved in Order in Council PC 1810, waiting to see the impact of the hearings.

The SCPA hearings offered the public a glimpse of the devastation that the wartime policies had wrought upon Japanese Canadians. Throughout May and June, the standing committee examined the Office of the Custodian's conduct, with testimony from representatives from the Office of the Custodian and the CCJC. The hearings concentrated on sales by the Custodian to the director of the Veterans' Land Act. The representatives from the CCJC – Andrew Brewin, Donalda MacMillan, and George Tanaka – presented shocking evidence of devaluation and sales at bargain rates. Particularly outrageous was the unapologetic testimony from Gordon Murchison, the Soldier Settlement Board administrator, who had helped to secure bargain basement rates for the valuable Fraser Valley farms. Following the testimony, *The Globe and Mail* reported that the "Fraser Valley land grab" was not an "accident of ineptitude and hate" but was "the result of deliberate policy."[71] The hearings revealed a miscarriage of process that resulted in the undervaluation of Japanese Canadians' property and, on 17 June parliamentarians recommended a commission to investigate the sales.[72]

The SCPA hearings impacted the proposed royal commission in two ways. First, they fuelled public support for the property issue. The many injustices revealed by this inquiry and a sympathetic press fuelled public sympathy for Japanese Canadians.[73] To those unaware of cabinet's existing plans to tackle the issue, it seemed like a watershed moment that ensured that Japanese Canadians' claims would be addressed. Second, the recommendation provided a last-minute opportunity for cabinet members to narrow the purview of culpability. Specifically, the SCPA recommended that a commission

> inquire into and report upon the claim of any person of the Japanese race now resident in Canada for alleged loss which resulted from the amount received by him being less than fair market value of his property *at the time of sale or loss.*[74]

Though the SCPA hearings brought to public attention the scandal of the forced sales and shaped public expectation for an inquiry, the specific phrasing of the recommendation worked in favour of the Office of the Custodian. Cabinet had already approved Order 1810, measuring loss according to market values *at the time of evacuation*. But the standing committee's recommendation was more reserved, in this fundamental regard, than what cabinet had approved: losses incurred after the uprooting but before sale were, by the SCPA wording, excluded.[75] This shift measured the market value of property after the over twelve months of vandalism and neglect that followed the uprooting of Japanese Canadians. Real estate values may have appreciated, but Japanese Canadians' property had suffered damage. Officials from the Department of the Secretary of State jumped at the opportunity to narrow the terms and changed the proposed order in council.[76]

In light of Japanese Canadians' claims to property loss and compensation, the order in council announcing the commission on 18 July seemed "totally ineffectual" to the CCJC.[77] Unaware of cabinet's prepared orders in council, those who followed the SCPA hearings were perplexed when the terms of reference appeared to be narrower than the recommendation.[78] The CCJC argued that the terms placed an "impossible burden" on claimants to prove their losses.[79] Japanese Canadians and their allies "laid siege to Ottawa" to expand the terms to fully match the recommendation made by the SCPA.[80] On 17 September, they achieved a small success: cabinet cut the requirement that claimants prove a failure of "reasonable care" from the terms of reference in an amendment, Order in Council 3737. Nonetheless, fundamental limitations remained. Extensive categories of loss were intentionally excluded from the commission: claims from the nearly 4,000 Japanese Canadians who had been deported, claims for losses arising out of the forced sale of more than 1,000 fishing vessels in early 1942, and claims from corporations. Rather than judging losses against the benchmark of value at the time of first uprooting, loss would be determined by the market value at the time of sale. Though the amendments relieved (some) of the burden of proof from claimants, the commission retained its fundamental design.

As of October 1947, the commission was set to run its course. Policy makers sought to define the issue of Japanese Canadians' losses. Losses were not a matter of unjust policy or discrimination but simply procedural error. Rather than an admission of wrongdoing, the commission was framed as an expected step of the government's (purportedly) successful wartime policies. The commission would teach Canadians how to understand Japanese Canadians' claims of property loss and, in doing so, would prove the state's accountability.

However, the commission still had the potential to exceed these limits. Despite the control the Cabinet Committee on Japanese Questions had over its design, the commission would run as an independent investigative body. In this capacity, the commission could veer from the course set by cabinet and address Japanese Canadians' claims more fully. It was an undetermined process that would require collaboration between Japanese Canadians, their legal counsel, and the commission staff.

Japanese Canadians' lawyers become entwined in the duplicitous commission

The deadline for Japanese Canadians to submit claims to the Bird Commission soon arrived: 30 November 1947. As government officials planned to put the property issue to rest, Japanese Canadians instead hoped to open it up for closer investigation.[81] *The New Canadian,* the sole Japanese Canadian publication permitted during internment, announced a collective strategy to submit claims "under strong protest," with the aim "that the Commission would uncover sufficient evidence so that the investigation would ... be enlarged before its termination."[82] Japanese Canadians' ambition to expand the terms of reference guided their counsel's legal strategy. As the government built a narrative of the dispossession through the lens of procedural accountability, Japanese Canadians called on the state to be accountable to them as citizens and property owners.

Since the intention of its framers could be challenged in the commission's proceedings, the hearings also reveal the processes required to uphold the state's preferred definitions of loss and narrative of the dispossession. Put simply, the commission continually resisted, silenced, and submerged Japanese Canadians' articulations of loss and value. The commission was meant to impart an impression of rule of law, of an orderly state correcting its own errors. However, it rested upon arbitrary decisions and ultimately was complicit in injustice. A close view of the commission in practice demonstrates how running the commission required continual exertion, and a rejection of the realities of the dispossession, in order to build a claim to justice in postwar Canada.

Caught in this fray were the lawyers for Japanese Canadians. Having campaigned for a different commission, the solicitors now needed to cooperate with the government to deliver successful results for their clients. Representing a large number of claimants, the CCJC lawyers balanced the interests of individuals with those of the entire body of claimants, in addition to those whose claims were excluded from the commission. Simultaneously, they leveraged their legal expertise to shape the commission in their clients' favour. Japanese Canadians' lawyers became mediators within the commission structure, yet, in the process of representing claimants in good faith, they became implicated in a much larger process that silenced Japanese Canadians' perspectives on the losses they had suffered and the compensation they deserved.

Representing hundreds of claimants required substantial organization. In late August 1947, the National Japanese Canadian Citizens Association (NJCCA) and the CCJC formed a coalition to represent Japanese Canadian claimants. Together, the NJCCA and CCJC set up the technical, legal, and financial machinery to represent Japanese Canadian claimants.[83] The CCJC represented most claimants, in addition to presenting expert surveys, analyses, and valuations. Neither organization acted alone: in campaigning for and participating in the Bird Commission, the organizations drew upon the network of Japanese Canadian and allied groups across the country that emerged during the campaign against deportations.

The CCJC assembled a team of legal representation for Japanese Canadians from this network.[84] Two lawyers would represent claimants in each province. The lawyers had a range of connections to Japanese Canadians: the Ontario lawyers came to represent Japanese Canadians through civil rights advocacy, for instance, while those from British Columbia, like J. Arthur MacLennan and Robert McMaster, had direct prior experience representing clients against the dispossession and the deportations. George Tamaki, working in Saskatchewan, was the only lawyer of Japanese descent. The CCJC formally represented just more than 1,100 claimants. Gladstone Virtue, a solicitor from southern Alberta with longstanding connections to Japanese Canadians in the region, represented two hundred clients and the remaining hundred claimants hired legal representation individually.[85] Though the NJCCA and CCJC prepared the

Figure 9.4 Japanese Canadians fundraise for the NJCCA, which was formed in summer 1947 to prepare for the Bird Commission.

legal arguments for the claimants, effectively representing Japanese Canadian claimants entailed the cooperation of a team of solicitors across the country.

The tensions that prevailed throughout the commission were on display in the first round of hearings. The Bird Commission officially began on 3 December 1947, when Commissioner Justice Henry I. Bird, the Dominion counsel, and Japanese Canadians' counsel met in Vancouver to establish the opening arguments. They then travelled to Kamloops, where the hearings opened on 8 December. The first claim belonged to Ito Imada, an Issei (first generation) mother who had built a life in Canada over the course of thirty years.[86] She had lost her family's farm in the Fraser Valley and with it all her belongings. She claimed the value of her farm at $7,935, more than double what the VLA paid for it in 1944.[87] In front of the intimidating audience, she testified that the government had sold her property for less than fair market value.[88]

For claimants like Imada, the Bird Commission hearings were simply another step in their ongoing engagement with the Canadian state. Claimants had registered with the Office of the Custodian and provided the necessary details to facilitate the office's management. They had requested their belongings delivered to them and often, in turn, learned of property destruction or theft. They had received cheques for their property in the mail and, in some cases, replied in disbelief, outrage, and anguish. They had launched a test case against the dispossession orders. Only a year earlier, they had steered through the debacle of coercive "repatriation" forms circulated through the internment camps. For half a decade, claimants like Shimo Kameda, Toyo Takahashi, Rinkichi Tagashira, Eikichi Nakashima, Dr Kozo Shimotakahara, Kaoru Atagi, and Katsuyori Murakami had navigated and protested their bureaucratic dispossession. Submitting their claims to the Bird Commission, they once against asserted that the Canadian state was culpable for their losses. Indeed, their pursuit of compensation was entwined with a vision of what a just government should be: a government that acknowledged and compensated for the violation of their rights as property owners and citizens.

Imada's case should have been straightforward: the director of the Soldier Settlement Board had publicly admitted underpricing the Fraser Valley properties earlier that year at the SCPA hearings. But Imada's hearing stalled and was postponed. Unable to understand the interpreter, Imada could not answer the questions put to her.[89] Despite her intimate familiarity with her home and property, she could not provide the details deemed necessary to specifying market value. The claimants who followed in this first round of hearings proved similarly "unsatisfactory" to the commissioner; they could not respond to the pointed questions about market value, could not understand the translator, and spoke against the line of inquiry.[90] The press reported on "tangled," "confusing" claims and "applications confused and intricately based" that threatened to put the Commission behind schedule.[91] "Jap Commission May Set Record," announced the *Vancouver News Herald*, predicting it would last three years.[92] It was a disconcerting start to the Bird Commission.

When the hearings opened, critical elements of the commission were still open to change. Negotiations over terms and how they should be interpreted continued throughout the initial months of hearings. Well into February, for instance, Bird considered recommending to the Department of Justice that the terms of reference be changed to evaluate loss from the time of uprooting (rather the time of sale).[93] Further, the CCJC persistently tried to bring additional categories of claims into the purview of the commission. They achieved early success in January 1948 when the commissioner agreed to hear corporate claims.[94] The CCJC's attempts to expand the terms to include losses for accounts receivable and goodwill, however, were unsuccessful. For the fishing vessels sold by the Japanese Fishing Vessel Disposal Committee, prior to vesting in the Office of the Custodian, the CCJC strategized carefully. Throughout the first year of hearings, the claimants' counsel submitted claims in this category, knowing that they would be rejected in the hearing. With the submission, however, the counsel built a body of evidence to which they would later refer in appeals to the minister of justice.[95] In this case, the claimants' counsel used the hearings to demonstrate the inadequacy of the terms.

The task of hearing and evaluating more than 1,400 claims presented a different challenge. Japanese Canadians' counsel and the government staff alike feared that, were the hearings to continue at the rate of the first proceedings, they faced a multiyear inquiry. For Japanese Canadians, this would have meant delay before they received compensation. For the government, it threatened a costly (and potentially embarrassing) inquiry. Given these exigencies, all parties agreed that the hearings would have to be streamlined. In this process, Japanese Canadians' lawyers became mediators between their clients and the commission staff, challenged with adapting the commission in the claimants' favour while appeasing the interests of the government officials.

After the initial hearings, the CCJC lawyers reported on Bird's reaction to their arguments but also his preferences and interpretations in court. Bird seemed sympathetic to the claimants, but the solicitors cautioned the team to respect the purview of the commission. "It appears that you did an excellent job in convincing the Commissioner that a generous view should be taken of all the claims submitted," one lawyer wrote to Andrew Brewin, "and that the utmost informality should prevail in hearing these claims." But he warned that the "questions of the propriety of the actions of the Custodian in his Office" were not the subject "at hand" and that they must work under the terms as established.[96] Tamaki also warned Brewin that Bird would "not be interested in claimants who seek to take this opportunity to criticize the evacuation."[97] Cautious not to overstep the commission's patience, the solicitors coached the claimants to testify only to the realm of the commission: was their property sold below market value? That winter, the CCJC was hopeful about the judge hearing Japanese Canadians' claims but wary of the limited arena in which they worked.

The limits of the commission meant that Japanese Canadian testimony, too, would need to be constrained. This meant restricting the range of topics addressed in testimony and also sometimes prompting claimants to consider their property in new ways. As most Japanese Canadians had not planned to sell their property when they were uprooted, few were certain of what its sale value might have been.[98] By adapting their presentations to answer this question, Brewin hoped the commissioner would discover that their

> representations [were] more and more useful to him and that he will come to recognize that his task would have been absolutely hopeless if it had not been for the work of [the CCJC]. This may well put him in a friendly mood in respect to the claims.[99]

From the perspective of the CCJC, adapting the commission procedure was a way to maintain open negotiating relations with the commissioner. They hoped that as a result of their cooperation, he would be more likely to be sympathetic to Japanese Canadians and consider expanding the purview of the commission.

Figure 9.5 In February, the Bird Commission travelled to the court house in Vernon, British Columbia.

An early solution to the problem of lengthy hearings was to shift claimants' testimony to forms.[100] After discussing strategy with representatives from Japanese Canadians' legal counsel, Brewin instructed the CCJC to create forms wherein claimants could provide information on their property. "At the original hearings in Kamloops," Brewin reported, "considerable experience was gained looking to the shortening of the proceedings. One suggestion that was made was that certain evidence could be put in writing and prepared, before oral evidence is taken."[101] The forms limited claimants' testimony, their opportunity to interject, and eliminated the complications of the forced uprooting in which many of their claims were tangled. The fields limited the submissions to the details of market value and the Custodian's management.[102] With this streamlining, the claimants' counsel hoped to present Japanese Canadians' claims more effectively for Bird.

As a further measure to streamline the hearings, McMaster proposed reading from the claimants' forms, which were completed in advance.[103] This circumvented the challenges of language and complicated testimony (Bird was reluctant to hire Japanese Canadian translators, instead using translators who were trained only in classical Japanese). The "Additional Comments, if any" section in the forms, where claimants and their legal aids recorded historical accounts of the claimants' property ownership and dispossession, were particularly useful in this regard. The claimants' counsel hoped to create a format in which all claims would be heard in a timely fashion. Although this was an efficient strategy to gather evidence, the forms further marginalized Japanese Canadians' testimony from the hearings.

By the second month of hearings, the adjustments seemed to be working. McMaster remarked that "Mr Justice Bird was good enough to comment at the hearing that he very much appreciated the statement as a time saving device." "He also indicated privately," McMaster continued, "that he could appreciate the continued use of the forms not only in the Province but in the other Provinces."[104] As the commission travelled across the country, the forms became a standard operating procedure. When the commission arrived in Toronto that spring, Bird chastised Brewin for not completing the forms like the lawyers in British Columbia and Manitoba. "However," Brewin recounted, "although the complaint was made that we were less efficient in Toronto than in any other part of Canada, on the whole we were able to get through the month fairly satisfactorily, certainly without any serious eruptions."[105] Although the claimants' counsel and government staff felt the pressure of time, the CCJC had to both represent their clients effectively and ensure the commission ran smoothly. They were, at times, contradictory tasks.

Despite their limitations, the forms offered subtle opportunities to include Japanese Canadians' narratives of the property value in their hearing evidence and case files. In the "Additional Comments, if any" section, claimants and their counsel took some liberty in expressing the complex value of their property and the chaotic conditions of their dispossession. When McMaster read Japanese Canadians' evidence in the hearings, he often affirmed their narratives and ensured their place on record. In Fujino Yamamoto's hearing, for instance, McMaster read directly from her entry, which the legal aid wrote in first person:

> Although we were getting old for operating the farm, we did not want to sell but had the idea that some day we might subdivide for residential holding so we could keep our home … We always cared for the house and property well and in later years had the assistance of our young grandsons and a nephew who lived with us and kept the farm up.[106]

In addition to a narrative of investment, family, and anticipated future benefit, McMaster entered into the commission record that Yamamoto's property was sold without her consent. In Hideaki Hirowatari's hearing, McMaster explained that the farmer disclosed that he had "no special knowledge of the value but states that it maintained their family, which was rather a large one."[107] Likewise, Ino Sasaki's standardized claim form testified to value beyond the market:

> [Sasaki's property] supported a prosperous greenhouse and nursery business from which the claimant and her husband and four children made a reasonably good living. It represents an investment of time and labour over a period of ten years.[108]

Having little to do with market value, these stories made claims for value that evoked loss beyond the restricted terms of reference. The stories of investment, sacrifice, family, and future aspirations conveyed loss beyond market value.[109] The solicitors recognized the breadth of their claimants' losses and included their narratives to craft compelling cases for compensation. The standardized forms and evidence offered a narrow window to submit narratives that extended beyond the terms of reference.[110]

Yet these were only small glimpses into the extent and significance of the dispossession for Japanese Canadians. Overwhelmingly, the concessions to streamline the hearing process marginalized Japanese Canadians' perspectives. In many hearings, claimants' testimony is nearly absent, appearing simply as "yes" and "no" answers by the translator.

Familiar with rumours that Japanese Canadians over-valuated their property and over-claimed their losses, the CCJC was cautious to craft claims in a way that seemed "reasonable" to Bird and the subcommissioners. Over the course of the hearings, the solicitors rejected claims with sparse evidence and carefully edited others down (often in the hearings themselves) to a reasonable valuation.[111] Saul Cherniack, the lead legal counsel in Manitoba, later described this element of strategy, saying that although the CCJC recognized that Japanese Canadians' losses extended beyond the metrics of market value, the solicitors "very diligently tried to bring people down to a realistic [claim]."[112] Cherniack explained his threefold rationale. First, he sought to discourage any preconception that "these people [Japanese Canadians] are being unreasonable in their claims." Second, he sought to avoid unrealistic expectations on the part of his clients: "no lawyer," he explained, "would let a client have expectations that were way beyond his means." Third, and mainly, Cherniack explained, "we didn't want to turn Bird against this whole thing by hearing claim after claim that was exaggerated."[113] The rational had merit: in a report to Commissioner Bird in spring 1948, a subcommissioner laid out his judgment of whether each claimant was "truthful," "reliable," or "demanding excessive sums."[114] Anticipating such judgements, the CCJC edited Japanese Canadians' claims to be legible and legitimate to the state. In the already limited commission, the CCJC further narrowed Japanese Canadians' claims.

As the counsel for the claimants strategized to maintain open lines of negotiation with Commissioner Bird, they were attentive to the influence of defence lawyers on his decisions. In February, McMaster noted what he saw as a particularly troubling intervention from Glenn McPherson, the former director of the Custodian's office. "To my sorrow," McMaster wrote, he found that he could not

Figure 9.6 The CCJC advised their clients to submit photographs of their property. These photographs express the diverse values Japanese Canadians attributed to their property and the complexity of their losses.

> talk frankly to him off the record – it ends up in the judge's ears; he's a good rationalizer; he's a loyal defender of the Department; he's interested in the political aspects of this deal not in justice; and a few other things. As far as he is concerned he looks on this as a game of poker.[115]

McMaster's encounter with McPherson shook his trust in the commission process. If there was sometimes a sense of good faith collaboration with the commissioner, McPherson's politicking suggested that there were concealed factors influencing the proceedings. "From now on my cards will stay close to my chest," McMaster concluded.[116]

While the claimants' counsel adapted claims to the hearings, the government sought to eliminate them altogether. Despite the commission "proceeding with greater rapidity than in the past," McPherson reported, government consul was "greatly disturbed at the magnitude of the problem of presenting 1400 defenses." He proposed his own solution to the problem of a prolonged commission.[117] In February 1948, McPherson met with Bird to address the matter, and they determined two potential solutions. The first was to hear 1,400 individual defences, a task that would likely last into late 1949. The second was to make general recommendations relating to the various categories of claims, drawing from statistical information "extracted from the files and the transcripts of evidence." He proposed that the commissioner "make a recommendation as to a percentage to be paid across the board" to various categories of claim. Bird would propose a similar solution later that year. For the government officials, shortening the commission would hasten putting the issue to rest.

Initially, the CCJC guarded against significant refinements proposed in the name of efficiency. In March 1948, CCJC lawyer J. Arthur MacLennan reflected on an exchange that had "shaken [his] faith" that "Bird intended to make a fair and impartial survey and recommendation." In discussion of the commission's workload and the difficulty of further streamlining claims, Bird proposed to dispense with hearings. MacLennan recounted that Bird said that "he had been through about the first fifty claims and he had come to the conclusion that in about one-half of them at least there was really no claim at all against the Custodian."[118] MacLennan was astonished that "such a procedure should even be considered" and that the commissioner could arrive at this conclusion, "without any rebuttal evidence that there was no claim in any case before him."[119] To Brewin, informed of Bird's proposal, the suggestion was "very disturbing." It indicated, he wrote to MacLennan, "a lack of understanding of what is involved in a public inquiry, in which it is the duty to procure all the facts." Nonetheless, he advised staying the course. The best approach, he said, was to "change [Bird's] opinion through the evidence as to valuations ... and the analysis of individual claims when all the evidence is in."[120] The CCJC declined Bird's proposal. The hearings were integral to building a case for the claimants.

Meanwhile, Bird was attentive to the claimant's growing distrust of the commission and of the streamlining of their testimony from the process. In May, a commission staffer reported "that the Japanese claimants were getting the idea that their claims were not, perhaps, being given the attention which they formerly received." Though claimants were informed that the streamlining was for the sake of early compensation, the staffer worried that the approach might undermine the "feeling of confidence and fairplay" in the commission.[121] Bird relayed the concern to his subcommissioners. An advocate for expedited hearings and categorical compensation, Bird nevertheless emphasized what he saw as value of the individual hearings: "I feel," he wrote,

> from a point of public relations between the Japs and the white people in Canada, as well as the Government, that it is desirable that the Jap be sent away from the sessions of the Commission with the impression that he has had his day in court and consideration will be given to his claim.

To foster the impression of interest, he encouraged the subcommissioners to put in some "local knowledge" to convey to the "claimant the idea that the Commissioner knew what he was talking about."[122] If he recognized the commission's place in a broader process of reconciliation that extended beyond material compensation, Bird also suggested a duplicity at the heart of the commission.

Over the summer of 1948, the CCJC and NJCCA continued to reject Bird's proposals to shorten the commission.[123] In June, Bird proposed that the Veterans' Land Act sales could be settled for a common percentage. The CCJC declined. McMaster, for one, could not "frankly see how it is possible to make such overall arrangement." In his view, the discrepancy between claims was too large to achieve fair compensation, but he did recognize the practicality of the proposal.[124] Bird suggested the strategy a second time in August, this time outlining a full schedule of categories that they would assess. It was the NJCCA's turn to block the proposal. It reiterated the importance of having each claim heard.[125] The claimants' counsel and the NJCCA insisted on the importance of the hearings. The hearings were the arena in which was built a body of evidence against the government's claim of accountability and a record of the dispossession; they were an avenue for future compensation.

By the end of September, however, the CCJC and NJCCA conceded to assessing the claims in aggregate according to category of property. Representing each individual claim was costly and the CCJC was already running out of funds from the initial amount they charged their clients.[126] Reluctant to ask the claimants for further fees and lacking confidence that they could continue the amount of work required to present the claims, the CCJC eventually agreed to this approach in September 1948. The government had outlasted the claimants' resources.[127]

The commission continued over the next two years. First, the claimants' counsel, government counsel, and Commissioner Bird negotiated how to sample the claimants' case files to determine property loss.[128] The final decision to award compensation through categories of claim had some advantages. In addition to saving time, the agreement bolstered weaker claims that otherwise might have been dismissed for lack of evidence.[129] Overall, the results were uneven. The commission awarded 5 per cent of the original sale price for claimants who had owned in the Greater Vancouver area; for real estate in rural areas (excepting those sold under the Veterans' Land Act), 10 per cent; and for sales under the Veterans' Land Act, 80 per cent of the original sale price. Claims for motor vehicles were awarded 25 per cent of their original sale price and those boats sold by the Office of the Custodian, 23.5 per cent of their original sale price. In all, the claimants received only 56 per cent of the amount they had claimed. The settlement spurred protests from Japanese Canadians, particularly the Toronto Claimants' Committee (with membership of 245), who protested the recommendations and dissent over the CCJC's representation.[130]

In their efforts to secure timely compensation for Japanese Canadians, the claimants' counsel became entwined in the state's broader project of sidelining accounts of the broad injustices of the wartime years. As they made Japanese Canadians' claims legible to the Bird Commission, the CCJC lawyers reinforced the state's definition of property loss and became complicit in producing a body of evidence that supported the government's claim to accountability. But they did so in good faith and, within the context of the Bird Commission, were able to achieve some success for their clients. They expanded the terms of reference from their initial form in July 1947 and succeeded in achieving some compensation. Tasked with mediating the multiple pressures within the commission, however, the CCJC reinforced the overarching silencing of Japanese Canadians. Ultimately, claimants and their counsel were faced with an inquiry designed to put the "property issue" to rest. As Japanese Canadians' lawyers tried to navigate the commission structure – in appeasing Bird, in modifying claimants' presentations – they were repeatedly drawn into the task of streamlining, simplifying, and moving on.

The federal government concludes a contrived commission and submerges (for the time being) Japanese Canadians' calls to fair compensation

The final report of the Bird Commission, published in April 1950, can be read as the conclusion to the approach cabinet had set in motion three years prior. Written from Bird's perspective, the report is worth quoting at length:

> I am satisfied with the evidence adduced before me that the very onerous task imposed upon the Director of the Custodian's Office at Vancouver … was competently performed, with due regard to the interest of the owners of such property … The fact that I have found that in certain respects fair market value was not realized in sales made by the Custodian in no sense reflects upon the work of the Custodian's organization. On the contrary, the evidence brought out on this Inquiry strongly supports the conclusion that this organization, in spite of the magnitude of responsibilities imposed on it, had substantially succeeded in administering and subsequently selling the property of evacuated persons with due regard to the owner's interest.[131]

Bird's report was an incongruous response to Japanese Canadians' calls for fair compensation, but it provided an answer to whether Japanese Canadians had been treated fairly. In the view of Justice Bird, they had. By defining the issue of loss as a matter of procedural accountability, the Bird Commission built a narrative that the government was fair and just, and abdicated responsibility for other losses that (in its account) were beyond its control. In doing so, the Bird Commission produced a history of the dispossession that, founded on the evidence of an extensive inquiry, vindicated the state's actions and portrayed the dispossession as legitimate state intervention.

By the late 1940s, even cabinet members who were fully committed to the forced uprooting, dispossession, and dispersal of Japanese Canadians were uneasy with the public discussion of the policies. In late 1946, they faced the task of moving past the wartime treatment of Japanese Canadians without undermining their own legitimacy. As government officials debated how to address the issue of property compensation, they engaged in a contest over the meaning of the internment era in public narratives. Faced with the challenge of addressing complex and extensive losses, officials steered the conversation of loss and compensation to a terrain where state accountability, they felt, could be proved.

This path was born out of a familiarity with Japanese Canadians' claims: activism was appropriated for state purposes. The officials at the Office of the Custodian and the Cabinet Committee on Japanese Problems crafted their recommendations from an understanding of Japanese Canadians' claims for fair compensation. The cabinet committee further consulted with the Department of Justice to strategically limit their accountability to claims Japanese Canadians were likely to bring. Determining a route to address Japanese Canadians' claims to property loss and compensation posed a profound challenge for the Canadian state. Certain losses would be impossible to reconcile. A recognition of Japanese Canadians' hardships may have been the most effective tool for addressing the loss of community, security, and a sense of home. The breach of property rights opened a similar, messy terrain. Yet, there were types of loss that could be measured (or compensated for) through market exchange. As they debated the grounds of the proposed inquiry, the cabinet committee narrowed its purview to categories wherein loss could be easily quantified and under which the Office of the Custodian's accountability could be proved.

The limited terms of the commission were not the inevitable outcome of government parsimony. Key officials and cabinet showed some willingness to consider losses in income or for the damages to chattels that did not pass through the Office of the Custodian's direct management. This path, however, also threatened to open the door to the broader condemnation of injustice, an accusation that the state was not ready to engage. Instead, government officials limited conversation of loss to a purview wherein settlement was (conceivably) achievable. Cabinet followed a route that conceptualized the state's responsibility to citizens as one of procedural accountability and narrowed the conversation of loss.

But it was not so easy to separate process (appraisals and sale prices) from the broader policies of which they were part (the forced uprooting and dispossession of Japanese Canadians). Japanese Canadians claimed that their losses resulted from both. The growing public criticism centred on the larger injustice. Injustice and material loss inseparable and government officials elided these two to build their claim to accountability. Having called a commission and awarded compensation, government officials could claim that government officials had investigated and addressed injustices against Japanese Canadians.

This effort succeeded in significant part. "Paid in Full," one editorial announced: "Mr Justice H.I. Bird has disposed of the Japanese property claims with honor to the nation, credit to himself and benefit-of-the-doubt generosity to the aggrieved applicants."[132] *The Vancouver Daily Province* quoted the final report directly, crediting the Office of the Custodian's good work, and saluted the commissioner for his "unlimited patience and clear thought."[133] The government had looked back into the operations of the wartime years and, where needed, made the appropriate corrections. Evading Japanese Canadians' most significant claims, government officials relied on the act of compensation to signify justice more broadly.

Looking back on the Bird Commission, we know that it constituted an additional betrayal of Japanese Canadians, suppressing their calls for compensation and justice. Yet in overlooking the Bird Commission proceedings, we risk reproducing that silencing. The Bird Commission records reveal that in the late 1940s, Japanese Canadians, of different backgrounds, seized the federal forum to push for a different postwar era, one in which the violation of their rights as citizens and property owners was recognized and compensated. But their claims were disregarded. If Japanese Canadians pushed the state to a higher level of accountability, their calls were silenced in a commission structured against their interests.

As they worked the commission, Japanese Canadians' solicitors negotiated between the government's paradigm of loss and the greater claims of their clients. Their task was to expand the purview of the commission to recognize all claims, but they also contributed to the state's broader project of silencing and moving on. The solicitors became entangled within the broader structure of domination in which they worked.[134] Attention to their strategies and rationales helps us see more clearly how three years of activism by Japanese Canadians and their allies, became entwined in state priorities.

This contest over the meaning of loss and injustice offers a pathway into understanding the legacy of the state violence against Japanese Canadians in the 1940s. It reveals something of Canada's uncomfortable transition from a series of explicitly racist state policies towards new approaches to pluralism. Japanese Canadians' calls for compensation, supported by their allies, offered government officials grounds to address the issue of property loss on their terms. Cabinet chose, however, to address their claims only indirectly, through a frame focused on fair procedure and established accountability. By redefining the issue of injustice, Cabinet carefully distanced itself from the larger injustices of the 1940s. Canada moved past the wartime treatment of Japanese Canadians through an act of silencing. With the Bird Commission, Japanese Canadians entered the postwar years, their claims to fair treatment under Canadian law largely dismissed, displaced from their homes and robbed of their investments, and citizens of a nation that, after three years of investigation, reported that what it had done was fair and just.

NOTES

This chapter first appeared in my MA thesis and draws from its overarching arguments. Kaitlin Findlay, "The Bird Commission, Japanese Canadians, and the Challenge of Reparations in the Wake of State Violence" (MA thesis, University of Victoria, 2017). As before, my sincere thanks go to Jordan Stanger-Ross, Penny Bryden, Eric Adams, Lynne Marks, Nicole Yakashiro, and Will Archibald for their help with that project.

1 Letter from Shears to Wright, 31 July 1947, file 55908, pt. 3: "Japanese Property Claims Commission," vol. 2817, RG 117-A-3, LAC.

2 Ibid.

3 Letter from McPherson to Shears, 4 November 1943, file 59010: "Chattels (Japanese)," vol. 2826, RG 117-A-3, LAC.

4 Sometimes referred to as the Royal Commission on Japanese Claims, the Bird Commission was officially titled the Royal Commission to Investigate Complaints of Canadian Citizens of Japanese Origin who Resided in British Columbia in 1941, That Their Real and Personal Property had been Disposed of by the Custodian of Enemy Property at Prices Less than the Fair Market Value.

5 Chapters 4 and 8.

6 Ken Adachi, *The Enemy That Never Was: A History of the Japanese Canadians* (Toronto: McClelland and Stewart, 1976), 325; Ann Sunahara, *The Politics of Racism* (Toronto: James Lorimer and Company, 1981), 13; Patricia Roy, *The Triumph of Citizenship: The Japanese and Chinese in Canada, 1941–67* (Vancouver: UBC Press, 2007), 242. Miki briefly notes this earlier development. See Roy Miki, *Redress: Inside the Japanese Canadian Call for Justice* (Vancouver: Raincoast Books, 2004), 112–4.

7 Jane Jensen, "Commissioning Ideas: Representation and Royal Commissions," in *How Ottawa Spends, 1994–95: Making Change*, ed. Susan D. Phillips (Montreal & Kingston: McGill-Queen's University Press, 1994), 49.

8 Ibid., 48.

9 Gerald E. Le Dain, "The Role of the Public Inquiry in our Constitutional System," in *Law and Social Change*, eds. Jacob S. Ziegel and Harry William Arthurs (York: Osgoode Hall Law School, York University, 1973), 85.

10 Stephanie D. Bangarth, *Voices Raised in Protest: Defending Citizens of Japanese Ancestry in North America, 1942–49* (Vancouver: UBC Press, 2008); Ross Lambertson, *Repression and Resistance: Canadian Human Rights Activists, 1930–1960* (Toronto: University of Toronto Press, 2005); Miki, *Redress*; Peter Takaji Nunoda, "A Community in Transition and Conflict: The Japanese Canadians, 1935–1951" (PhD diss., University of Manitoba, 1991).

11 Miki, *Redress*, chapter 5; Nunoda, "A Community in Transition and Conflict," chapter 8.

12 In this regard, this chapter continues from Eric Adams and Jordan Stanger-Ross's portrayal of Japanese Canadians' resistance to the forced seizure and sale of their property, beginning when the policies were first announced in 1942 (chapter 8). More generally, I build on rich scholarship that attends to Japanese Canadians' reactions and resistance to the state violence of the 1940s: Chapter 4, Jordan Stanger-Ross, "Telling a Difficult Past: Kishizo Kimura's Memoir of Entanglement in Racist Policy," *BC Studies* 181 (9 April 2014): 39–62; Jordan Stanger-Ross and Pamela Sugiman eds., *Witness to Loss: Race, Culpability, and Memory in the Dispossession of Japanese Canadians* (Montreal & Kingston: McGill-Queen's University Press, 2017); Peter Neary, "Zennosuke Inouye's

Land: A Canadian Veterans Affairs Dilemma," *Canadian Historical Review* 85, no. 3 (September 2004): 423–50; Michiko Midge Ayukawa, "Bearing the Unbearable: The Memoir of a Japanese Pioneer Woman" (MA thesis, University of Victoria, 1990).

13 Allan Manson and David J Mullan eds., *Commissions of Inquiry: Praise or Reappraise* (Toronto: Irwin Law, 2003), 3.

14 Thomas R. Berger, "Canadian Commissions of Inquiry: An Insider's Perspective," in Manson and Mullan, *Commissions of Inquiry*, 14.

15 Gregory J. Inwood and Carolyn Johns, *Commissions of Inquiry and Policy Change: A Comparative Analysis* (Toronto: University of Toronto Press, 2014), 10.

16 Maryka Omatsu, *Bittersweet Passage: Redress and the Japanese Canadian Experience* (Between the Lines, 2010), 75, 118.

17 Adachi, *The Enemy That Never Was*, 321–34; Sunahara, *The Politics of Racism*, 137; Miki, *Redress*, 114.

18 In this respect, this thesis contributes to Laura Madokoro's claim that liberalization in postwar Canada was "far from certain" (though Madokoro writes in relation to immigration policy, this study of the Bird Commission shows that change in attitudes and policies toward domestic racialized groups was also equivocal). Laura Madokoro, "'Slotting' Chinese Families and Refugees, 1947–1967," *Canadian Historical Review* 93, no. 1 (2012): 25–56. For closer examination of the debates over the meanings of Canadian citizenship, identity, and values in the immediate postwar, see Patricia Roy, "Lessons in Citizenship, 1945–1949: The Delayed Return of the Japanese to Canada's Pacific Coast," *The Pacific Northwest Quarterly* 93, no. 2 (2002): 69–80; Roy, *The Triumph of Citizenship*; Ivana Caccia, *Managing the Canadian Mosaic in Wartime: Shaping Citizenship Policy, 1939–1945* (Montreal & Kingston: McGill-Queen's University Press, 2010); Franca Iacovetta, *Gatekeepers: Reshaping Immigrant Lives in Cold War Canada* (Toronto: Between the Lines, 2006); Heidi Bohaker and Franca Iacovetta, "Making Aboriginal People 'Immigrants Too': A Comparison of Citizenship Programs for Newcomers and Indigenous Peoples in Postwar Canada, 1940s–1960s," *Canadian Historical Review* 90, no. 3 (2009): 427–62.

19 Press release, 24 January 1947, file 3851, vol. 361, MG26 J4 (William Lyon Mackenzie King fonds) LAC.

20 Adachi notes that this statement did not begin the process of redress but rather, "merely served to accelerate, channel and organize the agitation and resentments that had been mounting since 1942." Adachi, *The Enemy That Never Was*, 321. See "Govt. to Pay Indemnity for Property Losses," *The New Canadian*, 1 February 1947; "Deportation Plans Dropped in Revised Japanese Policy," *The New Canadian*, 1 February 1947; "Hope lifting of Jap Ban to End Race Restrictions," *The Toronto Daily Star*, 24 January 1947; "No More Japs Will Be Deported, Ottawa Says," *The Toronto Daily Star*, 24 January 1948; "Retreat Under Pressure," *The Globe and Mail*, 28 January 1947; Co-Operative Committee on Japanese Canadians News bulletin # 10, 10 February 1947, file 5: "CCJC: News bulletins, 1946–48," vol. 1, MG30 D200 (M. Grace Tucker fonds), LAC.

21 Previous scholars agree that by early 1946, the Canadian public had turned against the extension of the deportation orders in council. Fuelled by public education campaigns of the Co-Operative Committee on Japanese Canadians, civil liberties groups, church leadership, unions, and student organizations rallied against the discriminatory policies. A shared explanation across these accounts is the importance of postwar awareness of Nazi atrocities and the emerging discourse of human rights and citizenship.

Whatever it was, Sunahara writes, "It was sufficient that the anti-deportation campaign of January and February 1946 produced the strongest outburst of spontaneous public reaction in the long career of Prime Minister William Lyon Mackenzie King, an outburst King knew better than to ignore" (Sunahara, *The Politics of Racism*, 122–3). See also, Roy, *The Triumph of Citizenship*, 188, 202–32; Bangarth, *Voices Raised in Protest*, 101; Lambertson, *Repression and Resistance*, 140; Adachi, *The Enemy That Never Was*, 311.

22 Memorandum, 3 December 1946, file: "Japanese in Canada 2 of 6," vol. 1, MG 31 E87 (Gordon Robertson fonds), LAC; Minutes from the Cabinet Committee on Japanese Problems, 13 December 1946, file: j-25-1: "Japanese in Canada. 1946," vol. 249, RG 2 B2 (Central Registry files of Privy Council Office), LAC; Minutes from the Cabinet Committee on Japanese Problems, 10 January 1947, file j-25-1: "Japanese in Canada. 1947–49," vol. 84, RG 2 B2, LAC. The Cabinet Committee on Japanese Problems consisted of representatives from the Department of Labour, undersecretary of state, Department of Justice, Department of External Affairs, Veterans Affairs, the Privy Council Office and the prime minister's office.

23 Minutes, Cabinet Committee on Japanese Problems, 13 December 1946, file j-25-1: "Japanese in Canada. 1946," vol. 249, RG 2 B2, LAC; Minutes, Cabinet Committee on Japanese Problems, 10 January 1947, ibid.; Minutes, Cabinet Committee on Japanese Problems, 13 January 1947, ibid.

24 Memorandum for King by R. Gordon Robertson, 9 January 1947, file: "Japanese in Canada (2 of 6)," vol. 1, MG31 E87, LAC.

25 Memorandum for Arnold D.P. Heeney by R.G. Robertson, 6 December 1946, ibid.

26 Memorandum, 3 December 1946, ibid.; Letter to Brown from R.G. Robertson, 9 January 1947, ibid.

27 Press release (draft), 23 January 1947, ibid.

28 Ibid.

29 The Cabinet Committee remained deeply divided over the repeal (some called for the continued deportation of Japanese Canadians, regardless of citizenship), but others expressed concerns over the appearance of "ill-Liberal treatment of different persons" and the appearance of "inhumane" policy now that the war was over. Diary entry by William Lyon Mackenzie King, 22 and 23 January 1947, "Diaries of William Lyon Mackenzie King," LAC, accessed 16 September 2019, http://www.bac-lac.gc.ca/eng/discover/politics-government/prime-ministers/william-lyon-mackenzie-king/Pages/diaries-william-lyon-mackenzie-king.aspx. Later, Robertson described the arguments to end the deportations as the "new liberalism" within cabinet. Letter to Norman A. Robertson from R.G. Robertson, 29 January 1947, file ar 23-16: "Treatment of Japanese," vol. 2089, RG 25 (Department of External Affairs fonds), LAC.

30 For a discussion of public memory of parallel policies in the American context, see Caroline Chung Simpson, *An Absent Presence: Japanese Americans in Postwar American Culture, 1945–1960* (Durham: Duke University Press, 2001).

31 Different societies take different paths in memory of historical injustice, weaving very different narratives for their publics. See, for instance, James Edward Young, *The Texture of Memory: Holocaust Memorials and Meaning* (New Haven: Yale University Press, 1993). Roy Miki writes that, for many Japanese Canadians, "the fact that the government had never acknowledged the injustices meant that their innocence had never been publicly declared, which in effect also meant that they were still assumed guilty." The silence engendered "inward feelings of guilt that they had somehow brought the

wrath of Canadians upon themselves" (*Re-Shaping Memory, Owning History: Through the Lens of Japanese Canadian Redress* [Burnaby: Japanese Canadian National Museum, 2002], 26); Likewise, Sunahara describes how, being told by the government that they were uprooted, dispossessed, and dispersed "because they had failed to assimilate," the Nisei "blamed themselves for what had happened to them" (Sunahara, *The Politics of Racism*, 149). This compounded the silences of the traumas of the internment era that, as delicately portrayed by oral historian Pamela Sugiman, continue to have lasting consequences on survivors and their families: Pamela Sugiman, "Memories of Internment: Narrating Japanese Canadian Women's Life Stories," *The Canadian Journal of Sociology* 29, no. 3 (2004): 359–88.

32 Memorandum for Heeney by R.G. Robertson, 23 January 1947, file J-25-1: "Japanese in Canada. 1947–49 (2)," vol. 84, RG 2 B2, LAC.

33 Press release, 24 January 1947, file 3851: "WWII Japanese Canadians (3)," vol. 361, MG 26 J4, LAC.

34 Ibid.

35 Memoranda for King by R.G. Robertson, 11 January 1947, file: "Japanese in Canada 2 of 6," vol. 1, MG 31 E87, LAC.

36 Letter to Colin Gibson from King, 13 February 1947, file 55908 part 2.1: "Japanese Property Claims Commission," vol. 2817, RG 117 (Office of the Custodian of Enemy Property fonds), LAC. Following the 24 January announcement, Japanese Canadians and their legal representatives wrote to the Office of the Custodian and to cabinet, inquiring as to the nature of the proposed mechanism. Examples include Letter to Department of the Secretary of State (Office of the Custodian, Japanese Evacuation Section) from Alfred Best on behalf of Kenkichi Nagata, file 55908, pt. 2.1, vol. 2817, RG 117, LAC; Letter to Kenneth W. Wright from Shears, 5 February 1947, ibid.; Letter to King from Andrew Brewin, 30 January 1947, ibid.; Letter to Director, Department of the Secretary of State, Office of the Custodian from George T. Tamaki, 3 February 1947, ibid.; Letter to Frank G. Shears from J. Arthur MacLennan, 5 February 1947, ibid.

37 Letter to Wright from Shears, 15 February 1947, ibid.

38 Ibid.

39 Letter to Mathieu from Wright, 13 February 1947, ibid.; Letter to Wright from Shears, 15 February 1947, ibid.

40 Ibid.; Letter to O'Meara from Shears, 15 February 1947, ibid.

41 Letter to Wright from Shears, 27 February 1947, file 55908, pt. 2.2, vol. 2817, RG 117, LAC.

42 Memorandum for Secretary of State by Wright, 3 February 1947, file 55908, pt. 2.1, vol. 2817, RG 117, LAC.

43 As of 1942, Japanese Canadians "were required to surrender their businesses and positions … and generally speaking," he wrote, "their chances of earning a livelihood were cut off." Memorandum for Gibson by Wright, 17 February 1947, ibid.

44 On property destruction, see chapter 7.

45 Ibid. The issue of chattels, however, was delicate. According to the orders in council that vested Japanese Canadians' property in the care of the Office of the Custodian, the office was accountable for *any* property left in the protected area. PC 1942-1665, 4 March 1942, file 2516G, vol. 1750, RG 2-A-1-a, LAC. For an account of the Office of the Custodian as a trustee, see chapter 8.

46 In one letter he presented a summary of letters from Japanese Canadians protesting the forced sale of their property. Shears explained to Wright that, though the office

had received more than 200 "such letters," "it must not be thought ... that the above figures indicate that other Japanese are satisfied." Shears then described the conditions under which the properties were sold, offering context. The protests expressed outrage, betrayal, shock, and disbelief. Comparing his selections to the complete collection he drew from, Stanger-Ross and Blomley suggest that Shears selected letters that conveyed the "anger simmering in almost all of the protests" (chapter 4, 131).

47 Letter to Wright from Shears (2), 27 February 1947, file 55908 pt. 2.2, vol. 2817, RG 117, LAC.

48 Under the subheading "Real Estate," Shears elucidated: "It is possible of course that the Japanese idea of value might not coincide with the market value, but in my opinion a property established market value should be the only basis for a claim in this Commission." Regarding equipment, he explained: "Certain types of equipment in use by the Japanese were definitely old fashioned and while capable of producing revenue in the hands of Japanese, do not have value equivalent to the Japanese idea of its worth." Likewise, for greenhouses, according to Shears, "quite a discrepancy exist[ed] between the Japanese valuation and the amount at which some of the property was sold" (ibid).

49 Letter to O'Meara from Wright, 15 February 1947, file 55908, pt. 2.1, vol. 2817, RG 117, LAC.

50 The Cabinet Committee on Japanese Claims was created 10 March and then promptly amalgamated with the Committee on Japanese Problems on 17 April into the Cabinet Committee on Japanese Questions.

51 The Undersecretary of State Ephraim H. Coleman and the Secretary of State Colin W.G. Gibson transformed the briefs into reports and draft recommendations to the Cabinet Committee on Japanese Problems for a potential inquiry. These reports echoed the warnings of "thousands of claims" that could not be "substantiated in the court of law" and that Japanese Canadians had "inflated ideas as to the value of their assets" and, thus, "grossly exaggerated" claims. Memorandum for Cabinet, 28 February 1947, [edited 3 March 1947], file 2203: "Special Cabinet Committee on Claims by Japanese Evacuees – 1947," vol. 35, RG 36 27 (Department of Labour fonds, Japanese Division series), LAC; Memorandum for Gibson by Wright, 27 March 1947, file 23-2-2-5 pt. 2, vol. 641, RG 27 (Department of Labour fonds), LAC.

52 The committee comprised of Ian Mackenzie, James L. Ilsley, Humphrey Mitchel, Arthur MacNamara, and Wright.

53 Familiar with the dispossession policies from their development, Deputy Minister of Justice Frederick P. Varcoe developed this document. Minutes, Cabinet Committee on Japanese Problems, 24 March 1947, file 50076 40, vol. 470, RG 25, LAC; Report, "JAP 5," undated, file: "Japanese in Canada 1 of 6," vol. 1, MG 31 E7, LAC.

54 Later, when Japanese Canadians and their allies called for the claims to be expanded, Gibson explained that compensation must be considered in the broader landscape of Canadian politics. Veterans, he explained, had also abandoned their businesses during the war when they went to fight for Canada. To compensate Japanese Canadians in an analogous circumstance, he argued, would be perceived as privileged treatment. He said that, in this light, their claims were not realistic. Letter to Henry I. Bird from Gibson, 11 July 1947, file 55908 part 8: "Japanese Property Claims Commission," vol. 2817, RG 117, LAC; Letter to Bird from Gibson, 23 July 1947, ibid.

55 Report, "JAP 5," 27 March 1947, file: "Japanese in Canada 1 of 6," vol. 1, MG 31 E87, LAC. These edits were likely made at the Cabinet Committee on Japanese Questions meeting,

2 April 1947 (Minutes, Cabinet Committee on Japanese Questions, file J-25-1, vol. 84, RG 2 B2, LAC).

56 Minutes, Cabinet Committee on Japanese Questions, file: "Japanese in Canada 1 of 6," vol. 1, MG 31 E87, LAC.

57 Letter to Minister of Justice from Varcoe, 22 April 1947, file 55908, pt. 2.2, vol. 2817, RG 117, LAC.

58 Ibid.

59 Ibid. (my italics).

60 Memorandum for the cabinet by R. Ranger, 28 April 1947, file C-20-5: "Cabinet documents from between 1944–1949. [nos. 416–520, 1947]," vol. 66, RG 2 B2, LAC.

61 Memorandum, Frederick P. Varcoe, 18 July 1947, file J-25-1, vol. 84, RG 2 B2, LAC.

62 Letter to N.A. Robertson from R.G. Robertson, 13 May 1947, file: "Japanese in Canada (1 of 6)," vol. 1, MG 31 E87, LAC.

63 Chapter 8; Adachi, *The Enemy That Never Was*, 324–5; Sunahara, *The Politics of Racism*, 136; Bangarth, *Voices Raised in Protest*, 145.

64 The organized campaign for property compensation began in 1946. It built on the momentum garnered in the fight against the policy of deportation of Japanese Canadians that emerged in the year prior. Riding the wave of opposition, the CCJC prepared a campaign to demand compensation. They collaborated with the Japanese Canadian Committee for Democracy, who designed a survey to evaluate property losses in the Toronto area. Letter campaigns against the discriminatory policies had long included calls for fair compensation for economic harms. The evidence from the survey would prove their losses. When the Privy Council in London announced that the deportation orders in council were legal on 2 December 1946, the CCJC called on the government to rescind the orders, end restrictions, and announced that "fair compensation will be made for the grievous property losses that [Japanese Canadians] have sustained through no fault of their own" (Co-Operative Committee on Japanese Canadians news bulletin, "A Call to Action," 14 September 1946, file 5, vol. 1, MG 30 D200, LAC; "Economic Loss Survey of British Columbia Evacuees," 30 November 1946, file 10: "File 10 Memoranda: Japanese Canadian organizations 1946–1950 NJCCA, Slocan Valley Nisei Organization, JCCD," vol. 1, MG 30 D200, LAC; Press release by the Co-Operative Committee on Japanese Canadians, undated, file 2, vol. 1, MG 30 D200, LAC. Sunahara, *The Politics of Racism*, 136. For examples of claims submitted by property owners in the Slocan Valley in 1946, see file 23-2-6-9, pt. 1: "Compensation for Japanese Evacuees," vol. 653, RG27, LAC.

65 Letter to King from Brewin, 30 January 1947, file 55908 pt. 2.1, vol. 2817, RG 117, LAC; Letter to Shears from Brewin, 17 February 1947, file 55908 pt. 2.2, vol. 2817, RG 117, LAC.

66 Ibid.

67 Letter to Gibson from Brewin, 2 March 1947, file 4: "Canadian Civil Liberties Union, 1947," vol. 2, MG 28 V1 (Co-Operative Committee on Japanese Canadians fonds), LAC; Letter to Gibson from Brewin, 19 March 1948, file 55908 pt. 2.2, vol. 2817, RG 117, LAC; Letter to Gibson from Brewin, 24 March 1947, ibid. On the US claims process in comparative perspective, see Greg Robinson, *A Tragedy of Democracy: Japanese Confinement in North America* (New York: Columbia University Press, 2009), 274–83.

68 For examples, see Letter to T. Tamaki from R.G. Robertson, 10 February 1947, file 55908 pt. 2.1, vol. 2817, RG 117, LAC; Letter from Canadian Legion of the British Empire Service

League, 21 February 1947, file 55908 pt. 2.2, vol. 2817, RG 117, LAC; Roy, *The Triumph of Citizenship*, 242.

69 Adachi, *The Enemy That Never Was*, 324.

70 18 February, 14 April, 18 April, and 22–24 April, file 2: "Canada. Parliament. House of Commons. House of Commons Debates. [v. 86-87], February, 1947–December, 1947," box 14, F.G. Shears Papers, Thomas Fisher Rare Book Library, University of Toronto (hereafter Shears Papers).

71 "Not as Ordered," *Globe and Mail*, 19 June 1947, file 23: "Misc. Clippings 1945–53," vol. 3, MG 28 V1, LAC.

72 Sunahara, *The Politics of Racism*, 137.

73 Roy, *The Triumph of Citizenship*, 243.

74 Standing Committee on Public Accounts: Fourth Report, 4 June 1947, file 55908 pt. 3: "Japanese Property Claims Commission," vol. 2817, RG 117, LAC (my italics).

75 Such losses were significant. See chapter 7.

76 Enclosing a copy of the report to Glenn McPherson, the original director of the Vancouver Office of the Custodian of Enemy Property, Wright wrote that the "acquittal is pleasing to us all." On Saturday, 26 June, Wright, Coleman, and Gibson signed off on a revised order in council, striking out "at the time of evacuation" and replaced it with "at the time of sale, disposition or loss." Wright commented, "I doubt if this will please the Japanese claimants." Council approved the change later that week (Letter to Glenn W. McPherson from Wright, 18 June 1947, file 55908 pt. 3, vol. 2817, RG 117, LAC; Draft letter to Ilsley (unsigned but likely from Wright), 23 June 1947, ibid.; Letter to Coleman from Heeney, 27 June 1947, ibid.; Letter to E.A. Driedger from Wright, 30 July 1947, ibid.; Memorandum from Varcoe, 18 July 1947, file j-25-1: "Japanese in Canada. 1945–49," vol. 249, RG 2 B2, LAC.

77 Sunahara, *The Politics of Racism*, 137.

78 Letter to Thelma Scrambler from Donalda MacMillan, 4 August 1947, file: "Thompson, Grace 1," MG 30 C160 (Grace Thompson collection), LAC.

79 Press release by the Co-Operative Committee on Japanese Canadians, 24 July 1947, ibid.

80 Sunahara, *The Politics of Racism*, 137. For a description of the CCJC's correspondence with King and Ilsley that summer, see Letter to Scrambler from MacMillan, 14 August 1947, file: "Thompson, Grace 1," MG 30 C160 (Grace Thompson collection), LAC.

81 Though there was initially a considerable push to boycott the restrictive terms, Japanese Canadians agreed to go forward with the commission.

82 "Property Owners Will File Claims 'Under Protest,'" *The New Canadian*, 11 October 1947; "The Question of the Moment," *The New Canadian*, 13 September 1947; Adachi, *The Enemy That Never Was*, 326.

83 This included setting up a common fund into which claimants paid, if possible, one per cent of their total claim. This went towards legal costs and assured an adequate presentation of all claims. Sunahara, *The Politics of Racism*, 138. See also Miki, *Redress*, 112–14; Bangarth, *Voices Raised in Protest*, 146.

84 Roy Miki and Peter Nunoda ascribe (at least partial) culpability for the commission's failings to the CCJC. Miki and Nunoda simultaneously critique the CCJC (and particularly Andrew Brewin) for domineering leadership and the Nisei leadership for their submission to the committee's advice. Drawing from the meeting minutes and regular bulletins of the CCJC, Roy Miki and Peter Nunoda emphasize the hierarchical leader-

ship and paternalism of the organization in negotiations around compensation and commission process. Miki, *Redress*, 106; Nunoda, "A Community in Transition and Conflict."

85 Representing this group of claimants, Virtue attended many critical meetings with the CCJC and commission staff.

86 Michiko Midge Ayukawa, "Bearing the Unbearable," 16.

87 That is, $3,004.46.

88 Imagining Imada standing at the Bird Commission after the traumatic upheavals of internment and dispossession, Ayukawa writes that "it took a great deal of courage for Mrs Imada with her deep-seated resentment and disillusionment to appear before such an intimidating audience." Ayukawa, "Bearing the Unbearable," 16, 26.

89 Hearing transcript, 8 December 1947, case file 1: "Imada, Mrs Ito (Kamloops)," vol. 1, RG 33 69 (Bird Commission fonds), LAC, 10–12.

90 See RG 33-69 volumes 1 and 2, LAC.

91 "Confusing Jap Claims Delay Probe," *The Province*, 10 December 1947; "Japanese Claims Bring Tangled Problems Before Commission," *Victoria Daily Times*, 10 December 1947.

92 "Jap Commission May Set Record," *Vancouver News Herald*, 12 December 1947.

93 Letter to McMaster from Brewin, 26 January 1948, file 1–18: "Corr. Jan 1948," vol. 1, MG 32 C26 (Francis Andrew Brewin fonds), LAC; Telegram to Brewin from McMaster, 9 February 1948, file 1–19: "Corr. Feb 1948," vol. 1, MG 32 C26, LAC.

94 PC 1942-242, 22 January 1948, file 3738G, vol. 1988, RG 2-A-1-a, LAC. Sunahara, *The Politics of Racism*, 139.

95 Letter to Ilsley from Brewin, 30 June 1948, file 1-24: "Corr. June 1948," vol. 1, MG 32 C26, LAC; Letter to St Laurent from Brewin, 26 August 1948, file 1–26: "Corr. Aug 1948," vol. 1, MG 32 C26, LAC; Letter to Brewin from McMaster, 8 September 1948, file 1–27: "Corr. Sept 1948," vol. 1, MG 32 C26, LAC.

96 Letter to Brewin from Schumatcher, 22 December 1947, file 1–18, vol. 1, MG 32 C26, LAC.

97 Letter to Brewin from Tamaki, 30 December 1947, ibid.

98 Notes on Joint Committee Meetings of the Following Stated Committees on the Matter of Evacuation Losses Claims, 4 February 1950, file 10: "Memoranda: Japanese Canadian organizations 1946–1950 NJCCA, Slocan Valley Nisei Organization, JCCD," vol. 1, MG 30 D200, LAC.

99 He continued to remark on Bird's preferences as a judge: "I have also come to agree with you that he does not seem to be a judge who likes technical arguments and I think we should keep these to a minimum." Letter to McMaster from Brewin, 26 January 1948, file 1-18, vol. 1, MG 32 C26, LAC.

100 Another was the creation of subcommissions to hear hearings. These, heard by two subcommissioners, amounted to approximately 390 hearings. See Bird Commission Finding Aid, RG33 69, LAC.

101 Brewin circulated copies of this report to all CCJC lawyers. Letter to Ritchie and Huckvale from Brewin, 13 January 1948, file 1–18, vol. 1, MG 32 C26.

102 Memorandum for Mr Tanaka, undated, file 1–2, "Correspondence October- December, 1947," vol. 1, MG 30 E266 (Saul Mark Cherniack fonds), LAC.

103 The legal aids sat with the claimants, often in a hotel room, to record what they knew of their property's value and dispossession. Throughout the commission proceedings, the lawyers circulated notes on how best to prepare the files. Letter to Fred Nichikawa from Cherniack, 1 April 1948, file 1–4: "Corr. April 1948," vol. 1, MG 30 E266, LAC. For

examples of how Leckie prepared claims, see RG33 69 case files 6, 195, 99, 78, 86, 83, 119, 1053, 1056, LAC.

104 Letter to Brewin from McMaster, 27 January 1948, file 1–18, vol. 1, MG 32 C26, LAC.

105 Letter to Brewin from McMaster, 1 June 1948, file 1–24, vol. 1, MG 32 C26, LAC.

106 Hearing transcript, file "181 Yamamoto, Mrs Fujino (Vernon)," vol. 10, RG33 69, LAC, 3. Yamamoto's case file contained several photos of her family's home. One photo is an outlier, wherein the building is barely visible behind a group of thirty people. With elders sitting in front, it is a formal portrait of a family, dressed in formal wear. Rather than market value, the photo connotes establishment, prosperity, and community. Paired with her narrative of loss read by McMaster, Yamamoto's case file composed a claim for loss that extended beyond market value.

107 Appraisal form, case file: "69 – Hirowatari Hideaki (Kamloops)," vol. 4, RG33 69, LAC.

108 Appraisal form, case file: "1058 – Sasaki, Mrs Ino (Toronto)," vol. 53, RG33 69, LAC.

109 Chapters 3 and 4.

110 For a fuller account of claimants who pushed against these restrictions, consider the claims and Masue and Rinkichi Tagashira: Findlay, "The Bird Commission," chapter 3.

111 In correspondence with Japanese Canadians about their claims, Brewin, McMaster, and Cherniack's records contain evidence of this process. The hearing transcripts also show the process of amendments. Of seventy-two claims sampled (six of which were abandoned), the claimants' counsel amended thirty-six claims when they came before Commissioner Bird. See NNM, Campbell, Brazier, Fisher and McMaster Barristers and Solicitors fonds, series: "Japanese Claims: List of Claims Heard at Centres"; Files 1.3 and 1.4, vol. 1, MG 30 E266, LAC.

112 Saul Cherniack, interviewed by unknown, 1976, Vancouver, BC, tape 2010.23.3.4.29, pt. 1, Japanese Canadian Oral History Collection, Simon Fraser University Digital Collections, accessed 16 September 2019, http://digital.lib.sfu.ca/johc-413/interview-saul-cheriak.

113 Ibid.

114 "Japanese Property Claims Commission, Lethbridge Sub-Commission. Notes of Sub-Commissioner, His Honour Judge R.M. Edmanson," October 1948, file: 55908 part 7: "Japanese Property Claims Commission," vol. 2818, RG117, LAC.

115 Letter to Brewin from McMaster, 14 February 1948, file 1–19, vol. 1, MG 32 C26, LAC.

116 Ibid.

117 McPherson posited himself as an interlocutor and mediator who could aid Commissioner Bird and report to the Departments of Justice and of the Secretary of State. Letter to Coleman from McPherson, 4 February 1948, file 2–7: "Correspondence, memorandum, newspaper clippings, 1939–1948, 1985," box 2, McPherson Fonds, UBC RBSC; Letter to McPherson from Coleman, 13 February 1948, file 2–7: "Correspondence, memorandum, newspaper clippings, 1939–1948, 1985," box 2, McPherson Fonds, RBSC; "Report re Japanese Property Claims Commission," Glen McPherson, undated, ibid. For a fuller portrait of Glenn McPherson and his role as the executive director of the Office of the Custodian, see chapter 5.

118 Instead of continuing the hearings, Bird proposed that he give the Crown counsel a list of cases where he had discerned "no claim" and have Crown counsel "argue the question of a non-suit at the present stage." Letter to Brewin from MacLennan, 16 March 1948, file 1–20: "Corr. Mar 1948," vol. 1, MG 32 C26, LAC.

119 Adachi also noted that, as early as February, the "CCJC lawyers had been worrying that

the entire issue would be determined on the basis of expediency." Adachi described the federal government officials' concern to "whitewash" the Office of the Custodian (Adachi, *The Enemy That Never Was*, 406, n53).

120 Letter to MacLennan from Brewin, 18 March 1948, file 1-20, vol. 1, MG 32 C26, LAC.

121 Letter from Gordon Upton to Bird, 22 May 1948, file 55908 part 6: "Japanese Property Claims Commission," vol. 2818, RG117, LAC.

122 Letter to Colgan from Bird, 27 May 1948, file 55908, pt. 6, vol. 2818, RG117, LAC.

123 Letter to McMaster from Brewin, 1 June 1948, file 1–24, vol. 1, MG 32 C26, LAC; Letter to McMaster from Brewin, 2 September 1948, file 1–27, vol. 1, MG 32 C26, LAC; Letter to Brewin from McMaster, 13 September 1948, ibid.

124 Letter to Brewin from McMaster, 1 June 1948, file 1–24: "Corr. June 1948," vol. 1, MG 32 C26, LAC.

125 Sunahara, *The Politics of Racism*, 140–1.

126 McMaster expressed reluctance to ask claimants for further funds. Letter to Brewin from McMaster, 9 August 1948, file 1–26, MG 32 C26, LAC. Independently, Hunter and Bird approached the CCJC lawyers with the suggestion to shorten the hearings, and they began to consider opening negotiations. Hunter approached Brewin with the proposal in early September. Bird made a similar suggestion to McMaster around the same time. Letter to McMaster from Brewin, 2 September 1948, file 1–27, vol. 1, MG 32 C26, LAC; Letter to Brewin from McMaster, 13 September 1948, ibid.

127 Report for Varcoe by John W.G. Hunter, 7 May 1948, file 55908 pt. 6, vol. 2818, RG 117, LAC.

128 Despite the decision to treat the claims categorically, the commission eventually did hear the testimony of all the Bird Commission claimants. Following the agreement to determine loss and award claims according to categories of property, the hearings were further restricted to testifying to the Custodian's management of Japanese Canadian's property. If the Bird Commission was Japanese Canadians' opportunity to testify directly to the state, it was under severely restricted circumstances.

129 Sunahara, *The Politics of Racism*, 142.

130 Many claimants were unhappy with the settlement. Adachi describes the final signing of the release forms in 1951 as an "acrimonious, often vituperative confrontation" with the CCJC. The Toronto Claimants' Committee, a group of approximately 256 property owners, laid blame for the paltry compensation at the hands of the CCJC, for their advice to accept the terms of reference, to accept the settlement early, and their interpretations of law (Adachi, *The Enemy That Never Was*, 333. See also: Miki, *Redress*, 126).

131 Report, file 1, box 5, Shears Papers.

132 "Paid in Full," *The Vancouver Sun*, 14 June 1950, 4.

133 "Japanese Given Over $1 Million," *The Vancouver Daily Province*, 13 June 1950, 1.

134 Tina Loo, "Dan Cranmer's Potlatch: Law as Coercion, Symbol, and Rhetoric in British Columbia, 1884–1951," *Canadian Historical Review* 2, no. 73 (1992): 165.

PART FOUR

Dispossession Is Permanent

CHAPTER 10

The Economic Impacts of the Dispossession

Jordan Stanger-Ross and the Landscapes of Injustice Research Collective

Figure 10.1 Griffin Lake Road Camp, 1942. Tsunetaro Murakami with cane in hand, Peter smiling in foreground.

In the spring of 1942, the Canadian government uprooted Tsunetaro Murakami from his twenty-seven-acre farm on Salt Spring Island. Officials took him to the Griffin Lake road camp, near Revelstoke, in the interior of British Columbia. His son Peter, who worked on the mainland as a millhand but listed Salt Spring as his home, was interned with his father. At Griffin Lake, the two toiled alongside other Japanese Canadians to build provincial highways. Tsunetaro, who was almost sixty, might well have found it back-breaking labour. In a surviving photograph of the road camp, the farmer stands closed-lipped at the edge of a work crew comprised for the most part of men decades his junior, a light wooden cane clutched in his right hand. His son, Peter, smiles, seated cross-legged on the rocky foreground (figure 10.1).

A naturalized Canadian, resident in the country for more than three decades, Tsunetaro had purchased his Salt Spring Island property in two transactions in the early 1930s. He grew hay, asparagus, raspberries, and strawberries on the farm, logging its back acreage. Located on the main road to the island's central village, his farm's close proximity to a school, stores, and local churches made the land particularly valuable. Tsunetaro likely imagined soon passing the property to Peter, the sole survivor of his two children.[1]

Instead, the Murakami property was badly mishandled by the Custodian of Enemy Property. It was initially leased to a Mr Jaggs, who, despite renting two separate internee-owned properties on the island, refused to pay rent to any Japanese Canadian (on the grounds of "what the Japanese had [purportedly] done to his sister"), threatened officers of the Custodian with physical assault, and stole belongings from the Murakamis when he was finally evicted.[2] The Custodian subsequently sold the farm without the permission of its owner to the director of the Veterans Land Act, one of hundreds of properties acquired for the benefit of returning soldiers. Stripped of his home and lands, Tsunetaro boarded a ship in exile to Japan in 1946, leaving half of his remaining estate (just over $700) to his son who remained in Canada, still barred from the Pacific coast.[3] Peter should have inherited far more.

This chapter tells the subsequent history of the dispossession of properties like the Murakami farm, tracing the history of real estate transactions following the dispossession, analyzing what happened after the lands of Japanese Canadians were sold by the Custodian of Enemy Property. This analysis can provide only a limited perspective on the legacies of the dispossession: the value of homes and property, as we have argued throughout this volume, cannot be reduced to a market of exchange. But this perspective is important. The monetary losses of Japanese Canadians give material expression to the state's disregard for their value as people, citizens, and communities. For their part, Japanese Canadians have sought since the 1940s to comprehend and express the economic impacts of the policy.[4] Historians have not attempted an analysis of Japanese Canadian losses. This failure leaves an additional gap: the history of benefit.[5] When Japanese Canadians lost their lands, others gained. While some scholars have gestured to this flipside of property loss, none has undertaken its study. This chapter proposes a new analysis of the dispossession in which economic losses and benefits are counted.[6]

I begin by examining the question most commonly asked about the dispossession: Did the Custodian sell Japanese Canadian–owned properties for less than market value? This question has been answered before, most notably by a postwar royal commission inquiry into Japanese Canadian losses.[7] Using title histories assembled by Landscapes of Injustice researchers, I test the conclusions of the Bird Commission, and largely, to my surprise, corroborate its conclusions, even with respect to urban real estate that it hardly investigated. Having examined the question of market value

I then turn to the longer-run legacies of loss, which, I argue, are both quantifiable and significant. This chapter emphasizes that the most significant losses of Japanese Canadians came not by comparison with the wider market at the time of the forced sales but rather by comparison with the people who purchased their lands and benefitted over time. The costs of the loss of freedom – the freedom not to sell and, barring that, to at least reinvest – can only be appreciated within history.

"Fair market value"

From the time that state officials sold Japanese Canadian–owned property, the prices they received have been controversial. Hundreds of Japanese Canadians immediately insisted that their property had been sold far below its worth.[8] Their protests encouraged federal officials to create the Bird Commission, whose terms of reference made "fair market value" the focus of its analysis. Before Landscapes of Injustice, the two historical studies most attentive to property loss – Sunahara's *The Politics of Racism* and Adachi's *The Enemy That Never Was* – assessed the public and archival records of the Custodian and of the commission, both concurring that the sale prices were too low.[9] At the same time, both Sunahara and Adachi, and other scholars, criticize the Bird Commission for using an analysis of market value to divert attention from larger questions of injustice and harm.[10] Still, it matters whether officials sold farms, homes, and businesses for pennies on the dollar. Sales below market value, especially deliberately so, would seem to evidence a particularly stark form of state malfeasance. Absent detailed analysis, this kind of wrongdoing has sometimes, indeed, been assumed.

The most systematic analysis of "fair market value" to date remains the Bird Commission.[11] The commission's formal mandate was to inquire into the claims of Japanese Canadian property owners that "real and personal property vested in the Custodian ... was disposed of ... for less than the fair market value thereof at the time of sale resulting in loss to the claimants."[12] Though rightfully maligned for these limited terms of reference and its failure, even within those terms, to fully consider the material harms of the internment, the commission did take seriously the prices paid, examining sales to the director of the Veterans' Land Act (VLA sales) with particular rigor.[13]

Operating between 1947 and 1950, the commission compiled more than 25,000 pages of transcript collected in hearings across the country, including testimony by Japanese Canadian claimants, state officials, real estate agents, and appraisers. It included 8,996 exhibits filed, among these the contents of Custodian of Enemy Property case files, which had been made available to counsel for the claimants. It considered both real estate – which will be discussed in this chapter – and other forms of personal and moveable property. Justice Bird concluded that federal bureaucrats performed their tasks unevenly. He found that 741 VLA sales (which constituted almost half of all sales by the Custodian of Enemy Property and the majority of claims brought to the commission) "were substantially lower than the fair market value of the lands."[14] By contrast, he was most confident that urban property in Vancouver had been sold at "prices substantially equivalent to the market value," a determination he made in considering the appraisal and sale process, the assessed values of the property sold, and expert testimony.[15]

In the case of the VLA sales, administrative failures had already generated public controversy, so Justice Bird was compelled to carefully examine claims in this category.[16] The commission considered (1) appraisals of the farms conducted by the Soldier Settlement Board, which provided the basis for the VLA sales prices, (2) alternative appraisals of a small number of properties made by an advisory group at the time, (3) prices paid for forty-three comparable properties that the Custodian sold to other purchasers, (4) prices paid for eleven comparable properties sold by Japanese Canadians prior to their uprooting, (5) a reappraisal of the properties by Fred Clement, dean of Agriculture at UBC, and (6) a comparative analysis of the ratio between assessed values and sale prices, with forced sales to the VLA tested against hundreds of free market sales of comparable properties in the same period, complied by Anthony Corbus (a lawyer for Japanese Canadian claimants) and reviewed by UBC economist George Drummond.[17] Based on these combined methods, Justice Bird concluded that the VLA sales netted Japanese Canadians just over half of their real value: he recommended that all claimants in this category be awarded a standard supplement of an additional 80 per cent of the original sale prices, and in many individual cases the commission recommended still higher payments.[18]

No similarly rigorous approach was adopted for the other categories of real estate.[19] Instead Justice Bird largely trusted what he regarded as sound administrative process and accepted the narrative of government officials that, when the process went awry, it was as a result of factors outside of their control. The report, in general, followed the commissioner's conviction that "the very onerous task imposed upon the Director of the Custodian's office at Vancouver … was competently performed, with due regard to the interest of the owners."[20] Where he found the administrative process unhampered, as in the city of Vancouver, Justice Bird concluded that Japanese Canadian–owned real estate had sold at fair market value. Where he saw minor impediments, as in rural lands sold to buyers other than the VLA, he suggested minor awards (10 per cent). Justice Bird undertook careful study and proposed significant payments only for VLA sales, where he saw serious administrative problems.

Justice Bird's perspective on the Custodian of Enemy Property is not supported by the larger body of research reported in this book, which finds instead that the Vancouver office was directed by a thinly veiled racist, could have done much more to protect the property of Japanese Canadians, and played an active role in making the destructive decision to force sales without consent.[21] Rather than a well-intentioned state agency suffering at the mercy of external circumstances, we see the Custodian as unprepared and improvisatory but very much complicit in the harms of the dispossession.[22] Our analysis is thus much closer to that of Thomas Shoyama, a Japanese Canadian leader of the time, who, in his 1948 brief for the Bird Commission, described the Office of the Custodian as:

> Caught unprepared ... [by a task] of such magnitude and complexity that it was not able to find personnel capable of realizing all the programme entailed ... [and] unable to formulate policies and procedures adequate to cope with the problems as they arose. As a consequence, there was unnecessary suffering and hardship on the part of the people and loss of economic resources on a large scale.[23]

With access to the internal documents of the Custodian, historians can observe that the government lacked not only the capacity but also the will to adequately protect the property of Japanese Canadians. Even without such proof, Shoyama offered a precise analysis: the realities of the Custodian's activity mean that all of it, not just the VLA sales, should be subjected to rigorous testing, a task at which the Bird Commission fell short.

Not trusting, as Justice Bird did, the Office of the Custodian to have sought fair outcomes for Japanese Canadians in cases other than the VLA sales, our project conducted comparative analysis of the real estate market in the Powell Street neighbourhood, comparing sales by the Custodian to free market sales in the same area. Here Justice Bird claimed that sound administrative process meant that Japanese Canadian–owned properties sold at market value. What would analysis show? We also compared the Custodian's VLA sales with a sample of free market rural sales, replicating a key category of evidence considered by the Bird Commission, but analysing differently.

In both cases, our analyses largely confirmed the conclusions of the Bird Commission with respect to market value. Take, to begin, the Powell Street neighbourhood, where no prior comparative analysis has been conducted. The neighbourhood had been home to Japanese Canadians since the start of the twentieth century: a bustling area of stores, boarding houses, restaurants, schools, and modest houses. Japanese Canadians owned diverse property there, ranging from the large and iconic Tamura building to small and even dilapidated structures.[24]

Japanese Canadians were never alone in the neighbourhood, as either residents or property owners. They owned 122 (39 per cent) of the 312 properties that sold between 1942, when the Custodian assumed control of their real estate, and 1949, when restrictions were finally lifted.[25] The prices paid by purchasers in the 122 forced sales were lower than those paid in 190 free market transactions over the same period.[26] The free market sales in the neighbourhood netted an average price of $149 per square metre

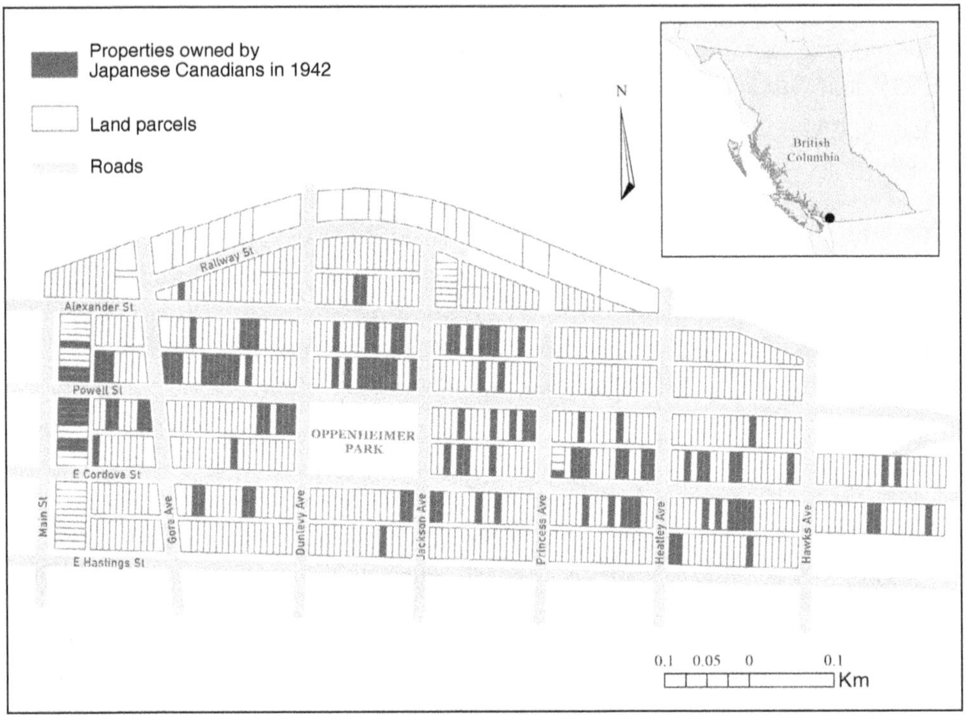

Figure 10.2 The Powell Street Neighbourhood Study Area. Researchers collected data for all properties in a twenty-three-square-block area, within which Japanese Canadians comprised at least 40 per cent of the residential population in 1941.

of land (prices in 2018 dollars), whereas forced sales by the Custodian generated an average price of $135, seemingly a discount of just over 9 per cent.[27] But this straightforward comparison overlooks pertinent information about the value of the lands in question: even before the state seizure of Japanese Canadian–owned real estate, their lands tended to sell for less. Indeed, at prior dates we see a much larger gap between the prices of the properties in question. Japanese Canadians had paid an average of $248 per square metre to buy their properties, whereas other purchasers had paid an average of $456.[28] Taking into account these prior prices, analyses revealed no material disadvantage for having the Custodian of Enemy Property as the seller, as against selling in the free market.[29] Our analyses support Justice Bird's conclusion that the Custodian sold Vancouver properties for market value at the time of sale.

Another approach to the question of "fair market value" may be useful in testing this observation. Real estate market data permit not only analysis of earlier transactions – those exchanges antecedent to internment era sales – but also subsequent ones. We are able to ask what happened to properties after their sales by the Custodian and, by comparison, what happened to properties sold within the free market.[30] If sales by

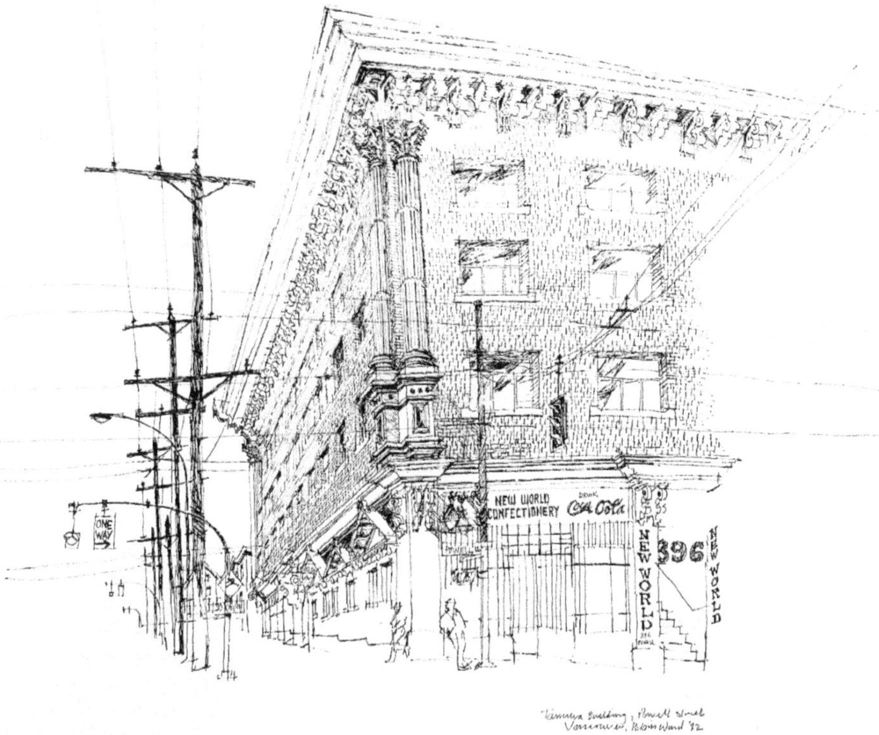

Figure 10.3 Tamura Building on Powell Street. Japanese Canadians owned diverse kinds of real estate in the neighbourhood. This iconic building was commission by Shinkichi Tamura in 1912 and later depicted by artist Robin Ward. With the New World Hotel above and commerce at street level, the Tamura building was perhaps the most expensive Japanese Canadian–owned property in the city.

the Custodian were significantly below market value, then we might expect to see particular subsequent advantage to those purchasers. We might see people who bought low from the Custodian holding properties for just a short period of time and flipping them for gain or, failing that, to at least have made particular windfall profits when they did sell.

Analysis of the real estate market in the Powell Street area, however, reveals no such evidence. Buyers from the Custodian, in short, gained no special advantage over other purchasers, that is, people who bought during the same period of time but in free market transactions.[31] For the properties on which subsequent sale data are available (118 lots sold by the Custodian and 179 comparison lots) no statistically significant differences could be discerned between people who bought from the Custodian and those who bought from other sellers. The timing of resale provides little evidence of "flipping." All purchasers resold on a wide range of subsequent dates: a small number held their properties for a just a few months before reselling, others held onto their properties for decades. On average, purchasers from the Custodian tended to sell somewhat sooner – just over eight years after their initial purchase, as against almost ten years for other buyers. With so much variability among resale dates, however, this mean difference was not statistically significant. When buyers from the Custodian did sell, almost all made substantial profits, gaining an average $185 (2018) per square metre in value. In a span of eight years, on average, they more than doubled their initial investments. But such gains were not particular to them; their free market counterparts also profited, selling for $304 (2018) more per square metre than they had paid, tripling their initial investments. The difference between gains achieved by the two sets of buyers (again, due to great internal variability) is not statistically significant.

Purchasers from the Custodian in Powell Street benefited greatly from their investments but not because they had gained a special advantage over other buyers. Instead, they did well because they bought at an advantageous time for all purchasers – a point to which I will return below. For the moment, however, observe that the real estate data do not allow us to sharply distinguish buyers from the Custodian from those in the free market in the Powell Street neighbourhood.

An important caveat is necessary. The Custodian of Enemy Property sales comprised a large proportion of the market in the neighbourhood in 1940s, so we must assume that those sales impacted the prices of other nearby properties. A comparison with price trends in the wider city, which is beyond the scope of this analysis, might yield different conclusions. However, that approach would require its own caveats because the East End neighbourhood had always been distinctive within Vancouver, as it remains to this day. Extrapolation from the wider city to a marginalized neighbourhood could yield only tentative conclusions. The presumed impact of custodial sales on the local market means that unequivocal conclusions cannot be reached. Nonetheless, the fact remains: contrary to my expectations when I began this work, there is no conclusive evidence here for disputing Justice Bird's conclusions about the sale of Vancouver properties.

As in the case of the Powell Street neighbourhood, retrospective analyses of VLA sales in an important area of Japanese Canadian rural settlement, Maple Ridge, largely corroborate the conclusions of the Bird Commission. Japanese immigrants began farming in the Maple Ridge area in the first years of the twentieth century, pioneering berry cultivation, especially of strawberries. In 1906 Jiro Inouye, an immigrant from Saga prefecture, bought twenty acres in the area becoming the first Japanese Canadian to own farmland. Over the next generation, more than one hundred fellow immigrants and their children followed him to Maple Ridge, as moist alluvial soil and the Canadian Pacific Railway line on the north flank of the Fraser River made it ideal for growing, processing, and moving berries to a mass market. In 1942 Japanese Canadian farmers – organized together into a mutual association – occupied an important

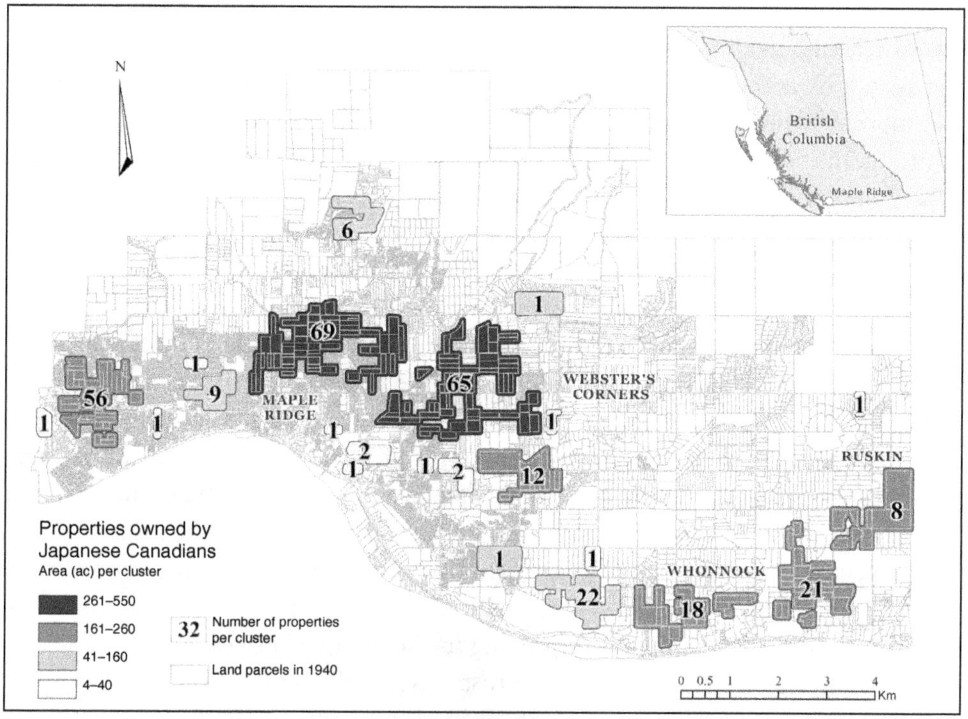

Figure 10.4 Maple Ridge Farms. The first site of Japanese Canadian farming, Maple Ridge was also the most popular among members of the community. Japanese Canadian–owned farms are highlighted, with darker shading indicating a larger acreage in a given grouping of Japanese Canadian–owned farms. The numbers indicate the count of Japanese Canadian farmers in each grouping. Our data come from two clusters on this map, the one indicating sixty-nine Japanese Canadian–owned properties in centre and the one indicating twenty-two Japanese Canadian–owned properties to the southeast.

position in the market and owned hundreds of valuable parcels of land in Maple Ridge.[32] Even as the farmers packed their belongings to internment, agents of the Soldier Settlement Board began to circle the farms, planning their acquisition for soldiers returning from war. In 1944, when the director of the Veterans Land Act acquired virtually all of the Japanese Canadian–owned farms in Maple Ridge and elsewhere in the lower mainland, he did so, Justice Bird concluded, at prices far below "fair market value." The commission recommended that all claimants in this category be awarded significant supplements to the original sale prices. Our analyses in Maple Ridge support the commission's course of action.

The market in Maple Ridge bore little resemblance to its urban counterpart. Large farm properties – averaging more than 7.5 acres (the largest among them almost sixty acres) – changed hands in the 1940s for much lower prices per square metre than land in the city, just as they had in decades prior. The number of transactions in this analysis is much smaller than the Powell Street neighbourhood: in this case I contrast fifty-three sales by the Custodian against thirty-five comparison sales between 1942 and 1949.[33] Nonetheless, the difference between the Custodian and the free market was more evident in Maple Ridge than in Powell Street. Other vendors sold their farms for an average price of $3.60 per square metre of land. The Custodian sold for a fraction of this price, netting only 40 cents, just over 10 per cent of the free market sale price per acreage.

As in the case of the Powell Street neighbourhood, it is important to take into consideration prior land prices, and, as in the city, Japanese Canadians had tended to purchase more affordable real estate. They had paid an average of just 30 cents per square metre when they bought their farms whereas the comparison properties had been purchased for an average of $1.43 per square metre (prices in 2018 dollars). But here an important difference seems to emerge, confirming the analysis of the Bird Commission. The sellers in the comparison sample, who had bought their land within a very similar timeframe to Japanese Canadians and then sold in the 1940s, saw much greater gains, with prices rising, on average, by 150 per cent.[34] In his testimony to the Bird Commission, UBC's dean of agriculture explained that the market for lower mainland farms was strong and improving in this period: "Prices had begun to advance about 1939," he testified, "but the prospects picked up materially in '41 and very materially in '42 and '43."[35] Records of the federal government offer further confirmation of this price trend, with one Soldier Settlement Board official urging a hasty purchase from the Custodian because "I do not look forward with any pleasure to the prices that will have to be paid," at later dates in the bull market.[36]

Forced to sell, Japanese Canadians did not benefit appropriately from rising land prices. Instead, based upon what the Bird Commission found to be demonstrably flawed assessments by the Soldier Settlement Board, Japanese Canadians in Maple Ridge earned only 33 per cent more (40 cents per square metre) when their farms sold than what they had paid upon purchase (30 cents). Had the sale of their properties reflected the wider market of exchange, they might have been expected to earn approximately 75 cents per square metre, almost twice what they had received from the VLA. Justice Bird's standard recommended adjustment, applied to the average sale price of the sample properties in this analysis, would have brought them close to 72 cents per square metre.[37]

Many of the Japanese Canadian owners of our sample of fifty-three properties received significantly more than the standard recommended awards from the Bird Commission, perhaps reflecting adjustments for inflation in the intervening years, the recognition that prices were continuing to rise in real dollar terms, and/or acknowledgment that in some cases the government's appraisals of the properties contained errors. For example Kankichi Onagi, who purchased a Maple Ridge farm in 1924, received an award of 110 per cent ($810 for a property sold to the VLA for $736). Saul

Cherniack, his legal representative at a commission hearing in Winnipeg, Manitoba in 1948, argued that the Soldier Settlement Board appraisal had undercounted the cleared acreage and fruit trees on the farm and misdated the farmhouse.[38] The commission heard the claim of Sakiye Takasaki, another owner in our sample, at New Denver in June 1948. The Takasakis, who had also farmed in Maple Ridge since the 1920s, argued that the Soldier Settlement Board had undervalued their fruit trees, overlooked two structures on the property, over-estimated the age of the buildings on the farm, and mischaracterized the quality of its soil. Takasaki, whose lands had been forcibly sold for a total of $1,433 in 1944 was awarded $2,176, or 152 per cent of the original sale price.[39] In both instances, Japanese Canadians estimated their farms as worth far more than they received, even including the award amounts. They described their investments of labour and insisted they would not have sold by choice. The Bird Commission did not compensate them for their loss of autonomy, a loss that had, as I will argue below, quantifiable material consequences. And yet, narrowing our view to contemplate the market at the time of the sales, our comparative analyses reinforce the claims of Justice Bird that he had accurately assessed "fair market value" and made appropriate awards in this respect.

The process by which the Bird Commission came to be defined by market value at the time of sale – rather than the broader economic impacts of the uprooting and internment – have been detailed elsewhere.[40] Nonetheless, it is important to note that, despite its limitations, the question of "fair market value" at the time of sale is necessary to an assessment of the material harms of the dispossession. Our data suggest that the commission was competent in this task. Further analysis would be necessary to determine whether other urban markets and other rural sales were accurately portrayed. However, the two categories analyzed here cover the majority of the sales and provide no grounds for disputing the commission's conclusions in respect to securing the "fair market value" of seized real estate for its dispossessed owners.

Where the commission erred, and erred gravely, was in declaring this analysis sufficient to capture the whole story of material loss. Clearly this was not the case. Shoyama's brief for the commission, for example, suggested that valuations of property include analysis of "earning value assuming the parcel is to be developed to the highest usefulness possible in its location," along with other future-oriented factors normally taken into consideration by potential investors in land.[41] That the commission ignored such considerations means that it cannot have the final say on material losses.

Choice, opportunity, and loss

We can only understand the losses suffered by Japanese Canadians by going beyond the market at the time of sale. Take, for example, Tsunetaro Murakami's farm on Salt Spring Island. In 1944, when the Custodian sold the property to the director of the

Veterans' Land Act, it was comprised of two separate lots. The first, 1.7 acres nearest the main road, was forcibly sold for $174 (the funds, minus a $3 registration fee, were credited to Tsunetaro's account with the Custodian).[42] The small plot would soon be worth much more. In 1963, when Donald and Edna Francis McLeod completed their lease payments to the Veterans' Land Act and assumed title for the farm, it was valued at $15,000. Another decade passed, and, following the death of her husband, Edna sold the property for $52,500.[43] Consider these exchanges in "real" dollars, compensating for inflation. In 1944, Tsunetaro had received just over the equivalent of $2,500 in 2018 currency, whereas Edna sold for more than $220,000 (2018). The price of the property had increased almost one-hundred-fold, or an astounding 9,000 per cent, in one generation.[44]

An even more dramatic story unfolded on the other parcel, the twenty-five-acre lot comprising most of the farm. In 1944, the Custodian sold it for $988.[45] After a small rebate on his property insurance and payment of the $3 fee, Tsunetaro received $986, or the equivalent of $14,465 (2018). By the 1970s, this area had been subdivided into thirty-three separate properties, with a small roadway, including two culs-de-sac (figure 10.5). In the time since Tsunetaro's dispossession, those thirty-three lots had been repeatedly exchanged. Indeed, the bits and pieces of land that once comprised his farm had changed hands in more than one hundred separate transactions. As rural land became subdivided, its value skyrocketed. Between the late 1960s and the mid-1970s, each of the thirty-three properties sold at least once and some as many as six times.

What was the former farm worth, a generation later? A precise value is difficult to ascribe because as the property splintered it branched into many separate histories of exchange, with each property changing hands at the preferences of its various owners. Using 1976 as an outer benchmark – thirty years after Tsunetaro's departure for Japan and a date by which his son Peter might have contemplated his own retirement – we can query the value of each parcel at its most recent sale. Taking this approach, twenty-nine separate transactions between 1967 and 1976 provide a rough value of the farm one generation after dispossession. The raw sum: $571,150. Converting each transaction to 2018 dollars, the total value of the lands comprising the back lot of the farm was $2,759,904. Counting Tsunetaro's smaller roadside lot as well, the total value of the 1944 farm was almost a full $3 million. Had Peter retained but one subdivided lot of the farm that should have been his inheritance, for example a 0.4-acre house plot at the turnoff for what became Fairview Road, he might have possessed a property worth a quarter of a million dollars. Instead, a massive profit on that particular lot was reaped by Mervyn Gardner (the son of a prominent island family and a leading member of Salt Spring Island Credit Union) and his wife Edith, who purchased the lot in 1973 for $5,500 (equivalent to $30,092 in 2018) and then sold two years later for almost ten times the price, possibly having developed it in the interim.[46]

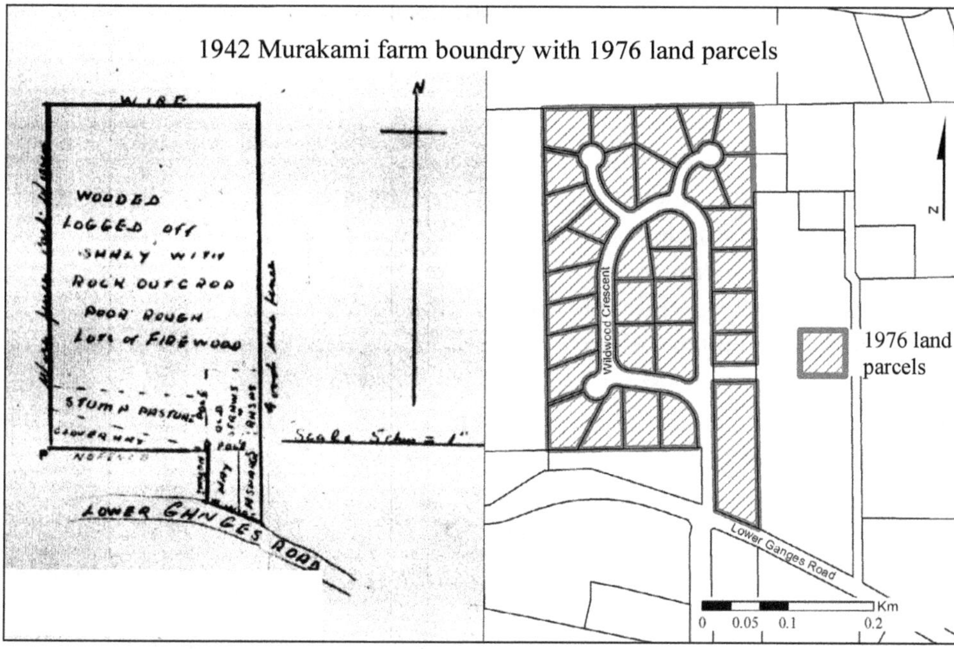

Figure 10.5 The Murakami farm before and after subdivision.

To understand such losses, we need to situate the market of the 1940s in history. The forced sales must be contextualized not by contrast to the wider market at the time of sale but rather within the passage of time in the market for land. Such analyses exceed the capacity of the Bird Commission, which ran from 1947 and 1950. They also exceed the standard considerations of eminent domain cases, which typically restrict themselves to market value at the time of property taking. But this is a particular history. Leaving aside the lawfulness of the dispossession, the wider policy context – in which Japanese Canadians were mostly confined to remote areas of limited opportunity (and low property values), forbidden, in any case, from purchasing new property, required instead to expend their capital to support themselves in confinement, and then forcibly relocated again to eastern destinations – made its effects particularly enduring. Many Japanese Canadians had to rebuild in the postwar era from virtually nothing. The material effects of these federal actions cannot be assessed without a view to their intergenerational impacts.

The results of this analysis will be anticipated, in broad strokes, by anyone familiar with the subsequent history of real estate in coastal British Columbia. Japanese Canadian real estate owners were astoundingly well situated in 1942. Fortunate and successful immigrants and their children – most of them labourers or small business owners – had struggled across the Pacific and through the Depression, some of them managing to gain a foothold in the market for land by 1942. They stood on the precipice of life changing and heritable economic benefit. Their dispossession, and the draconian rule that they use the equity resulting from the sale of their property to meet their basic needs, meant that they were deprived of gains that should have been theirs. Instead, others reaped those rewards.

Even if we know this "ending" as we begin, the details should matter. They mattered to Japanese Canadian landowners. More broadly, they promise to ground in evidence new analytic insight. Previous work in this area has tended to fall into two camps: those who seek to express property losses in monetary terms and those, on the other hand, who focus on interests in property that are abstract, ineffable, and difficult to measure – the identity-constituting value of property to its owners. The division between such perspectives has often been contentious. From his side of the battle lines, geographer J.D. Porteous (whose insights into the loss of home are foundational to this wider volume) laments that "attachment, grief, [and] loss" are "immeasurable" and "thus easy to ignore by the cost-benefit brigade."[47] From the opposite perspective, Frank Shears, in the Office of the Custodian in the 1940s, advised that compensation for Japanese Canadian losses should exclude their claims of harm to self, citizenship, and community, maintaining instead strict focus on the "tangible and specific."[48] Representing opposite poles in the politics of dispossession, Porteous and Shears seem to agree: quantification cannot capture the deeper meanings of loss.

By specifying the material impacts of forced sales in the context of the prior and subsequent sales, the following section attempts a third path: emphasizing the economic significance of *choice,* particularly in the context of dynamic markets. By placing the sales in historical context and emphasizing the importance of the deprivation of choice, this analysis expresses loss in material terms without reducing it to a simple assessment of "fair market value." The loss of freedom – a large measure of the injustice of the internment and dispossession – has quantifiable material dimensions. This analysis will not, of course, convey the full emotional impacts as articulated variously in other chapters of this book. But it does draw two disparate ways of thinking about loss somewhat closer together and communicate material harms in terms of the enduring legacies of injustice.

In some senses, this approach offers a reframing of a key prior analysis of the dispossession, the Price Waterhouse report of the 1980s, commissioned by the National Association of Japanese Canadians as part of their campaign for federal acknowledgment of harm and redress. Conducting title searches on fifty properties, Price Waterhouse estimated the worth of Japanese Canadian holdings in 1949 when government restrictions were finally lifted. Rather than accepting the market at the moment of sale as the benchmark of fairness in the handling of property, Price Waterhouse shifted perspective, detailing the material harms of the whole internment era. The study emphasized the prohibition against real estate purchases by Japanese Canadians, which meant that they were divested from the market as prices were rising. By the time those few with the funds to do so could contemplate investing again, they had already paid a steep premium. Within the Price Waterhouse analysis, 1949 stood for the end of the internment policy and hence the end of documentable harms, a sensible strategy in pressing the government for compensation.[49]

From a wider historical perspective on the real estate market, however, 1949 is an inadequate end point. Extending only slightly the logic of the Price Waterhouse study, we can inquire more expansively into the value over time of the lands that Japanese Canadians owned in 1942. We can ask what the properties were worth in the 1950s or, indeed, the decades that followed. Given the opportunity, many Japanese Canadians would have chosen to keep their property well beyond the first moment of their return to Pacific Canada. They might have leveraged what they already owned as security for further investment or sold and reinvested otherwise. This analysis encourages a counterfactual imagining. We conjure a history in which Japanese Canadians had not been forced to sell but rather retained their lands not just to 1949 but also beyond.[50] If such reflections are counterfactual, however, the analyses are not – rather, they can be grounded in the actual values of the lands that Japanese Canadians owned in 1942 but were forced to sell against their wills and over their protests.

This analysis will follow two principal branches, both offering descriptions of the market over time. The first approach is to reexamine the two important markets that I have discussed so far, taking into account the values of all properties transacted for the entire time period for which our project was able to collect data. The result of such a perspective is straightforward and stark. In the Powell Street neighbourhood, there was never a worse time to sell than the internment era (figure 10.6). For the most part, Japanese Canadians had purchased in the 1920s and 1930s, buying into a market that – in real dollar terms – was temporarily declining in value. They bought low, but then were forced to sell even lower, as the market reached a nadir in the 1940s. Then, in the years after their dispossession, prices skyrocketed. Forced to sell in the 1940s, Japanese Canadians parted with real estate at prices lower than the prevailing rates at any other time in the span of almost a century.

Other people also sold at the same time, but they did so by choice. We cannot trace for certain what they did with their money; many likely reinvested, either in real estate or elsewhere in the economy that was on the verge of booming. Japanese Canadians were deprived of this opportunity, which should, by law and right, have been theirs.[51] One consequence was deprivation from the remarkable investments they had made in the decades prior. Prices in the market where they invested doubled in the subsequent decade and again by the 1970s and again by the start of the 1980s. During a period of exponential returns, Japanese Canadians were instead, for the most part, rebuilding their lives in Eastern Canada or deported to war-ravaged Japan. Such losses have multigenerational impacts.

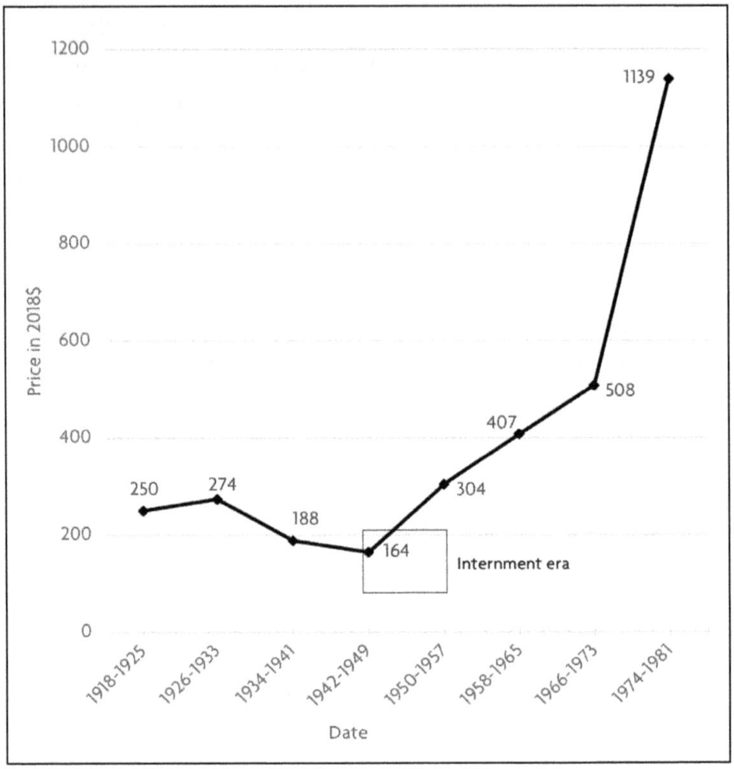
1200
1000
800
600
400
200
0
Price in 2018$
250
274
188
164
304
407
508
1139
Internment era
1918-1925
1926-1933
1934-1941
1942-1949
1950-1957
1958-1965
1966-1973
1974-1981
Date

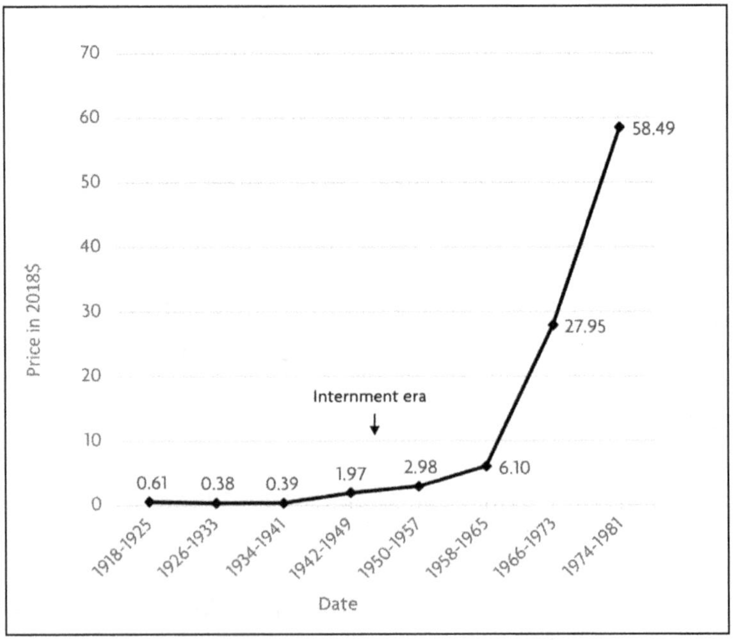
70
60
50
40
30
20
10
0
Price in 2018$
0.61
0.38
0.39
1.97
2.98
6.10
27.95
58.49
Internment era
1918-1925
1926-1933
1934-1941
1942-1949
1950-1957
1958-1965
1966-1973
1974-1981
Date

In Maple Ridge, too, Japanese Canadians were dispossessed of remarkable investments in land. Indeed, owners of land in the vicinity of Vancouver's expanding suburban periphery were even better situated than their city-owning counterparts, and markedly so. As farms became suburban developments, the "real" price of a metre of land in Maple Ridge rose at a rate enviable even for Powell Street owners. Lands selling for two dollars per square metre in the 1940s sold for three times that price by the late 1950s and early 1960s, fourteen times as much a decade later, and reached thirty times their original prices by 1981. When the VLA purchased Maple Ridge farms at artificially depreciated prices and transferred them to returning veterans, they handed over a virtual goldmine (figure 10.7). In one sense, Japanese Canadian owners in Maple Ridge fared somewhat better than their Powell Street counterparts. Whereas prices in Powell Street dipped in the 1940s (so they were dispossessed at an historic low point in the market) in Maple Ridge land prices had already begun their meteoric rise by the time of the dispossession. As a result, in real dollar terms, Maple Ridge owners received on average more in the dispossession sales than they had paid in the decades prior (although, as noted above, they received considerably less than the prevailing market of the 1940s would have dictated). Nonetheless, from a broader perspective, the forced sales in Maple Ridge can only be regarded as a travesty. Rather than starting from nothing, former Maple Ridge farmers ought to have been weighing their remarkable opportunities in the postwar era.

A final descriptive analysis in a third locale reinforces and expands these observations of Japanese Canadian losses in historical perspective. We return to the place where the chapter began – Salt Spring Island. Once our researchers had completed data collection in our two principal sites of study (Powell Street and Maple Ridge), sufficient resources remained to do more limited analyses at several additional sites.

Figure 10.6 *Opposite top* Average price (in 2018 dollars) of a square metre of land, Powell Street, 1918–1981 (in eight-year segments). N = 1139 (1918–1925 = 250, 1926–1933 = 274, 1934–1941=188, 1942–1949 = 164, 1950–1957 = 304; 1958–1965 = 407, 1966–1973 = 508). For the segment from 1942 to 1949, sales by the Office of the Custodian have been excluded to reflect changes in the free market of exchange. Note that the price per square metre figures in this analysis differ somewhat from those reported in the prior section of this chapter due to selection criteria in each analysis (see https://loi.uvic.ca/realestate for a fuller explanation).

Figure 10.7 *Opposite bottom* Average price (in 2018 dollars) of a square metre of land, Maple Ridge, 1918–1981 (in eight-year segments). N = 1474 (1918–1925 = 34, 1926–1933 = 29, 1934–1941=57, 1942–1949 = 232, 1950–1957 = 200; 1958–1965 = 315, 1966–1973 = 513, 1974–1981=94). For the segment from 1942 to 1949, sales by the Office of the Custodian have been excluded to reflect changes in the free market. Note that the price per square metre figures in this analysis differ somewhat from those reported in the section above due to selection criteria in each analysis (see https://loi.uvic.ca/realestate for a fuller explanation).

Of these, the most reliable and important data pertain to Salt Spring.[52] On the island, we were not able to collect comparison data from the free market and instead searched only the transactions on properties owned by Japanese Canadians in 1942. The result is an analysis of a much smaller number of initial properties: we found thirteen sales by the Custodian on Salt Spring Island, although they were subsequently subdivided into many more parcels. We traced subsequent transactions on the original thirteen titles for thirty years. In instances of subdivision, we followed all descendent properties whenever possible. The result is a portrait of Custodian-sold properties one "generation" after the forced sales. In contrast to the graphs just above, which excluded Custodian sales from analysis of free market trends, this analysis builds specifically from Custodian sales to a subsequent history of exchange. The results reinforce the story told thus far but also point to the local specificity of the dispossession. The material impacts of forced sale were at a basic level common across all areas that we studied: Japanese Canadians would have been much better off retaining their lands. But the extent of the benefit of which they were deprived varied by locale. In this sense the legacy of the dispossession is both common and highly differentiated.

Among the localities for which we collected data, none saw so rapid an increase in postwar values as Salt Spring Island. Tsunetaro Murakami's farm was in this sense typical: in the three decades after their sale by the Custodian of enemy property, the real value of Salt Spring Island lands increased at a remarkable rate. The Custodian sold low on Salt Spring Island, dispossessing Japanese Canadians for just sixteen cents per square metre. By the early 1970s, the same areas were selling for more than sixty times as much (figure 10.8).[53] Sales by the Custodian brought a Japanese Canadian farmer, working eighteen acres of land, the average holding in 1942, $12,750 (in 2018 dollars); a generation later the same areas sold for an average of more than $750,000 (2018).

Price gains on Salt Spring brought tremendous benefit to the purchasers of forcibly sold property. Indeed, the island was the site of one of the most notorious single land acquisitions of the entire dispossession: the sale, on 1 March 1945 of the 600-acre property of Tozaro Iwasaki. This transaction later became the subject of a challenge that reached the Supreme Court of Canada, where its legality was affirmed, in part on the basis of the misguided Nakashima case of the 1940s.[54] The transaction was a boon to the purchasers, the prominent Salt Spring Island Mouat family. Troublingly, Gavin Mouat was the local agent of the Custodian on Salt Spring Island, responsible for the safekeeping and management of Japanese Canadian–owned property. It was Mouat who rented the Murakami property to the unreliable Mr Jaggs. He also surely played a role in ensuring that the sprawling Iwasaki lands – ultimately one of the most valuable of the Japanese Canadian–owned properties in coastal British Columbia – went not to the director of the Veterans Land Act but rather into the hands of his own family company, Salt Spring Island Lands, for the sum of $5,250 ($76,825 in 2018).[55]

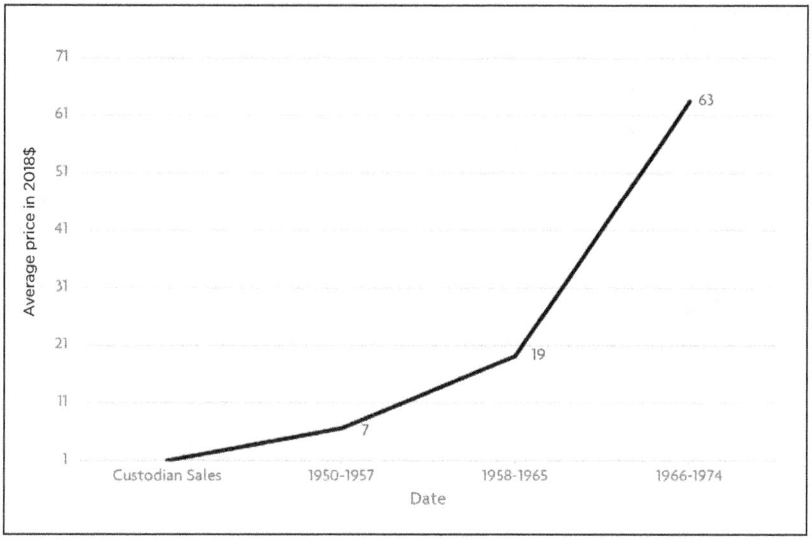

Figure 10.8 Salt Spring Island sale prices (average cost per square metre) for one "generation" of sales after the Custodian sold, expressed as a multiple of Custodian sale prices. N = 6 Custodian sales and 114 subsequent transactions (see https://loi.uvic.ca/realestate for a fuller explanation).

Three years later, at the Bird Commission hearings, Iwasaki claimed the lands were worth \$60,000 (\$870,000). This valuation was ridiculed. "I do not think I will allow this claim to pass," exclaimed Commissioner Bird, "without making some comment on the extravagance of the claim. I know something of Salt Spring Island and anyone who came up with a proposition that … [its] lands were worth a thousand dollars an acre would make it ridiculous." In fact, Iwasaki was claiming \$100 per acre. "Probably," opined, Iwasaki's lawyer, Robert McMaster, "the problem is that the claimant is expanding his idea of the development of the land into the future rather than the present time." Bird replied: "Very far into the future." Iwasaki, present but testifying through an interpreter, was asked nothing about his valuation. Acknowledging, nonetheless, that land values were indeed rising, the commission recommended an award of \$6,750 in consideration of Iwasaki's losses on Salt Spring and another piece of real estate on the mainland.[56]

In fact, all of the participants to the conversation massively underestimated the future value of the property, but Iwasaki was closest. Over the subsequent years, the Mouats subdivided the lands into dozens of parcels. Parts passed to Gavin's children, Winnifred and Norman, some sold decades later. By the 1970s, the Mouats made enormous profits. As Salt Spring Island properties splintered, our researchers were forced to subselect rather than follow all branches of title history, so we cannot report

Figure 10.9 The Mouat family's sprawling oceanside property, circa 1970.

all of the transactions on the immense property, but we were able to trace the sale of seventy-three acres, or 12 per cent of the total Iwasaki lands. These the Mouats sold in twenty-seven transactions, stretching from the early 1950s to 1970: small parcels, sold one-by-one, to various buyers. Gavin made back the family's entire initial investment, and more, on 2 February 1953, selling two small parcels: Olga and William Napper paid $4,000 ($37,362) for 2.5 acres while Ralph Guilbride paid $6,000 ($56,043) for 3.2 acres nearby. Thus, five years after Iwasaki's valuation was ridiculed by Justice Bird, Mouat sold seven acres for $10,000 ($93,405), even more than the supposedly fantastical price – $1,000 per acre – that the commissioner had derided. In September of the same year, Gavin sold another lot, this time for $8,000 ($74,723). And so it went: Gavin made another sale in 1954. One the next year. At least three each in 1957 and 1958. In seventeen years of subdivision and sale, the Mouats netted more than $1.2 million (2018) by selling just seventy-three of the 600 acres. Tracing the rest of their gains would require sustained further research, but we can be certain that Iwasaki's losses considerably enriched one of the island's wealthiest families.

Conclusion

In February 1943, the editors of *The New Canadian*, the only Japanese Canadian newspaper permitted to publish during the war years, expressed a concern shared by many of its readers: that members of the community would see their investments in land "dwindle and vanish" by the end of the internment. A month had elapsed since cabinet's passage of Order in Council 469, which explicitly affirmed the Custodian's power to sell property without their consent. This breach of the prior promise of protection threatened to extinguish a fragile hope to which many property owners still clung: "that no matter how their cash and other assets might dwindle and vanish during the war, they were assured at least of a house or a piece of land which might see them through."[57] For property owners in coastal British Columbia, their investments in real estate promised much more than this. Their homes, farms, and businesses should have been foundations of remarkable opportunity.

Forced to sell, real estate owning Japanese Canadians lost intergenerational wealth: wealth that been accumulated at great pains and that could have changed the lives of their children and grandchildren. The most significant material harms of the dispossession followed from the abrogation of choice as well as the barriers, including legal prohibition, to timely reinvestment. Those who owned in Powell Street were forced to sell at a uniquely inopportune time: prices had never been lower. Those who owned in Maple Ridge and Salt Spring were divested of lands that stood on the verge of historic price increases. The losses of Japanese Canadians were not confined to the moment of sale or the era of the dispossession. Their losses increased over time. The scope of the dispossession became apparent in the legacies of benefit and loss that it generated.

No more clairvoyant than we are today, British Columbians could not have foretold the future of the market. Other people of the 1940s also sold land. But they did not move to the remote interior of British Columbia, or the other internment sites, forced to exhaust their equity for mere subsistence while law prohibited them from reinvesting in land. They did not suffer multiple forced displacements while officials limited their access to their own money. The implications of forcing Japanese Canadians to do so cannot be reversed. The dispossession – in its unearned benefits and unwarranted losses – is permanent.

NOTES

Thanks to readers Eric Adams, Nicholas Blomley, Michael Ross, Hildy Ross, and Eric Sager.

1 Custodian of Enemy Property Case Files 3277 and 8118, RG 117, C-3, LAC, Ottawa. The death of Tsunetaro's other son was reported to me anecdotally by Mary Kitagawa, also a resident of the island before the war. I conclude that Tsunetaro had lived at least three decades in the country due to the birth, thirty-one years prior, of his son in Canada.

2 In response to Jaggs's rant about "Japanese" people, about which only this cryptic line in an official memo remains, F.G. Shears claimed to have "admitted that our opinions might possibly agree [i.e. in strong antipathy for Japanese Canadians] but that this was quite aside from the question at issue [i.e. that people who fail to pay rent are evicted]." This exchange, aridly reported in official correspondence, simultaneously denotes the pervasiveness of racism and its insufficiency as an answer to questions about the dispossession (why were officials insistent that Jaggs pay rent, given that their "opinions … agree[d]" on the topic of "the Japanese"?) that has been noted more broadly in this volume. See F.G. Shears to G.W. McPherson, 13 January 1943, Custodian of Enemy Property Case Files 3277, RG 117, C-3, LAC.

3 Ibid.

4 At least 300 Japanese Canadians wrote to the Custodian between 1943 and 1947 to protest the sale of their property. Among these, more than 70 per cent indicated that the sale price was too low. More broadly, see chapter 4.

5 As Matt James and I argue in chapter 14, some forensic examination of the beneficiaries of injustice is necessary to the democratic learning that we hope will follow from studying (and teaching) such histories.

6 This chapter is based upon the Landscapes of Injustice Real Estate Database, which is presently available for consultation at www.loi.uvic.ca and will eventually be integrated into our project's full digital research collection. After consultative discussions within the Landscapes of Injustice Research Collective – taking into account both academic and community-based priorities – five sites of study were selected for real estate research: (1) Vancouver's Powell Street and (2) Kitsilano neighbourhoods, (3) Maple Ridge, (4) Steveston, and (5) Salt Spring Island. Working with the support of the Land Title and Survey Authority of British Columbia, researchers directly accessed plans (legal maps of properties), land titles (deeds of ownership), and transfer documents (conveyances) pertaining to properties in each of these areas, entering information into a purpose-built database codeveloped by myself and Martin Holmes of the Humanities Computing and Media Centre at the University of Victoria. In all five sites, the search process involved tracing the transactional history of individual selected properties. We adopted specialized search protocols in the various sites, due to the nature of the data and the constraints of time and resources, as documented at www.loi.uvic.ca.

7 Chapter 9.

8 Chapter 4.

9 Ann Gomer Sunahara, *The Politics of Racism: The Uprooting of Japanese Canadians during the Second World War* (Toronto: J. Lorimer, 1981), 95; Ken Adachi, *The Enemy That Never Was: A History of the Japanese Canadians* (Toronto: McClelland & Stewart, 1976), 329–30.

10 See Kaitlin Findlay, "The Bird Commission, Japanese Canadians, and the Challenge of

Reparations in the Wake of State Violence" (MA thesis, University of Victoria, 2018). See also chapter 9.

11 Another major systematic analysis of Japanese Canadian losses, the Price Waterhouse Study of the 1980s, will be discussed below. However, that study deliberately avoided the question of "fair market value" at the time of sale, preferring instead to benchmark losses against values in 1949, when Japanese Canadians were permitted to return to the Pacific coast.

12 Justice Henry Irvine Bird, Report Upon the Investigation into Claims of Persons of the Japanese Race Pursuant to Terms of the Order-in-Council P.C. 1810, 18 July 1947, as amended, File 1, Box 5, Series 2, F.G. Shears Papers, Thomas Fisher Rare Books Library, Toronto (hereafter Bird Commission Report).

13 Chapter 10.

14 Bird Commission Report, 38. Bird also considered "other" rural sales – that is sales other than those to the VLA – and sales of other urban properties. Neither of these additional categories of real estate are discussed at length in this section of this chapter. The VLA sales and the Vancouver area sales constituted a majority of properties sold and the two poles of Bird's conclusions. Of an approximate total of 1,740 sales by the Custodian of Enemy Property of Japanese Canadian–owned real estate, 741 (40 per cent) were VLA sales. The Bird Commission heard claims in relation to 884 of these properties, 486 relating to the VLA sales (Vancouver Office Report, undated [circa 1948], File 16, Vol 2, RG117, LAC).

15 Bird Commission Report, 23.

16 See chapter 9.

17 Throughout this discussion I will use "free market" to designate sales that were not compelled by the federal government as a result of dispossession. Free thus contrasts with the forced sales by the Custodian. Of course there are a variety of ways in which free market transactions may be compelled in various ways (by debt, etc.), but, for the purposes of this discussion, all transactions except those compelled by the Custodian of Enemy Property will be described as free.

18 Bird Commission Report, 39.

19 Both the reassessment of property values (by Clement) and the comparative analysis of market sales (by Corbus) were conducted only with respect to VLA sales (see Transcripts, 1220 and 1414, General Evidence 1–4 February 1949, Volume 77, RG 33-69, LAC).

20 Bird Commission Report, 14.

21 Chapter 5.

22 See also Jordan Stanger-Ross and the Landscapes of Injustice Research Collective, "Suspect Properties: The Vancouver Origins of the Forced Sale of Japanese-Canadian-Owned Property, WWII," *Journal of Planning History* 15, no. 4 (2016): 271–89.

23 National Japanese Canadian Citizens Association, Submission to the Royal Commission on Japanese Canadian Property, written November 1948 and entered into evidence 1 January 1949 (20) General Exhibit 97–131, Vol 79, RG 33-69, LAC.

24 Audrey Kobayashi, *Memories of our Past: A Brief History and Walking Tour of Powell Street* (Vancouver: NRC Publishing, 1992); Beth Carter, *Monogatari: Tales of Powell Street* (Burnaby, BC: Nikkei National Museum, 2011); Adachi, *The Enemy That Never Was*, 131–2, 151–2.

25 Determining the "granularity" for analyses of real estate data requires choice among imperfect options. In the discussion that follows, I take two distinct approaches.

Examining "fair market value," where it is especially important to trace individual properties longitudinally over time, I use legally described lots, or parcels of real estate, as the unit of analysis. It is important to note that individual "properties," as colloquially understood and encountered in the world in the form of buildings, homes, or farms (for example), often occupy more than one legally described lot or parcel. In many cases therefore, a given lot (A) is packaged with others (B and C) in one or more transactions (say, when a large building is sold). Subsequently, if, for example, the building is demolished and a number of smaller edifices take its place, each of the lots might be sold individually. Further, any or all of the original lots can be packaged with still others (D, E, or F) in subsequent transactions. In addition, various forms of redevelopment result in the original lot (A) being extinguished, subdivided, and replaced by new legally described properties (1, 2, and 3), which might then be transacted together, separately, or in combination with other preexisting lots. As a result data analyses (and even database construction and management) required many long and complex deliberations between our programmer, Martin Holmes, and myself. We chose to begin our longitudinal datasets with each legally described property, linking those with antecedent and descendent exchanges of properties that occupy the same geographic location (as determined by a protocol regarding geographic overlap). As a result, in the analyses reported in this section, an individual transaction (of, say, lots A, B, and C conveyed together in one transfer) can appear three separate times within the three separate property histories of lots A, B, and C. The price agreed upon in a single transaction thus establishes the price for three different properties/lots. From the standpoint of statistical analyses this approach has drawbacks – ideally all individual rows of data would be completely independent of one another – but the reality of real estate transaction made this, in our view, the only feasible approach to tracing transaction histories over time. For fuller documentation of the files used in this analysis, see www.loi.uvic.ca/realestate.

26 Note that these are first transactions on each property after 4 March 1942.

27 Here square metre refers to lot size only. This analysis does not take into account the buildings on the properties, only the lot parameters.

28 The complexity of transactional histories means that these figures can be reported in various ways, with slightly different results. The figures reported in the text are for prior transactions (T1) of the properties subsequently sold (T2) by the Custodian of Enemy Property and 190 comparison sales. An alternative approach leaves aside the question of Custodian sales and instead compares prices paid by Japanese Canadians as opposed to non-Japanese Canadians for all properties exchanged prior to 4 March 1942. This approach yields 283 purchases by non-Japanese Canadians and 148 purchases by Japanese Canadians. The price discrepancies using this approach are slightly larger than those reported above; Japanese Canadians purchased at an average of $244 per square metre, non-Japanese Canadians at $465 per square metre (2018 dollars). Going still further back in time (to what we might call T0), to the prices of properties even before Japanese Canadians purchased them, we find that the properties that that they would subsequently buy, and then later lose to the dispossession, were already significantly less expensive, on average, than comparison properties in the neighbourhood.

29 This comparison was conducted as analyses of variance, for the effect of the Custodian as a seller (independent variable) on the price per square metre (dependent variable),

controlling for prior (T1) price per square metre and the date of the T1 transaction. These analyses found no statistically significant effect for the Custodian as seller.

30 This form of analysis is much more straightforward in the case of the urban market than in the VLA sales discussed below. Because the VLA as a purchaser was not seeking profit (and because VLA sales were often completed through lease-to-own arrangements with veterans that are not visible within the records of the market) analyses of what the purchaser from the Custodian did with their property (as against the purchasers in free market sales) is strained at best. Various attempts to circumvent this challenge yielded results largely corroborating the findings in the urban market: purchasers from the VLA did not make special profits. However, such analysis is indirect and somewhat speculative and is not reported here. In the urban market, by contrast, we are able to directly compare purchasers from the Custodian to purchasers in free market sales.

31 The comparison examines sales from 1942–49.

32 Yasutaro Yamaga, *History of the Haney Nokai*, trans. W.T. Hashizume (Beamsville, ON: History Editing Committee of Haney Nokai, 1963).

33 This difference results from our research process, which prioritized Powell Street as the largest node of Japanese Canadian life in the prewar period, as well as the considerable difficulties involved in rural research, where subdivision meant that these properties splintered into hundreds of descendant lots. As a result, in Maple Ridge we selected fifty-three Japanese Canadian–owned properties and one comparison property for each. Because not all of the owners in the comparison sample chose to sell in the 1940s, we have fewer comparators in our sample, somewhat reducing the statistical power of our analysis.

34 In contrast to Powell Street, Japanese Canadians and non-Japanese Canadians had purchased within a similar timeframe in Maple Ridge (with similar mean and median purchase dates ranging from the mid-1910s to 1941). We might expect, therefore, their returns on their investments to be roughly similar.

35 Transcripts Volume 6, 2334, File 1, Box 7, Series 2, F.G. Shears Papers, Thomas Fisher Rare Book Library, University of Toronto.

36 Letter to Gordon Murchison from Ivan T. Barnet ("Barney"), 28 March 1943, File V-8-10 Part 3: Japanese and their Farm Properties, vol. 403, RG 38, LAC.

37 This analysis was conducted as a repeated measure, testing the effect of the Custodian as a seller and time (as independent variables) on the price per square metre (dependent variable), controlling for prior (T1) price per square metre and the date of the T1 transaction. The Custodian sold properties for less, by comparison with prior values, than other sellers in the market. Depending on the restrictions placed on this analysis (which cases were included) this comparison hovered around the standard test of statistical significance. In the most restricted analysis, in which only the thirty-five comparison sales that occurred between 4 March 1942 and 1 April 1949, the test indicated a 94 per cent likelihood that the Custodian had an independent and significant effect on changes in property values over time. In a more open analysis, in which the number of comparison sales was increased, the analysis passed the test for statistical significance, with a greater than 95 per cent likelihood that the effect was not produced by chance. In the text above, I have reported the most conservative use of comparison data (only the thirty-five transactions).

38 Kankichi Onagi, Bird Commission Hearing Transcripts, 20 September 1948, File 923, Vol. 46, RG33-69, LAC.
39 Sakiye Takasaki, Bird Commission Hearing Transcripts, 24 June 1948, File 429, Vol. 20, RG33-69, LAC.
40 Chapter 9.
41 Thomas K. Shoyama, Submission to the Royal Commission on Japanese Canadian Property, 12 November 1948, National Japanese Canadian Citizens Association, File 5, Box 7, Series 2, F.G. Shears Papers, Thomas Fisher Rare Books Library, Toronto.
42 Custodian of Enemy Property Case Files 3277, RG 117, C-3, LAC, Ottawa. This parcel was legally described at the time as Lot 2 of Section 4, in Range 2 East of the North Division of Salt Spring Island, Cowichan District, Plan 3805.
43 All land transaction data, unless otherwise cited, is derived from the Landscapes of Injustice Real Estate Database, compiled at Land Title and Survey Authority of British Columbia offices. For details on the database, as well as access to data, see www.loi.uvic.ca. Donald McLeod died in 1970; see "Last Rites for Donald McLeod at Ganges Church," *Gulf Islands Driftwood*, 5 February 1970. Thank you to Ceridwen Ross Collins at the Salt Spring Island Archives.
44 Currency conversions using the Bank of Canada Inflation Calculator (https://www.bankofcanada.ca/rates/related/inflation-calculator/), 25 December 2018.
45 Lot 3 of Section 4 and 5, in Range 2 East of the North Division of Salt Spring Island, Cowichan District, Plan 2183.
46 Mervyn Gardner chaired a meeting of the Salt Spring Island Credit Union in March 1964, *Salt Spring Island Driftwood*, 12 March 1964; on his family's pioneer status on the island see Richard Mouat Toynbee and kindred souls, *Snapshots of Early Salt Spring and Other Favoured Islands* (Ganges: Mouat's Trading Company, 1978), 19.
47 J.D. Porteous, "Domicide: The Destruction of Home," in *Home: Words, Interpretations, Meanings, and Environments*, ed. David N. Benjamin (Ashgate, 1998), 153.
48 F.G. Shears to K.W. Wright, 27 February 1947, file 55908, part 2.2, RG 117, LAC (2nd of two letters of that day).
49 National Association of Japanese Canadians and Price Waterhouse, *Economic Losses of Japanese Canadians After 1941: A Study* (Winnipeg: National Association of Japanese Canadians, 1985).
50 Landscapes of Injustice research coordinator (and contributor to this volume) Kaitlin Findlay suggests that there is, more broadly, an inherent counterfactuality to the study of loss. To study loss is to study what is not or can no longer be. Another collaborator, David Mitsui, sent me an advertisement for his dispossessed family home, recently listed in Port Coquitlam for almost $700,000. The history of real estate loss has retained symbolic importance to Japanese Canadians perhaps because public expressions of market value repeatedly convey the opportunities lost in dispossession. Every real estate advertisement and every newspaper spread on the unaffordability of housing in coastal British Columbia puts a number on the enduring loss of what might have been.
51 For the claim that the sales were illegal, see chapter 8.
52 We also collected data for sales by the Custodian in Vancouver's Kitsilano neighbourhood (where we found twenty such sales) and Steveston, a fishing settlement at the mouth of the Fraser River (twenty-one such sales). The title searches collected in these locales are useful for case studies of individual properties and may enter into some future analysis. In broad strokes, both seem to confirm the observations reported in

this chapter. However, given the particular analytic approach taken here and the subselections of property that it entailed neither of these locales yielded reliable and reportable results.

53 From 1966 to 1974, lands traced on Salt Spring sold for an average of $10.45 per square metre.

54 Chapter 8.

55 For details on this purchase, including the transaction of additional lots, see Brian Smallshaw, "The Dispossession of Japanese Canadians on Saltspring Island," (MA thesis, University of Victoria, 2017).

56 Torazo Iwasaki Bird Commission Hearing Transcripts, 2 March 1948, File 252, Vol. 13, RG33-69, LAC

57 "A Statement Is in Order," *The New Canadian*, 20 February 1943, 2.

CHAPTER 11

Remembering Acts of Ownership

Kaitlin Findlay, Heather Read, Jordan Stanger-Ross, and the Landscapes of Injustice Research Collective

The history of the dispossession must include the voices of Japanese Canadians. As we have seen in previous chapters, these voices can be heard in many sources. From the moment of their arrival in Canada – indeed, even before – the perspectives, interests, and experiences of Japanese Canadians are expressed in archival sources.[1] In recent decades, particularly since the 1970s, more than a thousand Japanese Canadians have conveyed their memories and stories in interviews. Major collections include a repository of more than 400 recordings at the Nikkei National Museum in Burnaby and more than 200 preserved at the Japanese Canadian Cultural Centre in Toronto.[2] Part of the work of the Landscapes of Injustice project has been to compile a database of all existing interviews of Japanese Canadians. In addition, we conducted a major oral history project of our own, comprising 148 interviews, under the leadership of Dr Pamela Sugiman.[3]

The oral history collection of Landscapes of Injustice differs in four key respects from prior repositories. First, it was conducted with explicit interest in the dispossession of property. Second, it was undertaken as part of a national project, with interviews concentrated in Ontario and British Columbia, and recorded also in Alberta, Saskatchewan, and Manitoba. Third, it is deliberately multigenerational. Like many interview projects, we sought to preserve the voices of narrators who lived through and remember the dispossession (Isabel Hiroto was the first born, in 1915, of all of our narrators, ninety-nine years of age when she was interviewed), but our collection also preserves the perspectives of forty people born in the 1940s or after (the youngest, Emma Nishimura, born in 1982). These younger narrators have no living memory of the dispossession; they convey history and memories passed down across generations. Finally, almost a third of our interviews record the views and experiences of non-Japanese Canadians. While those interviews are not the focus of this chapter – we have chosen instead to explore the life histories of Japanese Canadians – the Landscapes of Injustice oral history collection comprises the first significant repository of the views of bystanders, witnesses, and beneficiaries on the meanings and memories of the internment.[4]

The interviews were conducted using a life history approach. Rather than narrow our focus to any one theme or experience – including the dispossession of property

– Landscapes of Injustice interviews situate internment era experiences within a wider context. As Sugiman notes both in her publications and in her guidance of the cluster, Japanese Canadians are more than their internment narratives.[5] The interviews explore such topics as childhood, school, coming to adulthood, work, marriage, and parenting. They are long, many among them more than an hour, some more than two, their transcripts commonly reaching more than one hundred pages in length. Some narrators met more than once with researchers. To a significant extent, the emphases and interests of the narrators steered the interviews. Nonetheless, narrators did participate in the project with knowledge of its thematic foci and within a wider politics and culture of memory that have emphasized the midcentury denial of Japanese Canadian citizenship. They tend to emphasize the internment era and the dispossession of property in their narratives. The resulting collection of interviews complements and extends the information gathered in other facets of project research by providing a view of Japanese Canadian lives that passes through, but is not limited to, the era of dispossession.[6]

This chapter takes a dialogical approach. Henry Greenspan, noted Holocaust scholar, describes a good oral history interview as "a process in which two people work hard to understand the views and experiences of one person: the interviewee."[7] Oral historian Ronald Grele describes an oral history interview as a "conversational narrative … [conversational] because of the relationship of interviewer and interviewee, and narrative because of the form of exposition – the telling of a tale."[8] In a field manual for oral history, Edward Ives reminds prospective interviewers they are not holding a dialogue with a narrator but rather a "trialogue, with the tape recorder itself as the third party" standing in for future listeners.[9] In keeping with these understandings of oral histories we strive together – and in our own conversation – toward understandings of the Landscapes of Injustice collection. We embark on this analysis from different perspectives and have each focused our contribution on a different subset of the interviews.

Jordan Stanger-Ross, who conceived of the Landscapes of Injustice project and participated in the design, administration, and direction of the oral history initiative, focuses his reflections on narrators who were young adults during the uprooting and internment. Born in 1928 or earlier, the youngest among them was twenty-one years of age when the internment ended. Heather Read, whose comments will focus on narrators born in the 1930s (children of the internment era), was the oral history cluster's postdoctoral fellow in 2015. She conducted interviews and trained and supported research assistants who conducted most of the interviews in the collection. The oldest person in Heather's group would have been eleven or twelve at the time of the initial uprooting, and the youngest would have been too young to remember this first disruption but old enough to have formative childhood experiences during the internment era. Kaitlin Findlay focuses on narrators born in the 1940s and beyond, whose knowledge of internment is largely received from others. Kaitlin worked in a variety of capacities with the project before becoming its research coordinator. Elsewhere, her writing has focused on the experiences and perspectives of Japanese Canadians as conveyed in archival sources.[10] Collectively, we have decided to explore three themes that emerge from the interviews: ownership in the face of dispossession, making home in the aftermath of loss, and return trips. In this layered conversation – a conversation about conversations – we strive to understand a complex history richly remembered, finding that stories about property are most often also about human relationships, that Japanese Canadians strove for generations to rebuild a sense of ownership and belonging, and that returns – both conceptual and physical – carried enduring significance.[11]

Origins, authority, and motive

JORDAN

Before we begin our analysis of the interviews, it may be worthwhile to discuss a question of identity and authority: none of us is of Japanese Canadian descent. Are we in a position to write this chapter, conveying the voices and experiences of Japanese Canadians? In her book on memories and narrations of internment, *Cartographies of Violence*, Mona Oikawa urges anyone working and writing in the area to interrogate "their relationship to the Internment and to the people they claim to be representing." Her questions for non-Japanese Canadians are particularly pointed: "Why are you writing about Japanese Canadians? Do you consider the effects of your representations on Japanese Canadians?" For Oikawa, these questions are especially necessary because scholars outside the community might otherwise operate with impunity, in ignorance of impacts of our work upon the people who suffered the harms of the original policies. By contrast, she argues, Japanese Canadians studying the internment "live and work in relation" to the community that they represent and hence "live with the consequences" of what they write.[12] Elsewhere, feminist scholars have explored related themes, but from a different perspective, emphasizing the importance of a continuity of experience between the authors of history and the subjects that they study. Hence the "spark of feminism" within historical writing (as in other contexts), according to Ruth Roach Pierson, is "ignited in a woman's consciousness at that moment when she senses a discrepancy between a cultural definition of 'woman' and her own experience."[13] Pierson herself expresses concerns about the ultimate conclusion of an argument that ties authority to personal experience – "Must we conclude that the only legitimate feminist women's history is autobiography?" she asks – but her emphasis on experience nonetheless resonates today within scholarship and a wider culture concerned about the appropriation of voice.[14]

HEATHER

I think these are very important considerations. Why am I participating in writing this chapter? For me, this chapter is a primer to the oral history collection, a series of thoughtful explorations I hope will prompt people to listen to or read transcripts of some of the interviews with Japanese Canadians. In that spirit, I feel like the three of us can write this, as long as we are open about who we are and how our lived experiences influenced what we heard or read.

I often turn to Ruth Behar when thinking about authority and subjectivity. She encourages writing where authors are forthcoming about how their backgrounds shape choices in research and writing. In *The Vulnerable Observer*, she argues that to "assert that one is a 'white middle class woman' or a 'black gay man'" within a study is "only interesting if one is able to draw deeper connections between one's personal experience and the subject under study." Researchers should be reflexive about "aspects of the self [that] are the most important filters through which one perceives the world, and most importantly, the topic being studied."[15] I know for me, my personal ethnic background and my personal circumstances at the time I was doing active oral history research influenced my perspectives on this history.

My ethnic background is predominantly English, Scottish, and Irish Canadian. My mother's family immigrated to Canada in the late 1800s. My paternal grandmother's family has been in Canada for a similarly long time, but my paternal grandfather was born in England. When I started interviewing, I was often asked if I was partially Japanese Canadian because I have dark hair and eyes. At times, this question made me feel awkward as I had to answer no, I am English Canadian, and then go on to ask Japanese Canadians about how English Canadians harmed their families.

I find it interesting that Sugiman's work with Landscapes of Injustice focuses primarily on non-Japanese Canadian narrators. As a Japanese Canadian, she is trying to understand the choices, memories, and experiences of non-Japanese Canadians during a time that fundamentally affected the life of her family. This chapter inverts that perspective, and I hope emphasizes this interview collection as one where cross-cultural views on history can be explored. When I think about myself, trying to understand the choices, memories, and experiences of Japanese Canadian narrators, I know I was most affected by stories from narrators who were children during the era. I was pregnant with my first child throughout my research work. Narrators I spoke with often told powerful stories about how their parents had protected and shielded them from the worst of the experience, maintaining family life as best they could. For me, the power of these narratives was amplified when, stepping away from an interview, I could not help but compare their stories with my own imaginings of my future child's life. The stark, awful discrepancy between challenges I might face as a parent and what their parents had gone through continues to influence my research perspective. It crystallized the injustice for me.

Figure 11.1 Research assistant Momoye Sugiman and Dr Heather Read interviewing Aiko Murakami.

JORDAN

In this work I have often thought about the story of my own family. Jewish immigrants from Eastern Europe in the era of Japanese Canadian arrival, our story is in many ways typical: one of striving across generations toward the economic and cultural mainstream of Canadian society and carrying with us, along with many other immigrants, a sense of having slowly remade that mainstream.[16] Throughout my childhood, my great-uncle Frank, the family storyteller, wove together tales of astute decisions that carried his immigrant father from precarity to security and, ultimately, some measure of wealth. Frank came of age in Toronto in the 1940s, as Japanese Canadians displaced from British Columbia streamed into the city. Listening to interviews of his Japanese Canadian contemporaries, I have been reminded of Frank. He grew up in an anti-Semitic Canada, but Frank never saw the accomplishments of his own parents ripped away. Instead, his father, after whom I am named and whose initialled ring I inherited, was the hero in Frank's adventure narratives. I have been drawn to the familiar and the unfamiliar in the stories told by the oldest narrators in our collection. Their stories sometimes sound much like where I come from, but an era of state violence walled-off Frank's experiences from theirs. It is hard for me to imagine Frank having peered over that wall to try to understand Japanese Canadians.

And so, I think we have an ethical responsibility, as non-Japanese Canadians writing in this area, to grapple deeply with the life histories of the Japanese Canadians who spoke with our researchers, to strive toward understanding, and to present that understanding as best we can. I think we have a responsibility to listen with care and to engage with conviction. Our research team has done so in ongoing dialogue with Japanese Canadians – inside and outside of the academy – and the organizations that represent them. Active engagement with pasts other than our own is not only permissible in scholarship but also necessary. Striving toward understanding across difference is, to my view, essential to the mission of the humanities.

KAITLIN

Like you, Heather, I am often asked if I am Japanese Canadian. I've thought of this question as being one about motivation. In other words (and echoing Oikawa), "Why are you doing this?" Perhaps there is something intuitive about researching your own past that brings the question to mind. I try to use the discomfort of the question constructively. It offers an opportunity for reflection and clarification that often is too easily deferred. The question is one reason I enjoy the community-engaged process: it forces me to continually check my intentions and expectations in writing on Japanese Canadian history.

Listening to Japanese Canadians' stories, I am most often struck by differences between them and me, including how we relate to place and experience belonging.[17] My father's family owned a foundry in small-town Ontario. Though the business was sold by the 1960s, this heritage meant that for Christmas dinner we drove to my grandparents' house on High Street, Carleton Place, amidst a line of brick houses with old trees and large lawns. When I sat in the passenger seat of my grandfather's dusty Jeep, he would tell stories of the relatives and neighbours who lived on that street over the years. Today, as in many small towns across the country, the town has painted murals commemorating its heritage, including one dedicated to the foundry. When I visited the town in my youth, I felt secure, nestled in a history of importance.

Reflecting on difference, an exchange between Ellen Crowe-Swords and Kyla Fitzgerald comes to mind. When, at the end of their interview, Kyla asked Ellen if she had a final message for those listening, Ellen replied, "probably I should say that we are more alike than we are different. [Pause] So hang on to the part that says that, 'We are more alike' and let go of the 'we are different' part."[18] I believe there is value in continuously moving between Ellen's two clauses. I can relate to feelings of fear, turmoil, and distance. I have my own intuitive feelings of home. I believe it is vital that we continue to recognize and be moved by our narrators' tribulations, their tough decisions, and their resilience. But recognizing differences allows me to understand Japanese Canadians' stories more clearly. Of all the Japanese Canadian business owners, industrialists, and community builders of British Columbia's prewar years, very few have the privilege of seeing their contributions recognized in public ways. Very few grandchildren had the opportunity to spend afternoons running errands while learning the geographies of their family's past.

Shared heritage can bring insights that I cannot replicate (or compensate for), but I think it is imperative to learn from Japanese Canadians' stories in other ways. For me, interrogating difference opens space for honesty and learning. As I move along the spectrum of Ellen's statement, I see myself as someone learning from this past, starting from my own circumstance.[19]

HEATHER

As we consider why we are engaging in this work, I think we should also consider why our narrators agreed to speak with the Landscapes of Injustice researchers. No oral history collection should be assumed to be completely comprehensive of the range of experiences for a group of people, and this one is no different. During the year I was helping to manage the cluster's interviewing, there were people, both Japanese Canadians and non-Japanese Canadians, who declined our interview requests. Sometimes people say no to talking to researchers, regardless of the subject. Telling personal stories is not something everyone wants to do or feels safe doing. Some people asserted they had no story to tell, because their family had not talked about it, so they knew nothing. Others told me they believed that what happened in the past should stay in the past. And still other people just never replied to initial contact efforts.

That being said, 148 people did participate in conversations with researchers. Thinking about the question of why anyone gives an interview at all, Sean Field, known for his work on apartheid in South Africa, suggests that oral histories can offer "support to interviewees' efforts to recompose their sense of self and regenerate agency."[20] For some people, the interviews were a chance to tell a story never previously shared. For others, a Landscapes of Injustice interview aligned with a larger life history of advocacy and work on behalf of Japanese Canadians. Others shared their stories in the hopes that they could prompt parents or grandparents to participate as well, creating an intergenerational learning experience. Some spoke to our researchers because they saw similarities between current world events and Canada's 1940s.

JORDAN

It seems to me Heather that you are reflecting on the motives of all the participants in our layered conversation, rather than just the three of us as authors. I think you are right to urge careful and sustained attention to motives and past histories on all sides of the discussions. Many of our interviews took place in the homes of Japanese Canadians, as interviewer, narrator, and other family members often gathered around the kitchen table or settled in chairs around a coffee table. Our thinking about these interviews is greatly enriched by careful consideration of everything that each participant, including future listeners, brings to the table.

Theme 1: Ownership in the face of dispossession

JORDAN

Among the core questions of our oral history interviews – and one in which I had a great deal of interest – was a simple one: what did you take with you when you were forced to leave your home? Displaced people can carry only vestiges of their material lives. In the case of Japanese Canadians, the federal government severely limited what they could bring on the trains and trucks to government-administered internment camps: 150 pounds of personal effects, clothing, and kitchen items per adult (including mattresses), seventy-five pounds per child, one crated pedal sewing machine per family, thirty pounds of carry-on, food "for at least three days," and $1.00 per person for the purchase of food.[21] Under such circumstances, Japanese Canadians made one of many cruelly constrained choices of the internment era. Asking Japanese Canadians what they (or their families) took with them, we hoped to learn something about value in the context of dispossession.

Whatever we anticipated in conceiving the research topic, the interviews led in unexpected directions. These directions comprise the first major theme of our analysis. In the section that unfolds below, Heather, Kaitlin, and I explore complex responses to our researchers' questions about what Japanese Canadians families packed when they were uprooted, a topic that interweaves with discussion of what they were forced to leave behind.

a. What did you take?

JORDAN

The narrators born in the 1910s and 1920s, young adults at the time of internment, seldom describe in detail the possessions that they packed or left behind. This surprised me. Given their age, I expected that they might remember packing their bags for internment and making difficult decisions about what to take and what to leave behind. Instead, I was struck that, in response to our questions, many young adults of the 1940s had relatively little to say. While it is tempting to focus on those who evocatively convey the value of what their families retained, many of the oldest narrators do not dwell on the topic, even when prompted. The interviews contain many exchanges like these:

> Alexander: "When you went to the camp, did you take many things with you?" / Frank Moritsugu: "We were only allowed in our case 1 kit bag and one suitcase. So whatever you could cram into that. For instance, I took my Judo outfit."[22]

> Erin: "When you had to leave to be evacuated, what did you take with you?"[23] / Bob Hori: "Just … one … suitcase. That's about it. That's all your clothing you know, there's one thing I remember taking with me was my Indian siwash sweater."[24]

> Joshua: "Was there anything else that you distinctly remember your mom saving?" / Mary Kimoto: "No, she didn't save not much stuff." / Joshua: "Yeah." / Mary: "No, yeah." / Joshua: "Yeah." / Mary: "Because you can only take so much, you know."[25]

In each of these cases, I am interested in the examples that the narrators provided; the Judo outfit, the sweater, and Mary's story about the groceries that her mother took each have a place in our analysis. Yet, specific articles of property seem of secondary concern and even difficult to recall.

Similarly, questions about the particulars of the property that was lost during the dispossession tended to generate only minimal exchange. For example, asked what his family left behind, Frank Moritsugu, who was twenty years old in 1942, answers, "I'm a bit unclear about what happened."[26] In another case, one of our interviewers, Joshua Labove, notices a prewar photograph of a fine tea set during his conversation with Mary Kimoto (another twenty-year-old in 1942):

> Joshua: "What am I looking at there? Is that a tea set down there?" / Mary: "Tea set down there, yeah" … / Joshua: "Did your family have one before the war?" / Mary: "Oh, I think we had it but I don't think we brought it with … when we packed we just left stuff like that behind. I got a few things of my mother's, but it was mostly groceries from the store that we loaded onto the truck. Anything else we just left behind."[27]

Some vagueness about the specifics is to be expected seven decades later, as narrators understandably struggle to recall details (and some narrators lament everything they have forgotten).[28] But the oldest interviewees vividly recall a wide range of experiences. Indeed, their lengthy discussions with our researchers are highly specific. Thus, these vague exchanges suggest instead that particular possessions left behind (along with what they packed and took with them) are seldom foregrounded in their own recollections of these events. I should emphasize that this is not always the case. There are also narratives in which detailed stories of property come forward (as discussed below).[29] But interactions like these, in which specific possessions seem only a passing concern, are common.

KAITLIN

I am also surprised, in part because today the question "If you could bring one suitcase, what would you take?" is a regular part of education about the internment era.[30] If the question is a powerful educational tool, however, it risks historical flattening. I suspect that narrators do not talk about property and value as much as you anticipated because, when they were forced from their homes, they did not have full knowledge of the impending dispossession. In 1942, when Japanese Canadians were being uprooted, the federal government assured them that their property would be protected.[31] Even those who doubted the veracity of this promise had little choice but to undertake their decisions in hopes of ultimately returning to their homes and belongings. This might help explain why older Japanese Canadians' answers to this question are unexpected. In the context of the uprooting, practical items – that might not warrant later mention for their ordinariness – were of heightened value.[32]

In some instances, younger narrators – born during or after the 1940s – recall these decisions with considerable specificity. Vivian Wakabayashi Rygnestad, born in 1943, relates her paternal family's decision to bury their valuables:

> [My father's] parents did very much what many families did. Because they could only take what they can carry, and they were told they were coming back, and that everything would be looked after, they buried – and most families buried – things like their really good china and their silver that they knew they weren't going to need in the next two years. So, my father said that his mother and father, in those, you know, those tin cans that they used to have for, for rice? They buried a lot of dishes and things like that. And ... they had, sort of like a shed. And ... they couldn't bury it in the house, and so they went out to the shed, they dug down deep, and they buried it. And they thought they'd come back.[33]

The Wakabayashis intended their valuables to be protected from theft in their absence but accessible when they returned. Certainly, many Japanese Canadians brought items for reasons other than practicality, as I will discuss below. I think we must remember that Japanese Canadians made these decisions in a pretense of temporary displacement rather than permanent dispossession, which may account for aspects of how property losses are later recalled.

What comes into view in the interviews of the youngest narrators, however, is that the possessions Japanese Canadians brought became meaningful in subsequent generations. These possessions became rare tangible ties to family histories prior to the forced uprooting. Mark Sakamoto, born in 1977 in Medicine Hat, Alberta, for instance, reflects on the "terrible decisions" his family was forced to make because of the weight restrictions on luggage when they were uprooted. He imagines choosing, "Do we bring the family kimono, do we bring our wedding pictures. Or do we bring rice? Or do we bring water?" Decades later, when cleaning out his grandfather's garage in Medicine Hat, Mark found a big tea box ("about two feet by three feet") at the very back, "probably because it was one of the first things that was put in the garage in 1952, when he moved into the house." It was the box his family used to bring rice from coastal British Columbia to Alberta. Mark shipped the box to Toronto, had it cleaned up by the Royal Ontario Museum, and now displays it prominently in his house. The cover of his acclaimed book, *Forgiveness*, features a picture of the box. He explains that it serves as a "wonderful and terrible reminder of the sacrifices that they made during that period. The sacrifices that they were forced into, the dilemmas they were forced into." For Mark, the box represents his family "forced to choose between the sentimentality of their life or their life," that is, between mementos and sheer necessities: "I kept it because, it shows what they're made of and how they could survive and how strong they were."

For Mark, an ordinary item like a box of rice became a poignant link to his family's past, emblematic of their hardship and the injustice they endured.[34] Other younger Japanese Canadians remember specific objects of value. Ellen Crowe-Swords, born in 1941, recalls that her mother, married in 1940, brought the tea set and silverware she received as wedding gifts.[35] Sachiko Okuda, born in 1958, remembers that her father brought a "big block" sweater that he won at UBC in recognition for his excellence in athletics, which he wore on special occasions after the war.[36] Many of the Japanese Canadians in the youngest cohort also showed interviewers objects tied to their family's past. They showed photographs, a sewing machine, sewing patterns, and a chest. When Japanese Canadians packed for their internment in 1942, they could not have known that they would lose what they left behind. The dispossession, however, ensured that the belongings they brought with them would become younger generations' only material ties to prewar life.

JORDAN

I'm interested to learn that younger Japanese Canadians seem more likely than those who lived through the uprooting to ground their understandings of the dispossession in particular possessions that survived. This may, of course, be a matter of individual differences among members of relatively small groups of people (each of us working with about thirty interviews) or perhaps differences between how you and I approach the material. But I wonder whether there may be a larger difference here, having to do with how memories are transmitted within families. Perhaps as younger Japanese Canadians sought to understand the dispossession of their parents and grandparents – an effort that required them to imaginatively bridge differences of generation, experience, and time – they tended to do so in connection with material heritage. For younger Japanese Canadians, heirlooms that survived the dispossession may become

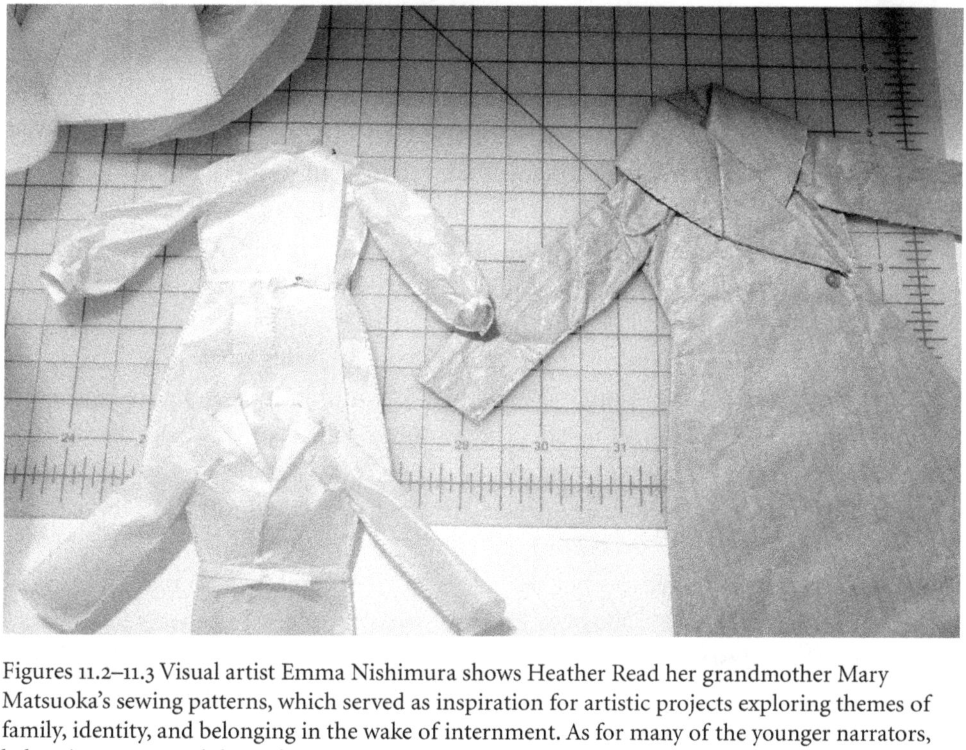

Figures 11.2–11.3 Visual artist Emma Nishimura shows Heather Read her grandmother Mary Matsuoka's sewing patterns, which served as inspiration for artistic projects exploring themes of family, identity, and belonging in the wake of internment. As for many of the younger narrators, belongings preserved through internment and dispossession facilitated Emma's connection to and exploration of her family's past.

mementos of a larger history of loss, while the generation that lived through the dispossession instead carries the more diffuse memory of direct experience.

HEATHER

This discussion is calling to my mind the writing of Barbara Kirshenblatt-Gimblett, when she describes "objects of ethnography" – objects from a particular cultural context that are meant to represent the culture of origin in some way. What we consider ethnographic objects today are typically removed from their context for purposes of study, preservation, and often, display.[37] This excision is fraught and can be extremely complex, since it most often occurs in academic and museum collections with tendencies towards an othering of non-European cultures. However, this discussion has me wondering if this concept could apply to the personal possessions of Japanese Canadians in present day. People who were adults at the time of the dispossession have lived experience and memory of what it meant to be Japanese Canadian in prewar coastal British Columbia. Most of their prewar belongings may not be remembered as meaningful because they were everyday objects. By contrast, for those who only have inherited memories of life before the dispossession, such possessions can become fragments of a family culture that can no longer be experienced in its original context. Think of a one-dollar coin or a cup in your kitchen; these are average things, which someone might see and use every day in Canada. But if they were all one of our descendants had from our lives in twenty-first-century Canada, they would provide glimpses into larger cultural codes and understandings. Perhaps more importantly for our descendants, they would be tangible connections to the people we once were. Objects excised from context come to represent a culture, and that is a powerful concept in the aftermath of an attempted cultural genocide.

The narrators born in the 1930s, fall between the generations you are discussing. Interestingly, it seems to me they straddle both groups in the ways they remember and speak about dispossession. These narrators, in many ways, express a child's perspective on property, with specific memories of treasured objects. In these instances, they are reminiscent of the youngest narrators, for whom physical objects had great meaning. At other times, narrators tell general stories, conveying loss broadly without rooting memories in objects.

Of the narrators who reveal very specific memories of objects, several recall treasured dolls. Some survived the era and some did not. Jean Kamimura, eight years old in 1942, remembers her mother packing a "wet'em doll," which had an internal tube connecting its mouth to its "rear end [so] when you feed it, he wets the diaper." The doll was later destroyed in Tashme by her brother so he could make a slingshot.[38] Blanche Kishi, nine years old at the time, describes being able to bring decorative dolls that her father had acquired in Japan, which she showed to interviewer Carolyn

Nakagawa.[39] Harry Hamade, also nine, remembers dolls used for girls' and boys' day celebrations were "one of the things we had to leave behind."[40]

Two narrators, Grace Omoto and Joanne Maikawa, describe their discovery, well into adulthood, of dolls their parents had secretly taken from coastal British Columbia; despite the dolls not figuring in their childhoods, both recall delight at being reunited with them. Grace Omoto talks about finding the stash of dolls her mother had brought from Vancouver:

> I discovered, I went through her boxes and I came across some of those dolls that you use on girl's day and on boy's day. But you know my mom never brought them out during the war, or even in Beamsville … I had never seen them until I ruffled through all of her boxes. So, she must have tried to keep something, but then she never observed the holidays [laughs], so the dolls never came out.[41]

The dolls took up space that might otherwise have been devoted to items of practical use. Their inclusion suggests they were deeply valued. And yet, Grace explains that the dolls were not used in Beamsville, Ontario where her family lived for a time postwar, perhaps because of her mother's desire to assimilate into mainstream Canadian society. Similarly, Joanne Maikawa, who has no recollection of what she herself packed, recalls that once her family moved to Toronto her father "presented me with my dolls." She was surprised they were saved and brought from British Columbia. It was momentous to have them reappear, thanks to the efforts of her father.[42]

Other possessions are described by this group of narrators. Elmer Hara, nine years old in 1942, recalls his mother gave him "one suitcase," told him to put in "all your things that you want to take" and not to worry about clothes. He took his electric train, his "treasure," and some other toys; his sister, he believes, chose her dolls.[43] Fred Koyama's parents gave a prized scooter and tricycle to a friend who helped the family leave Ucluelet. Koyama, six at the time, recalls it "really hurt" to have those given away.[44] Sisters Blanche and Florence Kishi (nine and five, respectively, in 1942) remember, in separate interviews, that their parents brought a gramophone from Vancouver. Blanche says the music provided youth with a social outlet during their internment at Christina Lake.[45]

Kaye Hayashida, ten years old in 1942, vaguely remembers his parents packing. He was not included in family decision making but has clear memory of his own plans about a prized fishing rod:

> The thing that I remember, that strikes in my mind, was that I had my fishing tackle, right? And there were talks, I heard discussion vaguely that the Japanese people were not going to be turfed out of their houses for long … I remember

> my Mom and Dad packing up stuff, and taking it over to my cousin's place, who had just built a new house … I don't remember that packing and … indecision … of what to take and that. I do remember my decision. What was I going to do with my fishing rod? I couldn't take it. But I thought we're going to come back, anyway, so, as you go from the main floor to the next level, there's that open stairway. And I thought, I'll screw it up there, and I know where it is and I'll come back and get it. But that was the last of it. It never happened.[46]

This is, for me, a strongly evocative example of a child's memory of the era; I can picture hazy parental figures orchestrating the family move and young Kaye wanting to protect what he found most dear. Similarly, Mary (née Murakami) Kitagawa's account of her older sister noticing the family dog on the day they left Salt Spring Island also provides a child-focused perspective on trauma. Mary's sister saw the dog on their way to the boat to take them off the island; it apparently escaped from the home where the family had left it. A family friend, "Mervin Gardiner, who was taking us to the boat … said 'Don't worry … I'll take the dogs home and I'll look after them.'" Mary, seven years old in 1942, notes Gardiner's kindness gave her family "a bit of peace," on a deeply traumatic day.[47]

I found the question of what did you take, for this age group, certainly provided a wider ranging set of answers than I might have anticipated. The narratives include parents working out details largely unknown to their children, as well as extremely specific perspectives about personal treasures, both of which perhaps reflect the viewpoints of children. They are, however, children's memories narrated by people who are now adults. Even when specific, poignant memories of dolls and toys come up, narrators often broaden discussions to touch on what was lost to the Japanese Canadian cultural community.

KAITLIN

These powerful stories of loss remind me of a story that Vivian Nabata, interviewed with her husband Tony, recalls being told by her grandmother:

> Vivian: "So … yeah. I know my grandmother kept telling me this story over and over whenever she had the grandkids around and she said that you'd know during that time because you only had – what? Twenty-four, forty-eight hours to pack up and leave?" Tony: "Yeah." / Kyla: "Mhm." / Tony: "One suitcase each."
>
> Vivian: "She said that she remembers, you know, they had a pickup truck that they could take up things going to Magna Bay. And she says, 'We had to pack that truck,' and she said, 'I remember driving away from my home in Steveston and just being broken-hearted because she said that stuff was falling out of the truck because they'd overloaded it [quietly laughs].'" / Kyla: "Oh…"

> Vivian: "So you know, as you're driving away from your home you're seeing, I mean it's only things but it was a part of their life, I guess is just that, you know? Having being forced to leave right that day. She said she'll never forget … that's her lasting … her last impression, I guess … of having to leave her home in Steveston was that they had to rush, it's chaotic, terrible and … just things falling off the truck."[48]

The story of Vivian's grandmother is about possessions in the context of the forced uprooting and it conveys the heart-wrenching emotion that accompanied these events. Vivian's grandmother was "broken hearted" because of what she was leaving behind: "I mean it's only things, but it was part of their life." I wonder if Vivian's grandmother continued to tell the story of that event because it so powerfully encapsulated the broader feelings of loss that came with the forced uprooting.

b. Intangible Losses

HEATHER

Questions about what was taken and what was lost are complicated by narrators' emphasis of intangible losses. Mary Kitagawa phrases this eloquently, noting that while it can be common to focus on the material aspect of loss, for her, "The loss was, greater, on the psyche. We lost friends, we lost … our community … We lost … education … our dreams were shattered."[49] Other narrators also express education as their most intense experience of dispossession, such as Peter Kurita (twelve years old in 1942). Peter, who went on to become a teacher as an adult, declares the "worst thing" was "that the government, both governments, decided not to educate Japanese Canadians." He notes he "never saw a professional teacher from December 1942 to when I left the camp in 1946."[50] Tosh Kitagawa, nine years old in 1942, whose siblings worked to stave off extreme poverty while living on sugar beet farms, also describes education as "the biggest loss."[51]

Discussion of these intangible losses seem to differ in relation to the varied sites and forms of internment.[52] Several narrators, such as Sam Matsuo, Arthur Miki, and Tosh Kitagawa, were in rural prairie communities on sugar beet farms after the uprooting, attending local schools with non-Japanese Canadian children. Both Arthur (six in 1942) and Sam (twelve in 1942) recall having to walk great distances in cold winter conditions.[53] Tosh explains that, while he attended school as often as he could, he thought the teachers were not "really qualified," recalling they were mainly high school graduates. His bus to school would frequently get stuck in grooves on muddy roads when it rained, and children would have to get out and push.[54] People, like Peter, who lived in larger camps, instead tend to recall the ways in which the community worked together. Jean Ikeda-Douglas, ten years old in 1942, missed "almost two years [of education]," but she emphasizes the accomplishments of older children working together to create a school in Slocan: "it's amazing that everybody pitched in." The government, she recalls, only supplied building materials after receiving petitions from Japanese Canadians concerned for the welfare of their children.[55] Florence Kishi recalls that at the self-support camp in Christina Lake, adults "decided that the children should have an education." She remembers that some "got in touch with the Department of Education [and] … They got a room down the basement of the hotel painted." Despite a lack of trained teachers, the community "did have one person who had gone to university and we also had a lady who had graduated from high school, so they were hired." Florence speaks highly of the school, noting, "Everybody was really smart. So, we did well."[56]

I think the frequent mention of education likely results from the age of narrators I focused on (so the disruption in school life was, for them, a very noticeable loss). We can also learn a great deal about the adults of the same era from these recollections. Adults realized the potential for severe disruption of future generations and created schools out of nothing. These seem to me acts of quiet resistance. For some, like Florence and Jean, internment-era schools are an enduring source of pride. George Takashima, seven years old in 1942, concurs, recalling that in New Denver "there happened to be two Japanese Canadians who were qualified teachers from the prewar days," who supervised instructors in various internment sites. George proudly notes,

> Obviously, obviously, they had done a good job because after the war when we spread out across the country and we went into the mainstream schools we were rated high or, in many instances, we could skip … a grade. So that said something.[57]

The education was not perfect, however, and for some narrators the makeshift schools were challenging and provided inadequate preparation for future education. Jean Kamimura describes the makeshift school at Tashme as unbearably noisy. She notes the barn where classes were held was "divided into two," with the other side serving as a "regular community hall" where funerals were often held during school hours. She also recalls, despite the efforts of her community, it was difficult for her to integrate into mainstream schools in the late 1940s.[58]

c. Remembering Decision Makers

JORDAN

So far, we have discussed a wide range of responses to our questions about what Japanese Canadians took with them to internment and what they were forced to leave behind. The narrators differ – it seems on generational lines – in how closely they tie their answers to specific material objects. Some, in response to these questions, explain that their families and communities preserved intangible (or perhaps communal) possessions such as schooling. What they took with them was an education. For others, this was precisely their greatest loss.

Before we conclude discussion of this theme, I want to note another pattern in my interviews: many people born in the 1910s and 1920s recall the material constraints of the uprooting, in significant part, through the responses of their parents and their families to the circumstances it imposed. Their stories often revolve around decision makers, people who made key choices. While the hardships imposed in policy are certainly remembered, the ways in which Japanese Canadians anticipated and navigated these challenges often receive at least as much attention.[59]

I am struck, for example, by the stories Betty Toyota told in 2016 when she was interviewed along with her daughter Joy and cousin Mike. Aged ninety-one when she shared her memories, Betty lived in Vancouver until she was seventeen when she and her family were interned in Slocan City. Betty remembers other Japanese Canadians in terms of the losses they suffered, including a "young bachelor" neighbour whose boat was confiscated: "I remember [him] coming over one night, just crying. He said that his boat was his wife. It was like a wife to him." By contrast, Betty describes her own family anticipating and carefully steering through the challenges of the dispossession. "When the war started dad knew right away," she recalls, "so naturally, the first thing my dad thought was the money. So he took all the money out of the bank … [and] got all the money out of the insurance policy … he lost quite a bit right? But at least he had the cash." Having drawn down his accounts, he moved quickly to liquidate other assets: a piano, a "real big dining room set," Noritake chinaware, "everything, just to get the money." Betty recalls these sales with a sense of pride; rather than telling a story of "panic" or "fire sales" forced upon Japanese Canadians, her story is about her father's fast thinking, which advantaged the family in the years that followed. After her father was separated from them and incarcerated in Ontario, Betty's mother carried the cash with her, always clutching a purse that – unbeknownst to her daughters – contained the family's inheritance.[60] Other narrators also convey family members who anticipated or were able to mitigate some of the harms of government policy. Yoshiko Hasegawa, born, like Betty, in Vancouver in 1925, recalls that her family sold everything they could, "like the chesterfields and the pianos and whatever," concealing their money in the hollows of a Japanese doll and a miniature clay chest of drawers.

HEATHER

A striking story of this kind is of Aileen Yokota's father. Aileen did not experience life in an internment camp; despite being born in British Columbia, she spent most of her early childhood in Toronto. Her father, she describes, anticipated that racial tensions were mounting in the province and decided to move his family to Ontario before Pearl Harbor even happened.[61]

There are others with more similarities to Betty Toyota's narrative. Mary Kitagawa discusses her mother's decision to sell the chickens on their farm on Salt Spring Island. She recalls the local representative from the Office of the Custodian, a family friend named Gavin, came and "told my mother that she had to get rid of the chickens."[62] There were "Chinese people, in Victoria," who were interested in purchasing them for a "low price." Mary recounts that her mother had worked to incubate the chickens and that they were in "their prime egg-laying period." Her mother had "a business head…[and] negotiated a much higher price." Mary also describes how her mother (parenting five children alone because her husband was forced away to a road camp) safeguarded the family's funds in a "money belt that she wore around her waist" and procured food to keep her children well fed.[63] Doris Kimura relates her father's quick decisions about property in Port Islington. Following advice from "[h]is friends, the Caucasian friends," who "told him to sell it," Doris's father sold the family restaurant and home, which he had owned since approximately 1918. Jordan, you were the interviewer and you asked whether she thought her father sold under duress. She replies no, "he felt it was a good move, business wise … because the whole community is going to be lost."[64]

KAITLIN

Tony Nabata explains that his father and grandfather liquidated their holdings for cash in two short days. After selling the supplies and equipment of their small business, he recalls, "they were left with close to ten thousand dollars. Now ten thousand doesn't sound like a lot today," Tony explains, but "back then … it was quite a bit of money … it was still a lot for them considering they only owned this barbershop and shoe repair shop."[65] Tony tells the story with pride, while still recognizing the injustice of the broader context in which the sales took place.

JORDAN

Some narrators describe smaller but still valuable decisions. Bob Hori, twenty at the time of the internment, remembers that his mother anticipated the cold of the British Columbia interior and encouraged his purchase of an "Indian siwash sweater."[66] Frank Moritsugu treasures his collection of prewar family photographs. He attributes the good fortune of having the album to the wisdom of his mother who "made sure that she brought all the photographs that she already had, that the family had, with us. Things like this [referring to an album]. Some other people, a lot of the other people said they don't have pictures of the old days because [they] stored them away and they are gone."[67]

Other narrators describe efforts to bend, as much as possible, official regulations to mitigate their harms. Yoshiko Hasegawa explains, "we were allowed a trunk each and a suitcase and a canvas bag, so we went to buy a trunk for each of us and the biggest suitcase you could find. Everybody had that. It was a big paper suitcase ... and then we bought the biggest canvas bag that you could find [laughs]."[68]

Somewhat similarly, Mary Kimoto, twenty years old in 1942, and her family avoided the official internment process by quickly escaping, under cover of night, from Vancouver with two truckloads of goods – food and personal belongings – and relocating to Kelowna:

> My [future] husband was on the west coast and they had to leave. They were given, what, forty-eight hours' notice to pull out. My husband's mother was living in Vancouver and she told my mother that this is what's happening, that we're all going to have to move and, of course, my mother, she really got frantic and she decided that we better leave before we're going to be all separated ... so she hired two friends that had a truck ... and we pulled out at about 2 am in the morning and we headed for Kelowna ... Of course, it was in January so we hit snow in Hope and it was a scary trip.

Mary conveys the menace of the uprooting and the panic it induced. She also reveals the networks of information among friends and the fast thinking of her mother, who anticipated, correctly, that her children could find work in the orchards of the Okanagan. She feels "lucky that my mother made a decision pretty quickly" before the officials had time to organize and regulate the uprooting and dispossession.[69]

These recollections describe subtle assertions of ownership in a context of dispossession. They convey the agency that Japanese Canadians retained, as well as the importance of their choices about property and material well-being. Despite their subtlety (by comparison, for example, with the legal challenge mounted by property owners), such acts of ownership were meaningful, as families used available resources to meet their needs at a time of violent disruption. These acts of ownership also suggest the limits of state power: officials could announce precise weight limits and proclaim a maximum allowable cash in hand, but they lacked the capacity, in the makeshift uprooting process, to weigh every bag and inspect every purse. Officials could not mobilize quickly enough to control all movements of people and goods.[70] As a result, Mary's family made it out of coastal British Columbia on their own terms, Betty's mother had a stash of money in Slocan City, and when Yoshiko arrived in Greenwood "everybody had to help ... hauling our trunks."[71]

Even as they teach about the subtlety of resistance and the limits of state power, these narrators are also telling another story: one about the smart decisions, luck, and hardship that comprise family history (here the narratives often remind me of those told by my great uncle Frank). In these stories the state's decision to uproot and intern Japanese Canadians is formative: it sets the boundaries or contours within which Japanese Canadians undertake their lives. But, at least at these points in these stories, state malevolence is consigned to the background. The real message that a narrator is trying to convey is a genealogical one, a story of family that steers through the 1940s and all the way to the moment, decades later, of narration, when, because of those choices, Betty, Yoshiko, and Mary could each sit to reflect on their lives.

HEATHER

I like thinking about the narratives as depicting what you call "decision makers," and I wonder how our project, as an audience, shaped this narrative content. Why did Betty, Yoshiko, and Mary tell these stories in these ways to our interviewers? Had they told them before in other ways? What does it mean to Betty, Yoshiko, and Mary to be able to tell a story of smart decisions?

JORDAN

If I am right that stories about decision makers in the context of dispossession convey subtle resistance to state power while also providing an alternative narrative, in which family choices are foregrounded, then I would think that they could be empowering to tell, both privately and in public. It may be also that the emphasis on decision makers, rather than what they lost, reflects the passage of time since the dispossession and the personal positions from which our narrators tell their stories. Japanese Canadians recalling the dispossession today know that, despite the dispossession, their community recovered remarkably in the postwar era. Most did not live the rest of their lives destitute. They know that, decades later, the federal government apologized. They know that this history continues to be studied and understood as a major breach of Canadian citizenship. Although the past is never neatly closed and the dispossession, as this book argues, is permanent, the narrators tell their stories from a vantage point almost unimaginable in the 1940s, when Japanese Canadians had no idea how they would rebuild their lives, educate their children, regain some measure of citizenship, or, indeed, when the internment would ever end. Perhaps in this context, looking back across remarkable personal and familial journeys since the 1940s, many Japanese Canadians find that the smart decisions of the 1940s, rather than harms suffered, carry the most significance.

KAITLIN

Some narrators refer to a wave of storytelling that followed the redress settlement. I wonder if this also reflects what you are suggesting, Jordan – that a narrator's sense of security can shape their testimony. I wonder, however, about a different reading of these narratives. Some experiences are difficult to put into words; perhaps, for some narrators, the most bitter losses are unworthy of retelling. Those might be stories below the surface, which we might not hear.[72] The stories of quick thinking and quiet resistance – of survival – are, perhaps, the slim positive glimmer in what was likely an overwhelmingly difficult time. I see something similar in your example, Jordan: along with the ring you inherited from your great uncle Frank, you received a heritage – of resilience and astute decision making – in which you could have pride. Those stories are perhaps simply the easiest to tell, a part of experience the narrator can comfortably remember and to convey in public storytelling.[73]

HEATHER

Jean Ikeda-Douglas's interview also focuses on relationships that sustained her family through considerable hardship. Jean's family remained in Vancouver longer than most Japanese Canadians because her sister was severely ill with tuberculosis. As a result Jean, at ten years of age, watched "crazy mob[s]" descending upon homes vacated by Japanese Canadians in her neighbourhood: "they had hammers and axes, and they would just crumble the window or the door glass ... and you'd see every stick of furniture or anything that was left in the house. It was a grand melee of people. They stripped the place clean."[74] Her life story is full of grim realities: before the internment era began, Jean lost her father at a young age. Then, she spent time in multiple hospitals with an ill sister as her mother tried to care for the family, a situation compounded by the hardships of internment.

Despite this, Jean's account is peppered with anecdotes about people who helped her family. For example, she recalls the kindness of their Chinese Canadian friends. Although, in general, "Chinese and Japanese did not really mix that well" in the Vancouver area, her mother had a close relationship with the owners of a local Chinese grocery. In the 1930s, the relationship was warm: in return for free haircuts at her mother's store (where she both made dresses and cut hair), the grocers gave the Ikedas discounted produce and fish. With the coming of war, and the imposition of restrictions on Japanese Canadians, these friends gave the Ikedas badges prepared by the City of Vancouver to identify Asian people of non-Japanese descent, allowing them greater freedom of movement. Jean also recalls neighbours, the Hiroshita family (a white woman named Alice who was married to a Japanese Canadian man Jean only remembers as "Mister"), who were close enough with Jean's mother that they offered to adopt Jean after the sudden passing of her father before the war.[75] In 1942, the Hiroshitas stored the Ikeda's belongings in their basement. Jean recalls "all the boys from the Ishi family [cousins] came over and moved everything," commenting "we were very lucky." In the following months, the Hiroshitas shipped these possessions to Slocan. Later, the Hiroshitas visited Slocan and convinced the RCMP to allow Jean's mother to open a hairdressing salon to improve morale.[76]

The theme of decision makers has given me a fresh perspective on Jean's interview: earlier, I had not seen these narratives as examples of people deciding to resist norms. But, Jean depicts multiple decision makers, a cross-cultural network of people, working together to make life bearable for Japanese Canadians. To me, Jean's emphasis on the community's decisions to resist state actions seems deliberate, like she is choosing to remember a version of history that emphasizes goodness within a common human family. There are also multiple layers of decision making within her storytelling; she is deciding to resist a binary division between Japanese Canadians and the rest of Canada, and she is also choosing to frame her life story positively, rather than as tragic or traumatic.

d. Property Destruction as an Act of Ownership

JORDAN

There is a final form of decision – or perhaps a final assertion of ownership in the face of dispossession – that may be relevant as we consider complex forms of resistance and empowerment. Some of the narrators describe responses to the dispossession that defy altogether a straightforward binary of losing property, on one hand, and retaining or preserving it, on the other. For example, some Japanese Canadians destroyed their own property rather than allow it to be seized. Yoshiko Hasegawa describes her family's destruction of the dishware from the restaurant that they operated in Vancouver: "You couldn't sell it. It was all Japanese china. Oh, and the lacquered tray." Since the dishes couldn't be sold, the family shattered them instead. Having broken the dishes, Yoshiko also burned them: "We just had a small stove in the kitchen. I had to break it all up and burn it in there."[77]

HEATHER

Jean Ikeda-Douglas has a striking story of destruction. As I described earlier, Jean's mother arranged to hide most of the family's possessions in the basement of the Hiroshita's house. However, her mother refused to hide a precious family heirloom:

> the only thing that my mother vowed was that she did not want to give up the, the sword that had been in our family. Because we had come originally, way back, from a warlord family of samurai. And so, we had, you know, like armour and a sword that had always been on the wall. And she said there's no way she was handing that in after all these generations. And so, although Japanese people were not supposed to be out after dark, my mother and our relatives that lived in North Vancouver, that were boat makers, they came over and said "Ok, we're going to row out into the straits." Where all the big ships would come through. And she threw it overboard.[78]

Jean remembers her mother's determination to maintain agency over her family's prized possessions.[79]

JORDAN

The exertion required in each instance – breaking china into pieces small enough to fit into a stove where it could be lit, a perilous traversal of the straits at night – speaks to the depth of resolve on the part of some owners to avoid the unjust seizure of their property. There is, in each instance, an almost ritual dimension to the destruction. The plates were not merely broken but then burned. The dropping of the sword into the ocean feels to me powerfully ritual, perhaps even funereal. These acts ensured the finality of the property destruction but surely did more than this. They must have offered some catharsis transforming inevitable loss into a powerful exercise of ownership.

HEATHER

Along a similar line, perhaps, is the act of burying property. Ken Nishibata, eleven years old in 1942, remembers his parents buried some possessions prior to leaving Steveston. The Nishibatas were fishermen before the uprooting and eventually worked on sugar beet farms on the prairies:

> I believe they did hide things … They may have dug and put something underground, they may have I think they did put some things underground because they were thinking they would be back maybe within half a year or so, so they could retrieve it. But I really don't know where all the goods went to.[80]

To me, burial seems like such a complex decision, imbued with both scepticism (that things would not be safe if left in the homes) and hope (that people would be able to return home to retrieve them). Since so many people were never able to go back home, in retrospect, acts of burying seem almost funereal.

KAITLIN

Surprisingly, some Japanese Canadians did manage to retrieve buried property. David Mitsui, born in 1954, for instance, recalls going to elementary school show-and-tell in postwar Smithville, Ontario, with the wakizashi sword of his great-great-grandfather, which his father had buried and then dug up after the war.[81] Burial was not always a futile means of preserving property.

Two stories from the youngest narrators connect with these complex acts of ownership. In both cases, Japanese Canadians discarded property that symbolized their belonging in Canada, but in each instance a second party intervened to prevent its loss. David Mitsui recalls the bitterness of his grandfather Masumi Mitsui, who was a decorated veteran from the First World War, in 1942:

> Well when he had to report to the security commission at Hastings Park, that's where everybody had to report to, he said, "Well, what good are these medals [for meritorious service]?" And he threw them down at the officer and left. My Aunt Lucy apparently had gone with him to report in and retrieved the medals.[82]

Similarly, Kelvin Higo recounts an act of his father-in-law on the day he was deported to Japan: "[H]e was so upset with how he was treated he was getting into a boat and threw his Canadian citizenship papers down at the foot of an RCMP officer." Kelvin describes his father-in-law's subsequent gratefulness for the officer's response: "He says, 'Fortunately, the officer picked it up and says "You may need this sometime in the future."' My father-in-law says, 'Thank God he picked it up and gave it back to me.'"[83]

Like stories of destruction and burial, these can be interpreted as powerful acts of ownership in a context when Japanese Canadians' actions were severely restricted. By publicly discarding Canadian military medals and citizenship papers, Japanese Canadians protested the failure of key symbols of citizenship to carry the meaning they should have in the 1940s. I wonder if these stories were passed on because they communicate the severity of betrayal felt by many Japanese Canadians. The second parallel between the stories – how a bystander bent down to pick up and return the property to the men – is fascinating to me. Perhaps by placing the act of anger and rejection in this arc, the storytellers both convey and diffuse the passion of the moment.

JORDAN

We have covered fascinating ground by trying, initially, to answer questions about what Japanese Canadians took with them to sites of internment and what they were forced to leave behind. Answering our questions, Japanese Canadians tell stories in which specific material objects sometimes play a leading role and sometimes fade into the background. We hear stories about quiet resistance and open defiance, about stinging losses, but also about smart decisions to preserve what was possible in extreme circumstances. These narratives offer no straightforward account of what was valued in the context of loss. Instead, reflections on this topic are indirect. They are accounts of people making do, acting as property owners and also as members of families and communities. And through all of this, the narratives convey the hard work of assimilating an era of political violence into larger narratives of family and personal life. More than finding out what was cherished and preserved in a moment of state-sanctioned theft, we found out how Japanese Canadians chose to remember and to narrate family history and loss.

Theme 2: Making home in the aftermath of dispossession

HEATHER

My research prior to coming to Landscapes of Injustice was based, broadly, in material culture studies. So, I had spent time thinking about why and how people make things, and the networks of places, people, and materials layered into objects. When I first came to do oral history research with Japanese Canadians, I found the question of what people made in the aftermath of overwhelming material loss poignant and important. For me, the idea of "making" is a lens through which we can consider how people rebuilt their senses of self, home, community, and place in the aftermath of uprooting, internment, and dispossession. Rebuilding usually began with basic, material things like tables and food and clothes. As we have already noted, material possessions are bound up with immaterial aspects of personal and group identity. So, when you are making things, you are also influencing and expressing your identity.

Jane Dusselier has been informative for me in this regard. In her studies of Japanese American internment-era craft making, she takes a broad view of material culture, using words like art and craft to describe the creation of very simple objects many people would consider utilitarian, as well as objects created solely with aesthetic purpose. Her purpose is to demonstrate the range of creative and constructive work required to rebuild lives in the context of incarceration and dispossession. She also often frames this work as an act of resistance and empowerment.[84] When I write about "making" I am even broader than Dusselier and refer to all the various ways in which Japanese Canadians reestablished their lives. So, narratives that explicitly explore material culture, which I discuss below, fit in this category. Narratives about how the community reestablished education, Scouting, dances, and sports also relate; for all those activities, people needed objects, many of which had to be physically made, but narratives about these activities are also narratives about rebuilding community bonds in the wake of trauma.[85]

Gilly Carr and Harold Mytum, in the introduction to their essay collection *Creativity Behind Barbed Wire* (which explores diverse examples of making in prisoner-of-war camps and internment camps worldwide), explain that for all the people whose stories are represented in their book "creativity of one form or another was a central form of survival."[86] They seek to "reposition" creativity as a source of information that can sit alongside oral and written testimony, conveying subtlety and richness in lived experience.[87] Gilly and Mytum found "no situation where civilian or military POWs were unable to use creativity to both improve the conditions of their internment and as statements of spiritual resistance to the conditions in which they found themselves."[88] Similarly, I see "making" as a necessary practice in the aftermath of the uprooting, internment, and dispossession of Japanese Canadians. It relates, perhaps, to the theme of decision makers: by recognizing Japanese Canadians as makers, whether the making was of physical things or intangible identities, and whether it was done out of a sense of communal strength or individual coping, we can better understand the (sometimes limited) agency they maintained in the face of dispossession.

a. Making Things

JORDAN

Japanese Canadians immediately began to make/remake their material lives (broadly conceived, as you have explained) in response to the dispossession. For example, Betty Toyota details complex stove making, an ingenious response to deprivation. She, her sister, and their mother were separated from the rest of their family and forced to live in a tent in Slocan for the first months of their internment. This was a particular hardship as autumn wore on, because "you know how cold it gets?" But, Betty quickly explains, "Japanese are smart. They think of something." What follows is a somewhat technical explanation of "making" that also demonstrates the role of community networks in mitigating the loss of home:

> We got to know this one young fellow … And he was a carpenter. So you know the nail kegs, they used to come in a keg … [and he] made a little foundation made of wood and filled it with gravel and put this nail keg upside down and made a hole in the front and then made a hole on top. And by that time the commission would give us stovepipes … and there was this Japanese man … He was a tinsmith and he made these things called roof jack … So we were allowed to go to the commission, the warehouse, and get two pipes and a roof jack. So that roof jack would go out from the flat of the tin. So we had enough little fuel to burn in this little nail keg with the smoke going up the room. And that kept our little tent warm enough.[89]

The invention and construction of the stoves provided basic necessity of shelter – protection from the elements – while relying upon and reinforcing community. This making of home seems also a reassertion of ownership. Deprived of meaningful shelter, Japanese Canadians came together to produce for themselves what they needed. These stoves were their own. Betty also describes women establishing craft businesses in the camps, which provided a source of income and reinforced community:

> there were two or three women that set up a dressmaking store, but then there were individual women that knew how to sew. And they had classes in their house. They would take about two or three women and teach dressmaking. Or there was another lady that taught Ikebana, flower arranging. Or some ladies taught cooking, Japanese cooking.[90]

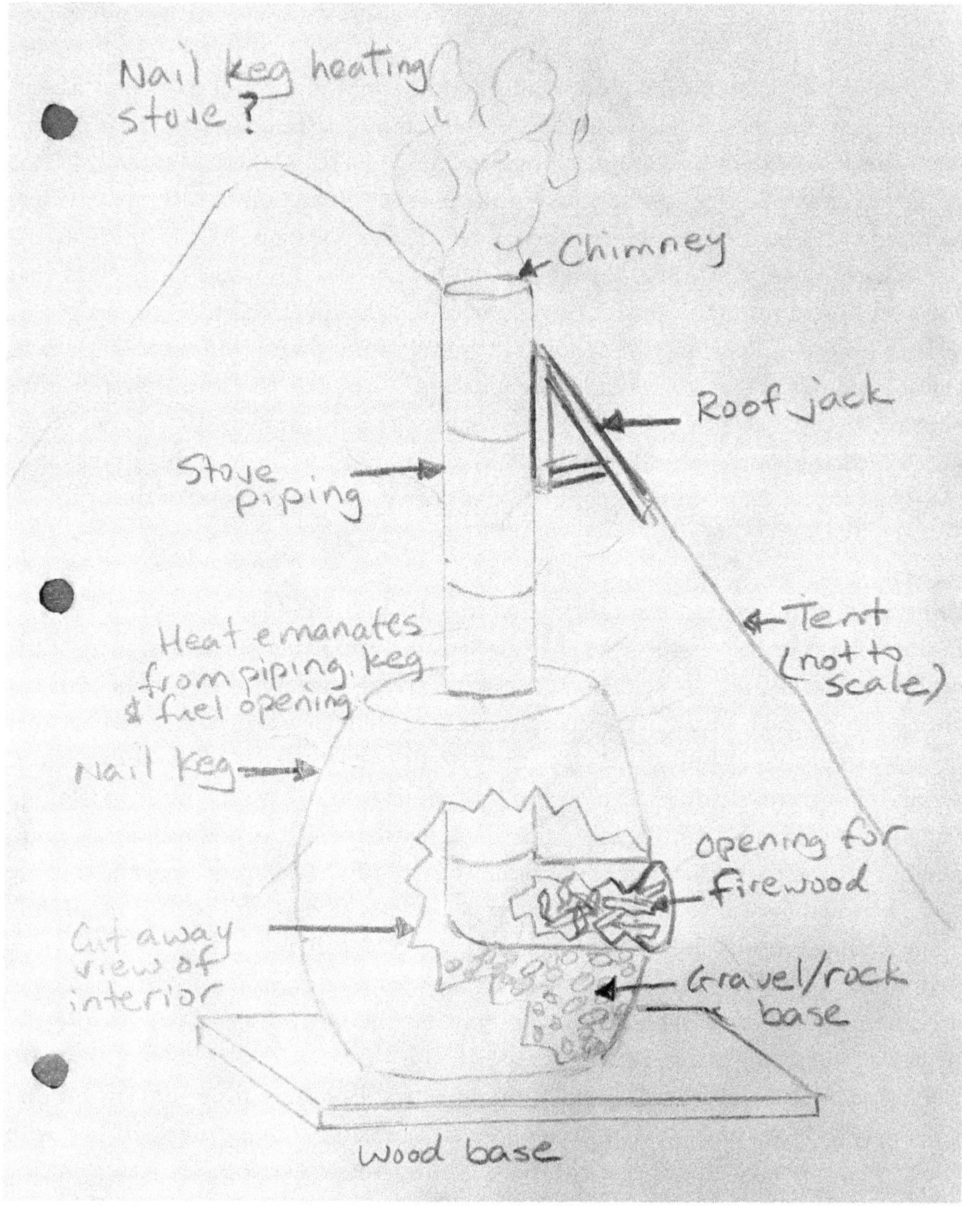

Figure 11.4 Betty Toyota's younger cousin, Mike Abe, drew the stove that she describes as he imagined it in 2018.

Although she explains that the women established these businesses "just to make side money," Betty situates her description of them in a discussion of community, sandwiched between communal baths ("every night we went for a bath and, yes, sit around") and reminiscences of Saturday night movies and dances.

Complicating such portrayals of making is the story of Yeiji Inouye, who was seventeen years old when he was separated from his family to build shacks at the internment site of New Denver. Working alongside other men his age, and eventually joined by his father as well, Yeiji participated in the hasty construction of some 150 shelters required to house internees before the winter of 1942. Kyla, one of our interviewers, expresses some admiration at this work: "Oh my god. So this is an actual shack that you built?" Yeiji responds, pushing against her sentiment, "I know … it's terrible … terrible housing." Recalling the spare inadequacy of the shacks and the violations of privacy and family that they entailed, he reiterates, "it was terrible, but anyway, we got nothing we could do."[91] The exchange was a striking reminder to me that not all "making" served as a source of pride or a buttress to community. The hardship of displacement and the necessity of makeshift could also be part of the terrors of the era.

HEATHER

I wonder if we might notice another generational difference in remembering here. As in the answers to the questions of the previous section, many of the narrators in the group that I studied seem to express making through the lens of childhood. For example, George Takashima, who learned to craft wood in New Denver, remembers that there was a group for boys there who made "sleds and bobsleds." In the summers, he recalls building rafts from which he and his friends would "try their hand at fishing." He also remembers catching wild rabbits, taking them home, and building "rabbit pens, only to discover that they could escape quite easily." Food gathering and making was a key memory for George as well. Everyone had a garden, and George recalls foraging for mushrooms and fiddleheads. Since there were no refrigerators, "what many people did was dig deep into the ground to keep the food cool."[92] George's memories are narrated in a very matter-of-fact way; for him, this was not necessarily positive or negative but rather just the reality of his early life.

Norman Takeuchi, five years old at the time, recalls leisure time with his brother playing with boxes and making his own toys: "I remember being very satisfied with what we could make out of scraps of wood, making toy trucks, logging trucks, cutting large branches." He also tells a wonderfully descriptive story about the making required for his family to supplement their income in the self-supporting camp where they lived. The family bought "a few hundred chicks" and Norman remembers his father building a chicken pen. Once eggs were laid, the family would transfer them into "these little cardboard forms which we are all familiar with, piled on the wagon, and we would walk down the highway to this chicken farm," where his father would sell them. Norman recalls feeling embarrassed but as an adult, reflects, "we had no choice, we had to do that."[93]

JORDAN

One of the older narrators, Yoshiko Hasegawa describes similar work and its benefits to the family in the postwar. During the internment, her family also raised chickens, selling their eggs, and made a variety of traditional products, including oboro and kamaboko fish pastes. In addition:

> We used to make those little boxes by hand. My dad used to buy the ends of the lumber from the sawmill and then he bought a little table saw and he could make little boxes and we would nail it together. He made the three yokan [red-bean-based jelly desserts]. We sent that across the country, too. My dad said "In a place like Greenwood, if you want to save X amount of money it's quite easy because there's nowhere else to spend it other than your life, what you spend for your daily expenses."

Indeed, the family saved enough to purchase a house in Vancouver immediately after internment, where Yoshiko's sister still lived in 2015: "she's thinking of moving and selling the house but there's too many memories. I think it's hard for her to get rid of everything."[94]

HEATHER

Harry Hamadea, nine years old in 1942, describes making skis in Lemon Creek: he would pick up lumber, two to three inches wide, build a bonfire, "get a bucket, fill it up with water … and soak the, boil the heck out of the lumber to get the bend, and then we'd squeeze it in somewhere and bend it to get the toe, and build our own little skis."[95] Ed Kimura notes that interned shipwrights "built sleighs for all of us" at Christina Lake.[96] In her narratives, Mary Kitagawa offers one of the most complex depictions of making in the context of internment. She recounts in harrowing detail the hardships of life in Rosebery, describing the unbearably cold first winter and the inadequacy of the housing. She goes on to reflect that "it's amazing, how people in this kind of condition … persevere and try to create community … so that the children will feel as if it's normal." She recalls women created sewing groups, men played board games, and the community, "after about a year," demanded schools, so, "the fathers built these desks … desks and bench." Mary remembers fathers in the community helped to "build this great big bath house, so that at least we can keep ourselves clean, instead of bathing in that tiny tub," which had been the government issue. She also describes food gathering in great detail, from foraging strawberries and hazelnuts, to the numerous "productive gardens" in the camps.[97]

Figure 11.5 Joshua Labove interviewing Keo Shibatani.

b. Making Community

HEATHER

Making is about much more than things. Children of the 1940s who were in internment and self-supporting camps recount a rich community life and a precious freedom that was established, in addition to the material creations already described.[98] These narratives sit in tension with the lived realities of the adults and seem to me to exemplify the strength of quiet resistance taking place. Roy Uyeda describes it well: "I had a grand time, always romping in the hills, you know? Watching these wild deer and all that … I don't think the adults were thinking the same thing. They lost all of their property."[99] Roy's brief comments communicate the stark discrepancy between the realities of the wider world and the protected world of childhood.

Similarly, Keo Shibatani recalls community life in Tashme in contrast with an early life of poverty in Vancouver during the 1930s. His father was a labourer and they moved frequently. But during the 1940s in Tashme, Keo actually "experienced a very stable lifestyle for the first time." Keo describes a wealth of activities at Tashme, recalling that there were twelve blackbelt judo teachers (which he believed "represented almost one hundred per cent of the black belt holders in Canada"), as well as a thriving Scouting community. Keo and a friend played baseball. Members of the community also played hockey:

> [W]e played on a lake. So, there's no boards, no nothing. The puck would go sliding way across the lake to where the ice was not that thick and, unless you're careful, you'd fall in. So we always made a fire before we put our skates on so that if somebody fell in ... you'd have a fire going right there. I remember falling in once.[100]

Henry Shibata recounts rich life in Lemon Creek. In addition to a primary school, for activities "we'd ski, skate sled, fishing, all that; and then we had communal baths where people would congregate and talk to each other." He also recalls watching movies in camp, remembering an "enterprising guy" who travelled between camps, "taking reels of movies" for local screenings.[101] In Roy, Keo, and Henry's narratives, we glimpse a network of adults working very hard to protect children's lives and remake community ties and connections.

For some reason, a biological metaphor comes to mind here: a forest fire is one of the most devastating things that can happen to an ecosystem, but almost immediately after a fire, life begins again, as pioneering species start to take root in the soil and regrow the forest. I make the comparison here as a way of suggesting that human beings make objects and make lives together as a natural impulse and that it is almost impossible to cut that impulse off. Despite the Canadian government's extreme efforts to eradicate Japanese Canadian communal life and due to the incredible efforts of Japanese Canadians during the era, aspects of community and cultural life persisted, albeit in forever altered forms.

KAITLIN

The challenge of rebuilding continued after the internment. Though cabinet repealed the last policies of internment in 1949, their effects lingered in postwar Canada. Impoverished and displaced, Japanese Canadians grappled with the legacies of internment and dispossession while facing continued discrimination in housing and employment. For fear of renewed hostility, many Japanese Canadians raised their children in mainstream Canadian culture. Japanese Canadians faced continued challenges in the decades following the war.[102]

Rose and Richard Murakami's account of their reestablishment on Salt Spring Island and attempts to commemorate Japanese Canadian history there point to the continued enmity against which they struggled.[103] Rose, born in 1937, and Richard, born in 1940, describe the explicit hostility that their parents faced when they returned to Salt Spring Island in 1949. Practicing Anglicans, they were shocked when the bishop bluntly excluded them from the church on the island; Richard recalls that the archdeacon "came here and told our mother that 'you can never, ever come to church again' because we were evil people." Rose adds, "He came on behalf of the congregation." The incident was one of many. The siblings describe a phone call from a representative

Figure 11.6 Kyla Fitzgerald with Richard Murakami.

of the Islands Trust informing them of the federation's intention to get the "god damn Japs out of the island," and the explicit rejection, on grounds of race, when Rose and her sister Mary sought employment. They describe businesses refusing to serve them. They remember hostility from government officials. They recall that when their family donated money to include a weeping cherry tree in a commemorative garden for Canada's centenary in 1967, the organizer told them that "the park committee decided that they didn't want people of your race to donate to the park." The stories of the Murakami family are jarring. They are unique in certain ways, reflecting their experience on Salt Spring Island, but they are not dissimilar from other narrators' stories of reestablishment across Canada, especially in the immediate postwar period. Though the internment had ended, Japanese Canadians encountered continued prejudice as they sought to rebuild.

In this context, the reestablishment of the Japanese Canadian community stands as resistance and resilience. Working within a hostile society, Japanese Canadians created community in their new locales. In Toronto, Aiko Murakami became involved with the Nisei Ladies Women's Club.[104] Mel Tsuji initially became involved "because there were some dances being held and it was a good way to meet girls" but throughout his life remained connected to community initiatives through sport, being a longtime member of the Japanese Canadian Hockey League, and even serving as the president of the Japanese Canadian Sunday Baseball League.[105] Japanese Canadian community life emerged and reestablished in the postwar period, in the new locals.

These networks laid foundations for the remarkable achievement of the 1988 redress settlement between the government of Canada and the mobilized Japanese Canadian community.[106] Although, this is not an emphasis of this chapter, redress was frequently discussed in the interviews as narrators described how it touched their lives in varying ways. Some narrators were directly involved with the strategic team (like Tony Nabata), while others were involved through local organizational branches (like Vivian Wakabayashi Rygnestad). As we contemplate the "makings" of the wartime and immediate postwar era, I think it is important to consider the foundations that this work provided for subsequent mobilization. Japanese Canadians rebuilt homes within which their tradition of political assertiveness could reemerge.[107]

If the rebuilding of home sometimes took communal and political form, it also served private and personal ends. Akemi Kobayashi's interview reminds us that Japanese Canadians rebuilt lives away from community associations. Born in Toronto in 1947, Akemi describes her parents as being of "that generation ... [who] accept[ed] things for how they were, didn't dwell on the past." Instead, they focused more on the "present and the future." Her parents worked constantly to make ends meet; her father held three jobs and her mother worked as a seamstress. Each week, the family sat for a "very traditional British Sunday dinner" with "roast beef, Yorkshire pudding," and "several different kinds of cakes and pastries and pies" that her mother made. Akemi explains that her mother's love of "everything British" was "just the influence of working for these families and living in Vancouver." Given this environment, Akemi grew uncertain in her cultural identity: "I don't know growing up that I really, I mean I knew I was Japanese heritage but ... I didn't always just self-identify as Japanese." At the time of her interview, Akemi explains, she did not "really strongly identify being of Japanese heritage." Nonetheless, she was "proud" of her "cultural background" and "very grateful" to her parents, explaining that she felt "French, not Japanese." Since a trip to France after university, she had immersed herself in that culture: "I love the culture ... the arts, there's parts of France that I love to spend time in."[108] Japanese culture was not completely absent from her life – she and her siblings loved when her father made Japanese food and she enrolled her son in Japanese language lessons – but her story is different from those narrators who invested in Japanese Canadian organizational life. It is an important reminder that Japanese Canadians rebuilt varied material and cultural lives in the postwar era. Reestablishment of community – building security and lives after internment – could take different forms, depending on the interests and life-paths of the individuals.[109]

HEATHER

The oral history collection is filled with joys and surprises but also with the trials and traumas of making in a context of dispossession. The achievements of Japanese Canadians in rebuilding their lives are remarkable. Stories of Japanese Canadian creativity and invention during internment and thereafter offer inspiration. At the same time, the life narratives in the Landscapes of Injustice collection also convey overpowering material and psychological hardship. It is vital to remember that their creations did not emerge from their own free expression but rather from the violence of the killing of home, in all its complexity.[110]

Theme 3: Returns

KAITLIN

When I was working through the interviews, I started taking notes on what I thought of as "return trips."[111] In the interviews that you are writing from, Heather and Jordan, there is a chance that these trips were "returns" in the most literal meaning of the word. Many Japanese Canadians born before the 1940s have lived memories of the places from which they were displaced. They could knock on the door of a house from which they had been uprooted and meet its new owner. These stories are often poignant and are sometimes surprising.

The question of returns is different for those who were born after the uprooting in 1942. When these narrators visited sites of prewar Japanese Canadian life, they often came to them for the first time. Their stories of "return" are part of their relations to the legacies of the 1940s. The youngest narrators' return trips were shaped by their family cultures of storytelling and often by their silences. Visits to sites of prewar Japanese Canadian life were a way to connect with a past that was often difficult to discuss.

Listening to the stories of the youngest narrators, I noticed that the silences they describe had limits and contours around which children caught glimpses of past lives. Terry Watada and Michiyo Jean Maeda each describe similar narrative disjuncture in their understandings of their own family histories. Terry, who was born in Toronto in 1951, recalls growing up with the knowledge that "my parents are in Vancouver and then they came here [to Toronto]. I don't know what happened in between [laughs]." Similarly, Jean, born in 1946, recalls that her mother

> once said to us, "You know, we used to have some really nice furniture when we lived in Vancouver." And I always thought, "Well that's stupid, why didn't you just bring it to Winnipeg?" … It's like, I had no idea … that they were evacuated and that they couldn't take anything, you know? She just, she just mentioned that and then that was it. And then I never asked her. [Laughs][112]

For these narrators, the internment was a missing link in their family history – an absence that grew increasingly conspicuous as they grew older. Yet the silence around the internment years was not always absolute; in some families, the difficult memories

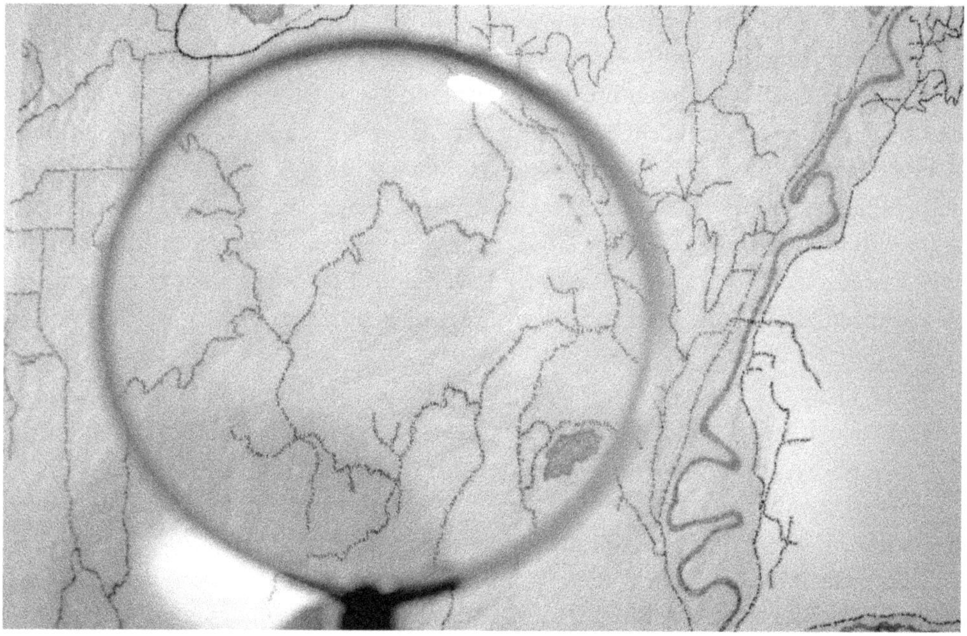

Figures 11.7–11.8 Emma Nishimura ties together notions of research, memory, and place in art. Sometimes too tiny to discern, the lines in Emma's etchings for the series *Constructed Narratives* are actually printed text from fiction, nonfiction, and audio recordings that connect to what her family lived through in those places. In this piece, Emma suggests that places hold evidence of their family's past, a common theme among narrators in the youngest group.

made uneven storytelling. In Sachiko Okuda's family, the harm of the internment years remained palpable and shaped her knowledge of her family's past. Though her father would tell stories of internment in "unconnected anecdotes," her mother preferred to "put the past behind her" and rarely spoke of those years. If she ran into friends from internment, Sachiko's mother would vaguely introduce them as "friends from camp" but tell Sachiko, "I don't like to talk about those times." Despite this reluctance, however, Sachiko had glimpses into her mother's past. For instance, when her mother criticized schooling in Montreal, she would tout the benefits of a BC education. Or, when her mother instructed Sachiko and her brother on how to address envelopes, she referenced her experience working in a post office during internment: "She had told us about being in the post office in order to justify her criticism of our handwriting," Sachiko explains, "but she was always very cagey about where this post office was, which was in Bay Farm."[113] Visiting their family's prewar homes offered a chance for some narrators to explore the terrain opened by such silences.[114]

In their returns, the youngest narrators imagined their family's pasts. David Mitsui, who grew up in southern Ontario, describes his unexpected opportunity to walk through his family's former home in British Columbia. Until the "last few years" of their lives, he explains, his parents did not speak "a single word" about their internment experience. Instead, commemorations of his grandfather's First World War military service drew David into researching his family's past. When he was planning a Thanksgiving visit to his daughter's new home in Coquitlam, a real estate advertisement popped up on David's internet browser: "It had this house for sale, 1945 Laurier Avenue, formerly owned by World War I veteran Sergeant Masumi Mitsui," David recalls. He and his wife contacted the real estate agent and arranged a visit. The following week, David found himself on his family's former property, in the house his grandfather had rebuilt in 1941 after a fire: "There were four bedrooms and the kitchen was modernized but the rest of the house was basically the same," David recalls:

> It was an eerie experience … it was just, I don't know, an unreal experience to … especially just walking … The downstairs was pretty much [the same], the kitchen was modernized, the living room area and dining room … you know the spaces were the same but it had been upgraded a bit. Going upstairs to the bedrooms, the ceiling was rounded and it had like cedar planks, thin planks and four bedrooms and I'm thinking, "Hmm … I wonder which one my dad had and which one was my aunt Lucy and my aunt Amy."

Walking through the house, David recalls thinking, "if things were different and this property was still owned by my grandfather, what it would have been like?" David's wife encouraged him to pursue historical designation for the site, but he demurred. When it sold, for more than $600,000, she said, "that should be your place."

But David thought, "No, that's history. That's a long time ago and I'm not into digging up old wounds like that and you know that's my history but it's not my history. It's my grandfather's and my father's place, or was their place ... It just made me, I guess, very sad."[115]

Leslie Uyeda describes a similarly complex reaction to seeing her family's prewar home. Her family was reticent to talk about the internment years, but their reservations about returning to British Columbia made the history present in Leslie's life in Montreal. One of her aunts was vehemently against returning to the coast: "I believe the quote was, 'they threw me out once and they will never do it again' and, indeed, she did not come back here to visit." Leslie undertook her own research to learn about her family's past and in the late 1980s she first drove past her family's prewar home in Dunbar, a neighbourhood of Vancouver. Like David, she imagined her family in the home:

> So, I would drive up there and just look at it and see my family, imagine my family there on those steps. It has a very particular front, this house, it's on a corner overlooking a park. It's probably worth gazillions now. Part of why that house means something to me is that my rage is involved in that house because it's still there ... I wonder how the present owner has got it and the previous owners, how did they get it? And the previous owners, how did they get it? And did the first owners, after my family had had to leave, did they know how they came to acquire that house?

Leslie was reluctant to pursue answers to those questions, unsure of her place to do so. "I feel that," she explains, "it was not my sorrow, in a way ... It certainly wasn't my direct sorrow, but these things are passed on whether it's through stultified silence or through rage or through verbalization or anything." Leslie describes her relationship to the home as "unfinished business," saying she "didn't have the courage" to knock on the door and felt it would be unfair to residents.[116] Despite the emotional impact of witnessing their family's prewar homes, and the connections that they felt to these places, Leslie and David share a similar reluctance to express publicly their feelings of connection and ownership. Their reluctance reflects some uncertainty over both culpability (was it fair to hold the current owner responsible for the harm of the dispossession?) and victimhood (was it their place, as descendants of the former owners, to pursue that sort of justice?).

HEATHER

In my group of narrators, Arthur and Keiko Miki, based in Winnipeg, Manitoba, discuss broadly the idea of Japanese Canadians returning to British Columbia, in the context of their work in redress. Keiko reflects that, "a lot of people ... who moved

East … didn't want to go to BC again because they had all these bad feelings about it." She mentions after redress, they had "reunions and a celebration" but some people declined attending. Art concurs, recalling a conference called "Home Coming" that they organized in Vancouver, which people refused to attend. Both Keiko and Art are almost at a loss to explain why people declined, saying "they hadn't dealt with it," and "they hadn't really discussed [it]," referring to the trauma of the past.

Arthur and Keiko also tell personal stories of return. Keiko was born in Steveston. Asked about returning to her family's former homes, Keiko implies she would not know where to go, expressing confusion about whether her parents had owned property. She recalls addresses for several rental properties that she has seen in family records and muses that she needs to seek more information. Arthur was born in Vancouver but grew up in Haney. Art is more discursive, recalling that he and Keiko took their kids to see his grandparents' farm in Haney, "to just show them." As he talks, he recalls multiple return visits to the former home:

> the first time we went there … the kids weren't there. You [Keiko], my mother, and I and Roy I think we went and saw the house that we lived … my grandfather's house was still there but this other house was the one … that we'd lived in [and it] was being boarded up and they were going to tear it down and I remember my mother going through it and saying this was where this was and oh they moved this … But … we were told that that part of the property was sold and that it would be converted. So the next time that we went to the same property that building was gone and there was a huge house on there, yeah big house. But our farm was still there and so the guy who owned … my grandfather's house allowed us to go and visit so we took our kids there and so that they could see.

Art later heard the house was "boarded up" and "was being demolished," and now, "it's gone." After making that statement, gently directed by the interviewer, Art recalls specific details about the house and refers to photos he inspected before visiting, noting "nothing's changed." While it is gone in a physical sense, the property lives in Art's memories.[117]

In Art's personal story, there is a tale of literal return, of knocking on a door and meeting a new owner. It is a journey that members of the family make multiple times. Within Art's narrative, too, there are glimpses of returns made across generations: Art's mother, who could relive the past in more detail, returns to a house that for her would have been full of remembered experience. Art's children are also present in the narrative, but they were returning to a place of family heritage, making a pilgrimage to history, rather than retracing their own steps. And Art, his brother Roy, and his wife Keiko are present in the narrative as well, bridging the generations. Art's narrative suggests a rich avenue for future research to bring multigenerational families together to explore how each might narrate the experience of returning differently.

In his interview, Henry Shibata describes two kinds of return trips. Henry was born in Vancouver and lived through internment in Lemon Creek. After the war, his family was deported to Japan, a new place for Henry but a return for Henry's parents, both from Hiroshima. The journey by boat took ten days. Henry recalls the trip was not bad, but when they got to Japan, "it was a different story." He describes Japan as "a battle ground," that people were "going hungry … [and] dying on the streets." His father had told Henry positive things about Japan, in stark contrast to what they found; the discrepancy prompted Henry to ask his father, "why the hell did you bring me to this godforsaken place?" Henry's parents sent telegrams once they landed to determine if any relatives had survived the war; thankfully they had all been evacuated before the bomb and were able to take care of Henry and his family as they adjusted to life in Japan. Henry finished school in Japan, becoming a doctor and working, for a time, for a US-led research institute studying the effects of the atomic bomb on humans. Henry often "thought about trying to find a way to come back to Canada" and eventually did return (going first to Beverly, Massachusetts in 1957 and eventually ending up in Montreal in 1961). Later in life, he went to find his prewar home in Vancouver:

> Yeah, I've gone to look at the house where we used to live. It's on 308 Cordova Street. It's gone now. They made some kind of an apartment or condominium complex there now but it used to be there and the distinguishing feature of that house that we lived in was that it had a cherry tree in the front yard … Anyways, that house, I used to go back there and every time I'd go to Vancouver I'd go and see if that was still there and it was still there. The last time we went, which is about 1989 or 1990, it was gone.[118]

I find Henry's story compelling because it reveals tension and division between the generational experiences of home in Henry's family. Henry's parents decided to accept exile, according to Henry's understanding, to take care of any aging relatives who might have survived the war. After living through severe discrimination in Canada and watching their hometown get bombed from afar, Henry's parents attempted to return to an anchor point, in both a personal and geographic sense. But Henry's anchor was in Canada. He spent a decade and a half plotting a return to his country of origin and eventually succeeded. Finally, like Art Miki, he describes multiple returns from Montreal to his family's former home in Vancouver.

In both Art and Henry's narratives there is a sad finality to their statements when the old properties are discovered to be "gone." They are simple words, simply spoken, but there is considerable emotion behind them. They seem to be describing a final moment of loss for each family, where there is perhaps an understanding that the last vestige of an old home has finally been destroyed; as Porteous and Smith describe, a sense of home is bound up in the physical space of home, as well as "the meaning and social texture of community that is inextricably interwoven with the physical fabric." For Art and Henry, the meaning and texture were long gone, but the "physical manifestation" at least facilitated or generated memories that connected them to the past.[119] I find myself wondering where do they now go when they want to remember or to prompt memories in others?

JORDAN

The oldest narrators speak relatively seldom about return trips. I am not sure what to make of this. In some instances, these interviews include brief exchanges about returns, somewhat reminiscent, in their terseness, of those that I noticed in relation to specific possessions. In her interview of Tom Matsui, for example, Heather asks, "did you ever go back and visit ever?" Tom replies, "Ah yeah, I did. I did in '68, and then very recently my son went back and he was looking for that house 617 Powell Street." Tom says almost nothing about his own return, moving quickly to his son's experience, which included a tour of the interior of the house with its present owners.[120] Min Takada answers the same question similarly, "yeah. It was all gone. There was somebody else living there. So, yeah, well, we went by the old house but that's about it." Min then reflects briefly on the motives of officials who forced the sales in the 1940s, never elaborating on his experience of return.[121] Yeiji Inouye heard from others the fate of his family's apartment in Vancouver, "yeah, well it's torn down."[122] Perhaps, in such exchanges, and in the ellipses that they seem to imply, we catch a glimpse of the absences that motivated return trips within your cohorts and rendered them so meaningful. In the context of so little being said, a return trip by a younger relative had vast silences to fill. Certainly, it is also possible that such exchanges convey the pain of loss.

KAITLIN

I agree, Jordan; it does seem like the older narrators showed some of the reticence that the youngest narrators describe in the interviews I studied. Their relative terseness also reminds me of our earlier reflections on the generational differences in relation to property salvaged during the forced uprooting. Following that line of thinking, we might consider that it was because the older generation could relate to the landscapes of their past in memory that they were more ambivalent about visiting those geographies than their descendants (for whom, in contrast it is an opportunity to learn). Unlike stories about belongings, stories about returns also provoke descriptions of repulsion, anger, and lingering harm. I think this is an important distinction. Whereas belongings could sit firmly within narratives about family and resilience, the landscapes of British Columbia, which remained in the ownership of others, recall their displacement.

Further complicating the question of returns were the experiences of narrators who lived in British Columbia. Some of our narrators describe returns undertaken in the immediate aftermath of the internment as their families – a minority among the uprooted – stayed in the province. Several explain that their families returned to British Columbia after deciding that it offered better economic prospects than the east. Suzy and Kelvin Higo (mother and son, respectively) explain that their family's decision to return was largely made by Kelvin's father. When they initially resettled in Winnipeg, he found work in a foundry. Despite welcome job security, the work nearly consumed him: describing long hours, night shifts, and concerning weight loss, Suzy explains that the "job was too much for him." When Kelvin asks his mother if they were concerned about racism upon return to British Columbia, she suggests that the opportunity for employment outweighed any such worries:

> I don't think so because I felt, well, my husband's choice was to come back to be a fisherman. He felt that working in a foundry was not going to be a good job and when they allowed ... From the time he was little he knew fishing. His dad took him out fishing so from the time when he was old enough, maybe ten or twelve years old, he'd be rocking for his dad so he knew nothing but rock fishing.[123]

Similarly, Shig Ugeyama's father attempted to settle in eastern Canada before returning to British Columbia. When the family returned to Canada from exile in Japan in 1956, they began a business in Toronto. When it failed, Shig's father moved the family to Nanaimo where he resumed salmon fishing "like he did when he was a kid." In Nanaimo, the family rekindled old relationships where they had left off: "Nanaimo was the type of place where they had good relations before the war," Shig explains, "so my dad had kept those friends and in fact he went fishing with the guys he went fishing with before the war."[124] In Kelvin and Shig's stories, reestablishment in the fishing industry, which contained its own world of codes and community, overshadowed the history of animosity and any remaining hostility. For their fathers, returns to prewar work enabled them to rebuild, if partially, their former lives.

For some in British Columbia, postwar life brought them into close proximity with sites of dispossession. Vivian Wakabayashi Rygestad, for instance, describes her family driving past their prewar home on several occasions. The Wakabayashis had stayed in Blind Bay after the internment orders lifted and returned to Vancouver in 1960 so that Vivian could pursue a university degree. Back in Vancouver, their father often brought his daughters to see his childhood home, recalling to them where he and his father buried silverware and china before their uprooting. Vivian laughs and remembers how she and her sister would always say, "Let's go knock on the door and see if it's still there!" Her father, however, always declined. "He wouldn't let us. I don't know what his reasons were."[125] Vivian's story, like many of the others we have mentioned, points to a generational difference. Whereas she and her sister were eager to recover the family's belongings, her father refused. Despite this, the building remained part of his personal landscape in Vancouver twenty years after his forced uprooting, a landmark to point out to his daughters. For the Wakabayashis, and a few other narrators in our collection whose families returned to their prewar locals, their former homes remained meaningful landmarks in painful stories of the past.

Together, these stories of return suggest that, simultaneous with the tremendous rebuilding and success of the postwar, sites of dispossession remained meaningful to Japanese Canadians. For some, painful reminders of the injustices of the 1940s foreclosed any potential visit to former homes. For others, returns were necessary to the telling of such harms and to the wider story of their family histories. Parents brought their children, in Art's words, "to just show them," to bear witness. Other narrators sought out these sites to fill gaps in what their families could share. For these returnees, witnessing the homes offered an opportunity to connect the fragments of their family's stories, to somehow link the disjointed ends of before and after internment.

Inevitably, the injustices the families endured were part of the experience. When his family walked into their former single-room apartment on Princess Avenue in 1994, for instance, Ed Tanaka's older sister "burst out crying." Her memory of the room, he explains, was from the perspective of a seven- or eight-year-old, "and what she saw there was so different."[126] Narrators express simultaneous connection with and estrangement from the sites of their dispossession. In highlighting this unsettled dynamic in family storytelling and memory, the stories of return help us see the legacies of displacement and dispossession.

Conclusion

JORDAN, HEATHER, AND KAITLIN

At the start of this chapter, Heather described it as a "primer" to the Landscapes of Injustice oral history collection soon available to a wider research community. We hope it will indeed serve this purpose. The oral history cluster produced an invaluable archive, one that should enrich both scholarly and communal understanding of this history for years to come. The collection testifies to the breadth and diversity of Japanese Canadians' experiences before, during, and after internment. The dispossession lives on as part of thousands of families in thousands of ways. To convey the scope of the collection, we choose an approach that touches only briefly on each interview, leaving much of each narrator's life unexamined. We all hope that future researchers will enter into this rich collection to dwell at depth on individual stories, learning and writing new accounts that will surely challenge our own.

Here, we have emphasized several key patterns in the collection. We observed generational differences in how Japanese Canadians narrated loss and in the role that particular material possessions played in their memories. We encountered striking stories of outrage in the face of dispossession, and heartening evidence of resilience and of the capacity of individuals, families, and communities to mitigate state violence through careful decision making and remaking their homes and communities. We explored the legacies of loss in a landscape pockmarked by the scars of dispossession, sites of loss sometimes avoided and sometimes visited in a search for meaning and history.

The Landscapes of Injustice collection will soon sit beside other oral history projects with Japanese Canadians. In the 1970s, when government records remained restricted and the internment forgotten in public commemoration, oral histories were part of a vital attempt to document this past. Since then, Japanese Canadians have mobilized remarkable initiatives to achieve public and state recognition and to prevent similar injustices from repeating, including major oral history projects. One of the achievements of redress was to infuse energy (and funds) into community institutions so that these initiatives could snowball. The narrators in our collection contributed to, engaged with, lived and grew-up in the context of these achievements of the Japanese Canadian community. The Landscapes of Injustice interviews stand in conversation with the history that followed the 1940s as much as they recall the details of those years. Japanese Canadians' stories today allow us to ask questions about what it means to have grown up with memories of injustice, what it means to ask questions, to tell this history, and to listen, as firsthand knowledge becomes intermixed with and supplemented by community initiatives and historical research.

The oral history collection also affirms, in its complex and varied ways, that the history of property is a history of relations among people, the lives of families, and forms of belonging, rather than merely a history of people in relation to material objects.[127] The decoration of an apartment, the dishes we eat from, our clothes, farms, and the business we create become bound up with our sense of self because our ownership is situated in a web of human relations unfolding over time – family, community, professional, political – that imbue at least some objects and lands with special meaning. This reality of property ownership was powerfully expressed by Japanese Canadians in the 1940s as they tried to communicate to officials the harms caused by the seizure and sale of their property.[128] In very different ways it is expressed also in these memories. The Landscapes of Injustice oral history collection expresses the varied ways in which property becomes a meaningful thread in the fabric of self-understanding. It conveys complex multigenerational relationships. It reveals how the harms of property dispossessed endure in the ruptures of lives lived.

NOTES

Thanks to readers Mike Abe, Tosh Kitagawa, Mary Kitagawa, Lynne Marks, David Mitsui, Vivian Wakabayashi Rygnestad, and Eric Sager.

1 Chapter 1.

2 The NNM's oral history collection – the largest and to date most accessible archive of interviews of Japanese Canadians in the country – is available online through the Simon Fraser University Library: http://digital.lib.sfu.ca/johc-collection.

3 The count of 148 refers to the total number of people interviewed. In total, our researchers recorded 132 separate conversations.

4 Pamela Sugiman, "Acts of Kindness and Complicity," unpublished paper presented at the Royal BC Museum, 28 January 2018.

5 Pamela Sugiman, "'Life Is Sweet': Vulnerability and Composure in the Wartime Narratives of Japanese Canadians," *Journal of Canadian Studies* 43, no. 1 (Winter 2009): 186–218.

6 The reflections on the relationship of the oral history component of the project to the broader whole can add to a growing body of Canadian scholarship reflecting on the methodological challenges of larger scale oral history research. See Steven High, *Oral History at the Crossroads: Sharing Life Stories of Survival and Displacement* (Vancouver: UBC Press, 2014).

7 Henry Greenspan, On Listening to Holocaust Survivors: Recounting and Life History (Westport, CT: Praeger, 1998), xvi.

8 Ronald J. Grele, *Envelopes of Sound, The Art of Oral History,* 2nd edition (Westport, CT: Greenwood 1985 [1975]), 135.

9 Edward D. Ives, *The Tape Recorded Interview: A Manual for Fieldworkers in Folklore and Oral History*, 2nd edition. (Knoxville, TN: University of Tennessee Press, 1995), 39.

10 Kaitlin Findlay, "The Bird Commission, Japanese Canadians, and the Challenge of Reparations in the Wake of State Violence" (MA thesis, University of Victoria, 2017).

11 With the division of research established, our writing process resembled a relay. In the first round, each author introduced a theme and offered preliminary reflections. With each theme introduced, we then took turns with the draft. We made edits, left comments, and added new material each turn. As one author introduced new material, the other authors adjusted their analysis in other sections of the chapter accordingly. Thus, analysis occurred in the process of writing with and in relation to each other. Where our names are attached to certain segments that reflect our research and thinking, the sections undoubtedly benefited from the perspective and review of the other coauthors.

12 Mona Oikawa, *Cartographies of Violence: Japanese Canadian Women, Memory, and the Subjects of the Internment* (Toronto: University of Toronto Press, 2012), 250.

13 Ruth Roach Pierson, "Experience, Difference, Dominance, and Voice in the Writing of Canadian Women's History," in *Writing Women's History: International Perspectives*, eds., Karen Offen, Ruth Roach Pierson, and Jane Rendall (London: MacMillan Press, 1991), 83.

14 Pierson, "Experience, Difference, Dominance, and Voice," 90.

15 Ruth Behar, *The Vulnerable Observer* (Boston, MT: Beacon Press, 1996), 13.

16 For a more extended discussion of my own family, see Jordan Stanger-Ross and Pamela

Sugiman, "Preface," in *Witness to Loss: Race, Culpability, and Memory in the Dispossession of Japanese Canadians*, eds., Stanger-Ross and Sugiman (Montreal & Kingston: McGill-Queen's University Press, 2017), xiii–xvii. More broadly, see Richard Alba and Victor Nee, *Remaking the American Mainstream: Assimilation and Contemporary Immigration* (Cambridge, MA: Harvard University Press, 2005).

17 I am conscious that I have less in common with Japanese Canadians than with the people who perpetrated the dispossession. Does that enable me to understand their motivations and decisions? I am not sure. But, if we are serious about learning from this past, I think it is valuable to imagine (and recognize ourselves) as agents of change with the capacity to inflict harm upon others, even in complacency.

18 Ellen Crowe-Swords, interviewed by Kyla Fitzgerald, 27 July 2015, Ucluelet, British Columbia, LOIOH, University of Victoria .

19 I am inspired by the words of Alessandro Portelli, "Let [our history] show how historians themselves grow, change, and stumble through the research encounter with other subjects," he writes. "Speaking about the "other" as a subject is far from enough, until we see ourselves as subjects among others and we place time in ourselves, and ourselves in time" (*The Death of Luigi Trastulli and Other Stories: Form and Meaning in Oral History* [Albany, NY: State University of New York Press, 1991], 76).

20 Sean Field, "'Beyond Healing': Trauma, Oral History and Regeneration," *Oral History* 34, no. 1 (2006): 31.

21 Important Notice, 19 May 1942, Personal Archives of Masako Fukawa (figure 5.2, chapter 5). The allowances differed slightly for those uprooted to the sugar beet farms of Alberta and Manitoba (permitted $2 for food each) and those sent to work camps (less baggage, blankets explicitly suggested). Japanese Canadians uprooted to so-called "self-support" camps, who paid privately for their own removal, could take with them what they could afford, aside from confiscated property, such as radios, fishing vessels, and automobiles. After the initial internment, Japanese Canadians could request other belongings be shipped to them, though often at their own expense (see chapter 9).

22 Frank Moritsugu, interviewed by Alexander Pekic, 28 July and 4 August 2015, Toronto, Ontario, LOIOH.

23 Here Erin's terminology runs against the principles of our project, which identify "evacuation" as a deceptive government euphemism for the uprooting and internment of Japanese Canadians. However, it must be remembered that the interviews aim to allow narrators to speak about their lives in their own terms. Bob Hori introduced the term "evacuation" in his response to Erin's first question, "Would you like to start with your family history?" and she mirrors this language back in subsequent moments of the interview.

24 Bob and Sue Hori, interviewed by Erin Yaremko, 16 June 2016, Regina Saskatchewan, LOIOH.

25 Mary and Suzy (Shizuyo) Kimoto, interviewed by Joshua Labove, 12 July 2015, Ucluelet, British Columbia, LOIOH.

26 Frank Moritsugu, interviewed by Alexander Pekic, 28 July and 4 August 2015, Toronto, Ontario, LOIOH.

27 Mary and Suzy (Shizuyo) Kimoto, interviewed by Joshua Labove, 12 July 2015, Ucluelet, British Columbia, LOIOH.

28 Thomas Hiroshi Madokoro interviewed by Rebeca Salas, 17 July 2017, Langley, British Columbia, LOIOH.

29 Indeed, at other moments in their interviews, both Mary and Frank speak in much greater detail about property, as will be explored later.

30 The question is a way to get at the centre of a tumultuous moment, for students (young and old) to put themselves in the shoes of Japanese Canadians and to understand something of their hardship. Rather than a lesson about possessions, it helps participants empathize with the feeling of displacement. Kayla Isomura's recent, and acclaimed, photography exhibit *The Suitcase Project* beautifully displays the reflective power of this exercise: https://www.suitcaseproject.ca/.

31 See chapter 8.

32 Thus, for example, the Hasegawa family filled the bottom of their suitcases with rice, sugar, and salt, unsure of what awaited them in the interior (Yoshiko Hasegawa, interviewed by Kyla Fitzgerald, 17 October 2015, Steveston British Columbia, LOIOH). Likewise, Ken Morisawa, born in 1934, explained that his family took "the bare necessities of what you could put in a suitcase." Laughing, he continued, "So I mean there wasn't much that we, the children, brought of their favourite toys or whatever" (Ken Morisawa, interviewed by Alexander Pekic, 18 November 2015, Georgetown Ontario, LOIOH).

33 Vivian Rygnestad, interviewed by Rebeca Salas, 27 August 2017, Richmond, British Columbia, LOIOH.

34 Mark Sakamoto, interviewed by Alexander Pekic, 18 December 2015, Toronto, Ontario, LOIOH.

35 Ellen Crowe-Swords, interviewed by Kyla Fitzgerald, 27 July 2015, Ucluelet, British Columbia, LOIOH.

36 Sachiko Okuda, interviewed by Joshua Labove, 4 August 2015, Ottawa, Ontario, LOIOH.

37 Barbara Kirshenblatt-Gimblett, *Destination Culture: Tourism, Museums and Heritage* (Berkeley and Los Angeles, CA: University of California Press, 1998), 17–78; Kirsten Emiko McAllister applies a similar argument to "mundane objects of everyday life" transformed by memorialization of the internment into "a status akin to a relic" (*Terrain of Memory: A Japanese Canadian Memorial Project* [Vancouver: UBC Press, 2010], 117).

38 Jean Kamimura, interviewed by Carolyn Nakagawa, 27 January 2018, Vancouver, British Columbia, LOIOH.

39 Blanche Kishi, interviewed by Carolyn Nakagawa, 10 January 2018, Richmond, British Columbia, LOIOH.

40 Harry Hamade, interviewed by Erin Yaremko, 19 November 2015, Winnipeg, Manitoba, LOIOH.

41 Grace Omoto, interviewed by Alexander Pekic, 24 November 2015, Newmarket Ontario, LOIOH.

42 Joanne Maikawa, interviewed by Momoye Sugiman, 18 August 2015, Toronto, Ontario, LOIOH.

43 Elmer Hara, interviewed by Erin Yaremko, 15 June 2016, Winnipeg, Manitoba, LOIOH.

44 Fred Koyama, interviewed by Joshua Labove, 23 July 2015, Toronto, Ontario, LOIOH.

45 Blanche Kishi, interviewed by Carolyn Nakagawa, 10 January 2018, Richmond, British Columbia, LOIOH. Florence Kishi, interviewed by Joshua Labove, 19 November 2015, Port Coquitlam, British Columbia, LOIOH.

46 Kaye and David Hayashida, interviewed by Heather Read, 18 November 2015, Waterloo Ontario, LOIOH.

47 Keiko Mary Kitagawa, interviewed by Rebeca Salas, 17 June 2017, Tsawwassen British Columbia, LOIOH.
48 Vivian and Tony Nabata, interviewed by Kyla Fitzgerald, 15 July 2015, Vancouver British Columbia, LOIOH.
49 Keiko Mary Kitagawa, interviewed by Rebeca Salas, 17 June 2017, Tsawwassen British Columbia, LOIOH.
50 Peter Kurita, interviewed by Heather Read, 10 April 2015, Cobourg, Ontario, LOIOH.
51 Tosh Kitagawa, interviewed by Rebeca Salas, 26 June 2017, Tsawwassen, British Columbia, LOIOH.
52 It is important to note that there was another group of narratives about education from people whose families were deported to Japan during this era. Their stories also provide a compelling perspective on what life was like in Japan during the Second World War. I have excluded their narratives due to the brevity required when writing collaboratively. Researchers interested in pursuing this particular theme further can explore interviews such as those with Doris Kimura and Henry Shibata.
53 Sam Matsuo, interviewed by Erin Yaremko, 11 February 2016, Winnipeg, Manitoba, LOIOH; Keiko and Arthur Miki, interviewed by Erin Yaremko, 9 August 2016, Winnipeg Manitoba, LOIOH.
54 Tosh Kitagawa, interviewed by Rebeca Salas, 26 June 2017, Tsawwassen, British Columbia, LOIOH.
55 Jean Ikeda-Douglas, interviewed by Heather Read, 13 August 2015, Toronto, Ontario, LOIOH.
56 Florence Kishi, interviewed by Joshua Labove, 19 November 2015, Port Coquitlam, British Columbia, LOIOH.
57 George Takashima, interviewed by Joshua Labove, 1 October 2015, Lethbridge, Alberta, LOIOH.
58 Jean Kamimura, interviewed by Carolyn Nakagawa, 27 January 2018, Vancouver, British Columbia, LOIOH.
59 For reflections on the complexity of agency and resistance in the context of the internment, see Jordan Stanger-Ross, "Telling a Difficult Past: Kishizo Kimura's Memoir of Entanglement in Racist Policy," *BC Studies* 181 (2014): 39–62.
60 Betty Toyota and Joy Trapnell, interviewed by Kyla Fitzgerald and Mike Abe, 12 October 2016, Duncan, British Columbia, LOIOH.
61 Stan and Aileen Yokota, interviewed by Heather Read and Peter Hur, 30 October 2015, Scarborough, Ontario, LOIOH.
62 On Gavin Mouat's problematic role as both the local agent of the Custodian and a major beneficiary of land transfers on Salt Spring Island see chapter 10.
63 Keiko Mary Kitagawa, interviewed by Rebeca Salas, 17 June 2017, Tsawwassen British Columbia, LOIOH.
64 Ed and Doris Kimura, interviewed by Jordan Stanger-Ross, 26 June 2015, Vancouver, British Columbia, LOIOH.
65 Vivian and Tony Nabata, interviewed by Kyla Fitzgerald, 15 July 2015, Vancouver, British Columbia, LOIOH.
66 Bob and Sue Hori, interviewed by Erin Yaremko, 16 June 2016, Regina, Saskatchewan, LOIOH.
67 Frank Moritsugu, interviewed by Alexander Pekic, 28 July and 4 August 2015 Toronto, Ontario, LOIOH.

68 Yoshiko Hasegawa, interviewed by Kyla Fitzgerald, 17 October 2015, Steveston, British Columbia, LOIOH. Hasegawa grew up in Vancouver.

69 Mary and Suzy Kimoto, interviewed by Joshua Labove, 12 July 2015, Ucluelet, British Columbia, LOIOH.

70 See James Scott, *Domination and the Arts of Resistance: Hidden Transcripts* (New Haven: Yale University Press, 1990).

71 Yoshiko Hasegawa, interviewed by Kyla Fitzgerald, 17 October 2015, Steveston, British Columbia, LOIOH.

72 Marlene Epp, "The Memory of Violence: Soviet and East European Mennonite Refugees and Rape in the Second World War," *Journal of Women's History* 9, no. 1 (1997): 58–87.

73 These reflections connect to Dr Sugiman's writing on composure and dignity in the stories of Nisei women. See Pamela Sugiman, "'Life Is Sweet': Vulnerability and Composure in the Wartime Narratives of Japanese Canadians," *Journal of Canadian Studies* 43, no. 1 (Winter 2009): 186–218.

74 Jean Ikeda-Douglas, interviewed by Heather Read, 13 August 2015, Toronto, Ontario, LOIOH.

75 According to Jean Ikeda-Douglas, the Hiroshitas were given special permission to stay in Vancouver. In her interview, Jean relates that Alice went to the RCMP and asserted that she would not be moved from her home and that the RCMP allowed them to stay as long as she became responsible for her husband's behaviour. While there has been some discussion of the small number of Japanese Canadians exempted from internment (most of them in mixed marriages or the children of such marriages) the area demands further research. See Ken Adachi, *The Enemy That Never Was: A History of the Japanese Canadians* (Toronto: McClelland & Stewart, 1976), 235 and Oikawa, *Cartographies of Violence*, 145–7.

76 Jean Ikeda-Douglas, interviewed by Heather Read, 13 August 2015, Toronto, Ontario, LOIOH.

77 Yoshiko Hasegawa, interviewed by Kyla Fitzgerald, Steveston, 17 October 2015, British Columbia, LOIOH.

78 Jean Ikeda-Douglas, interviewed by Heather Read, 13 August 2015, Toronto, Ontario, LOIOH. Quoted in Heather Read and the Landscapes of Injustice Research Collective, "The Legacy of a Hidden Camera: Acts of Making in Japanese-Canadian Internment Camps During the Second World War, as Depicted in Tom Matsui's Photograph Collection," *Material Culture Review* 84 (Fall 2016): 29–30.

79 Thanks to Doug Harris for his contributions to our thinking around these acts of property destruction.

80 Ken Nishibata, interviewed by Erin Yaremko, 2 September 2015, Winnipeg, Manitoba, LOIOH.

81 David Mitsui, interviewed by Joshua Labove, 22 September 2015, Edmonton, Alberta, LOIOH.

82 Ibid.

83 Kelvin and Suzy Higo, interviewed by Joshua Labove, 6 May 2016, Richmond British Columbia, LOIOH.

84 Jane Dusselier, *Artifacts of Loss: Crafting Survival in Japanese American Concentration Camps* (New Brunswick, NJ: Rutgers University Press, 2008). The discussion that follows is also influenced by Katherine Teresa Yamashita, "Finding Home After Internment: A

Seven-Sided Story-Art Practice, Memory, and Engaged Response" (PhD dissertation, York University, Toronto, 2011) and Gilly Carr and Harold Mytum eds., *Cultural Heritage and Prisoners of War: Creativity Behind Barbed Wire* (London: Routledge, 2012).

85 Many narrators also talked about redress, a phenomenal example of making in the aftermath of trauma, which we only discuss briefly. We limit our commentary to the internment and the more immediate postwar periods due to space constraints and a sense of where we can most contribute to scholarship. On redress see Roy Miki, *In Flux: Transnational Shifts in Asian Canadian Writing* (Edmonton: Newest Press, 2011), 63–90 and *Redress: Inside the Japanese Canadian Call for Justice* (Vancouver: Raincoast, 2004); Maryka Omatsu, *Bittersweet Passage: Redress and the Japanese Canadian Experience* (Toronto: Between the Lines, 1992); Cassandra Kobayashi and Roy Miki, eds., *Spirit of Redress: Japanese Canadians in Conference* (Vancouver: JC Publications, 1989).

86 Carr and Mytum, *Cultural Heritage*, 3.

87 Ibid., 4.

88 Ibid., 13.

89 Betty Toyota and Joy Trapnell, interviewed by Kyla Fitzgerald and Mike Abe, 12 October 2016, Duncan, British Columbia, LOIOH.

90 Ibid.

91 Yeiji Inouye, interviewed by Kyla Fitzgerald, 17 July 2015, Victoria, British Columbia, LOIOH.

92 George Takashima, interviewed by Joshua Labove, 1 October 2015, Lethbridge, Alberta, LOIOH.

93 Norman Takeuchi, interviewed by Joshua Labove, 24 January 2016, Ottawa, Ontario, LOIOH.

94 Yoshiko Hasegawa, interviewed by Kyla Fitzgerald, 17 October 2015, Steveston, British Columbia, LOIOH.

95 Harry Hamade, interviewed by Erin Yaremko, 19 November 2015, Winnipeg, Manitoba, LOIOH.

96 Ed and Doris Kimura, interviewed by Jordan Stanger-Ross, 26 June 2015, Vancouver, British Columbia, LOIOH.

97 Keiko Mary Kitagawa, interviewed by Rebeca Salas, 17 June 2017, Tsawwassen British Columbia, LOIOH.

98 There were making narratives in the life histories of people who moved to sugar beet farms as well, but they often focused on the physical adjustments to homes that were necessary and the food gathering work that they were engaged in. The narratives were less explicitly about remaking community bonds until much later in their lives, often when people became involved in or aware of redress, involved in a Japanese Canadian church, or some other explicit community building efforts.

99 Roy Uyeda, interviewed by Rebeca Salas, 15 July 2016, Burnaby, British Columbia, LOIOH.

100 Keo Shibatani, interviewed by Joshua Labove and Heather Read, 19 November 2015, Toronto, Ontario, LOIOH.

101 Henry Shibata, interviewed by Joshua Labove, 29 February 2016, Ottawa, Ontario, LOIOH.

102 Adachi, *The Enemy That Never Was*, 356–538, 362; Oikawa, *Cartographies of Violence*, 35–7, 237; Patricia Roy, *The Triumph of Citizenship: The Japanese and Chinese in Canada, 1941–67* (Vancouver: UBC Press, 2007), 211.

103 Richard and Rose Murakami, interviewed by Josh Labove and Kyla Fitzgerald, 26 July 2015, Salt Spring Island, British Columbia, LOIOH.

104 Aiko and Michael Murakami, interviewed by Momoye Sugiman and Heather Read, 26 June 2015, Toronto, Ontario, LOIOH.

105 Mel Tsuji, interviewed by Alexander Pekic, 3 September 2015, Woodbridge, Ontario, LOIOH.

106 Chapters 13 and 14.

107 On the history of Japanese Canadian activism, see for example chapter 2 and Adachi, *The Enemy That Never Was.*

108 Akemi Kobayashi, interviewed by Alicia Fong, 24 August 2015, Toronto Ontario, LOIOH.

109 Ken Morisawa (born in 1934) offers another example of the myriad directions Japanese Canadians' lives could take after internment. In his interview, Ken recounted his lifelong passion for tennis. When he moved to Toronto in the 1960s, local tennis organizations became the foundation of community and friendship in his life. Ken Morisawa, interviewed by Alexander Pekic, 18 November 2015, Georgetown, Ontario, LOIOH.

110 See Douglas Porteous and Sandra Eileen Smith, *Domicide: The Global Destruction of Home* (Montreal & Kingston: McGill-Queen's University Press, 2001) and the introduction to this volume.

111 Though not included in the original Landscapes of Injustice question list, the theme of returns quickly emerged when the research team began conducting interviews. Mona Oikawa also noted trips to prewar sites of Japanese Canadian life in the stories of Nisei women, describing them as a way to prevent the internment era from being forgotten. Oikawa, *Cartographies of Violence*, 251–4.

112 As mentioned above, researchers in the Landscapes of Injustice collective recognize the term "evacuation" as a harmful euphemism for the uprooting and internment, but many Japanese Canadians continue to use this language, and the interviewers chose to allow narrators to speak on their own terms.

113 Sachiko Okuda, interviewed by Joshua Labove, 1 January 2016, Ottawa, Ontario, LOIOH.

114 On the topic of returns to British Columbia, Sachiko explained, "My parents never went back to BC and my mother, I feel, had a real resentment or she just wanted it to be behind her." Later the interview, Sachiko describes her own journey to Qualicum Beach, the place where her mother grew up but refused to return. Poignantly, Sachiko describes visiting the place to learn something about her mother and her past, which was too difficult for her to describe. Sachiko Okuda, interviewed by Joshua Labove, 1 January 2016, Ottawa, Ontario, LOIOH.

115 David Mitsui, interviewed by Joshua Labove, 22 September 2015, Edmonton, Alberta, LOIOH.

116 Leslie Uyeda, interviewed by Joshua Labove, 4 August 2018, Vancouver, British Columbia, LOIOH.

117 Keiko and Arthur Miki, interviewed by Erin Yaremko, 9 August 2016, Winnipeg Manitoba, LOIOH.

118 Henry Shibata, interviewed by Joshua Labove, 29 February 2016, Ottawa, Ontario, LOIOH.

119 Porteous and Smith, *Domicide,* 183

120 Tom Matsui, interviewed by Heather Read, 7 April 2015, Toronto, Ontario, LOIOH.

121 Min Takada, interviewed by Joshua Labove, 25 September 2015, Calgary, Alberta, LOIOH.

122 Yeiji Inouye, interviewed by Kyla Fitzgerald, 17 July 2015, Victoria, British Columbia, LOIOH.

123 Kelvin and Suzy Higo, interviewed by Joshua Labove, 6 May 2016, Richmond, British Columbia, LOIOH.

124 Shig Ugeyama, interviewed by Rebeca Salas, 18 July 2016, Burnaby, British Columbia, LOIOH.

125 Eventually, Vivian and her sister visited the house on their own and, peeking into the garage window, found that the new owners had laid down a concrete floor. Vivian Rygnestad, interviewed by Rebeca Salas, 27 August 2017, Richmond, British Columbia, LOIOH.

126 "My sister thought it was a huge room at that time," Ed explained. "When she looked at the actual room, it was so small" (Ed Tanaka, interviewed by Erin Yaremko, 15 June 2016, Regina, Saskatchewan, LOIOH).

127 In this respect, the oral histories converge with an interdisciplinary scholarship that situates property ownership very broadly within lived experience. For a discussion of this scholarship, see chapter 4.

128 Chapters 3, 4, and 6.

CHAPTER 12

The Politics of Honorific Naming: Alan Webster Neill and Anti-Asian Racism in Port Alberni, British Columbia, Canada

Ian G. Baird

Introduction

On 23 January 2017 the city council of Port Alberni (on Vancouver Island in British Columbia, Canada) convened a formal meeting. Early on, knowing that the proposal of whether or not to change the name of Neill Street was on the agenda (raised by city councillor Chris Alemany), a member of the Tseshaht First Nation, Hiʔhunkennis (Robert Watts), spoke. He noted that Alan Webster (A.W.) Neill spent much of his life opposing people like him "as well as other races" (apparently referring to Asian Canadians). He supported the idea to change the name of Neill Street, which had been named in honour of Neill more than sixty years earlier.[1] Then Rosemarie Buchanan, a school board trustee for School District 70 Alberni, summarized many of Neill's racist views, backing up her findings with Neill quotes taken directly from Hansard, the official record of the Canadian House of Commons. She too suggested that it was time to change the name of Neill Street. However, Cameron Stefiuk responded by providing information about the positive contributions of A.W. Neill. He opposed the idea to change the name of the street and was also opposed to moving toward reconciliation in relation to the past.[2] As far as he was concerned, no recognition or reconciliation was necessary.[3] Instead, he advocated for the following: "We should not forget the past but learn from it and not repeat the same mistakes going forward."[4] Nevertheless, before long the following proposal was moved and seconded: "That Council for the City of Port Alberni, in the spirit of Reconciliation, work with the Hupacasath and Tseshaht First Nation Councils, the Community and any affected property owners to potentially rename Neill Street."[5] However, the council voted down the motion, five to two, thus retaining the name of the street.[6]

There was still the matter of the school. A.W. Neill was said to have been particularly proud that the first junior secondary school (later an elementary school) in Port Alberni – which opened in September 1957 – had been named after him. The *Alberni Valley Times* reported that "Among the honors he [Neill] cherished in the later years of his life were the fact that the district's first junior high school was named for him."[7] Tonkin wrote in a newspaper article thirteen years after Neill had passed away, "the A.W. Neill School in Alberni perpetuates a name which surely should be remembered

Figure 12.1 Photo of the sign for Neill Street in Port Alberni, August 2018.

best as belonging to one who never forgot he was a servant of the people."[8] However, as indicated above, some have argued that he was only the servant of some people (whites), while working actively against others (Asians, people of Asian descent, and First Nations). Thus, on 24 January– the day after the motion to rename Neill Street had been defeated by city Council – Chris Alemany petitioned the Alberni 70 School Board to rename A.W. Neill Elementary during the 2017–18 school year.[9] The school board did not initially agree to change the school's name, with some trustees voicing strong opposition to the proposal, maintaining that local memories are attached to the school and thus to the name as well.[10]

Questions related to honorific naming and renaming can clearly be controversial. In this case, how should A.W. Neill be viewed? What are the implications of the effort to change the names of places that honour him? More broadly, it raises the question of how we should understand the role of honorific naming in constituting and co-producing particular places and landscapes. This chapter reviews the history of A.W. Neill and the controversy that has emerged regarding honorific naming associated with him. In particular, it documents Neill's longstanding views regarding Japanese Canadians. This chapter contributes to our consideration of the legacies of the internment era by drawing inspiration from a wider scholarship on the contentious politics of honorific naming. In British Columbia, as elsewhere, the names given to public spaces and facilities convey important societal values, linking people and spaces and constituting inclusion and exclusion through imbuing landscapes with the names of people who symbolize particular values.[11] Indeed, naming constitutes an important part of how spaces are produced.

My research regarding Japanese Canadians

In the summer of 2016, I started conducting focused research regarding white racism against Asians on Vancouver Island during the twentieth century, initially concentrating on my own family's involvement in racist organizations in Nanaimo, British Columbia, particularly the Native Sons and Daughters of British Columbia. I endeavoured to develop an anti-racist methodology that involves investigating and interrogating one's family's own past links to racism.[12] However, in the summer of 2017, when I returned to Vancouver Island to conduct more research, I learned that some of my relatives – who had been small-scale fishermen in the Nanaimo area – had developed close relationships with some Japanese Canadian fishermen who also fished out of Nanaimo, both before and after World War II. This inspired me to theorize that an important part of my antiracist methodology should be to not only expose and challenge family racism from the past but also to investigate how and under what circumstances good cross-cultural interactions occur.[13]

In the summer of 2018, I continued my research regarding Japanese Canadians on Vancouver Island. Work done at the Nanaimo City Community Archives in 2016 and 2017 had been rewarding, not just with regard to gaining access to important documentation but also for what I learned from people whom I met at the archives. These people helped direct me in my research, put my research in historical context, and recommended and helped find people for me to interview. This being the case, I was interested in learning what was available at the community archives in Port Alberni. In preparation, I emailed with one of the volunteer archivists at the Port Alberni Historical Society, which manages the archives. Then in early August 2018 I visited the archives, even though I had been informed by an archivist that, "We do have a clipping file of newspaper articles relating to the Japanese 'problem' … internment, and redress, but nothing of a more personal nature." Still, it seemed worth visiting the archives.

When I arrived at the archives, a volunteer archivist helped me access the files I was looking for. We talked and I provided some background information about my research regarding the history of Japanese Canadians on Vancouver Island. I also mentioned my interest in learning more about the racism directed towards Asian Canadians in the past. She asked me if I had heard about the controversy associated with proposals to rename Neill Street and A.W. Neill Elementary. Up to that point, I knew nothing about either, so she explained the controversial proposals, particularly that Neill had been accused of being strongly racist against people of Japanese descent (both Canadians and non-Canadians) and that his racist views were the main reason for proposing the name changes. I was surprised that my historical investigations seemed to be suddenly converging with present-day controversy in Port Alberni. I decided to shift my immediate focus from generally looking at the history of Japanese Canadians in the area to investigating how A.W. Neill was linked to racism against Japanese Canadians and how his legacy is associated with present-day naming and renaming controversies. I found a considerable amount of documentation about A.W. Neill at the Port Alberni Archives, and before long I realized that Neill was one of the key anti-Asian Canadian politicians of the twentieth century, a member of the Anti-Asiatic League. I also sought out and interviewed Chris Alemany, Rosemarie Buchanan, and others with an interest in the issue, as well as some Japanese Canadians who were either living then in Port Alberni and Ucluelet or had been previously.

My research and Landscapes of Injustice

In 2017, I first became aware of the Landscapes of Injustice project. The project's research seemed relevant to my own investigations regarding racism against people of Asian descent on Vancouver Island. Soon I was officially affiliated with the project and maintained dialogue with its director, Jordan Stanger-Ross. My research has occurred outside the scope of the project itself, complementing, rather than directly emerging from, the activity of the research collective. As Landscapes of Injustice grapples with the enduring legacies of the dispossession, controversies over the present-day landscapes of the province help to illuminate one of the ways in which this history remains unfinished. I now turn to recounting relevant parts of A.W. Neill's history, in order to provide the appropriate context for thinking about the honorific naming controversy.[14]

Who was Alan Webster Neill?

Alan Webster Neill was born in Montrose, Scotland, on 6 October 1868.[15] His father was a Scot and his mother was English.[16] In 1885, when Neill was just sixteen, he traveled to New Zealand where he farmed, logged, and worked as a sheep shearer on a large farm.[17] Neill immigrated to Canada in 1891 at the age of twenty-three. He ended up acquiring a quarter section (160 acres) of land in the Alberni Valley, but he was restless and soon joined the military. After a few years, he left the service and returned to Scotland to assist his ailing father. However, Neill decided to return to Canada and the Alberni Valley in 1897.[18]

Neill unexpectedly became nominated to run for office, and in 1898 was elected as a member of the Legislative Assembly of British Columbia, representing Alberni, a position for which he was twice reelected.[19] From the beginning of his political career,

Neill lobbied to have all people of Asian ancestry expelled from Canada and, crucially, he did not distinguish between Canadian citizens (or British subjects of Japanese descent) and Japanese nationals. Neill was persistent, and by his own admission, during his time in the BC legislature he voted "for each and every anti-Chinese law."[20] Neill's scrapbook from the period includes many newspaper articles critical of Asian immigration, indicating his considerable interest in the topic.[21] Neill decided not to run in the 1903 election, apparently due to the high cost of financing frequent election campaigns. Once he left politics, Neill was appointed stipendiary magistrate for Nanaimo and Victoria. From 1903 to 1913 he also served as federal Indian Agent in the Alberni area, and between 1911 and 1927 Neill operated the Pioneer Feed, Coal and Oil Store in Alberni.[22] He was a school board trustee from 1912 to 1914 and an alderman on Alberni's first city council in 1913. Beginning in 1916, he served as mayor of Alberni for a year.[23]

In 1921, Neill launched his first federal election campaign as a strong advocate for the "Absolute exclusion of Asiatics" from immigrating to Canada. He also argued that fishing licences should only be issued to "White British subjects."[24] In all, Neill appears to have been able to take advantage of post-World War I racial tensions to advance his political career.

Within a few weeks of being elected to federal Parliament for the first time as a member of the Progressive Party, Neill pledged his support for Prime Minister William Lyon Mackenzie King's Liberal Party. Later, Neill would become an Independent, apparently so that he could work with different parties depending on the issue. He was the only member of Parliament from Vancouver Island who supported the Liberal government at the time. He often supported policies that, in his view, advanced the interests of the working class.[25]

In 1922, Neill took his concerns about Japanese domination of the fishing industry to the Fisheries Committee of the House of Commons, since Canada did not yet have a Ministry of Fisheries.[26] In his first speech in the House of Commons, delivered on 16 March, Neill demanded "Asian exclusion," and he also advocated for heightened restrictions on the issuance of fishing licences to people of Japanese descent. Neill stressed, "on these matters particularly I want action – not talk, and legislation – not lengthy debate."[27] Within just three months of becoming a member of Parliament (MP), Neill had contributed to a 33 per cent decrease in salmon trolling licences for Japanese fishermen, and he had gained the reputation for being the chief anti-Asian member of the House of Commons.[28]

In 1922, the federal British Columbia Fisheries Commission (also known as the Duff Commission, chaired by William Duff) was established, of which Neill was one of the commissioners.[29] The Duff Commission – undoubtedly influenced by Neill's strong anti-Asian views, along with those of two other well-known racist members of Parliament from British Columbia – recommended that the number of fishing licences allocated to nonwhites and non-Indigenous peoples be reduced by 40 per cent, a decision that, Neill boasted, caused 800 Japanese Canadians to be barred from fishing.[30] In line with this, Fukawa and Fukawa reported that throughout the years of fishing licence reductions for Japanese Canadians, between 1922 and 1927, when the courts prohibited such discriminatory behaviour, 1,253 people of Japanese descent lost their fishing licences.[31]

Neill explained it in a letter, writing, "The recommendation of the Commission of 40% was only for this year and did not extend beyond this year. On the trolling it was made 25% reduction this year because there had been a 33% cut the year before making a total cut of 58%." Neill also claimed success for reducing trolling licences to people of Japanese descent by 10 per cent more.[32] Neill recounted, "If I asked 40% I would have got nothing."[33] Then, in 1925, there was another 15 per cent cut.[34] Neill also wrote that he planned to ask for a 40 per cent reduction of handline cod licences to Japanese, the same reduction as there had been on salmon trolling licences for Japanese. Neill wrote, "Cod hand line fishing was not licensed until this year, I got the dept to licence them so we would know how many Japs fished as they went into it heavily after being cut out of the salmon licences."[35]

For the gillnet fishery, Japanese fishermen were allocated 40 per cent fewer licences in 1922, and there was a further 15 per cent reduction in 1925. For the newly proposed pilchard fishery, everyone involved had to be white, since Neill insisted on it.[36] In fact, Neill claimed that he would not allow the industry to commence operations until there was agreement regarding this matter.[37]

In 1924, the so-called "Neill's Law" was introduced. It mandated a reduction in the number of Japanese who could work in sawmills, canneries, and dry salt herring plants, reserving those positions for either white people or "Indians" (First Nations). The idea was to reduce Japanese Canadian employment by 25 per cent per year until no Japanese Canadians were employed after the fourth year, 1927.[38] As Neill put it, "This law is now working out to restore to the white race an important industry on this Coast … It will add greatly to the population of our Coast and result in the building up of little communities of hardy, white fisherfolk."[39] Neill's efforts to reduce Japanese Canadian involvement in fisheries were quite successful.[40] In 1929, however, the courts determined that fish plants were under the jurisdiction of the provincial government, not the federal government.[41] This caused people such as Neill to fear that this might lead to the rehiring of Asian Canadians to work in fish plants on the coast.[42]

Neill's committee created political campaigning materials that stated, "Mr Neill's efforts on behalf of the fishermen have caused him to be recognized as the friend and the representative of the fishermen from the whole of British Columbia."[43] In line with this, on 14 October 1925 the *Port Alberni News* published an article titled, "Made White Man's Chances Better is What Fishermen Say about Neill."[44] The reporting was mainly devoted to describing the content of a letter sent by the West Coast Fishermen's Association to L.A. Hanna, Neill's campaign manager for the western part of the Comox–Alberni electoral district. The article reported that the association had praised Neill for reducing the duty on gas engines that the fishermen needed to operate their boats and compete with the Americans.[45] More importantly, however, the association praised Neill as follows:

> Before the last Dominion election it was felt that it was only a matter of a few years and there would be no white fishermen on the coast of British Columbia, especially considering the rate at which the Japanese were increasing and the white fishermen decreasing. Mr Neill has been instrumental in changing these conditions, with the result that more and more white fishermen are being employed in the fishing business from year to year.[46]

Neill clearly put a lot of effort into reducing the involvement of Japanese Canadians in various fisheries along the coast of BC. Indeed, the number of Japanese Canadians working in fisheries declined significantly during the 1920s.

Although Neill put a lot of his energy into undermining Japanese Canadian fishermen and fish workers, he also supported various other important initiatives, albeit ones specifically designed to benefit white Canadian fishermen. For example, Neill assisted white Port Alberni fishermen in changing the gillnetting boundary to enable netting for salmon going up the Somass River, and worked to prevent discrimination against small seines in relation to larger ones.[47] He also advocated for reducing the licence fees for white fishermen. Seine licences went down from $500 to $20 each, and gillnet licences declined from $5 to $1.[48] Neill also became well known and popular in the Alberni Valley, and more generally in British Columbia, for advocating the adoption of the Canada Pension Act in 1927. He also promoted legislation in support of what eventually became known as Remembrance Day.[49]

Despite these other areas of activity, the politics of race never receded from Neill's view or his interventions in public discussion. In 1928, Neill wrote a letter to the *Port Alberni News* in which he bemoaned a 1927 Supreme Court decision regarding the Fisheries Act of Canada, which stated that, "the Minister has no power to discriminate between British subjects, whatever their origin." In other words, "a naturalized Oriental could not be refused one [a fishing licence]." In Neill's view, "The result would threaten to be very serious for the white fisherman of British Columbia." However, the court did not state that the Fisheries Act could not be amended to grant powers to the minister to discriminate, and not surprisingly, Neill advocated "to get the government to amend the law at this session" (a proposal that did not succeed).[50]

In the same letter, Neill explained his views on immigration, particularly Japanese immigration. He praised the government decision to abrogate the 1908 "Gentlemen's Agreement with Japan," which emerged following the 1907 anti-Asian riots in Vancouver and stipulated that in order to reduce anti-Asian tensions in Canada, Japan would issue a limited number of passports, and Canada would only accept immigrants holding those passports.[51] The agreement significantly reduced immigration of Japanese, to about 500 a year, but that was not sufficient for Neill, who claimed that under the agreement Japanese authorities had been allowed to interpret Canadian immigration laws as they saw fit and that "we were bound to accept their recommendations." Abrogation of the agreement, Neill believed, would allow Canadian authorities to handle the immigration of Japanese as a matter of domestic priorities.[52]

Neill's anti-Asian views dominated his political campaigns. In 1930, a newspaper advertisement paid for by Neill's reelection campaign stated, "Who has been big enough to tackle the Oriental question and worked hard to improve the lot of the fishermen? A.W. Neill."[53] Four years later, Neill's committee asserted that Neill "regards the constant and increasing encroachment of Orientals in many fields of endeavour as one of the greatest problems in BC and a peril to the coming generation that cannot too often be emphasized."[54] In 1938, Neill continued to try to find ways to make it more and more difficult for Japanese to immigrate to Canada.

Neill's ongoing vocal racist position in the 1940s

Not surprisingly, Neill was a strong supporter of the early March 1942 order to relocate all Japanese nationals and Japanese Canadians living within one hundred miles of the coast and intern them far into the interior of British Columbia. Prior to that decision, in early February Neill wrote to Norman Robertson, the powerful deputy minister of external affairs, arguing against a policy that would differentiate between naturalized Japanese Canadian citizens and Japanese nationals. He wrote, "I maintain the naturalized Japanese [i.e. the British subject of Canada] is very often more dangerous," without providing any evidence in support of this view. He suggested that all people of Japanese descent be subjected to the same restrictions on the use of cameras and radio sets as Japanese nationals. He asked what the government had done since confiscating Japanese Canadian fishing boats and strongly argued for relocating all Japanese Canadians away from the coast, suggesting that this would ensure the safety of those of Japanese descent.[55]

Just over two weeks later, on 19 February 1942, Neill delivered a speech in the House of Commons on "The Japanese Situation in British Columbia" in which he called for stricter restrictions on all people of Japanese descent, whether they were British subjects of Canada or not. He praised the government for quickly confiscating the fishing boats of Japanese Canadians in British Columbia but criticized it for not moving more quickly to restrict their freedom of movement, places of residence, and their possession of cameras and radios. He also recommended that the government deport all people of Japanese descent from Canada once the war was over:

> I do suggest – perhaps it is too early to talk about it now, but it is well to get it started – that we should make an arrangement that when peace time comes, we expatriate all the Japanese; do it on fair terms, buy them out, pay them liberally … Let us settle once and for all this canker in the life of Canada which prevents us from being a united white Canada. And that is what British Columbia wants.[56]

It was a view that Neill would repeat as the war continued. He also appealed to Christianity when arguing against Japanese Canadians even though many were Christian. He even wrote to the United Church's general secretary in order to protest their resolutions supporting Japanese Canadians. He also claimed that Japanese Canadians bred three to one compared to whites, so as to justify his proposal to exile Japanese Canadians from Canada as part of a peace agreement with Japan once World War II ended.[57]

As World War II progressed, Neill continued to insist that advance arrangements were needed to deport all people of Japanese descent immediately after the war ended. Indicative of Neill's view, he said the following in the House of Commons in 1944:

> I have not said anything about race or creed. I have not attempted to raise the issue at all. But we say, as the hon. member of New Westminster said, that these people will not assimilate and cannot assimilate. They do not want to assimilate. The real test of assimilation is marriage. You cannot get anything else without that. They simply do not want to do that. They approach you and say that it made their heart bleed on Election Day when they see white men going to vote and they cannot. That is all poppycock. When the war broke out we had to close sixty-nine Jap schools, entirely Jap staffed, where they taught the Japanese language, Japanese culture and Japanese doctrines. We got some of their stuff. It was written in Japanese, of course. We got some of their textbooks translated. It was anti-white man stuff. They used to leave the white schools where they got all they could out of our culture, and go across the road to their own schools.[58]

The above quote clearly indicates that Neill was indeed strongly racist, even if he did not want to think of himself in such a way, instead imagining himself as a protector of the vulnerable white people, a position that many white supremacists endorsed.

In 1945, at the age of seventy-seven, A.W. Neill resigned from Parliament due to age and failing health. At the time, he was the only MP in British Columbia to have held his seat continuously from as far back as 1921.[59] Not surprisingly, at the end of

CANADA

House of Commons Debates

OFFICIAL REPORT

"JAPS MUST GO"

SPEECH BY

Mr. A. W. NEILL

MEMBER FOR COMOX-ALBERNI

DELIVERED IN THE HOUSE OF COMMONS ON FRIDAY, MAY 5, 1944

Figure 12.2 Front page of the "Japs Must Go" speech in the House of Commons by A.W. Neill, 5 May 1944.

World War II, Neill once again proposed that "everyone of Japanese origin be deported from Canada," and almost 4,000, including many who were Canadian citizens, were indeed deported in 1946.[60]

In 1945, Neill returned to Alberni to set up a notary public business, which he ran for a number of years. He was ninety-one years old when he died on 7 July 1960. *The Western Advocate* reported that Neill had been "one of Alberni's greatest men, respected and admired by all who knew him," but "all who knew him" was undoubtedly not intended to include Asian Canadians.[61]

A.W. Neill honorifics in Port Alberni

The two local politicians who initiated name-changing efforts related to A.W. Neill in Port Alberni were Chris Alemany, city councillor of Port Alberni, and Rosemarie Buchanan, a school board trustee. However, it was Chris Stevenson, a former resident of Port Alberni, who inspired them to push for changing the names of the school and the street. In 2002, Stevenson wrote a university paper about World War II injustices associated with the internment of Japanese Canadians. At that time Stevenson identified Neill as a key white racist from Alberni, and Alemany and Buchanan learned about this through a social media post.[62] On 11 May 2016, Stevenson wrote the following on Facebook:

> Speaking of possible renaming of things ... how many people are aware that one of the schools in the [Alberni Valley] district and a street are named for one of the most vocal political aggressors against the Asian-Canadian community in the late 1930s and 1940s – the MP for this area, who was one of the most vicious and ardent proponents for Japanese internment, who had the power, authority and voice, and made it his mission to make internment happen? You know, where all people of Japanese descent (some third generation) were forced to leave their homes, businesses and property (property that was subsequently stolen from them)? Talking about AW Neill of course. If we're looking to rename things, let's start with these things. I'm surprised that his name still smears a SCHOOL, and a street ... How about renaming the school with a First Nations name, in the spirit of reconciliation?[63]

This post sparked discussion about changing the names. However, the idea did not gain traction until December 2016, six months later, when more focused discussions started to occur and Alemany and Buchanan began to seriously consider the possibility of name changing. Some First Nations people got involved, writing letters in support of name changing, but, despite some effort, Alemany and Buchanan were unable to find any Japanese Canadian families in town who would speak to the negative impacts of Neill's racism.[64] However, Lorene Oikawa, vice president of the National Association of Japanese Canadians, sent a letter to Port Alberni Council to support the idea to change the name of A.W. Neill Elementary School and the street named for Neill. She pointed out that, "tributes to A.W. Neill are tacit support for his racist actions" and that changing the names would constitute "the first step towards reconciliation."[65]

While Alemany and Buchanan were receptive and willing to act once they learned about Neill's racist history, many others in Port Alberni strongly objected to their efforts. When Alemany's plan to change the street name was leaked to a local radio station, *the Peak*, many in Port Alberni strongly criticized him on social media. The controversy particularly erupted on a Facebook page devoted to Port Alberni politics called AV (Alberni Valley) Chatter Box. Brian Calm, an administrator for the site, criticized the idea heavily. Critics made comments including, "These people need to get a life, and talk about real issues."[66] One commenter wrote, "waste of time [and] taxpayers money! Move on to something more constructive!" Others, however, such as Shelley Shenton supported Alemany, writing in response to Cameron Stefiuk, "We can work harder on lessening it [racism]. That is the whole point of cross-cultural, inter-cultural work." The controversy polarized Port Alberni.[67] A former Liberal Party candidate for Member of the Legislative Assembly in Port Alberni, Darren DeLuca, was particularly critical of removing Neill's name as an honorific.[68] DeLuca has remained critical of these name changes, and on 26 October 2018, after local elections took place in BC, he criticized, via Facebook, politicians "who prefer to desecrate the names of our national leaders, people like John A. McDonald or A.W. Neill, rather than learning from them."[69] His comment, in some ways, mirrors the comments that Cameron Stefiuk made at the Port Alberni City Council meeting on 23 January 2017.

More than fifty letters were submitted to city council with regard to the name changing issue, indicating the interest that the public had in the issue. Not surprisingly, many who took the time to write were strongly supportive of name changing, pointing to the symbolic value of doing so, and the need to do so in order to work toward reconciliation. Others, however, wrote forcefully against name changing, arguing that moving ahead with such changes would cause division in the community and "open up old wounds." Still others argued that there would be considerable costs associated with changing the name of Neill Street, such as changing letterheads, etc. Some felt it was a waste of taxpayer's money to even consider name changing.[70]

Although initial efforts to remove Neill's name from honorifics in Port Alberni were not successful, the proposal to change the school's name, unlike that with respect to the street, was not actually defeated in a vote. Instead, a decision was postponed, as there was no policy in place to deal with proposed name changes. In the fall of 2017 the school board announced that it had decided to develop a policy for addressing potential school name changes.[71] This set up the possibility that the name of the school could be changed in the future, once procedures for dealing with such questions have been established.[72] Indeed, Rosemarie Buchanan told me, when we met in August 2018, that if she was reelected in October 2018 (and she was), she would push for changing the name of A.W. Neill Elementary School in 2019. She explained that the new policy for school naming states that it is generally better to not name schools after individual people and that it is preferable to name schools after particular areas or landscape features, such as streams, hills, etc. Since approximately 50 per cent of the students who attend A.W. Neill Elementary are First Nations, it is possible that in the future the school could be given a local First Nations name to replace A.W. Neill.[73] That would be symbolically important. Buchanan has also been in touch with a Japanese Canadian in town, Marlene Mortensen (née Madokoro), whose parents were interned during World War II and who is willing to speak in front of the school board when the time comes to again petition to have the name of A.W. Neill Elementary School changed.[74] More recently, the school board publicly indicated their interest in changing the name of A.W. Neill Elementary School, and called for public input into this proposal, including possible new names for the school.[75]

While none of the Japanese Canadians from Port Alberni have any direct memories of A.W. Neill – as is apparently the case with First Nations as well – their families were all affected by Neill's racism. One elderly Japanese woman, Terry Hamagishi, who lives in Port Alberni and was uprooted from Port Alberni during World War II, told me that her late husband Eugene, who was also interned, also did not know anything specifically about Neill, but like other Japanese Canadians of their era, he did know about Neill's part-time ally, Prime Minister William Lyon Mackenzie King. Eugene remained angry with King for his whole life for ordering the internment of Japanese Canadians in 1942. Therefore, he always refused to cash a Canadian $50 bill, since the bill honours King by having him on it.[76] I doubt that many white Canadians look at the $50 bill in this way.

Conclusions

This chapter began with a discussion of the ongoing controversy surrounding efforts to rename Neill Street and A.W. Neill Elementary in Port Alberni. Some people feel that it is unproductive, divisive, and a waste of time to try to remove honorific names associated with blatant racists such as A.W. Neill. Others, however, clearly believe that removing problematic honorific names from the landscape is an important step towards reconciliation with those victimized by such racists in the past, whether they be Japanese Canadians or Indigenous peoples. Moreover, removing such honorifics clearly indicates that real change is desired. In this sense, such efforts can be very important for the present. Indeed, Keiko Mary Kitagawa – the leader of a related and successful campaign to convince the Canadian government in 2007 to name a federal building in Vancouver after Douglas Jung, the first Canadian MP of Asian descent, rather than Howard Charles Green, a prominent Canadian anti-Japanese politician – has recently been awarded the Order of British Columbia for her contributions to public life in the province.[77]

Those involved in the controversy associated with A.W. Neill honorifics in Port Alberni, including Chris Alemany and Rosemarie Buchanan, were not aware of the Landscapes of Injustice project when I first met them in August 2018. However, their efforts demonstrate the types of struggles that are occurring to try to transform landscapes of injustice, places named in honour of blatant racists such as A.W. Neill, into places that symbolize reconciliation and justice. One of the first steps in that direction should be to remove A.W. Neill's name from the street and the school, so as to make it materially and symbolically clear that real efforts at reconciliation are underway, whether it be with Japanese Canadians or First Nations.

Indeed, projects like Landscapes of Injustice – and other research efforts – can help contribute to understanding more about how injustices have emerged and who was responsible for them. This work is crucial, as honorific naming has important space-making value for people and tends to demonstrate societal values. It is also an important indicator of the types of things that people support and the types of things that they do not. No wonder that honorific naming and renaming is often highly controversial wherever such name-changing efforts occur. But make no mistake, this issue is far from trivial; honorific naming is important for representing societal values.

In the particular case of A.W. Neill, there is more than sufficient evidence to suggest that he was a strong racist against Asian Canadians, particularly Japanese Canadians, and that over many decades he consistently looked for ways to undermine Asian Canadians. It would be appropriate to include exhibits about Neill in museums, where the good, the bad, and the ugly can all be assessed and scrutinized. We certainly should not forget Neill and what he stood for. However, honorific naming is about honouring someone, elevating that person because he or she is seen as being worthy to stand as an example to others, even as a role model. I do not think that Neill reaches that bar; not even close. Name changing is nothing new. Rather, it represents a reevaluation of societal values, something that periodically occurs, and should not come as a surprise. That is why it seems to me that it is now time to stop honouring A.W. Neill.

NOTES

1 City Council Minutes, 23 January 2017, Port Alberni, 1, accessed 14 September 2019, https://www.portalberni.ca/sites/default/files/council_mtg/Jan23_Updated_opt_tf.pdf; *Alberni Place Names* 2nd ed. (Alberni: Alberni District Historical Society, 1988).
2 Wawmeesh Hamilton, "One Town, Two Worlds: Reconciliation in Port Alberni," *The Discourse*, 20 January 2018, accessed 14 September 2019, https://www.thediscourse.ca/urban-nation/one-town-two-worlds.
3 Chris Alemany, personal communication, Port Alberni, 15 December 2018.
4 City Council Minutes, 2.
5 Ibid.
6 Ibid.
7 "Neill Mementos Displayed Here," *Alberni Valley Times*, 13 May 1970.
8 D.F. Tonkin, "A Servant of the People," *The Daily Colonist*, 16 September 1973.
9 Board of Education Minutes, 24 January 2017, School District 70, Port Alberni, British Columbia, accessed 14 September 2019, https://www.sd70.bc.ca/Board/MeetingsMinutes/Board%20Meeting%20Minutes/2016-17/01-24-17%20PUB%20min.pdf; "Changing Name of A.W. Neill School," School District 70, Port Alberni, British Columbia, Alberni (unpublished document, 2017), 14.
10 Rosemarie Buchanan, personal communication, 23 August 2018, Port Alberni, BC.
11 Derek H. Alderman, "Naming and the interpretation of cultural landscapes," in *The Ashgate Research Companion to Heritage and Identity*, eds. Brian J. Graham and Peter Howard (Farnham, UK: Ashgate, 2008): 195–214; Reuben S. Rose-Redwood, "From Number to Name: Symbolic Capital, Places of Memory, and the Politics of Street Renaming in New York City," *Social & Cultural Geography* 9, no. 4 (2008): 431–52; Reuben S. Rose-Redwood, Derek H. Alderman, and M. Azaryahu, "Geographies of Toponymic

Inscriptions: New Directions in Critical Place-Names Studies," *Progress in Human Geography* 34, no. 4 (2010): 453–70.

12 Ian G. Baird, "An Anti-Racism Methodology: The Native Sons and Daughters and Racism against Asians in Nanaimo, British Columbia, Canada," *The Canadian Geographer* 62, no. 3 (2018): 300–13.

13 Ian G. Baird, "Developing an Anti-Racism Methodology: Considering Japanese and White Canadian Fishermen Relations in Nanaimo, BC, Canada," *Canadian Ethnic Studies* 51, no. 2 (2019): 107–30.

14 It so happened that at the same time as I was learning about Neill and his past behaviour, another divisive controversy associated with historical honorifics was developing on the southern tip of Vancouver Island, in Victoria which brought my work into further dialogue with Landscapes of Injustice researchers. There, city council had set up a reconciliation process with local First Nations, and as part of that work, they decided to remove an honorific statue of John A. MacDonald from in front of city hall, since it was identified as intimidating by some First Nations people. Although MacDonald was the first prime minister of Canada and is considered to be "the father of confederation," he also had a very poor record when it came to the treatment of First Nations, including having played a key role in the establishment of residential schools for First Nations children. Many felt that it was not appropriate to continue honouring MacDonald. The statue was removed, taken away, and stored. However, the removal triggered considerable public criticism of the Victoria city council and particularly the mayor of Victoria, Lisa Helps, for supporting the removal of the statue. Some people felt that "history was being erased." Others complained that the removal should not have occurred before additional public discussions. Some argued that the statue should not have been removed but that it would have been appropriate to have relabelled it to reflect the range of opinions of his legacy. There were strong feelings on all sides, with protests and counter-protests. Landscapes of Injustice coinvestigator Dr Reuben Rose-Redwood, an associate professor of geography at the University of Victoria and a proponent of removing the statue, pointed out that there is the need to distinguish between putting a statue of a controversial figure in a museum, in order to interrogate the historical record associated with that person, and erecting a statue for largely honorific purposes. For Rose-Redwood, the statue of MacDonald might be better housed in a museum than situated in front of city hall.

15 Jan Peterson, "Valley in Review," *Alberni Valley Times*, 15 February 1990.

16 Tonkin, "A Servant of the People."

17 George Nicolson, "Alberni Man First in All Canada to Get Age Pension," *Daily Colonist*, Victoria, 29 July 1956.

18 "Neill Mementos"; Peterson, "Valley in Review"; "'Comox Alberni Member Has Had a Colourful Career': Mr A.W. Neill Has Been in Public Life for over 40 Years; 18 in House at Ottawa," file "A.W. Neill," Port Alberni Historical Society.

19 "Neill Mementos"; "Upper House Appointment for Neill? Island Endorses Perennial Independent Member for Vacancy," file "A.W. Neill," Port Alberni Historical Society Archives.

20 Alan W. Neill, "To the Electors of Alberni District" (1921), file L.54.17, Port Alberni Historical Society Archives.

21 A.W. Neill's scrapbooks, books 157 and 158, Port Alberni History Society Archives.
22 "Neill Mementos."
23 "Neill Mementos"; Neill's Committee, "Why We Are Supporting A.W. Neill," 1940, West Coast Advocate, file L.54.17, Port Alberni Historical Society Archives; "Council Cancelled in Respect for the City's Ex-Mayor," *Western Advocate*, 15 July 1960.
24 Neill's Committee, "Mr Neill's Platform" (1921), file 71.8, Port Alberni Historical Society Archives.
25 Peterson, "Valley in Review."
26 Alan W. Neill, "Letter to N.E. Lyche, Esq. Secretary of West Coast Fisherman's Association, Alberni," file L.54.17, Port Alberni Historical Society Archives.
27 Canada, House of Commons Debates, vol. 1, 16 March 1922 (Ottawa: King's Printer), 169.
28 Patricia Roy, *The Oriental Question: Consolidating a White Man's Province* (Vancouver: UBC Press, 2003), 105–10; "A.W. Neill," 1945, file 71.8, Port Alberni Historical Society Archives; Neill's Committee, "Why We Are Supporting Mr Neill."
29 Duff, W. et al. (1922). *British Columbia Fisheries Commission* (Ottawa: F.A. Acland).
30 Canada, House of Commons Debates, 22 June 1936 (the other two vocally anti-Asian members of Parliament were W.G. McQuarrie [New Westminster] and C.H. Dickie [Duncan]), Neill, "Letter to N.E. Lyche," L.11.7, A.W. Neill Clippings, Port Alberni Historical Society Archives.
31 Masako and Stanley Fukawa, *Spirit of the Nikkei Fleet: BC's Japanese Canadian Fishermen* (Madeira, BC: Harbour Publishing, 2009), 112.
32 Neill, "Letter to Lyche."
33 Ibid.
34 "Made White Man's Chances Better Is What Fishermen Say about Neill," *Port Alberni News*, 14 October 1925; Neill's Committee, "Why We Are Supporting Mr Neill."
35 Neill, "Letter to Lyche."
36 Neill's Committee, "Why We Are Supporting Mr Neill."
37 Ibid.
38 "To Further Reduce Japanese Licenses," *Port Alberni News*, 6 December 1925.
39 "Orientals Ousted from Fisheries: New Neill Law Now in Force Putting White Men into Coastal Industries," *Victoria Daily Times*, 4 December 1924, 9.
40 Patricia Roy, *The Oriental Question*, 108–10.
41 Neill's Committee, "Letter to Voters," 1930, *Courtney Free Press*, file L.54.17, Port Alberni Historical Society Archives.
42 "Federal Member Takes Stock of Lumber and Fish Industry," *Port Alberni News*, January 1930.
43 Neill's Committee, "Why you should vote for A.W. Neill Independent Candidate," *Weppen Press*, undated, file 71.8, Port Alberni Historical Society Archives.
44 "To Further Reduce Japanese Licenses."
45 Neill's Committee, "Letter to voters."
46 "Made White Man's Chances Better Is What Fishermen Say about Neill," *Port Alberni News*, 14 October 1925.
47 "Dominion Member ets extension of boundaries," *Port Alberni News*, 13 January 1926.
48 Jack Gibson Campaign Committee, "Great Record of Alberni Electoral Representation," undated, file L11.7, Port Alberni Historical Society Archives.

49 Hamilton, "One Town, Two Worlds."
50 "Matters of Importance to BC Given in a Report by A.W. Neill," *Port Alberni News*, 21 June 1928.
51 John D. Meehan, "From Ally to Menace: Canadian Attitudes and Policies toward Japanese Imperialism, 1929–1939" (PhD diss., University of Toronto, 2000).
52 "Matters of importance to BC."
53 Neill's Committee, "Advertisement for 1930 Federal Elections," *Cumberland Islander*, 25 July 1930.
54 Neill's Committee, 6 October 1934, file L.54.17, Port Alberni Historical Society Archives.
55 Alan W. Neill, "Letter to N.A. Robertson," 3 February 1942, file 3464-b-40c, vol. 2978, RG 25, LAC.
56 A.W. Neill, "The Japanese Situation in British Columbia," Canada, House of Commons Debates, 19 February 1942 (Ottawa: King's Printer), 9.
57 Alan W. Neill, "Members Rights in Parliament – Old Age Pension Reform – Japanese Exclusion," 1 March 1943, House of Commons Debates Official Report, 7. Fukawa and Fukawa. *Spirit of the Nikkei Fleet*, 162.
58 A.W. Neill, "The Japs Must Go," 5 May 1944, House of Commons Debates Official Report, 5–6.
59 Anonymous, "Upper House Appointment for Neill? Island Endorses Perennial Independent Member for Vacancy," file "A.W. Neill," Port Alberni Historical Society.
60 Peterson, "Valley in Review," *Alberni Valley Times*, 4 October 1990; Tatsuo Kage, *Uprooted Again: Japanese Canadians Move to Japan after World War II* (Toronto: TI-Jean Press, 1998); Baird, "Developing an Anti-Racism Methodology."
61 "Council Cancelled."
62 Chris Alemany, Rosemarie Buchanan, Chris Stevenson, personal communication, August 2018.
63 Chris Stevenson, Facebook, 11 May 2016.
64 Chris Alemany, personal communication, Port Alberni, 15 August 2018; Rosemarie Buchanan, personal communication, Port Alberni, 23 August 2018.
65 Lorene Oikawa, Letter to Mayor Ruttan and Council, National Association of Japanese Canadians, 16 January 2018, accessed 14 September 2019, https://www.portalberni.ca/sites/default/files/council_mtg/Jan23_Updated_opt_tf.pdf.
66 Hamilton, "One Town, Two Worlds."
67 Chris Alemany, personal communication, Facebook, 5 November 2018; Chris Alemany, personal communication, Port Alberni, 15 August 2018.
68 Ibid.
69 Darren DeLuca, Facebook, 26 October 2018.
70 City Council Minutes, 19–81.
71 Hamilton, "One Town, Two Worlds."
72 Rosemarie Buchanan, personal communication, 23 August 2018, Port Alberni, BC.
73 Ibid.
74 Marlene Mortensen, personal communication, Port Alberni, 21 August 2018.
75 On 11 February 2020 the school board trustees for School District 70 Alberni voted to rename the school. The process of determining a new name is under way.
76 Terry Hamagishi, personal communication, Port Alberni, 27 August 2018.
77 Keiko Mary Kitagawa, personal communication, 13 September 2018; D. Heidt, "Howard Charles Green and Japanese Canadians," *BC Studies* 164 (2009/10): 31–50.

CHAPTER 13

The Road to Redress: A Presentation to the Landscapes of Injustice Spring Institute, 2018

Art Miki and Audrey Kobayashi

Early in the morning of Sunday, 27 April 2018 (the year marking the thirtieth anniversary of the federal government's acknowledgment of wrongdoing and its redress settlement with the Japanese Canadian community), Arthur Miki and Audrey Kobayashi, key members of the National Association of Japanese Canadians negotiating team in 1988, spoke to a gathering of the Landscapes of Injustice Research Collective, of which they are both a part.

AUDREY

Good morning everyone. I am honoured and delighted to be able to have a conversation with Art Miki. You can just think of it as two seniors getting together to reminisce. [crowd laughs] So if we get too far into the reminiscence, then let us know. I want to start by going back to the 1970s when we were not exactly kids but young. Earlier, we saw a photograph of Gordon Kadota and his presentation to Parliament in the early 1970s. I'm not sure how many Nikkei knew that that presentation was going on, but it really was a turning point almost spiritually in the understanding of Japanese Canadians as an organized group and in their place in Canadian history. Everyone knew, of course, about the experiences of the 1940s – at that time most living people had experienced the 1940s, but this was the start of a different time when Japanese Canadians as a community had a new sense of their place in the geography and history of this country.

I want to start with that turning point. The Japanese Canadian centennial marking the arrival of Manzo Nagano, believed to be the first immigrant to Canada from Japan, was coming up and it was a tremendous, symbolic time. The whole country got together in planning that centennial in 1977. I was a graduate student at UBC at the time, and I remember I wasn't very excited about the celebrations because, you know, I was a radical at UBC (to the extent that UBC is radical), and I was concerned about redress. And there were a bunch of us who were concerned about redress. We had meetings at restaurants, and we were really determined to do something in order to make the Canadian government accountable. But it was still a sort of disparate thing.

I remember Gordon Kadota standing on the stage at the first Powell Street Festival in Oppenheimer Park or Powell Street Grounds as we call it. Gordon was one of the first Nisei to speak out strongly for a redress settlement, and he encouraged the audience to think about 1977 as the beginning of a new century devoted to justice.

The Powell Street area was once a vibrant Japanese Canadian community prior to the 1940s, the largest centre of Issei culture and the economic hub. Although there had been little Japanese Canadian presence since the uprooting, the centennial was an opportunity to encourage community presence and to reawaken a sense of Nikkei identity. This festival first began in 1977 and is held annually in August celebrating Japanese Canadian arts and culture, traditional and contemporary. It has become an important tourist attraction in Vancouver.

During the festival, Gordon Hirabayashi, a Nisei who later waged a successful lawsuit against the American government, met with a group of Sansei in a nearby restaurant and discussed with us what it would mean to start a redress campaign.[1] And I remember the passion, the fire, and the way he got everybody excited. So, Art, I want you if you can, I know you can, to start in 1977, and maybe start by just telling us what it was like and how you got involved. Not too long after that you became president of the NAJC, and the rest is history.

ART

Well thank you, Audrey. Well again, welcome everyone this morning. It's a pleasure to be here and to share this story. For the people here, this year is the thirtieth anniversary of the Japanese Canadian Redress Settlement. And when you said two old people, you're right – that was a long time ago. But it's interesting, something that I will certainly never forget. My involvement with the Japanese Canadian community nationally began with the Japanese Canadian Centennial Society. I was representing Manitoba. And the idea was to get people from across the country together to celebrate this occasion of one hundred years, the arrival of the first immigrant in 1877. That landmark date is in question now, but at that point it became a focus for our community to get together. And it was interesting because through the gathering, there were certain projects that developed. I can remember the Japanese Canadian Centennial Project Redress Committee project, a national history photo exhibit called "A Dream of Riches: Japanese Canadians, 1877–1977" that was developed in Vancouver and had traveled across the country. In Winnipeg, we had it set up in the Hudson's Bay Company store, and so the public was able to come and visit and look at the information. And so in a way that was the beginning, really, of unveiling our history to the public.

And also it gave an opportunity for many people in our community to speak about their experiences. I had invited Thomas Shoyama come to Winnipeg in 1977, and he gave a lecture on his experience and what happened to him in his early years. Tom Shoyama was the former editor of *The New Canadian*, a Japanese Canadian newspaper, and later became the deputy minister of finance in the federal government. That

Figure 13.1 Art Miki and Audrey Kobayashi at the Landscapes of Injustice Spring Institute, 2018.

type of thing awakened a lot of the young people because many of them said that they never knew that happened, and they didn't realize that their parents came to Manitoba as a result of being forcibly removed. Many of them thought that their parents made a choice, and they often questioned, "Why did you come *here*?" [crowd laughs] But they didn't realize the real story behind it. And some of them after meetings were very angry at their parents for not telling them because it was something they had not really discussed in their homes.

And the same applies in my family as well. I began to learn all about this around 1977 and '78, when Ann Sunahara spoke about her research in her book *Politics of Racism*. That book gave information about what happened to the community and showed that there was certainly a wrong done as revealed through the documents uncovered in the government's archives. The following year, in '78, the National Association of Japanese Canadians (at that time it was called the National Japanese Canadian Citizens Association) established the Redress Committee. In 1980 the committee reported indicating that one of the ways of rectifying the wrongs of the past would be for the government to make an apology and also to create a foundation or a community fund: as a symbolic gesture on the part of the government. And that was the position that the NJCCA first adopted.

Not everyone was happy with that. I became president in 1984. Before that, in 1983, there had been a meeting of the NAJC national council. We were all invited to Toronto for discussion of a proposal put forward by the Redress Committee. Without involvement of the communities, the Redress Committee had already made an informal deal with the government that they would accept an apology and a community fund or foundation, whatever those might be. We all gathered in Toronto, and we had this discussion. The committee wanted us to endorse their plan. But people began to question: first of all, you didn't consult with the wider community, and now you're putting forward a position? Many people questioned the fact that no consideration had been given to individual compensation: that is, compensation to be paid to individual Japanese Canadians who lived through the internment and their families. And so, as a result, the council rejected the proposal.

Meanwhile, the Redress Committee had already gotten funding from the federal government, separate from the national association, of $100,000 dollars to conduct the meeting with the intention that they would deliver the agreement, or they would deliver our support for it. Well that fell through, and the Redress Committee at that time talked about resigning. Although many representatives were upset, there was hesitancy to accept their resignation. Anyways, that committee stayed on, and I became president in 1984.

At that point, the national association adopted an official position that we would seek an acknowledgment – not an apology, an acknowledgment – some form of compensation, and a repeal of the War Measures Act. That was the position that national council adopted. The council also made a stipulation that the Redress Committee was now accountable to the executive, to the president, to the national council, because up to this point, they were operating independently of each other. And so to tighten the relationship, that was adopted.

Well, the same people who had sought a quick agreement with the government, that same Redress Committee, remained in place. So we had a conflict within our organization. The committee continued to oppose individual compensation. What we found out is that these people had very close connections with the government, and they made a deal, silently, and they were trying to push it regardless of where the wider community stood. And so that became the big issue.

It came to a point where the Redress Committee without the endorsement of the national council, or the executive, had arranged to have an apology given in the House of Parliament, and they began to contact people in our community. One of the members of our national council phoned me one day and [said], "Did you know that we were invited to Ottawa for an announcement?" I said, "No. I have not heard anything about it." The Redress Committee had decided that they would go ahead without consulting us or even letting us know, despite the fact that they were accountable to us.

When I found out about that – Henry Kojima and I, both from Winnipeg, contacted Honourable Lloyd Axworthy, a Liberal cabinet minister, to express our concerns.

And we met with him and told him "First of all, this is not something that this association has endorsed. It is something that's being done within our own community but the national association has not endorsed it or approved it." Mr Axworthy took this message back to his cabinet. So that day that they were going to bring in all of these people was cancelled. But the government, because they had indicated that they would do this, Honourable David Collenette expressed regret in the House of Commons on behalf on the government for what happened to Japanese Canadians. Meanwhile we had indicated to the press that we rejected the action of the government.

This was the summer of 1984, and the Liberal government was going to prorogue Parliament. It was the second or last day of Parliament, and that's when Mulroney was now opposition leader, and he questioned the government about redress for Japanese Canadians. Prime Minister Pierre Trudeau responded, "I don't think it's the purpose of government to right the past. It cannot rewrite history. It is our purpose to be just in our time." His message implied that this government would not be compensating Japanese Canadians. Fortunately for us, Mulroney stands up in retaliation, and said, "If it were the Conservative government, we would surely compensate Japanese Canadians." Great news! [crowd laughs]

Right away we sent a letter to Mulroney, expressing our support. And, lo and behold, he becomes the prime minister that following election. He becomes the prime minister, and the first thing we do is send him a letter: "Reminder." [crowd laughs]

And you know what? He reacted very quickly, appointed a minister of state for multiculturalism, Jack Murta, and within a month or so we had a meeting arranged. It was authentic. And so, in December of 1984 a meeting was arranged to bring the national council to meet with the government. It was mainly run by the bureaucrats from Minister Jack Murta's office, and in the end we agreed to a negotiation process. A press release was jointly prepared by the National Association of Japanese Canadians and the government agreeing to a negotiation process to rectify the wrongs of the past. We were extremely happy. And so in January, a few weeks later, the process of negotiations began. We met four times in January – once a week. After a few meetings we began to realize that they're not negotiating. They've basically adopted the same position as the previous government except the quantum had been increased to six million dollars from five for the community funds and an apology. They were not prepared to consider individual compensation.

One of the things that really frightened us is that when one of the government officials hinted to us that the minister might take action by saying, "Well if you don't agree to it, we're going to put a bill through the House of Commons." That is when we decided to go to Ottawa. So we take the negotiations team to Ottawa and set up meetings with the opposition parties: because, in government the opposition plays an important role. When we met with Liberal parliamentarians we were very careful about what kind of support we wanted. What we said to them is, "We want you to support us in a negotiated settlement. Negotiated means that both parties agree." And we knew at that point there were a number MPs that if they heard a quantum of even $100,000 or whatever, they would react negatively. A few years after Sergio Marchi confirmed that, "if you had come in asking us to support individual compensation, the Liberals would not have supported you."

We also met Ed Broadbent and the NDP caucus. While we were meeting with him his staff member comes in and states, "We just had a note from the House leader. The Conservatives would like to put forward a motion tomorrow morning on the Japanese Canadian Redress." While we're sitting there, Ed Broadbent turns to me and says, "Do you know anything about this?" I said, "No." I said, "There's no way that we've come to any agreement with the government." So he told his staff person to tell the House leader they would not support it. That action died.

I often wondered, had we not been there at that exact moment, [crowd murmurs] whether it would have gone through because the government had planned to put it through. That's when we realized that the negotiation process was not a negotiation process. Right after that, the CBC picked up the story because it became a press item that there was dissatisfaction within the NAJC with the negotiations process. I was asked by CBC *The National* news to appear on the program with Barbara Frum, for those who are older or remember her, she was the host. She had the minister and myself on there. And she said to Minister Murta, "Did you not agree to a negotiation process? Didn't you send out a press release?" "Oh yes, we did that." But then in the end he comments, "But, we didn't really mean negotiate. We wanted to consult." That statement lost him his job. Otto Jelinek was then appointed as minister for Multiculturalism. He would be the next person that we would meet in the negotiations process.

I'm going to get back to the political part because within my own community there were divisions and dissatisfaction. As I told you, there was a group of people who were trying to put through a redress position that did not have the approval of the national council. In the end, after the attempt of the apology with the Liberal government, we had a council meeting and we disbanded the National Redress Committee. Those same people would form their own group and began to lobby the government saying, "We agree to your proposal." And they're saying, "We represent the silent majority." That was the term they used. The silent majority. That was the term they used to try to discredit the NAJC and show the government that we were not the true representative organization for Japanese Canadians.

AUDREY

Radicals. [crowd laughs]

ART

Right, we were radicals, actually. So as a result, they formed their own group after we disbanded the Redress Committee. So we established the Redress Strategy Committee, which I was on, and Audrey and a number of our committee people were a part of it. So we began to develop a process. Through our experience of negotiations with the government in January, we recognized a few things. First of all, Minister Murta asked us in our meeting, "What did your community really lose?" Simple question. What did your community really lose? You know what, we couldn't answer that question. We could say, "Well they lost their property, education, all of those things." He then asked, "Can you quantify how much your community lost?" That's when we realized that we didn't have an answer and so the need for a study of economic losses became a priority.

We undertook a fundraising campaign in our community, and at this point there wasn't that much support by our community members. A lot of people, especially the first generation people, were not supportive at all, they kept saying, "*Shikataganai.* Just leave it alone, don't bother." There are other people that said, "You know we've established ourselves, and by entering into this discussion with the government and asking for compensation, we're going to get backlash. Our neighbours will turn against us." There was this fear. I can understand that concern. So we didn't have much support. So our problem was how are we going to raise enough funds to conduct an economic losses study. We checked with some accounting firms and the cheapest we could get one done was for $150,000. So we started fundraising.

Well, when you have a very small portion of your community supporting you, you couldn't raise that much money. We did get funds from the City of Toronto – $5,000 – and the City of Lethbridge gave us $3,000 for research. But, in our own community we only raised about $28,000–$29,000. Henry Wakabayashi who was helping us said, "You know what? I know the president of Price Waterhouse." So he set up another meeting with Price Waterhouse because they were the ones who quoted $150,000. We met with Phil Barter, the president, and he listened to our plight, and in the end he said, "You know my father was president of Price Waterhouse at the time of the internment, and he often said that shouldn't have happened." It might have been that he had a friend or someone who was sent away, and he said, "This is wrong." And so Phil Barter said, "You know what? Maybe we could do something. We are prepared to do your study if you can just pay the upfront cost of sending someone to research in Ottawa in the archives. We'll do it for you." And he said, "If you *ever* get Redress, you can pay us then." So that's how the study came around. And so 1986 we released the Price Waterhouse report or study quantifying the losses to the media. This study measured minimal losses because they couldn't measure pain and suffering. Price Waterhouse quantified losses of property and wages, and it worked out to $443 million dollars, in 1986 dollars. That was the result.

The second project that we did was to conduct a national survey on forms of compensation because up to this point this group who is opposed to individual compensation kept telling people, "No one wants individual compensation. People don't want it. And we're being greedy by asking for it." So we did a national survey [and got] 2,000 responses: the majority supported individual compensation, and there were a number who preferred community funds. But when we put it together we recognized that individual compensation was a very important component about what we should be seeking – it confirmed the importance of seeking individual compensation even though the government was not willing to consider it at all.

The division in our community began to disappear once this particular group stationed out of Toronto did something that was pretty unethical. They had met with the minister responsible for multiculturalism, Otto Jelinek, who was certainly not a supporter of NAJC. In fact, the first time that I ever met him he made a big boo-boo because he was also minister of sport. He says, "Well I'll meet you at the airport." And so we met at the airport, and his chief of staff was there waiting for him, and the first thing he said to me was "How are you, Mr Oki?" [crowd laughs]

Mr Oki was one of the people leading the other group, so obviously Jelinek and staff had already met with him and that other group. I didn't know. This was the first time meeting Otto Jelinek. We met in this room at the airport. I brought a number of our community members along, and Otto Jelinek says to us in his opening, "Yes, I understand your issue. You know, I understand your problem very well." He says, "You know what, I was an immigrant, too."

And one of our seniors just stood up and said, "We're not immigrants. We're Canadian citizens. Obviously you don't understand this at all." And so we just walked out of the room because at that point there's really no point in discussing it. But later on, we get a call to meet Otto Jelinek in Ottawa. So we go down there. We get to this meeting in this office, and when we walked in and there's a whole slew of press there. There were cameras and reporters waiting for us. Mr Jelinek says to me, "Do you mind if the press takes some pictures before our discussion?" After taking the pictures the media disappear. We were wondering what that was all about and then we have this meeting. We thought there were some important developments that he wanted to discuss. Then he says to us, "We don't think that you represent Japanese Canadians, officially." He said, "We have word that you're not the real representative. We're holding a press conference after this meeting, would you like to join me in the press conference?" I said, "No." But we go attend to the press conference to curiously find out what he will say. He announces to the media that the National Association of Japanese Canadians is not the true representative of the Japanese Canadian community. And then he reads out a list of all the organizations in Toronto who indicated that they supported the other group. About ten or fifteen Toronto organizations.

Fortunately that same list had been given to the City of Toronto when we were applying for a $5,000 grant, and the same group was opposing the grant to the National Association. But at that time, our supporters went through the list and checked every organization, contacted them. None of them had ever been contacted by this group and they didn't even know their name was on this list. There were two or three organizations that were defunct. As Otto Jelinek is reading this list we're thinking, "Oh my god." So the next day we called a press conference and we denounced his statement and his accusations. We encouraged the reporters to contact some of the organizations themselves to find out the validity of Jelinek's statements. It became a national story. The *Toronto Star* reporter contacted these organizations, and, true enough, none of them had heard of this at all – it was all a sham. And so, in that sense Minister Jelinek's credibility went down the drain. We knew that he was supporting the other group because we heard that he had funded some event for them to garner support. When I met him and accused him of that, he would not say, "We didn't do it." He just skated around the issue like his figure skating career did, I guess. [crowd laughs] When I said, "Did you arrange to support this group, did you fund it?" He never said no through the whole thing, so we assumed that he did.

One of the interesting things during Jelinek's time was that the government was very conscious of the fact that if there was a press conference and if the prime minister was there, the question of redress would come up. So one day I am attending the National Conference for Mathematics Teachers, and in the middle of the session that I'm chairing, two people open the door and they stand there and say, "Is Mr Miki here?" So I say, "I'm here." "We have to see you; it's an emergency."

So I go out the door, and I apologize for the disruption to all those people in the session. I meet them outside the door and they say, "Minister Jelinek wants to meet you. It's urgent that we meet." And I tell them, "Well I have a press interview with CBC at 4:30." They reply, "We'll have a taxi there waiting for you. As soon as you finish, the taxi will take you over to the Fort Gary Hotel, where the meeting is going to take place."

I phone one of my colleagues, Harold Hirose, and I say, "Harold, you have got to join me because there's an emergency meeting, and I want to have another person there with me." So we get to this meeting and Jelinek comes and shakes our hands and says, "excuse me, I will be right back." Disappears for about ten minutes, comes back, and we sit down. And I ask, "So, what's the issue?" He says, "Well our position hasn't changed." So I asked, "Well, why did you call me?" He just shook his head, and then we walked away. Interesting, that night, I phoned my brother in Vancouver, and I said to him, "The strangest thing happened today." And he said he attended a press conference in Vancouver with Mulroney and the question of redress was raised about what the government was doing. Mulroney's response was, "At this very moment, in Winnipeg, the minister is meeting with Mr Miki." My meeting in Winnipeg was orchestrated to ensure that Mulroney's response would not be challenged. And so it was the ploy to ensure that contact was made.

Shortly after Jelinek was removed from the portfolio, and David Crombie became the minister for Multiculturalism. Initially there was optimism because he had been the minister for Indian Affairs. People were quite pleased that we had him, but in the end it turned out that he was no different than the rest. And we gave him about a year, and then when we finally met in Winnipeg he gave us an ultimatum when he said to us, "This is the final offer. If you don't take it, negotiations are finished." And we decided at that point that we would walk away and say, "Fine. Negotiations are over."

And we did. We walked away. I said to him, "one of the issues that we are concerned about is individual compensation. You're not even willing to consider these things?" He said, "Oh yeah, why don't you take the thirteen million?" He was referring to community funding. He asks, "Why don't you take that and give it to individuals?" And I said, "Well that's $800 per person. I don't think that would even buy anything in our community. That is an insult." So anyway, we walked away. And so the negotiations process became dormant.

But it became an issue for us because then we didn't know what to do. We had to change our strategy. Up until now, it was the Japanese Canadian community against the government. We went back and forth, but there was very little progress. Eventually we were at a standstill. And so NAJC Strategy Team gathered in Vancouver and brainstormed how we should restrategize. We decided that what we needed to do was to broaden our approach by forming a National Coalition for Japanese Canadian Redress. And the national coalition meant that we would include Canadians who generally wanted to support us. We asked Justice Thomas Berger as the honorary chair from Vancouver, and we recruited a number of prominent Canadians: Pierre Berton, Margaret Atwood, and June Caldwell. Joy Kogawa was able to get some of the top writers to join. We had other politicians join, mayors of cities, eventually we got the major unions to support us, we got all the churches in Canada except for one, which was the Buddhist Churches of Canada. [crowd laughs] But I can defend their position because if you know their philosophy, they don't question what happens in the past. That's part of living, is that when you face difficulties, you move on. One of the things the church did say is that, "if individuals want to support you, that's fine. But as the church, we cannot endorse you." Even when we met with the veterans' organization Cliff Chatterton of War Amps, who said as an organization they couldn't support us, but they said to us, "We'll let the individual veterans decide on where they stand on this issue, but we will not dictate to them."

AUDREY

Assembly of First Nations was also great.

ART

The NAJC hired David Murata from Toronto to coordinate the coalition and recruit supporters. Eventually we had over 4,000 individuals and many organizations in support of a negotiated settlement. Committees in Toronto and Montreal organized buses to take supporters to Ottawa for the protest rally. So the idea of a coalition, of getting other Canadians involved, was effective. We had a postcard campaign where we gave postcards out to people and had them sign it. We had gathered about 4–5,000 postcards. The culminating event for the coalition was the Ottawa rally on 14 April 1988 where many of the internees and friends marched on Parliament Hill. I recall even within our own community some people were against the rally as they said, "Japanese people do not march; they don't protest; that is not the Japanese way." [crowd laughs]

AUDREY

April 1988, right?

ART

Yeah, April 1988. And they were pretty offended, some of the people. But we decided that the Canadian way is that we do this, and we did it. And we had over 4–500 people who came from different parts of Ontario, some came from out West, and they marched on Parliament Hill. All of the people who had gone through the internment; it was quite the show. Very solemn – quiet. No loud shouting or anything like that. And we held a session in West Block where coalition speakers came and spoke, representing the churches, the libertarian groups, and so on. And even Gerry Weiner, who was the new minister of multiculturalism, attended despite the fact that he was warned by his staff not to go.

AUDREY

I think it was his first public speech.

ART

Yeah, his first public speech and he was warned not to go. His staff warned him, "Look what happened to your three predecessors." [crowd laughs] But he told us he felt obligated to go. At that point there may have already been a change taking place in the government that we didn't know about. The rally was a success. We had national coverage. We had the victims of the internment in the face of cameras. It was important. People – the Canadian public – began to recognize, "These are people right here who had suffered." It wasn't just some abstract group of people. And so it was very powerful.

Shortly after I received a call from the minister saying … Well, I should go back a little bit. We had all these postcards, there were about 500, and we had mailbags full of them, and Minister Weiner offered to walk with our group of supporters to the prime minister's office to dump off these postcards. I thought that was quite a thoughtful gesture on his part, that he would do that for us.

AUDREY

From the west wing to the prime minister's office carrying massive bags of yellow postcards. But I just wanted to challenge one thing. I don't think it was that quiet. Okay, so we had taiko and Indigenous drummers. And on one of the few occasions I have seen, we had this drumming jam session that was really fantastic and *really* loud. It reverberated all over Parliament. Maybe you forgot that part? [crowd laughs]

ART

Well, remember I'm partly deaf. [crowd laughs] I'm just kidding. Well certainly there were activities there, and the night before the rally we had a big get-together in the hotel. We had big celebrations. Several MPs came, and it was exciting, really. So that set the tone for the next day. As I said, it was a powerful, powerful impact that I think for the campaign because shortly after, the minister of multiculturalism called me and said, "We have to meet." I said, "Well, first off all, we are not meeting unless we can discuss individual compensation." He said, "I've talked to the prime minister. He said everything's on the table." So that is when we said, "Okay, we'll go and meet." In the end, the rally created national awareness and proved to be the vehicle that eventually led to a settlement.

The NAJC Strategy Team met with the minister and his staff in Winnipeg in July 1988. The biggest concern that the prime minister's office had was – because they had already rejected our negotiation process and we had walked away – that they wanted to save face and they're wondering how can we begin the talks again. We made suggestions such as, "Why don't you set up a three-man committee made up of representatives and they'll make a recommendation? Or get one individual, someone we can both agree on, to make recommendations."

We waited to get a response, and the difficulty for them was the payment – the financing of it. Because if they had to pay out, they would have to go to Privy Council, and going to Privy Council meant that you'd have to let other politicians know that you were doing. The prime minister was very coy about this; he kept everything quiet. So as a result, he decided not to do the Privy Council because they were afraid if he went to Privy Council someone would raise that question of "Why are you doing this?" He might raise negative reactions against redress from his party colleagues. In the end, the Minister Gerry Weiner told us, "The prime minister has found some money from his own slush fund." I'm not sure how large it is. [crowd laughs] Anyways, we were given the go ahead to hold the negotiation meeting. So we had a secret meeting in Ottawa for three days in late August.

AUDREY
Montreal.

ART
Montreal. Sorry, Montreal. And we were at what hotel?

AUDREY
Well, we were at the Delta later, but we started out at the Ritz Carlton.

ART
Ritz Carlton.

AUDREY
And they took us in through the kitchen so that the press wouldn't see us. [crowd laughs]

ART
That's right. We went through the kitchen, up the back stairs, and we finally arrive at the room where the meeting will be held. And interesting enough, the person there waiting for us is Lucien Bouchard. [crowd murmurs] Lucien Bouchard sits down with us. He was very close to the prime minister at the time because he was appointed by the prime minister to be secretary of state in cabinet. He said to us, "The government is willing to offer $15,000 individual compensation." That's the first thing he says. And we said, "Oh my god. You know, this is serious."

That was the starting point. So he laid it right on the table that individual compensation was a go. So in the end, we hammered back and forth for a couple days. They wanted all kinds of details about what we would do with the money if we had a community fund. And we brainstormed as a group … it was just a process. We ended up at $20,000 individual compensation. And I forget what the community fund was; it was a little higher than what we had. And they agreed to all the terms that we had laid out, except that the quantum was different. So we're at $20,000, and then we do a little history lesson with the minister and his officials about the treatment the Japanese Canadians. We explain it was even more severe than in the United States and explained some of the differences between the treatment. I remember saying, "Wouldn't it be nice if ours was a little higher, symbolically?" The minister said, "Oh wow, maybe we can do that?" And so we agreed to reduce the community fund a bit and shifted the money to individuals. So that's how we arrived at $21,000. People often ask why $21,000? Instead of twenty or twenty-five or whatever. And so we explained the rationale behind it.

The government agreed to $21,000 individual compensation, to a $12 million community fund, and to the formation of the Canadian Race Relations Foundation. And the reason for that foundation is the fact that when we tried to do the study of economic loses, we had applied or asked the government to fund it, and they rejected us. They said, "Why would we fund you and have you use this study against us?" [crowd laughs] Well I said, "That's logical, too." [crowd laughs] We accepted that and so we had to fund it ourselves. That's when we recognized that there must be other groups such as us in similar situations. Where would they get support? If the government won't support them, where would they go? And so that's the genesis for formulating the Canadian Race Relations Foundation: to help other groups. And so that was accepted. In fact, the way we worked that out is that $12 million was contributed on behalf of all those Japanese Canadians who had already passed away before the redress settlement. Symbolically, it represented them. And the government contributed $12 million. So the endowment for that organization was $24 million. Unfortunately, at the time that we were looking at this, the interest rate was running 10 per cent. So we figured two-and-a-half million a year for operation should work out. Well, the interest rate went down, and now they're having difficulty surviving. Well they are surviving, but it's more difficult. They can't do the programs that they should be doing, I guess.

AUDREY

What Art isn't saying is that he was an exceptionally canny negotiator. Very, very smart, like a fox. And just kept coming back: hammering, hammering, and hammering. And the rest of us, well, we all had different jobs. And mine was numbers, right? I was the numbers person. I was the one who worked with Price Waterhouse and did the demography and everything. And so, the government doing their math, you can see their heads turning, right? And they're saying, "22,000 people, how is that going to work out?" And I would say to Art, "But Art, it was 27,000 people." Because 22,000 was a number of people who were actually moved out of their homes, but they forgot all the ones who were already outside, and they forgot that you know, people get *born*. And between 1942 and 1949, a bunch of people had been born. I say to Art, "Art it was 27,000. You've got to tell them." And Art's saying, "Shut up." [crowd laughs]

ART

That's right. We said to the press that about 14,000 would be eligible for payment, not to quantify it so high that they would back away from considering individual compensation. We tried to keep it down, but we knew it was higher than 14,000. It turned out to be eighteen in the end. The final payment was to approximately 18,000 people. But, we knew things like, we checked the insurance company projections studies and other information and felt that about 14,000 was reasonable. Meanwhile, we're lying a bit. [crowd laughs] I think Audrey gets her notes higher, but we said, "No, no. It's okay."

The rest is pretty much history in a sense: 22 September. The end part is really interesting. By the time we concluded the negotiations only four people knew in government. And that was the minister of multiculturalism [Weiner], Lucien Bouchard, the prime minister, and Deputy Prime Minister Don Mazankowski. The prime minister asked his staff to have us agree that we say nothing about the settlement to anyone until the prime minister's office lets us know when there will be an announcement in the House of Commons. So we kept quiet. The reason for that is because they had to convince the cabinet that they would have their support. It's strange, the politics that goes on. Because prior to that – and I've heard one of the staff people that I dealt with that whenever Mulroney raised redress for Japanese Canadians, he was shot down in his caucus but mainly by one of the cabinet ministers, George Hees, who was the minister of veterans affairs. A well respected politician, and every time Mulroney raised the issue he would speak against any redress for Japanese Canadians.

AUDREY

He said, "Japanese, no."

ART

Japanese, no, because he was likely thinking of the Hong Kong veterans who were opposed to redress, and so he supported their views. Well you know what happened? In about April, George Hees becomes ill. And he's hospitalized. And so he has to resign from cabinet. It was shortly after that the tenor of Mulroney's approach changed. Up to that point, it was always a roadblock – they weren't ready to move. And then when we met in July, Minister Weiner says, "Everything is on the table, we are ready to negotiate." The tide changes quickly, well. That's politics. And so here we are, four politicians have to go to cabinet and convince the rest of their colleagues that they support the redress motion.

And it was 22 September. A month later, because we met on 25 to 27 August. On 21 September, I receive a call around 11 am, while I'm working at school, from the minister's office saying, "Come down to Ottawa tomorrow morning. We're having the redress announcement. We have tickets for you at the airport. All of the members of the Strategy Team have tickets waiting for them." We are to be in Ottawa for that evening so that the announcement would be made the following day. Meanwhile, earlier in the morning I did get a call from the press saying, "I understand there's going to be an announcement." At that point I said, "No, I don't know about any announcement." But what happened was they let the press know that the announcement was going to happen before anyone else just to alert them. So the press knew before we did. But anyways, we did get the phone call and the rest is history.

AUDREY
Art, the real hard negotiating of course was over the money. But a lot of the discussion was over principles.

ART
Right.

AUDREY
And that's one of the things that will always stick in my mind. One of those principles was acknowledgment rather than apology, which has a lot of resonance with groups today. And I heard you speak so many times, so eloquently, about how we would not accept an apology. Can you briefly just give that speech again?

ART
Well I give you credit, but you're right, we've always talked about this thing. Apology is – I mean anyone can say I'm sorry to you. It may not have much meaning. But acknowledgment means admission, which is the important part – to have the government admit that they made a mistake was important to us. So we've always said acknowledgment rather than apology. But usually apology is the word that is so often used, but it was not the main issue.

There were other principles, too. One of the things that we really wanted to make sure is that whatever happened, we were involved because we kept saying, "When the Japanese Canadians were removed from the West Coast, they had no say. They had no say in the actions taken by the government." We wanted to insure that the community participate in the redress process as part of the healing process and that we would have a voice. That's why when we pressed the opposition parties and supporters for a negotiated settlement, it meant that *we* are agreeing to eventual result. That was a key point, and I think if you look at all the things that we did during the implementation process, we were involved. Once the agreement was made, the application form for redress was created by the NAJC. It was a one-pager. And we deliberately made sure that the bureaucracy was not involved in having a two- or ten- or twelve-pager. We said, "One-pager. Make it simple. Make it easier for the people to apply." And they agreed to it, which was great. They also agreed to help fund some offices so that we could help our own community seek redress. So they put in $3 million to help set up centres where we could provide lawyers and community support workers to help individuals with their application forms and also to send individuals out to remote areas to seek out people.

They also funded for us to go to Japan because there were 4,000 people who were sent to Japan in 1946 and were eligible. So we had a ten-city meeting schedule where the exiled Japanese Canadians were invited to come. We had about 800 or 900 people who attended these meetings. So everything was done to try to facilitate the victims, and part of that was we were being involved. It was important that having the power and the responsibility made the settlement and apology more meaningful. [There are] a lot of settlements today where a group receiving compensation has no say in the final outcome. I think the Chinese Head Tax apology was that way. It was just given one day to them without involvement and consultation. The Ukrainian internment – same thing. So for any apology by government to be meaningful, the victims of the injustices must be involved in the redress process.

One of the things that really hurt me was the fact that at the very early stages, this particular group out of Toronto, they were meeting with the government on the side and they kept saying to us, "We know the politicians; we have these contacts. You don't." This was a disadvantage for us because we were being used, and it prevented the community from being consulted. So this is why I always argue that community consultation regardless of what the outcome is, is always more important in the process than just getting something in the end.

AUDREY

Art, I want to give time because I think people have lots and lots of questions. Just very quickly, what did the whole thing mean to you? How do you feel as a Canadian? Was it a vindication? Or was it something different?

ART

Well, for me, I was extremely proud of the fact that I was involved with the redress movement. I have always said through whole process, whatever happens, the biggest benefit was educating other Canadians on what happened to us. Even if redress was to never happen, I still felt that we had to do this. It was important for us. The fact that it came to fruition was certainly a surprise for me and certainly a joyous event. I mean, we sat there after the negotiation, in the corner of the hotel room floor saying, "We can't believe it, it happened. It happened!" You know, people were in tears. I remember Roger Obata, he was just in tears. I was that way too. It was just overwhelming, and a very proud day for us and for Canada. [crowd applauds]

AUDREY

That's exactly what it felt like, and I remember it very well. I mean we were six people who were working hard; we were practically living in the same place, eating all our meals together for those number of years that all of this went on in the sense of not just the camaraderie, which of course happens when you have a joint project, but the sense of belonging to a larger community and working with that community, to me was a game changer. It changed the understanding of the country. It changed, for me personally, an understanding of what it means to be an academic, a researcher, a writer,

Figure 13.2 Art Miki (at desk to the right of Mulroney) and Audrey Kobayashi (glasses, behind Art) at the signing of Redress, 1988.

and the responsibilities that come with it. There was the responsibility of the government; Art just kept pressing and pressing and pressing: "Take responsibility, acknowledge that you were wrong." And they did that. But there was also this sense of responsibility, I think, within the community that has carried on.

ART

Well, I think certainly the redress has revitalized our community to a great degree. We have a lot of seniors' residences now that all received funding from the foundation. Nearly all the cultural centres in our country received funding. It sort of helped stimulate the communities. So I think it was very important, the community fund. When I compare it to the American Redress Settlement, it did nothing to help develop these communities at all. Their proposal was just individuals. Whereas we built in the fact that the Japan Town in Vancouver was destroyed and we have to revitalize our dispersed community. So while we were doing it, we needed to provide funds for different projects, for writers – we funded a lot of writers to write about our history ...

AUDREY

Scholarships.

ART

Scholarships, yeah. We've established a fund that's available today, the NAJC Community Development Fund. But that was part of the agreement that we made to help stimulate and maintain, sustain our community in a way. So it was important. One of the interesting things about the early days is whenever we met in Ottawa, reporters would ask for my card to contact me at the office or where our office was located. I had to admit that my office, our office, was my living room table. [crowd laughs]

AUDREY

It's an amazing story – a fantastic story. And one that we treasure, partly because of you – mainly because of you as the centre of this whole thing – but also because it's such an important contribution to this country, however we think of it. So thank you. [standing ovation]

NOTES

1 "Sansei" refers to third-generation Nikkei. On Hirabayashi's long-delayed vindication by American courts, see Peter Irons, *Justice at War: The Story of the Japanese-American Internment Cases* (Oakland: University of California Press, 1993); Gordon K. Hirabayashi, *A Principled Stand: The Story of Hirabayashi v. United States* (Seattle: University of Washington Press, 2013). For a discussion of the troubling legal legacy of the Hirabayashi decision, see Eric Muller, "Hirabayashi and the Invasion Evasion," *North Carolina Law Review* 88, no. 4 (2010): 1333–88.

CHAPTER 14

Social Accountability after Political Apologies

Jordan Stanger-Ross, Matt James, and the Landscapes of Injustice Research Collective

On 22 September 1988, a Thursday at 11 o'clock in the morning, Prime Minister Brian Mulroney rose in the Canadian House of Commons: "I know that I speak for members on all sides of the House today … in offering to Japanese Canadians the formal and sincere apology of this Parliament for … past injustices against them, against their families, and against their heritage."[1] Mulroney's words, in offering Canada's first political apology, spoke the day into significance. Three decades later the National Association of Japanese Canadians, which negotiated the government's apology and redress settlement, observes an annual tradition of meeting in the third week of September. In contradistinction to more straightforward anniversaries of state heroism on the one hand and malfeasance on the other, the 22 September date commemorates an apology for state wrongdoing and a community's remarkable struggle for justice.

The apology was a core component of the 1988 Japanese Canadian Redress Agreement, which provided for a spoken expression of regret by the prime minister in the House of Commons, a formal written acknowledgment of wrongdoing, individual and community reparations, and the establishment of the Canadian Race Relations Foundation, an organization that has gone on to do considerable public education work on matters of racism and racialization.[2] The written acknowledgment of wrongdoing articulated the harms of the internment era with specificity, naming (1) the disenfranchisement of Japanese Canadians; (2) their detention; (3) the confiscation and, subsequently, sale of their property; (4) the use of the revenue from those sales to pay for the internment; (5) the postwar expulsion of Japanese Canadians; (6) the restriction of their movement; and (7) the continuation of these policies for almost four years after the war. Ottawa recognized that this treatment of Japanese Canadians "was unjust and violated principles of human rights as they are understood today." It pledged to "ensure … that such events will not happen again," and it praised the "fortitude … of Japanese Canadians who, despite great stress and hardship [retained] their commitment and loyalty to Canada."[3]

A statement of regret and a recognition of harm, the apology also took responsibility for wrongdoing.[4] However, in contrast to its specificity about the harms that Ottawa's internment policies had caused, the apology gestured imprecisely toward *who* was responsible, *what* they did, and *why* they did what they did. This chapter draws on archival and secondary sources to outline what we believe is a more satisfactory account of responsibility for the actions perpetrated against Japanese Canadians in the 1940s. It is crucial to emphasize that our objective is not to establish the inadequacy of the original apology. Rather, we aim to develop a kind of dialogue between that somewhat limited instance of official responsibility taking and a fuller account of unjust decision making, which we offer in the following pages. This dialogue, we hope, will help to advance what we see as the ongoing democratic potential of Canada's initial regretful acknowledgment of wrongdoing, as well as contribute to scholarly and public knowledge on the role of political apologies in present- and future-oriented processes of public accountability.

Our approach in this chapter follows from our work on the "impermanence" of political apologies.[5] In that writing, we argue that engaging political apologies retrospectively tends to lay bare their factual and interpretive inadequacies. We view this process of critical retrospectivity as building upon (and enhancing) the democratic work of political apologies rather than as a straightforward matter of denouncing the weakness or hypocrisy of political apology as a genre. Our research suggests that political apologies often fail to provide the final word on historical injustices; apologies may even contribute to subsequent critical inquiry and engagement that reveals their own flaws. For example, the 1988 apology to Japanese Canadians did so by providing funding for community organizations that went on to press their own inquiries, by sparking heightened social attention that led to further probing of the wrongs, and even by containing specific failings that helped to motivate subsequent calls for more meaningful forms of responsibility taking. In these ways, the 1988 apology helped to make possible this book and our chapter within it.[6]

The present chapter builds on this "impermanent apologies" perspective by taking seriously the potential role of political apologies as mechanisms of accountability that can be used to place official accounts of injustice and responsibility under further critical pressure. It does so by contrasting the responsibility claims in Canada's 1988 apology for the internment of the country's population of Japanese descent with what we have learned from historical sources. The primary aim of this comparison is to pursue further the democratic potential of Canada's high-profile 1988 act of apology and redress. A secondary aim is to develop the impermanent apologies perspective in explicit relation to considerations of accountability.

Accountability and political apologies

Perhaps many of us have the intuition that apologizing (admitting wrong, stating regret, and promising nonrepetition) is a way of making ourselves accountable, either directly to those we have harmed or to those with whom we have relations of responsibility or trust.[7] While the literatures on apologies in medical settings and in interpersonal relations are explicit in treating apologies as mechanisms of accountability, the political apology literature lacks any direct and sustained treatment of the topic.[8] Accountability is multifaceted, a "radial" concept that resists simple binary judgments of absence-versus-fulfillment.[9] Standardly, to be held accountable means being made answerable for our actions and, alternatively, or in addition, being compelled to face some form of sanction for misconduct.[10] While these are in themselves complex concepts and processes, our treatment of accountability in relation to political apology rests on a distinction between two overarching ways in which the topic might be approached.

The first considers accountability as a specific relation between a wrongdoer who is called to account and some determinate actor or individual to whom accountability can be said to be owed. The public administration literature refers to this as the "principal–agent" model, while scholars in psychology and management studies sometimes speak of accountee–accountor relations.[11] More broadly, holding wrongdoers directly to account is perhaps the primary accountability focus of the global phenomenon that political scientist Kathryn Sikkink calls the "justice cascade": the worldwide pursuit by victims, activists, and prosecutors of individual leaders and state authorities accused of having committed gross violations of human rights.[12]

From this essentially dyadic perspective on accountability, the 1988 apology would seem to fare reasonably well. The Japanese Canadian redress movement demanded that the Canadian state take responsibility and make reparation for the injustices of the internment. The 1988 agreement, negotiated between the state and community representatives, satisfied the movement's main demands.[13]

But there is also a distinctively different perspective from which to view accountability in relation to political apology, one that focuses more on diffuse processes of civic exchange and learning than on dyadic relations of demand and response. Law scholars tend to describe the goals of these more diffuse processes in terms of social accountability; political scientist Michelle Bonner treats similar concerns under the rubric of what she calls discursive accountability.[14] To highlight social accountability in political apology is to look beyond processes of demand and institutional response and to think more broadly about how official apologetic accounts might be used to help publics learn about past injustice in ways that promote the more responsible exercise of democratic power in the future.

Formal institutional processes can also engage publics, promote civic learning, and therefore serve social accountability goals.[15] Canada's 2009–15 Truth and Reconciliation Commission (TRC), which addressed this country's century-long policy of separating Indigenous children from their families and forcing them to attend residential schools, is one recent example. Although the TRC's mandate prevented it from making findings of fault or law, rendering it weak as a forum for residential school survivors wishing to hold government, churches, or school personnel directly to account, the commission promoted new civic languages of historical trauma and cultural genocide for public education and engagement.[16] Bonner's conception of discursive accountability suggests that this kind of institutional contribution can be important in helping activists and reformers to find effective and usable languages, symbols, and frames with which to denounce wrongdoing and advocate change.[17] At the same time, and in the specific case of the TRC, political scientist Rosemary Nagy notes that Canadian publics will have a crucial, ongoing social accountability role to play in trying to help ensure that such languages get developed in transformative rather than colonial ways.[18]

These and other distinctions between different kinds of accountability are overlapping and blurry. Formal institutional processes can serve social accountability goals; social accountability will involve not only discourses of wrong and harm but also concrete interactions and struggles for institutional and legal reform; discursive framings of wrong and harm are central both in social accountability processes and formal institutional settings. Nevertheless, and without neglecting this necessary messiness, we want to keep squarely in view the distinction between the dyadic aspect of political apologies as institutional responses to politically mobilized victim and survivor groups and more diffuse social accountability concerns. We argue that these latter concerns can and should be brought to bear on the apologetic responses that victim and survivor groups elicit from states.

This chapter highlights the underacknowledged potential of political apologies as ongoing mechanisms of social accountability, considering them as acts whose retrospective engagement can help stimulate processes of civic learning. For example, we might engage an apology to establish linkages between its account of wrongdoing and present-day structures or attitudes; we might probe it to pursue questions of agency, asking how people in analogous potential situations of wrongdoing might "act otherwise"; or we might take its account as a springboard for exploring more general questions of public responsibilities in fighting and righting injustice. Political apologies cannot be expected to perform this work on their own but rather require our ongoing critical engagement.

Judging the 1988 apology

Although criticism is crucial to this chapter's project of retrospective analysis, it should not detract from recognizing the significant achievements of the 1988 apology. The apology and redress package emerged from direct negotiations that, after several years of high-stakes political contention and many setbacks, satisfied the core demands of the mobilized Japanese Canadian community.[19] The apology was regarded as meaningful by many recipients, particularly those elderly community members who had sought the sense of personal closure that official Canadian repentance might bring. It led to support for institutions that continue to engage the history of internment, such as the NAJC and the Nikkei National Museum, each of which has helped in turn to motivate and guide the historical research on which much of this book rests.[20] The apology embraced key community demands, making the Canadian federal government and state accountable to a wronged constituency of citizens. It set a precedent that encouraged other communities in Canada to press their own demands for historical redress.[21] It helped to promote the dynamics of impermanency that we have argued are important to longer-run processes of social accountability in historical justice.

Yet taking a social accountability perspective also makes the limitations of Ottawa's 1988 apology more apparent. Drawing in particular on the work of philosophers Nick Smith and Cindy Holder, we identify three expectations of responsibility assignment in political apology that were unmet in 1988 and that seem particularly important from a social accountability perspective.[22] These expectations are as follows: an apology for a specific wrongful policy or act should (1) link the wrongs, where relevant, to longer-run structural and historical factors and contexts, (2) probe questions of individual and institutional agency, and (3) examine the responsibilities and complicities of wider publics. Mulroney's apology to Japanese Canadians disappoints on each of the three expectations.

From the perspective of social accountability, the apology's denial of structural racism demands our attention. The written acknowledgment described the actions of the 1940s as "unprecedented," thus effacing decades of discriminatory treatment, such as the disfranchisement of Japanese Canadians, which lasted until 1949. For its part, Mulroney's apologetic speech in the House of Commons eulogized a Canadian past significantly at odds with historical reality:

> the treatment inflicted on Japanese-Canadians during the War … went against the very nature of our country, of Canada. We are a pluralistic society. We each respect the language, opinions and religious convictions of our neighbour. We celebrate our cultural diversity … That is the Canada of our ancestors. That is the Canada our ancestors worked to build.[23]

Although denial and euphemism may have helped to enable the apology by making it palatable to white electorates, a social accountability perspective demands that these manoeuvres be addressed. Put simply, the apology's account of the "Canada of our ancestors" is irreconcilable with a history of settler colonialism and racial and religious inequality in immigration, housing and labour markets, schooling, political participation, and the application of the law. This failure to name the racist context and structures that enabled the more specific injustices directed at Japanese Canadians seems typical of political apologies. For example, apologies in Australia and Canada to Indigenous peoples for the injustices of the "stolen generations" and residential schooling, respectively, failed explicitly to discuss the systems of colonial dispossession from which those wrongs sprang and that continue to oppress Indigenous communities in those countries today.[24] Thus, social accountability demands that we challenge official apologetic accounts by linking the relevant injustices to the large-scale patterns of wrongdoing that apologies tend to ignore and whose ongoingness officialdom seeks to efface.

The social accountability perspective also draws our attention to the importance of conveying adequately the individual and institutional agency directly responsible for the wrongs. One might find a minor nod in this direction in the 1988 written acknowledgment of wrongdoing, which noted that "despite perceived military necessities at the time … [the treatment of Japanese Canadians] was unjust," or in Mulroney's House of Commons speech, which observed that Canada committed the wrongs "[in] the crisis of wartime." These statements, crafted in close collaboration with representatives of the Japanese Canadian community, were not intended to suggest that Japanese Canadians posed a security threat; instead the apology indicated that the government had acted out of proportion to real risk: the "military necessities" were perceived, not real. The "crisis" was not of Japanese Canadian making.[25] Nonetheless, by emphasizing the "crisis of war" and its effects, the acknowledgment and apology of 1988 came close to explaining racism away as a kind of collective stress or distraction. Neither the text nor the speech offered any further account of government agency or intention involved in the wrongs. If this limited form of apologetic responsibility taking is familiar (most of us will have forgiven some wrong or another on the basis of a wrongdoer's stress, distraction, tiredness, error, and so forth), it is hardly a robust explanation of nearly a decade of governance.[26] The internment era in Canada did not involve one impulsive or panicked moment of decision but rather dozens, even hundreds, of choices to sustain ongoing violations of human and constitutional rights, even long after the war had ended. Although the government took responsibility for its actions in 1988, it left important work to be done in specifying who was responsible for what and why they did what they did.

Even when government falls short in this way, more specific accounts of responsibility can play an important role in ensuring the ongoing relevance of political apologies. As Smith writes, "precise attributions of blame identify the need for reform at various levels." Careful accounts of culpability can promote "awareness of how individual actions aggregate to cause large-scale harm"; in turn, ongoing sensitization to this dynamic may help individuals to behave more ethically, thus increasing "our chances of preventing further harm."[27] Understanding causal and moral responsibility can be a difficult undertaking in the context of modern states, which are complex agglomerations of branches, institutions, and agencies, involving thousands of different individuals of different roles and inclinations, and presided over by governments with their own complex internal relations of faction, personnel, and party. Nonetheless, taking the opportunity of a political apology to at least attempt some kind of anatomy of the choices and agency involved in the injustice can help attune decision makers, officials, and even publics to how wrong is done; this kind of ongoing individual and collective learning, we believe, is crucial to vindicating the basic democratic presumption that political communities can improve on their past choices.[28]

Finally, both the written acknowledgment and the House of Commons speech avoided what we have identified as the third and final core requirement of responsibility taking in political apology: engaging questions of public responsibility in relation to the wrongs. The written acknowledgment stated that the policies of the 1940s were "influenced by discriminatory attitudes." This statement might have implicated the public or perhaps it referred merely to officials: no further direction was offered. Readers today might reasonably infer that the "attitudes" noted in the statement were those of officials because the remainder of the text referred exclusively to harms perpetrated by the government and never gestured toward a wider Canadian public.

But calling publics to account, as Holder has recently argued, is important if we expect political apologies to engage the present-day political community as opposed merely to impugning the (all-too-conveniently) abstract and impersonal state.[29] In examining political apologies she urges us to consider the identity of those on whose behalf apology is made, how these people are implicated in the wrongdoing, and what kinds of moral and reparative responsibility, if any, members of the public are assigned and take for that wrongdoing. Thus, Holder leads us to ask in an apology for some act of past official racism, does the apologizer identify civil society racism as part of the circumstances that gave rise to the wrong? Do they talk about the historic character, nature, modalities, and carriers of that civil society racism? Do they name any of its key individual proponents and agents? Do they draw connections between it and contemporary racism? Do they talk about beneficiaries of injustice? As Holder explains, even if the account in the apology of the state's wrongdoing is relatively robust, if that account ignores what she calls these problems of "public-ness" it may fail to "spur self-reflection within the population at large and [therefore] not contribute to the transformation of social, cultural and political attitudes and structures."[30]

In sum, Canada's apology to Japanese Canadians, in spite of its significant successes and the remarkable community initiative that brought it about, demands critical reexamination with social accountability goals in mind. First, the structural and contextual dimensions of the harms perpetrated against Japanese Canadians demand articulation. Second, the individual and institutional decisions of the internment require further explanation. Finally, the role of civil society must be illuminated. Absent these analyses, the apology leaves current readers and audiences to imagine the internment era as a damaging and regrettable departure from the larger path of Canadian history, explicable only as a reaction to the heat of war and antiquated attitudes.

A more robust portrait of responsibility enhances the potential of retrospective engagement with political apologies to help the democratic work of civic learning, while at the same time conveying a more accurate history. In the next section, we sketch a history of the era that pursues the "specificity in moral causation" that Smith sees as important in political apology, considering also some of the questions of "publicness" stressed by Holder.[31] We then return to questions of democratic process and the relation of impermanent political apology to social accountability.

Responsibility and Canada's internment era

The research of the Landscapes of Injustice project discussed throughout this book is particularly suited to engaging existing accounts of responsibility for internment era policies. Because the dispossession of Japanese Canadians brought long-term economic consequences, obliterating the Japanese Canadian property ownership that had arisen from multigenerational migratory strategies, its significance is only comprehensible within a longer historical context in which property had been acquired in the years before internment and benefits and harms of dispossession continued to reverberate over succeeding decades.[32] Similarly, the forced sale of all Japanese Canadian–owned property, which was authorized only after Japanese Canadians had been uprooted from coastal British Columbia and which continued in the postwar, cannot be explained as an act of panic under the crisis of war. Instead, we need a fuller account of the institutional and individual agency involved in the decisions to intern, dispossess, and exile Japanese Canadians.[33] Finally, the dispossession of property required buyers and sellers, as well as appraisers, agents, auctioneers, clerks, and lawyers.[34] It cannot be understood without an account of public involvement and complicity. We now consider more fully each of these factors – structure, agency, and public involvement – drawing significantly on the material presented in prior chapters and concluding this book with a call to democratic engagement.

a. Structural context

Canada's internment era policy choices had complex origins. The federal government's actions during the 1940s were shaped by British Columbia's relation to the geopolitical and strategic position of Canada as the British Dominion in North America and Ottawa's own longstanding use of legislative racism in support of "white Canada" and anti-Indigenous policies. Particularly relevant was the tendency of support for provincial rights and even separatism to erupt in the so-called "white man's province" on those occasions when Canadian foreign or economic policy goals had led Ottawa to block or disallow racist provincial legislation. This historical background made racist discontent on the Pacific coast particularly concerning to the federal cabinet in a time of war.[35] From the perspective of articulating responsibility for the discriminatory treatment of Japanese Canadians in the 1940s, several relevant prior events stand out. Perhaps the most significant was the provincial disenfranchisement of 1895, which, in addition to preventing Japanese Canadians in British Columbia from voting in provincial and federal elections also precluded them from holding public office, serving on juries, taking provincial or municipal employment, working in law, pharmacy or policing, or holding liquor licences.[36] The 1902 decision of the Judicial Committee of the Privy Council in the case of *Cunningham v. Homma*, which declared the British Columbia disfranchisement a valid exercise of provincial legislative authority, gave explicit constitutional affirmation to this far-reaching act of legislative racism.[37] This decision was followed by further provincial and municipal laws that segregated schools and neighbourhoods and restricted Japanese Canadian business opportunities.[38] In another significant prior event, anti-Asian political mobilization spiralled into street rioting in Vancouver in 1907, a manifestation of racist discontent in the province that Ottawa chose to accommodate by moving to establish a *de facto* ban on immigration from Japan.[39]

From the standpoint of structure, these prior rounds of historical struggle combined cumulatively to create "Japanese" as a racialized category in Canadian law, to establish anti-Japanese measures as familiar pacificatory devices in federal–provincial relations, and – as one might suspect in a state founded on Indigenous dispossession – to confirm the continued constitutional validity of legislative racism. Thus, when the federal cabinet met to specify the internment and dispossession in law, the relevant regulations – including the dispossession of property – could be applied to all "persons of the Japanese race." By contrast, "persons of the German race" or "persons of the Italian race" were not mobilized as policy categories. For example, on 7 December 1941, when Canada declared war on Japan and extended the key Defense of Canada Regulations to include Japanese Canadians, it revised the law to apply to all persons: (1) born in territories under the sovereign control of the German Reich as of 3 September 1939; (2) born in territories under the sovereign control of Italy as of 10 June 1940; or (3) "of the Japanese race." The racialized treatment of Japanese Canadians under the law necessitated further elaboration in their case: "For the purposes of these regulations 'persons of the Japanese race' shall include a person not wholly of the Japanese race if his father or mother is of the Japanese race."[40] By contrast, German and Italian Canadians were always understood as internally differentiated. Canada interned Germans (including naturalized Canadians) suspected of some enemy interest but never contemplated the internment of all Canadian-born people of German descent or the seizure of all of their property on the basis of their purported race; federal policy interned particular Italian Canadians who, however unjustly, were considered to be fascists or fascist sympathizers, but it undertook no blanket Italian Canadian internment.[41] A subset of those populations was most vulnerable to the full force of wartime regulation: those who were not British subjects and were suspected of some direct connection or involvement with enemy powers. "Persons of the Japanese race" existed as a potential and then actual policy category because of a prior Canadian history that – in spite of the formal status that Japanese Canadians possessed in law as British born, naturalized subjects, or residents of a British Dominion – had explicitly placed them beyond the circle of equal membership or, in post-1946 terms, had denied them full citizenship.[42]

For the purposes of taking responsibility for the harms of the 1940s, these less laudable aspects of the "Canada of our ancestors," rather than its purported inclination toward the celebration of diversity, demand articulation. That the apology failed to articulate this wider context is fully understandable given the circumstances of its production: both the federal government and members of the Japanese Canadian community had reasons to emphasize the singular and exceptional dimensions of the internment. For Japanese Canadians, the campaign for an apology was not a campaign for connective historical analysis (or indeed historical analysis of any kind) but rather for the acknowledgment of a specific harm perpetrated at a particular time. However, critical consideration of the apology requires understanding the internment as a consequence, as indeed redress campaigners themselves did, of the longstanding vilification of Japanese Canadians, their exclusion from equal membership and voice in the Canadian political community, and their explicit racialization through numerous acts of state.[43] The internment era should not be understood, and nor should responsibility for its harms be articulated in such terms, as a temporary lapse amidst the paranoia of war. We need to push beyond an apologetic account that repudiated and took responsibility for the specific policies and harms of internment. We need to relate these policies and harms to structural racism. We need to emphasize that this structural racism was legitimated and entrenched by prewar policy that racialized Japanese Canadians in a broader constitutional context in which racism was normal and acceptable government business.[44]

b. Institutional and individual agency

Attention to context is necessary but not sufficient in pursuing what Smith calls specificity in accounts of moral causation. Structural racism and existing policy made possible the internment of "persons of the Japanese race," but individuals and groups operating within specific institutional settings made the many choices of the internment era. As noted at the outset of this chapter, the 1988 apology was specific in articulating the wrongs of internment. These wrongs included three policies that, in light of the apology's emphasis on the "crisis of war," deserve particular attention: the seizure and sale of property; the exile, in 1946, of almost 20 per cent of the prewar coastal population; and the extension of the internment to 1949. Any effort to articulate responsibility for the policies of the internment era should at least attempt to account for these decisions, which bore little (if any) relation to defending the country. The sale of property continued well after any crisis had passed (the final sale of Japanese Canadian–owned real estate in Vancouver's historic Powell Street neighbourhood occurred in 1950), and the latter two policies were crafted and executed as postwar measures. Here a contrast with the United States is instructive: although both countries shared a history of racism against people of Japanese (and other Asian) descent and the US experienced much more directly the security threat of the Pacific, US officials refrained from seizing and selling all of the property left behind by incarcerated Japanese Americans, deported less than 1 per cent of the prewar population, and ended the internment upon the war's conclusion. How did the choices of Canadian officials lead to more extreme policies in these respects? To answer this question, we need an account that understands the institutional dynamics of the wartime decisions and attends to the individuals who played pivotal roles within them.

When the federal cabinet chose to uproot and intern all people of Japanese descent in Pacific Canada, it unleashed an almost immediate cascade of difficulties and harms: at every step of its implementation, policy generated its own administrative problems, which in turn required solutions. Those solutions, concocted for the most part by bureaucrats (in chains of correspondence that generated thousands of pages) and then passed into law by their political masters, created further problems that demanded further resolutions. Understanding what political scientists and public administration scholars would call these path-dependent decisions is essential to a fuller account of responsibility in the internment era.

Indeed, as the notion of path dependency suggests, students of policy and government have known for generations that public decision making is seldom a matter of clear sighted command from the heights of reason (or indeed the depths of racial animus); rather, it involves juggling among suboptimal alternatives shaped by preexisting choices and constraints.[45] The internment era is understood poorly as a singular plan devised in government and then implemented by public servants. Instead, the initial uprooting created a variety of problems, real and perceived, leading officials to improvise various solutions. Pivotal within this process was the decision, in March 1942, to entrust the property of Japanese Canadians to the federal government. The decision to seize all property in coastal British Columbia set the Canadian government on a path toward the creation of a problem of Japanese Canadian placelessness, whose multiple ramifications officials would then eventually try to "solve" through dispossession, exile, and the extension of the internment.[46]

The original version of Order in Council PC 1665 of 4 March 1942, which specified the administrative mechanisms of the uprooting, made no mention of property nor was the Custodian of Enemy Property envisioned as a key federal body within the internment process.[47] However Austin Taylor, the business magnate named to the helm of the British Columbia Security Commission, read the draft order and demanded some provision for property. In hasty response Ian Mackenzie, the British Columbia representative in the federal cabinet and a politician who for decades had positioned himself as a champion of white British Columbia, made a phone call to Ephraim H. Coleman, the bureaucrat responsible for staffing and administrative oversight of the Custodian of Enemy Property. The details of their conversation are unknown, but its results were consequential to thousands. In a hasty revision to the internment orders, the two agreed that all of the land, homes, businesses, and personal belongings (in short, everything) that Japanese Canadians owned in coastal British Columbia would be administered by the Custodian of Enemy Property. This was perhaps the pivotal decision on the path to Japanese Canadian placelessness.

As noted in the introduction to this volume, the vesting of property in the federal government, which led to some of the most draconian measures of Canada's internment era, could be rationalized at the time as a form of responsible public administration. Although they surely reflected the amoral machinations of what scholars now call administrative racism, the decisions involved were also instances of attempted problem solving that could, however strangely, be understood by those involved as reasoned responses to a mess not of their own making.[48] For example, some officials, Coleman included, defended the property transfer as a genuine protection of the interests of Japanese Canadian owners; the offices of the Custodian were indeed organized initially for this purpose. In the highly constrained context created by the uprooting, vesting the property in the protective authority of a federal office could plausibly be argued to be the decision most likely to safeguard the constitutional rights of Japanese Canadians as property-owning British subjects and Canadian residents.

Officials soon perceived new problems created by the vesting itself. Taylor commented that the vesting had exacerbated a "complete lack of confidence" on the part of Japanese Canadians in the trustworthiness of the government. This crisis of confidence might, he felt, jeopardize the orderly cooperation of Japanese Canadians with internment policy that he had been entrusted to implement. Taylor believed that Japanese Canadians were especially anxious about their long-term futures. Was the uprooting a temporary wartime measure or a permanent disruption of lives and communities built over generations? Left unchecked, such uncertainty would "add tremendously," Taylor argued, "to our present problem [of uprooting and interning Japanese Canadians]."[49] To solve the problem of mistrust, the federal government specified in law that the property of Japanese Canadians would be protected for the duration of the war and returned as soon as possible. A new order in council, passed at the end of March, stipulated that all property (real and moveable) left behind by Japanese Canadians during their uprooting would be administered "for the [owners'] benefit" and that the government would "release such property" back to those owners as soon as possible.[50]

The mandate to protect and preserve the property of Japanese Canadians thrust considerable responsibility on the Custodian, whose operations in Vancouver were directed by Glenn McPherson. In 1942, under his direction, officials opened files for each Japanese Canadian property owner and kept running ledgers of the debits and credits against estates (particularly real estate) as rents were collected, taxes and insurance paid, and repairs made. These responsibilities, along with those of ascertaining the extent of the vested property, assessing the condition and value of that property, establishing title, and translating and typing communications with Japanese Canadian property owners, rapidly overwhelmed the staff of the Custodian. Even as officials came to grips with the extent of the property under their control, they were inundated by more than 10,000 claims by creditors against that property. Property management was soon perceived as its own policy problem.

The forced the sale of all Japanese Canadian–owned property in coastal British Columbia could thus be imagined, at least in part, as a solution to a difficult problem. The dispossession emerged from other interests as well, including those of other British Columbians in acquiring Japanese Canadian–owned lands and belongings and those of elected officials who, like Mackenzie, had committed publicly to preventing Japanese Canadians from ever returning to their former homes. Pressure from such sources mounted. The City of Vancouver, which sought the redevelopment of a large Japanese Canadian neighbourhood in the east end of the city, and the Soldier Settlement Board, which hoped to acquire Japanese Canadian–owned farms for distribution to returning soldiers, both pressed for forced sales. These pressures, combined with the burden of property management helped to make dispossession an appealing policy choice. In January 1943, overcoming the objections of those within the bureaucracy who remained committed to the protection of Japanese Canadian assets, McPherson convinced cabinet to permit the sale of everything his office had formerly struggled to manage.

The move to forced sales solved problems for staff in the Office of the Custodian of Enemy Property but generated new challenges for other branches of government, especially the Ministry of Labour, which was responsible for the internees as the war in the Pacific ground to a close. Here again, a contrast with American policy is instructive. In the summer of 1945 Robert Gordon Robertson, in External Affairs, commented that the Americans were dismantling their internment and permitting internees to return to their former homes and communities. "We might" he proposed, "adopt a plan similar" and free Japanese Canadians "as soon as possible after examination and vetting."[51] No, explained Arthur MacNamara, deputy minister of labour, "I do not believe the situation in the United States is a parallel one." Canada was already on its own policy path: "In the first place the property of Japanese on the United States west coast was not sold except with the consent of the owner." For this reason, and others, MacNamara felt "it would be impracticable" for Japanese Canadians to return to the coast "before the end of the war and probably for a long time to come."[52] The impossibility of "return" was a result of the dispossession, itself a consequence of the vesting of property in the federal government, which was in turn a consequence of the uprooting. Officials had manufactured, in a series of steps, Japanese Canadian placelessness. As the war drew to a close, officials sought alternatives to resolve this problem of their own creation.

To say that Japanese Canadian placelessness was, in some ways, an unforeseen creation of prior policy is not to deny its reality as a practical problem for public servants. Thousands of people could not remain indefinitely in sites of internment; yet they had no homes to which to return. In any event, key federal politicians remained steadfastly opposed to the return of Japanese Canadians to the coast. As the war drew to a close and Japanese Canadians and their allies began to generate widespread public unease about the internment their placelessness became an increasingly pressing political problem. Canadian officials needed to extricate themselves from the spiralling cascade of injustice they had unleashed. They needed a way out of what had quite quickly become an increasingly unpopular suite of policies, policies created by the decision to uproot and dispossess thousands of people on the basis of race – a decision resting firmly within the still more longstanding policy and constitutional grooves of using race in general and, in this case, Japanese ancestry as a ground for the allocation of public burdens and benefits.

Officials devised a two-pronged solution. They would exile as many Japanese Canadians as possible to Japan, a country that many internees had never visited, and disperse most of the rest to points east, leaving only a minority to reintegrate into British Columbian society. Chairing a major interdepartmental meeting regarding Japanese Canadian internment in April 1944, Norman Robertson, under secretary of state, External Affairs, articulated "basic assumption[s]" that were to guide future policy. "Ultimately," he explained, "we should aim at getting rid of restrictions which rest on the basis of racial discrimination." To achieve this end, the myriad regulations of "persons of the Japanese race" – including but not limited to their internment, their disenfranchisement, and a federal prohibition on their purchase of real property – would have to be eliminated. Exile was a means to this end: in order to extricate Canada from the consequences of its own racist policies, it "would be necessary to aim at a fairly substantial reduction in the Japanese population of Canada after the war." Such a reduction, Robertson explained, "would make it possible to give freedom from restriction to those who remained after the 'winnowing' process." "The difficult problem" for officials, even ones well accustomed to the problem-solving/problem-making dynamic of statecraft, "was to determine the basis on which the reduction should take place."[53]

This approach won the support of cabinet, which expressed the political appeal of winnowing and then normalizing with particular lucidity. Days after Robertson's interdepartmental meeting and in consideration of reports on its proceedings, cabinet anticipated an ultimate "settlement of the problem of Japanese in Canada" and embraced "the underlying assumption" that had guided bureaucratic discussions:

> it was felt that only by ... selection and removal would it be possible to enable an elimination of the restrictions which at present apply on a purely racial basis to a section of persons of British status, as well as to aliens of the same race. It was also felt that if such selection could be made, it would be much easier to approach the provincial governments ... with a policy for re-settlement, which would be just to the Japanese remaining in Canada, defensible in the interests of Canada, and at the same time acceptable to the provincial authorities.[54]

This policy direction would take time. By contrast with simply disbanding the camps and letting Japanese Canadians go free, exile and resettlement were in themselves complex undertakings. The exile required the federal government to specify its parameters, to battle a court challenge to its legality, and to arrange its logistics. The "second uprooting" of Japanese Canadians to Eastern Canada required consideration of provincial and local authorities. And so, as it pursued this path, the government extended the internment, carrying into the postwar period not the "crisis of war" but rather the cascading injustice of policy that flowed from the internment in general and from the vesting of Japanese Canadian property in the federal government in particular. At the same time, this policy approach gained the grudging support even of progressive civil servants who had previously objected to the excesses of Canadian policy. Henry Forbes Angus (a UBC professor and External Affairs staffer who had objected vociferously to the forced property sales), for example, seemed to accept winnowing and normalizing as an unfortunate reality, describing it as "in essence not ungenerous."[55] In November 1945, as drafts of the deportation order circulated to key staffers, John Erskine Read (another progressive member of External Affairs who had protested the mishandling of property and would later object more forcefully to the deportation) similarly accepted exile as a necessary evil. While lamenting that "there is not the slightest possibility of any Order with which I would be in sympathy being acceptable to all of the members of the [federal] Government," Read cautioned against too limited a deportation program. Proposals to "whittle" the deportation process down to an "inconsiderable number" would risk "giving rise to a reaction which would result substantially in a 100% deportation policy."[56] Both Read and Angus were concerned about how the policy would be applied, wondering who precisely would be exiled, but by 1945 both had concluded that, given both popular and political will, some "winnowing" would be necessary for the policy outcomes they desired: the removal of racism from Canada's law books and the normalization of Japanese Canadian citizenship. For them, the exile was indeed a solution to the problem of internment, which had become a matter of increasing discomfort for progressives in cabinet as well.[57]

By acquiescing to what they saw as the best of bad alternatives, figures like Angus and Read abdicated responsibility in ways that should remain instructive today. Both in some sense knew better, but they nonetheless failed to push against the constrained boundaries of the policy discussions that led to mass exile. In the United States, no similar deportation was necessary to reintegration. Nor should it have been in Canada, despite the difficulties imposed by the forced sale of property. This reality was already visible before a single Japanese Canadian was deported, when American camps disbanded. Voices of reason and justice failed.

This failure resulted in part from the power of racism and malice within officialdom and among the politicians of the era. Indeed, racism was constitutive of, entrenched in, and legitimated by Canadian law. Further, key figures such as Ian Mackenzie saw the war as an opportunity to permanently obliterate Japanese Canadian communities in British Columbia. Such visions did ultimately come to fruition, at least in the short term; racism, on the part of individual actors and hard-built into Canadian law, mattered in this history. At each moment of choice, an institutional process not infected with racial animus might have turned out otherwise. In this respect the apology was right to point to the "discriminatory attitudes" underlying the internment. However, a fuller account of responsibility (and one more likely to have social and political force today) must also comprehend that the federal state of the 1940s was an institutional context in which officials of diverse ideological inclination found ways of working together to solve the problems of administering Japanese Canadian lives. Past decisions created contexts within which draconian policies that would wreak long-term damage could seem like reasonable solutions to pressing administrative problems, even to individuals who regarded themselves as antiracist.

The preceding account of individual and institutional agency in the internment goes well beyond anything considered in the 1988 apology. We saw in the earlier discussion of responsibility and structure that the apology obscured the context of preexisting state-sanctioned racism that made the categorical race-based internment of Japanese Canadians thinkable and actionable. We have now seen in this section on individual and institutional agency that the apology's blanket admission of federal government responsibility fell short of the reckoning with moral causation that Smith and others believe political apologies should at least endeavour to provide. The point here is not only that key individual politicians and civil servants, such as Mackenzie and McPherson, bear particular responsibility for the internment, dispossession, and ethnic cleansing of Japanese Canadians. It is also that the improvisatory, path-dependent character of agency in public administration gave particular decisions a consequential importance that their individual authors could not at the time have predicted.

Problems involving interconnected causes and informational opacity – difficult to resolve in the best of situations – are particularly vexing in contexts of ill institutional intent.[58] We now turn to the last of our three sections on responsibility in relation to political apology, addressing Holder's concern with questions of "public-ness."[59]

c. Public responsibility

Retrospective engagement with matters of responsibility in relation to apology encourages scrutiny of another consideration overlooked in 1988: social complicity. Broadly speaking, responsibility for the harms of the 1940s cannot be adequately addressed without an understanding of public roles and responsibilities. British Columbia newspapers demanded internment policies and then publicly supported those policies as they unfolded. Petitions and letters to politicians also demonstrated considerable public knowledge of and support for many of the major harms of the internment era. Finally, in the last year of the war, and then in the years that followed its conclusion, the Canadian public, press, and opposition parties began to push against the ongoing internment policies. Public involvement has been described, rather than analyzed, in the scholarship to date, and, given the complexity of this public involvement, ours can only be an initial, rather than final, critical discussion of the matter.[60] However it may be useful to specify categorically the kinds of public responsibility entailed in the internment era: members of the public were culpable as political constituents, as direct unlawful actors, and as beneficiaries.

In the first instance, members of the public were implicated in internment era policy as constituents, advocating as individuals and in groups for policies directed against Japanese Canadians. For example, Vancouver Centre Liberal MP Ian Mackenzie found ample support for his racism among constituents. Letters advocating the government's first pivotal decision of the internment era – the choice to uproot and intern the entire population of Japanese descent – poured into the minister's office in the critical first months of Canada's war in the Pacific. On 21 December 1941 one constituent resented "cocky" Japanese Canadians and predicted trouble: "I would not be surprised if Riots should break out. The protracted Black ants [by which he seems to have meant Japanese Canadians] get on the nerves of the people."[61] With less vitriol but greater authority, the Anglican Diocese of New Westminster wrote Mackenzie in the same period to affirm that the "present National peril" took clear priority, in the view of British Columbia Bishops, over the secondary value of "British … justice and fair play."[62] In February 1942, as orders in council specifying the internment circulated among officials, A.G. Duncan Crux, partner in the Vancouver law firm of Crux, Kennedy, and Paine, advised Mackenzie that "generally speaking the population here will not be satisfied until all Japanese are moved out of the coastal areas." For their part, members of the Vancouver Real Estate Exchange forwarded to Mackenzie their resolution that "such removal should apply to and include all Japanese born or naturalized in Canada regardless of age or sex."[63] Writing on Valentine's Day in 1942, W.J. Tregidga, of Vine Street in Vancouver, anticipated the wider direction that would soon be assumed by federal policy: "I urge you," he wrote,

> to remove all Japs – man, woman, and child ... Take away all arms, radios, camera + *Vehicles* ... + send them away by train to the *Dust* Bowl in Saskatchewan – Let them take away only their clothing and cooking utensils ... *Confiscate* all *money* + *property* owned by *Japs* to be used to carry on our war against them + make it unlawful for them to acquire any land or property from now on.[64]

Mackenzie, who replied to Tregidga with thanks for his interest and "for the suggestions in your letters," would help to ensure that much of this vision was, in fact, carried out.[65]

Additional forms of public complicity in the harms of the internment era are especially evident regarding the dispossession of property. The dispossession (or, in the terms of the apology, the confiscation and sale of Japanese Canadian–owned property and its use to pay for the internment) required the ongoing involvement of thousands. The dispossession happened in downtown Vancouver, in weekly auctions of goods in the Fraser Valley, and in the homes and neighbourhoods of many British Columbians.[66] Members of the wider public were directly implicated in the harms of the dispossession, even before officials decided upon property sales. Records of the widespread theft and destruction of Japanese Canadian property leave little doubt of a broader responsibility for injustice than has been officially acknowledged. For example, in some small British Columbia towns, former neighbours desecrated Japanese Canadian graveyards after the internment began.[67] In Vancouver, a ten-year-old Japanese Canadian, Jean Ikeda-Douglas, watched as "crazy mob[s]" ransacked the vacated homes and businesses in her neighbourhood; touring the area in the wake of the "melee," Glenn McPherson confirmed that thieves had made off "with everything moveable."[68] Eileen Carefoot, whose family moved into a home previously occupied by Japanese Canadians in Steveston, recalled a neighbourhood besieged by looters: "at night, you could hear the trucks coming up down the road from Vancouver and they were taking everything of value from the houses and nothing was being done."[69] In Victoria, officials were appalled by the public destruction of the historic Japanese garden and teahouse in Esquimalt, the first of its kind in Canada and a longstanding public attraction. Inspecting the site in May 1944, one official described the premises as "just a wreck. Practically everything of value has been removed, doors broken down, electric wires cut ... in fact the place has been ravaged and wanton destruction has taken place."[70]

Partly in response to the public plundering of Japanese Canadian–owned property, officials relocated all chattels to centralized warehouses. There, inadequate security allowed the pillaging to continue. Officials in Vancouver explained that, "our central storage places have been broken into several times." Yet the "worst feature of this," in their view, was "not so much the amount stolen, but [that] the throwing of the contents of boxes on the floor in the search for valuables makes it difficult or impossible to identify the goods belonging to various owners."[71] Officials could and should have done more to prevent such harms by the wider public. But the historical record is not one of government responsibility alone and nor can these acts be understood as instances of panic in the "crisis of war." Rather, the opportunism and misconduct of a wider public became one of the problems that the forced sale of property was intended to solve.

As the forced sales began, purchasers benefited. The market for dispossessed property was broad and diverse, with some buyers (migrant farmers from the Depression-ravaged prairies, Chinese Canadians in East End Vancouver) suffering their own forms of economic and social marginalization and perhaps seeing few other options. Returning from the war, hundreds of veterans took advantage of the availability of the former farms of Japanese Canadians, which had been transferred in 1944 from the Custodian of Enemy Property to the Veterans Land Act Administration at a fraction of their value. In the decades that followed, most of the farms in the Lower Mainland were sold and subdivided into suburban lots for the expanding Vancouver metropolitan area, a financial boon to owners.[72] Some powerful British Columbians were able to take particular advantage of the opportunity presented by dispossession. Forestry magnate H.R. MacMillan, who during the 1940s also served terms as Canada's timber controller and as chairman of the Wartime Requirements Board, acquired the lands and lumber of a former competitor, Eikichi Kagetsu, one of the wealthiest Japanese Canadians on the eve of the internment. Acquiring for $93,000 (1.4 million in 2018 dollars) lands that Kagetsu valued at twice as much, MacMillan went on to be a principal in one of the largest forestry companies in the world. Meanwhile Kagetsu struggled in postwar Toronto, eventually dying without assets beyond his own modest home.[73]

Members of the wider public also benefited from employment opportunities created by the dispossession. For example, dispossession required real estate agents who managed properties before their sale and then clamoured for the opportunity to represent them on the market.[74] Jack Walker, manager of Vancouver's Pemberton Realty Company, toured federal officials through Japanese Canadian–owned properties, helping to convince them that forced sale, rather than management, was the preferable policy path.[75] Appraisers were employed to assess values and then to testify in defence of state actions.[76] Auctioneers worked charged commissions on sales.[77] Lawyers represented both Japanese Canadians and the government in the legal proceedings and challenges of the dispossession (chapter 9). Employment opportunities arose also in the burgeoning offices of the state itself. At its peak, the Vancouver Office of the Custodian employed more than one hundred people, most of them women. Alma Graham McArthur, for example, worked in the Vancouver office from March 1942 to December 1949 and was awarded a certificate for her outstanding contributions to the dispossession.[78] Frank Shears who ran the Vancouver office, recommended her for a subsequent posting in the Citizenship Branch, writing: "no one has sought more to safeguard the Custodian's interests or been more loyal in seeking to carry out the responsibilities of this office."[79] The letter of recommendation was typed and posted by another employee-beneficiary, Shears's secretarial assistant.

There were dissident voices throughout and immediately after the internment.[80] Among the letters to the editor praising internment or advocating still harsher measures, we can find, albeit in significantly smaller numbers, ones opposing the uprooting on civil libertarian or antiracist grounds. In later years, advocates of an entrenched constitutional bill of Canadian rights would point to the internment as the master exemplar of the kind of injustice that they hoped to prevent.[81] But opposition to internment and dispossession in midcentury Canada had its limits. For example, even the civil libertarian representatives on the 1949 Senate Special Committee on Human Rights, Canada's first parliamentary inquiry on the topic, chided Japanese Canadian witnesses for wasting the committee's time with talk of internment.[82] For its part, the key white organization that opposed the internment, the Christian-affiliated Co-operative Committee on Japanese Canadians, never embraced the right of the dispossessed to return to the West Coast; in Roy Miki's words, although the organization professed to support citizenship rights, it also believed "that dispersal and assimilation would solve the 'Japanese problem.'"[83] In short, even the progressive advocacy of the period was complicit in the climate of racialized power surrounding it.

We are not arguing that responsibility for the injustices of internment was equally shared. The point instead is that social accountability goals are ill-served by following the 1988 apology in ignoring these tough questions of public responsibility and complicity. In particular, it seems important to emphasize that the injustices emerged from the interaction of constituent activism and official response; that otherwise normal, law-abiding Canadians committed numerous acts of destruction and hate; and that, through the intergenerational transfer of wealth, thousands of mainstream British Columbians continue to materially benefit today from these injustices.

Conclusion: Political apologies and social accountability

We have treated questions of responsibility in relation to the 1988 apology under the three rubrics of structure, agency, and publicness. First, structural racism, entrenched and legitimated by decades of Canadian policy and constitutionalism, was the foundational condition of possibility for the policies of internment, dispossession, dispersal, and exile – policies that are too often misunderstood as results of the crisis of war. Second, advocated by specific individual public representatives and bureaucratic actors, the dispossession and ethnic cleansing policies were parts of an injustice cascade unleashed by seemingly "normal" public problem solving by individuals in a context of institutional wrong.[84] Some of these individuals, such as McPherson, bear special responsibility for particularly egregious conduct and decisions. Finally, individual members of the public engaged in acts of racist hate, lobbied for injustice, and then benefited from it directly; public officials heeded and encouraged some of their constituents' worst instincts and wishes.

The apology can surely be faulted for ignoring these structural, agential, and public dimensions of responsibility. But it is important to remember that its historical accounting was shaped by the political circumstances of its production. The redress movement in its insistence on a direct acknowledgment of state wrongdoing was not in the first instance seeking a complex probing of casual and moral responsibility; it was seeking a definitive federal government admission of responsibility for the injustices in order that Canada might acknowledge the suffering, moral equality, and right to reparation of the victims and survivors of internment. This concession was hard won over years of activism. The acknowledgment of wrongdoing was a major break with the silence, denial, and defensiveness that Japanese Canadians first encountered when the redress movement began, and the results of the apology were, by many accounts, transformational for the individuals who had suffered the policies and for the wider political community. It is the accomplishment of the apology that makes the present analysis possible.

At the same time, we are insisting that critical scholarship and activism needs to identify, engage, and reengage the limitations of official acts of historical justice. We believe that this insistence has particular relevance beyond the immediate case because acts of historical justice are almost congenitally likely to suffer limitations and omissions stemming from the circumstances of their production. For example, historian Brian Gettler has recently argued that key limitations of the account of residential schooling in the final report of the Canadian TRC – such as its relative inattention to perpetrators, agency, and regional variation in residential schooling – can be traced in part to the way in which earlier battles of residential school survivors for public recognition and respect shaped the operating assumptions and mandate of the commission.[85] The assumptions and mandate flowed directly from the class-action lawsuits launched by former residential students, who were seeking a forum that would acknowledge their experiences, amplify their voices, and force Canada to acknowledge its collective responsibility for the individual, intergenerational, and collective harms of residential schooling. Much like the internment survivors, former residential school students did not mobilize for a complex forensic probing that would assign varying levels of responsibility for the policies and choices of the residential schools era.[86]

The point here is not to fault justice seekers for the limitations of official responses, such as truth commissions and political apologies, which are better regarded as real-life exemplars of the point that knowledge is sociologically produced. From the standpoint of social accountability, taking this point about knowledge production seriously means recognizing that the interests of survivor groups may intersect with the preferences of officialdom and dominant social groups in ways that make historical justice responses inadequate as assignments of responsibility.[87] Redress-seekers, particularly in instances where the government has previously denied any wrongdoing, may insist on straightforwardly categorical, buck-stops-here visions of accountability. For their part, governments fear offending mainstream sensitivities and dislike forensic probing of their pasts. Despite their official character and occasional pretensions to finality, then, truth commissions and political apologies cannot provide the last word on wrongdoing. At the same time, we do not dismiss these types of official response as instances of historical regret serving a manipulative theatrics of power. We say instead that such responses will have inevitable biases and limitations that actors concerned with historical justice must consider how to address.

The impermanent apologies approach is our admittedly limited and partial response to these realities and concerns. Treating questions of structure, individual and institutional agency, and public responsibility, we have explored the tension between the ideals aspired to in theories of political apology and the limitations of what has generally been regarded as an exemplary Canadian instance of the genre. The result has been an exploration of wrongdoing that differs considerably from Canada's official account. But our exploration cannot be seen as a flinty-eyed demolition of untruth, either. The research and findings summarized in this chapter have depended significantly on the research funding, ongoing survival of key community organizations, and heightened climate of civic awareness that have all been provided or promoted by the Japanese Canadian Redress Agreement. Further, our account has benefited directly from the opportunity to engage the factual admissions and normative commitment to nonrepetition contained in the apology. This chapter is predicated on the productive impermanency of political apology.

We have framed our goal in terms of social accountability, which, in Stanton's words, means "reflect[ing] upon [our] society and acknowledge[ing] [our] own responsibility in creating a greater democratic good."[88] Further guidance comes from the comprehensive recent work of public administration scholar Mark Bovens and his coauthors, who observe that accountability processes require dialogue and scrutiny. By this they mean not only the one-time "provision of explanations and justifications" but also the "possibility for [a] forum to interrogate … and to question the adequacy of the explanation" afterwards.[89] Political apologies do not usually afford immediate space for these kinds of dialogical opportunities.[90] Thus, we argue that critical research can help fill the gap, capitalizing on apologetic impermanency and contributing to social accountability by subjecting the original act to new rounds of criticism and questioning.

To this end, we have scrutinized, critically but not unsympathetically, the account of state wrongdoing in Canada's 1988 apology to Japanese Canadians. What have we learned from this dialogue between the compact and limited account of responsibility in the 1988 apology and the research findings discussed in this chapter? The apology depicted a single moment of crisis that drove a monolithic state apparatus to initiate a deliberate singular policy that lacked antecedents, advocates, and beneficiaries. But the internment, dispossession, and exile were not inexplicable crisis responses without precedents. They were within the constitutional mainstream of a federal settler polity built on Indigenous dispossession and of a province that pursued white domination through decades of anti-Asian policy. This production and reification of race by Canadian authorities, well documented by scholars, was a key cause of the crisis that internment purported to solve.[91]

The internment, dispossession, dispersal, and exile also required choice making on the part of specific public actors and officials. Vancouver Centre Liberal MP Ian Mackenzie built a career as an advocate of white supremacy, a battle he was only too eager to continue in cabinet. Glenn McPherson was instrumental in turning the decision to hold the internees' property in trust into the wholesale and deceitful dispossession of an entire community. In the postwar period, Norman Robertson and Henry Angus provided respectable justifications for the dispersal and exile of Japanese Canadians, justifications formally in tune with the new, more egalitarian times. But a different kind of agency was also important. This was the improvisatory, path-dependent agency of officials dealing with the unforeseen consequences of prior decisions. One particularly notable instance of this dynamic and its consequences was the supposedly protective and reassuring decision to hold the internees' property in trust.

Finally, the internment, dispossession, dispersal, and exile involved publics. These measures were, in part, accommodative official responses to letters-to-the-editor, to missives from constituents, and to public interventions by religious and civic leaders: the routine flow of citizen input and public output in a so-called liberal democracy. Publics also benefited from the dispossession, particularly through their purchases of individual items, homes, farms, and even business empires. The profound intergroup transfer of wealth involved, a transfer perpetuated across subsequent generations through inheritance and investment, is a concrete demonstration of racialized patterns of benefit and loss that persist on Canada's West Coast.

One way to understand the broader import of this chapter's more expansive account is in terms of analogical historical learning. As historian Gerda Lerner observes, "history is not a recipe book"; the constant change over time of collective human experience means that no past lessons can be directly applied in the present. But, she continues, "we can learn by analogy."[92] Historian John Tosh elaborates: "the whole point of an analogy is that it notes similarities in things which in other respects are unalike." Rather than learning from the past because the present replicates historical circumstances, we can derive insight from careful observation of both "contrast and convergence." "Provided we are open to both," writes Tosh, "the effect is to liberate our thinking from the rigidities of current discourse, not by prescribing a course of action but by expanding our sense of the options."[93]

What kind of analogical learning might emerge from this chapter's attempt to pursue social accountability concerns by placing the official 1988 account in dialogue with a more expansive treatment of responsibility? Emphasizing the deep constitutional, political, and social roots of racialization in this country helps us to understand why the criminalization and legal assault on Others has been an all too frequent Canadian crisis response.[94] Moreover, this fact suggests that better crisis responses depend not only on situational vigilance but also on the longer-run production and maintenance of critical public memory.

Emphasizing the agency and influence of key leaders and public servants at specific moments of decision is both a reminder of the immense importance of leadership and character in tough situations and a warning to present-day holders of public trust that their actions and reputations may someday be subject to similar scrutiny. At the same time, emphasizing the disastrous outcome of the property trust decision reminds us that no choice in public decision making is *a priori* innocent. Being aware of these facts and concerns means that what critics might ridicule as politically correct timidity may simply be the circumspection that minimally decent public administration demands.

Indeed, this chapter's account of the path-dependent and improvisatory character of the dispossession, which flowed almost inexorably from the difficulties that attended the decision to hold internees' property in protective trust, holds particularly resonant lessons for public servants. Illustrating the banal modalities of what critical and antiracist public administration scholars call "administrative racism" or "administrative evil," the path-dependent dispossession involved countless minor instances of individual problem solving that were well within the established confines of institutional routines and roles. As the recent Canadian case of Maher Arar attests, this ethic of technocratic neutrality – which directs public servants to ignore the moral implications and human impacts of the countless individual decisions they must make to execute policy – remains a reality of the contemporary administrative state.[95] At the same time, emphasizing the internment, dispossession, dispersal, and exile as in some ways routine products of the marketplace of public demand and official response reminds us that democracy itself requires clear limitations. These limitations will not only be constitutional ones but informal discursive and symbolic restraints on what kinds of claims and concerns are legitimate candidates for public accommodation.

In summary, therefore, our analysis shows the relevance of critical public histories to social accountability. Times of crisis; legacies of structural racism; policy entrepreneurs peddling hate; unforeseen consequences stemming from minor decisions; constituencies courted for electoral or career advantage – these are not idiosyncratic or remote one-time considerations. They are recurrent political and sociological facts whose ongoing management requires critical historical inquiry and awareness.

The more specific purpose of this chapter has been to develop and demonstrate an approach that might militate against political apologies as instruments of finality that reify injustice. Such use is certainly widespread: for instance, museum exhibits on the Japanese Canadian internment at the Museum of Canadian History, Canadian War Museum, and Canadian Museum of Human Rights, visited by one of the present authors in 2014 and 2015, all cleaved in their substance to the account of responsibility contained in the 1988 apology, and each concluded its exhibit by giving the apology the last word.[96] Indeed, one former curator reports that it is the explicit policy of the latter institution, where possible, to end every treatment of a Canadian injustice by quoting from or pointing to its corresponding apology.[97] Moves like this are natural targets for critics who denounce the pacifying and normalizing thrust of the contemporary emphasis on the official regretful memorialization of historic injustice. But the museums might also be pushed to contribute to social accountability by, rather than sanctifying the official apologetic accounts, using other interpretations and voices to place the accounts under renewed pressure.

The dynamic of apologetic impermanency should not be seen as an assault rendering worthless the original statements of responsibility and contrition. Apologies may be valuable precisely because they invite scrutiny of their admissions and accounts and because they help to stimulate processes of activism and redress that, however inadequate and partial, may serve in turn to encourage further critical engagement. Public institutions, such as museums, news media, and schools, might ask how they could further this kind of scrutiny as well. More generally, now that Canada has what has become a rather lengthy catalogue of actually existing political apologies, there are numerous opportunities for activists and researchers to engage the official regretful accounts in the continued critical dialogue that they both encourage and deserve.

NOTES

1 Canada, House of Commons, Debates, 33rd Parl, 2d sess., vol. 15, 1988, 19499, accessed on 15 September 2019, http://parl.canadiana.ca/view/oop.debates_HOC3302_15/1037?r=0&s=3.

2 Audrey Kobayashi, "The Japanese-Canadian Redress Settlement and its Implications for 'Race Relations,'" *Canadian Ethnic Studies* 24, no. 1 (1992): 1–19.

3 Formal acknowledgement accessed in 2019 at the NNM, courtesy of archivist Linda Kawamoto Reid.

4 On the standard expectations of adequacy in political apology, see Ąžuolas Bagdonas, "Historical State Apologies," in *The Palgrave Handbook of State-Sponsored History after 1945*, eds. Berber Bevernage and Nico Wouters (London: Palgrave, 2018): 775–99.

5 Matt James, Jordan Stanger-Ross, and the Landscapes of Injustice Research Collective, "Impermanent Apologies: On the Dynamics of Timing and Public Knowledge in Political Apology," *Human Rights Review* 19, no. 3 (2018): 289–311; Matt James and Jordan Stanger-Ross, "Cross-Disciplinary Perspectives, the Impermanent Apologies Approach, and the Politics of Political Apologies," *C4E Journal: Perspectives on Ethics* 13 (2017), accessed 15 September 2019, https://c4ejournal.net/2018/01/26/matt-james-jordan-stanger-ross-the-landscapes-of-injustice-research-collective-cross-disciplinary-perspectives-the-impermanent-apologies-approach-and-the-politics-of-political-apologies/.

6 Contrary to critics who see political apologies as neoliberal tools for domesticating unruly pasts and smothering dissent, we argue in the works cited above that apologies often fail, sometimes quite spectacularly, to achieve officialdom's cherished goal of "closing the books" on injustice. We maintain instead that apologies are best seen as unstable and politically charged moments in longer-run processes of historical justice, acts with an often-unwitting potential to amplify the voices of justice seekers and to motivate subsequent enterprises of questioning, reinterpretation, and exposure. This dynamic of impermanency is key to the capacity of political apologies to help promote more satisfactory collective confrontations with historical injustice.

7 On these basic requirements of apology, see Nicholas Tavuchis, *Mea Culpa: A Sociology of Apology and Reconciliation* (Stanford: Stanford University Press, 1991).

8 Karine Levasseur and Fiona MacDonald, "Mea Culpa: Apology Legislation, Accountability, and Care," *Canadian Journal of Political Science* 51, no. 4 (2018): 749–69; Aaron Lazare, *On Apology* (Oxford: Oxford University Press, 2005).

9 Andreas Schedler, "Conceptualizing Accountability," in *The Self-Restraining State: Power and Accountability in New Democracies*, eds. Andreas Schedler, Larry Diamond, and Marc F. Plattner (Boulder: Lynne Reimer 1999).

10 On more recent innovations in accountability practice, see Peter Graefe, Julie M. Simmons, and Linda A. White, eds., *Overpromising and Underperforming? Understanding and Evaluating New Intergovernmental Accountability Regimes* (Toronto: University of Toronto Press, 2013).

11 Mark Bovens, Thomas Schillemans, and Robert E. Goodin, "Public Accountability," in *Oxford Handbook of Accountability*, eds. Mark Bovens, Thomas Schillemans, and Robert E. Goodin (Oxford: Oxford University Press, 2014), accessed 14 September 2019, doi: 10.1093/oxfordhb/9780199641253.013.0012; Harald Bergsteiner, *Accountability Theory Meets Accountability Practice* (London: Emerald Books, 2012).

12 Kathryn Sikkink, *The Justice Cascade: How Human Rights Prosecutions Are Changing World Politics* (New York: Norton, 2011).

13 Chapter 13. Maryka Omatsu, *Bittersweet Passage: Redress and the Japanese-Canadian Experience* (Toronto: Between the Lines, 1992).

14 Kent Roach, "Canadian Public Inquiries and Accountability," in *Accountability for Criminal Justice: Selected Essays*, ed. Philip C. Stenning (Toronto: University of Toronto

Press, 1995), 268–94; Kim Stanton, "Looking Forward, Looking Back: The Canadian Truth and Reconciliation Commission and the Mackenzie Valley Pipeline Inquiry," *Canadian Journal of Law and Society* 27, no. 1 (2012): 81–99; Michelle D. Bonner, *Policing Protest in Argentina and Chile* (Boulder: First Forum Press, 2014).

15 Roach, "Canadian Public Inquiries"; Stanton, "Looking Forward."

16 Ronald Niezen, *Truth and Indignation: Canada's Truth and Reconciliation Commission on Indian Residential Schools* (Toronto: University of Toronto Press, 2013). On the mandate, see Matt James, "Uncomfortable Comparisons: The Truth and Reconciliation Commission in International Context," *Les Ateliers de l'éthique* 5, no. 2 (2010): 23–35.

17 Bonner, *Policing Protest*. Of course discursive considerations are important in dyadic or formal accountability settings as well, but here we pursue them only in relation our specific focus on political apologies and social accountability.

18 Rosemary Nagy, "The Scope and Bounds of Transitional Justice and the Canadian Truth and Reconciliation Commission," *International Journal of Transitional Justice* 7, no. 1 (2013): 52–73.

19 Chapter 13. Ottawa had also responded earlier to the redress campaign by replacing the War Measures Act, which had provided the former legal basis for internment, with more rights-conscious emergency legislation. See Roy Miki and Cassandra Kobayashi eds., *Justice in Our Time: The Japanese Canadian Redress Settlement* (Vancouver: Talon Books, 1991), 121.

20 Arthur Miki, *The Japanese Canadian Redress Legacy: A Community Revitalized* (Winnipeg: National Association of Japanese Canadians, 2003).

21 Kobayashi, "Japanese-Canadian Redress Settlement."

22 Nick Smith, *I Was Wrong: The Meaning of Apologies* (Cambridge: Cambridge University Press, 2008); Smith, "Political Apologies and Categorical Apologies," in *On the Uses and Abuses of Political Apologies*, eds. Mihaela Mihai and Mathias Thaler (Houndmills, UK: Palgrave Macmillan, 2014): 32–51; Cindy Holder, "Whose Wrong is it Anyway? Reflecting on the Public-ness of Political Apologies," *C4E Journal 8* (2017), accessed 15 September 2019, https://c4ejournal.net/2017/11/03/cindy-holder-whose-wrong-is-it-anyway-on-the-public-ness-of-public-apologies-2017-c4ej-8/.

23 Canada, House of Commons, Debates, 33rd Parl, 2nd sess., vol. 15, 1988, 1999, accessed 15 September 2019, http://parl.canadiana.ca/view/oop.debates_HOC3302_15/1037?r=0&s=3.

24 Jennifer Balint, Julie Evans, and Nesam McMillan, "Rethinking Transitional Justice, Redressing Indigenous Harm: A New Conceptual Approach," *International Journal of Transitional Justice* 8, no. 2 (2014): 194–216; Francesca Dominello, "The 'Apology to Australia's Indigenous Peoples' in its Historical Context," in *The Palgrave Handbook*; Sheryl Lightfoot, "Settler-state Apologies to Indigenous Peoples: A Normative Framework and Comparative Assessment," *Native American and Indigenous Studies* 2, no. 1 (2015): 15–39.

25 Some scholarly debate persists on this topic, but the matter is generally settled.

26 See introduction and for a similar reflection on the incarceration of Japanese Americans case, see Eric L. Muller, *American Inquisition: The Hunt for Japanese American Disloyalty in World War II* (Chapel Hill: University of North Carolina Press, 2007).

27 Nick Smith, "Political Apologies," 36.

28 Karl Deutsch, *Nationalism and Social Communication: An Inquiry into the Foundations of Nationality*, 2d ed. (Cambridge, MA: MIT Press, 1966).

29 Holder, "Whose Wrong."

30 Ibid.
31 Smith, "Political Apologies," 36.
32 Chapters 1 and 10.
33 Chapters 5, 7, and 8.
34 Chapters 7 and 10.
35 Patricia Roy, *A White Man's Province: British Columbia Politicians and Japanese Immigrants, 1858–1914* (Vancouver: UBC Press, 1989) and *The Oriental Question: Consolidating a White Man's Province, 1914–41* (Vancouver: UBC Press, 2003).
36 The BC legislation meant federal disfranchisement because voting federally depended on being on a provincial voter's list. Explicit federal enfranchisement came in 1948 and the province followed suit the next year.
37 Andrea Geiger, "Writing Racial Barriers into Law: Upholding BC's Denial of the Vote to its Japanese Canadian Citizens, Homma v. Cunningham, 1902," in *Nikkei in the Pacific Northwest: Japanese Americans and Japanese Canadians in the Twentieth Century*, eds. Gail Nomura and Louis Fiset (Seattle: University of Washington Press, 2005): 20–43.
38 James W. St G. Walker, *"Race," Rights, and the Law in the Supreme Court of Canada* (Waterloo, ON: Wilfrid Laurier University Press, 1997); Constance Backhouse, *Colour-Coded: A Legal History of Racism in Canada, 1900–1950* (Toronto: University of Toronto Press, 1999); Timothy Stanley, *Contesting White Supremacy: School Segregation, Anti-Racism, and the Making of Chinese Canadians* (Vancouver: UBC Press, 2011).
39 Michael Barnholden, *Reading the Riot Act: A Brief History of Riots in Vancouver* (Vancouver: Anvil Press, 2005).
40 PC 1941-9591, 7 December 1941, file 2463G, vol. 1741, RG 2-A-1-a, LAC.
41 Robert H. Keyserlingk, "Breaking the Nazi Plot: Canadian Government Attitudes Towards German Canadians, 1939–1945," in *On Guard for Thee: War, Ethnicity, and the Canadian State, 1939–1945*, eds. Norman Hillmer, Bohdan Kordan, and Lubomyr Luciuk, (Ottawa: Government of Canada, 1988), 53–69. Franca Iacovetta, Roberto Perin, and Angelo Principe eds., *Enemies Within: Italian and Other Internees in Canada and Abroad* (Toronto: University of Toronto Press, 2000).
42 The 1946 Citizenship Act became operational in 1947, establishing for the first time citizenship as a formal Canadian category. See Robert Craig Brown, "Full Partnership in the Fortunes and in the Future of the Nation," *Nationalism and Ethnic Politics* 1, no. 3 (1995): 9–25.
43 Miki and Kobayashi eds., *Justice in Our Time.*
44 Backhouse, *Colour-Coded*; Walker, *"Race," Rights and the Law.*
45 Perhaps the classic source is Herbert A. Simon, "Rational Choice and the Structure of the Environment," *Psychological Review* 63, no. 2 (1956): 129–38.
46 On placelessness in Japanese Canadian narratives of the internment, see Mona Oikawa, *Cartographies of Violence: Japanese Canadian Women, Memory, and the Subjects of the Internment* (Toronto: University of Toronto Press, 2012), 183.
47 The following discussion draws upon chapter 8, chapter 5, and the introduction.
48 Anthony M. Starke, Nuri Heckler, and Janiece Mackey, "Administrative Racism: Public Administration Education and Race," *Journal of Public Affairs Education* 24, no. 4 (2018): 469–89
49 Austin C. Taylor to Ian Mackenzie, 4 March 1942, file 67-25(1), vol. 24, MG 27 III-B5, LAC.
50 PC 1942-2483, 27 March 1942, file 2531G, vol. 1752, RG 2-A-1-a, LAC.

51 Robertson to MacNamara, 9 July 1945, file 104(s), pt. 2.1, vol. 5761, RG 25, LAC.
52 MacNamara to Robertson, 17 July 1945, file 104(s), pt. 2.1, vol. 5761, RG 25, LAC.
53 Robert Gordon Robertson, Policy with Regard to Japanese in Canada (meeting minutes), 12 April 1944, file 12, vol. 1, MG 31 E87, LAC.
54 A.D.P. Heeney, 18 April 1944, file 104(s), pt. 1.1, vol. 5761, RG 25, LAC.
55 HFA [Henry Forbes Angus] Memorandum on Mr R.G. Robertson's note on policy with regard to Japanese in Canada, 22 March 1944, file 104(s), pt. 1.1, vol. 5761, RG 25, LAC.
56 John Erskine Read Memo, 1 November 1945, File 104(s), pt. 2.2, vol. 5761, RG 25, LAC.
57 Sunahara, *The Politics of Racism*, 101-116.
58 Cf. C. West Churchman, "Wicked Problems," *Management Science* 14, no. 4 (1967): 141–2
59 Holder, "Whose Wrong."
60 See chapters 7 and 10.
61 [Ham L. Phelan?] to Ian Mackenzie, 21 December 1941, file 70-25, vol. 25, MG 27-IIB5, LAC (hereafter Mackenzie Fonds).
62 Sir Francis Heathcote to Ian Mackenzie, 9 January 1942, file 70-25, vol. 25, Mackenzie Fonds.
63 A.G. Duncan Crux to Ian Mackenzie, 10 February 1942 and the Vancouver Real Estate Exchange Limited, 23 February 1942, file 70-25(2), vol. 25, Mackenzie Fonds.
64 W.J. Tregidga to Ian Mackenzie, 14 February 1942, file 70-25, vol. 25, Mackenzie Fonds.
65 Ian Mackenzie to W.J. Tregidga, 19 February 1942, 1942, file 70-25, vol. 25, Mackenzie Fonds.
66 Chapter 7.
67 Eric Adams, "Constitutional Stories: Japanese Canadians and the Constitution of Canada, *Australasian Canadian Studies* 35 (forthcoming).
68 Chapter 11. Letter from Glenn McPherson to E.H. Coleman, 9 December 1941, file 70-25c: Liquidating Lands in the Fraser Valley that are Jap Owned, vol. 25, Mackenzie Fonds (quoted in Stanger-Ross, "Suspect Properties").
69 Her own family could not resist joining in the fray, stealing a sewing machine from a neighbouring home. Eileen Carefoot, interviewed by Pam Sugiman, 26 April 2015, Richmond British Columbia, LOIOH, University of Victoria.
70 Japanese Tea Garden, P. Doucet, 11 May 1944, case file #1426, RG 117-C-3, LAC.
71 F.G. Shears to Norman McLarty, Report, 28 January 1944, image 288, microfilm reel C-9469, Office of the Custodian of Enemy Property: Vancouver Office, Héritage, http://heritage.canadiana.ca/view/oocihm.lac_reel_c9469/228?r=0&s=1. Quoted in Stanger-Ross, "Introduction," in *Witness to Loss: Race, Culpability, and Memory in the Dispossession of Japanese Canadians*, eds. Jordan Stanger-Ross and Pam Sugiman (Montreal & Kingston: McGill-Queen's University Press, 2017), xxxiii.
72 Chapter 10.
73 Introduction and Tadashi Jack Kagetsu, *The Tree Trunk Can Be My Pillow* (Victoria: University of Victoria, 2017).
74 Agents for Evacuee Properties, undated (Spring 1943), file 5, b ox 513-E-2, fonds AM199-Advisory Committee on Japanese Properties in Greater Vancouver, CVA. See Stanger-Ross "Suspect Properties."
75 Memo to McPherson from Wright, 16 October 1942, file 59008, pt. 1.1, vol. 2536, RG 117, LAC; Letter from McPherson to Coleman, 9 December 1942, file: 70-25c: Liquidating Lands in the Fraser Valley that are Jap Owned, vol. 25, Mackenzie Fonds. See Stanger-Ross "Suspect Properties."

76 See Kaitlin Findlay, "The Bird Commission, Japanese Canadians, and the Challenge of Reparations in the Wake of State Violence" (MA thesis, University of Victoria, 2017), 119–33.
77 Chapter 7.
78 Certificate of appreciation to Mrs A.G. McArthur, file 2: Canada. Office of the Custodian of Enemy Property, box 17, F.G. Shears Papers, Thomas Fisher Rare Book Library, University of Toronto. The quote is from Francis's 1751 play "Eugenia." Nicole Yakashiro, "Women in the Archives" (Landscapes of Injustice Working Paper), July 2018, https://landscapesofinjustice.com/wp-content/uploads/2019/09/Working-Paper-6-Women-in-the-Archive-Yakashiro-Nicole_July-2018.pdf.
79 Letter to A.H. Mathieu from F.G. Shears, 12 October 1949, file 1, pt. 1: Correspondence Re Various Staff Members, RG 117-C-1, LAC.
80 Stephanie D. Bangarth, *Voices Raised in Protest: Defending Citizens of Japanese Ancestry in North America, 1942–49* (Vancouver: UBC Press, 2008).
81 Matt James, *Misrecognized Materialists: Social Movements in Canadian Constitutional Politics* (Vancouver: University of British Columbia University Press, 2006).
82 Ibid., chapter 4, "The Postwar Identity Emphasis: Rights, Universalism, and Virtue."
83 Roy Miki, *Redress: Inside the Japanese-Canadian Call for Justice* (Vancouver: Raincoast Books, 2005), 128.
84 Sikkink, *Justice Cascade.*
85 Brian Gettler, "Historical Research at the Truth and Reconciliation Commission of Canada," *Canadian Historical Review* 98, no. 4 (2017): 641–74.
86 Rosemary Nagy, "The Truth and Reconciliation Commission of Canada: Genesis and Design," *Canadian Journal of Law and Society* 29, no. 2 (2014): 199–217.
87 Matt James, "A Carnival of Truth? Knowledge, Ignorance, and the Canadian Truth and Reconciliation Commission," *International Journal of Transitional Justice* 6, no. 2 (2012): 182–204.
88 Stanton, "Looking Forward," 97.
89 Bovens, Schillemans, and Goodin, "Public Accountability," 10.
90 But note the landmark insistence of Indigenous leaders on responding to Canada's 2008 residential schools apology in the House of Commons immediately after delivery, some of whom declared at the time their scepticism that words would be followed by action. For critical discussion, see Eva Mackey, "The Apologizer's Apology," in *Reconciling Canada: Critical Perspectives on the Culture of Redress*, eds. Jennifer Henderson and Pauline Wakeham (Toronto: University of Toronto Press, 2013), 47–62.
91 Rita Dhamoon and Yasmeen Abu-Laban, "Dangerous (Internal) Foreigners and Nation-Building: The Case of Canada," *International Political Science Review* 30, no. 2 (2009): 163–83; Nisha Nath, "Defining Narratives of Identity in Canadian Political Science: Accounting for the Absence of Race," *Canadian Journal of Political Science* 44, no. 1 (2011): 161–93; Debra Thompson, "Is Race Political?," *Canadian Journal of Political Science* 41, no. 3 (2008): 525–47.
92 Gerda Lerner, *Why History Matters: Life and Thought* (New York: Oxford University Press, 1997), 202–3.
93 John Tosh, *Why History Matters* (London: Palgrave MacMillan, 2008), 62.
94 Dhamoon and Abu-Laban, "Dangerous (Internal) Foreigners"; the authors examine the cases of Japanese Canadian internment and the 1970 FLQ and 1992 Oka crises.
95 On the Syrian imprisonment and torture at Canadian behest of the innocent citizen

Maher Arar, which flowed from routine bureaucratic information sharing in the so-called War on Terror, see Pauline Wakeham, "Rendition and Redress: Maher Arar, Apology, Exceptionality," in *Reconciling Canada*, 278–98. On administrative evil and administrative racism, see Guy B. Adams and Danny L. Balfour, *Unmasking Administrative Evil: The Dynamics of Evil and Administrative Evil* (Thousand Oaks, CA: Sage, 1998) and Starke, Heckler, and Mackey, "Administrative Racism."

96 Matt James visited the first two institutions on 8–9 August 2014 and the third on 25 November 2015.

97 Tricia Logan, "National Memory and Museums: Remembering Settler Colonial Genocide of Indigenous Peoples in Canada," in *Remembering Genocide*, eds. Nigel Eltringham and Pam Maclean (London: Routledge, 2014), 112–30.

EPILOGUE

Jordan Stanger-Ross

During the years when *Landscapes of Injustice* was being conceived and written, the questions at the heart of this history seemed to grow more urgent. With tens of millions of people displaced and the politics of security, migration, and race perpetually entwined, members of our research collective connected the work we were doing to the challenges of the present.[1] How will states and citizens protect human and civil rights at times of national insecurity? What response will democratic institutions make to tribalism? Who is harmed by a politics of fear, and who benefits? Such questions seem likely to bedevil the coming century, just as they did the past. History will not save us, but it is, perhaps, a tool, among many, in answering some of our most pressing questions.

We should value our contested, critical histories, in which hard questions are asked and past injustices interrogated. The alternatives are not good. The great feminist historian Gerda Lerner, jailed in 1938 for her resistance to the Nazi take over of Austria before escaping from Europe, later reflected:

> To those in power, history has always mattered. In fact, recorded history began as a means of celebrating the accomplishments of military chieftains, usurpers, and kings … Similarly, usurper regimes of the 20th century used history for their own purposes. Mussolini's gangs legitimized their accession to power by boasting of Roman roots … German National Socialism created an elaborate official history extolling the mostly mythical deeds of Teutonic ancestors and rewriting more recent history to fit their version of "Aryan" racial superiority. The Communist regimes in Russia … went to inordinate lengths to create "official" histories … The United States, in its rise as world power … used the doctrines of American exceptionalism and Manifest Destiny … as a legitimizing explanatory system.[2]

Absent critical histories, power too easily co-opts the past, in Canada as elsewhere.[3] Japanese Canadians of the 1940s, Lerner's contemporaries and, like her, victims of a politics of race, knew better than most the impacts of being pushed outside the story of a nation.

They said so at the time. In 1948, Thomas Shoyama, then president of the National Japanese Canadian Citizen's Association, attempted to convey the dispossession of Japanese Canadians within the lives that they lived. "When, early in 1942 and under the grim compulsion of global war, the federal government finally decreed the complete removal of the Japanese Canadian minority from the British Columbia coast," he wrote:

> it brought to a drastic and disruptive end a half-century's advance towards economic security and success. The story of the struggle of that half century, beginning with the early arrival of eager, though bewildered young men, is an intensely human one, beneath all its political, social and economic ramifications … a story of extravagant hopes and prospects quickly deflated by the press of unexpected reality; a gradual acceptance of and adjustment to actual conditions; a transformation from hopes of easy and quick success into the determination to build for the future … it is against a background such as this that … [internment] may be properly assessed.[4]

This book has attempted to follow Shoyama's lead, and that of many Japanese Canadian storytellers since, in conveying the "intensely human" story of their confrontation with "unexpected reality."

At the same time, we have worked to investigate the processes of injustice. We have sought to understand who was responsible, why they did what they did, and how so many were complicit. We have examined the possibility of alternatives: of paths not taken and voices unheeded. Hannah Arendt, reflecting on the mid-twentieth century, suggested that "under conditions of terror most people will comply but some people will not." "No more," she proposed, "is required, and no more can be reasonably asked, for this planet to remain a place fit for human habitation."[5] Our project has sought to understand the undertaking of political violence, the compliant majority, and those who thought and acted otherwise.

We have done this work in partnership. A large grant from the Social Science and Humanities Research Council of Canada enabled, and required, that we work in connection with one another. Some seventy people, from seventeen varied institutions, met regularly to discuss, debate, and struggle over this history. We benefitted from two advisory committees, one comprised of senior scholars and the other made up of leaders within the Japanese Canadian community. Our collective is diverse: ranging from people who lived through the dispossession to those who came to it for the first time in answer to an advertisement for a summer job. We have benefitted also from the presence, at all of our meetings, of varied academic perspectives as well as the contributions of museum curators, in-service teachers, and archivists already working to translate this history for new audiences and to ensure its long-term preservation.

Many who are not represented as authors in this volume nonetheless made essential contributions to its creation; this is truly the result of a research collective.

Connecting across differences of experience, discipline, and perspective, we developed an approach to historical analysis that was for me, at least, novel, challenging, and exciting. I came to imagine our collective as a wheel: our work meets at a hub in the centre, in discussion of the dispossession of Japanese Canadians, but each of our contributions – life histories, analyses of land titles and law, the lessons necessary to teach fifth graders to think in new ways about fairness and loss – radiate out from that core in their own direction, each with its own theories, methods, and objectives. Student researchers on our project have carried this history into projects of their own, reshaping the topic to fit their urgent questions and pressing concerns.[6] The work of partnership is to hold these varied initiatives together in the same room, to work together but not in unison, to integrate without flattening.

Years ago, when Landscapes of Injustice remained in its infancy, I was walking with my wife toward the central square of a historic city when people, mostly young men, began to stream toward us. They had on black armbands and combat boots. They saluted passing traffic, drivers serenading them with honks. My wife Ilana, who is from Brooklyn, favoured confronting them, asking what they wanted, what they believed. I, having always lived in small Jewish minorities, urged instead that we divert to another street. Afterward I struggled with what we had seen and how we had each responded. I had a feeling of helplessness but also reassurance that at least I, and many others, were working hard to understand the histories from which such present hatreds emerge. Our history may not save us but working hard to draw it to light, together and across difference, is an essential task of our times.

NOTES

1 Some sense of the present relevance of this past is conveyed in newspaper op eds that I have written along with other members of the collective in recent years: John Lutz, Jordan Stanger-Ross, Kaitlin Findlay, and Tsugio Kurushima, "Teahouse Plan Offers a Vision for Esquimalt," *Times Colonist*, 14 April 2019; Jordan Stanger-Ross and Matt James, "A Political Apology Is Just a Beginning," *Globe and Mail*, 1 December 2017; Jordan Stanger-Ross, "A Cautionary Tale from Canada's Past," *Toronto Star*, 22 November 2017; Jordan Stanger-Ross and Eric Adams, "Remembering Promises-Lessons from the 75th Anniversary of the Dispossession of Japanese Canadians," *Vancouver Sun*, 19 January 2016 (carried also in the *Calgary Herald*, the *Montreal Gazette*, and the *Edmonton Journal*); Jordan Stanger-Ross, Eric Adams, and Laura Madokoro, "Lessons from the Japanese Canadian Internments: Policies Built on Fear Won't Make Us Safer," *Globe and Mail*, 19 January 2016. See also Jordan Stanger-Ross and Lynne Marks, "Attack on Niqab a Backward Step for Canada," with Lynne Marks, *Victoria Times Colonist*, 8 October 2015.

2 Gilda Lerner, *Why History Matters* (New York: Oxford University Press, 1997), 202. Lerner is also discussed in chapter 14.

3 See Ian McKay and Jamie Swift, *The Vimy Trap: Or, How We Learned to Stop Worrying and Love the Great War* (Toronto: Between the Lines, 2016).

4 National Japanese Canadian Citizens Association, Submission to the Royal Commission on Japanese Canadian Property, written November 1948 and entered into evidence 1 January 1949, General Exhibit 97-131, vol, 79, RG 33-69, LAC, 3.

5 Hannah Ardent, *Eichmann in Jerusalem: A Report on the Banality of Evil* (New York: Viking Press, 1964), 233.

6 For example, Nicole Yakashiro, "Daffodils as Property: Settler Colonial Renewal and the Dispossession of Nikkei Farmers in the 1940s" (MA thesis, UBC, 2019); Camille Haisell, "Systemic Racism & Mental Health: Effects of the 1940s Canadian Policies of Dispossession and Internment on Japanese Canadians in BC Psychiatric Care" (JCURA Project, University of Victoria, 2019); Rebeca Salas, "Spatial Narratives of Property Loss: A Geographical Perspective of the Relationship Between Memory and Property" (MA thesis, Simon Fraser University, 2018); Kaitlin Findlay, "The Bird Commission, Japanese Canadians, and the Challenge of Reparations in the Wake of State Violence" (MA thesis, University of Victoria, 2017); Kate Siemens, "Witnessing Internment: Captain V. Best's Letters to Ottawa" (Honours thesis, University of Victoria, 2017, a website project available at: https://witnesstointernment.wordpress.com/); Martin Strong, "Japanese Canadians and Internment: The Role of *The New Canadian* as an Agent of Resistance, 1941–1945" (Honours thesis, University of Victoria, 2017); Ariel Merriam, "'Our Appreciation for All Your Goodness and Kindness': Power, Rhetoric, and Property Relations in the Dispossession of Japanese Canadians" (Honours thesis, University of Victoria, 2016); Eiji Okawa, "Community Records and the Human Experiences of the Uprooting of Japanese Canadians," *The Bulletin*, 7 October 2016, accessed 16 September 2019, http://jccabulletin-geppo.ca/community-records-and-the-human-experiences-of-the-uprooting-of-japanese-canadians/; Heather Read, "The Legacy of a Hidden Camera: Acts of Making in Japanese-Canadian Internment During the Second World War, as Depicted in Tom Matsui's Photograph Collection," *Material Culture Review* 84 (2016): 26–48. Many smaller projects have been undertaken and several theses are presently in progress.

CONTRIBUTORS

ERIC M. ADAMS is a professor at the Faculty of Law, University of Alberta, where he researches and teaches in the fields of constitutional law, legal history, and labour and employment law. The recipient of multiple awards for his research and teaching, including a Killam Annual Professorship, Professor Adams has led the legal historical research on the Landscapes of Injustice project. A frequent national media commentator on a range of constitutional topics, he is also the author of legal histories of some of Canada's most important cases including *Christie v York*, *Roncarelli v Duplessis*, and *R v Drybones*. Professor Adams is currently completing a book with Professor Jordan Stanger-Ross on the exile of Japanese Canadians from Canada after the Second World War.

WILL ARCHIBALD is a specific claims researcher at the Union of BC Indian Chiefs and an MA candidate in the Department of History at the University of Victoria. Their research focuses on the intersecting histories of settler colonialism, Indigenous dispossession, and the racialization of Asian Canadians and Asian migrants in the lands currently known as British Columbia.

IAN G. BAIRD is an associate professor of geography at the University of Wisconsin-Madison. He is also the director for the Center for Southeast Asian Studies at UW-Madison. Most of his research is focused in southern Laos, northeastern Cambodia, and northeast and northern Thailand and is related to political ecology and political geography. His most recent book is *Rise of the Brao: Ethnic Minorities in Northeastern Cambodia during Vietnamese Occupation* (University of Wisconsin Press, 2020). Over the last few years he has also been conducting research on the Japanese Canadians of Vancouver Island, British Columbia, Canada, where he originally comes from. In particular, he has been working in Nanaimo, Hilliers, Port Alberni, Ucluelet, Tofino, and Cumberland, considering the ways that racism and anti-racism operated in the past. He is presently conducting research on Japanese Canadians living in Nanaimo before World War II and what happened to the community during and after internment.

NICHOLAS BLOMLEY is professor of geography at Simon Fraser University. He has a long-standing interest in legal geography, particularly in relation to property. He is interested in the spatiality of legal practices and relationships, and the world-making consequences of such legal geographies. Much of his empirical work concerns the often-oppressive effects of legal relations on marginalized and oppressed people. Recent and current research projects, in addition to Landscapes of Injustice, include a) the analysis of "rental precarity" in Greater Vancouver; b) the study of court-mandated "red zones" imposed on street-involved people and protestors in Montreal and Vancouver; c) a community-based project creating tenant-led research into precarious housing conditions in Vancouver's most vulnerable population; and d) the governance of poor people's possessions by private and public regulators in Canadian cities. He is also trying to unpack the relationship between territory and property, and is interested in the practice of urban commoning. Past research has focused on topics such as gentrification, panhandling, urban gardening, and indigenous–state treaties.

KAITLIN FINDLAY is research coordinator for the Landscapes of Injustice project. She completed her BA history (honours) at McGill University and her MA thesis at the University of Victoria. Her MA research examined the social and political history of the Bird Commission and received an honourable mention as best MA thesis in the Canadian Studies Prize from the Canadian Studies Network. Since then she has served as a research consultant on two public history projects, the virtual exhibit "Writing Wrongs" and the augmented reality game "East of the Rockies," and as a curatorial assistant at the Nikkei National Museum for the exhibit *Hastings Park, 1942*. She is the standing chair of the Research Assistant Committee and the editor-in-chief of *The Scholarship and Activism Forum*, which publishes monthly.

MATT JAMES is associate professor in the Department of Political Science at the University of Victoria. He holds an honours BA in political studies and history from Queen's University and an MA and PhD in political science from the University of British Columbia. He studies the politics of reparation and transitional justice and has expertise in the fields of constitutionalism and social movement studies. He is the author of *Misrecognized Materialists: Social Movements in Canadian Constitutional Politics* (University of British Columbia Press) and has published on reparation, memory, and political apology in journals such as the *Canadian Journal of Political Science*, *Citizenship Studies*, *Human Rights Review*, and *International Journal of Transitional Justice*. He has also produced for the Truth and Reconciliation Commission of Canada the research report "Victim- and Perpetrator-Centred Truth Commissions: Choices and Tools."

AUDREY KOBAYASHI has a long history of research on Japanese Canadians and, in addition to her participation in the Landscapes of Injustice project, is involved in the "Right To Remain" project that includes a number of university researchers and graduate students in partnership with community advocacy organizations in the Downtown Eastside of Vancouver where rapidly increasing property prices and gentrification threaten precarious residents in hundreds of single occupancy residences (SROs). Many of these buildings were erected by Japanese Canadians who were forced from their homes during the 1940s. They have used activist art as well as more conventional research such as housing surveys and interviews to document this new uprooting. A native of British Columbia, Audrey Kobayashi completed a BA (1976) and MA (1978) at the University of British Columbia and a PhD (1983) at UCLA. She taught geography and East Asian studies at McGill University from 1983 to 1994. She came to Queen's initially as head of the Department of Gender Studies (1994 to 1999) and thereafter as professor of geography. She has spent time as a visiting professor at the University of British Columbia, University College London, and, most recently, Canterbury University, Christchurch, New Zealand. In 1994, Audrey was a Fulbright fellow at the Migration Policy Institute in Washington, DC. Other positions include president of the Canadian Association of Geographers (1999–2001) and editor, *People Place and Region, Annals of the Association of American Geographers*. She is also a former president of the Association of American Geographers.

ARIEL MERRIAM received her BA in history from the University of Victoria in 2016. She worked as a research assistant on the Landscapes of Injustice project from 2015 to 2016. In addition to her chapter in this manuscript, her work on the Nagata correspondences has included an honours thesis and an online article published by The Champlain Society. She is currently an MPA candidate at the University of Victoria.

DR ARTHUR KAZUMI MIKI, CM, OM is an active leader in the Japanese Canadian community having served as president of the National Association of Japanese Canadians from 1984 to 1992. He led the negotiations to achieve a just redress settlement for Japanese Canadians interned during the Second World War. He and his family were forcibly relocated to Manitoba sugar beet farms in 1942. For his efforts nationally, provincially, and locally he has received the Order of Canada, this country's highest recognition, as well as the Order of Manitoba, and recently the Order of the Rising Sun from the government of Japan. Art is a member of the Community Council and a representative on the Steering Committee for the Landscapes of Injustice project. He is a director for the Japanese Cultural Association of Manitoba and the Asian Heritage Society of Manitoba and the NAJC representative to the Canadian Race Relations Foundation. Art is a former teacher and principal, citizenship judge, author, and a lecturer at the University of Winnipeg.

EIJI OKAWA worked with Landscapes of Injustice as a postdoctoral fellow from 2016 to 2018, after completing his doctorate in Asian studies at the University of British Columbia. Currently he teaches Japanese history at Western Washington University. His areas of research include the history of Japanese migrants in early- to mid-twentieth-century Canada and the social and cultural history of premodern Japan. He is especially interested in thinking about how members of historical communities thought of themselves, related to one another and their surrounding landscapes, and dealt with challenges. He is as fascinated by the textual records of the Issei, or the migrant generation of Japanese Canadians, as he is by the documents of religious institutions in medieval and early modern Japan.

YASMIN AMARATUNGA RAILTON is the postdoctoral curatorial fellow in the Landscapes of Injustice project. She holds an honours BA in art history, an MA in art business, and a PhD in contemporary art from the Courtauld Institute of Art, London, UK. She has more than ten years' experience in major art museums and auction houses in London, UK. An art historian and curator, she specialises in contemporary art with a focus on conservation and new media. Bridging object-based studies, public history, and museum studies, her interdisciplinary research focuses on the display and archiving of ephemerality of contemporary art within the art market and public museums. She has lectured extensively internationally in English and French.

HEATHER READ was the Rebanks postdoctoral fellow in the Canadian decorative arts at the Royal Ontario Museum (ROM) from 2017 to 2018. There, she spearheaded the creation of the ROM's 2019 exhibition, *Being Japanese Canadian*, which featured works by eight multigenerational Japanese Canadian artists from across Canada. The show thematically evolved from her work with Landscapes of Injustice. In 2015, she was the oral history cluster postdoctoral fellow for Landscapes of Injustice, where she conducted her own interviews and assisted with the training of students, archiving of data, and overall management of the cluster. Her doctoral degree is in adult education and community development from the Ontario Institute for Studies in Education at the University of Toronto (OISE-UT), and her master's degree is in folklore, from Memorial University in Newfoundland and Labrador.

JORDAN STANGER-ROSS is associate professor of history and the project director of Landscapes of Injustice at the University of Victoria. His research and teaching focus on immigration, race, and inequality in twentieth-century North America. He is, along with the Landscapes of Injustice collective, the recipient of a Canadian Race Relations Foundation award of excellence. Throughout his career, his publication and teaching have been inspired by the changing places he has lived. In Philadelphia, he wrote on immigration and residential segregation. After living in Toronto, he published on the geography of poverty in Canadian cities, and since moving to British Columbia in 2005 he has studied municipal acquisitions of Indigenous lands in Vancouver as well as the social, legal, and political history of the dispossession of Japanese Canadians. In all of this work, he has been fascinated by how people and societies seem to get stuck, their choices constrained by ideological, institutional, economic, and social patterns.

JOSH VAN ES is a coauthor and editor at Landscapes of Injustice. Bringing ten years of experience in writing and website management to the project, Josh's work focuses on the development of content for the public-oriented narrative website. The website will present a curated analysis of more than five years of multidisciplinary research by the Landscapes of Injustice collective. He holds a BSc in psychology and BA in history from the University of Victoria and expects to pursue graduate work in 2020.

TREVOR J. WIDEMAN is a PhD candidate in the Department of Geography at Simon Fraser University and a research assistant with the Landscapes of Injustice project based at the Nikkei National Museum. He is currently involved in organizing the Landscapes of Injustice museum exhibit after spending three years researching with the project. His master's thesis in geography at Queen's University examined how Japanese Canadian heritage was used in a recent local area plan to promote neighbourhood transformations in the Downtown Eastside of Vancouver. His ongoing PhD work in urban geography attempts to advance a nuanced theoretical understanding of the historical links between land use, property, and planning in Canada.

INDEX

www.ingramcontent.com/pod-product-compliance
Lightning Source LLC
Chambersburg PA
CBHW080323170225
21928CB00002B/3
9780228001720